D0546280

The Pantheon Asia Library

New Approaches to the New Asia

No part of the world has changed so much in recent years as Asia, or
awakened such intense American interest. But much of our scholarship,
like much of our public understanding, is based on a previous era.
The Asia Library has been launched to provide the needed information
on the new Asia, and in so doing to develop both the new
methods and the new sympathies needed to understand it. Our
purpose is not only to publish new work but to experiment with
a wide variety of approaches which will reflect these new
realities and their perception by those in Asia and the West.

Our books aim at different levels and audiences, from the popular
to the more scholarly, from high schools to the universities, from
pictorial to documentary presentations. All books will be available
in paperback.

Suggestions for additions to the Asia Library are welcome.

Other Asia Library Titles

The Japan Reader, edited by Jon Livingston, Joe Moore, and Felicia
Oldfather
    Volume 1 *Imperial Japan: 1800–1945*
    Volume 2 *Postwar Japan: 1945 to the Present*

A Chinese View of China, by John Gittings

Remaking Asia: Essays on the American Uses of Power, edited by
Mark Selden

Without Parallel: The American-Korean Relationship Since 1945, edited
by Frank Baldwin

Chairman Mao Talks to the People: Talks and Letters, 1956–1971, edited
by Stuart Schram

A Political History of Japanese Capitalism, by Jon Halliday

*Origins of the Modern Japanese State: Selected Writings of
E. H. Norman,* edited by John Dower

China's Uninterrupted Revolution: From 1840 to the Present, edited
by Victor Nee and James Peck

The Wind Will Not Subside: Years in Revolutionary China, 1964–1969,
by David Milton and Nancy Dall Milton

The Waves at Genji's Door
JAPAN THROUGH ITS CINEMA

By the same author

The Battle of Algiers
Marilyn Monroe
Women and Their Sexuality in the New Film
Voices from the Japanese Cinema

The Waves at Genji's Door

JAPAN THROUGH ITS CINEMA

Joan Mellen

PANTHEON BOOKS
New York

Copyright © 1976 by Joan Mellen

All rights reserved under International and Pan-American Copyright Conventions. Published in the United States by Pantheon Books, a division of Random House, Inc., New York, and simultaneously in Canada by Random House of Canada Limited, Toronto.

Grateful acknowledgment is made to the following for permission to reprint previously published material:

The Film Society, Lincoln Center: Quotation from "Susumu Hani Interviewed by James Blue" from *Film Comment*, vol. 5, no. 2, spring 1969. Copyright © 1969 Film Comment Publishing Corporation. All rights reserved.

Kinema Jumpo Co. Ltd.: Quotations from interviews with Mikio Naruse (December 1960); Matsuo Kishi, "A Talk with Mizoguchi" (April 1, 1952, no. 35); Akira Iwasaki and Shinbi Iida, "A Talk with Ozu" (August 15, 1958, no. 212), all published in *Kinema Jumpo Motion Picture Times*.

Macmillan Pub. Co., Inc., and Macmillan Company of London & Basingstoke Ltd.: Two lines of poetry from "The Second Coming" from *The Collected Poems of William Butler Yeats*. Copyright 1924 by Macmillan Publishing Co., Inc., renewed 1952 by Bertha Georgie Yeats. Reprinted by permission of the publishers on behalf of M. B. Yeats and Miss Anne Yeats.

New Directions Publishing Corp. and J. M. Dent & Sons, Ltd., and the Trustees for the Copyrights of the late Dylan Thomas: Two lines of poetry from "There Was a Saviour" from *The Poems of Dylan Thomas*. Copyright 1943 by New Directions Publishing Corporation.

The author and publishers wish to thank the following for permission to reproduce photographs:

Kiichi Hoshi
Imamura Production
Yoichi Matsue
Museum of Modern Art Film Stills Archive
Ogawa Productions
Seirinsha Co., Ltd.
Toho International

Special thanks are due to the Japan Film Library Council, who made available most of the photographs in this book.

Design by Irva Mandelbaum

Library of Congress Cataloging in Publication Data

Mellen, Joan.
  The Waves at Genji's Door.
  (The Pantheon Asia Library)
  1. Moving-pictures—Japan. I. Title.
PN1993.5.J3M4   791.43'0952   76-9592
ISBN 0-394-49799-6
ISBN 0-394-73278-2 pbk.

Manufactured in the United States of America

First Edition

For Donald Richie

. . . it seemed as though the waves were at Genji's door. Night after night he lay listening to that melancholy sound and wondering whether in all the world there could be any place where the sadness of autumn was more overwhelming. The few attendants who shared the house with him had all gone to rest. Only Genji lay awake, propped high on his pillow, listening to the storm-winds which burst upon the house from every side. Louder and louder came the noise of the waves, till it seemed to him they must have mounted the fore-shore and be surging round the very bed on which he lay.

Lady Murasaki, The Tale of Genji

Wandering between two worlds, one dead,
The other powerless to be born.

Matthew Arnold, "Stanzas from the Grand Chartreuse"

Foreword

I confess to a missionary purpose. In writing this book my major aim has been not only to analyze but to champion that magnificent body of Japanese films for Western audiences so they might discover and experience for themselves the finest national cinema in existence. With respect to the Japanese film, Western critics have been singularly negligent. Some have been intimidated by the degree to which Japanese films are concerned with a national history at once unfamiliar and even unappealing, given the plethora of what appear to be endless civil wars engaged in by samurai swordsmen.

In this study the Japanese film is placed in its historical, social, and political context in the hope of dispelling the myth of inaccessibility which has denied the Japanese film its due. I have sought to elucidate that history which appears to many, Japanese and non-Japanese alike, so directionless. To the casual observer, Japan appears to have exploded in sudden modernization, following an equally sudden rejection of feudalism, an overnight pre-war militarism, and a miraculous postwar recovery. None of these events was as "sudden" as it appeared; the seemingly instantaneous disappearance of feudalism never occurred! Samurai abandoned their swords by decree, but feudal ideas continued to prevail in this culture, becoming an unseen if intrinsic component of daily life in Japan.

To understand Japanese life requires a grasp of Japanese history. Considering the brief existence of cinema itself, the Japanese film has accomplished a re-creation and reflection of an entire national past with uncommon brilliance. Contrary to the pattern of Western movies in their sporadic examinations of history, the Japanese film has been in quest of the inner dynamic of Japan's ancient culture, its unavowed patterns of industrial development, and the crisis of identity that flowed from these. Above all, the Japanese film has captured the trauma of a culture in transition. No other national cinema has so unhesitatingly and so feelingly recorded the historical tensions of the society it describes. And in no other country has film become the premier expression of a nation's cultural life. The consistent level of Japan's film art and its agonizingly honest quest for new values and mores, at once true to the national identity and free of its afflictions, have created in Japan a socially conscious cinema of the highest aesthetic attainment.

To Western audiences I would reintroduce the Japanese film.

Acknowledgments

I wish to thank the many people whose help to me in this project has been immeasureable. They made it possible for me to tread the arduous path of a foreigner in Japan attempting to interpret Japanese history, culture, and society. In availing me of the facilities and archives of the Japan Film Library Council and the Film Center of the Tokyo Museum of Modern Art, Mme. Kashiko Kawakita became my guiding spirit. Without her kindness and the overwhelmingly generous assistance afforded me by Akira Shimizu, general secretary of the Japan Film Library Council, I would have been unable to complete this work. Ms. Hisako Aoyama shepherded me on my path. To these people I owe an unrepayable debt.

I should also like especially to thank my friend Masahiro Shinoda for his help and for all the good talk we have had about Japan and its cinema. My gratitude must go as well to Shinsuke Ogawa and his staff, to Noriaki Tsuchimoto and his colleagues, and to Shohei Imamura and his co-workers for the many, many hours we spent together. I would also like particularly to thank Ms. Momoko Cho of the Seirinsha Company, who arranged many screenings, discovered stills, and made certain I found my way.

Yoshikata Yoda spoke to me generously of his collaboration with Kenji Mizoguchi. Kazuo Kuroki, Koichi Saito, Yoichi Higashi, and Kiichi Hoshi gave unstintingly of their time. And once more I must thank those directors with whom I passed long hours when I first began this project in 1972. Among them are Susumu Hani, Kon Ichikawa, Tadashi Imai, Daisuke Ito, Masaki Kobayashi, Akira Kurosawa, Toichiro Narushima, Nagisa Oshima, Kaneto Shindo and Hiroshi Teshigahara.

There are many other people in Tokyo who contributed to this work in small ways and large: among them Ichiyo Muto, and Frank Baldwin, who assisted me with written materials and gave of his time. I was also fortunate enough to have special friends in Japan, like Hajime Seki, whose encouragement and support have been unceasing. Setsure Tsuru-shima has been a kindred spirit whose humor, wry wit and political shrewdness were qualities second only to the trust one can place in his judgments. Kyushiro Kusakabe, who introduced me to many directors during my initial trip, continued his sympathetic help.

Keiko Mochizuki, of the University of California at Santa Barbara, most generously and kindly translated the script of Kurosawa's *Dersu Uzala*, as well as many articles and interviews, from Japanese into English. Without her help, my understanding would have been far less.

Facilities within the United States for viewing Japanese films are singularly poor, but I would like to thank my friend Charles Silver, head of the Film Study Center of the Museum of Modern Art, Dan Talbot of New Yorker Films, Martin Bresnick of Macmillan Audio-Brandon, and John Poole of Janus Films for their cooperation.

Leonard Schrader deserves special appreciation for making his own work on the Japanese film available to me in the most comradely of spirits.

Professor Martin Collcutt of Princeton University was also most helpful.

To Jim Peck of Pantheon Books I owe the special delight of working with an editor in an atmosphere of sympathy. With his help, the antagonism so frequent between author and publisher has been replaced by a spirit of enlightenment, mutual collaboration and trust.

Finally, I would like to express my gratitude to Donald Richie and to his books about the Japanese film. If I have not always given him credit for insights he discovered first, it is because they have been unconsciously assimilated. It is to this remarkable person that my book is dedicated.

Contents

Illustrations

PART 1

PART 2

PART 3

PART 4

PART 5

PART 6

Introduction

This is a book about Japan, the land of Prince Genji of Lady Murasaki's tenth century novel, a world of recalcitrant traditional values eroded by steady intimations of change. Like the waves moving upon Genji's very doorstep, these murmurings seem to approach from sources so deep as to presage a transformation of the entire society. At times they recede and Japan, Genji's household, appears to return to stasis, a place where the psychology of a tenth century inhabitant is reasserted every day on the streets of the twentieth century megalopolis.

Of late, long-denied currents, forebodings of the ineluctable need for a transformation of this neo-feudal society, are flowing again. Latter-day Genjis may not yet be lying awake at night, tormented by shifting tides which threaten their very existence. But Japan since the Second World War teeters on the verge of a real confrontation between unanswered needs of people and modes of life which date from before the time of Lady Murasaki. These involve a social code designed to repress rather than avow the urgings throbbing beneath the surface of national life. Japan, as Western commentators have stressed so often, is a country where change has been a cause of dread, accommodation the norm, and popular control reduced to untested consensus. Yet there is ferment—portents of discontent, if not full-bodied dissent.

This book explores Japan through film, its most vital and thriving art in this century. From its beginnings in the 1920s, the Japanese have used their cinema as a rite of passage, a means toward discovering who they are and the kind of culture they have produced as a people. Their subjects, like those of the films of any country, may vary widely. At times they focus on the nuances of family relationships in this still staunch patriarchy, as in the films of Ozu, Naruse, and the younger, more rebellious Hani and Oshima. The passing of the noble samurai class into extinction has provided Kurosawa with one of his great themes. Other directors refuse to make historical films, preoccupied as they are with the traumas of this century, as in Kon Ichikawa's unfolding of the barbarism coloring the period of the Second World War. And perhaps the greatest number of fine Japanese films reflect upon the bittersweet turmoil of life amidst the ruins of postwar society, a theme pursued by directors as diverse as Ozu, Imai, Kinoshita, Kurosawa and Imamura.

The directors whose work is emphasized here are those who have been most concerned with the spiritual fate of Japan: Naruse, Mizoguchi, Ozu, Kurosawa, Kinoshita, Imai, Kobayashi, Ichikawa, Shinoda, Imamura, Oshima and Hani. To describe the spiritual stagnation afflicting Japan, it is they who often use the term "feudal," indicating that the Japanese, despite their country's modernization, remain enmeshed in relationships remarkably similar to those which enslaved its people in medieval times. In *The Man Who Left His Will on Film* (*Tokyo Senso Sengo Hiwa*, 1970) one of Oshima's characters speaks, with the director's sympathy, of being "mired in the feudal and the modern" that is Japan. And even the conservative Ozu, who finds much to be cherished in the old ways, recognizes the validity of the argument of one of his young women in *Equinox Flower* (*Higanbana*, 1958) who calls her father "feudalistic."

No longer supporting the economic structure that existed during feudal times, Japan might be called a "neo-feudal" society because the culture continues to partake so overwhelmingly of feudal responses to authority, retaining the priority of superior to inferior, determinedly perpetuating the status quo. Many of Japan's outstanding directors attribute the injustice and repressiveness continuing in their society to a retention of feudal ideas. It is with their work that this study is concerned. And several Japanese films familiar to Western audiences, such as Kinugasa's *Gate of Hell* (*Jigokumon*, 1954) and Teshigahara's *The Woman in the Dunes* (*Suna no Onna*, 1964), have in fact been omitted because they do not especially illuminate this quest of national and self-discovery to which the Japanese director has so persistently dedicated himself.

The touchstone of Japanese cinema, more than that of any other nation, is its constant preoccupation with history. The dominant impulse has been to re-create the Japanese experience almost obsessionally, as if only in this way might catharsis result and, through the creative effort, film itself uncover what went wrong and where uniquely Japanese values were lost. Japanese films reconsider repeatedly the social institutions of Japan: the workings of the family, the status of women, the nature and effects of the educational system, the uses to which the press, police, and military have been put. For its mass audience Japan's films have sought to elucidate what is authentic in Japanese life, as if this question had never been properly posed, let alone answered. They forever plumb the Japanese past to unfold how it may provide a purer definition of what is distinctive in the culture. They sift among their findings to decide which of Japan's past ways should be revived and cherished if the nation is to discover its true character and destiny.

Through the Japanese film we, as well as the Japanese, are able to penetrate this society and its history. The body of film work in Japan is incredibly large, more so perhaps than that of any other nation, reflecting how seriously the Japanese have taken this art form. They have invested film with a spiritual authority, always experiencing it as far more than casual entertainment. Cinema in Japan has become a mirror into the hearts of a people in impatient and, at times, frantic search for values in which to believe. It is a sometimes angry admission that such values have not yet been identified.

Film in Japan has often functioned as the great dissident art form. We find in this cinema a very different image of the Japanese from that widely imagined in the West and in the rest of Southeast Asia. The view of the Japanese as "economic animals"—people voluntarily chained to factory and office, refusing even paid vacations in frantic devotion to productivity—is a surface view which fails to perceive the quest consuming the Japanese beneath a seeming impassivity.

If feudal norms and institutions continue to bind the individual in Japan, and they do, Japan's cinema also reveals formidable energy and vitality, people willing to devote their lives to the struggle against feudalism. Populating these films, and making them, are people who have suffered less than willingly the trauma attendant upon the march of the ruling order to wealth and power by the use of feudal dictates of loyalty and obedience. Japan's cinema has offered a distinctive arena in which Japanese intellectuals explore the moral direction of their society through ideas appropriate, not to a feudal hierarchy, but to a post-capitalist era. The history of the Japanese film unfolds an effort heroic, noble, and often no less than quixotic in its daring.

PART 1

AT GENJI'S DOOR

The Feudal and
the Modern

But you must not think that K's inability to discard his old ways and begin his life anew was due to his lack of modern concepts. You must understand that to K, his own past seemed too sacred a thing to be thrown away like an old suit of clothes. One might say that his past was his life, and to deny it would have meant that his life thus far had been without purpose.

Natsume Soseki, *Kokoro*

In sympathy with K, his emotionally paralyzed friend, Soseki's hero, Sensei, ironically named "teacher" or "master" because he can find no answers himself, exposes the "heart" (*kokoro*[1]) of Japan. K finally commits suicide and, with the death of the Emperor Meiji in 1912, Sensei does so as well. Alienated and sickened by what they view as a Japan profaned by the twentieth century, Soseki's characters—and the Japanese—too often find no remedy except a despairing reach into the feudal past. Outwardly a republic, "democratized" since the Second World War, Japan and the Japanese obsessively return to feudal ways.

There is also a pervasive sense in Japan that the identity of the nation and the feelings human beings have for each other (these, to the Japanese, are one and the same) can be truly expressed only through a hierarchy of relationships established during Japan's eight centuries of warrior rule. Employer and employee respond as lord to vassal; man and woman interact as in the patriarchal American South of the nineteenth century, in a relation of master to slave. Appalled by the injustices that are integral to their culture, even the most outspoken and dissident Japanese retain in their personal lives the forms and manners of feudal times toward which Soseki's Meiji intellectuals felt so attached. Japan today is beset by overwhelming pollution and a despoliation of the environment that, because of its confined area, exceeds that of all other industrial nations. The countryside is ravaged, while a claustrophobic overcrowding suffocates the cities. The denial of individual rights is exacerbated by an industrialism without regard to social need. The racism directed toward Koreans, toward *burakumin* (an outcast group treated much like India's untouch-

[1] Literally *kokoro* means "heart," but its significance has to do with the power to feel emotion toward things, or the actual emotion which is felt.

ables), and toward aliens in general complements Japan's exploitation of the less technologically advanced peoples of Southeast Asia in the pursuit of cheap raw materials and markets for Japanese conglomerates.

In their protest against these evils, Japanese intellectuals, and those film artists who have been among the most effective social critics since the War, have frequently been able to project moral alternatives for Japan only in terms of the past. Japanese filmmakers have charted the nation's social history, moving freely among its most significant moments. Constantly they ponder how to respond to the moral vacuum at the heart of Japanese culture, a lacuna exposed beyond question at the moment of the Meiji Restoration of 1868. It was said that when the last Tokugawa shogun departed, feudalism was defeated in Japan. Yet little changed. The Emperor Meiji ascended the throne and, through the sanctity of his person (for it was believed that he was a direct descendant of the gods), old codes of behavior were perpetuated. The living presence today of an Emperor in Japan itself preserves the values of the past.

Within the consciousness of this culture, amidst the crying need for greater social justice and concern for the individual, the precarious marriage between the feudal and the modern continues. There is a hunger in Japan among many reflective people for radical and structural change, but the terms of that transformation continue to derive from a formal past, a period when national identity and sense of place were attached to rigid and hierarchical institutions.

Minamata: The Victims and Their World: The thousands of victims and their families have so far confined their protest to demanding of Chisso that it assume its proper role of benevolent protector.

When the residents of Minamata City found that they were suffering from mercury poisoning caused by wastes poured into the ocean by Chisso, a chemical company, and consumed by the fish they ate, they did not overtly challenge a feudal paternalism which the *zaibatsu*[2] pretend to practice. "Minamata disease" results in the deterioration of the entire nervous system, causing an inability in its victims to control their physical and mental functions; they are rendered completely helpless. Yet the thousands of victims and their families have so far confined their protest to demanding of Chisso that it assume its proper role of benevolent protector, accusing it of violating its obligations. They did not challenge Chisso's *right* to operate without restraint, but demanded that Chisso explain why it did not regulate itself in accordance with those duties which accompany complete authority.[3]

One of the most radical moments in the Minamata case occurred when the victims confronted the president of Chisso at an annual stockholders' meeting. This dramatic encounter is brilliantly conveyed in Noriaki Tsuchimoto's documentary, *Minamata: The Victims and Their World* (*Minamata: Kanja- sans to Sono Sekai,* 1972). In it, he captures Japan looking forward and backward simultaneously. The corporate officers sit impassively in a row on the stage. Their retainers try to restrain a seething crowd of banner-wielding families and victims. No dialogue is attempted by the executives; it would be as out of place as the mass upheaval is unseemly. For the issues are only part of the drama, as the formal relation between rulers and ruled becomes a matter of decorum.

But the people themselves, in their rage and anguish, then surge forward, seemingly demanding a dismantling of the corporate structure of Chisso. "We don't want your money," a woman screams into the face of the shaken president. Yet the rebellion, despite its passion and fury, translates itself finally into a form of pleading with the enemy. The corporate officers are addressed as if they were feudal lords who, in their harshness, have pushed the people too far. In demanding of Chisso that it regulate or change itself, the people simultaneously, if unconsciously, resort to a demand to brutal authorities for a refurbishment of old feudal norms. Natsume Soseki, one of Japan's greatest novelists, was prophetic in 1914 when he spoke of the past, for the Japanese, as "too sacred a thing to be thrown away like an old suit of clothes."

Japan's adoption of industrial technology and its entry into a world market dominated by the West have brought unavoidable penetration by foreign cultures. That industrialization has been destructive of the spiritual and physical well-being of Japan's people is not solely the result of the day in 1853 when Commodore Perry arrived in Tokyo Bay with his "black ships." The economic development of Japan epitomizes the

[2] The *zaibatsu* are the giant corporations which make up Japan's financial oligarchy, such as Mitsui, Mitsubishi, Sumitomo, Yasuda.

[3] On May 4, 1976, the former president of the Chisso corporation, Kiichi Yoshioka and Eiichi Nishida, former head of the Chisso factory in Minamata City, were formally charged with involuntary manslaughter in causing seven deaths through negligence.

development of all capitalist societies. Japan perceived that only the rapid acquisition of technology could forestall colonial conquest. Inevitably, the Western control of this technology resulted in a Western penetration of Japanese culture, even as the acquired technology was the sole means of preventing not merely penetration but the loss of national independence.

That many Japanese associate the ravaging of their country with its response to the Western threat, the real danger that Japan would be carved up into spheres of influence by the British, Russians, and Americans in the way that China was, has prevented the Japanese from perceiving that their problems are not merely the result of emulating foreigners and of being forced to choose between mastering Western technique or losing national autonomy. In its drive toward capitalist modes of production and defense, Japan, with a feudal culture, has reproduced all of the ills of Western industrial society. Japanese tend to attribute these deformities to the Western character of the industrialization. And the strong impulse in the culture is to return to the Japanese past in reaction to this Westernization, an impulse epitomized in much of Japan's art, particularly in the films of Shohei Imamura and in the novels and essays of Yukio Mishima. Were it not for the convenience of blaming the despoliation of Japan upon "the West," the Japanese might not so frequently look to feudal forms as a palliative for present decay.

The very concept of "progress" has not permeated Japanese culture as it has ours, if only in theory. It was also absent in Western Europe until the industrial revolution brought both social mobility and an ascending standard of living. Yet, although Japan has industrialized even more rapidly and dramatically than the West, the absence in the culture of a belief in progress points clearly to the persistence of both feudal values and sensibility. The philosophic traditions of the West suggest that people have the opportunity to make the future better than the past. Westerners believe that it is their own fault if they are taken so unawares that tragic events recur. In their personal sense of purpose and value, they believe they can shape not only themselves, but also their society. The Japanese seem convinced that they can influence neither.

Industrialization unfolded in East and West within very different traditions. Westerners still live and dream under the impact of a bourgeois revolution typified by the French Revolution of 1789, which granted the individual the right to be protected from the State, and, indeed, to be held in higher value than the State when basic freedoms were threatened. Without such an expectation of the State, there cannot even be the facade of democracy. Democratic life in Japan has been rendered stillborn because the culture inculcates above all the subordination of the individual to the hierarchy. Not only must the individual submit to the superiority of those above—in job or in government—but this submission has been sanctified, because the highest position in the hierarchy is occupied by a figure still thought of by many as a descendant of the supernatural. The Emperor continues to embody the "Japanese spirit" (*kokutai*), which permeates every level of political life in Japan. And the continuing existence of the old *kokutai* enforces the use of the past as the only authentic source for understanding the present.

In the West, the theory of the divine right of kings was rendered anachronistic by the bourgeois revolution. There could not be justice for the individual were justice to be defined absolutely, arbitrarily, and without recourse. Through the existence of the Emperor, justice in Japan is still perceived, if by now unconsciously, as a matter of birth and status rather than of equity and right. The Japanese revitalized the role of the Emperor in 1868 with all his "divine right." In their official histories, they may call the Meiji Restoration a "revolution" because power changed hands. But in actuality, and this is one of the most profound themes developed in the Japanese film, the Meiji Restoration brought the political and ethical structure of feudal times intact into the new in-dustrializing, modern Japan. In the bureaucracy of the new government, three-fourths of all office holders were samurai—feudal warriors now attached to a new master, the Meiji government.[4] Samurai constituted only five percent of the total population; yet by 1871, eighty-seven percent of officials in the nine ministries of the central government were from the ex-samurai class. In 1880, that class comprised eighty percent of all officials in both central and provincial governments as well as the majority of policemen and schoolteachers.[5] Only lip service was paid to the idea of the "rights" of the individual. The Popular Rights Movement (*Meiji jiyu minken undo*) that did exist, feeble as it was, in practice often meant *shizoku minken*, protecting the rights of the samurai class.[6] And many of the uprisings in the early years of Meiji were *against* such re-forms of the new government as the legalization of Christianity or the emancipation of the *Eta*[7] caste.

The introduction of industrial capitalism to Japan meant that property inheritance laws had to be changed to allow individual family members to exercise personal property rights. The educational system was tempo-rarily liberalized and suffrage was extended, although by 1880 Confucian-ism was re-established as the basis of the ethics taught in the schools. A host of reforms were enacted between 1870 and 1873 which seem, on the surface, to have abolished feudalism. The legal equality of all social classes was declared, feudal dress abolished, Buddhism disestablished and Christianity legalized. Attacking the feudal economic structure in those areas where it was not compatible with the growth of industrial cap-italism, freedom of occupation of the land and of choice of crop was declared, and fiefs dismantled. There was a removal of the ban against the sale of land, a freedom necessary for the growth of a new landlord class.

[4] Jon Halliday, *A Political History of Japanese Capitalism* (New York: Pantheon Books, 1975), p. 24.

[5] Keizo Shibusawa, ed., *Japanese Life and Culture in the Meiji Era* (Tokyo: Obunsha, 1958), p. 312.

[6] Halliday, *Japanese Capitalism*, p. 30.

[7] Slang for people "full of filth," supposedly because, as slaughterers and executioners, these outcast people traditionally worked in trades held in contempt by the Japanese. The more acceptable term is *burakumin*.

But in no way did a previously embattled class, like Europe's bourgeoisie, and one which, in Japan, would have had to include the peasantry, alter the balance of power in the new society. The aristocracy, through the samurai, retained power. And in exchange for continuing to command the state, this aristocracy aided the merchant class in its ruthless drive to transform Japan from a rural society into a modern superstate. Government holdings were sold to the growing *zaibatsu* for very little, and the close relationship between these corporations and the government which exists to this day was established from the first moment. Previously ostracized merchants now derived the status appropriate to their already secure place in the economy, but the masses remained as peripheral to the center of power as they had been under official feudalism. The peasantry continued to be severely taxed. Rural discontent, expressed as always in peasant uprisings, was handled by suppression.

The bombing of the Mitsui Corporation's head offices in the autumn of 1974 dramatizes how the modern trading company, far from "Westernizing" Japan and democratizing its institutions through bourgeois constitutionalism, in fact recapitulates Japan's feudal history in microcosm. After the bombing, Mitsui's private, yellow-helmeted security force, many in number, revealed itself. Parallel to the State, corporations like Mitsui retain private armies. Arm in arm, the security force stood in front of the Mitsui building, blocking the press from entering, offering the explanation that "there are secret documents in the communications room."[8] The riot police. from Japan's Self-Defense Force, a refurbished army over 300,000 strong by 1971, was no match for these Mitsui "samurai." Mitsui thus functions like a modern clan, armed by paid retainers loyal to a feudal lord (daimyo)—not the particular president of the company, but the company itself.

In the end, the Meiji Restoration provided only a pause during which Japanese feudalism could reconstitute itself, taking into account the growing power of the merchant class, which had long outgrown its ridiculously low rank, somewhere below peasants and artisans, on the social scale. Thus, Meiji kept Japan closed to liberalizing ideas. When dissent arose during the 1920s, it was suppressed with little effective resistance. Trade unions never had a chance to develop as an independent force. In the consciousness of the culture, and in the social institutions in which that consciousness is expressed, feudalism stretches to the present in an unbroken line.

Japan's social history is enacted in her magnificent cinema. The tension between the feudal and the dissident, which is entwined in the texture of everything Japanese, has found expression in film, the most social of the arts. Rooted in an immediate physical existence, and insistently confronting us with things as they are, film seems best able to express contradictions in daily life which one would not ordinarily perceive. Japanese

---

[8] *Mainichi Daily News,* October 15, 1974.

directors have produced great works of art in a process of exposing ailments lurking beneath the pragmatic surface of Japanese culture. No more, perhaps, than Japanese intellectuals as a whole have film directors been successful in posing solutions. But coming to an art form whose origins lie in the free-wheeling America of the first quarter of this century and in revolutionary Russia (the two principal influences on Japanese film), the Japanese film artist has been able to express a sense of his culture outside of models feudal in form and therefore invariably feudal, to some degree, in content.

The two major traumas of Japan's recent history—the defeat of the warrior clans and the fall of the shogunate in the middle of the nineteenth century, and the Second World War—are recorded over and over again in its films as the Japanese director, like all Japanese artists, faces questions that seem to plague this culture as they do no other: (*a*) what does it mean to be a Japanese? (*b*) what identity shall Japan and the Japanese assume? and (*c*) what is unique about Japan and how shall it be preserved?

Precisely because the Japanese seem not to have resolved the meaning of their history, and because they find it so problematic to separate the past from the present, to distinguish the feudal from the progressive, many Japanese films are set in feudal times, when values and relationships seemed unambiguous. Kon Ichikawa has said that there are so many *jidai-geki* (period films) made in Japan because Japanese filmmakers "are somewhat unable to grasp contemporary society."[9] Surrounded by a long-familiar history characterized by the unmistakable clarity that only feudal relationships can have, the Japanese director struggles with difficulty to elucidate, as Ichikawa puts it, "certain themes which have implications for modern society."[10] In battle with what they have been, with what they are, and with what they will or can become, Japanese directors have produced an extraordinary array of films from 1946 though the 1960s.

This use of the act of creation as a vehicle for understanding their culture has proven to be an energizing phenomenon for Japanese intellectuals and artists. And this quest for the meaning of "Japan" has become the theme of nearly every major Japanese film ever made. Such a search for spiritual redefinition, not surprisingly, proceeds in manifold directions. It led that most Westernized of Japanese novelists, Yukio Mishima, to a vision of a reconstituted *bushido* (the code of the samurai) and to dreams of an army that would be much more rigorous in its obedience to the martial code than it had been in the recent past. In Mishima's fantasy, it was to be a far cry from the absence of discipline among late Tokugawa samurai—indolent, impoverished, and bored, restless within privileges no longer economically real and no longer protectable by the sword. "We watched Japan become drunk on prosperity and fall

[9] Joan Mellen, "Interview with Kon Ichikawa," *Voices from the Japanese Cinema* (New York: Liveright, 1975), p. 121.
[10] *Ibid.*

into an emptiness of the spirit," Mishima lamented,[11] speaking for
Japanese of both left and right. In his very person, Mishima conveyed
the dualism between the feudal and the radical that characterizes Japan
today. He wrote novels Western in structure, while looking back nostal-
gically toward a pure Japanese spirit lost in Westernization. What is
interesting about Mishima's notorious death by *seppuku* (hara kiri) is
not that he chose to die—this successful novelist, still in his prime at forty-
five—but the metaphor he selected. If Japanese take Mishima's *seppuku*
seriously, it is because they, like Mishima, recognize in his submission
to the warm blanket of a long-familiar feudalism a choice to which they
too may succumb when faced with the vacuum at the heart of the culture.

In the West, the decadence of the culture does not prevent us from
feeling spiritually intact as individuals because we do not believe that we
derive our values totally from the society at large. We can still believe
that institutional corruption, as in the Kennedy assassinations, Vietnam,
or Watergate, only confirms the *differences* between ourselves and those
in power. In Japan, there is strong cultural pressure against the arrogance
of assuming that one can be "oneself" without being affected by what
it means at a given moment in history to be "a Japanese." Flaunting
before the Japanese this image of a marriage between fascism and feudalism, Mishima—his personal idiosyncrasies aside—was seeking Japanese
integrity in "the true spirit of the samurai." His personal need for this
solution is forgettable, of minor and prurient interest only. What is of
significance is that Mishima could believe that he sacrificed himself to
show the Japanese what they are. Had Mishima thought there was any
value or promise of political or moral success in reviving such an anomaly,
had he really believed in it, he would have lived to make it happen. The
bloodbath of his last moments must not then be seen as a Tojoesque
parody, but rather as Mishima holding up a mirror to a people lacking
in either self-knowledge or purpose, as if he had irrevocably, completely,
and in full desperation turned his aesthetic away from the parables of
art to social existence—to life in Japan.

Some of Japan's finest filmmakers, people who would be instantly
critical of Japan's feudal past—and present—nonetheless share with
Mishima the idea that a return to the traditions of old Japan, when it was
a primitive island insulated from the rest of the world, would allow a
revitalization of the culture. These include Imamura (and those who
emulate him, like Koichi Saito) and Shinsuke Ogawa. Imamura has
launched virulent attacks in his films on the American military presence
in Japan and its influence on the shaping of postwar society. *Pigs and
Battleships* (*Buta to Gunkan*, 1961) is an expose of life in the environs
of the American naval base at Yokosuka, and A *History of Postwar Japan*
(*Nippon Sengoshi*, 1970) treats of how American influence affects one
woman, a bar madam. Ogawa has devoted the last years almost exclusively
to filming the struggle of the Sanrizuka peasants.

[11] Quoted in John Nathan, *Mishima: A Biography* (Boston: Little, Brown & Co.,
1974), p. 270.

Thus it is not only the would-be fascists like Mishima who, disenchanted with the directionless materialism of contemporary Japan, search for meaning in a past still seen as a repository of value. Many of Japan's most radical directors continue to regard interruption by alien forces as the reason why the continuities of tradition seem no longer able to sustain the culture in the present. Conventional political solutions have been abandoned by most directors since the Communists, Socialists, and the Neo-Buddhist Komeito Party often seem to differ only in their rhetoric from the ruling Liberal-Democrats. People like Imamura have sought the uniqueness of Japan and the definition of what it means to be a Japanese (which all agree is a good in itself) in the origins of the Yamato, the original tribe populating the archipelago. These were an island people: insular, collective in their social impulses, and, like peasants everywhere, resistant to change and bound to custom as a means of survival.

Given the roughly similar behavior of peasants in most cultures, this rather romantic view has not been one indulged in by a director as shrewd in his understanding as Akira Kurosawa. The last scene of *Seven Samurai* (*Shichinin no Samurai*, 1954) should stand as at least a partial corrective to all those who, like Imamura and Ogawa, search among the peasantry for the revolutionary spirit of which the rest of the Japanese, led as they are by merchants as selfish as they are energetic, seem defiantly incapable.

At the end of *Seven Samurai*, Kurosawa's peasants turn their backs on the good-natured *ronin*[12] who have risked their lives to ensure the survival of the village besieged by bandits who came with each harvest to rob the villagers of their food and women. The bandits, themselves hungry *ronin*, are demolished (along with four of the heroic seven samurai). The peasants then burst into song as they plant the next rice crop. Bamboo flutes begin to play. As the women bend over their plants, they move together in physical harmony. Because they are egocentric in their very fiber, thankfulness would be as gratuitous for these peasants as concern for how the homeless *ronin* will now themselves manage to survive. The film is set in the sixteenth century, but already history has rendered the samurai class obsolete. Warriors will no longer be needed in the merchant-dominated days ahead. The peasants, however, will remain. In silent acceptance of this fate, in homage to it, they sing and they plant. They would no more rebelliously challenge the political organization of the society, or the movement of history, than they would the passing of the seasons. Still an animistic people, it is with nature that they feel most at home.

The island, a frequent setting for so many recent Japanese films, is often treated as a metaphor for Japan. But many of the directors who set their works in areas still retaining pre-Meiji traditions are by no means as convinced as Imamura that the pure Japanese spirit of the rural past contained anything but the same violence enacted against the individual today. They consider it a form of nostalgia to sanctify tribal

---

[12] Homeless samurai who, through social upheaval, had lost the feudal masters to whom they had been attached as retainers.

traditions for their own sake. Toichiro Narushima in *Time Within Memory* (*Seigenki*, 1973) and Masahiro Shinoda in *Himiko* (1974) unfold the tribal roots of the Japanese sensibility while at the same time registering its highly destructive workings.

Yet, torn by a sense of their own powerlessness to do anything to halt the decimation of traditional life styles and the alienation of everyone in the new Japan, directors like Imamura discover an escape from the confusions of the present in isolated areas where a basic Japanese culture still thrives. The heroine, Toriko, of his *Kuragejima: Tales from a Southern Island* (*Kamigami ni Fukaki Yokubo*, 1968) is promiscuous, inarticulate, and secretive. She appears demented to our eyes, but this is as Imamura intends. For Imamura, our view has become so jaded and corrupt that what is pure seems insane. It is our rationality that has prevented us from discovering the freedoms rooted in the past, which may be our only answer, deformed as we are, and rendered mad ourselves by urban life. Near the end of *Kuragejima* a railway locomotive, the symbol of progress here as in the American film *The Man Who Shot Liberty*

Kuragejima: Tales from a Southern Island: It is our rationality that has prevented us from discovering the freedoms rooted in the past.

Near the end of *Kuragejima* a railway locomotive, the symbol of progress, chases the ghost of this girl, once wild and free. She embodies the spirit of the island, the life of Japan, now pursued to its very destruction.

Valance and in the films of Satyajit Ray, chases the ghost of this girl, once wild and unrestrained. She embodies the spirit of the island, the life of Japan, once free but now pursued to its very destruction. "It's more painful here," says one of Imamura's characters, returning to the island, "but in Tokyo I don't feel I'm myself; I'm all in pieces." Like a girl waiting for her lover, Japan, represented by this wild girl, Toriko, sits in expectation of a redeemer who doesn't come.

Imamura's response to the laissez-faire destruction of Japan is essentially religious. It is Buddhist in its distance from social injustice. Rather than attacking social ills, it seeks to provide solace. It assumes and accepts the continued existence of suffering. "If you think of life as an unending cycle," Imamura has said, "it is less threatening."[13] It is a view suffused with patience; it believes it has time on its side—a parodox, since Buddhism begins with the notion of the inevitable transitoriness of the things of this world. But Imamura suggests that abiding values will outlast the present.

Imamura's is the voice of a Japanese Nietzsche convinced that "imported rationalism is not congenial here."[14] It is Nietzschean as well in its endorsement of a folk culture at a time when, as the locomotive in *Kuragejima* suggests, society has moved on to another stage of its development. But Imamura is a man of the left, not in any sense a fascist. No

[13] Conversations with the author, Tokyo, October 1974.
[14] Conversations with the author.

film director has been as vehement as he in denunciation of Japanese imperialism in Southeast Asia. And he has been the most effective satirist of the American manipulation of Japanese politics since the Second World War. This same man, in *Kuragejima*, locates his central image of freedom in a communal life where everyone is related through blood. More particularly, freedom is expressed in *Kuragejima* in the relationship of incest. That Toriko sleeps with everyone indiscriminately, including her own brother, seems negative to our eyes. But Imamura wants us to perceive that the insular Japanese, who for centuries kept all foreigners, with very rare exceptions, from entering—and their own people from leaving (the punishment for which was no less than death during the Tokugawa reign)— lived in harmony with nature. Their homogeneity expressed their naturalness and their oneness with the outside world. The continuity of interrelated generations evoked the "Japanese spirit." It is perhaps a measure of Mishima's own corrupting Westernization that he should have called Imamura's films "dirty."

Shinsuke Ogawa, unlike Imamura, is an activist. His political documentaries are based on, and in support of, actual uprisings. Yet, like Imamura, he believes that the revolutionary energy accessible to the Japanese people can come only through the ancient customs of the peasantry. The abiding theme of all his Sanrizuka films is that through the rural traditions of cooperation and mutual action, originally forged in the service of feudalism, Japan can be transformed. In the rural folkways of the same conservative peasantry depicted by Kurosawa, Ogawa finds the only consistent strength with which to combat the power, cunning, and vagaries of corporate rule and its state power.

To other directors, such a view appears naively romantic. It willfully ignores the fact that Japan, like England, reveals a history sprinkled with peasant uprisings, but that neither can boast of a major revolutionary upheaval. It is interesting that, in England as in Japan, the aristocracy merged with the bourgeoisie instead of being overthrown by it. If the Japanese traditionally identify the needs of the village with those of the self, a view which made the Sanrizuka demonstrations so successful, and are therefore culturally more capable than other peoples of sustained collective action, it is no less true that a religious caution suffuses these people. They doubt the permanent gain of changing society and, as Masahiro Shinoda has said, they believe it is purer (in a society where purity is one of the cardinal virtues) to sacrifice oneself for an invisible ideal than for a political cause.[15]

A revolution for the Japanese so rooted in feudal ways would thus have to create something eternal and unchanging, an image of Utopia. Shinoda argues that there is small faith in political revolution among the Japanese because the impulse which would move toward this end resolves itself in the quest for an absolute, a god.[16] And this, once again, is why the

[15] Joan Mellen, "Interview with Masahiro Shinoda," *Voices from the Japanese Cinema*, p. 244.
[16] *Ibid.*

Emperor system, far from having been rendered obsolete, stands as a bulwark against true social change in Japan. Shinoda is quite right when he says that the political power structure in Japan today uses the Emperor for its own protection.[17] It keeps the Emperor sacred as a means of ensuring its own power by immobilizing dissent before it can be born.

For the Emperor as an institution to continue to exist is for the Japanese to be ever reminded that the unchanging, the status quo, takes precedence over revolt against what is. Buddhism suggests that it is pointless to expend one's efforts to change society since social change can do nothing to obviate the sufferings endemic to the human condition. Shintoism argues that it would be wrong to amputate traditional loyalties because these alone sustain and render to the collective whatever identity it has. Together, the Imperial institution, Buddhism, and Shintoism keep careful watch against the very whisper of dissent, or any hint at the desirability of change.

In *Himiko*, set in the second century at the time of the birth of "Japan," Shinoda uses the same image endorsed by Imamura, that of incest. The goddess Himiko falls in love with her brother, and it is in part this love that makes it no longer possible for her to share her communications with the sun god. The people reject her. Incest may be the primal emotional response of the Japanese, but Shinoda, departing from Imamura, believes that the insular inbreeding of a people shut off from the rest of the human race has produced a nihilistic, self-devouring culture, even as Himiko, out of jealousy, finally has her brother mutilated and cast from her kingdom.

Shinoda considers the present Emperor, with his silence in the face of the massacres and genocide characterizing the term of his reign, a symbol of this nihilism.[18] In the Japanese cinema of the 1960s and 1970s, directors like Shinoda, Susumu Hani, and Nagisa Oshima have insisted upon a theme drastically new and unsettling: in the Japanese past, there is nothing to go back to.

---

[17] Conversations with the author, New York, April 1973.
[18] Conversations with the author, Tokyo, October 1974.

The Warriors
of Meiji

A merchant wearing silks is an ugly sight. Homespun is not only
more suited to his station, but he looks smarter in it.

Saikaku Ihara, *The Japanese Family Storehouse
or The Millionaires' Gospel Modernized*[1]

In Japan today, intellectuals, leftists, salaried men, blue collar workers,
students, and "liberated" women continue to accept in obeisance their
place in the social hierarchy. Despite a thunderous and violent student
movement, which at its height attracted hundreds of thousands, and the
life-and-death anti-pollution struggles dotting the country and epitomized
by the peasants of Sanrizuka and the victims at Minamata, change eludes.
Those traditionally scorned in the culture—Koreans, *burakumin*, foreigners, and women—continue to be objects of unabated discrimination. Only one historically abused group, the merchants, have escaped the
social onus they suffered during Tokugawa times. And today the multinational corporations over which they preside are among the largest in
the world.

The merchants began their social ascent when they were courted in the
last days of the Edo or Tokugawa period by low-ranking, impoverished
samurai who, through intermarriage, sold the merchants respectability
in exchange for ready cash. By 1868 the Osaka merchants alone possessed
seventy percent of the national wealth,[2] and it was their economic
hegemony that gained them what no other of the outcast groups has
achieved. They were more than willing to share political power with
the Meiji samurai, who rewarded them by selling nationally held assets
dirt cheap to private enterprise. During the period of the Second World
War the merchants exhibited no uneasiness about allying themselves
with the military. Unlike other middle classes, they were untroubled by
the absence of a democratic facade. They had never challenged feudal
authority by creating truly representative institutions through social

---

[1] Cited in Jon Livingston, Joe Moore, and Felicia Oldfather, eds. *The Japan Reader*
(New York: Pantheon Books, 1973) 1:73.

[2] Yasuzo Horie, "An Outline of the Rise of Modern Capitalism in Japan," *Kyoto
University Economic Review*, 11 (July 1936): 101, quoted in Halliday, *Japanese
Capitalism*, p. 9.

struggle. Hence, any demand for human rights in the culture at large not only had been unnecessary for the merchants, but the absence of such rights suited their purposes well because it allowed them to exploit their factory workers, particularly women, without transgressing any institutionalized liberties or laws.

The intelligentsia of the second half of the twentieth century, a group that includes Japan's film directors, however occasionally nihilistic in their outlook and hopeless of change, have recorded a particular distaste for the merchant. The merchant as a figure has been a target of abuse and outrage, as if he and his class alone were responsible for the moral ruin in which Japan now finds itself. This satire of the merchant forms an obvious and direct link to the plays of one of Japan's greatest playwrights, a *ronin* named Mozaemon Chikamatsu, who already in the late seventeenth century was ridiculing this class because he felt it vulgarized the true Japanese spirit. Feudal distaste for the merchant, born of aristocratic snobbery and privilege, has been assimilated, along with other feudal attitudes, into the modern era, even when it passes as social protest.

Chikamatsu's revulsion for the merchant was that of a samurai who believed that it was vulgar per se to touch money and that ignorance of the value of different coins was a measure of good breeding. Should he have anything to do with trade, the samurai was always to see that the profit went to the other side. A samurai, speaking of his son's education, had said in the Tokugawa period, "it is abominable that innocent children should be taught the use of numbers—the tools of shopkeepers. What will the teachers do next?"[3] And in late Tokugawa times those samurai already too poor to have servants would wrap their faces in small hand towels and go out in the dark when they had to do errands, so humiliated were they to be seen handling money. Yukichi Fukuzawa, in his autobiography, naively but without tongue in cheek, feels he has to justify the spending of money. " 'This is my own money,' I would say to myself. 'I did not steal it. What is wrong with buying things with my own money?' "[4]

The scorn of the merchant which comes down to the twentieth century reflects the confusion between the feudal and the progressive in Japanese culture. It expresses the disdain of an aristocrat like Chikamatsu even as it serves the point of view of anti-capitalists who propose, not a return to a pre-industrial value system, but a transformation of Japan which would be at once post-capitalist and post-feudal.

Certainly the finest film of Kenji Mizoguchi, Japan's greatest director, *A Story from Chikamatsu* (*Chikamatsu Monogatari*, 1954), nowhere suggests a return to pre-merchant days. Mizoguchi's aristocrats are as dishonest and unattractive as his merchants, and the film implies that a society that would care for the needs of human beings can be ruled by neither. But, at the center of *A Story from Chikamatsu*, is the merchant Ishun, relentless, hypocritical, and clearly representing the class that will

[3] G. B. Sansom, *The Western World and Japan: A Study in the Interaction of European and Asiatic Cultures* (New York: Alfred A. Knopf, 1968), p. 427.
[4] *The Autobiography of Yukichi Fukuzawa* (New York: Schocken Books, 1972), p. 11.

dominate the Japan of the future. Ishun runs his scroll-making factory
for profit alone. He cares little for the well-being of his workers, not even
for that of the hero, the artisan Mohei (Kazuo Hasegawa), from whose
great skill Ishun derives boundless profit. Ishun attempts to seduce the
maid-servants. He drives ailing workers to a level of productivity that
deprives them of their health (Mohei, at the beginning of the film, is
already coughing and feverish). Ishun, in fact, is one of the most con-
temptible figures in the Japanese cinema and is symbolic of a ruling
order in embryo.

The year is 1683. In a single, deep-focus shot Mizoguchi, varying the
direction of motion of the characters, and portraying people behind
people, reveals the daily life in the factory. Four layers of laborers are
frantically at work on the annual calendar. A foreman orders the workers
to hurry. The merchants are already in the employ of the government,
and the calendar is a symbol of the onrush of time that will catapult them
to the top of the social order. Ishun has striven hard for a monopoly on
Imperial calendar production by bribing the requisite officials. In a later
scene, in a ceremony honoring Ishun's completion of the calendars,
Ishun sits side by side with his arch-competitor, Isan. Their placement
in the shot allows Mizoguchi to display visually their parallel characters.
For Mizoguchi, Ishun's evil is one intrinsic to his class rather than a
personal psychic configuration.

One of Mizoguchi's central concerns is to show that the new prosperity
accruing to the merchants has not brought either well-being or human
rights to the community. An employee at the scroll establishment asks

At the center of A Story from Chikamatsu is the merchant Ishun, relentless,
hypocritical, clearly representing the class that will dominate the Japan of the
future.

how one can preach morality, defined as loyalty to the master, to starving people. Mizoguchi depicts how feudal relationships have been transported intact into the new capitalist world. It is in this context that the plot of A *Story from Chikamatsu* unravels. Ishun's wife, Osan, a woman of a better family and much younger than he, is pressured by her mother to ask Ishun for a loan of five *kan* of silver which is owed on a mortgage. Ishun has already paid the family for the "purchase" of Osan herself, and she is reluctant. This demand by her family for further money leads ultimately to the deaths of Osan and Mohei at the end of the film.

More importantly, it is the inhumanity of the merchant which causes the disaster. Ishun refuses her the loan and Osan is forced to ask Mohei for help. He, who has been selling his labor for subsistence alone, has no money. To help her, he forges the merchant's signature and is caught. In feudal fashion, Ishun has him locked in the storehouse. The merchants, in their greed, perpetuate all the worst abuses of the dying aristocracy.

When Osan is later compromised, having been found alone in the company of Mohei, the two flee Ishun's house together. Adultery ensues, and at the end of the film the lovers are crucified; unfaithfulness by a wife brought capital punishment in Tokugawa times. Earlier in the film, in a foreshadowing image, Ishun spies a pair of adulterous lovers being led to their crucifixion outside his window. "A samurai must kill illicit lovers himself," he says, "or lose his rank." Ishun is no samurai, despite the fact that he obviously identifies with his social superiors. Ishun, Mizoguchi and Chikamatsu repeatedly remind us, is one of the lowest of the low. He will later beg for the return of Osan, willing to forgive her even this transgression so that he can keep the favor of the Premier and avoid the disgrace caused by her scandal that will result in the ruin of his thriving business.

Money has supplanted value. For Mizoguchi, the merchant mentality has accomplished the destruction of the Japanese cultural heritage, a destruction that began with the decadence of the aristocracy. The Imperial emissaries, members of the dying samurai class, hate Ishun because, although they are more valuable in the system of rank, they are starving and he is rich. "Merchants are making money while nobles like awake at night worrying," one of them says in fury. These samurai must sell or pawn their family heirlooms to Ishun to pay the interest on the loans he has made them, for he is also a usurer charging exorbitant interest rates. That they must beg for his favor is so humiliating to them that they are very happy to accept the bribes of his foreman, Sukeymon, now in the service of a competitor, and take away Ishun's title as "Grand Scroll-Maker."

It is still the seventeenth century and while the merchant's influence is growing, he does not yet enjoy the absolute power he will wield in the twentieth. Mizoguchi hates Ishun for his exploitation of women— as with his wife, Osan, and the servant, Otama, whom he tries to seduce— and for his exploitation of his workers, exemplified by Mohei. But mer-

Sancho the Bailiff: The son confides that he found it incompatible to hold an official position in the society and simultaneously serve the cause of good.

chants like Ishun, he reveals, replaced those whose corruption differed from his only in terms of their capacity for survival.

Japanese directors like Mizoguchi have been well aware of the evils attendant upon the commercialization of Japan. The absence of a tradition of human rights founded on a popular revolution has, however, often stopped them at the point of discovery. There has been little support in the culture at large for any faith in the defeat of the Ishuns. Mizoguchi, therefore, chooses to halt at the moment of revelation, leaving us at the onset of the merchants' ascent to power. He allows his films to pass into aestheticism at the moment when they have reached the ineluctable question: "what then?", a result which, his screenwriter Yoshikata Yoda believes, flows from Mizoguchi's personal and deep commitment to Buddhism.[5]

This withdrawal is also apparent in the last scene of *Sancho the Bailiff* (*Sancho Dayu*, 1954), another of Mizoguchi's great films. After suffering inhuman torture, a son who had been made a slave is reunited with his mother, who had been sold into prostitution. They weep in each other's arms. The son confides that he found it incompatible to hold an official position in the society and simultaneously serve the cause of good. He had miraculously gained the position of Governor of Tango and had tried to abolish the institution of slavery in the very province where he

[5] Conversations with the author in Kyoto, November 1974.

had been a slave throughout his childhood and young manhood. Yet, even as he seemed to achieve power, he was faced with the truth that slavery was so entrenched in the culture, so bureaucratically protected, as to place it beyond the reach of any individual, regardless of his position.

At the final moment Mizoguchi abandons the political theme, moving into an extreme long shot. The camera bypasses son and mother until they are tiny specks on the landscape. It travels high above the barren island where the two have found each other until they are entirely removed from the shot. Only a minuscule fisherman in the left-hand corner of the frame testifies to a human presence in the universe. We are powerless before the "all," and there Mizoguchi leaves us.

No less at an impasse than Mizoguchi concerning a direction for Japan, Shinoda, too, has adapted a Chikamatsu play, one written for the Bunraku Puppet Theater, to express through a petit-bourgeois merchant all the weaknesses that presaged today's Japan. A paper merchant during the Tokugawa period, Jihei, the hero of *Double Suicide* (*Shinju Ten no Amijima*, 1969), is a victim of obsessional love that renders him weak, irrational, and destructive. Married, he has fallen in love with a prostitute named Koharu. By having Jihei's wife, Osan, and his lover, Koharu, played by the same actress, Shima Iwashita, Shinoda points to the absurdity of Jihei's obsession. That a merchant should feel so much passion that he destroys the lives of everyone, including himself, is incongruous and pathetic in Chikamatsu's eyes.

Almost the way a racist play of the American South might cast amused, scornful, condescending eyes on the presumptions of black people toward sensitivity, Chikamatsu patronizingly and sardonically chronicles Jihei the Paper Merchant's "grand passion" for a courtesan. Such is the quality of aristocratic disdain for the values of the bourgeoisie. In the absence of any real rebellion against these values, contemporary intellectuals like Shinoda find satisfaction in rendering anew and revitalized Chikamatsu's horror of the merchant-besotted new culture.

Unable to ransom Koharu from the house of prostitution to which she has been indentured and unable to face his wife, who is all-dutiful and obedient to the norms of a woman of her time, Jihei loses all control. He wrecks his paper shop in childish frustration after spending days in bed, inert and impotent. He stands by helplessly as his wife is humiliated and carried off by her father in shame.

At the end, when he and Koharu choose double suicide as their only means of union, Jihei must be aided by *kuroko*, the puppeteers of the Bunraku Theater, whom Shinoda makes omnipresent. Partly they are there because it is a merchant who is attempting a heroic end; as a merchant, and unlike, of course, the samurai class, he is forbidden by law from dying by the sword. The *kuroko* must nail up the scaffolding and slip the noose around Jihei's neck, so incapable is he made, even at this last moment, of acting decisively as a man.

Throughout, the merchant is seen as a figure of contempt. Jihei's brother, a flour merchant, must disguise himself as a samurai before he can gain entrance to the house of prostitution to meet Koharu. Jihei's own merchant status is compounded by poverty, as a richer merchant named Tahei, a rival for Koharu, is quick to point out. "There's nothing money can't buy," shouts Tahei, "money's everything." Jihei, he sneers, is "like his own torn paper." Tahei, in his arrogance, even scorns the would-be samurai, asserting the power of wealth which the merchant class felt entitled them to the privileges of the upper class (and which the Meiji Restoration would ultimately grant them): "Samurai or merchant, what's the difference?" He threatens to possess both the samurai (Jihei's disguised brother) and Koharu: "Any sword will break before my money." Jihei himself escapes the full force of Chikamatsu's hatred only because of his weakness, the author preferring that the merchant continue as a pathetic figure.

If the satire is obvious, the vulgarity and energy combined in these men symbolic of Japan's future express both Chikamatsu's and Shinoda's outrage. Directors like Shinoda, standing before the organized and indefatigable power of this class, have felt able to choose only between nihilism—a sense of hopelessness before the ethical bankruptcy these merchants have engendered—and an aestheticism that was still credible during the fifties, when Mizoguchi made his best films, but which seems obsolete in the late sixties and seventies.

Reflecting the discontent with the changes wrought by the Meiji Restoration, the anti-merchant theme runs as a leitmotif through the history of the Japanese film. In Shiro Toyoda's *Wild Geese*, sometimes called *The Mistress* (*Gan*, 1953), a young girl has been forced to become the mistress of a moneylender so that she can support her old father, a common enough theme. But she falls in love with a student. He, personifying Japan's future, has an opportunity, upon passing his exams, to go to Germany as a doctor's assistant. A foreign education means more to him than anything else, as it did for so many during the Meiji period.

Toyoda moves easily into allegory. Japan sacrifices her identity, seduced by the power of an alien Western science and technology. The young woman stands in the doorway of the house rented for her by the merchant usurer, looking with longing after the student, a future "merchant" of a different kind, as he passes with a friend. "Her world's different," they conclude. The future leaders of Meiji Japan are ruthless and selfish. In their drive for success they are unmindful of those less fit for survival in the new society, and they pay no heed to the devastation of Japan's sense of self which their frenetic foreshortening of the process of industrialization will wreak upon their land. The woman, representing the "old" Japan, feudal and dependent, can only look passively after them as they make the choice of entering the race for industrial strength and, ultimately, global hegemony.

The most brilliant of Japanese films in defiance of the ethos that led to merchant-dominated Japan is Kurosawa's *Yojimbo* (1960). The time is 1860 and the merchants are no longer willing to tolerate feudal laws

Wild Geese: Japan sacrifices her identity, seduced by the power of an alien Western science and technology.

that decree how much they can spend on a wedding, a funeral, or, for that matter, the umbrella they may carry. A homeless *ronin* (Toshiro Mifune), now in the full ripeness of middle age, wanders into a town looking for someone to whom to sell his services as a bodyguard (*yojimbo*) in exchange for his next meal. He personifies the fate of samurai caught in a transitional era when feudal relations are decaying but the crass merchant order has not yet come fully into its own. He is also a forerunner of the contemporary *yakuza* (gangsters) hired today by big corporations to do their bidding by force.

In this miniature metropolis two factions of incipient merchants have created a reign of terror in their competition for the silk market. The town itself has become a microcosm of nascent capitalism. The haste with which everyone struggles to pass into the new age is ridiculed and satirized through the life-and-death battles waged daily; even the local brewer is a silk broker.

In one scene, a dog runs past, gripping a human hand in his mouth, thus initiating the canine imagery which pervades the entire film. Dogs bark intermittently on the sound track. Someone says, "the smell of blood brings the hungry dogs," indicating the *ronin* who is so desperate that he will sell himself to anyone, no matter their purpose or how they behave. "Not even a dog fight," someone else says during a rare peaceful moment. "Lucky dog," Ushi-Tora, one of the belligerents,

Yojimbo: Kurosawa expresses the hopelessness of all the intellectuals of Japan who have watched their country pass into its modern technological stage guided by nothing but the pursuit of profit.

calls an enemy who has eluded him. It is the dog-eat-dog world soon to be imposed upon Japan by these vicious and amoral, albeit endlessly energetic and exasperatingly inventive, merchants.

Ushi-Tora has had a government inspector killed so that his successor would leave the town quickly out of fear, without examining Ushi-Tora's lack of legal adherence to the Tokugawa rules of trade. Murder is the means of these merchants, economic control their end. Guided only by an ethic of relentless cutthroat competition in which any perfidy is permissible if it leads to success, they believe the world will be theirs. The coffin maker cares only about the rate at which he uses his materials, as he, too, profits from the internecine warfare between the two merchant groups struggling for the silk monopoly. Kurosawa passes judgment on the morality of them all; the coffin maker becomes distressed only when the fighting becomes so extensive—with bodies multiplying geometrically— that the rival merchants, as with rival merchant nations at war, no longer bother with coffins.

Yojimbo reflects the upheaval experienced by all strata of the society at the moment when Japan passed from a feudal to a capitalist social order. In the first sequence, a peasant's son leaves home to seek adventure and money in the town. "Who wants a long life eating mush?" he asks. The temptation to join the fray is very great indeed. "Everybody's after easy money," laments the boy's father, speaking for Kurosawa. Later, caught in the life-and-death competitive struggle between the two warring factions of merchants, this peasant boy screams for his mother. The *ronin* spares his life. He is, after all, only an innocent who has been seduced by the promise of luxury offered in the Japan of 1860 solely to the merchants. The film allows him to survive because he is not of the merchant class. "A long life eating mush is best," Mifune tells him. He runs home, his adventure a presage of the future when Japanese farmers would (as they had begun to by 1700) abandon the countryside in droves to seek survival in the swelling cities.

The *yojimbo* feels no qualms in choosing to fight for one faction or another, as both sides represent the same aspirations, morality, and cause. With the loss of his own feudal master, he has been deprived as well of his personal identity and must improvise a name. He chooses "Kuwabatake Sanjuro" (Mulberry Field) on the basis of the local terrain, for all is now ludicrous and without moral sense. Neither feudal honor nor rational purpose remains. "Better if all these men were dead," Kuwabatake Sanjuro declares.

The *ronin*'s contempt for the traders is both absurd and justified, for the feudal world of samurai, if fixed in its values, was no less harsh. Kurosawa is also well aware of the nihilism and futility of such an "answer." It is the merchants who are in ascendance. They cannot be wiped out; it is too late. The *ronin* is a member of a dying class whose nobility is anachronistic because he cannot save Japan. He can save one woman, who has been kidnapped and made the concubine of one of the merchant traders, but he cannot save the society from its inevitable fate. He can kill every one in the town by the end of the movie (he leaves alive only the innkeeper who has been kind to him, the coffin maker, and one madman). But we know that the massacre is a wish-fulfilling fantasy and that with the Meiji Restoration only eight years off, merchants will re-emerge from behind every post and doorway.

"Now it will be quiet in this town," says the *ronin*, but the calm is no more permanent than his own survival. With the skill of centuries of warrior power expressed in his person, none of the upstart merchants could compete with his sword. But Ushi-Tora's younger brother, Nosuke (Tatsuya Nakadai), has bought a gun on his travels. The Dutch after all, have had their outpost near Nagasaki. Commodore Perry has come and gone. The gun is a symbol of the passing of the warrior culture, of Kuwabatake Sanjuro's incipient obsolescence. Cut down by the *ronin*'s sword, Nosuke asks to die with his gun in his hand. The samurai proffers it to him, accepting Nosuke's word that the weapon is now empty (which it is not). Because the film is a fantasy, a wish-fulfillment of the defeat of technology-ridden, pollution-drenched Japan, Nosuke dies before he can fire the final shot and kill the *ronin*.

Yojimbo is one of Kurosawa's darkest films. It does not, as some of Kurosawa's most voracious Japanese critics contend, substitute the "superman samurai" for a solution of the problems of contemporary Japan. Kurosawa, rather, expresses the hopelessness of all the intellectuals of Japan who have watched their country pass into its modern technological stage guided by nothing but the pursuit of profit, even as feudal relationships persist. And it is the descendants of the merchants of *Yojimbo,* now directors of multinational corporations, who have so ravaged the countryside that, as in the case of the town after the *ronin* departs, little of value remains.

The Japanese Woman

Onna-hideri wa nai.
(There is never a dearth of women.)
Japanese proverb.

Despite the anguish of artists and intellectuals from Chikamatsu's time to our own, the merchants continue ensconced smugly in the seats of power in Japan. Women, their polar opposite in social station and access to decision-making, are virtually as fully oppressed as they have been since the victory of the warrior culture in the Kamakura period of the twelfth century. They continue as unrecognized and under-valued servants of Japan's prosperity. In 1972 women comprised 57.5 percent of all factory workers, yet their average wage was 48.2 percent of that of the average man, and frequently they faced forced retirement at the age of thirty or younger.[1] In 1973 a Tokyo High Court judge approved Nissan Motors' policy of retiring women at the age of fifty, maintaining that the physical functioning of a fifty-five-year-old woman equals that of a man of seventy.[2]

The oppression of the Japanese woman began with the creation of the Emperor system, in the fourth and fifth centuries A.D., and its imposition of a patriarchal society on Japan. A Chinese history of the Wei dynasty reveals a second-century woman ruler named Himiko (about whom Shinoda made his film). She was succeeded by a man, under whose power the country fell into disarray. Her adopted daughter, Toyo, succeeded him, but she, too, was followed by a man. The *Kojiki*, the oldest history of Japan, written several centuries later, records the rule of Japan at its beginnings by a female: Amaterasu, the sun goddess. It was she who was commanded by her supernatural parents to rule the islands of Japan.

The paradox of the Heian period (782–1167) lay in the fact that, while the culture had long succeeded in putting woman in her place, women authors, the only writers working in the vernacular (cultured men wrote in Chinese), produced lasting works. During the Heian period,

---

[1] Halliday, *Japanese Capitalism*, p. 224.
[2] Yoko Akiyama, "The Hidden Sun: Women in Japan," *International Socialist Review*, March 1974, p. 24.

as well, women could inherit and own property, a right lost during the reign of the Tokugawas; Heian law even prevented a husband from beating his wife. But Lady Murasaki's *Tale of Genji* still tells us more of the oppression than the liberation of women, notwithstanding the fact that Heian women might be authors. By Murasaki's time, Amaterasu had long become part of the national mythology and was no longer experienced as a woman. Himiko had never been heard of.[3] Other influences tempered the discontent of Murasaki and women like herself, aristocrats of the lower orders who chronicled the court life of their time. Buddhism encouraged them to acquiesce in their own oppression, to display a calm acceptance of the inevitable. It reminded them that there were no women in Buddha's Western Paradise. In order to enter it, they would first have to be reborn as men. The "five drawbacks" of being a woman meant that she could not, in her future incarnations, become Brahma, Indra, Yama, a Wheel-turning Monarch, or a Buddha. Shinto demanded of women loyalty and filial piety; Confucianism, which would become the true state religion upon the ascendance of the Tokugawas in the seventeenth century, expected of them the "three obediences": toward father, husband, and son.

And because she was a woman, even if the author of the greatest work of literature of her epoch, Lady Murasaki was unable to escape profound feelings of contempt for herself from the moment she set foot in society. Thus does she confide in her diary: "Although an unimportant person I had passed my life without feeling any sort of contempt for myself until I went to Court—since then, alas! I have experienced all the bitterness of it."[4]

Alongside her elder brother (and proving far the better scholar) Murasaki had studied Chinese, a subject forbidden to women. Later, at court, she had to pretend not to be able to read Chinese characters, although she was enlisted in secret to teach the Empress parts of Chu-i's collected works. In *Genji* she would write: "Sometimes indeed a woman should even pretend to know less than she knows, or say only a part of what she would like to say."[5] Gossips labelled her "proud" and Murasaki was stung by contemptuous references to her as "the Japanese Chronicle Lady."

Given how deep and pervasive is the feudal spirit retained in Japan, it is not surprising that women have internalized the degrading cultural assessment of their value. For many centuries the majority of Japanese women have accepted an estimate of their worth invented and enforced by those who profit from this total lack of any adequate sense of themselves in women. Murasaki's *Tale of Genji* functioned as escape literature for the frustrated aristocratic women of her time. This is revealed by the woman who wrote anonymously a work which has come to be known as *The*

---

[3] Letter to the author from Masahiro Shinoda, December 23, 1974.

[4] "The Diary of Murasaki Shikibu," *Diaries of Court Ladies of Old Japan* (Tokyo: Kenkyusha, 1961), p. 111.

[5] *The Tale of Genji* (Boston and New York: Houghton Mifflin Co., 1935), 1:43.

Sarashina Diary. It was composed in the eleventh century and the author has come down to us only as an unnamed daughter of one of the powerful Fujiwaras:

> The height of my aspirations was that a man of noble birth, perfect in both looks and manners, someone like Shining Genji in the Tale, would visit me just once a year in the mountain village where he would have hidden me like Lady Ukifune. There I should live my lonely existence, gazing at the blossoms and the Autumn leaves and the moon and the snow, and wait for an occasional splendid letter from him. This was all I wanted; and in time I came to believe that it would actually happen.[6]

Later in her life, when experience rendered her more sanguine about herself, she refers in this diary to her husband as "the man I depended upon" and, more tellingly, as "the sorrow of the World," a most revealing euphemism.

Throughout the centuries of warrior rule, from the end of the twelfth century through 1868, women were instructed according to the *Onna daigaku,* a book of learning by which samurai girls learned of their place in the world. "Approach your husband as you would heaven itself," they read, "for it is certain that, if you offend him, heaven's punishment will be yours." "Let her never even dream of jealousy," intoned this catechism; "should she show emotion over her husband's dissoluteness, she will only make herself intolerable in his eyes." Women were taught to isolate themselves from men, and that part of the lack of value in women lay in particular in the fact that they suffered from the defects of disobedience, anger, speaking ill of others, jealousy, and ignorance. If it would permit father, husband, or son better to serve their feudal master, women were instructed and expected to sacrifice their lives. It is no wonder, then, that the Japanese cinema, as part of its examination of social life in Japan, should have embarked upon so ardent a rebellion against this reduction of women to a slave caste.

Rebellions among women against such a definition of themselves did, of course, occur. The *Tsutsumi Chunagon Monogatari* of the twelfth century contains a picture of an angry young woman who finds that she has enemies not only in the patriarchy, but also among her own sex; her experience must have echoed that of many:

> She thought that people's artificial manners were hateful and refused to pluck her eyebrows. She declared that teeth-blacking[7] was even more harmful and dirty . . . and her smile displayed astonishingly white teeth . . . people were scared and ill at ease before her and shunned her [and another lady of the household said of her]: "Even her eyebrows look like caterpillars and her teeth as naked as a skinned animal. . . ."[8]

---

[6] *As I Crossed a Bridge of Dreams: Recollections of a Woman in Eleventh-Century Japan,* trans. Ivan Morris (New York: Harper Colophon Books, 1971), pp. 71–72.

[7] Expected of married women.

[8] Cited in Louis Frédéric, *Daily Life in Japan at the Time of the Samurai, 1185–1603* (London: George Allen & Unwin, 1972), p. 84.

The Meiji Restoration brought only superficial changes in the status of Japanese women. In the Civil Code of 1898 a husband, but not a wife, might use adultery as grounds for divorce. That the wife could no longer immediately be put to death, as were Mizoguchi's Osan and Imai's Tane in *Night Drum* (*Yoru no Tsuzumi*, 1958), constituted, of course, an enormous change. But the wife divorced on grounds of adultery in Meiji Japan was still forbidden legally from marrying her partner in adultery.

Women in Meiji Japan found it necessary to form a Ladies' Society for Foreign Hair Styles to agitate against the traditional haircomb, which made use of so many pins and ornaments that it caused chronic dizziness and a rush of blood to the head. And Meiji was an era, as well, in which a superstition flourished that the newly arrived telegraph wires were coated with the blood of unmarried women. It awaited the post–World War II American Occupation for women to be granted the right to vote, and to coeducation with men, and thereby the legal right to an equal education. For "separate but equal" had worked no better in Japan than in the American South in justifying segregation, in this instance, of the sexes. The Occupation also brought women in Japan the right to a claim on their husband's property. But perhaps because these social advances were imposed by a conquering power with the increasingly obvious motive of restoring Japan's former ruling hierarchy, the attitude towards women went largely unchanged, as it might not have done had these transformations been the result of indigenous social upheaval.

Until 1945 the Japanese woman thus bore a relation to the Japanese man as slave to master. The pattern was parallel in striking ways to the patriarchy of the American South. The man had the right to keep the children, should he choose to send his wife back to her family for whatever reason. He could at whim decline to enter her name in the family registry (an important theme in Imamura's *Intentions of Murder—Akai Satsui*, 1964) or to delay its entry, thus depriving her of any of the rights accorded a member of the family—the only rights, in fact, which any Japanese could claim. Like the American slave, she was treated as well as the economic situation of her master allowed. That a woman in an aristocratic household might be as well-dressed, fed, or housed as the rich in any Western country never meant she had transcended her caste.

Women in Japan today, even when they are seemingly treated as equals, are done so with noblesse oblige—and unmistakable traces of condescension, discomfort, and fear. The issue of women's rights is approached with such caution by so many Japanese, men and women alike, because it is implicitly recognized that, far from being frivolous or susceptible to marginal reform, it requires radical change in the very structure of the state. Were women to assume positions of responsibility and control in government, corporate offices, factories, or communications, the patriarchal system, which derives its authority from the Emperor himself, would be undone. In a society faced for the first time since the War with mass unemployment, the male merchants who rule are unable to welcome women as equals or to countenance their participation in the running of the society.

Japan's rulers are confronted by both economic and psychological challenge because, now as before, the rigid society they command requires relationships in which all know their place. It accords status and role on the basis of who is above and who below. The certitude and stability of the established order flows from defining who one is by his place in the hierarchy. As a male-dominated hierarchy, it would certainly be shaken by the appearance of large numbers of women in positions of power, for women have only occasionally been decision-makers or rulers in the culture. The Japanese male seems not only unaccustomed to but uncomfortable in a role subservient to a woman. In addition, the inadequately recompensed labor of women has been essential in building Japan's present prosperity. Despite the appearance of great wealth in Japan, there has not been enough to go around.

Lamenting the contemptuous attitude and low evaluation assigned by Japanese men to their relationships with women, Chie Nakane, the only woman full professor at Tokyo University, cites the eighteenth-century story of *The Forty-seven Ronin* as continuing to express and define sexual politics in Japan.[9] *The Forty-seven Ronin*, a great national favorite which has been adapted in several motion pictures, concerns forty-seven samurai left masterless *ronin* by an unjust incident which forced their master, Lord Asano, to commit *seppuku* in disgrace. Because Asano had not given him the appropriate bribes, Lord Kira retaliated by failing to instruct Asano in the etiquette necessary to receive an Imperial ambassador. In anger, the severely provoked Asano later drew his sword against Kira in the castle itself, a forbidden place. For this act, he was ordered to kill himself. Led by Asano's chief retainer, Kuranosuke Oishi, the forty-seven wait, carefully disguising their intention by leading dissipated lives, entering trades, and seeming to disperse. When the opportunity arises, they attack and behead Lord Kira, avenging their dead master at last.

The plans and enactment of the revenge require the men to share their deepest feelings and commitments, renouncing, like Christ, all personal and family ties. No relationship with a woman could approximate the spiritual communion these men discover together as they act in concert in a common cause. United in a struggle they know will lead to their deaths, the forty-seven find solace and comfort in being pledged together to the same noble end.

In Hiroshi Inagaki's film version of the story of the forty-seven *ronin*, *Chushingura* (1962), Asano's chamberlain, Kuranosuke Oishi, is shown leaving his wife and children to frequent the Yoshiwara, the prostitute quarter. He assumes the life of a philanderer and drunkard to allay suspicion and deflect attention from his plan for revenge, particularly since Kira's allies expect just such retaliation from Asano's men. As in the original story, Oishi divorces his wife, mercilessly sending her home with

[9] *Japanese Society* (Berkeley and Los Angeles: University of California Press, 1970), p. 71n.

Chushingura (The Forty-seven Ronin): In anger, Asano draws his sword against
Kira in the castle itself, a forbidden place.

neither explanation nor even an affectionate farewell. Their son, who is
old enough to participate in the coming attack on Lord Kira, declares to
his father in feudal pride: "As your wife, she must have understood."

Inagaki does not even, as in some versions of the original, allow the
wife her moment of attack upon Oishi's cruelty when she begs for
mercy, as if even this meager protest might momentarily distract the
audience from its proper admiration of the samurai hero. The true
samurai wife must "understand"—and in silence. And any emotional en-
tanglements the forty-seven have must be severed because their first and
only attachment will be to their swords. In Inagaki's flamboyant spectacle,
flawed by visual excess, after the killing of Kira the forty-seven march
triumphantly through the town, tired, wearing their dirty, bloodstained
clothes, but supremely dignified. Nakane seems quite accurate in her
suggestion that the sexual and emotional energy of the Japanese man is
epitomized in the choice of feudal brotherhood over heterosexual love,
the theme which informs and suffuses *Chushingura*.

In Kenji Mizoguchi's two-part version of the story, *The Loyal Forty-
seven Ronin of the Genroku Era* (*Genroku Chushingura*, I, 1941; II, 1942),
he retains the original story, but the traditionally beloved elements interest
him least. The two films proceed routinely and without much invention as
the director goes through the motions of pleasing the wartime government,
creating a film which is to exalt the feudal past. Only at the end of

Part II, when the theme of the relationship between men and women is introduced by the director, immediately altering the spirit of the original, is Mizoguchi's heart in the project.

Unlike Inagaki, who does not include this aspect of the story at all, Mizoguchi focuses on the fifty days following the death of Lord Kira, but preceding the mass *seppuku*. Men have been sending their sons to the house where Oishi and his *ronin* are quartered, so they may learn how to be samurai, an undertaking which Mizoguchi himself disdains, as he does all feudal values and codes.

One day a woman appears. She had been engaged to one of the forty-seven, and her father had spent all his money in arranging the details of the marriage. He now feels betrayed by the *ronin*'s decision to join the expedition. The camera dollies one hundred and eighty degrees around the woman for the entire duration of her explanation to Oishi of her predicament, adding an emotional intensity lacking in the film before now. The woman seeks to discover what her former fiancé really feels, and whether he has chosen this course because he simply did not love her enough. Inagaki's woman, the ideal of her time, suffering indignity

Chushingura: The forty-seven march triumphantly through the town, tired, wearing their dirty, bloodstained clothes, but supremely dignified.

in silence, would have breached all etiquette had she uttered the unspeakable. But Mizoguchi, depicting the feudal period from an anti-feudal point of view, creates a young woman bold enough to assert her right to an explanation. The film is sympathetic toward her desire not to suffer in doubt for the rest of her life. The camera keeps moving, signalling that the most sincere of human feelings are now being revealed without hypocrisy.

Oishi requests that she not see her lover because the young man might weaken at the last moment; he might doubt that he loves honor best, and be unable to accomplish the *seppuku* to which he has been sentenced. The young man is, however, finally permitted to appear. And although he says, pro forma, that he doesn't love her, he reveals that he has retained a small strummer used for the playing of the *koto*, a token of their relationship. He must renounce all feeling for her, or he will not be able to accomplish his final act in honor. But in preserving the token, he has revealed his continuing love. "Tell your father I am still his son-in-law," he concludes.

He turns to go, and the woman is left alone in a room replete with paintings, amidst the empty splendor of a feudal age. Mizoguchi then violates all Japanese expectations of *Chushingura*. The only *"seppuku"* we are permitted to witness is that of this girl, who kills herself to prove her sincerity. The act of ultimate sacrifice, of honor and nobility, belongs to the woman. Further, Mizoguchi grants the suicide of the woman not merely no less value, but even more value than that of the *ronin*. Hers alone is allowed to appear on camera. The film stresses that her family would not have been permanently lost because the *ronin* abandoned her. She could have married another man and the family fortune been rebuilt. In this way, in stark defiance of the implicit ideal of male love, which suffuses the story of the loyal forty-seven *ronin* as it does the entire value system of feudal Japan, Mizoguchi elevates the sacrifice of a woman. The names of the forty-seven are read out as each is called for his final act, but we are not permitted by Mizoguchi to witness these deaths, heroic or otherwise. The sacrifice of this lonely and chastened woman is Mizoguchi's answer to the exaltation of male love for which *Chushingura* is beloved by so many Japanese.

As Nakane argues, the involvement of Japanese men in relationships with each other epitomized in the story of the forty-seven *ronin* has rendered their emotional involvements with women gratuitous. Under official feudalism, men's emotions were expended so completely in devotion to their masters that very little room was left for relations with women. But Nakane's more interesting point regards how fully this samurai mentality still permeates Japanese life. In warrior times it was felt to be demeaning and weak for a man to be in love with his wife, and almost shameful to be seen with her in public. Families appear abundantly in public on weekends in Japan today, but a relationship with a woman seems rarely to be seen by men as the sustaining one of their lives.

Two of the finest directors in the history of Japanese cinema, Yasujiro

The Loyal Forty-seven Ronin of the Genroku Era: Mizoguchi
violates all Japanese expectations of *Chushingura.* The only
seppuku we are permitted to witness is that of this girl, who
kills herself to prove her sincerity.

Ozu and Akira Kurosawa, said to be at opposite political poles, ultimately
share an estimation of women as *bushido,* the samurai code, would have
us see them. Ozu's attitude is expressed typically in *Tokyo Story (Tokyo
Monogatari,* 1953), perhaps his finest work.

The plot concerns an old woman and her husband, who journey to
Tokyo from the countryside to visit their grown children. The old lady,
shrewd and perceptive, is a living example of all that is beautiful and
becoming in the manner and behavior of the past. In her person, woman
at her most splendid and feudal values at their apogee are conjoined.
These have been rendered an anachronism in modern Tokyo, and by the
end of the film she must die. Her male children are indeed as selfish and
inconsiderate as her daughter, Shige, but Ozu focuses his disapproval
most particularly on Shige, a beautician as vulgar and obsequious as her
trade connotes. It is through the women of the film that Ozu unfolds his
moral sense, and it is in the measure of their definition of what it means
to be a woman that he values them.

In Tokyo the old lady actually encounters three women—her daughter, Shige, who is cold and domineering; the wife of her doctor son, Koichi; and another daughter-in-law, Noriko, who is the widow of a son who died in the Second World War. Koichi's wife is subservient in the presence of her husband's selfishness toward his parents. Alternately tyrannized by husband and two bratty sons (the third generations in Ozu films are invariably male and, in the postwar films, self-centered little animals), she is a faceless, non-individualized human being. The first shot of her occurs as she sweeps the house in all-suffering silence, preparing for the arrival of the old couple. If she is not explicitly cruel to them, neither is she particularly kind. Ozu does not blame her for the subservience that makes her attend to her husband's wishes, but neither does one believe that she could be better or different than she is. The strains of family life in Tokyo have dehumanized her, as they have everyone. She has been unable to retain any of the old *kokutai*, and, consequently, Ozu has no particular interest in her.

The old lady represents all that was of value in the Japan of the past. As such, she is not so much expressive of her sex, being far beyond the age of sexuality, as she is a presence who reminds Ozu and us of what has been lost. The ideal *woman* in the film is the widowed Noriko (Setsuko Hara): gentle, yielding, always correct and considerate, always thinking first of the feelings and comfort of others.

Noriko is poor, and must work as a typist. But although in this new, deformed Japan such a woman must support herself, Noriko never complains, nor does she allow the world to perceive her suffering. Through her, Ozu expresses how the ideal woman behaves, even in these troubled and chaotic times. The director's affection for Noriko is apparent. It records his nostalgia for the passing of an ideal that includes a passive acceptance of one's station and fate, an ideal that is becoming ever more difficult to sustain in a corrupt, industrialized Japan which is out of touch with both nature and human feeling. In *Tokyo Story* the dignity of forbearance is allied to the nobility of doing one's duty in accord with obligation, both quintessentially feudal values.

As soon as the old lady arrives in Tokyo, Shige tells her she has grown even heavier, and dredges up a childhood tale of how the mother, visiting at her school, was so fat that she broke a chair, to Shige's great embarrassment. In contrast, Noriko tells her that she "hasn't changed." Shige, counting every penny, decides that her parents needn't see a show and can do without expensive cakes. She offers the old lady her most worn *geta* (wooden sandals) with which to go to the baths. Koichi's wife cannot take them on their day tour of Tokyo because the house would be left unattended; Shige is, of course, too busy. It is Noriko, she who can least afford to lose a day's pay, who shows them the town by taking the day off from her job.

The tour of Tokyo is meaningless because the concrete and glass environment, with chimneys spewing poisonous gases over all, cannot provide any aesthetic pleasure. The bus bounces the old couple up and down, their eyes unnaturally forced from left to right. In such a world they can register nothing of beauty or of merit. For Ozu, there is nothing of value to see. Yet all is not lost, because Noriko contains within herself the harmony that has been trampled in the society at large.

Ozu cuts from the bus tour to a woman, whom we have not yet seen, folding laundry. She is a person totally insignificant to the action, and the sudden focus on her takes us by surprise. Ozu has introduced this discordant moment to contrast the absurd guided tour of Tokyo with the harmonies about to be established in Noriko's humble room where she will offer her parents-in-law rest and dinner. The woman quietly folding laundry provides a necessary pause. She is in the film as well because she will be asked by Noriko for the loan of sake to entertain her guests.

The extreme poverty of Noriko is a further measure of the incompatibility of so fine a person with the postwar confusion of Japan in the 1950s. She must even borrow the cups out of which the old couple drink their sake. Noriko is like the Japanese woman of old who accommodated herself silently to her lot in life, and her graciousness is directly associated with her reverence for the past. She has refused to remarry (as no well-bred samurai woman would ever do) and a photograph of her dead husband is still prominently displayed. She and the old woman, kindred spirits, share the feeling that he is "alive somewhere."

This common emotion expresses a sense of the continuity between the living and the dead shared by all sentient Japanese but vulgarized in English by the expression "ancestor worship." It is possible, in *Tokyo Story*, only for Noriko and her mother-in-law. They naturally adjust their emotions to an unspoken hierarchy of relationships that once represented the Japanese spirit at its best, and which includes Noriko's dead husband. The only meal eaten in harmony in this film, which contains so much talk of food, is in Noriko's room. The peace of the moment, as Noriko sits fanning the old people, is broken, however, by the sound of a train whistle; such respite can be only furtive and transitory. The world of such good people, like the "good people" referred to in Lady Murasaki's *Tale of Genji*, has ceased to exist and can be re-created only temporarily and in such unlikely quarters as Noriko's shabby flat.

In contrast is the inn at Atami, a hot springs town, where Shige sends her parents to get rid of them for a few days. Noisy and uncongenial, the place expresses Shige herself. While Mah-Jongg games last into the early hours of the morning, the tiles rattling across the table, the old couple lie awake in their beds, unable to sleep. The next day they flee— back to Tokyo—having been unable to find a place for themselves anywhere in the contemporary world, a presage of the old lady's death at the end of the film. "Greeting" them, Shige abandons even the facade of politeness. "Why are you home so soon?" she demands querulously. Ashamed of her parents, she goes so far as to tell a customer that they are "friends from the country." Ozu finds that Japan's women have been rendered coarse and cruel, vulgarized by their entrance into the

Tokyo Story: Both recognize, each agrees, that "it's not like the old days."

world of commerce. Even Shige's husband is appalled by her lack of civility, let alone generosity, toward her parents.

The night of this return finds the old lady with no place to stay. She is beholden once more to Noriko, and the two women spend the night together. Her mother-in-law advises Noriko to remarry, well aware that the ideal Noriko represents, while infinitely superior and desirable, can no longer be sustained in the dissolute and decadent Japan of today. Pitying Noriko's loneliness, the old lady, in direct contradiction to her own moral sense, urges her quite strongly to marry again.

It is "a treat to sleep on my dead son's bed," observes the old woman, as Ozu in this way subtly suggests that it would be best and most in keeping with the purity of things for Noriko to remain a widow. But with the breakup of the family and the ensuing selfishness of a world inherited by the Shiges, it is more practical, and ultimately kinder, that Noriko submit to expediency. We somehow doubt, however, whether she will ever be able to bring herself to so impure a choice.

Noriko massages the old lady's neck as they share this evening of communion. Both recognize, each agrees, that "it's not like the old days." "I'm happy. I like it this way," says Noriko. It is both the correct thing for her to say and the truth. All the older woman can reply in tribute is "you're so nice," and, as she leaves the next morning, "thank you very much." In a culture where feelings cannot be encompassed by something as impure as language, the moment must contain enough of harmony and fulfillment to say it all.

Scarcely having left Tokyo, the old lady takes ill and her death follows shortly. Again Ozu uses the responses of the children, particularly of the women, to express his own sense of how human dignity may best be sustained. Shige is full of platitudes: "Isn't life too short? . . . she died peacefully, without suffering and full of years." For all her financial ability, the modern independent woman, whose very soul has been commercialized, has lost the power to feel and, instead, replaces emotion with hollow words. A short moment later Shige, her mercenary sensibility ascendant, will request the old lady's grey sash and linen kimono as "keepsakes."

At this point begins the most significant conversation in the film. It is between Noriko and the old woman's youngest daughter, Kyoko, who has not figured very much in the action before now because she remained at home when her parents went to Tokyo. Appalled by Shige's behavior, Kyoko speaks out in anger, calling all the others "selfish," as indeed they are. Yet Ozu and Noriko correct her. "At your age I thought so, too," says Noriko. Women of grace, all people of quality and sensibility, adjust to inevitabilities without childish rebellion. Shige, says Noriko, "meant no harm . . . people have to look after their own lives."

The younger woman persists, hoping that life, not only for women, but for everyone, can be made better than it is. "I won't be like that," she bursts out. She is arguing, in a most un-Ozu-like way, that we can have control over what we become and that we can be better than those before us. But Ozu, through Noriko, considers this an illusion. "I may become like that—in spite of myself," says Noriko. She has tried so hard to live rightly precisely because she recognizes that there will be times when she cannot choose what she will be, one of Ozu's profoundest lessons.

"Isn't life disappointing?" concludes Kyoko, having learned enough from Noriko to be able to speak for Ozu. "Yes, it is," answers Noriko, and she smiles, a smile that expresses something no less than the peace that passeth understanding. The Japanese woman, for Ozu, must be ever conscious of her own deficiencies. She must not fill herself with the pride of being either different or successful. "I'm not as nice as she thought I was," Noriko tells the old man after he discloses to her that the old lady had said she "never saw a nicer woman than you." "I'm quite selfish," says Noriko, "I'm not always thinking of your son."

Noriko chastises herself because she is not perfect in her Buddhist resignation, because days go by when she does not think of her dead husband at all, and because, discontented with the dreariness of her existence, she cannot always accept her lot in life. "Sometimes I feel I can't go on like this forever," she admits. "My heart seems to be waiting for something." Ozu is too shrewd an observer to suggest that mere acquiescence in things as they are will destroy our dreams of something better. He advocates such acquiescence, nonetheless, because it is best and most graciously approximates the truth about our place in the universe, our role in an eternal order of things over which we have no control. Noriko, who expresses all that is truest and finest in the human response to our condition, is awarded a real keepsake, the old lady's watch. It is a gesture redolent of the continuities so loved by Ozu. Noriko cries, and the old man pays her Ozu's highest tribute: "I'm wishing you a happy future from the bottom of my heart." Our last look at Noriko constitutes another tribute. In a very close shot—rare for this film and for Ozu—as she sits on the train carrying her back to Tokyo, with all that the city-world has come to mean, Noriko looks pensively at the old woman's watch.

In films that critics have praised as the least didactic of all Japanese movies, Ozu is, in fact, stridently prescriptive. He is imperious in conveying how the Japanese woman ought to behave. She neither has potential for ruling society, nor should she try. Nor can women better themselves through education, since their truest self-expression will be realized only in their facing the modern world with as much of the feudal ideal as can be sustained in a disintegrative age. Ozu would never use the term "feudal" in defining himself, yet whenever, in his films, he accepts the right of characters to prefer freedom to the codes of the past, as sometimes happens, he and the film display discomfort. Ozu believes, reluctantly, that we must accommodate the world of Shige, if only because we may ourselves become like her in spite of our knowing better. But his heart is with the many Norikos he creates in an *oeuvre* dedicated, in part, to the ideal of such women.

Kurosawa's Women

Of course, all my women
are rather strange, I agree....
Akira Kurosawa[1]

Ozu is a traditionalist and through his films we perceive the feudal, pre–World War II evaluation of the Japanese woman. But Kurosawa has always respected the act of individual conscience, and from him we would expect a more sympathetic response to the psychic enslavement of the Japanese woman.

Kurosawa has made three films in which women figure significantly: *The Most Beautiful* (*Ichiban Utsukushiku*, 1944), *No Regrets for Our Youth* (*Waga Seishun ni Kuinashi*, 1946), and *Rashomon* (1950). *The Most Beautiful*, made during the war, is a propaganda film concerned with increasing factory output; *Rashomon* offers a stereotyped view of woman as a creature ruled by sensuality, an involuntary victim of her passions. But *No Regrets for Our Youth*, in sharp contrast, is one of the finest examples in the history of the Japanese film of a woman's struggle for personal liberation. It is also the first of Kurosawa's films to suggest that only in renouncing the ego and dedicating oneself to the suffering of others can a person be truly human; this is the only life for which there can be "no regrets." It was to be, as well, the theme of Kurosawa's two greatest films, *Ikiru* (1952) and *Seven Samurai*.

Miss Watanabe, the woman supervisor in *The Most Beautiful* (Yoko Yaguchi, soon to be Mrs. Kurosawa), exhibits the grit and determination that Kurosawa respects in people. She increases the productivity of the other women on the assembly line by setting an example of unrelenting dedication to one's work. In the climactic scene she remains at her machine in an optical factory the entire night, searching for a missing lens. Miss Watanabe does not bow before the governing prejudice that her women can do far less work than men. She argues that, given women's lesser physical strength, the fact that they produce two-thirds of the men's output reflects even greater effort on the part of the women. The production chief has asserted that women can only produce half of what the men turn out, and Miss Watanabe has proven him wrong.

Nonetheless, despite the film's approval of what appears to be feminism

[1] Cited in Donald Richie, *The Films of Akira Kurosawa* (Berkeley and Los Angeles: University of California Press, 1965), p. 40.

on Miss Watanabe's part, there is something unattractive and "unfeminine" about her. Her hair is pulled tightly back and it seems as though Kurosawa is accepting the essentially anti-feminist cliché that the strong woman must also look stern and forboding, as if physical vulnerability or sensuality and determined character are irreconcilable in woman. "When she's angry," someone laughs, "her left shoulder is higher than her right." While the other women can be playful in their moments of recreation, Miss Watanabe is always overly serious.

Miss Watanabe's courage is thus defined and measured solely in terms of the male ideal of *bushido*, the very code which subjugated women for centuries. When her mother falls ill, rather than go to her bedside, Miss Watanabe remains at her post in the factory. As she works, the sound track carries the cry of a child yelling *"okasan"* (mother) outside the building. We know that Miss Watanabe's thoughts are with her own mother; she is not unfeeling, but dedicated—in the warrior tradition, the *Chushingura* sense. Like a samurai, she hides her grief so no one may know of her personal distress. She would never inflict her suffering on others, nor allow herself to be an unnecessary burden.

Spending all night in search of the missing lens, Miss Watanabe sings military songs to keep herself awake: the good *bushi*, the good patriot. Finally, as she prays, Kurosawa cuts to the other women praying as well. The choral sounds of their voices overlap with her image. They are one, united in their effort on behalf of the fatherland—a dedication of which (for the moment) women are as capable as men. Her mother dies, but still Miss Watanabe does not wish to abandon her post. She is the true soldier.

The tribute granted Miss Watanabe at the end of *The Most Beautiful*, however, reminds us that although she may have exhibited the qualities of the *bushi* in these times of stress, she is still a woman, "a sweet and good girl." Tears fill her eyes and we perceive that the strain of the warrior life is not wholly compatible with her nature; it must be forced. She is finally *only* a woman, her character distorted by times which have demanded of her a warrior spirit. The last shot finds her bent over her machine once more, now vulnerable even in her pathetic, willed strength. The dichotomy between men and women is thus implicitly stressed all the while that Miss Watanabe is shown straining to be the good soldier, an unnatural posture for abnormal times. We can infer that, just as Kurosawa implicitly affirms the by no means obvious truth that men are physically stronger than women, so, as soon as the war ends, his Miss Watanabe will revert to a more "feminine" demeanor.

So obviously made on behalf of the war effort, *The Most Beautiful* offers a very limited vision of a woman's emancipation. Miss Watanabe's unhesitating efforts are, after all, for the purpose of producing more and more optical parts without questioning their intended use or for whom they are manufactured. A parallel development in the image of women occurred in the United States. The absence of men from factory production because of mass conscription required recruitment to the assembly lines of large numbers of women. Thus the image of woman as either sex object or housewife was modified in film, and Hollywood admitted Rosalind Russell, Katharine Hepburn, Joan Crawford, and Bette Davis to roles as independent career women. Their roles, however, were often qualified by obligatory marriages at the end and by such unfeminine touches as their wearing garments with padded shoulders and men's suits and ties. Miss Watanabe, too, is made to seem masculine in her appearance and in her cold, somewhat hard determination. Her tears at the end are designed not to much to soften the characterization as to stress how her natural yearning is to be soft, yielding, and passive. In any event, unquestioning service to Japanese imperialism, however dedicated and self-sacrificing, can hardly be a mark of personal liberation for a woman—or for anyone. With this Kurosawa would agree, as may be seen in *No Regrets for Our Youth.*

No Regrets for Our Youth is about a woman named Yukie (Setsuko Hara) in the process of discovering what it means to be human during the troubled times of the 1930s, when moral courage ensured official reprisal. Simultaneously, she is transformed into a mature woman. Yukie is the daughter of a well-known liberal professor, whose characterization is based upon a real-life individual named Yukitoki Takikawa, dismissed from Kyoto University in the early thirties for radical beliefs. Yukie is a middle-class young woman of her time, who expects to marry and assume a traditional life style. She is playful with her father's students, one of

No Regrets for Our Youth: Typically for women of her background, Yukie studies the piano and flower-arranging.

whom will probably become her husband. Typically for women of her background, she studies the piano and flower-arranging. Through Yukie, Kurosawa quite deliberately characterizes the life and expectations of Japanese women before the war.

As the film begins, Japan's descent into militarism and repression is already disturbing the carefree climate of Yukie's world. She objects to the predictions of Noge, one of her father's students, of a Japanese invasion of China, and drowns out his words by playing the piano. Yet, sensing the truth in what he says, she is troubled. Her manner carries intimations of a potential to respond fully and courageously to the historical trauma about to envelop Japan—and her own family. After her father is dismissed from the university because of his progressive ideas, Yukie slowly becomes appalled by the life which so suited Ozu's Noriko. Her parents would have her remain untouched by social upheaval, but such passive indifference becomes inconceivable to Yukie. In one scene she destroys her flower arrangement, to the horror of the other young women whom she has been instructing. A shot of the torn blossoms floating desolately in the basin of water where she has thrown them expresses the irreparable rupture in the life she has known.

Yukie, we learn, has always possessed a sensibility uncharacteristic of the Japanese woman of her time. Kurosawa shows her, as a child, painting airplanes and locomotives and involved with "other mechanical things," unlike other girls—suggesting, quite prophetically, that a non-sexist educational experience will produce a new kind of woman, one equal to men in every way. However, Kurosawa seems to indicate as well that Yukie's distinctiveness is congenital, since we are given no indication of how she came so vehemently to repudiate the expected role of woman from early childhood on. The only clue, and this may indeed suffice for the logic of the characterization, is the attitude of her liberal father, who had always defined freedom as self-sacrifice and responsibility. These ideas belonged to the atmosphere of her upbringing.

In any event, Yukie decides that she must become independent and financially self-sufficient, the first step toward her liberation from the passive norms imposed on women, although by no means the last. She goes to Tokyo and takes a job as a secretary in an import-export company. There she meets once again her father's disciple, Noge, who has been writing clandestine antigovernment articles. The two become lovers. When Noge is arrested and executed, Yukie must serve time in prison because of their association. The focus here, however, is not on Noge, but on Yukie, and it is rare in the cinema of any country that we are permitted to witness a woman experiencing the consequences of political beliefs and social acts. Only the Cuban film Lucia comes to mind as a comparable example of the treatment of history through the lives of women. But Lucia was made after a revolution, unlike No Regrets for Our Youth which, although it was made in the first flush of the reforms of the Occupation, nevertheless was produced in a country where the female norm would remain, in practice, the opposite of Kurosawa's ideal in this film.

For, at the end, Yukie unconditionally renounces her prospects for marriage. She will not, as she is expected to do, assume the role of a sensitive, well-educated Japanese wife. Instead, in her defiant quest "to find what it is to live," she joins Noge's parents, peasants living under the most extreme hardships of rural life. There the children hiss at her and call her a "spy." The rice fields she plants with Noge's mother are destroyed at night and she must begin again. The exhausting life has transformed her from a genteel young woman to an earthy and uninhibited peasant who drinks greedily from the spout of a kettle.

Yukie goes on, accepting as her life purpose "to do something for the women and young people there. The womenfolk are still unhappy and need help." She discovers that this can be achieved only by becoming one of them and living as they live. In the last scene, Yukie returns to the village of Noge's parents after a visit to her own. She accepts a ride from a truckful of peasants and is submerged in this mass of people; we can barely distinguish her face from the others as Kurosawa stays in long middle shot. Yukie chooses to merge her life with theirs, and in this lies her transcendence.

Yukie becomes a liberated woman because, at the historical moment in which she lives, she discovers that it is inconceivable to be at the same time a conscious, morally attuned human being and a woman in the traditional sense. To have continued the highly cultivated life she shared with her parents would have led only to marriage. In this film the confinements of traditional marriage are implicitly conceived by Kurosawa as a denial of the woman's humanity and experience, a repressive waste of the energy and potential talent which he shows as utterly unfulfilled in casual piano-playing, skilled or unskilled, or in flower-arranging.

Yukie rejects the comforts of this life because they prevent her from committing herself in a manner equal to that of the radical Noge. Because she is a *Japanese* woman, Kurosawa knows that she must choose between the selfishness of family insularity and the broader arena of the society itself. To reinforce his uncompromising point, he shows how Yukie's peasant existence results, within conventional terms, in her desexualization. Yukie's appearance changes with her conditions of life. The energy she expends as a farm woman in the hard times of the war years renders traditional views of "femininity" obsolete. To live as a human being in this Japan is to renounce all the previous indices of what it means to be a woman.

In fact, Yukie is at once more beautiful and vital as a bedraggled peasant, hair awry, than she was as a spoiled schoolgirl. The very aesthetic standard regarding "femininity" is called into question by a new social perception, for the image of the woman as painted doll becomes as vapid as it is dead when compared to the vitality of Yukie once she has discovered something for which "to live." If this theme does not quite

No Regrets for Our Youth: Yukie is at once more beautiful
and vital as a bedraggled peasant with her hair awry than she
was as a spoiled schoolgirl.

emerge in the case of Miss Watanabe of *The Most Beautiful*, it is clear
with Yukie. Her presumed defeminization not only expresses her value,
but rejects all previous standards of feminine beauty and demeanor.
It is rather ironic that Setsuko Hara plays Yukie as convincingly as she
did Ozu's Noriko. In *No Regrets for Our Youth* her face expresses the
very potential of the Japanese woman that has been so often, during all
these long centuries, left wasted and latent.

    Rashomon offers Kurosawa's last fully drawn portrait of a woman. The
two Akutagawa stories are set in the era of Lady Murasaki during the
end of the Heian period. These tales, upon which the film is based, are
by now legendary. A notorious bandit named Tajomaru rapes the wife
of a samurai in a forest which is the bandit's hunting ground. The
samurai is killed, or dies, and the bandit and the woman are hauled
to court to testify in the murder trial. On hand to tell the samurai's
side of the story is a medium in touch with the dead man's spirit. A
woodcutter has also witnessed the event, and he tells his version to a

priest as they sit huddled under the Rashomon Gate, a once impressive structure at the southern entrance to Heian-Kyo (Kyoto) and now, by the twelfth century, fallen into disrepair. Heian Japan is represented, not through the world of Murasaki's amiably promiscuous courtiers, but by the poverty and dissolution that have permeated the rest of the society. This misery is symbolized by the Rashomon Gate itself, haunted by beggars, thieves and outcasts of one kind or another, a convenient place for people to dump dead bodies at night.

Four versions of the story are told, none of them endorsed by the film and all differing, sometimes in detail and always in essentials. Each of the three principals claims to have killed the samurai. The woodcutter's version has the bandit Tajomaru killing a cowardly samurai screaming for his life at the last moment in a craven whine, the very antithesis of *bushido* and the samurai way. In none of the versions, including her own, is the woman (Machiko Kyo) granted self-respect, dignity, or spiritual value; the samurai (Masayuki Mori), in his own version, fulfills the demands of the warrior code with grace, and Tajomaru (Toshiro Mifune), in all versions, is vital, energetic, and physically magnificent.

Tajomaru's story is told first. Here the woman, Masago, appears as a victim of the fortuitous. As she passes through the forest on horseback, accompanied by her husband on foot, a wind blows her veil aside. Tajomaru, sleeping under a tree, catches a glimpse of her extraordinarily beautiful face. "I thought I saw an angel," he recounts at court. Attempting to rape her, he discovers that she is a demon as well ("she fought like a cat"). It is the feeling Kurosawa wanted Kyo to convey, as, in an oft-repeated anecdote, we are told how he instructed her to imitate the black leopard in a Martin Johnson jungle picture which the cast viewed during the shooting.[2]

Woman is angel outside and demon within, even as, in the culture at large, we are offered the choice of the "good" woman—the faithful wife—or the "bad" woman—the prostitute or whore from whom alone men derive sexual pleasure. Men may not marry the woman of sexual appetite because only absolute monogamy will assure them of reliable heirs, and because frigid, cowed women can be relied upon to accept their lot, no matter what the vagaries of their husband-mates. In the image of Masago in *Rashomon* Kurosawa implicitly expresses the double standard that continues today to define the lives of Japanese women.

As he raped her, the bandit tells us, Masago involuntarily responded. Wife on the outside, she is whore within, a demon more than a woman after all. The camera executes a three-hundred-and-sixty-degree pan of the sky with sun filtering through, in a technique that would only much later become a cliché of sexual response. The dagger Masago had been holding drops, penetrating the earth in a very short take, during which the camera does not focus on the weapon so that the sexual symbolism

[2] See, for example, Richie, *Films of Akira Kurosawa*, p. 77.

Rashomon: Woman is angel outside and demon within.

will not be overstated. Masago grips Tajomaru tightly and her eyes close. A few moments later she will insist that one of the men must die or she will feel "doubly disgraced." She must "belong" to the stronger. But after Tajomaru kills her husband, he, in his account, has her lose her nerve and run away. Looking back upon the experience with a philosophical eye, Tajomaru concludes, "About that woman—it was her temper that interested me, but she turned out to be just like any other woman." There is no one present to say otherwise.

It may be argued that this is how the woman was seen by a lustful bandit who could not possibly do justice to the character of his victim. All versions agree that the rape occurred. But lest we, doubting Tajomaru, are encouraged to value Masago too highly, Kurosawa follows with her account of the events. She emerges in her own testimony as pathetic. She tells us that after the rape (which she is too modest to describe), she wept before the scornful look of her husband and buried her face in the ground. Unable to bear his scorn, she begged him to kill her. Receiving no response, she killed him instead, fainted, and, upon waking, fled. At the trial she plays on the sympathies of the judge we never see, crying and pleading: "I tried to kill myself. But, I failed. What should a poor helpless woman like me do?" When all else fails, she sinks to the ground. Hearing about this from the woodcutter, a commoner huddled for warmth under the Gate doubts her immediately: "Women lead you on with their tears; they even fool themselves." Cynic though he is, his assessment of Masago's performance is too accurate for us to doubt that at this moment the commoner, as an "Everyman," speaks for the director.

Masago figures least in the version told by her dead husband, as if her existence had never been of much account to him. He tells us that she responded with radiance to the bandit's lovemaking and he had never in all their life together "seen her more beautiful." She begged Tajomaru to take her with him, but first to kill her husband. He refused because the worst man is better in character than the best woman, social class notwithstanding. It is a graphic example of why, in Japan, the liberation of women will necessitate a restructuring of the entire society. The husband, in keeping with the code of honor by which he had always lived in good faith, performs his own *seppuku*.

In the final story, that of the woodcutter, the woman is the most demonic. Laughing hysterically at her predicament, she calls both men fools, attacking their manhood in order to extricate herself from a situation in which she has lost all honor. She has accepted their judgment of her, internalized it, and now flaunts her baseness. Yet the men are reluctant to fight for her, another implication of the sense of true male supremacy which suffuses this film. To provoke the fight, she must spit on Tajomaru. And he, although a bandit and a murderer, is made the better human being by Kurosawa. He is allowed to forgive her; even the woodcutter feels a form of kinship with this ruthless bandit against the woman. "Women cannot help crying, they are naturally weak," says Tajomaru in the woodcutter's story.

In *Rashomon* woman is perceived as castrating female taunting competing males for not being "real men." "A woman can be won only by strength, by the strength of the swords you are wearing," she screeches near the end of the film. And it is with this view of her character that Kurosawa leaves us. He has given no grounds for belief in Masago's own story, the only one in which she does not respond passionately to the bandit. And even in that story, she is a murderess. Her punishment is presented implicitly as a just reward for her having assumed the role of docile wife under blatantly false pretenses.

After *Rashomon*, Kurosawa seemed to have abandoned his interest in the potential of women, as if repelled by Masago, that half-demon of his own creation. His response is parallel to that of the culture itself. Women are rendered powerless and subordinate and hence reduced, like Masago, to manipulation or deceit for influence and survival. Then the image of the feline woman is reified by male perpetrators into a stereotype. It is a classic example of the self-fulfilling prophecy and the prototype of all social victimization, unmediated in the Japanese film by the presence of women directors, with the exception of a few minor directorial efforts by the actress Kinuyo Tanaka. And once, of course, the stereotype is elevated to a symbol in the arts, presented as an image of truth, the impact of this perpetuated myth in turn conditions the view women have of themselves. It is indeed a vicious circle, as yet unbroken in Japan by profound social change.

Kurosawa has made two adaptations from Russian literary works, *The Idiot* (*Hakuchi*, 1951) and *The Lower Depths* (*Donzoko*, 1957). In both, the women fall into one of two summary categories. The sensual woman is portrayed as the castrating bitch and the "good" girl is devoid of any capacity for pleasure. Thus, in his version of Dostoevsky's *The Idiot*, Kurosawa's Nastasya, called Taeko Nasu (and played by Setsuko Hara), the woman whom Mishkin wishes to save, is reduced to the stereotype of the female who destroys men. Her destructiveness is so devastating that it pains Kameda (Mishkin) even to look at her. Further, her frenzied outbursts, which Kurosawa accepts from the Russian original to reinforce his sense of her "badness," are so out of keeping in a Japanese context that she causes embarrassment instead of serving as a suitable object for the hero's compassion.

Kurosawa's equally close adaptation of Gorky's *The Lower Depths* finds the two women who love the thief Sutekichi (Toshiro Mifune) again expressing the two sides of Masago; together they capture Kurosawa's now fixed sense of woman. The landlord's vicious wife, Osugi (Isuzu Yamada) is manipulative and malicious as a woman scorned. Sutekichi prefers Osugi's sister, Okayo (Kyoko Kagawa), who embodies woman as angel, sweetly obliging and therefore weak and unable to survive on her own. "Some day I'll end up like this," she says, observing the coughing old woman dying in pain and freezing under her thin blankets. It is a direct echo of Gorky's Natasha, who laments, "some day I will end up like that—in a basement—forgotten by everybody."

The Lower Depths: By the end of the film Osugi has beaten up her sister many times.

By the end of the film, Osugi has beaten up her sister many times and engineered, as well, Sutekichi's murder of her old, usurious husband. In Gorky's original she says, "I beat her so hard, I cry, myself, out of pity for her." Okayo, in panic, irrationally denounces both Osugi and the innocent Sutekichi: "They killed him [the landlord] and now they're going to kill me." She is too callow to perceive the sincerity of Sutekichi's love. In a hysterical fray, evil triumphs. Okayo disappears, and it isn't known if she is alive or dead. Osugi is in prison, as is Sutekichi. All has come to nought. The knowing whore, Osen, echoing the secret feeling of all oppressed women, exclaims, "I wish every man was banished from the town." Okayo is good and Osugi, evil, but both bring chaos and further disarray to a world already burdened by endemic poverty and disillusionment. Neither woman is worth a man's love.

In his great period films Kurosawa upholds without irony or distance the accepted feudal and samurai view of woman as possession and object. The only important female character in his otherwise brilliant *Seven Samurai* is the peasant girl, Shino, who seduces the youngest of the samurai, the innocent Katsushiro. The irony is that her father, out of fear that the samurai defending the village might rape her, forcibly cuts her hair so the samurai would not realize she is a woman. It is she who is the brazen seducer.

Seven Samurai: The only important female character is the peasant girl Shino, who seduces the youngest of the samurai.

Yet only because he is not yet an adult, not yet a mature samurai, does Katsushiro hesitate even for a moment, at the film's end, before leaving Shino behind. He will join the leader, Kambei, on the further adventures that will lead indubitably to their extinction. A samurai, even a disciple-samurai like Katsushiro, could no more allow love for a woman to be the central emotion of his life than he could become a peasant.

Sanjuro (Tsubaki Sanjuro, 1962), the sequel to *Yojimbo,* introduces a woman who is indeed a match for the *ronin* hero, and one of the rare women in the later Kurosawa films to possess an intellect. But she is merely a peripheral character, and Kurosawa gives her no name. We know her only as Mutsuta's wife. She is also a woman of late middle age, having long passed the time when she could use her sexuality against men.

Kurosawa's last period film, *Red Beard* (*Akahige,* 1965), is a love story between two men: the doctor, Kyojio Niide—Red Beard—(Toshiro Mifune), and his young disciple, Noboru Yasumoto (Yuzo Kayama). As in the deepest of love relationships, one learns from, and is profoundly changed by, the other. Red Beard, in winning Yasumoto over to serve the people with his talents as a doctor, gives him a meaning in life. The spiritual union between these two men is expressed even in the use of the music. The central motif from Brahms properly belongs to the great man, Niide. When Yasumoto begins to imitate him, and when he has learned from him how "to live," the sound track allows him this motif as well. It is a tribute to both, and an expression of intimate harmony between the two men before which the idea of mere sexual congress with a woman pales. Yasumoto marries finally, but it is clear that his new little bride, a shallow creature, cannot offer, even remotely, emotional or moral competition to the great teacher.

With *Red Beard,* women in Kurosawa have become not only unreal and incapable of kindness, but totally bereft of autonomy, whether physical, intellectual, or emotional. It is through men that understanding is reached. Women at their best may only imitate the truths men discover, as when Miss Watanabe had to behave like a *bushi,* a warrior, during the war. It takes men, and in hard times as our own, supermen such as doctor Niide, to teach us how to live.

Like the younger Shinoda and Imamura and so many of Japan's film directors, Kurosawa has been appalled by the lack of direction afflicting Japanese culture. From *Red Beard* on, he turns to basic and simple human virtues as the only response to an irremediable society: kindness towards one another, indulgence of human frailties, dedication to helping people, but now without the hope implicit in an early film like *Ikiru* that society can be changed if we care enough. When Red Beard says "there are no cures, really," he speaks not merely of the state of medicine in late Tokugawa Japan, but of social remedy in Kurosawa's time.

Kurosawa's *oeuvre* embodies the central angst, the defining crisis and experience of Japanese society and culture. As in Oshima, the true war is now being waged within the Japanese psyche. Obsolete feudal responses, however frantically the Japanese cling to them, are no longer effective, yet new values and a correspondingly more humane mode of behavior have not yet come into being. Kurosawa's work is set at moments of transition, when old ways pass before the new has coherently emerged. For the human being confronted by the chaos inherent in the disintegration of a once fixed and secure code of values and set of social responses, the absence of any clear, supportable, or understandable alternative brings a form of hysteria and madness. This is the mood which suffuses *Red Beard* perhaps more despairingly than it did earlier films like *Record of a Living Being* (*Ikimono no Kiroku*, 1955), set more literally amidst the postwar ruins.

In Kurosawa's late work, men and women alike are perceived as victims. Sexuality represents, now more than ever, a distortion of the humane, a point of view which, in *No Regrets for Our Youth*, seemed directly attributable to the frenzy and stress of the wartime setting. Yet, on closer examination, all the settings in Kurosawa are, in their deepest sense, "wartime." For Kurosawa has always accepted the *bushido* dichotomy—the choice between duty and love. "To live" is the central theme of *Ikiru*—which is the Japanese for that phrase. But it is, as well, the motif of *No Regrets for Our Youth* and it expresses in many of Kurosawa's films the necessity to choose between love between man and woman and love of humanity. To act meaningfully obliges one to reject the former. In *Ikiru* the old bureaucrat, Watanabe, had to be freed from a relationship with a young woman before he could begin to build the playground for slum children which became the redeeming act of his life. Only in experiencing the emptiness of seeking love from another individual could he make the choice that rendered his life worth living. And by making the young woman so much younger, and thereby unsuitable, Kurosawa rendered love and work incompatible.

The world Kurosawa has come to love is, finally, one in which women have become superfluous. The Soviet-sponsored *Dersu Uzala* (1975) is, like *Red Beard*, a love story between two men. In an allegorical encounter between the passing of a pure way of life and the "civilized" inauthenticity of the culture to come, the explorer, Arseniev, discovers the Soviet Asian hunter, Dersu Uzala, who still lives within nature. Dersu becomes Arseniev's guide through Siberia, teaching him what remains meaningful in life. Dersu is a human being who has since become lost to us, who died out with the advent of industry, technology, and the urbanization of the planet. Kurosawa must turn to the beginning of the twentieth century, and an exploration of remote Siberia where most of the film was shot, to locate a man capable of authentic communion with his natural environment. Finally, the theme of *Dersu Uzala* becomes the landscape itself, with Kurosawa seeming to have lost interest almost entirely in man and his plight.

Arseniev is quite demonstrably in love with Dersu, and Kurosawa includes several scenes in which the two men physically embrace. Not once do Arseniev and his wife even come close to touching or showing each other the physical affection Arseniev reserves for Dersu. And Arseniev brings Dersu home, at the end of the film, to live with him and his family in his house in Moscow. Dersu's eyes had begun to fail and, if he cannot hunt, he will not be able to survive. His fate intimates the closing of the wilderness that will convert his very existence into a tragic anachronism. Arseniev's wife is there to see to Dersu's comfort, although he does not live long in the city which is so alien to him. His flight back to a wilderness that no longer exists signals his death, as Dersu is murdered by a thief who covets the high-powered rifle that was Arseniev's

Dersu Uzala is, like *Red Beard*, a love story between two men.

final gift to make Dersu's hunting easier. Arseniev's family is rather awkwardly inserted in the film to soften the intensity of his feeling for Dersu, to deny his obsession and affirm his "normality." But the presence of his wife, because she is a genuine alternative, merely reminds us all the more that it is Dersu whom Arseniev cherishes.

Having long lost faith in the possibility of social change, Kurosawa elevates abstract qualities of personal power, evocative of his early samurai. In the script of *Dersu Uzala* these are ascribed to a Chinese character named Chen Pao. "The power of his personality," writes Kurosawa, in obvious admiration, "is evidently the result of his intelligence, self-control, and ability to make others obey his orders." Dersu, too, has the power to command when, as in a fierce blizzard, leadership becomes necessary. Such virtues at once express elitist and profoundly feudal values.

These qualities are not new to Kurosawa's work. They are the attributes exhibited to the highest degree by Kambei, the leader in *Seven Samurai*, by Sanjuro, and by Doctor Niide in *Red Beard*. At an impasse in his quest for an idea capable of liberating Japan, the prime object of concern to so many Japanese artists, Kurosawa reverts once again to the code of *bushido*, to the ethos of the samurai. In the world as it is now, however, only the "savage" Dersu is capable of approximating that ideal. Like a samurai of old, he retains the freedom to sacrifice money for friendship. Dersu gives Arseniev the valuable healing root he has discovered, a find which would have brought him much money. Like a true samurai, Dersu never mentions the one most loving moment of his relationship with Arseniev, the time he saved Arseniev's life, because "he thinks he has done nothing special." Like Imamura's Toriko, to our beclouded eyes and to those of Arseniev's fellow explorers, Dersu at first seems ridiculous. He calls a duck a "gentle man" and the sun "the greatest man"; he considers himself "various." Yet it is only he who is able to be friend, commander, and partner in adversity.

Dersu Uzala is, in fact, remarkably like Yeats' fisherman, whom the poet set apart from the merchant-besotted crowd and whose skill in living at peace within nature, justified by the skill with which he plied his trade, made him the primal person, a pure example of Rousseau's noble savage. The simple purity Yeats admired in the fisherman, the Platonic elegance expressed in 'the simple "downturn of his wrist as he dropped his flies in the stream," is contained as well in the person of Dersu.

Kurosawa had spoken of making a film "about pollution"[3] before doing *Dersu Uzala*. In a very real sense, this is what he has done. *Dersu Uzala* in an ideal sense would turn the Japanese away from what they have become, restoring them to that love of nature which has defined them as a people from earliest times. It was a love shared by peasant and aristocrat alike, as Ivan Morris reveals in his description of the closeness with nature felt by the noble denizens of Heian Kyo:

> The inhabitants of the shining prince's world never try to cut themselves off from their natural environment; rather they strive to blend themselves with the nature that surrounds them, believing that thus they can learn to understand themselves and those about them. Sensitivity to the subtle moods of nature, indeed, was an essential attribute of 'good people'.[4]

This nostalgia for lost values, of which *Dersu Uzala* is one more example, quixotic and escapist though it may be, is positive and real to many Japanese because it returns them spiritually to what they see as their lost, best selves. From one Japanese point of view, that Kurosawa should have been forced to go to the Soviet Union to create Dersu shames an industry and a nation that can no longer provide working space for perhaps the world's greatest living film director. Kurosawa's journey itself becomes one more effort to awaken a morally lethargic people.

[3] Conversation with the author, Tokyo, August 1972.

[4] *The World of the Shining Prince: Court Life in Ancient Japan* (New York: Alfred A. Knopf, 1964), p. 20.

PART
2

BEING JAPANESE:
THE QUEST THROUGH HISTORY

The Japanese director turns to the past in search of what it means to be a Japanese. It is a quest undertaken in the hope that its outcome will begin to fill the moral vacuum of the present. More Japanese films are set in the past than those of any other country, including the United States with its "Westerns." There is a faith in this culture that its history, if faithfully perceived, can be relied upon to reveal the way back to the *kokutai*, the national essence now lost. However, many directors, such as Kobayashi and Imai, are deeply critical of Japan's feudal history. Their purpose in setting many of their films in the past is not to exalt a set of values, now lost, but rather to uncover a route of escape from the rigid, restrictive, if compelling, definition of what it means to be a Japanese—a code which has been damaging to the individual and demeaning of the national dignity.

The historical Japanese equation of honor, both personal and national, with an unquestioning obedience to authority, has led to a profound self-hatred manifested most obviously in the degree of violence of so many of these historical films, both in the *chambara* (sword-play films) and in the *jidai-geki* (true period or historical films). Haunting the characters in these films is a constant, if unconscious, feeling of being insufficiently worthy, since the criterion of value is a total subordination of will to the demands of those above, even when no superior is present. Hence the person and the nation are forever subject to doubt about the sufficiency of their service and the real value of it. Forever to internalize the sternest judgments of harsh authority, always to act in such a fashion as to placate those who allow only the most grudging acknowledgment of one's value—this is a sensibility which will be constantly ill at ease with itself. The first indication of insufficient effort, the earliest sign of failure even after maximum effort—these induce Japan and the Japanese to condemn unrelentingly and to exact the ultimate punishment. The Japanese dance with death, a feature of nearly every one of the period films, reflects a fear that nothing in life will ever be sufficient to prove worthiness. Even the romance of self-destruction, symbolized by *seppuku* (the title of one of the best of these period films, directed by Masaki Kobayashi) as proof of nobility and devotion, betrays a conviction that to be a good Japanese is never enough. It is always to be tested and ultimately scorned by some sterner judge. The feudal code, which shaped the nation's past and its very sense of identity, has condemned Japan's children to a futile quest for approval as Japanese that can never be fully realized. As with Sisyphus, the greater the effort, the more vast the fall from grace upon failure. The anti-feudal director finds ultimately that to be Japanese is to embrace a credo of despair because the demands of the code of *bushido* can never be satisfied.

Even those most stridently critical of the feudal past have been formed by it and exhibit a love-hate relationship with what Japan has been, as Kurosawa exhibits in his admiration of the samurai character at its best. "My ideal style," said Yukio Mishima in his late neo-fascist mood, "would have had the grave beauty of polished wood in the entrance hall of a samurai mansion on a winter's day."[1] In this last phase of his life, Mishima admired "an intrepid fighting spirit, the power of dispassionate intellectual judgment, and a robust disposition,"[2] ideals exalted even in the most anti-feudal period films.

The Japanese director reveals simultaneous revulsion and attraction particularly for the Edo period (1603-1868) because, despite the brutalities of life under the Tokugawa Shogunate, a confident sense of the Japanese spirit had not yet been lost. If the stress of being "truly Japanese" was considerable, at least belief in a group identity remained untainted by doubt. Yet, in the last days of the Shogunate, there were also those who were in search of what had gone wrong with Japan and sought answers. Some of these figures, despite the failure of their quest, have become the most popular characters in Japan's best period films. In the uneasiness of men like Ryoma Sakamoto over what true changes the fall of the Shogunate would bring to Japan, these characters have inspired contemporary film directors who seek now to dispel the myth that the evils of feudalism were undone by the Meiji Restoration. Their aim is to challenge the myth that a "revolution" had occurred. As Shinoda has bluntly put it, there was "no change" from Tokugawa shogun to Emperor.[3]

---

[1] *Sun and Steel* (New York: Grove Press, 1970), p. 47.
[2] *Ibid.*, p. 27.
[3] "Interview with Masahiro Shinoda," *Voices from the Japanese Cinema*, p. 247.

Ryoma

Ryoma Sakamoto was a rebel whose dream was to bring down the oppressive Tokugawa rule and truly to emancipate people . . . making *Bakumatsu* in 1970 I was able overtly to show Ryoma discussing his real dream of revolution—establishing a society that doesn't separate people on the basis of social class.

Daisuke Ito[1]

The films exploring this insight frequently center around the figure of Ryoma Sakamoto. As Masao Maruyama writes, "what happened in the Meiji Restoration was that by the union of authority with power the preponderant role of force in feudal society was systematically incorporated into the structure of modern Japan."[2] When he registered the degree to which feudal values would continue into the Restoration, Ryoma was forced to the conclusion that his own samurai class had to be truly abolished if justice and concern for the rights of the individual were to be gained for the Japanese. The essential first step was a breakdown of traditional clan and family loyalties, an event Ryoma never lived to witness.

To the young rebels who fought the Tokugawa shogunate, the restoration to central power (in 1868) of a national figure, the Emperor, was a distinctly anti-feudal act. They assumed that a figure personifying the nation would represent a drastic challenge to the rigid hierarchy of clans characteristic of the warring feudal families. More importantly, particularly to a visionary like Sakamoto, the creation of a central authority was prerequisite for the modernization of Japan. It is in this context that one can understand such a declaration of support for the Emperor by Ryoma:

Surely you realize that one ought to put the Imperial Court before his own province, and ahead of his parents. The idea that putting your relatives second, your province second, and abandoning your mother, your wife, and children—that this is a violation of your proper duty—is certainly, considering our times, something that comes from the stupid officials.[3]

[1] Joan Mellen, "Interview with Daisuke Ito," *Voices from the Japanese Cinema*, p. 29.

[2] "Thought and Behaviour of Ultra-Nationalism," *Thought and Behaviour in Modern Japanese Politics*, ed. Ivan Morris (New York: Oxford University Press, 1963), p. 18.

[3] Letter to the parents of Kurata Ike, July 31, 1863, cited in Marius B. Jansen, *Sakamoto Ryoma and the Meiji Restoration* (Stanford, Calif.: Stanford University Press, 1971), p. 174.

In precisely the way that the establishment of a central monarch in
Europe heralded the rise of the nation-state, subordinating rival lords of
local feudal domains, the Meiji Restoration was intended, at least by
rebels like Sakamoto, to smash the feudal authoritarianism which had held
ordinary Japanese in thrall.

It must have come as a profound shock to Ryoma to discover, as he did
in his last days, that the Restoration movement had betrayed these expectations, and that instead of a new egalitarianism, the nation-state of Meiji
would simply elevate the feudal code and values of the shogunate to a
national imperative. Feudal lords were rendered Imperial functionaries
and the worst of feudal ways were granted a quasi-religious status through
the sanctity of the Emperor, a course of events Ryoma foresaw but did not
live to observe.

Near the end of his life Ryoma continued to struggle for a real democratization. He had looked to the representative governments of the bourgeois
era in the West as an answer, recognizing that the absence of mass involvement in the anti-shogun struggle would allow feudalism to remain intact.
In an "Eight-Point Program" Ryoma had called for a Council to "conduct
affairs in line with the desires of the people."[4] It would include not only
an upper house comprised of nobles, but also a lower body granting
decision-making "even [to] commoners selected from among those who
are just and pure-hearted."[5]

The historical Ryoma was a low-rank samurai of the Tosa clan. His
grandfather, a successful sake brewer, had *purchased* samurai status in 1771.
Like many revolutionaries, Ryoma began as a reformist, distressed by clan
corruption and by the invasion of Japan by foreign interests seeking her
subjugation. "How can our feudal lords continue on in the indulgences
of sloth and luxury?" he wrote in his treatise on clan reform, the *Han Ron*.[6]
Ryoma also signed his name to the statement of the Tosa Loyalist Party
dedicated to reactivating the "Japanese Spirit," even as, at different
moments in Japan's history, both radicals and traditional defenders of the
established order have embarked upon this same quest: seeking sanction
in Japan's past for future change. The statement asserted that "our magnificent and divine country has been humiliated by the barbarians," and its
signers vowed to "go through fire and water to ease the Emperor's mind."[7]

But finally, Ryoma remains one of the few authentic revolutionaries in
Japanese history. He foresaw the carry-over of feudal values with the passing of power from the Tokugawa shogunate to the Satsuma and Choshu
clans, those most active in the Restoration. And he recognized that the
Japanese people would be as subject to the decisions of a new Meiji ruling
class as they had been to the shoguns who had ruled Japan since the
twelfth century. Ryoma Sakamoto, unlike the majority of Japanese states-

    [4] *Ibid.*, p. 300.
    [5] *Ibid.*, p. 301.
    [6] Cited in E. H. Norman, "Feudal Background of Japanese Politics," *Origins of the
Modern Japanese State: Selected Writings of E. H. Norman*, ed. John W. Dower
(New York: Pantheon Books, 1975), p. 364.
    [7] Cited in Jansen, *Sakamoto Ryoma*, pp. 108–109.

men who came after him, defined "democracy" as the handing over of control to the masses, not as consensus among a small ruling group, the prevailing view even today. There are indications that he planned to create a mass movement that would challenge the new Meiji government at the moment of its ascent to power, calling for an insurrection that could best be compared to the French Revolution of 1789. Ryoma is beloved by so many in Japan because it is likely that he would have offered the Japanese people at last the basic rights promulgated by such men as Voltaire, Rousseau and Paine. It is therefore hardly surprising that on the eve of so crucial a moment in Japanese history, when the feudal stranglehold on the culture might have been broken by an incipient popular revolt, Ryoma Sakamoto should have been assassinated.

The Japanese film frequently reveals Ryoma Sakamoto as a man profoundly imbued by, and devoted to, democracy as a revolutionary creed. It chronicles his development from an anti-*bakufu* (shogun) samurai to a rebel who recognized presciently that the evils of the shogunate would persist in the new Japan unless an assault were made on all privilege.

Daisuke Ito's *Bakumatsu* (1970) places Ryoma in the context of the intense class warfare emerging in the last days of the shogunate. In the opening sequence a townsman wears wooden clogs, thereby violating edicts which the government had outlined for the wearing apparel legal for his class. In a pouring rain he grabs them at the last minute as he rushes outside on an errand. Immediately he is killed by samurai, vicious as well as decadent, and activated only by concern for the privilege of their class. Without a moment of wasted footage, Ito dramatizes how, in Tokugawa times, a samurai could kill a commoner without bringing upon himself so much as a legal inquiry; for others, however, as E. H. Norman points out, the law read differently:

> For a samurai to kill in cold blood a commoner whose only offense was an insult, imaginary or real, did not even require a legal investigation, whereas for a commoner to be guilty of a minor offense against a superior, such as an angry word, an improper petition or more serious, a blow, would expose him to the full rigors of feudal justice.[8]

This frequently entailed torture, most frequently by crucifixion carried out by a member of the *burakumin* or *Eta* class, the outcasts who were hereditary executioners for Japan's aristocracy.

Another member of the lower ranks in *Bakumatsu* compares Japan to London. There, he says, "they don't care if I used to be a baker." Ryoma is revealed as a man who, in loving Japan, must choose between nation and clan. He is shown admiring Western technology, even as radical intellectuals had done in Tsarist Russia, viewing it as a means toward national advance. The real Ryoma had even planned to send his wife abroad after the Restoration to acquire a modern education. The film ends, as in life, when Ryoma is assassinated with a fellow Tosa dissident, Shinta Nakaoka.

Bakumatsu itself, degenerating like many Japanese period films into

---

[8] Norman, "Feudal Background of Japanese Politics," pp. 334–335.

Bakumatsu: Ryoma is shown admiring Western technology, even as radical intellectuals did in Tsarist Russia, viewing it as a means toward national advance.

scenes of physical action for their own sake, does not achieve Ito's avowed aim. Its importance lies in what Ito wanted to say about Ryoma. Ito, who began his film career in the early twenties, and was the originator of the blood-and-gore samurai film, the *chambara*, has said that he was glad to have made *Bakumatsu* so late in his career since, before the War, he would not have been able to show how critical of the Imperial system Ryoma Sakamoto had been.[9] He perceives Ryoma as a rebel whose dream was not only to bring down the Tokugawas but to emancipate the Japanese people by "establishing a society which doesn't separate people on the basis of social class." Nakaoka, in Ito's vision, warns Ryoma that to advocate such a thing will ensure assassination by members of his own class, now about to assume positions of responsibility in the Meiji government. From Ryoma's writings, Ito had discovered the man's loneliness and his awareness that his ideas placed him far ahead of his time. "I have such crazy ideas," Ito quotes Ryoma as saying, "and they try to assert themselves. They must be locked up in a jail."[10] Ito, himself a descendant of samurai, pinpoints the importance of Ryoma in his recognition that the samurai

[9] "Interview with Daisuke Ito," *Voices from the Japanese Cinema*, p. 29.
[10] *Ibid.*

class and its perpetuation were at the root of Japan's failure, at this historically critical moment, to liberate its people from the tyrannical feudalism it had endured for centuries.

Heinosuke Gosho's *Firefly Light* (*Hotarubi*, 1958) pictures Ryoma in April of 1862, arriving at the Teradaya Inn where the Choshu and Satsuma *ronin* had gathered, preparing for one of a series of early unsuccessful risings against the Tokugawas (later to be known as the "Teradaya Incident"). The film itself is about Tose, the woman innkeeper of the Teradaya. Ryoma appears as a "guest" she must shield from the police, and her courage is expressed in her willingness to accommodate him. The anti-*bakufu* movement is seen through the eyes of this strong, silently suffering woman who runs the inn, who has survived despite her having been abused by a jealous mother-in-law and a weak husband. As Jansen describes the historical model for this character, "the Teradaya was run by a strong-willed woman whom Sakamoto praised in his letters as one who helps men who work for Choshu and the nation . . . she has a good deal of learning, and carries out projects worthy of men."[11]

At the beginning of *Firefly Light*, the Teradaya is invaded by a group of almost laughably serious samurai. A band of unruly *ronin*, historically followers of Kuniomi Hirano, they disturb everyone. Eventually Satsuma samurai arrive in a surprise ambush. Blood splashes on the walls of the Teradaya, which Tose's prissy husband had always demanded be kept immaculately clean. Swords slice the tatami mats; a body falls down the stairs.

These events are the prelude to Ryoma's striking arrival: "I am Sakamoto from Tosa . . . may I stay here and hide? I didn't do anything wrong . . . I want to improve the world and it depends on you." Actually, Ryoma was posing at the time as a Satsuma samurai. But Gosho is not as interested in historical detail[12] as he is in using the figure of Ryoma to delineate the character of Tose. Her heroism is revealed in her response to a momentous historical event: the choice, by an insurgent Ryoma, of the Teradaya as a hideaway. "Please feel relieved," she assures him, swiftly converting her inn into an asylum. She accepts him immediately, deciding to ally herself with this great man and his cause. Her husband insists frantically that she get rid of this dangerous guest, but, in contrast to Tose, he is indecisive and craven, confining himself to practicing songs from the *Bunraku* called *joruri*. He is too indolent to enforce his displeasure, although it is hardly unjustified, since a "wanted" poster of Ryoma earlier in the film had informed us that, at twenty-eight, he is already accused of planning a coup d'état.

In *Firefly Light* Ryoma spends most of his time studying Dutch. The book in which he is absorbed is, rather obviously, on the subject of "freedom." Tose draws the bath of the great man, but in his bath, Ryoma is transformed from historical legend to human proportions. He sings nursery

---

[11] Jansen, *Sakamoto Ryoma*, p. 227.
[12] Gosho prefaced a screening of *Firefly Light* in Tokyo in November 1974 with just this confession.

rhymes in the tub! His access to childlike feelings is complemented by private passion, with Gosho correcting any concept of Ryoma as an unrelievedly sober, single-minded leader.

Ryoma seduces Tose's adopted daughter, Oryo, regaling her with ghost stories in a charming courting sequence. As the "O" of Oryo is honorific, the lovers actually possess the same name. The historical wife of Ryoma, also Oryo, had been granted shelter in the Teradaya at Ryoma's request. Gosho alters historical detail for the purpose of making Oryo another vehicle for Tose's abiding humanity.

The Oryo of *Hotarubi* is a young, uninhibited eighteen-year-old who rushes out at night to view the fireflies of the film's title. The historical Ryoma had written of her, "she has more strength than I do."[13] In homage to Ryoma's own sense of his wife, Gosho mediates Ryoma's ideas through the consciousness of Oryo as she reports on their friendship: he wishes to eliminate poverty, the achievement of which, he believes, first requires the overthrow of feudalism and the destruction of the class system. Gosho and Ito arrive at an identical assessment of Ryoma's advocacy and social purpose.

The life of Tose, a lonely woman who must run the Teradaya by herself, is redeemed and fulfilled by her alliance with a person like Ryoma. When, at one point, he is discovered and shot (not fatally), he confides to her his own profound loneliness, the sense of isolation and danger to which his advanced ideas inevitably expose him. They are parallel, emotionally equal figures but, as a woman, she can serve only by aiding men of revolutionary dedication to prepare a future liberation of women. Gosho sees Tose as no less heroic than Ryoma, notwithstanding her middle-class life, because her acts and her free spirit align her with a struggle for change. Each plays a leading role in the demise of the feudalism of which they are both victims. Ryoma, at one with history, will play a more obvious part. But, behind the scenes, women like Tose do their part as well, even as the manifold humiliations of Tose's life express the very suffering which had inspired Ryoma to struggle against feudal Japan.

Shinoda's *Assassination* (*Ansatsu*, 1964) is set in the early 1860s. It opens with the assassination of the Tokugawa Premier, Ii, who decided to open Japan to trade for the purpose of fortifying his own power. The hero of the film is a *ronin* named Kiyokawa; Ryoma Sakamoto appears as his friend. During the period depicted in the film, which ends in 1863, Ryoma is presented as peripheral to the Restoration. The mood of Shinoda's characterization of Ryoma suggests, not the power of the man's vision but the director's own sense of helplessness before the failure of Japan's "revolution."

Ryoma and Kiyokawa, like dissident samurai everywhere in Japan, are in hiding at the beginning of *Assassination*. They were the radicals of the early 1860s and, like revolutionaries everywhere, they believed that their dissent should be reflected in their personal life styles. Jansen observes how the *shishi* refused to shave or wash, and clomped around in

[13] Cited in Jansen, *Sakamoto Ryoma*, p. 226.

螢火

Firefly Light: Gosho sees Tose as no less heroic than Ryoma, notwithstanding her middle-class life, because her acts and her free spirit align her with a struggle for change.

wooden clogs.[14] Their protest against accepted mores made them the hippies of their day. Ryoma and Kiyokawa also wear the deep straw hats, typically used to disguise identity and accessible only to men of the samurai class. They pause before two wall posters, one picturing each, announcing that they are wanted men. Kiyokawa tells Ryoma that he is in need of a bath.

Gosho and Shinoda would each demystify their samurai heroes, but for opposite reasons. Gosho places Ryoma in a tub to provide an outlet for more mundane, human, and, indeed, childlike emotions, to establish, in an appealing way, Ryoma's common humanity. Shinoda, of the next generation, would see Ryoma bathe because he is dirty and smells, seeking thus to deride the pretensions of charismatic and quixotic historical figures. And, indeed, the difference in their handling of this "hygienic" issue captures the purpose of each director. Gosho celebrates the humanism of his

14 *Ibid.,* p. 136.

rebel hero. Shinoda is not merely cynical, but a nihilist. In his eyes, Ryoma's pretensions are finally absurd because human beings cannot live up to the noble aspirations held for them. His Ryoma smells because he is no more than flesh and blood, and, equally, his dreams are chimeras. Clinging to them may only blind him to his own motives.

We have not yet been permitted to understand who is involved in the Restoration movement, or what is happening politically. Shinoda provides a close-up of a hat, and then of a foot. Ryoma tears down the "wanted" poster concerning Kiyokawa, but leaves the one about himself. Kiyokawa, although wanted for a murder he (we later learn) clearly committed, has been granted a dispensation, pardoned because the Tokugawa shogun wishes to make use of his sword against the Restorationists. Ryoma, on the contrary, is sought because he opposes the shogun politically. "I haven't been amnestied like you," Ryoma says with some irony, reflecting the fact that the Tokugawas indeed had more to fear from one who would overthrow their three-hundred-year-old dynasty than from a common murderer. It is, in any event, pointless for him to destroy his "wanted" poster because it will simply be replaced by another. A sense of helplessness pervades this Ryoma, far more so than Kiyokawa, who is about to raise an army of hungry samurai and whose problem is not that of taking action, but on which side to ally himself.

Later in the film, in the midst of a melee, we hear Sakamoto's name, but we don't see him, perfectly befitting an epoch when survival depended upon being elusive. Shinoda deliberately avoids a linear, chronological approach that would tell the audience who is who and where the action leads. But neither are the principals themselves certain of their next move. Style and substance conjoin.

Ryoma is also used by Shinoda to comment upon the character of Kiyokawa, the "mysterious Hachiro." Ryoma serves this purpose well, because he is a personage immediately recognized and respected by the audience. "None can understand him," Ryoma says of Kiyokawa; even he is limited in his perception by Shinoda. A flashback from Ryoma's point of view takes us to Kyoto; the action, out of focus, is pulled into clarity as Ryoma recognizes Kiyokawa on the street. They repair to an inn where Kiyokawa reveals that he has gathered a band of free samurai "to rise in revolt." The next day Ryoma returns to the inn to find the place a shambles, blood staining the torn screens. Everything is destroyed. Shinoda creates a stark metaphor expressing the futility of the entire anti-*bakufu* movement.

At this moment Ryoma drops his hat, picks up a *koto* and sings, "Why must you tie/Your colt to a tree/ Should the colt want to go free/ Blossoms will all die." Ryoma is made the conscience of *Assassination*, a sometime commentator who sees through the violence and chaos of the day, the bloodshed that only replenishes itself in more death, the loss of the goal in the course of battle. Shinoda finds that, in the course of history, we are restricted in what we can perceive. Worse, our acts may bring results we cannot possibly anticipate, let alone desire. Ryoma favored Western technique because he hated feudalism and desired a modern, democratic Japan. Kiyokawa hated foreign control and acted on behalf of his hatred, unaware that the Restoration would not be true to his objective of uncompromising resistance to foreign penetration. Both supported the Restoration for opposite reasons, and both were daring, brilliant men. By placing them together in the same film, Shinoda cleverly illuminates what for him is the irony of commitment.

Perhaps the most beautiful homage to Ryoma Sakamoto appears in Kazuo Kuroki's semi-farce, *The Assassination of Ryoma* (*Ryoma Ansatsu*, 1974). The mood is very much like that of Shinoda's *Assassination*, with its sense of pervading futility, especially because the action is confined to

Ryoma is made the conscience of *Assassination*, a sometime commentator who sees through the violence and chaos of the day, the bloodshed that only replenishes itself in more death, the loss of the goal in the course of battle.

Assassination: By placing Kiyokawa and Ryoma together in the same film, Shinoda cleverly illuminates what for him must be the irony of commitment.

the last three days of Ryoma's life in December of 1867. Convinced that his enemies (nameless, numberless, ubiquitous) are plotting his assassination, Ryoma is again in hiding. He wears the Western shoes he so favored in real life; by now, they have lost their laces and flap around his ankles; there are deep holes in the soles.

Kuroki uses titles to hasten the pace as the action moves toward Ryoma's murder. Ryoma, "moving out" from one hide-out to another in the first scene, has temporarily lost his clothing, and it is with a naked bottom that he makes his appearance. Kuroki's Ryoma is less the "hero" than the human being limited by the age in which he lived.

Kuroki intercuts scenes of hysterical mass festivals which occurred in 1867 just before the Restoration. With the fall of formal feudalism imminent, there is great disorientation and apprehension as the familiar passes. People imagine supernatural events as, through "acceptable" religious experiences and Saturnalia, they begin to break the bounds of the overwhelming political repressiveness of the entire Tokugawa era. The doomsday mood of the last days of Edo was reflected in this *"Eija nai ka"* (literally, "isn't it good?") movement. People suddenly believed that amulets from the great Shinto temple at Ise had fallen from the heavens. Dressed in brightly colored clothes, they poured into the streets, dancing and imbibing volumes of sake while playing drums, bells, samisen, and flutes. A local observer reported the mass hysteria at the time as follows:

About this time, on the road between Kyoto, Osaka and Nishinomiya, frequently these talismans fell out of the skies and the townsmen regarded this as a happy omen of a prosperous year, and cried out in refrain, *"Eija nai ka, eija nai ka,"* and they inserted at random many obscene and coarse lines into the verse and the rhythm of the song was droll and amusing. . . . The old and young, men and women, without distinction, put on gay flower-designed clothes and wandered about the city streets making a continual uproar.[15]

People thus donned costumes in masquerade, as if uncertain of the new identity they would have as individuals and as Japanese in the new era. Men dressed in women's clothes and women in men's. In Kuroki's film Ryoma goes out dressed in woman's garb, a disguise perfectly appropriate to the time and providing Kuroki with the means of showing how, in this climactic moment, when inhibitions could finally be discarded, even sexual barriers seemed to be breaking down.

And all the while the people ironically sang *"Eija nai ka, eija nai ka,"* isn't it good?. Holding red lanterns as in a religious festival, they behaved as though the age of the gods had descended upon them. Passers-by were offered sake; the streets were filled with noise and excitement. Politically, the chaos and uproar allowed the Satsuma and Choshu leaders to make contact with the Emperor in Kyoto and consolidate their forces. As E. H. Norman puts it, the frenzy "like a flood . . . swept away the fine-spun meticulous controls of the feudal authorities."[16]

Norman assesses the *Eija nai ka* movement in a manner very similar to that of director Kuroki. For Norman, it was "an instinctive groping of the people in a form of mass movement toward some goal *but not necessarily in a politically or socially progressive direction."*[17] Kuroki has said that Ryoma's natural constituency for a struggle that would have replaced both shogun and Emperor with a popular government was precisely this *Eija nai ka* movement which, however, he was unable to organize.[18] It could have provided him with that army which, in Kuroki's film, Ryoma speaks of creating. At no point in the film does Ryoma view these aroused people in the streets, casting off centuries of conditioning, as potential followers. And it is on this ground that Kuroki criticizes the historical Ryoma as unable to transcend his membership in the samurai class.

To play Ryoma, Kuroki chose a sensual, attractive man, Yoshio Harada. But it is in this very physical expressiveness that Kuroki locates his initial criticism of both Ryoma and the Japanese. Ryoma acts, first and always, on the basis of intuitive feeling and impulse. He is incapable of sustained analysis and, in this respect, is similar to the historical Ryoma, who was no more than half-educated. He's "good at being a voyeur," says one of the titles. This Ryoma is a man easily distracted. During these last three days of his life that are traced in the film, Ryoma, his passion unabated, devotes

---

[15] Cited by Norman, "Feudal Background of Japanese Politics," pp. 344–345.
[16] *Ibid.*, p. 349.
[17] *Ibid.*, p. 354.
[18] Conversation with the author, Tokyo, November 1974.

much of his energy, not to the exigencies of the Restoration movement, but to an affair with a beautiful prostitute.

Kuroki's film freely intermixes conventions from comic pornography in displaying Ryoma's rambunctious, haphazard, and experimental love-making. The director uses pop singers as actors in certain parts and evokes a generally disorderly atmosphere. All of these are qualities which attracted young people to the cheap, pornographic, farcical Japanese films of the 1970s designed to appeal to just this audience, as well as to rural and far less educated filmgoers.

But it would be a mistake to see *Assassination of Ryoma* solely as an allegory about the decline of the New Left in Japan, as Japanese critic Tadao Sato would have us believe. Sato seems anxious to obscure, and thus comfortably dismiss, the film's political thrust. Wilfully, he confuses its larger canvas with a narrow attack on the recent student movement.[19] There is, of course, a passing evocation of the present in the analogy between Ryoma Sakamoto's murder by members of both the Satsuma and his own Tosa clan and the internecine strife in Japan between rival student sects during the late 1960s and the 1970s. Just as Ryoma is shown to have been betrayed by right-wing elements within the Restoration movement, so the *"Chukakuha"* ("Middle Core Faction") and the *"Kakumaruha"* (self-designated "Revolutionary Marxist Faction") of the student movement have attacked each other with everything from bamboo spears to metal bars, rocks, and worse, inflicting death on leaders of rival radical tendencies.

Kuroki, however, ranges far beyond an allegory of the demise of the student movement. The pop conventions, the incidental evocation of Japan's New Left, the mock-heroic Ryoma moving his bowels five times a day—all serve the far larger theme of the betrayal of the revolution and of every revolutionary in Japanese history. The light, absurdist tone enveloping one of the celebrated and heroic stories of Japanese culture underlines Kuroki's sense of futility. It is a frustrated judgment, not merely on the students but on all Japanese who have failed to register fully and rise to moments in their history when a course of action leading to salvation was at hand. For there were crucial times when mass disaffection and a general casting-off of centuries of rigid feudal passivity were possible. The *Eija nai ka* movement was, of course, one obvious example. At such times, a clear revolutionary leadership might have been decisive. Its failure to materialize has caused the very hope of serious change to recede, creating a more severe passivity because these moments of opportunity have come and passed unrealized.

Ryoma's naked rear end and flapping Western shoes render him absurdly comic, but his condition is already the fruit of persecution and isolation. Finally, it is those who were incapable of protecting him and of valuing such a man who, Kuroki shows us, are the fools. He does not attack, as such, certain student groups any more than he is particularly concerned

<hr>

[19] Address to the Japan Society, New York, April 10, 1975.

with the betrayers among Ryoma's own clan. From such people, caught up in their struggles for power and personal influence, nothing more is to be expected.

It is those who should have known better, those who cared, who must bear the responsibility. The themes of *Assassination of Ryoma* and Oshima's *Night and Fog in Japan* (*Nihon no Yoru to Kiri*, 1960) merge as one. Much of the action of the former takes place in graveyards, because Kuroki is interested in the historical dimension of his subject as well as in its universal application to the Japanese experience. The mood of his film remains the death of the Restoration, decaying before it has even begun and, with its demise, the loss of any hope of social transformation in Japan for generations to come.

Kuroki treats humorously Ryoma's fascination with Western technology. Ryoma tries to use a gun, but it never goes off. At one point he fires accidentally, nearly blowing off his foot. "Better to use a sword," a friend tells him. A camera mistakenly arrives in place of the 5,000 guns he had ordered for a struggle to be waged, after the Restoration, against the victorious Choshu, Satsuma and Tosa samurai. *It* doesn't work either. Ryoma's Western shoes wear out and there is no one to repair them. Satsuma samurai are shown drinking red wine, which they detest, but which they believe they must imbibe as the new men of the future.

Kuroki thus argues that the Western technology upon which the real Ryoma relied could not, finally, help him, nor could it be an answer for Japan. What Ryoma had to do, and what events prevented him from achieving, was to forge a mass movement, an organization of his own people, the very farmers and fishermen appealed to by Ryoma near the end of the film. For Kuroki, only in such an effort could there be found a hope for the creation of a free and just Japan out of the defeat of the feudal shogunate. It is partly due to Ryoma's own lack of resolve that he does not create this movement. He turns, in his despair, to sexual indulgence (as, of course, did many contemporary students, easily distracted by personal whim and unresolved psychological need). Kuroki permits Ryoma to recognize this weakness. In the film he writes to his beloved sister (who was his real-life correspondent as well): "Women . . . make men forget patriotic duty . . . I must heed this."

Ryoma, however, also becomes immobilized, partly because, as with present-day cynics and nihilists in Japan whom Kuroki is satirizing far more than the students, his effectiveness is reduced by a feeling that life is absurd. He compares the Restoration to cutting down a large tree simply to rescue a small cat, accepting in despair the meager social result of Meiji as inevitable, when he himself had envisaged a democratic nation arising out of the defeat of feudalism. It is as if, because he has failed to forge the movement necessary to realize his revolutionary aspiration by the time the film opens, Ryoma turns away from his own social ideas as quixotic or unattainable.

Thus he spends too much time teaching his woman how to dance Western style. He seeks diversion at a time when action is urgently needed. The world is in tumult. Aristocrats in Kyoto have begun to keep pigs because they are starving. Under a title that calls for a "bloodless revolution," pigs grunt—Kuroki's image for the historical fact that much more was needed. Ryoma had been obliged to address himself to the power struggle precisely because the victorious clans did not intend to rid Japan of feudalism, but only to secure positions for themselves on the basis of the same hierarchical patterns of rule. Meiji 1868 was not merely a revolution aborted, but a new vehicle for an old order.

Unable to respond to this critical moment, Kuroki's Ryoma is over-whelmed by a sense of futility. He speaks of "nibbling the tits of his irresistibly warm sister." While the *Eija nai ka* dancers move through the graveyard, his woman makes love to *her* brother, Uta, who has been hired by the Satsuma clan to assassinate Ryoma. His fellow Tosa dissident, Shinta Nakaoka, has also been ordered to kill Ryoma, but he finally refrains, not because he particularly believes in Ryoma's vision of a mass movement, but out of homosexual attraction.

Ryoma locates Shinta by dressing up as a woman and going out among the *Eija nai ka* fanatics. That the men are all disguised as women adds humor to the scene in which they sleep in a field in each other's arms.

The Assassination of Ryoma: Ryoma becomes immobilized, partly because, like the present-day cynics and nihilists in Japan whom Kuroki is satirizing, he feels that life is absurd.

The Assassination of Ryoma: In his despair, Ryoma turns to sexual indulgence, as of course did many contemporary students, easily distracted by personal whim and unresolved psychological need.

The political discussion between them, when it does occur, takes second place to the sexual. Shinta Nakaoka would burn Edo (Tokyo) to the ground: "That's reform!" Ryoma now poses a question that shows him to be the serious revolutionary, but one who will fail because he has not yet formulated a program for the implementation of his ideas. "The problem's after that," says Ryoma, "who'll gain power? Who'll grasp it?" Ryoma foresees "swarms of men after power . . . I don't mind overthrowing the Shogunate. But then how do I get out of the rat race for power?" Here Kuroki evokes simultaneously the failure of the Restoration and the defeat of the Bolshevik Revolution. In both instances, leaders antithetical to the revolutionary goals which motivated people like Ryoma seized power and defeated the ideals of the revolution itself.

By placing in Ryoma's mouth these intimations of revolutionary betrayal, of power struggles consuming the protagonists, Kuroki reveals his own fear that there is something inherent in revolutionary power which leads to its degeneration. These anxieties are shown to be part of the reason for Ryoma's loss of nerve and temporary surrender to indulgence. Kuroki, in his evocation of the various revolutionary defeats and betrayals of the past century, provides an honest corrective to the craven support so often given to revolutions which became, once in power, vicious imitations of the older order. And by criticizing Ryoma's indulgence and despair, Kuroki suggests that it is within the capacity of people to preserve revolutionary ideals, even as it is within their means to build meaningful revolutions. Only Kuroki's ultimate belief in such an alternative possibility could warrant his ironies regarding Ryoma's failure.

Shinta, like most samurai of the time, does not consider these questions. Ryoma, naked, hairy-legged, absurdly made up as a woman, knows something about history many revolutionaries have yet to face. He sees that class relationships will not change with the Restoration. Powerful samurai, already strong, will form the new government. He and Nakaoka, members of a very low rank, will find no place in the new regime. Out of this knowledge Ryoma has tried to secure the 5,000 guns and, when this fails, 100 or 200 weapons with which he will try to form a new army and navy by recruiting farmers and fishermen. "They're no help," scoffs Nakaoka, an elitist like all samurai, scornful of the lower classes. "Any man can learn to use guns," replies Ryoma. His plan is to train his men and then to attack the Satsuma and Choshu victors. "No wonder Satsuma's after you," Shinta says in alarm, as well he might.

The sexual, equated by Kuroki with irrationality, finally defeats Ryoma. He has decided to take his woman with him to Nagasaki, where he will begin to build his revolutionary organization. As the daughter of a fisherman, she could be the cook for his group. His dream is "to gather all the women like that one." He would "pick up people like her and grow bigger and bigger." It is not in his character to abandon anyone, but the woman fears that he will cast her aside, and she betrays him to his assassins. Just as Nakaoka, out of sexual love of the man, finally says, "bring me, take me with you," Ryoma's woman betrays him for the same reason.

Ryoma's dream, of course, transcends sexuality, but not even those closest to him understand this. After Ryoma tells Nakaoka his plan, Kuroki gives us an extreme close-up of Ryoma's eyes and nose. He is a man larger than life, grand but finally too large for the Japanese people of his time. A moment later, his assassins enter and Ryoma's skull is split in half. Blood drips down through the tatami to the floor below, as Kuroki parodies Daisuke Ito's early period films. Then Kuroki offers a freeze frame of the dead bodies of Ryoma and Nakaoka lying side by side, the composition of the shot completed by Rorschach-like ink blots of blood. It is an image out of Shinoda. In the assassination sequence, out of an absurdist sense of irony and futility, Kuroki has given us a foreshortened history of the period film in Japan.

But what has happened is also taken seriously by Kuroki. Kuroki has said that the woman who betrays Ryoma represents the Japanese people as a whole who, through misunderstanding and a failure of trust, have sold out their true leaders.[20] Just as his woman did not understand that Ryoma really loved her, the Japanese have failed properly to cherish those who would dedicate their lives to delivering them out of feudalism. Near

[20] Conversation with the author.

the end of *Assassination of Ryoma,* during the *Eija nai ka* demonstrations, Ryoma yells furiously out of the window, *"what* is all right? *what* is all right?" Ryoma is made physically near-sighted in this film, but no less near-sighted are people who would leave a man like Ryoma to languish in his hide-out, so full of desperation that he is reduced to screaming, "anybody who wants to kill me, kill me!" He and Nakaoka disarm themselves on the night of their death so as to establish, at least, the closeness of two people within this murderous context.

The masses are just outside Ryoma's door, waiting to be liberated. Instead, they allow themselves to be distracted by imaginary charms falling from the heavens. Rooted in their animism, they remain locked into a primitivism which makes them incapable of deserving a man like Ryoma. The revolution is lost before it begins. And the woman, left alone, jumps out the window (in another *jidai-geki* parody), only to fall into the waiting arms of these *Eija nai ka* fanatics in their desperate, frenzied, aimless dance.

Mere Anarchy: *The Nihilist Period Film*

The best lack all conviction, while the worst
Are full of passionate intensity.
William Butler Yeats, "The Second Coming"

Some of the most brilliant of Japanese period films have been made to demystify the Meiji Restoration. Shinoda's *Assassination* and *The Scandalous Adventures of Buraikan* (*Buraikan*, 1970) both demonstrate the pointlessness of trying to build an anti-feudal Japan out of the degenerate leavings of the Shogunate. G. B. Sansom has described the moral and political chaos of this moment in Japan's history:

> The throne rebukes great officers for doing what it has already approved, or enjoins them not to do what it knows they have already done. . . . A fantastic ethos prevails throughout the land. Patriots assassinate other patriots for views they have never held or professed, and statesmen declare intentions that everybody knows to be contrary to their real purpose. Feuds become alliances, friendships become hatreds, and the whole nation is in a state of uncertainty and doubt.[1]

Such a passage could almost stand as a plot summary for *Assassination*, with its hero, Kiyokawa, assassinating a man for we know not what reason, and being assassinated himself by a jealous fencing competitor, whom he had once defeated, for petty and meaningless ends.

Shinoda offers Kiyokawa as a typical *ronin* of his time, energetic, intelligent, restless—a dissenter. If the fate of the nation remains uncertain, so Kiyokawa wavers, unsure of his direction. He chooses to ally himself with the Emperor because he believes that he, unlike the Shogunate and its Regent, Ii, will repel the foreigners. The principal issue of the day is to deal with those foreigners who had begun to penetrate Japan ever since 1853, when the American Commodore Perry arrived in Tokyo Bay with his "black ships" to "open" Japan to trade with the West. The Russians have been present as well. The problem is complicated for patriots like Kiyokawa because both pro-Shogunate and pro-Restorationist parties invoke the slogan of repelling the foreigners in order to recruit support. Meanwhile, many among these secretly arrange foreign backing for their

[1] *The Western World and Japan*, p. 281.

side even as they pretend to be unequivocally committed to a fight to the finish to oppose foreign control of Japan.

Thus, in Kiyokawa's case, the group he finally chooses on the ground that they, the Imperial Restorationists, seem most determined to preserve Japan's autonomy, are, in fact, colluding with the very enemy they purport to oppose. Because it became clear that, without technology, no amount of resistance could withstand foreign domination, the most prescient of Japanese (Kiyokawa *not* among them) concluded that to oppose foreign control required collusion with the foreigners, if for a purpose opposite to that of the real collaborationists. The Tokugawas may have courted the foreigners because they thought that foreign wealth and collaboration would give their group an edge in retaining power at home. The other "anti-foreign" movement behind the Emperor, however, concluded that the only real way to resist was to master foreign technique and technology. This latter course outwardly resembled collusion, but had as its objective the ultimate preservation of Japanese autonomy. It is this aspect of Japan's relation to the foreign threat that Shinoda's Kiyokawa, whom one historian has dismissed as merely one more "xenophobe *ronin*,"[2] seems not to have understood.

It is a historical paradox and dilemma. Feudal Japan desired to preserve its traditions and its insular culture from foreigners who not only wanted to colonize Japan, but whose post-feudal institutions and ideology would corrupt and weaken Japanese culture, mores, and institutional life. But Japan's leadership during Meiji would find that they had to adopt the very techniques they feared in order to preserve Japan from complete conquest. Kiyokawa, in Shinoda's *Assassination*, embodies the sense of betrayal inherent in this irony of history.

He fights for the Emperor because he believes the Emperor will resist foreign control. Secretly, those closest to the Emperor meanwhile conclude that, in order to gain access to foreign technology, they must seem to make friends with these very foreigners. Kiyokawa, the purer patriot if the inferior strategist, would indeed become a liability once the Emperor's position was secured. Meiji would have had to turn on him, having used him when he was needed, because his very anti-foreign determination would now be a threat to long-term anti-foreign designs. To Shinoda, men like Kiyokawa are always betrayed because their idealism cannot correspond to the real dynamics of power, the real, duplicitous, ambivalent behavior of people—and of nations. And his story well serves Shinoda's sense of the human condition. Although Kiyokawa doesn't know it, history is beyond the reach of individuals like himself, in spite of their sincerity. He is foredoomed, and in Kiyokawa's bewildering struggle Shinoda chronicles his own despair over the idea that political action can work lasting, meaningful, revolutionary change.

Shinoda presents Kiyokawa's motive for taking political action as

[2] Paul Akamatsu, *Meji 1868: Revolution and Counter-Revolution in Japan* (New York: Harper & Row, 1972), p. 158.

despair over the disparity between ability and reward in the old feudal society. Because he is a low-ranking samurai, his possibilities for advancement are meager. He believes, as did all the film Ryomas, that men should be promoted according to their abilities and he is bitter about the impossibility of his rising above the bottom rung of the samurai hierarchy, even though he had been the brightest student at the academy. Kiyokawa would democratize the old order, and like so many of the *ronin* of his time, feels that giving his life would be a small price for such an undertaking. Nor is he ashamed of his low rank. The seven-star, special sword he carries did not come to him through his family, but had been mortgaged by a poor samurai of more noble origins. "It isn't the sword that makes a man," Kiyokawa asserts, "it's his caliber."

But despite Kiyokawa's efforts, the new society will be no more democratic than the old. Near the end of *Assassination*, a vainglorious samurai dressed up in ridiculous Napoleonic military regalia asks if Kiyokawa is yet alive. "He is only a common samurai even if he received an imperial order," he sneers. Class distinctions will persist. This Frenchified, absurd Japanese is clearly one of the survivors who will dominate Japan for the coming century. He is one of those who will preside over her overtly militarist period. Reinstated after the perfunctory postwar purge of the hierarchy that presided over Japan during the thirties and forties, he will assist in her incursions into the rest of Southeast Asia after the Second World War. Shinoda can only despair.

Kiyokawa is a man and not a hero; Shinoda is not an elitist who elevates people, making them larger than life. He does not seek characters whom others should emulate, characters who possess a control and intelligence which is admirable and rare but out of keeping with human frailty. He is incapable, for example, of creating a figure like Kurosawa's samurai leader, Kambei, in *Seven Samurai*.

Thus Kiyokawa can also be tender and loving, as he is with the prostitute Oren, whom he purchases out of bondage. The first shot of Oren is through bars. Like Kiyokawa, she is imprisoned by feudal Japan. In liberating her, he reaffirms his own commitment. Yet Kiyokawa, because he does not fully register how he is being used and abused unawares, himself falls victim to the social disarray described by Sansom. Lacking an explanation of the contradictory and chaotic behavior of his allies, his confused sense of betrayal leads to personal psychosis. Thus suddenly, seemingly inexplicably, Kiyokawa kills his first person.

Shinoda gives us no indication that Kiyokawa even knew that this man had been following him or whether he was a political or personal enemy. It is as if Kiyokawa lashes out at random, seeking the nearest target for a wrath he cannot direct. The dead man is a surrogate victim who stands as well for Kiyokawa himself—an innocent victim. It is thus an act of self-hating despair.

Blood splashes all over him. As he beheads the man, the skull freezes in mid-air, telling us that both perpetrator and victim are severed from

Assassination: There is also a freeze frame of a rush of birds streaking skyward as they scatter before Kiyokawa's relentless path.

themselves, unanchored from any fixed physical reality by the instability of their lives. Goals are separated from viable modes of implementation. Personal action has been separated from rational expectation of result. We learn the skull was grinning when it was retrieved. There is also a freeze frame of a rush of birds streaking skyward as they scatter before Kiyokawa's relentless path. Kiyokawa's violence reveals his panic in the presence of his inability to comprehend what is happening, his utter confusion. To express this, Shinoda arranges that the film's events do not proceed in chronological order. In the beginning, we learn that Kiyokawa has been acquitted of this random murder because the Premier needs his sword. He is the only man capable of organizing a free-lance, mercenary samurai army. "In these turbulent times," one cynic calculates, "he may prove useful." Another assesses Kiyokawa's dedication and prowess as "a razor in skilled hands [that] works wonders," even if "you may cut your own finger."

And indeed Kiyokawa will be driven to self-injury by those who use him. In the face of events he cannot understand or control, he is manipulated and thus corrupted. After he beheads the man in misdirected rage, the inevitable fruit of impulse in the absence of comprehension or perception of the root of his anger, the horror of his act fills Kiyokawa with simultaneous self-loathing and terror. He now dreads not only what is happening, but himself, internalizing both responsibility and guilt.

Trembling in Oren's arms, Kiyokawa repeats "blood splashed, blood splashed." In such times the victors are those capable of neither shame nor guilt. Kiyokawa's future assassin, a pathetic little man named Sasaki, angry because Kiyokawa once beat him in a fencing tournament, reads in the diary of Oren, who has since died, of the moment when Kiyokawa revealed to her his terror, his sense of vulnerability. Only then does he perceive that Kiyokawa's head can be his: "I can, I can kill him," he exults. It is Kiyokawa's humanity which ensures his death in such a world.

Midway through the film, Kiyokawa decides to fight on the side of the Emperor. When, in the film, Ii is assassinated (as he was in real life on March 24, 1860 by angry Mito samurai whose hereditary Lord Nariaki had been humiliated by Ii), Kiyokawa's followers dance in glee. They, too, had been plotting Ii's death. Assassination is omnipresent and in the air, as in our time. Plotters are ubiquitous, expressive of the disintegration of social decency or coherence. Kiyokawa leads his army on behalf of the Emperor and celebrates at a victory party near the end of the film.

But now, joined by his carousing, masterless samurai, Kiyokawa feels no joy. The fight is over and yet he is overwhelmed by a feeling of emptiness as he begins to see that nothing has been won. Earlier, seduced by the spurious power he seemed to be accumulating, Kiyokawa had confided to Ryoma, "what a feeling it is to command an army!" Taking on the coloration of his surroundings, his character so deteriorates that he kills a man whose life he had once saved. And after the party he will personally behead a group of "enemies" when none of his followers will do it. In the rain, a sea of parasols lyrically open as if in opposition to Kiyokawa's violence. They seem to affirm that life, apart from obsessional struggles for power, is still wholesome. For Kiyokawa, however, killing has become easy, as his idealism turns to infatuation with personal glory; he speaks of a "Kiyokawa Shogunate," as if the bloodshed and the fervor were for himself alone. The Kiyokawa who had held onto his sword so tightly, as he waited for word from the Emperor, that his men had to pry his fingers loose in the morning, now, at this party, having achieved some measure of prominence, writes a *haiku* in homage to power:

> Heading the van I'll be
> Till I die in glee
> So straight is the path
> To the Imperial plea.

As his men, in soft focus behind him, dance and sing to the *haiku*, Kiyokawa stands at the window and lets fall from his fingers a message from a friend which reads, "forgive my willfulness." His mood is one of ennui. Emotionally fatigued, Kiyokawa, as Shinoda's surrogate, experiences a sense of the futility of all things. He is "victorious," but there is no gratification in his victory. He seems to have forgotten about restoring the Emperor and even about the foreign threat. Power brings no fulfillment; peace and enlightenment elude him. Oren has been tortured and killed by his enemies. At this moment Kiyokawa enters a life of dissipation.

Assassination moves to the fulfillment of its logic. In a brothel, drunk, Kiyokawa calls a prostitute by the dead Oren's name. Outside, he wavers from side to side, the hand-held camera expressive of his disoriented sensibility. The cowardly assassin emerges from the shadows, and Kiyokawa is an easy victim. The hat which was serving as his disguise bobs forward. Blood now splashes onto the face of his assassin, Sasaki, as once it had splashed onto his. The unbroken cycle of incoherent violence denies any value to the Meiji Restoration, as the destructiveness of the past is shown to be moving unthwarted into the new era. All the characters, including Kiyokawa, like the goldfish of Yamaoka, one of the conspirators, remain enclosed by the glass bowl of their time, an epoch no different from the past and exactly like the future.

Other films about the last days of the Tokugawa Shogunate reflect an anarchic mood with its abiding despair for the future of Japan. Throughout Kurosawa's *Sanjuro*, the hero, Tsubaki Sanjuro, has expended great effort and risked his life to rescue the kidnapped chamberlain. Near the end of the film, when all has been resolved, the fledgling samurai, who have been the *ronin*'s willing if inept pupils and a most appreciative audience, assemble. The chamberlain waddles in, annoyed that one person is late, one place at the table unoccupied. This place, of course, belongs to the homeless *ronin* who is to be honored at this feast for making the chamberlain's return to power possible.

The chamberlain's wife, who earlier had taught Tsubaki Sanjuro that good swords should be kept in their scabbards, now reprimands her husband for forgetting "Tsubaki's" ("Camellia's") name. The chamberlain jokes about his not being popular with the people because he has a "horse face" and repeats an anecdote in which someone once said about him, "the horse's face is shorter than the rider's." Clearly he lacks not only the charisma, but the largesse, the leadership potential, and the grandeur of the *ronin* who saved his life.

When Tsubaki Sanjuro still doesn't appear, the old lady sends all the zealous young "warriors" to search for him and bring him back. But the chamberlain, wiser, thanks Sanjuro for not returning: "an extraordinary man like him would prove too much for me." Those who will lead in the coming epoch of Meiji will be lesser men. Those, like the Kiyokawas and the Ryomas who enabled them to lead, will be destroyed by people on their own side who fear their unselfishness and their revolutionary ideas.

Their vision will be too large for the smaller-minded men epitomized by Kurosawa's chamberlain. And, like Ryoma and Kiyokawa, Tsubaki

Sanjuro is presented by Kurosawa as too broad-spirited a man to work for a clan. His sense of the world, like that of Ryoma, is vaster than the narrow, claustrophobic, and feudal clan sensibility which will rule the new Japan. A close-up of the unclaimed kimono which Sanjuro is destined never to wear reminds us of that absence of moral leadership which will characterize the coming age.

Celluloid Samurai: *The Protest Film in Disguise*

Every act of rebellion expresses a nostalgia
for innocence and an appeal to the essence of being.
Albert Camus, *The Rebel*

"The customs and usages of feudal times," wrote Yukio Ozaki in the early part of this century, "are so deeply impressed upon the minds of men here that even the idea of political parties, as soon as it enters the brains of our countrymen, germinates and grows according to feudal notions."[1] The democratic functioning of political parties, continued Ozaki, is by definition impossible in Japan since the relationship between leaders and members inevitably degenerates to one "between a feudal lord and his liegemen."[2] For the Japanese concerned with social justice, the problem becomes how to root out old patterns, how to alter radically the entire psychic configuration of the culture.

Film directors who have lamented the authoritarian nature of Japanese society have often turned to the past, seeking to expose and attack feudal remnants at their source. But the past has also been the arena in which directors have sought to resolve these issues because it appears less threatening, both to audience and to authority, when injustices against which they protest are not presented in contemporary terms. There has been, however, an important practical reason why directors like Masaki Kobayashi, protesting against feudal remnants in the culture, have turned to the period film. Setting their films in a safe historical context, they could not so easily be stigmatized as dissidents and radicals in the precarious film markets still controlled by the major companies, which are themselves corporate conglomerates steeped in feudal ways. At the same time, when these *jidai-geki* suggest that the brutalities inflicted upon people are fixed in some distant epoch, no member of the audience is fooled. During the 1950s and early 1960s the period film again became a surrogate for modern Japan and a subtle cultural device for simultaneously assailing modern Japan, with her current evils, while showing the ingrained historical, social, and structural roots of the problems at hand.

[1] Cited by Norman, "Feudal Background of Japanese Politics," p. 387.
[2] *Ibid.*, p. 388.

And yet one is brought back to the view that the indirection and the slight dissembling involved in setting anti-feudal films in the past enabled the Japanese to accommodate themselves to the film's ideas despite their frequently inflammatory nature. Attacking present society through the period film almost takes on the quality of ritual in which the rules of the game are honored. By placing current dissent in a historical mode, face is saved for those who know the issues are real but are discomforted by open criticism because the culture frowns upon it as a breach of decorum. In this sense the very phenomenon of the *jidai-geki* reveals the ongoing feudal norms of the culture, even as the same *jidai-geki* may attack feudalism.

Two of the most outspoken of the anti-feudal period films are Masaki Kobayashi's *Seppuku*[3] (1962) and *Samurai Rebellion* or *Rebellion* (*Joiuchi*, 1967). Both are set in the Tokugawa period. *Seppuku*, a far finer film and perhaps Kobayashi's best, argues that the conscience of the individual and his worth as a human being supersede in value the mentality of the clan. It denies the right of the clan to dispose of human beings as if they lacked all intrinsic worth. *Rebellion*, which degenerates too soon into swordplay for its own sake, draws on a tradition discussed by Masao Maruyama:[4] that the truly loyal servant in feudal times must, as in our own, himself be the judge of what was in his lord's interest. He has to decide for himself what constitutes benevolent rule.

Rarely invoked, and frequently provoking the most severe punishment, this tradition flourished nevertheless. According to Inazo Nitobe, it was part of the code of *bushido* to look down upon the man who sacrificed his own conscience to "the capricious will . . . or fancy of a soverign."[5] Such a man would be despised for fawning, and for servile compliance. It was nevertheless also true, as Nitobe has to admit, that the only means open to the samurai in making his last appeal to the conscience of his lord was the shedding of his own blood, for as both Kobayashi films reveal, such rebellions, necessary and just and valid as they were, also represented a dead end for the daring samurai. Paradoxically, this form of rebellion was itself feudal in nature: the rebel had merely internalized feudal values, and his revolt took the form of protest against the lord's or master's own departure from them. This, too, is why the rebel, however justified in his struggle, often ends in suicide by *seppuku*. For the feudal code still obliges that the lord be honored. Even when the person serving him must, through dissent, remind him of his transgression of feudal propriety, the highest and most sincere fealty to feudalism, in the very course of rebellion, is the self-immolation of the dissident, both as a final protest and as proof of *his* fealty to what is right.

[3] Inadequately rendered in English as *Hara Kiri*.

[4] "Chusei to Hangyaku," *Kindai Nihon Shisoshi Koza*, 6 (1960): 393–397. See as well, R. P. Dore, "The Legacy of Tokugawa Education," *Changing Japanese Attitudes Toward Modernization*, ed. Marius B. Jansen (Princeton: Princeton University Press, 1965).

[5] *Bushido: The Soul of Japan* (New York and London: G. P. Putnam's Sons, 1905), p. 92.

The individual act of conscience, then as now, validates the life of the man who would rather die than submit to being dehumanized, but it does not shake the foundations of authority or leave the world a less tyrannical place for coming generations. The *jidai-geki* too frequently ignores this, and thereby unwittingly exalts the single, heroic samurai (played in Kobayashi either by Mifune or Tatsuya Nakadai) who rises beyond the narrow privilege of his class. He becomes the defiant individual, a conscience-bearer for the many. The lone defier thus takes on the qualities of a superman in a conception at once elitist and feudal. The implication is that ordinary people are incapable of such feats, that it takes a leader. And thus do these films fortify the very notion of an elite that they appear to be challenging. Even the finest of Japanese period films, Kurosawa's *Seven Samurai*, which as Donald Richie has said, is perhaps the best Japanese film ever made,[6] is open to this charge.

Seppuku opens with the camera panning down the white wig and armor which represent the ancestors of the House of Ii. They are enshrined in a sacred room and symbolize the samurai spirit. By the end of the film these have become the empty accoutrements of an age cherishing mores empty of human value. When the hero, Hanshiro Tsugumo (Tatsuya Nakadai), must commit *seppuku* as the film draws to its gory finish, he pulls down these relics with him, as he would have done in a more lasting way had there been a political outlet for his rage against the destructiveness of *bushido* and the class spirit kept alive by samurai brutality.

When the action begins in May of 1630, the Tokugawas have been in power but twenty-seven years. Already corruption and hypocrisy within the samurai world foreshadow the demise of the Shogunate. The protagonist, Tsugumo, is a homeless samurai, unemployed in these times of peace. He has been a *ronin* since 1619 when his own lord fell victim to the Tokugawa consolidation of power through confiscation of the lands of rival feudal lords. Only halfway through the film do we learn why Tsugumo has chosen the House of Ii in which to commit the *seppuku* he claims to desire. At the beginning, he begs them to take him in, his only motive that he may die honorably.

The clan informs him that when a supplicant asks permission to commit *seppuku* in their compound, they take him at his word. The plight of the *ronin* forms the background to Kobayashi's film. For these masterless samurai are not merely without social function but are desperate and destitute. As a means of obligating the House of Ii, and other clans as well, to hire their services, *ronin* threaten to commit suicide at the house gates if they are not taken in and provided with samurai employment—or at least bribed with money, in exchange for which they would take their leave.

As it would be a disgrace to the House of Ii for samurai to commit *seppuku* on their steps because the clan had failed to take them in, it

[6] *Films of Akira Kurosawa*, p. 108.

is understood by both indigent *ronin* and clan alike that the threat to commit suicide is not meant literally, but is, rather, a ploy to obligate the clan towards them in order to avoid the disgrace and responsibility for the suicide. Thus it is understood, by both *ronin* and clan alike, that the samurai desires a means of survival and not, of course, disembowelment.

But this desire can only be expressed by a warrior within the convention of *bushido* and in the language of honor—which calls for *seppuku*. Knowing this, not only does the cruel House of Ii refuse these *ronin*, and even deny them an act of charity in the form of money, but the clan insists on the actual enactment of suicide. The unsuspecting *ronin* is forced to carry out the deed because the cynical clan takes him literally and informs him that, as a *ronin*'s word is his bond, he has no choice. Worse, these clans know that the destitute *ronin* often have had to pawn their swords, thus leaving them to carry out the ritual disembowelment with crude, makeshift weapons such as bamboo swords, subjecting the *ronin* to unspeakable pain. In *Seppuku* the clan tells Tsugumo the story of his own son-in-law, Chijiiwa, of whom they had made an example by showing him no mercy when he had come begging at their door.

Seppuku is characterized by sharp contrasts in black and white with stark and ascetic geometrical shot compositions, at once formalistic and cold. They express the hypocrisy of the clan order, a class structure with neither morality nor justice at its center. The geometrically composed shots convey, in their austerity, the absence of any softening humanity within the samurai code invoked by the House of Ii against a weak and helpless Chijiiwa.

Gloatingly informed that he must commit *seppuku* to prove he is worthy to be a member of their house, he is ensnared in a feudal "Catch 22." When he tries to flee, requesting two days' grace, they trap him with another empty samurai precept: "A samurai's word is sacred." When he reveals that he has only a bamboo sword with which to disembowel himself, they insist that he go through with the suicide because "a samurai's sword is his soul," and he must be taught a lesson for pawning his hallowed weapon. And despite the horror of his having to rend and tear himself with bamboo, they insist that he cannot be beheaded until his disembowelment is completed, in order to renew the decaying tradition of *seppuku*, which had been undermined because many samurai had ceased to adhere to the full violence of the ritual. Some, they observe, were even using a symbolic fan in place of a sword and, avoiding disembowelment, dying instantly, if unheroically, by decapitation.

The retainers remain seated in their positions around the courtyard, barely moving, the symmetry of the scene expressing Kobayashi's horror of codes devoid of compassion. Chijiiwa's *seppuku*, shown in flashback, takes intolerably long; finally the sword must be stuck into the mat in front of him with the man throwing himself upon it. So excruciating is the pain that he bites off his tongue, an act regarded as cowardly and shameful for a samurai.

Tsugumo has come not only to revenge his son-in-law but to undermine the code of *bushido* itself by forcing the clan to admit they were unjust in not granting Chijiiwa the two-day respite for which he had begged. Tsugumo has already robbed three Ii retainers of their topknots, a hair styling which symbolizes their value as samurai. By insisting that one of these three serve as his second, Tsugumo gains the time to force them to listen to the story of his life.

"Our lives are like unto houses built on foundations of sand," he tells them, vulnerable to any "ill wind." The 12,000 retainers of his Geishu clan had been considered threats to the Tokugawa and were left unemployed to survive as they might. He and his daughter had been obliged to make and sell umbrellas and fans. We are shown, in flashback, Tsugumo as an affectionate father—one who, atypically, refused to allow his daughter to be "adopted" by a rich family, a euphemism for concubinage. He would not sacrifice her, as others in his place might have done, although he would have thereby gained a position for himself.

Instead, she marries a poor samurai, a children's tutor named Motome Chijiiwa, and they have a child. Tsugumo is the doting grandfather, singing to the baby, and Kobayashi cuts rapidly from this scene to that of the narration as rows of unsympathetic samurai, assembled at the Ii garden, await Tsugumo's *seppuku*. A whistle links the two scenes through a sound overlap.

Tsugumo's daughter contracts tuberculosis and her baby falls ill. It is this tragedy which forces Motome Chijiiwa to go to the House of Ii and threaten to commit *seppuku* at their door. He had been prevented from working by the samurai code, which forbade his entering a trade. Feudal custom allowed him no choice but to present himself to the House of Ii and beg for mercy. After his body is brought home, Tsugumo, as a true samurai, had assumed responsibility for what happened, furious with himself because he had never thought of pawning his own swords. "I clung to these worthless symbols," he tells himself bitterly. It is a remark that moves out of the film to speak to the Japanese of our time. Unlike his young son-in-law, he "wouldn't have dared" thus to strip himself of his status.

Tsugumo tells the Ii clan that his son-in-law was right to place family need above samurai pride. The fault lies in the ruthlessness of the Shogunate in abolishing provincial lords with no concern for how their retainers are to live. It is the feudal prerogative itself that is held wanting in decency and honor. "Our honor merely adorns the surface," Tsugumo asserts to the assembled samurai. In mockery and scorn he tosses the topknots of the three samurai who facilitated Motome's death before the startled eyes of the chamberlain. The loss of their ridiculous topknots has necessitated the absence of these samurai from the clan gathering—eloquent corroboration of Tsugumo's derision of the emptiness and superficiality of samurai "honor."

The Ii leaders, of course, refuse to acknowledge the power and merit of Tsugumo's charges. To do so would gravely damage their prestige and undermine their very existence. The chamberlain (Rentaro Mikuni) will not even admit he was wrong not to ask Motome why he so desperately sought one or two days' respite before committing *seppuku*. Unless the Ii chamberlain requested him to tell his story, samurai etiquette prevented Motome from offering an explanation, so fixed were the rules defining proper samurai behavior and manner.

All that is left to Tsugumo is to kill as many as he can in revenge, and this he does in a brilliantly choreographed bloodbath. Before committing *seppuku* himself, he hauls down the relics of the ancestor, as if the sight of this symbol gives him renewed strength to fight. Unable to defeat him in the samurai manner, the Ii retainers must shoot Tsugumo with guns. And the very fact that they never get the opportunity to behead him according to proper *seppuku* ritual presages the end of the samurai class.

The clan log must deny the truth of its own history and therefore contains nothing of Tsugumo's story. It records that the four dead retainers died of illness, while Tsugumo died of a *seppuku* he himself had requested. A partial victory mediates the nihilism of the ending. One (Tetsuro Tamba) of the three who lost their topknots commits *seppuku* willingly; the other two are ordered so to die. The rest of the clan cannot fail to observe that the samurai code can now be retained only through lies. Tsugumo has not totally failed so long as the clan retainers have heard his story and know that the ancestor relic now has to be propped up through falsehood. The clan log may read with confidence that "the House of Ii will prosper throughout the ages" and may take delight in the fact that their heir, Bennosuke, has been praised at Edo Castle for his handling of this "difficult matter." But two centuries later, a descendant of this same house, the Tokugawa minister Ii (Naosuke), will himself be assassinated as if in retribution for the lack of mercy shown Motome Chijiiwa. "My fate today may be that of others tomorrow," Tsugumo had said. His ultimate victory would be the fall of feudalism itself.

Seppuku attempts gratification through the struggle of a superhuman individual rising to a superhuman strength derived from his purity and the inherent truth of what he believes. The feats of swordplay accomplished by actor Nakadai at the end tend to distract us from how little Tsugumo has achieved. The Ii clan survives at the expense of as many human lives as it takes. It can even spare its leaders should they prove to be an embarrassment. Built on lies though it may be, the feudal structure is unimpaired by this one man's brave attempt to hold up a mirror to the values of an age. That it will take centuries before even the formal trappings of feudalism will be dismantled—while their substance remains alive and well in contemporary Japan—cannot help but add an abiding pessimism to Kobayashi's film.

Kurosawa's *jidai-geki* are much more sophisticated than those of Kobayashi in their attacks on feudalism. They never set out a schema within which they explicitly assail feudal standards as such. Kurosawa's films create living alternatives against which the dead weight of loyalty, obedience, and subservience palls. His films never become outraged simplistic protests against "clan tyranny" as do *Seppuku* and *Rebellion*. The flow of Kurosawa's creative imagination dramatizes the felt life of people who make discoveries, who change and live by new values which permit them to be human. The *jidai-geki* of Kurosawa, if less explicitly prescriptive, reach further than Kobayashi's because they introduce alternative and anti-feudal values which work in the lives of his protagonists. Thus does Kurosawa show in embryo what life might be like, were feudal ways undone.

During the Second World War, Kurosawa made *Sanshiro Sugata* (1943), his first film, and *Men Who Tread on the Tiger's Tail* (*Tora no O o Fumu Otokotachi,* 1945), two *jidai-geki* which seem to betray an ambivalence towards feudalism. Each explicitly glorifies feudal values, although it must be said that the militarist government of the day would not have permitted films to be made which clearly offered any other point of view. Yet, into the interstices of these films, Kurosawa works a subtle rejection of the feudal encompassment of human life. He avoids direct challenge, but gives his intense focus to the indomitable spirit of individuals, a sensibility which feudalism will ultimately find it impossible to accommodate.

Indicative of this, both films, although they were allowed to be made, were severely censored by the Japanese wartime regime. *Sugata* was shown in 1944, but shortened by 1,856 feet. *Men Who Tread on the Tiger's Tail* was completely censored by the Japanese for being insufficiently supportive of feudal values. Interestingly, it was also banned by the American Occupation because of the film's portrayal of the loyalty and grace of the feudal lords, qualities which Kurosawa admires apart from their feudal context. That he conjoins these virtues to his sense of the evanescence of their power was a subtlety obviously beyond the perceptive powers of the Occupation authorities. And it may well be that *Men Who Tread on the Tiger's Tail* was feared by them because it evoked established Japanese ways and a sensibility compared to which the ideas sponsored by the American Occupation would have to be regarded as crude.

A dialectical ambiguity about Japan's past colors Kurosawa's greatest period film, *Seven Samurai.* Samurai are sharply contrasted with peasants and other commoners, as is feudalism with its replacement. Besieged by bandits, a peasant village decides on the advice of its ancient elder to defend itself by hiring *ronin,* masterless samurai now hungry and without work. This is a desperate resort, as samurai are known to both scorn and oppress peasants. It is a sign of the troubled times that villagers dare approach their normal social enemy, and that any *ronin* would even consider such a proposal.

The seven samurai train the peasantry to fight with them. By the end, through persistence and determination, they have killed every one of the marauding bandits, but this very victory, achieved through an alliance with their normal antagonists, serves to elucidate the real theme of the film, the passing away of the samurai class and the values by which Japan has lived and which it will be unable to maintain in days ahead.

In the tragedy of their decline, Kurosawa's sixteenth-century *ronin* become heroes and, seeking to surmount an era in which they have been rendered obsolete, emerge as larger than life. If, before, samurai warriors performed bloody feats of "honor" in service to a clan, now, cut loose from employment, meaningful social station, and the rationale for their existence, such men seek ways to recover purpose. The diversity of their unanchored activity reflects the central problem of which, in their time, they are an expression. An era is in rapid disintegration and passing, while new values and social arrangements have not yet been discovered. Hence these *ronin* roam the countryside, ghosts cut off from the body of the social structure. Like wraiths, most of them perform wild and rebellious acts, trumpeting their defiance into the night of obsolescence that closes upon them as they disappear.

Kurosawa, however, chooses in *Seven Samurai* to focus on six *ronin* who are good men, representing the best of their class. And he unfolds how only in violent moments of transition, when one epoch is passing but its successor has not yet appeared, can these *ronin* express the finest aspects of their natures. The very desperation of the times permits these *ronin* acts which can occur only outside of fixed feudal relations and their established world. They are properly no longer samurai, but *ronin*, masterless men whose disengagement from feudal life, although traumatic and destructive to them personally, is precisely what allows them to jeopardize their lives to save a peasant village and to perform gratuitious, selfless acts of generosity. Had they remained integrated within the *han* (clan) system in service to a feudal lord, their assignment could not conceivably have been one of saving an obscure, miserable village of ragged peasants from predatory bandits.

In contrast as well as in profound similarity to the six good-hearted *ronin* (the seventh, a former peasant, will be added later) are the bandits themselves, among whom there are also masterless samurai, driven by their condition to become scavenging predators. Bandit and defender alike are of the identical social group, driven by the same condition to opposite choices. Nothing better expresses the passing of the samurai, the fading of his social utility and *raison d'être*. Nor is it a samurai function, or even a reflection of their code, which leads some to defend the weak and others to prey upon them. In times so out of joint, men are thrust into decisions flowing solely from their own character. Kurosawa, in introducing the ideal of the noble samurai, grants the very model of feudal virtue an anti-feudal quality. Only functioning *outside* the system which gave them life allows his *ronin* to act nobly.

Most *ronin* whom they approach refuse outright to aid peasants, unwilling to work for a bowl of rice or to risk their lives in a cause demeaning of their dignity. To serve lowly farmers without rank is the ultimate degradation for such people. Yet it must be said that through his six *ronin*, who will transcend the confines of rank, Kurosawa sounds a paean to the samurai class which could produce so noble a set of men. As the film opens, the samurai class is rotting from within, degenerating to a rampant selfishness and arrogance that have rendered most of its members unworthy of rank or honor. Kurosawa, however, pursues a broader historical perspective.

Underlying his creation of six *ronin* at once so kindly, appealing, generous, and beautiful is the perception that even the most retrograde social order has its beginnings in forms of organization and in values superior to those preceding them. Feudalism represented an enormous advance over tribal life, wherein small clusters of village-based groups warred and nomadic bands preyed upon each other. The elaborate series of obligations, the social organization, and the value placed upon loyalty to larger clans granted a degree of social stability, and consequent productive activity, on a scale previously unknown.

At its inception, feudalism provided order, purpose, and a sense of higher responsibility. Personal pursuits were subordinated to higher goals. It was only with the deterioration of feudal society into tyranny, arbitrary repression, and constant warfare that its values came to serve destructive ends. Kurosawa, in portraying the disintegration of the feudal order, is also conscious that the best of its ideals had merit—merit already threatened by the social decay of a feudalism in rapid decline by the sixteenth century, the period in which *Seven Samurai* is set.

Kurosawa loves the six true samurai with an intensity that transforms this adventure film into an elegy. Each of the six *ronin* expresses a facet of the nobility of his class. The seventh—the former peasant, Kikuchiyo, played by Toshiro Mifune—who joins them later, is equally if not more beloved by the director, producing emotional moments which seem to absolve Kurosawa of any suggestion of elitism.

Kambei, the leader (Takashi Shimura), long bereft of parents and friends, is the samurai at his humanitarian best, a man whose hair has turned grey fighting in the service of his lord. As he listens to Kambei's story, Katsushiro (Ko Kimura), the youngest samurai and Kambei's disciple, weeps on the first of two occasions in the film, in homage to the heroic life Kambei has led. The master swordsman Kyuzo, listening unnoticed at the door, is confirmed in his commitment to the enterprise by this saga of sadness and the final emptiness of this old samurai's life, his long years of dedication having left him alone and insecure, with nothing ahead but harsher days.

Kambei is a rare human being because the externals of his samurai identity are, for him, of little moment. He is prepared, during his first scene in the film, to cut off the topknot that denotes a samurai in order to disguise himself as a priest and so to save a kidnapped baby from a thief, a gratuitous act that at once allows us—as it does the peasants searching for samurai—to know that he will help the village as well. The epitome of the traditional Japanese at his finest, Kambei is all-wise and equally modest. He rubs his head in embarrassment whenever he is praised and speaks only in understatement. His every word carries the weight of that sincerity of which only samurai seem capable in Kurosawa's work. "I'll always appreciate your sacrifice," he tells the peasants early in the film when they, themselves starving, hand him a bowl of rice. The words are incidental and inadequate to the feeling they convey, a fact apparent to all.

Seven Samurai: Each embodies one facet of the nobility of the warrior. Kyuzo, the swordsman, whose moves are so swift that they are
undiscernible to the naked eye, reveals the samurai's skill and
control.

In his concern for the disadvantaged, Kurosawa clearly rejects the feudal.
In so doing he also mourns the passing of those who lived by a code of
service and maintained the best of feudal tradition. At every moment in
Seven Samurai, even when Kambei speaks in such delicate understatement
as to comment on peasant sacrifice without once referring to his own,
Kurosawa reminds us that a world in which there are no longer men like
Kambei will not necessarily be a better place. Kurosawa's heart goes out to
this gentle yet totally effective man, for whom a thoughtless act or a
malicious world would be inconceivable. Kambei moves with grace and
purpose, his very carriage justifying the effort of living and the sufferings
wrought by history. Kurosawa's creation of samurai like Kambei and the
ideals he embodies simultaneously reflects the dismay of Japanese intellectuals over the crassness which settled on Japan with the onset of capitalist development. The lost ideal once embodied by feudal notions of dignity
and service has, of course, led many to look to the past as a source of

redemption, and beneath its surface *Seven Samurai*, too, partakes of this tendency.

Each of the other samurai also embodies one facet of the nobility of the warrior. Kyuzo, the swordsman, whose moves are so swift that they are undiscernible to the naked eye, reveals the samurai's skill and control. Heihachi, the wood-cutting samurai, reflects the inherently cheerful and simple good nature belying the stereotype of the two-sword-carrying belligerent. Gorobei, representing wit and intellect, accepts the assignment because Kambei's character "fascinates" him. Shichiroji, Kambei's old friend, joins immediately out of loyalty and comradeship, the constancy of devotion unaffected by years of separation—traits which characterize the most eminently civilized.

The youngest, Katsushiro, who wishes only that Kambei teach him how to be a samurai—an anomaly in this time when the samurai class is rapidly becoming extinct—is loved by Kurosawa almost as much as the leader is revered. This youth embodies samurai innocence, trust, faith, beauty, and spontaneity. Through his eyes we are permitted to admire each of the others for what they do best. Out of his youth and unselfconscious ability to express his feelings, he tells Kazuo, "you're great. I've always wanted to tell you that"; he finds Kazuo "fearless, skillful and gentle"—and awesome, as indeed he is.

It is also the young Katsushiro who most pities the peasants. When their store of rice, which they have brought to feed the samurai they enlist, is stolen in an early scene before they journey to the village, he rains a flood of coins on the floor so they may buy more. And, already a true samurai, he objects to even the smallest expression of thanks. Yet, still an adolescent, it is he who, picking flowers, discovers Shino, the village girl whose father, to protect his daughter, had disguised her as a boy. Far from intending rape, Katsushiro cannot even accept the girl's own advances and expectations. He is at once too shy and too committed to the service of the elder samurai he admires. None of the samurai has private passions or indulgences of any moment; all are as dedicated to their mission as saints.

Before such human beings, the peasants appear paltry, selfish, and weak. The helpless Yohei can barely hold a spear; Manzo is forever worried about his daughter Shino; Rikichi, whose wife has been kidnapped by the bandits, is under constant stress, his tension expressed in the large vein protruding from his forehead. Yet the linking figures among the peasantry are indispensable to the action, for they alone enable the samurai to make contact with this peasant class they have traditionally scorned. They remind us that, historically, samurai had been dependent on the peasantry: for centuries their feudal lords had, in fact, paid their annual stipends in the very rice exacted from farmers like these.

It will be the seventh "samurai," Kikuchiyo, born and bred a peasant, who will enable the samurai and the peasants to make contact. He alone is able to beckon the peasants from their hiding places when the samurai arrive because he understands their fear of the warriors. His vitality was

expressed in his first scene, as he watched Kambei rescue the child. Using
an extension of normal duration, Kurosawa employs two shots for Kikuchiyo's gesture of pushing ahead of the crowd to get the best view of
Kambei. Unlike the samurai, and despite his ineptitude at the skills they
have perfected, he has a natural self-sufficiency and capacity for survival
that proves indispensable to them. He can catch fish with his bare hands;
they cannot. He can fight as well as they, although it is when Kikuchiyo
sleeps in a barn, as he does with the peasant Rikichi, that he feels most
relaxed because it is "like old times."

In his most important scene Kikuchiyo speaks on behalf of the peasantry, denying passionately, and with historical detail, the view of the world
that Kurosawa has up to now presented through the eyes of the *ronin*.
The samurai have been elegant, noble, and graceful, while the peasants
have appeared weak, cringing, deviously selfish. When the samurai discover that the peasants have a cache of armor, swords, and other weapons
stripped from the bodies of dead samurai, they identify with these fallen
comrades and, in rage, consider dropping the entire enterprise. They seem
about to attack the very peasants they have pledged to help.

Kikuchiyo, in a rare close-up, speaks directly into the camera as he
defends the peasants as a class and as historical victims of the entire feudal
order. He enumerates the multiple abuses to which they have been subject
for centuries at the hands of the samurai class. If they are "foxy" beasts—
mean, stingy and murderous—it is samurai who have made them so. Theirs
has been the response of the weak to unending persecution. Their villages
have been burnt. They have been forced to labor. Their women have been
raped or kidnapped, their food stolen or gratuitously destroyed. Now the
very samurai who have preyed upon the poor of the countryside are themselves suffering the experience of extinction as a viable social entity and as
a class. Perhaps, Kikuchiyo's words imply, they have earned the disdain of
history. Immediately, the others recognize the peasant origins of Kikuchiyo,
whose flood of words bespeaks indisputable experience. The truths he
utters are validated as the film ends and the peasants return to their
planting.

Thus the admiration of Kurosawa, especially for the master-disciple
relationship between Kambei and Katsushiro, is tempered by unrelenting
exposure of the historical role played by samurai as a class. The samurai are
six good men who hark back to a tradition no longer viable or sustained
by feudalism itself. Ironically, those noble *ronin*, despite their superior
quality as people, are now able to act only as individuals, although they
are fervently opposed to individualism. It is the peasants who preserve
their group function. For the village to survive, the self must be subordinated to the community—the individual, however assertive, blended in
the group. The peasant experience shows that people tied to natural processes in productive labor will surmount all vicissitudes. The samurai are
cast off from the life process and from a productive social role. The very
communalism of the village reveals that, in working together, the peasants

endure. Social forms must derive from this experience or they will fade away, like the world of the samurai.

Only through collective struggle is survival possible or can society itself be sustained. The samurai, having ceased to participate in a collective identity, are vanishing as a class because they have become parasites on a community to which they have ceased to belong. It is tragic in terms of these six, because they are better people than samurai historically. But all seven regain their heroic role only in relation to what they can teach the villagers about a collective unity now gone forever from their own lives. "He who thinks only about himself will destroy himself too," says Kambei. The noble values, the selfless dedication which these good samurai preserve and represent, can now be granted social expression only by their connection to the defense of the village. This, Kurosawa tells us, is the legacy of feudalism which we would profit by accepting. The seven samurai can live on in the lives of the peasants if their example becomes part of the communal life. The samurai put their skills, perhaps for the first time, at the service of ordinary people and teach them how to call forth their own latent strength which has lain dormant through years of misery and abuse.

At the beginning of the film we have heard the lament of the women: "We don't have a chance. We're born to suffer. That's our lot." One says, "we might as well hang ourselves." Kambei teaches by example, creating the interdependence that sparks this film. By attachment to the cause of the village, the samurai regain fleeting meaning. In turn, the villagers

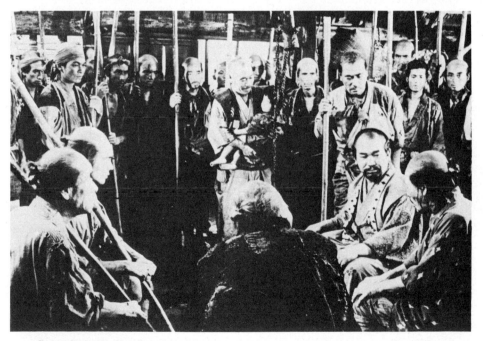

Seven Samurai: Kambei is teaching the peasants to overcome centuries of egoistic individualism as well as defeatism.

must master warrior skills previously the preserve of the privileged, the feudal elite, and turn these to their own ends. They must learn, as well, the self-esteem, confidence, pride, and defiance of the dying samurai order, yet use these qualities for productive, not destructive, ends.

Kambei is a stern and adamant instructor, even drawing his sword against the peasants when they refuse to accept his notion of collective struggle. As he holds a child through most of this scene, his humane purpose is clear. He is teaching the peasants to overcome centuries of egotistic individualism as well as defeatism. The lesson takes effect, and the man who had refused to sacrifice his house for the defense of the community later tells the others to forget "those worthless shacks" and remain at their posts. Kurosawa is careful to point out that "anyone can learn." As the action progresses, Kambei is decreasingly needed, and, as the peasants recover a sense of self and of collective confidence, the samurai begin to fade from importance in the structure of the film. This subtle process underlines the tragedy of the samurai. To survive, the samurai would have had to abandon their historical role and become peasants, tillers of the soil. Yet, the very psychology and social meaning of the samurai sensibility and sense of self precluded such a choice. Ironically, the samurai are finally less adaptable than the peasants themselves, for if the peasants can acquire samurai skills (to some extent), the samurai cannot acquire those of the peasants. Their class is truly obsolete and they must disappear.

Thus do the ways of the peasants begin to prevail, as in one scene a tottering old woman slowly approaches and takes her scythe to a bandit prisoner-of-war, helped by all to avenge her son's death. In keeping with the rules of combat, Kambei would have kept him alive, but in this village, fighting for its life, such scruples belong to an age when wars were fought for honor, like medieval tournaments, rather than for survival.

The prevailing of the peasant ethos is also manifested in the considerable attention Kurosawa gives Mifune in the role of Kikuchiyo, the rambunctious former peasant. In rescuing an infant, he sees his own life repeat itself, for he, too, had been saved as a child in similar circumstances, when his peasant parents were killed. In his personal history he carries the suffering of the peasant experience. In samurai terms, Kikuchiyo does everything wrong; still an egocentric individualist, he even leaves his post. Kurosawa is fond of him not alone because of the attractiveness and vitality of his spirit. His self-sacrifice flows not from a ritual commitment to a now obsolete *bushido* but from his own bitter experience, and hence from a humanity born of life in place of abstraction.

"Again we've survived—again we're defeated. The winners are those farmers, not us," says Kambei finally. As the famous planting scene of the ending proceeds in full force, the three surviving samurai look on, suddenly alien, severed from the flow of life of which these farmers are so intimate a part. The samurai are the "losers" because they have long since been cut off from participation in a productive life cycle.

To emphasize the simple truth of Kambei's insight, Kurosawa tilts up to the graves of the four dead warriors; samurai music at this final moment overlays that of the peasants at their rice planting which had been so sure, loud, and self-confident. Kurosawa leaves us with his sense that these samurai are magnificent men, full of grace and dignity. They recapitulate the positive content of a dying world. There is a profound sadness at the end of *Seven Samurai* because such as they have outlived their time. The peasants are the survivors, the carriers of a continuity that renews history, but something noble has been lost. Centuries will pass and it will not recur. It is as if the spirit of Japan, like a candle in the dark, had suddenly gone out. For Kurosawa, the Japan that follows has never since regained that beauty. It is perhaps a thing to be recovered in a future world increasingly remote and difficult to envisage. Kurosawa's films will never again be as lyrical as *Seven Samurai*. Nor does he ever again allow himself to feel so much for anything. The satiric works that follow seem, by comparison, like those of a person who has been hurt too deeply to allow himself to love again.

Kurosawa's remaining *jidai-geki, Throne of Blood* (*Kumonosu-jo*, 1957), *The Hidden Fortress* (*Kakushi Toride no San-Akunin*, 1958), *Yojimbo*, and *Sanjuro*, portray landscapes without faith. The underlying premise of all is that there is nothing left in which to believe. Remedy has eluded us. That we know the causes of suffering does not lead us out of the cycle of greed and brutality. The hope of the early postwar years, when it seemed that Japan might renew itself, led only to the moral darkness of resurgent neo-feudal power. Only *Red Beard*, with its willed message that good begets good, finds Kurosawa straining for some positive values in which we can all still believe. He can offer only a variation on the parable of the good Samaritan. But, by contrast with the hard brilliance of *Yojimbo, Red Beard* seems amorphous, even intellectually lazy, in its approach, as in Kurosawa's insistence through his main character that the insane murderess was born evil! Like Kurosawa in this film, the character Red Beard hangs on willfully to illusion, the only means he can discover of avoiding the nihilistic despair characteristic of *Yojimbo* or *Sanjuro*.

The Samurai Film
Without Samurai

Have you studied *Bu* [the warrior ethic]? Do you understand the way
of the sword? What does the sword mean to a Japanese? . . . I ask
you. Are *you* men? Are you *bushi*?
    Yukio Mishima addressing Japan's Self-Defense Forces immedi-
ately preceding his *seppuku*[1]

Some of the most anti-feudal of Japanese period films are those of
Kenji Mizoguchi, although samurai are never his heroes. When warriors
appear in Mizoguchi's work, they are weak and emasculated, brutalized by
the random violence which has occupied them for centuries and has
defined their manhood and reason for living. Samurai are never at the center
of Mizoguchi's films not, as Akira Kurosawa has remarked, because
Mizoguchi was better at portraying merchants and women.[2] Rather,
Mizoguchi's attitude is far less ambivalent than that of Kurosawa toward
the samurai class and toward Japan's feudal past. Mizoguchi is unreserved
in his welcoming of the demise of the feudal epoch. Unrelentingly he
shows in his period films how ninety-five percent of the population were
excluded from the samurai world except as victims, their lives under feudalism foreshortened and without the least recourse.

In a minor but lovely film, *Utamaro and His Five Women* (*Utamaro o
Meguru Go-nin no Onna*, 1946) Mizoguchi offers, in contrast to Kurosawa's *Seven Samurai*, his own paean, not to the noble warrior but to the
total rebel. He chooses a hero who is, like himself, an artist at once
deliberately anti-feudal and anti-traditional, a man of the Edo period who
preferred to live among the masses and who valued their strength. In the
life of the *ukiyo-e* (woodblock print) master Utamaro, Mizoguchi locates
a vitality submerged under the weight of centuries of feudal rule, but given
life in Tokugawa times by the burgeoning merchant class Mizoguchi would
himself later satirize in A *Story from Chikamatsu*. The merchants, more
cosmopolitan than the samurai if lacking in social status, began to demand
outlets for their flamboyant lust for life, a quality that would find expression in the popular arts. The *ukiyo-e* and the Kabuki Theater were both
derived from that new vitality.

[1] Cited in Henry Scott-Stokes, *The Life and Death of Yukio Mishima* (New York:
Farrar, Straus & Giroux, 1974), p. 47.
[2] Cited in Richie, *Films of Akira Kurosawa*, p. 97.

Utamaro and His Five Women: Utamaro is shown to be a revolutionary who writes inflammatory statements on the back of his prints, always a rebellious spirit.

Utamaro and His Five Women opens with a magnificent set piece, a procession of geisha down the main street of Kyoto during cherry blossom time. The camera travels faster than the people because the women, in their elaborate platform shoes, can barely walk. Immediately Mizoguchi's protest against the oppression and confinement of women is associated with the revolutionary spirit of Utamaro. Although the scene is characteristic of Mizoguchi, and could have appeared in any of his period films, it also happened that the theme of women's subjugation under feudalism was one of the subjects suggested to filmmakers immediately after the war by the Occupation authorities in their initial desire to dismantle Japan's pre-war institutions.

Utamaro is shown to be a revolutionary who writes inflammatory statements on the back of his prints, always a rebellious spirit. At one point we learn that his prints depicting Hideyoshi have so offended this shogun that he weighs exiling the artist. The merchants around Utamaro fear for the future of their lucrative sales of Utamaro prints; to their distress, Utamaro is finally confined to his house and handcuffed for fifty days.

Utamaro's rebellion takes both political and aesthetic form and Mizoguchi perceives each as integral to the other. Bright colors and fidelity to the details of ordinary life express the value Utamaro holds for the common person who never appeared in Japanese art; his choice of such subject matter lies at the heart of Utamaro's revolutionary aesthetic. Utamaro labels as "freaks" the women portrayed by other artists because they are so stiff and unreal. His women are portrayed smoking, visibly aroused and enjoying sex, or in emotional outbursts.

Above all, Utamaro opposes tradition. He refuses to duel with a student of the prevailing Kano school precisely in order to repudiate feudal custom. He wishes to embody direct opposition to the brute power of the age: "I would not make prints if I feared the sword or power," he says. "To settle things with the sword is cowardly." He argues that those devoted to revolutionary change must live differently from the oppressor. When Koide, the student who tried to engage him in the duel, eventually joins Utamaro's group as a convert, Utamaro's very *geta* squeak with pleasure over this victory, one he values in contrast to a cheap dueling triumph. As he walks out into the street with his new disciple, the image is overlapped by the sounds of the Yoshiwara, the prostitute quarter in which Utamaro seeks and finds subjects for his *ukiyo-e*.

As with all creative effort, and with revolutionary art in particular, Utamaro's work is fragile. The woman on whose back he creates one of his most glorious sketches, subsequently tattooed for "permanency," dies at the end of the film. Utamaro implies that his work must live or die with the people whom he celebrates and serves. As a revolutionary, instead of considering it beneath him to sketch for tattoos, he finds it as excellent a medium as any, indeed more so because it is so close to the personal, the actual lives of people. "I feel shut in conforming to tradition," he declares. Serious art, which Mizoguchi equates with truth, always necessitates a break with tradition, represented here by the Kano school where all is regular and follows rules set in the distant past.

Utamaro's answer to the question later posed by Yeats in "The Choice" —whether to choose "perfection of the life, or of the work"—is that only the latter falls within the realm of possibility. Utamaro feels free as an artist and is able to create only when he is not, like others, beset by passion. When his emotions are engaged outside of his art, he scatters his sketches. His work is particularly inferior when he is in love. When Utamaro is obsessed by personal desire, he expends himself aimlessly, suffers disorientation, and his work is depleted of that energy, discipline, and elan that made it vibrant. Mizoguchi, after Yeats, believes that the artist or the revolutionary, the truly dedicated person, offers his life as a sacrifice to his vocation. If the artist or innovator is exceptional, his total devotion, commitment, and concentration belong to his work as to a mission. It may be argued that obsessional need will undo what it serves—whether creative or political change—and the person whose vocation is a substitute for his or her life will end in distorting both. But Mizoguchi would not agree, although he is well aware that Utamaro, despite his resolve, cannot prevent his passions from recurring.

Thus what ennobles and elevates people is precisely that all-consuming dedication to a larger, transpersonal goal of which Utamaro is capable. His art and vision are beyond destructive passions. In one of the most powerful scenes in the film Utamaro, like a voyeur of life, is permitted the rare privilege of spying on a long line of pure and beautiful young women on a beach as they prepare to dive for fish. The camera travels past the line of women as they open their kimonos to us. Apart from the close-up of the betrayed prostitute, Okita, near the film's end, the first and only other close-up in the film belongs to Oran, the most beautiful of these young divers. Utamaro immediately insists that she pose for him, and, as she swims, Mizoguchi pursues her in a lovely underwater shot. A special point is made of the fact that, unlike the other divers, Oran is not the daughter of a samurai. The secret of her vitality and beauty, and her value as a subject for Utamaro, lie in her origins among the common people. She is a person of the future.

When Utamaro was confined to house arrest, his wrists were shackled with chains to prevent him from drawing. At the end, Utamaro's chains are removed. The shot is so composed that we observe everyone in the elated crowd of followers but the artist himself. His value is reflected in the jubilation of his friends. This contrasts with a slightly later shot of Utamaro, now alone in the middle of the room. He has decided not to celebrate, but to create. The deep-focus shot typical of Mizoguchi reveals Utamaro's three closest companions as they are served the victory dinner in the background. Set apart, in the shot as in his commitment to his art, Utamaro proceeds to draw. And as he vows to "draw the beauty of women," he speaks simultaneously for Mizoguchi, whose entire life's work can be seen as a tribute to woman and an impassioned unfolding of her persecution over centuries in a Japan demeaned by its feudal misogyny.

Although it is set in the same period as Kurosawa's *Seven Samurai*, Mizoguchi's *Ugetsu* (*Ugetsu Monogatari*, 1953) contains not a single *bushi* hero. Nonetheless, it functions as a parable of that epoch of civil war and disarray that was the sixteenth century. *Ugetsu* is the story of a potter named Genjuro, who lusts after the great profits possible during wartime inflation. Obsessed with money, he leaves his wife and child to journey to the city. There he meets a demon, Lady Wakasa, who holds him in thrall in a mansion constructed in the style of the Heian era.

It is to the horror of war that the mansion of Lady Wakasa offers such marked contrast. In the scenes with Lady Wakasa, Mizoguchi's style changes. He uses long, smooth dollies around the courtyard and garden as Lady Wakasa flatters Genjuro with words he longs to hear: "Beauty is the goal of your craftsmanship. Your talent shouldn't be buried in a village." Yet, as magnificent as the cinematography is in these scenes, it is always in the service of a surface elegance, a superficiality that has nothing to do with true human worth. By its very beauty, the exquisite camera work depicting Genjuro's sojourn with Lady Wakasa poses an implicit contrast to the rough scenes of samurai brutality depicted in earlier sequences. The implied comparison at once passes judgment on Genjuro's "escape." The lovely photography itself, seen in the context of the film as a whole, forms a moral judgment on this man who has sacrificed all responsibility for the sake of passion, a lust Mizoguchi parallels with his avarice. The splendor of *Ugetsu* bespeaks evil. During the erotic bath shared by Genjuro and Lady Wakasa the camera dollies away from them, swiftly moving through the garden until we come upon the two languishing on a blanket in the grass, a shimmering lake beyond them. At the very moment Genjuro expresses complete satisfaction, the camera becomes uneasy. It travels away from them at the peak of their pleasure, in moral judgment of their selfish love. At another point the camera dollies toward us while Genjuro moves in the opposite direction, subtly conveying the discordance of his surrender. Mizoguchi deploys diagonal traveling shots in the scene where Genjuro searches the house for Lady Wakasa to express the same malaise. "I don't care if you are an evil spirit. I never imagined such pleasure existed," the potter exclaims, while the camera movement carries Mizoguchi's judgment that this phantom fulfillment is the very evocation of mindless individual surrender to a social order in disarray.

Sancho the Bailiff even more clearly expresses Mizoguchi's hatred of the irresolvable, self-perpetuating feudalism of Japan's historical past. The setting is the late Heian period of Kurosawa's *Rashomon*. Mizoguchi opens with an ironic title, informing the audience that the film depicts "medieval times when Japan had not yet emerged from the dark ages." There is no suggestion anywhere in Mizoguchi's work, whether set in the past or present, of Japan's ever having so emerged.

Sancho the Bailiff centers on an aristocratic woman and her two children, all of whom have been separated by feudal tyranny from her husband, a fallen official. The two children, Zushio and Anju, are kidnapped and sold into slavery; the mother, captured at the same time, is forced into prostitution. Eventually the son escapes, although only the daughter's suicide allows him this chance for freedom. Coincidence, wholly plausible in an epoch characterized by such extremities of violence, allows Zushio to become Governor of the very province where Sancho's slave camp flourishes.

Sancho the Bailiff opens with a noisy scene of rebellion, a presage of many such outbursts in Japan's history to come. Peasants are revolting against the exile of their master, the father of Anju and Zushio. Rare for a period film, these serfs are individually characterized. In addition, they are politically active, unwilling victims of arbitrary power. Their revolt, however, must inevitably fail. Under feudal law, if a lord's subjects rebelled, it was the lord himself who would be accused of insurrection. In attempting to be kind to his peasants, the father of Zushio and Anju has gravely injured his own family. So debased is the feudal order that social justice and personal happiness have become incompatible under it, a theme which Kurosawa treats as equally applicable to the present age in Japan in *No Regrets for Our Youth*.

Because of the outbreak of this rebellion, originally inspired by the lord's opposition to the forced conscription of his subjects, his wife, Tamaki, must return with her children to her own family as if she had never married. The husband's violation of the feudal code has rendered his personal bonds illegitimate. Given Heian practice, the father's message to his son Zushio, in words which reverberate throughout the film, is pro-

Sancho the Bailiff: Those who try to escape are branded with a red-hot iron, but never in close-up, because the director wishes to stress the suffering of all rather than the tragedy of one.

foundly revolutionary: "Without mercy, a man is like a beast. Be sympathetic to others. Men are created equal."

Within the rigid class system of Japan which stretched from the Heian era to the Meiji Restoration and beyond, a span of over one thousand years, these words are tantamount to insurgency, even as were their counterparts during the French Revolution. To live by this simple injunction, Mizoguchi reveals in this film, requires the dismantling of the entire structure of this society. The peasantry and artisans, the majority of the Japanese people, would have to achieve political power and create their own institutions, something not yet accomplished in Japan in the twentieth century and the reason it was so important to Mizoguchi to make this film.

The slave camp is portrayed in all its barbarism, and yet in a manner that appears understated. Those who try to escape are branded with a red-hot iron, but never in close-up, because the director wishes to stress the suffering of all rather than the tragedy of one. The cruel Sancho is revealed to be under the protection of the Heian Minister of the Right, who comes from the court to be entertained. In return for this protection Sancho collects the Minister's rents in rice from hungry peasants of the area. The Minister is delighted by Sancho's methods and strong hand; here Mizoguchi is unveiling the real basis of feudalism and what it required to function at all. Simultaneously, he unfolds its impact on individual lives. Zushio is so corrupted and conditioned by the slavery in which he was raised that, as an adult, he himself administers the branding iron to a seventy-year-old man who, in the twilight of his life, has finally tried to escape. "It's better to be loyal to the Bailiff and look for his favor," a degraded Zushio proclaims. The life of a slave has brutalized him, coarsening his character as well as his appearance.

A revolutionary at heart, Mizoguchi combats the notion of a fixed human nature. His work opposes the easy suggestion that social evil flows from inherent human greed, aggression, or self-seeking. His people are capable of good or evil, depending on the social environment which gives them shape and forms their desires. It is this which most basically distinguishes Mizoguchi from more conservative students of the feudal era and of the Japanese experience. The social order he represents is never seen as an inevitable, eternal expression of weakness endemic to human beings. Nor does he believe that it could not be fundamentally or lastingly ordered in a manner other than it is.

As a loyal and cynical servant of the Bailiff, Zushio is assigned the most despicable chores. He must take an old woman, Namiji, into the woods where she will be left to die. Because she is too old to work, the Bailiff refuses to feed her, a feudal custom dramatized as well by Keisuke Kinoshita in *The Ballad of Narayama* (*Narayamabushi-ko*, 1958). Anju, unlike her brother, is pained by the cruelty, and wishes for Namiji that in her next life she will be born into a rich family. The irony is the director's, for Anju does not reflect on the fact that she and her brother had exactly that opportunity in their present life and have nonetheless become slaves. The brother and sister build a thatched shelter for Namiji's final hours.

The music of their childhood begins. Life moves in cycles and renews. The very act of doing something selfless, even if only that of providing shelter for an old woman cruelly abandoned, evokes their own need, and hence their humanity. Indeed, the more Zushio sought to harden himself, the more clearly he betrayed the effort necessary to push into unconsciousness his desire to escape all this horror. Zushio and Anju fall down together after the effort of taking down a large branch. The very same thing had happened in the woods the day before they were taken from their mother. An echo is heard on the sound track of their mother's voice calling "Z-u-s-h-i-o!" "A-n-j-u!" Brutalization will never be able wholly to deny us what we might otherwise be, because our own need for kindness remains, if only in the unconscious mind. Suddenly, in one of the film's few close-ups, one which suits the moment perfectly, Zushio bursts out, "Let's run away!"

He and the old woman Namiji leave first, and Anju stays to ward off their pursuers. Rather than submit to the Bailiff's torture, she commits suicide by drowning herself because "no one can make the dead speak." Raised in his slave camp, she knows well the methods of her oppressor. Mizoguchi allows a full shot of the pond only after it has engulfed her.

Zushio, now free, has an utterly fortuitous encounter which changes his life. The film until now has been starkly realistic. What might appear improbable is, in fact, another expression of Mizoguchi's sense of the arbitrariness of feudal ways. Zushio, for all his suffering, is of an aristocratic family; what would be impossible for another is at least conceivable for him. He meets a lord who, upon learning his identity, enables him to succeed his father. In a very ceremonious investiture he is made a Taira, the tormented slave now an overlord of the very region in which he, like so many, endured a living hell. But if the many would have to band together to overthrow the oppressor, Zushio, because of his origins, is afforded an opportunity to make a solitary, if temporary, moral gesture.

Sancho the Bailiff is by far Mizoguchi's most radical statement. Having become Governor of the very province in which Sancho the slave-keeper reigns, Zushio, despite a daring attempt, is still unable to abolish slavery. It is impossible to reform a decadent system from above or within. Nothing changes. Zushio, wishing to eliminate slavery from his province at least, is told that he is not authorized to invade private property; this is the prerogative of the Minister of the Right, whom we have already met. The cyclic sense of human experience re-emerges as Zushio repeats the experience of his father, who could only momentarily oppose the conscription of his serfs. Even the most enlightened feudal ruler will fail, his rebellion merely causing him to be assimilated among the oppressed. The feudal order is incapable of admitting compassion for the weak, for it is built upon their exploitation.

Zushio nevertheless issues an edict forbidding the sale of human beings on government lands and private manors. In a very deep-focus shot, reflective of Mizoguchi's sense of ubiquitous evil, Zushio marches with his men on Sancho's manor. Chaos ensues. Great fires are set and fear colors the faces of the slaves as they are told they are "free." Long traveling shots reveal the enslaved partying as if the end of the world has come. It is a set piece in which Mizoguchi partakes of wish fulfillment without judgment on the delirium sweeping the long-tormented slaves. The orgy following the fall of Sancho is fueled by the pent-up energy of those so long oppressed. Initially it is released in random outbursts. But if Zushio is able to "free" them, he lacks the power to create a world in which they can find a place to live as human beings. The finiteness of his power is expressed also by the limitations of his understanding. He is disappointed because his sister "didn't have the faith to wait," a misunderstanding that will endure because there is no one living to correct his error. In the next sequence, Zushio resigns his post.

Sancho the Bailiff was to be Mizoguchi's last passionate anti-feudal statement. In the year preceding his death he made one final historical

film, *New Tales of the Taira Clan* (*Shin Heike Monogatari,* 1955). Set in
1137 A.D., also at the end of the Heian period, it examines the decadence
of the last days of the Heian aristocracy.

Kaneto Shindo's *Onibaba* (1963) and *Kuroneko* (*Yabu no Naka no
Kuroneko,* 1968), his only two period films, are far more violent than
Mizoguchi's in their condemnation of Japan's feudal past. An expres-
sionist, Shindo employs broad, energetic strokes; what *Onibaba* and
Kuroneko lack in subtlety, they make up in vitality and passion. Like
Mizoguchi's, Shindo's samurai have no redeeming qualities. Nor are those
of the upper class capable of any sensitivity, a simplistic schema Shindo
feels essential to a treatment of the lives of the masses under feudalism.

Onibada, a *jidai-geki* from the point of view of the peasantry, is perhaps
Shindo's most remarkable film. It is the story of a peasant woman whose
son has gone off to war, enlisting in the service of one or another feudal
lord. She and her daughter-in-law inhabit a marshy area where they way-
lay and kill wounded samurai. They then strip these fugitives from warrior
battles, just as did Kurosawa's peasants in *Seven Samurai.* The two women
sell the clothing and armor of their samurai victims to a local usurer in
exchange for rice. It is thus that they are able to survive.

Shindo's people live like weeds amidst the tall grass which the eyes of
their rulers cannot penetrate. Shindo's focus is on his people as outcasts,
excluded from society's political protection. He seeks in his work to "capture their immense energy for survival."[3]

The opening shot is of the swaying reeds that dominate the environment. A samurai on horseback enters the marshy land. The sound track
intrudes a note of irony as birds begin to sing. When a second samurai
appears, the two engage in mortal combat. Time seems suspended. Suddenly, out of nowhere, the women peer through the reeds, readying themselves to finish off the samurai and strip their bodies. For both the murdered
samurai and these peasant women, mutilation and violent death have
become so endemic to their lives that they accept it without special notice.
Drums beat as the women drag the two bodies to a deep pit nearby.

Having returned to their hut, the two women eat rice with their fingers.
The condition of their lives has reduced them to an animal level of survival, even as it did their samurai superiors. Shindo has created a small,
brutish universe emblematic of its fourteenth-century setting, when
warrior clans decimated each other and the vast many starved and suffered
in misery, unnoticed and unrecorded in history. Shindo, above all, is concerned to place at center stage the anonymous masses of people, the generations who perished in despair, ignored in a history invented by their
superiors. Both art and history reflect the consciousness of the educated
and hence the privileged. Shindo seeks to re-create and celebrate the world
of the victims, the people whose voices were never heard.

The two peasants are victims of samurai, but also of merchants like

[3] Joan Mellen, "Interview with Kaneto Shindo," *Voices from the Japanese Cinema,*
p. 82.

Ushi to whom they sell their loot, and against whose cheating they have no recourse. "Nothing but junk," he declares, picking over their magnificent spoils. If the daughter-in-law would only sleep with him, he would give them one more bag of food. With no men around to aid in the planting, the farm women are starving.

We see the warriors through the eyes of peasants forever forced to fight for whichever side first captures them. When the least chance presents itself, these peasants desert and hunt for food. Hachi, one such deserter, returns and tells the old woman that her son had been beaten to death by farmers like themselves from whom Hachi and fellow conscript "warriors" had been stealing food. "It's sad," says the girl, so demoralized that even the news of her husband's death by torture fails to evoke much emotion; hers is a response dulled in part by the knowledge that she and her mother-in-law have survived exactly as have the peasants who murdered her husband—by killing hungry warriors. So encompassing is the oppressive evil of this system that people, rendered victims by their very separation from each other, survive by becoming predators on their own kind.

Among people living at so minimal a level of survival, sexual need becomes not only overpowering and uncontrollable but utterly indiscriminate. All else has been removed from these people, just as, in death, the samurai are stripped of their remaining armor. If, at any instant, violent death may come, all niceties become chimera, luxuries in which few can

Onibaba: Shindo views such driven sexuality as an expression of the human will to live, embodying vitality and an urge for survival.

indulge except in madness. Yet even in such pain, people so thrust upon their own resources and their will to survive acquire a certain power and beauty denied those protected by the labor of others.

Shindo seeks to portray human nature unaltered by urban existence, as in *The Island* (*Hadaka no Shima*, 1960). If he loathes the brutalization portrayed in *Onibaba*, he also admires the physical vitality released by the need to find an inner strength to survive. Shindo has called this the "primitive beneath the civilized veneer." And he sees it as positive, expressed by the magnificent body of Jitsuko Yoshimura, who plays the daughter-in-law. Her flesh has been darkened and made to glisten; her breasts are thrust outward, her eyes are aflame and her mouth is sensuous. Shindo views such driven sexuality as an expression of the human will to live, embodying vitality and an urge for survival.

The love that develops between Hachi and the girl disturbs the older woman, who fears now for her own survival. It takes two to kill and strip a wounded samurai and without the help of her daughter-in-law she may easily perish. In insular peasant fashion, jealous of her situation, the old woman has refused Hachi's offer to join them in this work: "We're us." Her disapproval, however, cannot overcome the sexual desire of the two young people, too powerful to be thwarted. At night Hachi and the girl race through the woods to meet. Their sex is frantic, involving affection indistinguishable from need.

Onibaba: The samurai immediately retreats behind the prerogatives of his class, incapable of viewing her as another human being, an equal: "It's not a face to show peasants."

A masked samurai enters the environment dominated by these three people. He has become lost among the marshes and seeks a guide. But he is no match for the old woman whom he asks to show him the way out. The samurai tells her that he wears his grotesque mask so as not to mar his beautiful face during combat. She replies in a winning and sympathetic manner, "I've never seen anything really beautiful since I was born." Her answer is pathetic and without guile. Shindo has drawn the old woman as expressing both the cruelty of the world and the remarkable capacity of some nonetheless to endure in it. It is evident why Shindo has remarked of her, *pace* Flaubert, "the mother is myself."[4]

The samurai immediately retreats behind the prerogatives of his class, incapable of viewing her as another human being, an equal: "It's not a face to show peasants." His class superiority turns us against him. When the old woman traps him into falling into the hole—one more of her samurai victims—he has lost our sympathy. "Men like you killed my son," is her ironic parting remark, which might as well be true, although her son died at the hands of fellow peasants. But the attitude towards peasants exemplified by the ensnared samurai is correctly seen by the old woman as the real source of the death of all her "sons."

Fearing now that unless she secures the girl's continued aid in hunting samurai, she will not survive, the old woman dons the samurai's mask. Thus she becomes a demon herself, emerging from the reeds to terrify her daughter-in-law into remaining home at night. In one such scene, lightning strikes behind her like a neon light. But Shindo does not long allow her the illusion that she can so control her world. People like these peasants are shown by Shindo as always acted upon and never the architects of their fate. Hachi surprises a starving, filthy samurai in his hut. The samurai's face is covered with beads of rice; he sits dribbling, then reaches for his sword and kills Hachi in a flash.

Meanwhile, the woman's mask has become stuck to her face. The girl agrees to chop it off, but only after the woman promises to allow her to see Hachi every night (she does not yet know that he is dead). The old woman cries in agony as the girl sadistically chops away. Blood trickles out between her face and the mask. "It's punishment," says the girl. Yet she does not blame the old woman for attempting to thwart her, because the old woman's will to survive is akin to her own.

When the mask finally falls away, the woman's face is a horrific mass of bleeding, leprous sores. The samurai had worn this mask to conceal the advanced infectious disease which had disfigured his face. Having put on his mask to terrorize her daughter-in-law, the old woman enacted his role even as she assumed his visage. The degenerative disease affecting him, as it did his entire class, was visited on the old woman when she took on his role, even if fleetingly and only to survive. It is not easy to remove the face of feudalism stamped on its victims. Even when they are successful, disfiguration will remain because the disease of the culture

[4] *Ibid.*, p. 81.

also afflicts its victims. Shindo does not condemn the old woman in so punishing her. The affliction is born of her momentary spiritual convergence with the repressive samurai role when she used the mask to coerce the girl into abandoning sexual joy.

The girl, horrified by the sight of the woman's face, flees into the night. The mother-in-law rushes after her, pleading melodramatically, "I'm not a demon. I'm a human being." The girl leaps over the pit. In the last shot, the old woman is poised at the brim; whether she can clear it is uncertain. Shindo has said, looking beyond the formal ending of the film, that after the leprous disease afflicting her was cured, she would become a survivor, escaping the old life she had led.[5] And her resilience may indeed carry her. However, even if she should summon the strength to leap across, Shindo has shown us how precarious life is under conditions of such pervasive ill-usage. Only this woman's extraordinary will and fierce determination have enabled her to survive this long. Such, for Shindo, was the lot of people during Japan's "glorious" feudal times, and such were the choices open to the victims of samurai hegemony.

Kuroneko, in many respects a companion film to *Onibaba*, is weaker because the grotesquerie of this ghost story at times obscures the central drama. Both films are unique as the *jidai-geki* of a director, himself of peasant origins, who, with Mizoguchi, refuses to concede any glory whatsoever to the *bushi*. Ordinarily not a director of period films, Shindo in *Onibaba* and *Kuroneko* seeks to set the historical record straight; they are paeans to the strength of the peasants whose history the chronicles of the exploiting few have sought to deny and suppress.

---

[5] *Ibid.*, pp. 82–86.

From *Chambara* to *Yakuza*

. . . when earth grew loud,
In lairs and asylums of the tremendous shout.
Dylan Thomas, "There Was a Saviour"

I prefer my sword to you. A man
has his way and a woman, hers.
Toshiro Mifune as Musashi Miyamoto
(*Samurai*, Part II)

It's my duty. What would you do in my
place?
Oryu, the Red Peony, in *The Hanafuda Game*

The typical Japanese sword film filled with the exploits of swash-buckling, sword-slashing samurai is called a *chambara,* to be distinguished from the true *jidai-geki,* or period film. Their similarity, however, is superficial. Both take place in the past, although *jidai-geki* more often range widely within Japanese history, going back as far as the Heian period (782-1167). The *chambara* are usually confined to the Tokugawa era (1603-1868), or to the decades of civil war immediately preceding it. The elements of each genre appear the same. Heroic warrior samurai—some of whom are noble adherents of the code of *bushido,* and others who abuse it—are at the center of the film; violent action and swordplay take precedence over psychology, a characteristic common to the Japanese film in general. They share as well a steady flow of blood and a wide panorama of recognizable historical events which unfold in the background of the film.

But whereas the *jidai-geki* is often a serious work of art (*Seven Samurai* would be an example of this genre at its best), the *chambara* rarely transcends American Western "B" film conventions. *Chambara* are unabashedly escapist entertainments. They do not pursue meaning and virtually concede their vacuity. *Jidai-geki,* in contrast, always have significant intent. They are interested in history not merely as a backdrop but as an illumination and a source of truth. Their premise is that through their discovery of what is uniquely valuable in Japanese history, the nation and the culture may be redeemed. The force of this quest ex-

A Tale of Genji: His character is submerged within a world haunted by fatalism and a Buddhist sense of the transitoriness of life. He never becomes more than a local aristocrat, never rises to symbolize an era.

plains why the *jidai-geki*, and even its imitator the *chambara*, have been, until the advent of the *yakuza* (gangster film) in the late 1960s, the most popular genres of the Japanese film.

When a *jidai-geki* abandons concern with the truths underlying history, it degenerates into a mere costume drama set in the past, possessing no more interest than the *chambara*. Such films, a typical example of which would be Kimisaburo Yoshimura's *A Tale of Genji* (*Genji Monogatari*, 1952), have little value beyond the decorative. Yoshimura's *Tale of Genji* presents Kazuo Hasegawa, then a matinee idol, as an effete, promiscuous courtier with none of the complexity of character found in Lady Murasaki's original. In the novel the "shining prince" was not only a brilliant aristocrat but epitomized what was best in the Japanese character of his time. His love of nature, his constancy, compassion, and effectiveness were the values most admired in Murasaki's world. Genji's life style expressed the height of the civilization achieved in Kyoto during the Heian period. Yoshimura's Genji is gentle, elegant, and compared by one of the court ladies to cherry blossoms. But his character is submerged within a world haunted by fatalism and a Buddhist sense of the transitoriness of life. He never becomes more than a local aristocrat, nor rises to symbolize an era.

Unlike *A Tale of Genji*, the true *jidai-geki* is concerned with how the past illuminates the present; its guiding impulse is always, in some form, a challenge to feudal norms. At its center it confronts the notion of loyalty so crucial to the feudal world, a theme at times borrowed by the *chambara* but pursued there without further implications and for its own sake. The *jidai-geki* rejects as irrelevant the dichotomy between *giri* (duty) and *ninjo* (individual choice or inclination) and poses, instead, the issue of justice. This it opposes to the typical feudal dualism because implicit in the acceptance of a conflict between *giri* and *ninjo* is the inevitable feudal choice of *giri*. The *jidai-geki* does not propose selection of *ninjo*, but rather a world in which honor and truth to one's own feelings are not irreconcilable. A film like Masaki Kobayashi's *Kwaidan* (*Kaidan*, 1965) would not be a *jidai-geki*, although it is set in the past, because, like *A Tale of Genji*, it sets out, not to challenge the past, but only to describe it. It never calls forth a definition of what it means to be a Japanese through an exposure of history and a challenge to feudalism, as Kobayashi does in a true *jidai-geki* like *Seppuku*.

The *jidai-geki* poses the question of what we should believe and how we should live, and is not, like the *chambara*, restricted to the conventional feudal conflict between *giri* and *ninjo*. Such concerns unite *jidai-geki* as varied as *Seven Samurai* and *Assassination*. While *Seven Samurai* presents the fall of the samurai class as inevitable, the efforts of its hero, Kambei, shine through the film as emblems of how we may live better.

The contrast between the *jidai-geki* and the *chambara* can be seen in a film like Hiroshi Inagaki's *Warring Clans* (*Sengoku Burai*). Carriers in the service of a clan transport its treasure across enemy plains, accepting the desirability of so doing without ever challenging the purpose of the action or the claims of the "enemy." (Adopting a remarkably similar plot in *The Hidden Fortress*, Kurosawa just barely manages to avoid making a pedestrian *chambara*; only the brilliant satiric overlay, in defiance of the value of transporting the treasure, raises *Hidden Fortress* to the level of *jidai-geki*.)

Most *chambara* display little cinematic merit. Their styles are as pedestrian as their one great theme the inspirational idcalization of the heroic samurai. The typical hero of *chambara* appears most blatantly in Inagaki's three-part *Samurai* (1954, 1955), which chronicles the adventures of a legendary historical figure named Musashi Miyamoto.

Like many heroes of *chambara*, Miyamoto begins as a rough peasant and learns "the way of the samurai." As with Kurosawa's Sanshiro Sugata, Musashi lacks discipline, constraint, and the wisdom that would enable him to integrate the controlled movements of swordplay into his life rhythm. His passage from crude, crassly ambitious warrior to contemplative man of experience seeking to perfect his craft, skill, and dedication to excellence constitutes a pilgrim's progress. The film unfolds the ethic appropriate to the man in command of self.

In *chambara* this theme is handled without question or implication. There is no historical distance that examines the moral or social meaning of such an ethos or social order. It is merely a morality play in which a novice, through arduous conformity, learns how to accept the values of the day and to embrace the status quo. In *chambara* we are presented with

Samurai, Part One: He longs for fame more than anything in the world and has a "healthy" samurai distaste and disdain for women.

received values and everything is a progression toward their implementation. It is the touchstone of authoritarian art, however cleverly disguised. *Jidai-geki*, on the other hand, are quests of a different order. They show what feudalism has cost Japan, exploring its damage and frequently seeking a better way.

Already as a peasant, Musashi is shown to have the requisite mettle. Although he is on the losing Toyotomi side at the Battle of Sekigahara (1600),[1] he refuses to admit defeat. He longs for fame more than anything in the world and has a "healthy" samurai distaste and disdain for women. When a girl tries to seduce him, Musashi proclaims, "I hate women!" Later, in a comparable situation, he turns away for a swim in a cold stream.

But if the young Musashi desires austerity and repression, his strength services an immature and impetuous spirit. He kills a man in a holy

---

[1] The battle at which the Tokugawa clan consolidated its power.

place and is admonished that lawlessness is leading his good heart astray. What is urged upon him is dedication to homicidal skill within the proprieties of the day; victory is viewed as a secondary result. Musashi must learn that it is the relative indifference to victory that, paradoxically, leads to it. Inagaki's *chambara* depict a feudal warrior code in which obsession with recognition or approval usually brings the opposite. Subordinating these desires to the perfection of a life or to dedication to a difficult task will often bring the very acknowledgment that ambition alone cannot produce. Indeed, the Zen Buddhist sense of life—which, under feudalism, was adapted to the samurai code and warrior ends— elevates indirection; by not seeking a goal at the expense of the way you live your life, you will the better attain it. For Zen and the feudal era, self-discipline is all.

Thus a Buddhist priest, aided by a girl named Otsu who falls in love with him, must civilize the wild Musashi. This is done, however, through the crudest means imaginable. The priest beats Musashi, drags him into town at the end of a rope, and hangs him from a tree. There, children throw stones at their pleasure and the rain beats down. The scene recalls Kurosawa's Sanshiro Sugata spending the night in penance in a lily pond, but with a world of difference, not the least of which is the absence of style, moral distance, ambiguity, or a visual articulation of these complexities. And in *Sugata*, the hero's purification was voluntary.

The *chambara* at its prosaic worst is replete with homilies. The onrush of plot is periodically halted in the service of declamation. Ideas are rendered trivial and the mode of expression is crudely didactic. The priest portentously advises Musashi, "could you but use that force for humanity's good . . . god and man would be moved." Musashi learns the requisite humility: "I saw that I, too, was bound by an unseen rope. And I couldn't cut the rope by myself."

Part One concludes with Otsu left behind to survive by selling cakes. For Musashi, loyalty to his vocation and duty to his elders, who have expectations of him, take precedence over any personal inclination, least of all one involving a woman. The samurai must wander, a novice submitting to the rituals of his training. Musashi literally walks into the sunset alone, like the latently homosexual hero of the American Western, of which the *chambara*, far more than the *jidai-geki*, is derivative. On the bridge which leads out of town Musashi has carved "forgive me," which Inagaki tritely frames in a close-up. The sunset is the symbol of Musashi Miyamoto's higher duty, unchallenged by the director.

It should not be surprising that, by the 1960s, an exhaustion of this typical *chambara* hero set in. His desire for noble connection appeared increasingly spurious, given his professed desire to help people and his presumed "good heart." The films featuring the blind swordsman Zatoichi, played by Shintaro Katsu in re-make after re-make, came to occupy the space previously held by Mifune and Nakadai.

Unlike the characters portrayed by them, Zatoichi proudly retains his proletarian and peasant sensibility. He comes unburdened by *giri* to a clan or a noble family. The Zatoichi movies acknowledge, unlike the earlier Inagaki *chambara*, that the society is changing so fast that what matters is not who you are but what you do. The Zatoichi films thus offer a far more comforting point of view for a declassé audience unsure of its own origins in a society still feudal in outlook. Zatoichi, the blind masseur, remains the ultimate swordsman of the *chambara* but, like us all and unlike the characters played by Nakadai or Mifune, he is vulnerable. He is also much more amiable and compassionate than they, his good heart and democratic spirit a foil for an appealing homeliness with which we can all identify. Zatoichi is often extremely sloppy and dirty, his rude manner nonetheless made appealing by both his earthy lack of pretension and his blindness. He often asks for a place in which to clean up. It rarely makes a difference, and he emerges as unkempt and homely as before. The irony is irresistible. In *Zatoichi at Large* (*Zatoichi Goyo Tabi*, 1972), directed by Kazuo Mori, the blind masseur delivers a baby; the act of childbirth is one more scene of violence, another disorderly and unseemly event enveloping the hero.

Blind, and therefore an unlikely master swordsman, Zatoichi is far more improbable, and his efforts less credible, than those of earlier *chambara* heroes. Thus do the Zatoichi films reveal the essence of the genre: its absolute despair before injustice and brutality. On the surface, these tired plots concern single-handed triumphs over banal evil, but the moral issues are simplistically offered and the clear implication is that they are not really formidable. Underlying this genre is a lack of faith in the possibility of changing anything. By reducing injustice to the uncaused evil-doing of individuals or random groups, and by assigning redress to a good-hearted, if bumbling, blind swordsman, the series slights oppression by its emphasis on escapist tales. Although social issues appear as a backdrop, and Zatoichi himself takes on the aspect of Robin Hood, these questions are not central or even important. They merely provide a means of defining Zatoichi as a hero who comes to the rescue of the deserving, while the resolution ignores all the social issues which have been incidentally raised.

The spirit of the Zatoichi series derives far more from the *chambara* where bloodshed, independent of any rationale, pervades the film. The plot is but the occasion for the violence; similarly, in the pornographic films, the reasons people meet are utterly incidental to the drawn-out, explicit physicality of the sex. In *chambara* the charge, arousal, and catharsis derived from the gore and bloodletting are equally orgasmic. The violence of the *chambara* is a sexual surrogate and also an emblem of sensuality in a repressed culture. In the grand guignol finale of *Zatoichi's Conspiracy* (*Shin Zatoichi Monogatari—Kasuma no Chimatsuri*, 1973) a leg is cut off at the knee, exposing a bloody stump. The evil magistrate wriggles and writhes as blood pours from him, spraying Zatoichi's hair. Blood soaks the rice sacks in the secret warehouse. The evil boss and magistrate then fall on their hands and knees and beg for mercy.

What characterizes all these sword films, although they appear to deny it, is a pervasive nihilism, a view of human nature as inherently corrupt and submerged in a kind of original sin. The benevolent heroics of a Zatoichi, the progress to self-mastery of Musashi, proceed in a world not only hopelessly cruel but inevitably so. The evil they combat is the furniture of our daily environment. The *chambara* imply that, naturally violent and destructive as humans are, it is far better that we bow to a *giri* that will restrain us. It is essential to preserve the world as it is rather than seek to change it because, given our bestiality, we would only make it worse by following our impulses or even our rational will. In films made one hundred years after the Meiji Restoration of 1868, the code of *bushido* can be exalted only by contrast with the false alternatives of disintegrative anarchy and violent chaos. The *chambara*, like the *yakuza* film which continues its aesthetic and ideological mission, is the most reactionary genre of the Japanese film, its values and perceptions akin to those of fascism. In the face of our impotence, brought home by the number of corpses left by the one superman samurai, we had best return to the strength of hierarchy, the dictates of leaders, and the force of tradition. Only these will save us from barbarism.

These films betray the cost to Japan of failing fully to overthrow feudalism. It is not only that they reinforce the established order but that they draw upon the feeling that collective struggle is futile and foredoomed. Above all, they reveal the absence of hope, of a vision of an alternative society. Even when the *chambara* appears to uphold "justice" and the defiance of *giri*, as in Hideo Gosha's *Goyokin* (1969), this defiance is portrayed as quixotic and self-destructive. The assumed incapacity of ordinary people is expressed in the premise that heroic feats are accomplished by men unlike any we have ever seen or imagined; we watch superhuman samurai cut down whole armies and a blind masseur, who emerges out of nowhere, do the same. Either the film acknowledges the unreality of such men by extreme exaggeration, as in the Zatoichi series, or they perish pathetically, because history is more powerful than even the most skillful samurai. When demonic culprits are demolished by the Mifunes, Nakadais, and Katsus, their places are immediately filled. *Chambara* exorcises evil through all-powerful figures, while suggesting that the supermen will never finish their tasks. Hence we will always need the strong leader to whom we must submit.

The feudal past is a pageant of blood and gore; the present is scarcely different. *Chambara* confirms us in a frustration that can find expression precisely in that senseless violence it both celebrates and declares to be absurd. Its underlying theme is that nothing can be relied upon but the strength of the moment, expressed in the easy movement of a sword—that "grace under pressure" so admired by Hemingway and other cynics.

Other *chambara* have attempted to be more sincere, right-minded, and anti-feudal. Paradoxically, these moralistic samurai films most clearly reveal the utter exhaustion of the genre. Despite their content, the anti-feudal *chambara* lack energy and are unrealized, relying on crude statement. The more "civilized" *chambara* seem most unable to integrate their social concerns, indulging instead in moral lamentations of which even Inagaki's *Samurai* series was not always guilty.

Goyokin, for example, is full of the noblest of sentiments. Magobei, a samurai (Tatsuya Nakadai) has left his clan in protest, appalled by the clan's slaughter of innocent fishermen. In addition, it had been stealing gold from a mine belonging to the Shogunate. When Magobei discovers that more fishermen are to be butchered, victimized solely because they live in proximity to the mines and hence are potential witnesses to the clan's thievery, his decision is made. Magobei returns to the clan in order to do combat with the clan leadership, and, in particular, his brother-in-law Tatewaki (Tetsuro Tamba). Magobei "wins" the duel, only to be left homeless and without purpose. To be dissociated from a clan or sanctioned group in a feudal order is to be cut off from life, to be an outcast, regardless of the rightness of one's choice. There is no place to go and no role to play. Survival becomes a function of one's wits, usually exercised in banditry (it was against the law for a samurai to become a peasant, so rigid was the class structure).

Giri is defined in *Goyokin* as loyalty to the clan, no matter what its morals; *ninjo*, as humanity and compassion for the weak. This, in Magobei's case, involves a direct violation of *giri*, so terrible an action that to save the fishermen he must lose his wife, the sister of his rival Tatewaki. Yet not to oppose clan brutality would make him less than a human being, and thus an unworthy husband. "Ever since I closed my eyes [to the first massacre]," says Magobei, "I forfeited my true worth as a man. I forgot that the samurai are supported by the weak masses."

The final combat is cinematically impressive. The great battle takes place on a hill. All of nature seems to participate. The sky fills with crows. Fires burn everywhere for both warmth and light. The sea rages; snowdrifts abound. The frost is such that the hands of the swordsmen must be continually warmed. As the fight proceeds, blood stains the snow. The peasants don masks and dance with great energy—an expression of their vitality as a class—in another image borrowed from Kurosawa. And of course the hero, Magobei, wins. It is an engaging film, full of the zeal of high adventure, yet finally empty and confined to the surface.

The *chambara*, which has faded as an important genre of the Japanese film, fell basically into two categories. The first and most prevalent were the sword-worshipping sagas that glorified *bushido* and the warrior life, films like Inagaki's *Chushingura* or his *Samurai* trilogy. The second consisted of nihilistic melodramas that reveled in gore, betrayal and the gratuitously vicious. Such films as Okamoto's *Samurai Assassin* (*Samurai*, 1965) or *Sword of Doom* (*Daibosatsu Toge*, 1966) served to underline the depravity of much of human history. Finally, there have been *chambara* that emulate the *jidai-geki* in their moral concerns, assuming anti-feudal themes and the struggle for justice, films like Gosha's *Goyokin*, Shinoda's *Samurai Spy* (*Ibun Sarutobi Sasuke*, 1965), or Imai's *Bushido* (*Bushido Zankoku Monogatari*, 1963). These are films that bridge the two genres, pursuing history and the social past, yet retaining a gratuitous fascination with swordplay and a mood of hopelessness even in the course of resistance.

The place of *chambara* in the Japanese film and with the Japanese audience has now been filled by a genre deriving directly from it, and with its point of view the polar opposite of Imai's concerns in *Bushido*. Drawing on the reactionary core of the *chambara*, whatever its overtly anti-feudal theme, the *yakuza*, a gangster genre, removes us finally to a world where not only is the struggle against feudalism deemed unnecessary, but feudalism's values, like long-lost brothers, are resurrected and embraced. "Nothing is more important," says actor Koji Tsurta in *Gambling House: Presidential Gambling* (*Bakuchiuchi: Socho Tobaku*, 1968), "than loyalty." The enormously popular, cultish *yakuza* films depict Mafiaesque goings-on within a Japanese version of the crime "family," a clan of gangsters presided over by a godfather, called in Japan the *oyabun*. The relationships within this collective are characterized by the traditional Japanese *oyabun-kobun* hierarchy. Inferiors (*kobun*) forever yield to their *oyabun* superiors, whose wishes they must always honor. Hack-formula potboilers all, generally displaying as little cinematic value as the most routine of *chambara*, the *yakuza* films are expected by their audiences always to contain certain essential ingredients. Ritual introductions ensure the gangsters of each other's sincerity and reinforce the legitimacy of clan relationships. As with poker in the American Western, gambling is ever-present and pursued with religious intensity. Prison sentences are taken for granted. Kidnappings, rescues, and assassinations, both attempted and realized, abound. There are also punishments peculiar to the *yakuza* world. Subordinates cut off their little fingers to establish sincere atonement after a "mistake." Failure or error by a *yakuza* warranting such punishment generally involves an egotistical or unilateral action taken without the approval of the *oyabun*. This severing of the little finger, along with other such details, establishes Masahiro Shinoda's *Pale Flower* (*Kawaita Hanna*, 1964) as a semi-*yakuza*. Shinoda originally filmed the amputation in such graphic detail, in mockery of the *yakuza* genre, that he was forced to remove the scene from the final version of the film as potentially too disturbing for the audience.

Grand and frequent swordplay and the throwing of daggers, as in the *chambara*, climax each *yakuza* film. When necessary, there is also the firing of guns. The gangsters themselves frequently bear scars of varying degrees of grotesqueness. Inevitably, they also come with tattoos, the more flamboyant the better. These are designed to set the *yakuza* apart from the rest of humanity. He is conceived as strong and silent, possessing the confidence of knowing always who he is and what he believes. It is a male image at once martial and feudal, and designed to cast aspersion on anyone less prone to violence and less subordinate to fixed authority. *Yakuza* are both superior to, and in greater peril than, the common lot of us.

Yakuza films are worthy of note not only because they have gained an inordinately wide audience among Japanese youth but, more importantly, because they reflect an agonizing sense among many Japanese of the

Pale Flower: Like poker in the American Western, gambling in the *yakuza* film is ever present and pursued with ritual intensity.

valueless state of their culture. Feudal mores as they operated in a pre-industrial era are glorified. Alienation is ascribed in modern Japan to departure from an authentic feudal code, and to insufficient fealty to the culture of the past which has granted Japan her unique identity.

In response to the moral vacuum they perceive in modern Japan, the *yakuza* films propose a return to the values of the past, particularly to those of the samurai culture that sustained itself by absolutes. Foremost among these was a loyalty to the clan and to one's superiors that took precedence over all other commitments, including those to loved ones. In the *yakuza* film, even more emphatically than in *chambara*, *giri* or duty is proposed as not merely necessary for the national and individual identity but as the most desirable means of carving out a life of merit within an amoral, corrupt social order. "*Yakuza*" is a gambling word which means both "winning" and "worthless," reflecting simultaneously the social trauma to which the *yakuza* film addresses itself and the relentless response it proposes to that "worthlessness." Physical combat and "winning" in mortal battle with one's opponents are the chief virtues in life. The presence of two contradictory meanings, "winning" and "worthless," itself reflects how deeply the *yakuza* code derives from the feudal era. The *yakuza* is worthless as an individual so long as he thinks, acts, or responds on his own. To "win"—or possess value—can occur only to the degree one subordinates oneself, accepts clan dictates, and is loyal to the *oyabun*.

The *yakuza* film is generally set after 1868, in assertion of the fact that something vital, which must now be retrieved, was lost with the Meiji

Restoration. Attempting in its initial stages to advance Japan by outlawing the rigid clan and class distinctions that thwarted the development of capitalism, the Meiji Government abolished the samurai class and outlawed the wearing of the long sword. Being a samurai, or continuing to behave with the samurai prerogative of settling one's scores through individual acts of violence, became impossible. Clans as such were abolished; the fiefs became lands open to bidding and sale, thereby creating a new, moneyed landlord class. To restore the Japanese to themselves, to replace the self-defining feudal norms that gave strength to the race, the *yakuza* gangsters attempt to emulate the outlawed samurai. They would bring to life, as best as they can in the new decadent age, the spirit of the Musashi Miyamotos. They would once more give the Japanese something in which to believe. Sacrificial death is a badge of honor, a small price to pay should it succeed in resurrecting the code of *bushido*. The very fact that *yakuza* films can draw upon widely felt feudal responses in the audience is a measure of the extent to which *bushido* still lives in the culture.

The effort of the *yakuza* films, not always successful, is to sustain the clan, its relationships intact, within an ever more dissolute Japan. *Yakuza* men are pictured as the last true opponents of a debased Western influence that has destroyed the country. They act like reincarnations of the *ronin* who were tricked into believing that their alliance with the Emperor, in the last days of the Tokugawa Shogunate, would ensure repulsion of the menacing foreigners. The *yakuza* films regard resistance through emulation—the beating of the opponent at his own game—as merely a disguised form of capitulation. One of the most influential admirers of these films was Yukio Mishima, who saw in them precisely the regeneration he sought for Japan in the code of *bushido*. The psychopathology of his last years was parallel to the behavior of the prototypical *yakuza* hero. Mishima welcomed the *yakuza* genre as a faithful expression of the sensibility needed to regenerate Japan.

The *yakuza* film always recognizes how difficult it is in today's Japan to sustain the samurai code; those who are able to achieve it are heroic, their rare dedication defined particularly by their determined effort to preserve proper *oyabun-kobun* relationships in the face of backsliding and betrayal. The bloody swordfights that climax so many *yakuza* films are in homage to the degree of bravery needed to maintain the samurai spirit against overwhelming social pressure.

The heroic struggle against odds, in which the prospect of defeat does not dismay (as Mishima was not deterred from his suicide by the imperviousness of the Self-Defense Force to his pleas), remains the leitmotif of all these films. It grants the protagonists a noble, tragic aspect, appealing implicitly for a violent struggle to restore Japan to what it once was. The great swordfight, even against overwhelming odds, provides indubitable evidence that men still exist equal to those who populated Japan's heroic past. The godfather, Nishi, in *The Hanafuda Game* (*Hibotanbakuto: Hanafuda Shobu*, 1969) says "my men are my treasures," an index of the popularity of the *yakuza* in a once closely knit society where people with no tradition of alienation now feel atomized and alone, unvalued and unappreciated in industrial Japan. Shinoda made his *yakuza* variant, *Pale Flower*, to reflect this same "mood of uneasiness"[2] at the moment Japan was preparing to compete industrially with the West; he even added heavy breathing to the sound track to convey this feeling. His *yakuza*-style hero, a gambler named Muraki, released from prison in the opening sequence, finds life equally futile in prison or out. Action born of conviction and devotion to the cause of a master is sorely missed. *Pale Flower* departs from the genre of the *yakuza because of its* psychological depth. Shinoda's Muraki finds relief not so much in devotion to a clan as in killing for its own sake, a far more accurate unfolding of the pathology of the real *yakuza in today's Japan.* "When I stabbed him" says Muraki of one of his victims, "I felt very much alive, happy." In the absence of feudal sanction that would connect his violence to an approved social purpose, such as the defeat of a neighboring clan, the act of murder itself, divorced from any "larger" objective, now constitutes an ecstatic moment.

Pale Flower, unlike any true *yakuza*, satirizes Muraki's gang, which makes peace with its rivals while he is in prison and fails to provide any moral sustenance to its members. The *oyabun* here is a ridiculous man who becomes a father for the first time in his fifties. His "beneficence" is reduced to humor as he repeatedly urges Muraki to have his teeth fixed upon his release from prison. The true *yakuza* does have inadequate, even corrupt, *oyabun* but, unlike *Pale Flower*, it always insists that good and true *oyabun* can and soon will supplant these traitors to the sanctity of the clan.

In the *yakuza* film the true alternative to loyalty is not—as in the *chambara*—*ninjo*, or humanity, but extermination for the individual who fails in his *giri*. While samurai functioned within the established order and were, in fact, sanctioned by it as members of private standing armies, the *yakuza*, illegal, are always threatened by disruption from outside their ranks, as well as by internecine clan warfare. The *yakuza* cannot see *giri* and *ninjo* as irreconcilables because the impulse of the *yakuza* film is not to challenge feudalism, but to endorse it. Even in *chambara*, not to mention *jidai-geki*, the obligations of *giri* are securely part of an accepted and unchallenged feudal order. Private desires, compassion, and humanity have a claim which often requires choice. In *Goyokin*, Magobei had to sacrifice his feelings for his wife in order to pursue his duty—his obligation to protest the clan's massacre of innocent fishermen. This was a duty to uphold the clan's honor by calling it to proper behavior in spite of itself. *Ninjo*, personal desire, becomes manifest in one's deciding for himself which duty—to clan or fishermen—deserves the higher priority.

But in *yakuza* films the samurai and feudal values exist within an outlaw context. The duty to clan proceeds in so threatened a general environment, with *giri* to the group so under siege from without, that the strongest personal desire of the *yakuza* must be to preserve feudal *giri* as a way of life.

[2] Joan Mellen, "Interview with Masahiro Shinoda," *Voices from the Japanese Cinema*, p. 251.

He can accommodate no other personal aim. *Giri* and *ninjo* become one. Because feudal institutions have passed into the corporate forms of industrial capitalism in Japan today, the *yakuza* warrior band must operate sub rosa. The reality upon which these films are based is that corporations constantly hire *yakuza* as thugs to threaten uncooperative trade unionists or dissidents in general. Given such tasks, the *yakuza*, unlike their samurai predecessors, cannot be openly avowed. And because social recognition for their efforts is impossible, the private passion of the *yakuza* becomes all the more to preserve *giri* to the "family." It is the only arena in which they can be wholly appreciated—among their blood-brothers and, in the best of circumstances, by a benevolently paternal *oyabun*.

There is another aspect to the *yakuza* code that goes to the issue of its outlaw origins. During pre-Meiji times there were many occurrences of murder or gross injustice inflicted by a lord on a vassal or peasant subject. Sometimes other vassals resorted to mutiny against the lord out of *giri* to the wronged victim. These vassals became members of outlaw bands, hunted because they had risen against an unjust master.[3] Such outlaw groups developed their own feudal structure with a master or *oyabun*. But their *giri* had a somewhat different character, reflecting their beginnings as mutinous rebels who had sided with a victim of injustice. Theirs was *giri* to the weak, to the helpless wronged. Acts of kindness to the disadvantaged became part of their tradition, almost as with the Western figure of Robin Hood. This, then, is also part of the *yakuza* mystique and accounts for no small measure of their popularity. With industrialization, the outlaw bands degenerated into gangsterism; ironically, because they failed to rebel against their original enemy, the feudal class system itself, they became part of the very system they had once resisted. Corporations took advantage of their illegal and, therefore, vulnerable status. Paradoxically, the populist beginnings of *yakuza* makes them even more useful as a repressive agency because their mystique earns them secret admiration from the population which remembers their romantic past. The appeal of the Mafia in the United States is similar. Immigrant groups forced by their station into outlaw status retain a tradition of generosity towards their own.

"Humanity" is rendered identical with the clan system. This is the *yakuza* answer to those who would assert that feudalism died precisely because the code of absolute loyalty entailed the sacrifice of justice and compassion. Paradoxically, there are many more instances of compassionate acts on behalf of the weak in the *yakuza* films than there were in the *chambara*. The poor and abandoned, particularly women and children, are occasionally the recipients of *yakuza* kindness, another reason for the immense popularity of the films. The *yakuza* tradition of *giri* toward women, regarded as prototypes of the vulnerable and defenseless, also accounts for the evolution of female *yakuza*, who were especially kind to weaker women and children.

In *The Hanafuda Game*, Oryu, the Red Peony, can wield her blade with

---

[3] For a useful discussion of this aspect of the origins of the *yakuza*, see Tadao Sato's essay "Reflex of Loyalty," translated by Leonard Schrader.

the best of men. But as Paul Schrader has observed, the Red Peony does not generally resort to a "man's job."[4] The values concerning women in the *yakuza* film remain those of Confucian times. Oryu advises a blind girl, Kimi, whom she rescues in the first sequence: "Study and become a pretty, soft-hearted bride." Later, with the aid of the best known *yakuza* star, Ken Takakura, Oryu helps Kimi recover her sight. The Red Peony herself looks sad and disconsolate as she counsels Kimi, for she herself has lost the chance of ever becoming a "soft bride," burdened as she is by the need, in these trying times, to sustain *yakuza* values. In 1972 Junko Fuji, who played the Red Peony, retired from *yakuza* films to marry. Accordingly, at the end of her last film, *The Cherry Blossom Fire Gang of Kanto* (*Kanto Hizakura Ikka*, 1972), she is allowed to marry Takakura and leave her clan with the *oyabun*'s blessing, a break with tradition.

The effort to sustain the *yakuza* spirit is relinquished by the Red Peony in life and in art. But such happy endings do not generally occur. Marriage is not endorsed by the *yakuza*, which, like the *chambara*, describe a male-centered world in which the most meaningful relationships are those among men. At a time when it is so difficult to keep the samurai spirit alive, goes the theory, marriage has become a luxury. Yet the departure of the Red Peony, who faces the camera and thanks the audience "for everything," suggests an affirmation of the genre rather than a violation of its ethic. The implication is that for Oryu to be allowed to abandon *giri* to the clan for the *ninjo* of marriage, the *yakuza* world must be flourishing. Others exist to take her place. Feudal values must be intact if so valuable a *yakuza* as Oryu can be spared.

In the typical *yakuza* film extreme circumstances are required to cast doubt on the value of loyalty to the *oyabun*—circumstances that imply an alternative obligation. Only the presence of an evil *oyabun* who undermines the blood brotherhood fortified by the rules of *bushido* would justify such rebellion. Of course, even a *bushi*, according to this code, could challenge a master who was pursuing a wrong course. Otherwise, duty is primary, as revealed in an advertising poster for one of the *yakuza* films: "The *yakuza* world—where duty is more important and humanity hangs in the balance."[5] More typical of the spirit of these films is the character in *The Cherry Blossom Fire Gang of Kanto* who begins to read the story of the Loyal Forty-Seven *Ronin*.

When *giri* and *ninjo* coincide, a choice between humanity and the entire system becomes otiose. Paul Schrader cites a number of seemingly contradictory statements within the same *yakuza* film:

(a) "We *yakuza* obey our code, no matter what happens."
(b) "Evil has no code."
(a) "We're outlaws but we're humane."
(b) "A friend is a friend, and a job is a job."[6]

[4] "Yakuza: Three Japanese Gangster Films," *The Museum of Modern Art Department of Film*, October 17, 1974.
[5] Cited by Paul Schrader, "*Yakuza-Eiga*: A Primer," *Film Comment*, January–February 1974, p. 12.
[6] *Ibid.*

But these statements are not at all in conflict. The life-and-death fight to preserve the samurai spirit in which lies the basic mission of the *yakuza* film admits no rules beyond the group obligation to preserve the fixed order. Whenever wrongs may be set right, they are so done in the strict context of sustaining the *yakuza* world. Precisely because the threat of Western colonial conquest destroyed the old samurai universe, all possible means must be used by the *yakuza* when their very survival is at stake. This sense of being threatened in the most total fashion, with their very identity as *yakuza* at issue, corresponds directly to the Japanese experience of the forced intrusion of Commodore Perry. It has governed the basic Japanese response to foreigners ever since, and the *yakuza* film reifies the sensibility that has come to define this danger to Japan's identity as a nation and people. Because a feudal order assumed the task of resisting foreign domination, even at the cost of mastering alien technology, when Japanese think of what constitutes their unique culture and identity, they turn to this feudal past. Had the nation not resisted foreign domination while remaining under feudal rule, the Japanese might not so readily identify being Japanese with ways of life peculiar to a feudal past, as in the *yakuza* film. It is this convergence of feudal forms with the preservation of one's identity that is celebrated by the *yakuza* and touches so responsive a chord in the audience. Upon being attacked with a sword, Oryu shoots her enemy with a gun, that symbol of Western influence. Any means, even despised Western techniques, must be employed to destroy betrayers of the code.

The most socially interesting of the *yakuza* films is *Presidential Gambling*, for it poses directly the choice between opening Japan to the outside or sustaining its preferred isolation. The plot is only superficially concerned with its ostensible theme, the problem of who is to succeed to the clan leadership. The real issue is expressed in the motives of the evil clan manipulator, Semba, who exploits a crisis in choosing a successor to the dying *oyabun* to seek control of the *yakuza* clan for the purpose of subordinating it to a large scheme for imperialist expansion in Asia.

Presidential Gambling becomes an allegorical attempt to argue that during the period of the Second World War, the clan (Japan) was temporarily usurped by a few evil leaders like Semba (Tojo and the other militarists) who were going against clan policy by calling for a Greater East Asia Co–Prosperity Zone. The good *oyabun* were opposed to this policy, but presumably were successfully, if only temporarily, displaced by a tiny minority. *Presidential Gambling* indirectly exonerates the culture as a whole from pro-fascist relationships, totally freeing the ruling class of blame for Japan's participation in the war. The film even sanctions the resurgence of the Old Guard after the defeat, since only a few individuals, like Semba, were evil. Nowhere, of course, does it suggest that the feudal structure of relationships, the *oyabun-kobun* mentality itself, had anything to do with the war.

The good characters in *Presidential Gambling* are on the side of the clan's confining its territory within domestic boundaries, since imperial expansion will entail a destruction of that past which the *yakuza* film is always trying to restore. The film agrees that Japan's desire for imperial expansion, necessitated by the period of capitalist development beginning with the fall of the Shogunate, lay at the root of her moral decay. The answer proposed, as it was by Mishima, is to return to a pure, pre-industrial form of feudalism, alive for the moment only within the sphere of the gangster clan.

As *Presidential Gambling* opens, it is 1934. At a board meeting, the leaders of the gang are assembled, as if they were executives of a giant corporation. Semba argues that "clinging to your home territory is absurd if there is a larger operation overseas." He is greedy, and avarice has always been in violation of the samurai spirit. The good characters, like Tokugawa shoguns, recognize that to maintain the integrity of the clan they must not go outside; the contamination of the West was precisely what led in Japan's past to the loss of the order they so prize—an order where succession is based upon seniority, rank, honor, and loyalty. That expansion outside will destroy the very essence of the clan is revealed as Semba, in order to effect these imperialist policies, has to upset proper succession to the position of godfather after the death of the good *oyabun*. He causes the two friends, the blood brothers Nakai and Matsuda, to become enemies, forced to choose between love for each other and clan duty. The *giri-ninjo* conflict is placed within a setting similar to that of the xenophobic debates of the 1860s, as if it were the moment of Western invasion that began the undermining of Japan's national identity.

Uncharacteristically for the *yakuza* film, *Presidential Gambling* ends with the deaths of all three principal characters: Semba, Nakai, and Matsuda. The very consideration of subordinating the clan to a "national front," whereby their operations would be extended to the "continent," has meant disaster. Thus does the *yakuza* exonerate itself of responsibility for the entire Second World War effort of the military and the industrialists, who felt that, for Japan's safety and continued prosperity, all of Asia had to be politically and economically subordinated to Japanese influence.

To achieve this end, Semba has to violate the proper succession rules of the Tenryu clan which would have made either Nakai or Matsuda the *oyabun*. Semba attempts to set up as *oyabun* a man named Ishido, a friend of Nakai and Matsuda and an unsuspecting pawn in Semba's hands. In the face of this threat to the clan, the bond of friendship between Nakai and Matsuda, symbolized by an actual vessel like the Holy Grail, is broken. Only if the clan continues to live in keeping with the sacred values of the past, says *Presidential Gambling*, can brotherhood be maintained.

Faced with Semba's violation of clan integrity, Nakai and Matsuda adopt different approaches. Nakai urges, in typical *yakuza* manner, that the clan as an entity be maintained at all costs, regardless of Semba's breach of clan ethics. Matsuda believes that the very integrity of the clan and the style of life it embodies are threatened by the upsetting of proper succession, and that all-out warfare must be waged. That

Ishido, the new *oyabun*, is actually not guilty of betrayal and that, nevertheless, he becomes one of the targets of Matsuda's rage, indicates that the film endorses the position of Nakai. Yet, although the *raison d'être* of the *yakuza* is, as Nakai believes, to preserve the clan no matter what, Matsuda is also right, for the *yakuza* must preserve what the clan stands for or the clan will cease to be an organization worth preserving. In principle, both men are correct.

In practice, however, Matsuda's impetuous behavior, his plot to kill both Semba and the innocent puppet *oyabun* Ishido, is shown to be destructive. Matsuda's quixotic idealism achieves nothing, becoming only a destructive force. He is insufficiently attuned to the traditional Japanese approach to such problems through compromise and the slow attempt to restore lost harmony. Childishly, he speaks in terms of how things ought to have been, unlike the true samurai who deals pragmatically with life as it is. "If you or I succeeded [to the status of *oyabun*]," he tells Nakai, "we wouldn't be where we are now." While these words are true, they are also, according to the *yakuza* ethos, those of a weak man, one who refuses to sacrifice his personal principles, which are seen as an egotistic form of self-indulgence, for the sake of the greater good, the clan.

Finally, in the *yakuza* world the hero is faced with the need to preserve the clan even when he is aware that it has ceased to embody the highest good, the values for which it once stood. This is the tragedy of the *yakuza*, a samurai forced to live in an environment inhospitable to samurai grandeur, a world whose corruption invades the very precincts of the *yakuza* clan itself. The moral dissolution of the clan forces Nakai to kill the tempestuous Matsuda, his blood brother, in order to preserve the clan from Matsuda's rage. Afterwards, Nakai calls himself a "cold-blooded murderer," aware that, like the clan, he personally has lost the integrity that made the *yakuza* world a refuge for true and noble men in corrupt modern Japan. It was not sufficient, as Nakai had originally thought, that, for the sake of preserving harmony, he forfeit the role of *oyabun* that should have been his. For, like the true samurai they were, neither Nakai nor Matsuda was personally ambitious to be an *oyabun*. What bothered Matsuda most, in fact, was that Nakai had been passed over despite his superior rank and service, a violation of feudal morality that was dangerous because it called into question the value of living on behalf of the clan.

The return to feudal values in the *yakuza* film means, inevitably, the resurgence and strengthening of patriarchal supremacy. In the *yakuza* world wives are expected to subordinate themselves to the obligations of their husbands, as were samurai women. When Matsuda disappears at one point, Nakai questions Hiroe, Matsuda's wife. She replies that she doesn't know the whereabouts of her husband, that "a woman has no right to know." Later, Nakai's own wife commits suicide because she has been unsuccessful in following her husband's instructions to prevent the flight of Matsuda and his follower, Ota, in their pursuit of Ishido and Semba. Her suicide note, read out in voice-over, expresses this woman's sense of her place within the *yakuza* moral hierarchy: "My female intellect told me what to do . . . I only hope my death will keep peace between you and Matsuda. I have been as happy a wife as any woman could possibly be." As in feudal times, a woman is expected always to be ready to sacrifice herself for the sake of clan harmony.

In the final scene of *Presidential Gambling*, Nakai, after he has killed Matsuda, hurls his bloody knife toward the audience, urging us to hold the murder weapon ourselves since it is we who are the real murderers, not the *yakuza* hero. We, as citizens of a corrupt Japan, are responsible for the undermining of the pure *yakuza* world. Our distorted values have endangered their more sacred ones. The implication is that even Semba's idea of a Greater East Asia Co-Prosperity Zone was originally ours. Now we support the State's murder of Nakai, who has just been sentenced to death by the Japanese courts; we are thrust back into our corrupt world, one lacking the redeeming values of honor and loyalty so much a part of theirs.

Rare for a *yakuza* film, there is no restoration of order at the end of *Presidential Gambling*. The despair over what Japan has become—a valueless society reduced to State murder of its finest men—goes unrelieved. Such an ending recognizes that the *yakuza* world flourishes only tenuously and in a corner of the real Japan. These films admit what the best of the *chambara* only implied: the sword-slashing finales, however successfully the hero defeats his enemies, are gestures of futility on behalf of something irrevocably lost. No matter how many victims are claimed, the samurai code has disappeared. It is the profundity of this national despair that allows the *yakuza* films, mediocre as they are, to become outcries of the culture, despite the fact that their styles are undistinguished and the motive of the Toei Company, the primary producer of these films, is exclusively commercial.

The more typical *yakuza* world is portrayed in *The Hanafuda Game*. The Red Peony, aided by Ken Takakura, saves the blind child Kimi and rescues a young couple caught, as children of the leaders of rival factions, in the middle of internecine clan warfare. At the end, the Red Peony is herself separated from Takakura, her obvious male counterpart and potential life companion. The train smoke billowing over a bridge in the last shot expresses the *yakuza* misery over modern industrial Japan, which swallowed up the values of the samurai and now threatens *yakuza* survival as well.

Oryu, the Red Peony, and Takakura, playing Itanaba, the "mysterious stranger" she meets, are both pariahs who long for a normality they find impossible in this Japan. All the *yakuza* in the film wish they did not have to live the lives of outlaws. Nishi, the *oyabun*, echoing Francis Ford Coppola's Godfather, wants his son Jiro to go to a university and be part of a generation that will find a satisfying life within the legal boundaries of the society. This is a fate inaccessible to Michael Corleone, but it is possible for Nishi's son because of the superhuman *yakuza* efforts of Oryu and Itanaba.

Nishi's son, Jiro, and his girlfriend, Yae, after being attacked by *yakuza* loyal to Yae's father, Kambara (a rival to Nishi), are first rescued by the mother of the blind girl Kimi. Blocking the door with her body so that the gamblers sent by Kambara cannot enter to separate the two young people, she is an easy mark for these *yakuza*, who plunge a sword into the door, running her through. Blood spurts like a geyser from her chest. Freedom, in the *yakuza* film, is the legacy of endless sacrifice.

The relationship between Oryu and Itanaba, one of love, is also a litany to the subordination of inclination to duty and loyalty, the pillars of the *yakuza* world. Itanaba is under obligation to Kambara, Yae's father. Oryu belongs to the side of Jiro's father, Nishi. Both tacitly agree that their obligations must always come first. Yet when *giri* can be accompanied by *ninjo*, the *yakuza* figure will always attempt their reconciliation because he has a good heart. Itanaba, violating his trust, lies to his *oyabun*, Kambara, when he says that he has never met Oryu. When Kambara demands that Itanaba kill Nishi, Itanaba does engage Nishi in a duel, but then deliberately wounds him only slightly. His true *giri* is to the well-being of the clan, of which Nishi is a much more valuable member than Kambara, despite the fact that he was hired by Kambara and should, by the sanctity of his agreement, support Kambara at every instant.

At the end, the conflict betwen the Kambara and Nishi factions can be resolved only through death. Nishi has seemed to be the victor in their dispute, but at the party over which Nishi presides, we find Kambara running off with the clan funds, still a willful disrupter of clan harmony. He must be finished off by Itanaba, since only his death will put an end to the chaos he has engendered.

Nishi, too, is wounded, and the camera focuses on his side, from which blood is flowing. But he won't lie down because this would be rude to his guests. Forms must be maintained at all cost. In the desperation with which the culture has turned to the *yakuza* film, adherence to manner is vital. Nishi dies seated in the position of honor at the party, like the good soldier who remains at his post.

While Nishi remains upright, though already dead, Oryu gambles in his honor while the music throbs, testifying to the glory accruing to the true *yakuza* hero. Itanaba tells Oryu that he loves her because "the warmth of your hand as we were by the river was like the touch of my mother's hand." This simplistic Freudianism is somewhat relieved by our knowledge that they are destined to part. Itanaba wishes Oryu "good luck" as he goes off to the police to assume the consequences of Kambara's death. His parting words are, "in the spring the flowers will blossom again." They will meet once more; their affection will remain as constant as that of the shining Prince Genji for each of his many mistresses.

In defiance of the insatiability of Japanese audiences for *yakuza* films, and contemptuous of the values for which these films stand, in 1973 Kon Ichikawa made The Wanderers (*Matatabi*), a minor work but of interest for its parody of *yakuza* values. Refusing to grant any glory whatsoever to the *yakuza* film's attempt to reinforce samurai codes, Ichikawa fills this work with the same emptiness and lack of direction characterizing Shinoda's *Assassination* and *Buraikan*. *The Wanderers* seems to have been made precisely to challenge the *yakuza* sentiment that a return to *bushido* would add meaning to Japanese culture.

Like the heroes of the earliest *yakuza* films, the characters of *The Wanderers*, called *toseinin*, live in the mid-nineteenth century. But unlike the appealing *yakuza* of the Toei movies, they are dirty, unkempt, and silly, as if these qualities characterized all *yakuza* heroes, whatever their façade. These *toseinin*, would-be outlaws who desperately desire to hire themselves out, are pathetic samurai imitators, lacking the grandeur and historical justification of that class, and lacking as well the altruism some might attribute to the *yakuza* to sanction their outlaw status and behavior. Ichikawa's characters, *yakuza*-apprentices, try to live by the elaborate codes and rituals of the *yakuza*, but invariably fail. They introduce themselves to would-be benefactors in the most elaborate, ritualized manner, but no one will take them seriously. The *oyabun* they approach are bored by their childish antics and indignant at the presumption of their very presence. While *yakuza* like the Red Peony are shown as benevolently enlisting their services on behalf of ordinary people such as the blind girl Kimi, Ichikawa attacks the hypocrisy of Japan's gangsters, the pretense that they are kind-hearted benefactors of the poor, by making his punk *yakuza* fear more than anything being confused with "ordinary people," whom they despise.

According to the mythology of the Toei films, the *yakuza* remain loyal to their code in the midst of external social confusion. Ichikawa's would-be *yakuza* define freedom as license; petty outlaws, period-film juvenile delinquents, their liberation from normal social restraints leads only to an outpouring of their worst impulses. The hero, Genta, kills his own father gratuitously. Once harmed by his parent, he retaliates by becoming a victimizer, which is what, for Ichikawa, the *yakuza* essentially is. Genta later sells his girlfriend to a whorehouse for food. Ichikawa shows that the true morality of the *yakuza* involves nothing more than self-interested lust and greed. Far from representing a resurgence of meaningful values for the culture, the *yakuza* reveals only a suppurating egotism concealed in samurai banners.

The ending of *The Wanderers* expresses Ichikawa's utter contempt for the *yakuza* and their aspirations. Genta quarrels irritably with his best friend, with no apparent issue at stake. Awkward beyond measure, with none of the grace of a real samurai, he trips over his own hat, falls into a ravine, hits his head on a rock, and dies. The entire incident occurs almost within a split second, as if these *yakuza* were worth no grand climax, no heroic death. The friend, who a few moments earlier had been stabbed in the arm by this same wild Genta during the course of their quarrel, looks for Genta and concludes that "he must be taking a shit somewhere." His call for Genta continues over the black

screen, chronicling not only the end of the film but an all-pervasive emptiness that renders absurd all *yakuza* film claims to a higher morality. A bleak
Japan, barren of purpose or of people who could change its downward
moral direction, will hardly be renewed through the hypocrisies of the
yakuza "code."

Yakuza films are inspirational, as *chambara* once were. They would
return the individual to the security of clan protection and, as long as
possible, keep him subordinated to its prior value through the force of
inviolable norms of duty. Taken seriously, which their popularity war-
rants, the *yakuza* films bespeak desperation and a hysteria that can
find an outlet only in the sword directed against any and all outsiders,
and, if one fails to meet the demands of the code of the *bushi*, equally
against oneself. The atrocities toward the individual in the name of
honor and loyalty with which Japan's history is dotted are, in the
yakuza film, preferred to the terrors of regeneration. In a flamboyant
failure of nerve, they face the moral vacuum engulfing Japanese society
armed only with the profound irrationality that in a return to feudalism
lies Japan's only hope for rebirth.

PART

3

THE SECOND WORLD WAR AND ITS AFTERMATH

The Japanese Film During the Second World War

We have no need of erudite historians and critics; we have need of brave souls ready for sacrifice. We must, we must create such souls, otherwise we are lost.

A Japanese teacher to Nikos Kazantzakis, 1938[1]

Japan was never a fascist country. Never having had a French Revolution to dismantle or even to interrupt its feudal institutions, the freedoms against which fascism moves never existed in Japan. Fascism is not merely a system of authoritarian repression. It involves a specific response by advanced corporate capitalism to the combined circumstances of an economic or political crisis and a large, mobilized, working-class opposition. Faced with an organized opposition to the State and economic turmoil like that occasioned by the Great Depression, an attempt is made to smash democratic rights and institutions.

In Japan the absence of a bourgeois revolution prevented truly representative government, democratic freedoms, and working-class organizations from coming fully into existence, whether through trade unions or political parties. Hence the authoritarianism of the 1930s was not a reaction to political freedoms already achieved but expressed in part the workings of a feudal order. Fascist repression was unnecessary; there was no need to suppress the individual and reject his claims for autonomy, since these had always taken second place to the needs of the collective. As General Koiso made clear at his war crimes trial, the insistence even upon individual responsibility was inconceivable in the Japanese context:

> The way of we Japanese is that no matter what our personal opinions and our own personal arguments may be, once a policy of state has been decided upon, it is our duty to bend all our efforts for the prosecution of such policy. This has been the traditional custom in our country.[2]

The decisive phrases are "we Japanese" and "bend[ing] all our efforts." Feudal values are equated with the national existence, loyalty to Japan, and one's very identity as a Japanese. Conformity calls for a greater effort of character than dissidence and rebellion, which are anathema.

[1] *Travels in China and Japan* (Oxford: Bruno Cassirer, 1964), p. 161.
[2] Cited in Masao Maruyama, "Thought and Behaviour Patterns of Japan's Wartime Leaders," in *Thought and Behaviour in Modern Japanese Politics*, pp. 105–106.

The subordination of the individual to the group had been a feature of Japanese life for nearly a thousand years. The brief human rights movements of the 1870s and 1880s, attendant upon trade contact with the democracies of the West, had been suppressed by the 1890s. The authoritarian, patriarchal family system, always a pivot of fascism, had been the dominant social institution in Japan since the establishment of feudalism itself. The prerogatives of the family were strongly reasserted in 1898. Lineage relationships were reaffirmed, with the eldest son once again regaining the exclusive right to inherit all family property. Thus even the limited anti-feudal measures of the early days of the Meiji Restoration were reversed.

It is true that, in common with Germany and Italy, the 1930s saw in Japan cynical, anti-capitalist appeals against "traitorous millionaires" to a populace affected by the world depression. There was, as well, a glorification of the peasant producer, the rapid growth of an expansionist army, and racist appeals on behalf of foreign conquest. But these emulations of European fascism were pre-emptive devices, not, as in Europe, a regression from existing political democracy and individual liberty. Even Japan's foreign adventures were seen in terms of an *Asian* dignity and self-assertion, repulsing colonial occupiers from Europe. It was the obverse of European fascist rationales, namely the duty to rule subject peoples.

Japanese feudal traditions were invoked. The country was made ready to assert its claims to an imperial role hitherto greedily monopolized by the Western industrial states. The spoils obtained through participation in the First World War had confirmed to the Japanese rulers that they would have to intensify militarization and fight for more. Japanese corporations were eager for such a course, well aware that their dependence on foreign raw materials meant that Japan's exclusion from imperial spoils would be fatal to the country's economic growth. Martial values, always latent in this feudal culture, were reasserted and found no serious opposition.

Communications and the arts were mobilized on behalf of the preparations for war. In the service of this goal, cinema as a mass art form was quickly seen as essential. The *Chuo Koron* magazine of October 1940 set out the demands which film and theater would be obliged to fulfill as Japan moved toward full-scale confrontation with the Western powers and the United States:

> Dramatic art must forget the old individualistic and class attitudes and must begin to realize that it has a new cultural role to perform in the total program of our new national consciousness. Actors are no longer to serve a class but the nation and they must act as persons who are part of the whole national entity. They must have the determination to make the cultural wealth of [their art] available to every group in the population. For this reason, the concentration of culture in the big cities should be eliminated.[3]

[3] Cited in Joseph L. Anderson and Donald Richie, *The Japanese Film: Art and Industry* (New York: Grove Press, 1960), p. 135.

In the war movies which follow, as in German National Socialism, a pseudo-classless approach is stressed. Although soldiers will be divided according to officer and rank-and-file status, these films also include the ideology that all are equally capable of devoting themselves to the Emperor's cause, the death of each in the service of the *kokutai* (national spirit) equally valuable. This myth of the equality of all was, of course, necessary to effect a unification of all Japanese for the national effort. Art must not be so esoteric as to raise philosophical issues or unsettle "the masses." In particular, the government dictated a list of film topics that would not be tolerated.

They prohibited "slice-of-life" films, which presumably would induce discontent with the squalor and poverty facing so many Japanese. Films exalting individual happiness were banned because implicit in this theme was the danger that some might default in their unquestioning duty to the national effort, substituting a quest for personal fulfillment. Nor were the lives of the rich to be filmed, because such descriptions might render intolerable the sacrifices demanded of, and necessary for, the war effort. As in many authoritarian countries, puritanism reigned, as if personal rebellion in the areas of sex or life style would seed that independence prerequisite to political rebellion. The first kiss would occur on screen in the Japanese film only after the War. Forbidden as well were scenes of women smoking or drinking in cafes.

It is instructive, however, that official puritanism during the war period drew upon a deep current in Japanese social life. Rigid repression of feeling had been instilled under feudal rule for so long that it had become a feature of the national character. The full significance of the failure to overthrow feudalism may be gauged by the inhibition of undisciplined spontaneous feeling still apparent in the Japanese film. Even in the anti-feudal and postwar films of such directors as Mizoguchi, Kurosawa, Kobayashi, and Hani, people rarely touch. Such formality presides even among husband and wife, parents and children. Generally, in the Japanese film, only children are permitted the unabated expression of their feelings, like Kon Ichikawa's defeated high school tournament baseball players shown weeping uncontrollably in his documentary *Youth* (*Seishun*, 1968). So much fervor has been attached to winning at these games that crying in public by the losers becomes accepted behavior.

Japan, shackled to this day by feudal inhibition, embodies the full extent to which social and political repression are first mediated by an authoritarian family, and then registered in physical rigidity and tension. The violent and hysterical modes of aggressive release of the samurai tradition reflect the extraordinary price paid in repression of self, of physical freedom, and of personal expression for those living under feudal and neo-feudal institutions.

After 1940 any semblance in films of unorthodoxy, or of life unruled by obligation and fixed tradition, were taboo. There were to be no foreign words permitted in Japanese films. Official propaganda during the war was devoted to exalting purely Japanese tradition while presenting Japanese militarism as a crusade to free Japan and Asia from Western imperialism and its cultural counterparts. The presence of foreign words suggested penetration by a "superior" culture and a recognition of the merit of foreign ideas. Such intimations of insufficiency were incommensurate with Imperial Japan's proclamations of its national destiny. All scripts were censored and, after Pearl Harbor, only "national-policy" themes were admitted.

Typical of such movies was Tomotaka Tasaka's *Five Scouts* (*Go-nin no Sekkohei*, 1938), set in China after the Japanese occupation. It does not have a "plot" with a beginning, middle, and end. There is no "hero" whose extraordinary feats of bravery signal a celebration of the Japanese cause. It does not suggest that personal glory is the fruit of battle. The most striking characteristic of this film and others like it, such as Tasaka's *Mud and Soldiers* (*Tsuchi to Heitai*, 1939), is a seeming indifference to the war itself. Yet they are masterpieces of propaganda for the Japanese *kokutai*.

In the background of *Five Scouts* Tasaka bombards the viewer with constant noise: loud gunfire, artillery, machine guns, bugles, explosions, the daily cacophony of life at the front. In the opening sequence a Japanese flag is planted on top of a bridge, but not in close shot and without particular fanfare. It is enough that we see it; its presence prepares us for the moment at the end of the film when soldiers will march out to battle under the same bridge. The flag is then always with us, seen and unseen. It provides the continuity, and hence the purpose, of our lives. And it is a more effective statement for its relative subtlety.

The camera tilts down to the line of soldiers standing at rapt attention. They have just captured the area and their commander thanks them for the bravery which has led to this success. He declares that he could not have done it alone, as only the "utmost effort" by the men of Japan can bring triumph; neither the superiority of the officer, nor his cleverness, creates victories in war. It is the opposite of the American approach in films about World War Two. In *Back to Bataan*, only the joint individual efforts of John Wayne and Anthony Quinn are able to thwart the Japanese. In *Five Scouts*, however, the officer refuses to grant that anyone is a "hero." Potential soldiers in the audience are thus encouraged and inspired. They are to be deeply moved by how profoundly needed, and hence fulfilled, each one of them will be, how the efforts of the Japanese nation are the sole result of the accumulated energies of every man at the front.

Despite its form, this ideology is the antithesis of either recognition of the value of individual expression or the social gain of collective effort. Characteristic of each would be the conscious determination of self-selected goals, either pursued personally or in common purpose through joining freely with others. But the real theme of such works as *Five Scouts* and *Mud and Soldiers* is that both individual and collective efforts are most highly realized through subordination to a preordained, mystical, national cause personified by the Emperor. Hence individual expression and collective purpose can be simultaneously invoked without contradiction or

Five Scouts: Life in the camp is shown to offer genuine joys, the result of men, like the warriors of old, participating together in a sanctified pursuit.

subversive implication because they are both subsumed by an a priori authoritarian ideal. All the responses that inspire people—heroic gesture, personal dedication, devotion to a cause larger than the self—are anticipated, neutralized, and pre-empted for the specific social order of Imperial Japan.

Before the Japanese army began to suffer large numbers of casualties, the war films did not focus on the exploits of supermen, moral or otherwise—individuals unafraid of death, whose courage was far beyond that of ordinary mortals. Rather, the characters of films like *Five Scouts* and *Mud and Soldiers* are presented as vulnerable and, like us all, humanly frail. Camp life on the front provides that satisfaction possible only when all work together for the same end, forgetting their individual selves. Being separated from the "main group" offers a more unpleasant prospect than being wounded or failing in a mission. Life in the camp is shown to offer genuine joys, the result of men, like the warriors of old, participating together in a sanctified pursuit. Some of the men whistle as they clean their guns. One does stunts with a sword, a literal resurrection of the *bushi.* Small pleasures suffice. If the water is of good quality, their rice will be tasty. Pedestrian comforts help the men get through trying moments. One pretends he can smell sukiyaki, another mushrooms. A third imagines that he is eating *sushi* (raw fish and vinegared rice). What is uniquely Japanese is good and valuable and a sufficient reminder of the meaning of the war, which need not be overtly discussed. Instead of hatred for the enemy, who rarely appears in *Five Scouts,* the soldiers concentrate on their shared Japanese identity, always to be cherished as something they possess that no enemy can emulate.

All the events which take place in *Five Scouts* are written up in a diary by the hard-working group commander. He is presented as psychically dependent on the men, rather than vice versa. When the battles seem not to be going well for the Japanese, he rereads his diary applauding the brave exploits of his men. From the accounts of these feats he derives his own strength.

The commander is also thoroughly humane. He feels "very bad" when he has to record a death. He won't eat unless he knows that his men are also eating. Sitting alone at night, illuminated by a kerosene lamp, he is photographed as if he were a saint. This sainthood stems in large measure from his ability to appreciate the men who died with the words "Long live the Emperor" on their lips, or those who perished in the act of calling to the others: "Advance, advance!"

The relationships in *Five Scouts,* as in all these films, are presented as egalitarian. All are sacrificing themselves for the sake of a greater good; the men treat each other as comrades in this effort. A close-up of a pair of hands holding cigarettes is followed by a shot of many hands reaching out. Tasaka dissolves to the entire group enjoying the cigarettes, which have been passed out equally to all. Death is despised and never exalted. It is seen as a necessary evil rather than as an avenue toward glory, despite the propaganda associated with the Japanese war effort and its *kamikaze* pilots.

In *Five Scouts,* as in so many of these films, the relationship between men and commander proceeds according to a formula. The commander is always solicitous when a man is wounded. He praises the injured man for having done a "good job." He is visibly upset when the man seems to be in pain. The wounded man, however, invariably refuses to go to the hospital even if this refusal means that one of his limbs will have to be amputated. His desire is to fight as long as he can hold a gun. The commander, humane and wise, knowing best, forces the wounded soldier to go to the hospital, a necessary but temporary suspension of his efforts. The man cries at this fate. By the end of the film the injured one is well enough to rejoin the group. At this point he is cheered and welcomed back by all.

At only one point in *Five Scouts* is the purpose of the war, and the presence of Japanese soldiers in China, suggested. The commander reads a letter, ostensibly sent by the Emperor, apologizing for the hardships of the war in China, which, we learn, was necessitated by China's alliance with England, thus threatening Japan's security. But that the Emperor personally endorses their efforts does not give these men greater courage and determination than they already had when they were fighting for "Japan," because they have already been giving their utmost. The Emperor's words are a reaffirmation, one which they don't really need. Thus do the five chosen scouts go off on their reconnaissance mission, moving through thick brush, slogging through endless mud, followed by a hand-held camera which adds greater immediacy to their travail.

These five are pitted against one hundred Chinese shooting at them, odds which make our heroes overwhelmingly sympathetic as they fiercely fire back. Tasaka takes one shot of the nasty terrain as if from the inside of a gun, dark and black, suggesting what the five scouts are up against. Yet these Japanese soldiers never hesitate. Nor are the Chinese caricatured as grotesque, as were the Japanese in American-made World War Two movies. When the leader of the five, Fujimoto, bayonets a Chinese, whose body then floats down a stream, it is done without fanfare and is presented, like all the events in these films, as more necessary than desirable.

When the scouts are two hours late for their return to the camp, everyone begins to look out for them. The men who are called to the front, says *Five Scouts*, will not find themselves fighting and dying alone, without the affection of others. Full light plays about Fujimoto's face when he returns with the required report regarding the whereabouts of the Chinese enemy. The fifth scout, Kiyuchi, fails to return. Only his helmet, embellished with the foliage with which he attempted to conceal his presence from the Chinese, is brought back.

In a dissolve we are brought together with the commander, his face once again illuminated by artificial light. He is engaged in the painful duty of recording that the fifth man died in battle, having fulfilled his duty. The men, however, refuse to give up hope that Kiyuchi will return, calling out into the night, "Come back if you are still alive. If you are suffering somewhere, I can't stand to think of it!" By now it is pouring, creating a muddy trough of the entire area.

Not content merely to wait, the men want to go out in search of Kiyuchi, but the commander refuses to permit this folly. He could not bear, he says, to lose any more of them, not because they are readying themselves for a major battle and he needs every man to fight, but because the pain of such a loss would be intolerable. At five A.M., his steps paralleled by the traveling camera, a man, slogging through endless mud, makes his way to the camp. It is, of course, Kiyuchi, his lost helmet replaced by a Chinese cap. All rush out, the camera panning their ecstatic faces. Kiyuchi himself sobs with joy. Such love and brotherhood are possible only when men live so closely together, united by a common effort that may cost their lives. At the front a human closeness is achieved that would be impossible except in such circumstances. Going to war has its compensations.

Such experiences allow men to exhibit their best qualities which, from the Japanese point of view, always involve the expression of self-effacement and humility. The returned Kiyuchi is ashamed to be reporting without his gun, which was lost during the mission. He apologizes for being late, for not being a "good scout," although we all know that a better scout could not be found anywhere. And the commander, of course, corrects him: "Yes, you were." To which Kiyuchi must reply, in extreme understatement: "Thank you very much." One is reminded again that for Japanese at such moments words become meaningless, bearing only the most tenuous relationship to the deep emotions felt by all. His comrades cover Kiyuchi with a warm jacket and inquire as to whether he is hungry. He keeps saying "*Arigato*" (thank you) over and over again. By now everyone is sobbing. In an overhead shot Kiyuchi sits by himself, crying uncontrollably, so overwhelmed is he by the beauty of the experience.

The last scene of *Five Scouts* finds the group going off at last to battle. The commander informs them that they must now be ready to die "for the Emperor, for the honor of the group, for the peace of the Orient," which will result from their efforts. The men stand at attention in a long line, the camera at a chest-high angle focusing on their bodies, in which has been incarnated the meaning of being a Japanese.

The commander requests, rather than orders, that the men die with him. Together they will say farewell to Japan. It is a beautiful moment, a paean to the consummate love expressed through life in the army. The men march out under the same bridge we saw in the opening shot, as a choral motif encourages them to "be ready to die," whether by land or sea. By now the men, through the mutual communion of army life, have experienced so much of the sweetness of human existence that death seems more an anticlimax than a trauma to be feared. Those remaining behind in Japan, and watching this film, learn that life at the front has more rewards than pain, and a deeper spirituality than the mundane life at home which lacks such magnitude and purpose.

Far more fully realized, both as a work of art and as successful propaganda, was Kimisaburo Yoshimura's *The Story of Tank Commander Nishizumi* (*Nishizumi Senshacho-den*, 1940). The Japanese had become aware of the overwhelming international criticism of their army's brutal behavior in China toward civilians, particularly in its march toward Nanking. In addition to its being a typical pro-army film, *Tank Commander Nishizumi* attempts to answer this criticism. A title indicates to the audience that the film has been made by the Japanese Army to dramatize realistically how life at the front really was, in honor of the 2,600th year of the birth of the Emperor's line. At once the lineage of the Emperor, upon which the Japanese *kokutai* was based, is reaffirmed. The Emperor's unbroken relation to the gods who founded Japan, his incarnation of the national spirit, will be symbolized in this film by the saintly commander, Nishizumi.

Unlike *Five Scouts* and *Mud and Soldiers*, *Tank Commander Nishizumi* attempts to offer the characterization of an individual, the hero of the film's title. But equally important remains the emphasis on group activities. "History makes people," says a narrator in voice-over at the beginning of the film. Students are shown at calisthenics, as the educational system is revealed to be in the service of the national effort. "The traditional spirit of the army remains in the people," continues this narrator, as if Japan's youth were preserving an unbroken line from the nation's past to its present participation in the war. All Japanese are said to possess a common spirit by virtue of their uniqueness as a race. Nishizumi himself is a second son. He will rise to a high position as an officer because in the

The Story of Tank Commander Nishizumi: As Nishizumi, Ken Uehara resembles a Japanese Errol Flynn, sultry-eyed with a pencil-thin moustache and a suggestive smile.

Japanese war film merit surpasses birth. One of the graduates of his high school was also a famous soldier and "our hero" was influenced by his example, just as the link of dedication to the Emperor's cause binds all Japanese to each other. In 1938, Nishizumi goes to war at the age of twenty-four.

The scene is the Shanghai front. The fighting has grown much fiercer than it had been in Tasaka's film, made only two years before. Men are shot and lie bleeding; their attempts to reassure each other are no guarantee against severe physical punishment. A huge number of Japanese tanks are on the scene, but technology does not ensure victory.

A tank top opens and Nishizumi emerges. As Nishizumi, Ken Uehara resembles a Japanese Errol Flynn: sultry-eyed, with a pencil-thin moustache and a suggestive smile. Chain cigarette smoking provides further testimony to his masculinity. But, like the Flynn of *Robin Hood*, he is cheerful beyond measure as the explosions resound behind him. Someone jokes, "Who is the hero today?" and the answer, so typical of the Japanese war film, comes back, "We are all heroes."

In the early scenes Nishizumi is submerged in army life, a man among men. At dinner the men quote Napoleon, who said that you can only fight when your stomach is full, as if to reassure the home audience that, however severe the trials on the Chinese front, the men were well fed. Huge jugs of *sake* are passed down the table, and army songs resound with gusto. Nishizumi, of course, joins in.

This camaraderie is interrupted by the arrival of corpses covered by Japanese flags. *Tank Commander Nishizumi* admits to heavy Japanese casualties in China and reveals, in the depictions of men being killed and wounded, the government's need to prepare the audience at home for bad news. Only an echo remains of the song the men had just been singing as Yoshimura cuts to a low-angle shot looking up into a machine gun. A huge tank breaks through a brick wall. By 1940 the war in China was posing unmistakable dangers to the Japanese soldier who, in Tasaka's films, seemed to be having a much easier time on the Chinese front. The need for a hero like Nishizumi, behind whom the others could rally, now exists in a way it did not when the war was going better.

Nishizumi emerges from his tank and plants a Japanese flag, an example of bravery that all might emulate. He is shown to be stronger and more heroic, if still, ideologically, no more valuable as a human being than the lowliest recruit. With impeccable style, he lights a cigarette. So devoted is he to his objectives that he can even use the Japanese flag irreverently, plunging it into a pond to test the depth of the water. When one of his men is shot, Nishizumi cradles him in his arms with a gentle reproach: "I told you not to come out." He is always capable of encouraging others, even at the most trying times.

Tank Commander Nishizumi also differs markedly from the earlier propaganda films in that its pace accelerates so rapidly. With the passage of time, the fighting has become more difficult. The horrors of war increase. Victory seems ever more distant.

By the time Nishizumi is actually promoted to the rank of Commander, we have witnessed a man afraid to go to the toilet because there are so many dead bodies heaped outside. Boxes of bones of the dead are lined up, as the men are instructed to ensure that they don't get wet. A Chinese comes close enough to land on top of Nishizumi's tank, and Nishizumi must kill him with a pistol. A wounded Japanese soldier lies in the path of the tank and Nishizumi jumps out and pulls the man to safety, himself suffering a wound in the leg. Every moment is fraught with danger. The *mise-en-scène* grows dark and, in most scenes, rain drenches everyone. When the sun does come out, it offers no respite.

Nishizumi, now on crutches, refuses to rest because he has assumed a position of responsibility. But, in his soft-hearted and gently loving attitude toward his men, he is like the commanders in the Tasaka films. A letter arrives from the brother of a dead member of the group, revealing that their mother didn't cry when she learned of the death of her son; she was content, as the Japanese Army urges all mothers to be, that her son could "do something for the country." But if the dead soldier's mother didn't cry, Nishizumi, as a surrogate mother, does. So overcome is he by emotion that he must pass the letter on to someone else to read. Crying in these films is never treated as a sign of weakness but of the strength of brotherhood and comradely feeling. Japanese soldiers have no need to demonstrate their masculinity, like the men in American war films, because it is so immediately taken for granted by all: director, actors, and audience.

The most important sequence in *Tank Commander Nishizumi* concerns Nishizumi's treatment of a Chinese woman who is found in their camp, having the night before given birth to a baby. In his treatment of this woman, more than at any other time, Nishizumi exhibits the Japanese spirit at its best, thus demonstrating what it means to be a Japanese. Every one of his responses to this incident testifies to his abiding humanity.

Nishizumi's first reaction is to call a doctor. Later, he pets the baby and speaks to the mother in Chinese, a language he mastered during his service in Manchuria, which the Japanese had invaded in 1931. He holds a candle in the darkness and the light illuminates his saintly face. "Don't worry," he consoles the mother in subtitled Japanese, "the Japanese soldiers won't hurt you." Yoshimura seems conscious of the reputation of the Japanese in China and has made this episode the pivot of his film as a means of answering the charges of unspeakable cruelty toward Chinese civilians leveled against the Japanese. One of the soldiers is made to remark, "mothers are the same everywhere," lest the Japanese be accused of racism toward this weaker people whose country they are decimating. And the woman responds by relaxing, indicating that she has found Nishizumi's concern sincere. When the doctor treats her, Nishizumi even holds her hand. He instructs his men to take good care of her.

Nishizumi's compassion, however, is not enough. The next day the Japanese learn that the woman has run away with her lover, abandoning the baby, who has died. The Chinese are thus revealed to be the heartless barbarians, and not the Japanese who burned, raped, and plundered their way across China. Undaunted, Nishizumi arranges a funeral for the baby, since religion decrees that it must not be allowed to remain unburied. Toward the mother he directs no blame: "She was grateful last night and that was enough." His tone indicates none of the condescension the words suggest. On a stick marking its grave Nishizumi has painted the word *Munako*, "Child with No Name."

Nishizumi thus displays the true Japanese spirit, kind and courageous, fearless before death and yet always mindful of his moral duty. By the end of the film he has become an inspiration to all, just as he personally had been motivated by the war leader who had attended his high school. All the commanders in these war films form a chain of unbroken kindness which is communicated to their men. On his wall Nishizumi writes, "in order to demonstrate the Japanese spirit, I will go anywhere."

As the Japanese move toward Nanking, the fighting becomes particularly fierce. At an unguarded moment, when he has stopped to smoke a cigarette, Nishizumi is shot by a Chinese. On his deathbed Nishizumi tells the men

The War at Sea from Hawaii to Malaya: Despite the heat and his having to carry a heavy suitcase, he doesn't sweat, so under control is his body.

to "become good soldiers so that the officers will be pleased with you." Overcome with grief, one of the wounded men wishes he could die in Nishizumi's place, so loved is Nishizumi by his men. His last words are, "What I have done is for the Emperor." He is a model soldier, a model man.

At this moment the Chinese arrive. Someone says that "people have to die. Even Nishizumi is a person . . ." But there is no time even for this platitudinous consolation. Rather, Nishizumi's death must be seen as part of the soldiers' service toward a greater end. Because he "was such a good man," they must defeat the Chinese. The men go determinedly out into battle, while the camera dollies in to the dead Nishizumi's candlelit face. A shot of the moon closes the scene. Nishizumi has died, but his spirit lives in the hearts of the troops. His ashes are carried in a box on his old tank as his spirit guides the men onward. The ending of *Tank Commander Nishizumi* is, however, the opposite of sentimental. The feeling we all by now share for the gentle Nishizumi reflects not sentiment, an excess of feeling toward an incommensurate object, but love. It is the only appropriate tribute to one who has so perfectly expressed the potential greatness of us all.

Typical of the Japanese war film, once full-scale fighting against the United States had begun, was Kajiro Yamamoto's *The War at Sea from Hawaii to Malaya* (*Hawai-Marei Okikaisen*, 1942). It is a film justly famous for its realistic re-creation, through the use of miniatures, of the attack on Pearl Harbor; later this skill with miniatures would be employed in Japanese science fiction and monster films, and in disaster pictures like *The Submersion of Japan* (*Nippon Chimbotsu*, 1974). *The War at Sea from Hawaii to Malaya* is much harsher than were the earlier films about the war in China, its propagandist intent less veiled. The people are more intense, even fanatic, and greater sacrifices are demanded of them.

The main character, not a "hero" even in the Nishizumi sense of the term because he is too young, is a naval cadet who returns home from the academy in 1936, having already been transformed by his training into a fighting man. Despite the heat and his having to carry a heavy suitcase, he doesn't sweat, so under control is his body. His sturdy peasant cousin must drop the suitcase, which he has offered to carry, every few feet. Impressed by his recruit cousin's having become so physically admirable a man, this peasant boy also wishes to become an aviator. Inspired by the Navy's cultivation of their manhood, says this film, all of Japan's young men should rally to the war effort and devote themselves to the glory of the fatherland. The two young cousins practice diving into the river off a very high cliff; it is the cadet's means of testing his peasant cousin. Unflinching courage is the first requirement. When the cousin survives this ordeal, our hero is convinced that he possesses those masculine qualities that will enable him to distinguish himself in the Japanese Navy.

The scenes at the naval academy stress discipline, omitting the alternation of moments of relaxation and harmony of the early war films. A pan down the hammocks of sleeping cadets is quickly punctuated by the blowing of a whistle, terminating their brief repose. All jump up en masse and make their beds. Energy itself becomes a testament to their dedication. Each morning the cadets recite in unison a poem to the Emperor Meiji, an overt expression of religious devotion deemed necessary here, but absent in earlier war films, where the love of the men for the Emperors was taken for granted and reciting their feelings aloud would have seemed a vulgarity. The recitation bespeaks a lack of confidence on the part of the official sponsors of this film, a doubt—unapparent in the earlier films—as to the sufficiency of Japanese support of the war.

Extreme long shots of the boys doing calisthenics are clearly placed in the film to dramatize how enormous were the numbers of young men preparing themselves for war, as if the entire country were involved. And so should be all is the message this film directs to the audience. Stressed over and over is "the spirit of absolute obedience" that all must manifest. Explicitly decreed, as well, is that every cadet is under the orders of the Emperor to struggle until death.

Yamamoto's smoothly traveling camera reminds us that he was the teacher of Kurosawa. It accompanies the cadets at their rowing exercises; the movements of the camera are in counterpoint to the rigor of their training. Those who lose a race are admonished, reprimanded for not trying hard enough. In training, the young cadets are encouraged to struggle until they have expended all their energy, until the moment of physical collapse. It is once again an evocation of the idea that through enough effort, as Jonathan Livingston Seagull preaches, anything can be achieved.

The instructors are kind but firm, believing too that exerting one's utmost will suffice to overcome all potential difficulties. While in the earlier films sadness at the death of a comrade was an approved emotion, here this sentiment is considered weak, debilitating, and unmanly. The cadet must harden himself against such emotions as pity and compassion, a theme which marks the Navy's premonitions of a Japanese defeat. Where there are family scenes in this film, they are presented in terms of the desire among the women left behind to do something for the war effort too, even if it means only baking cakes. When the peasant cousin, now a cadet, returns home for a visit, great stress is placed on cakes being left "for the ancestors." Dedication to the cause of the Emperor and obedience to Japanese traditions are overtly defined as one and the same. To observe proper rituals at home is the equivalent of expressing one's love for the Emperor at the front in the form of unflinching courage.

On the aircraft carrier bearing the men who will participate in the surprise attack on Pearl Harbor the training intensifies, as do the tensions. There is laughter, as the men gleefully identify from silhouetted drawings the American aircraft carriers *Oklahoma* and *California*. But this laughter reflects not a *joie de vivre* or the communality of their struggle, but a desperate will to believe that America is not so formidable an opponent after all. Yamamoto may not consciously have intended that this laughter reflect its opposite, but it does. A low dolly down the table of cadets as they drink the rice wine sent by their Supreme Commander, the Emperor, is typical of the predominance in this film of ritual observances, which supposedly strengthen the Japanese aviators for the arduous mission awaiting them. In long shot, as the carrier steams through the ocean, the men take off their hats, bow, and salute in the direction of the Imperial Palace. Solemnity accompanies the repeated assertion of Japanese superiority.

Thus dawns December 7, 1941. The men confined to the infirmary listen with pleasure to an American radio broadcast from Hawaii picturing the Americans as boozing and nightclubbing, totally unprepared for the attack, decadent and unmanly. Two Japanese, cheek to cheek, imitate "the way they dance there." Later the aviators in their planes will also laugh as they listen to American radio, revealing how unsuspecting they will find their adversary. With an extreme close-up of the propellers of their planes, the Japanese take off, having been told that they are offering their lives to the Emperor, and that their deaths will be a salute to the nation. At a surreal angle they run to their planes, the angle a comment on the transcendent glory of their cause. Those left behind wave their caps. Jubilation fills the air.

The actual attack on Pearl Harbor is dramatized through a brilliant miniaturization that allows us to witness the bombing at extremely close range, as if we were in the planes of the Japanese flyers fortunate enough to have been awarded this assignment. The clouds part. Scintillating in the sun is Pearl Harbor, viewed through the windscreen of one of the planes. At times the camera seems to be on land, looking up at the planes, an angle reflecting American vulnerability. As the bombs go down, the American ships blow up, exploding into a thousand pieces. There are extreme close-ups from under the planes, so that we can almost feel the water spraying up as the bombs fall. Sometimes the planes move in vertical descent, admirable in their regular formation. Aerial shots indicate huge airplane hangars being blown up. Bomb after bomb falls, until the American radio, which had been playing "Anchors Away," finally is interrupted by an announcement of the air raid. But by now the Japanese fighters have entered their second wave and victory is assured.

The attack on Pearl Harbor is re-created with panache and great bravado. The spectator cannot help but experience it as a marvelous *tour de force*, a fitting testament to Japanese readiness and the fruit of those long days of discipline at the naval academy. The last event in this spectacular enactment is symbolic of the theme of the entire film. One of the planes is hit by the Americans and, as a salute to his comrades, the pilot becomes a living torpedo, discharging his mission to the end, *kamikaze* style. His heroism is expressed in an unhesitating readiness to do what will be most effective for the Japanese cause. His fellow flyers admiringly remain confident that they would do the same, were the opportunity theirs.

The seriousness with which this film takes itself chronicles a fierce determination on the part of the Japanese military to train its cadre to do whatever would seem necessary in the service of the nation, even if it cost one's life. It asserts Japan's claim to be heard by exhibiting so unrelenting a fighting spirit. Yamamoto seems not to have been aware that the very rigidity and rigor he depicts suggest, as well, a painful sense of inferiority and vulnerability. Seen in retrospect, the urgency of the discipline imposed on the cadets in *The War at Sea from Hawaii to Malaya* fills the viewer with a sense of waste, futility, and pain. However exacting the discipline, one feels that it will never be sufficient to conceal self-doubt. The bravado of those who attacked Pearl Harbor, as portrayed in this film, illustrates most eloquently the quixotic character of the Japanese effort to impose its command on the rest of the world through will alone.

Not all Japanese directors were making war films or even overt propaganda films for the war effort. Ozu, for example, continued to make the same type of film about the small pleasures of family life that he had always made. One script he presented to the Censorship Office of the Home Ministry, *The Flavor of Green Tea over Rice* (*Ochasuke no Aji*), a title he would later use for an entirely different film, was rejected. The film concerned a couple taking this simple, typically Japanese meal together before the man leaves for the front. As Ozu has said, it was the spareness and ascetic quality of this uniquely Japanese meal that offended the Army:

> They objected to the fact that the soldier eats such everyday food instead of red rice to celebrate the special occasion of his departure. I wish I could have changed it, but it was ridiculous to rewrite it that way, so I forgot it.[4]

[4] "An Ozu Spectrum," *Cinema* (Los Angeles), 6, no. 1 (summer 1970), p. 3.

It would have been most unlike Ozu so cheaply to attach glory to the military exploits of Japan, especially in violation of his own sense of where the beauty in Japanese life lay.

During the war Ozu did make two films that suited government purposes quite handsomely: *The Brothers and Sisters of the Toda Family* (*Toda-ke no Kyodai*, 1941) and *There Was a Father* (*Chichi Ariki*, 1942). Of all Japanese directors, Ozu had been the staunchest supporter of the family system, implicitly approving of the subordination of all to a strong, benevolent patriarch. In *Brothers and Sisters of the Toda Family* disorder ensues upon the death of such a father; in *There Was a Father* the role of the patriarch, in exemplifying all that is noble, is clearer than in any other of Ozu's films.

At the center of Ozu's seemingly apolitical "home dramas" is the family as Wilhelm Reich has defined it, an "authoritarian state in miniature." Ozu's patriarchs are invariably gentle, if firm, and rarely use force to achieve their ends. But this only testifies to the absoluteness of their power, which is taken for granted by all. The Ozu patriarch can afford to behave with so much grace and elegance precisely because his point of view is, finally, indisputable. He may err in small matters, but he is never wrong on important questions. In every Ozu film the pattern Reich observed presides: "The child must learn to adapt himself as a preparation for the general social adjustment required of him later."[5] That the family has been the bulwark of reaction in Japan has long been recognized, and most succintly put by Masao Maruyama:

> Only by destroying the tenacious family structure in Japanese society and its ideology, the very place where the old nationalism ferments, can Japan democratize society from the base up.[6]

Thus it is not that Ozu was a propagandist—he is the least overtly didactic of any Japanese director—or that his works lack an artistic merit they would have enjoyed had their point of view been different.[7] *There Was a Father* is a very fine movie but, like Ozu's postwar films, it is as well an endorsement of the *kokutai*, the Japanese national spirit. Ozu evoked traditional ideas not because the militarists forced him to, but because he believed in them. He was not an Imperialist and saw no occasion for the serving of red rice when a soldier left for the front. He cared little for the expansion of monopoly capitalism in Japan, which the war party encouraged and which it argued necessitated expansion beyond the national frontiers. His frequent shots of industrial waste, chimneys pouring poisons into the air, aggressive railroads rushing over the landscape, and towering glass edifices, inhuman in their self-assertion, suggest that Ozu hated industrialization and capitalism. But his response to the despolia-

[5] Wilhelm Reich, *The Mass Psychology of Fascism* (New York: Simon & Schuster, 1974), p. 30.

[6] "Nationalism in Japan: Its Theoretical Background and Prospects," *Thought and Behaviour in Modern Japanese Politics*, p. 152.

[7] Even films with an explicitly fascist point of view can, of course, be great works of art, as Leni Riefenstahl's *Triumph of the Will* and *Olympia* make clear.

tion of the Japanese environment was not in seeking greater freedom for the individual, but in locating comfort and escape in the preservation of traditional forms of behavior.

The individual in Ozu's films functions best and expresses himself most completely within the context of the family. It is true, as Donald Richie has pointed out,[8] that Ozu managed not to be incorporated into the war effort, revealing himself to be somehow incapable of making a film commemorating the thirtieth anniversary of the South Manchurian Railroad— or film called *One Plane Has Not Yet Returned* (*Imada Kikan Sezaru Mono Ikki*) and *Far Motherland* (*Harukanari Fubo no Kuni*). But these were not appropriate Ozu subjects anyway. If Ozu was hard on directors who changed their themes after the war to fit the new *demokuratiku* ideas,[9] it was in part because Ozu had never valued a democratic philosophy and always found it a threat to the preservation of the old ways.

This reactionary aspect of Ozu's sensibility is conveyed most graphically during a relaxed moment in an interview he gave to critics Akira Iwasaki and Shinbi Iida for *Kinema Jumpo* magazine in 1958. Ozu, who at other times praises Western films and directors from Chaplin to Welles, reveals a xenophobia to which many Japanese seem addicted, a contempt for foreigners quite drastic in its stereotypic, racist approach. Ozu suddenly bursts out with an attack on foreign tourists whom he equates with Western critics who prefer the "high octave"[10] works of directors like Kurosawa to his own:

> "Something for damn foreigners" means something sold at souvenir shops in Yokohama, such as an embroidered red kimono with hollyhocks on it. I detest things like that. It's irresponsible to manufacture this junk just because "damn foreigners" will be happy with it. . . . We are Japanese so we should make Japanese things. If they don't understand them, there's nothing we can do about it.[11]

The embroidered red kimonos with hollyhocks on them are a scarcely veiled reference to the films of Akira Kurosawa which, Ozu is suggesting, were made to please foreigners; the "Japanese things" refer to his own films, whose failure to please foreign critics obviously irritates Ozu; only in the 1970s would his films gain a considerable following in the West. Interviewer Iida, delighted, replies with a Buddhist aphorism: "A lost soul is beyond redemption." A few moments later in the interview, Ozu speaks contemptuously of the inability of foreigners to understand his films: "They don't understand—that's why they say it's Zen or something like that." Beneath the placid surface of those "home dramas" of Ozu lies, in no small measure, the heart of a feudalist for whom the Japanese family

[8] *Ozu: His Life and Films* (Berkeley and Los Angeles: University of California Press, 1974), pp. 226–232.

[9] *Ibid.*, p. 232.

[10] In Japanese the word "octave" distinctly connotes tone and tension; thus "low-octave director" signifies a low-tone and low-tension director.

[11] Akira Iwasaki and Shinbi Iida, "A Talk With Ozu," *Kinema Jumpo*, June 1958. Translated by Leonard Schrader.

was the world. Rarely in his films does Ozu reveal himself so explicitly as in this interview. But, beneath its domestic surface, a film like *The Brothers and Sisters of the Toda Family* may be a more successful example of propaganda, and more typically express the wartime mode of Japan, than an obvious war film like *The War at Sea from Hawaii to Malaya*.

In *The Brothers and Sisters of the Toda Family* the harmony of a typical upper-middle-class Japanese family is disrupted by the sudden death of the formidable Toda patriarch early in the film. Lacking a home, since the father had lost all his money just before he died, the mother and unmarried sister, Setsuko, are shunted from the household of one brother or sister to another. First they enter the home of the eldest Toda son, whose wife abuses them and turns Setsuko into a household drudge. The benevolent if stern patriarch had demanded by his very presence that the selfish impulses of his children always be held in check. His authority had the salutary effect of bringing out the best in all and was justified by its results. Once he is gone, however, the greed and selfishness to which, for Ozu, the human being is ever susceptible emerge in his elder children. The selfish brothers and sisters, in their unkindness to the dependent mother and sister, are portrayed as violating the true Japanese spirit. At the end the youngest son of the family, Shojiro, the only child capable of real affection, takes his mother and sister back with him to China where he serves as a regional representative for the Japanese company for which he works.

The Toda patriarch had ruled firmly, but lightly. When his youngest daughter, Setsuko, had been born, he had first been displeased: "Another girl? Girls can't amount to much!" But when the maid replied that girls are needed for there to be sons, he had laughingly accepted Setsuko's arrival. His strength did not have to be expressed through brutality or obvious self-assertion. The film ends happily precisely because the patriarchy is so powerful that it can achieve miraculous effects even after the death of the father, such is his influence.

The youngest son, Shojiro, had always been a ne'er-do-well; he was even away on a fishing trip when his father died. When, in the first sequence, the patriarch sat at the center of the family on a throne-like chair for the picture-taking which would commemorate the mother's birthday, the whole family assembled with him, Shojiro was sleeping in his room, the only family member absent. The father grew angry but, significantly, this anger was expressed only off-camera, as if we were being permitted, as strangers, to see Mr. Toda only in the best possible light. As a boy, Shojiro had stolen and sold an expensive foreign book belonging to his father, who died just as Shojiro ceased to be afraid of him. Yet, as Shojiro admits, his father had pretended not to notice when his telescope and watch, also stolen by his son, were missing. He had taught his son to follow his example by patient forbearance, in the indirect and effective Japanese manner, rather than by punishments.

His father's death transforms Shojiro from a lazy playboy to a hard-working company man, from a careless, callow youth to the only member of the family willing to assume responsibility for his mother and sister. The first sign of his maturing came when he had been willing to join the company regional office in Tientsin, although it meant starting at the bottom and rising in the firm through hard work. Shojiro never breaks the habit of using his father's expensive works of art as ashtrays, but he ultimately reveals a character worthy of the patriarch with whom he had been so deeply in conflict, a struggle that turns out finally to have been only superficial.

Even in its few historical references to the war *The Brothers and Sisters of the Toda Family* is in perfect conformity with government policy. Although Japanese soldiers were ravaging China during this period, China is represented by Ozu as a favorable place of advancement for hard-working Japanese like Shojiro. There is no mention of the Japanese occupation of China, which was the result of a military invasion. Most of the time China is referred to neutrally as a country where the weather may be cold or it may be necessary to boil the water. There is not a single suggestion that it may be dangerous for Shojiro to live there. Implicit is Ozu's confidence that Japan's military control will permit Japanese like Shojiro to live relatively normal lives in China.

China, in *The Brothers and Sisters of the Toda Family*, is even seen as a place of refuge and salvation for the mother and sister. In Tientsin, Shojiro will find Setsuko a husband, a good, "sunburnt, well-built, but not handsome" man like himself, of course a Japanese. Shojiro returns for the first anniversary ceremonies of his father's death in Chinese clothes, as if he had indeed fully integrated himself into the Chinese environment, and as if this were a natural and morally acceptable thing to do. Ozu is the best kind of propagandist because he can so gently take the unthinkable for granted. He need present us with no chauvinistic soldiers nor flag-waving family members. The Emperor is never mentioned. Implicit behind the entire treatment of the China War in this film is the philosophy expressed by the Toda brothers and sisters as, early in the film, they react unanimously to the news that all the family possessions must be sold to pay a debt incurred by the father: "It can't be helped." It is too easy to say that such conformity, with its Buddhist suggestion of *mono no aware*, the sense of the inevitably sad passing of all things, expresses a typical Japanese response which Ozu is describing. Like that of his characters, Ozu's mood always reflects the smooth acquiescence of "it can't be helped." But, as directors like Kobayashi in films like *The Thick-walled Room* (*Kabe Atsuki Heya*, 1953) would point out as soon as the war ended, the repressive militarists aside and the threat of an artist being thrown in jail or not working at all notwithstanding, those who did not openly oppose the war were most responsible for its consequences.

Only two explicit references in *The Brothers and Sisters of the Toda Family* betray that Ozu's film was even made during the war. Near the end Setsuko agrees to marry if Shojiro does so as well. "I will," she says mischievously, "if Hitler does." The remark is made in fun, but without very much irony. For Setsuko will indeed follow the example of an authoritarian patriarch, replacing her dead father, whom the role, if not the personality, of Hitler well suits. Neither brother nor sister finds this comparison with Hitler offensive or outrageous. And a moment later, nervous over his imminent introduction to Tokiko, Setsuko's friend and a potential bride-to-be, Shojiro compares himself to "Siegfried" whose weakness, like his own, was that he was shy. Japanese culture had indeed been Teutonized. In the year that *The Brothers and Sisters of the Toda Family* was released, Japan would declare war on the United States as Germany's strongest ally.

There Was a Father, also directed by Ozu in the middle of the war, contains many of the attitudes encouraged during this period of extreme nationalism. It is set, "democratically," among the lower middle class, thus serving wartime propaganda about the "classlessness" of Japanese society. It exalts the patriarch and, like *The Brothers and Sisters of the Toda Family*, applauds the son's carrying on family traditions after his father's death. This approval is justified by the beauty of the father's character and his absolute devotion to his responsibility as a member of society. The subservience of women is implicitly endorsed in this film about a motherless family, which manages spiritually so well. It is as if a father alone can best pass on to his son all that is most noble in Japanese tradition.

There Was a Father opens with the father, Horikawa, a geometry teacher, lecturing his students. In the classroom sequence the typical low Ozu angle, looking up at the teacher from three feet off the floor, expresses and sanctions his power and value. It is as if we were sitting on tatami, gazing at him in awe, like his students at their desks. On a class trip, one of the students drowns. The teacher assumes complete responsibility for this tragedy, although he had forbidden the students to go boating, and is technically not at fault. When the students rush out, having heard that one of the boats has overturned, Ozu remains focused on their umbrellas lined up in the corridor. All those in the right row remain upright; the one stray umbrella, alone on the left side of the shot, represents the disorderly, disobedient student who drowned. In the ensuing confusion, this umbrella falls over.

Startling to Western eyes is the sight of a schoolteacher destroying his entire career as a result of an accident not his fault. Yet once the tragedy occurs, the issue becomes not one of individual responsibility in which someone who is "to blame" must be punished, but that collective good will among parents, students, and teacher has been irreparably damaged. The harmonious relationship previously enjoyed by these three groups is severed. Recognizing this fait accompli, the teacher has no choice but to resign, for he can no longer function for his students in a role in which each party implicitly trusts the other, as an infant would his mother.

The teacher and father of the film's title believes he must somehow not have done his best, introducing Ozu's main theme in this film, the need for us all to do our duty with the utmost effort. Ozu never suggests that this effort is to be in service of the war, and, in fact, stresses only that it is for the good of society in general. But in this advocacy of duty, Ozu could not have made a more subtle appeal to the Japanese to support the war, since in 1942 their utmost effort for the social good could only have been seen in the military context.

Everything to come in the film suggests that the father was correct to resign. However painful the decision, absolute responsibility must occasionally be assumed, even when one is not personally at fault. The individual must be ready obediently to submit whenever the situation demands that he do so.

Father and son return to Ueda, the father's home town. They are bound together in whatever life brings. At a local castle which they visit, the son lies about liking Ueda, throwing rocks off a height and manifesting the moral bravado characterizing all good Japanese men. "If you grew up here," he tells his father, "I can grow up here."

As a model father, Horikawa presses his son to study hard to pass his high school entrance examinations. Otherwise, in what would be an unpleasant fate indeed, he will be a "nobody." When the son, applying all his diligence, gets a mathematics problem right, the father rewards him first with praise, "Good! Wasn't that easy?" and then with a fishing trip. In a beautiful high-angle shot the camera looks down at their two figures standing in identical positions with their legs spread apart. They cast their fishing rods in parallel motion, in unison, first to the right and then to the left. The image expresses Ozu's message that the son fulfills his duty best by emulating this good father, who expresses his own value in providing so noble an example for his son.

The father returns to Tokyo to seek a better job in order to finance the son's education. From the boy, who must remain at school in Ueda, an extreme form of stoicism is required. The little son is told that he is no longer a child, although he clearly is, and that he should "act like a man" and not cry. "Both of us," says the father, "must do our best." Ozu has the son, as he cries, keep his back to the camera to avoid sentimentality, but that the son stands crying with his face to the wall, a posture he will once again assume later in the film when his father dies, only increases the pathos of the scene. "A man shouldn't cry," the father repeats. All Japanese, sons as well as fathers, may be called upon to make great sacrifices; it is for a good that they may understand only much later, and before which personal inclination must always give way. Although the subject is different, the import of these words bears directly upon the service of young Japanese in the war.

Although he resumes living with his parent only during the last week of the father's life, the separation has not prevented the son from growing up to be a strong, effective human being. For all along he has been guided by the advice of his father: "Once you choose a road, you must go as far ahead on it as possible." As the father spoke these words, on the wall behind him was a banner with the character for "morality." To Ozu, it represents the man.

The most important scene of *There Was a Father* takes place at a hot springs resort where father and son are able to meet briefly. The son announces his desire to leave his job at Akita in northern Japan in order to move to Tokyo where he can at last be united with his beloved father. The pain of living apart has proven unbearable. But the father opposes this plan. He talks about the son's job (he, too, is a teacher) as a "mission," his vocabulary coming close indeed to equating duty with support of the war. He lectures his son that there is no room in life for "personal sentiment," and, in another reference that applies as well to those participating in the war, "you can be at your best only when the task is difficult."

The father talks of the son's responsibility to his students at the school in Akita as a lifelong effort, instructing the Japanese audience that they will be happiest pursuing their duty. Father and son then go fishing again, casting identically as before, in a shot now expressing the harmony that will ensue once the father's advice is taken. And the next morning the father explicitly reiterates what his sermonizing has really been about: "A man has to serve his country."

There are two actual references to the war. The brother of one of the son's pupils has been drafted and the son tells him to study hard since his parents must be finding it difficult to manage without his drafted brother. Later we hear that the son has passed his "conscription test," although this is presented as a testament to his manliness and does not specifically indicate that he is destined for the front. Rather, Ozu suggests that his passing this test makes possible his marriage at the end to Fumiko, the daughter of one of his father's friends.

Ozu thus accomplishes his propaganda for the war through appeals to a traditional style of obedience, which is, however, only a brief step away from enlisting that obedience in the service of the State. The reference to the son's passing the "conscription test" suggests that, like all young men, he may indeed be drafted. What is important to Ozu is not that he may soon have to fight but that he be morally prepared, should the moment arrive. And it seems that, at least in part, Ozu made this film so that Japanese youths might be so readied.

Duty and ceremony replace individual and egotistic cravings in the young man who grows properly to maturity. The son, visiting the father in Tokyo at last, immediately rolls down his shirtsleeves, puts on his jacket, and offers incense before the funeral tablet of his mother. At this point the father says: "You've turned into a fine son." The dutiful person is the good one; those who live by their duty are rewarded with what is most valuable in life—the respect of others. To demonstrate this point Ozu shows that the father is still loved by his former students, who have never forgotten him. His life has been enhanced, not diminished, by his having chosen a higher duty in sacrificing his profession. All the former students marry, as will the son by the end of the film. All, as they were advised by the father, struggle to go as far in life as they possibly can. Conforming to established values is best. If the father could live to see it, he says, what would please him most is his son's having "a fine wife and nice children."

The typical Ozu clothesline blows in the wind, a portent of time and change. Unexpectedly and prematurely, although not surprisingly—given the hard life he has led—the father suffers a heart attack. Unaware of its seriousness, he says that he does not wish to indulge himself. He will go to work as always; he has never taken a day off!

But he can't get up. Wracked by horrible pain and convulsions, he cannot go on. Only such a trauma puts an end to the fulfillment of his duty. A lyrical shot of the garden where the attack occurred, a symbol of the moral quietude of their lives which no vicissitude can diminish, is followed by a cut to the hospital where the son and the father's former students wait for news.

The father's last words are in keeping with his character. Again he tells his son to "work hard" and not "be sad," since this would be only futile and debilitating. He says, "I did everything I could," which, as the film has amply shown, is true. The son, with Ozu's approval, turns away and cries, just as he did as a small boy when his father told him he was moving to Tokyo. Tears at such times are not unmanly but truly appropriate. Ozu's men thus sometimes partake of the Heian ideal of manhood, as exemplified by the emotional Prince Genji, rather than of the more severe samurai ethic of self-restraint. The father's friend, Hirata, is there to reiterate the propagandistic motif that consistently runs through this film. He asserts that the father was able to die so peacefully because he had accomplished his purpose in life.

Like *Tokyo Story*, *There Was a Father* ends not on the theme of death but on one of consolation. This is appropriate because the values and the traditions of the *kokutai*, on behalf of which the father has lived, survive him. His life has had meaning because he has contributed to keeping alive what it means to be a Japanese. He has produced a son "lucky to have such a fine father to remember," who will himself, now married to Fumiko, try to become such a man.

On the train returning to the village where the father was born, as if the son were a reincarnation of the patriarch, he remembers with pathos how, as a boy, he had so looked forward to seeing his father. The last week is one he will treasure as the happiest of his life. Like that of *Tank Commander Nishizumi*, despite the death of the hero, the ending of *There Was a Father* is not sentimental. However extreme the son's feelings on behalf of "such a nice father," they could not possibly be excessive. The train moves into the darkness, like the life of a person rushing to its end. With Fumiko, the son sits amidst his very good memories. By these he is sustained and made happy. His father's example has taught him to be something larger than himself.

Of Kurosawa's films, *Sanshiro Sugata*, *The Most Beautiful* and *Men Who Tread on the Tiger's Tail* were made during the war. The last-named was banned by the censors and only *The Most Beautiful*, a propa-

ganda film, escaped alteration and editing. To be released at all, even in
its cut version, Sanshiro Sugata required the intercession of Ozu on Kurosawa's behalf because of the film's individualism. That Sugata finds the
correct path through his own spiritual efforts, that no one but himself
could teach him how to be a man, must have made the censor uncomfortable. But it is also interesting that Ozu defended the film on the
basis of whether or not it was "good,"[12] rather than because of any sub-
stantive validity he recognized in its point of view.

The films directed by Mizoguchi during the war are interesting because
of their range. They reveal Mizoguchi's tactic of disarming the authorities
with potboilers so that he might acquire some measure of space to do
films in which he believed. In 1938 Mizoguchi made a film called The
Song of the Camp (Roei no Uta), about a military song which won a prize
in a contest organized by a newspaper. In 1945 he made two entirely forgettable films, Song of Victory (Hissyoka), and a version of the life of
that inventor of two-sword combat, Miyamoto Musashi, the Swordsman
(Musashi Miyamoto), which was completed in three weeks. Mizoguchi
also pleased the government with his Genroku Chushingura (1941-42)
which he said he made "so I wouldn't have to make anything else,"[13] but
which contains a marvelous ending.[14] To thwart the censors, he also made
several films about actors during the Meiji era, since such costume dramas
might seem to be politically innocuous. These include The Story of the
Last Chrysanthemums (Zangiku Monogatari, 1939), Woman of Osaka
(Naniwa Onna, 1940) and The Life of an Actor (Geido Ichidai Otoko,
1941). Seeming concerned "only" with the life of a performer, Mizoguchi
called the making of The Life of an Actor "my way of resisting."[15]

With all this subterfuge to confuse the militarists, and his choice of
seemingly safe and approved subjects, Mizoguchi managed to make one
of the most brilliant satires of the Japanese family system, The Story of
the Last Chrysanthemums. That it was made before the war with the
United States had begun and censorship was tightened still does not
explain how Mizoguchi accomplished so brilliant a tour de force in the
same year that Ozu was being censored for having his characters eat
green tea over rice rather than a richer substitute. Mizoguchi was aided
by the semi-period setting of his film, the Meiji era, and the fact that his
hero was a Kabuki actor. In many scenes he appears in costume and we
witness his performances, the theater an unlikely political arena. And yet
the Kabuki background and the difficulties the hero faces as he attempts
to rise in his chosen profession, which is also that of his father, are only
the film's ostensible subject.

The Story of the Last Chrysanthemums compares and finds similar

[12] Richie, Ozu: His Life and Films, p. 230.
[13] Cited in Peter Morris, Mizoguchi Kenji (Ottawa: Canadian Film Institute,
1967), p. 38.
[14] See Chapter 3, "The Japanese Woman," pp. 27–40.
[15] Morris, Mizoguchi Kenji, p. 37.

two hierarchies: that within the Kabuki theater, where the younger and less-established actors must wait patiently and work for years to achieve fame, with everyone ruthlessly jockeying for power behind the scenes, and that of the patriarchal family. Each operates according to absolute feudal principles decreeing that the individual subordinate his views to the demands of his elders; each is scorned by Mizoguchi, who implies that unless one rebels against established institutions, life will be rendered worthless, regardless of any worldly success one might achieve.

The hero of *The Story of the Last Chrysanthemums* is Kikunosuke, one of those Kabuki actors called *oyama*, actors who play the parts of women. As the film opens, Kikunosuke is revealed to be a failure at his art as well as the spoiled scion of a wealthy family. His character seems to change once he falls in love with Otoku, a household nursemaid hired to attend to his father's latest offspring. As soon as their affair is discovered, Otoku is banished by the family.

Kikunosuke follows her, and they live together for many years while he endures the life of a struggling, second-rate performer. Always she encourages him to give his best energies to improving his art, asking nothing for herself. The long years of practice and apprenticeship prove finally not to have been in vain. Kikunosuke at last has his triumph. Typically status-oriented and callow in their worship of success, his family, now that he is a credit to them, welcome Kikunosuke back into the fold.

But they refuse to permit Otoku, whose origins are lowly, to become his wife. Otoku, forcing his hand, disappears, preventing Kikunosuke from taking her home with him. But instead of stopping to look for her, he proceeds on his journey homeward, abandoning Otoku and relieved that he will not have to face the anger of his relatives. By default, Kikunosuke succumbs to the demand of his family that he leave behind the woman who for years had lived only to fulfill his needs and to help him excel at his profession.

At the end, Kikunosuke's troupe makes a triumphant tour of Osaka, where he briefly visits the now dying Otoku. As he parades beneath her window in pride before the cheering populace, she dies in her shabby room, a sacrifice not only to his art but to the family system. Kikunosuke's family is shown to be cruel and victimizing; its dictates are so inhumanely destructive that they make a mockery of the actor's triumph, and of all worldly success. *The Story of the Last Chrysanthemums* is a far cry from the *Kokutai no hongi* published two years before, and in fact can be seen as an outright defiance of the militarists' advocacy of the family as an institution.

Mizoguchi never romanticizes the life of the actor. The only lyrical moment in the film comes early, when Kikunosuke and Otoku share a watermelon in a very long take, Mizoguchi employing the one-shot, one-scene technique he would later perfect. Kikunosuke keeps Otoku company as she babysits. The watermelon they eat is the most pedestrian of foods, but the moment contains a resonance Kikunosuke will never forget.

When he returns home, having left Otoku behind, there is a large party for him, and again a watermelon appears, which serves, as did Proust's *madeleine,* to remind him of what he has lost and to fill him with despair and a sense of the emptiness of all he has achieved.

Most of the film depicts Kikunosuke's long years in cheap Kabuki theaters. He joins traveling troupes which perform in the provinces before peasant audiences. It takes a long time for Kikunosuke to achieve mastery of his craft, a very realistic touch. Through the many years of hardship Otoku is always present. To keep them alive, she sews. Their lives are not easy. Poverty, says Mizoguchi, turns even people who are in love against each other. At one point Kikunosuke slaps Otoku across the face because she has refused to give him money for "fun." Before his great triumph occurs, she has already begun to cough; tuberculosis, that disease of the poor and deprived, is already beginning to overtake her.

Haggard and breathing heavily, Otoku watches as Kikunosuke on stage at last fulfills his potential. When he chooses to return to his family in Tokyo, she deliberately hides, lying even to her sister, saying she was tired of their life together. Only when it is too late, and her life is nearing its close, does Kikunosuke's father allow him to thank her for aiding in his art. Overcome by the transformation in her appearance, Kikunosuke now promises to marry her.

But the festival that has occasioned his return to Osaka awaits, for there the Kabuki actors will be introduced to the public. As Kikunosuke stands at the head of a boat gliding through the canal, bowing to the crowds, Otoku lies dying in her bed. Mizoguchi cuts from one to the other, immediately rendering spurious the value of Kikunosuke's now apparent fame. The camera waits ahead for the boat to come into view. Kikunosuke bows as the boat passes the camera.

Only at this point does Mizoguchi allow one of his rare close shots, but it is not because he has any sympathy for Kikunosuke. Rather, it is a means of mocking his great triumph. Otoku has died. Kikunosuke is now viewed in full shot with his arms stretched out to his admirers, in total light, as if, once and for all, we were seeing through him and the social order that has encouraged his inhumanity and ruthlessness. Bowing to the crowds becomes synonymous with his surrender to the unspeakable dictates of his family, with his having sacrificed the person he loved for success and worldly approval. He prefigures Ohama in *Ugetsu,* who was forced to become a prostitute; she will tell her foolish artisan husband, who wants only to be a samurai, that "for success, somebody has to suffer." At the very moment that the world is proclaiming Kikunosuke's success, Mizoguchi's camera renders him small, demeaned, and pathetic.

Several other interesting films made during the war suggest the contrast in censorship and policy before and after Pearl Harbor.

Surprising in some ways was a film, *The Whole Family Works* (*Hataraku Ikka,* 1939), by a director later to be appreciated as one of Japan's most accomplished, Mikio Naruse. With the war against China in full swing, Naruse focuses on the suffering of a single Japanese family during the protracted Great Depression. The overwhelming implication is that any acceleration of the war would only make the lives of ordinary, already impoverished Japanese families like this one absolutely unbearable.

The family of the title has four grown sons in addition to a few toddlers. These boys are bright, clever, and full of energy and optimism. Each is eager to pursue his studies, each determined to have a "good life." Yet, instead of being able to develop their talents, all are forced to work at meaningless, routine jobs, from the eldest son, Kiichi, to the young Eisaku who, by the end of the film, is on his way to sacrificing middle school (junior high) for an apprenticeship. A photograph of Abraham Lincoln on the wall of the boys' room (frequent for Japan of the thirties) bespeaks the wider vision of the world of which these young men are capable, yet the experience of which will be denied them.

Their father is sympathetic but helpless, fearing above all that, should he permit the eldest, Kiichi, to go off on his own as he wishes, the others would insist on following suit. Their mother, shrewish and unsympathetic in a manner not uncommon for the women in the films of the early Naruse, cares only about survival, bereft as she is of any of the finer feelings. Totally selfish, she is even reluctant to permit the twenty-two-year-old Kiichi to marry, lest she lose the money he has been bringing in.

But Kiichi doesn't wish to marry. The conflict of the film concerns his ultimatum to his parents that he be permitted to leave his factory job to attend electricians' school. At the end, although everyone—including the teacher called in to mediate this family dispute, the father, Naruse and the audience itself—sympathizes with Kiichi, the outcome remains in doubt. The teacher tells him that there is no hurry, that he should "do what you must," and Kiichi replies, "I will." Kiichi's hesitancy clearly suggests that he may very well sacrifice his ambitions to his family's overwhelming needs.

Like the Ozu of *I Was Born, but . . .* (*Umarete wa Mita Keredo*, 1932) and *Passing Fancy* (*Dekigokoro*, 1933), also films of the 1930s, Naruse cares deeply for the younger generation, delighting in their desire for freedom, even if it is only the freedom to conform to society's definition of success. Naruse enjoys their cleverness and even their little eccentricities, such as not wanting to carry a lunchbox smelling of pickles, a motif repeated several times.

The war, however, looms in the background. One of the sons has a dream of being among "real soldiers at the front." Children play soldier with trumpets and flags. Another of the sons expresses the ambition to be a naval officer. Naruse's film gains a richness by being viewed after the war. One cannot help but wonder whether, in the full face of the Sino-Japanese war, and prescient about Japan's future military adventures soon to come, Naruse was adding an abiding irony to his last scene.

Upstairs in their room, the three youngest sons sit talking. They feel sorry for their beleaguered father, who cannot support the family on his own, and one son ventures a prediction that Kiichi won't leave after all. Each suddenly asserts that he wants to have a good life; they begin doing somersaults over and over, their good spirits surfacing despite the grim realities of their family situation. Uplifting music applauds their energy. Downstairs, puzzled by the noise and the tumult, the parents look up, unaware of what has caused this commotion and the ceiling to shake so. These are Japan's young people soon to be called off to battle, their problems perhaps to be solved, like those of Thomas Mann's Hans Castorp in *The Magic Mountain*, in death on a muddy battlefield. Underplayed, undidactic as it is, this last scene makes *The Whole Family Works*, produced as it was during wartime, almost an anti-war film. It was completed, of course, before Pearl Harbor, after which censorship became more stringent.

Perhaps the main reason that Naruse appears to have escaped the notice of the censors with this film is that it simultaneously remains in keeping with certain approved and highly conventional Japanese attitudes towards poverty and misfortune. It portrays a suffering family, but this did not tell the Japanese people who had lived through the hard times of the thirties anything new. More important, it fixes no blame for the fact that this family, no matter how hard its men work, cannot make ends meet. Naruse has his *deus ex machina*, the teacher, say, quite explicitly, "it's no one's fault," just as Ozu had the Toda brothers and sisters reply to their unhappy financial fate with a similar phrase: "it can't be helped." In *The Whole Family Works* the father also offers this cliche, so common in Japanese life, to the barber with whom he is playing *shogi*: "it can't be helped."

This neo-Buddhist philosophy of reconciling oneself to things as they are, implicitly rejecting the possibility that human effort might ameliorate harsh social conditions by attacking their cause, has been the means by which the Japanese people have always accepted difficult circumstances. By making it so strong a theme in this film, Naruse rejects what the militarists would have feared most, a collective effort on the part of the Japanese people to oppose their rule, an effort that might have been inspired by their having watched the family in this film refuse to tolerate its poverty.

It is also worth noting that while the sons chafe under the strain on their intellectual development caused by extreme poverty, the family does not break down. The sons pity their father and, we are confident, will do whatever is necessary to preserve the family. Naruse implies, by indirection, that they would even go to war should that father surrogate, the Emperor, deem it desirable. Small rebellions break out as they do in the Ozu families. Little Eisaku treats his brothers to dinner rather than loan his two yen to his mother, knowing she will never pay it back. But the real impulse reflected in Kiichi's becoming drunk every night, after a history of total abstention, is that sooner or later all must reconcile themselves to their duty. Heavy rain pours down in the last sequence, further evidence of the harsh fate to which, like the weather, we sometimes have no choice but to submit.

And yet there remains the irony of the ending, with its suggestion that Japanese youth should not have been destined for either poverty or war. Boys roll in acrobatic delight, dreaming of the day when they will be lawyers or officers, while the film's director, fully aware that such poor youths will be the first called up, not to be officers but recruits, cannot help but sadly wish them well.

By 1943, when Hiroshi Inagaki made *The Life of Matsu the Untamed* (*Muho Matsu no Issho*), censorship had increased so much that despite this film's obvious patriotism on behalf of the *kokutai*, it was criticized for the idea that a rickshaw man would presume even to think of loving a woman of a superior social class, the theme of the film. For such a relationship would suggest a full-scale rebellion against prevailing social standards, and the censors now firmly recognized that any dissent permitted in a film might instill in the Japanese people the courage at last to protest against the senseless losses inflicted upon them in a war not of their own making. Although the government, of course, concealed the extent to which the Japanese were suffering defeats, uneasiness remained.

The story of *The Life of Matsu the Untamed* is of the lifelong love and devotion, never even once articulated, of a rickshaw man for the widow of a general and her son, whom he helps to grow to manhood in the absence of the boy's natural father. To both woman and child he devotes his entire life. In return he receives only the joy of having loved them, a paltry reward perhaps, but one uniquely Japanese. As the old man of Keisuke Kinoshita's *She Was Like a Wild Chrysanthemum* (*Nogiku No Gotoki Kimi Nariki*, 1955) would say to his dead love, gone from him so many years before, "you understood how I felt. I don't ask more from love."

Inagaki probably never imagined that he was violating government policy which publicly articulated the "equality" of all Japanese in the united effort of the war. By this logic the militarists should have approved of the classless relationship between a rickshaw man and the widow of a general. Ironically, Inagaki's theme is exactly this classlessness of the Japanese, and his film asserts that the purest expression of the Japanese spirit can be expressed by a simple rickshaw man. At the end, never having told the widow of his love for her, Matsu dies in the snow, having deposited his life's savings in her name.

As a man, Matsu is wild and animal-like, a stereotype of the lower classes. He is so inarticulate that he can only grunt and gesture most of the time. Yet, unlike that of his superiors, his life is "free" enough that he can ignore wealthy customers when he so chooses; here Inagaki suggests a nobility in the poorest Japanese that was a theme of the war films as well. An angry, rich customer in a typical Meiji frock coat—the film has a Meiji period setting—gestures wildly with his umbrella. Matsu, unknotting the boy's kite, pays him no mind.

The climax of the film is the Gion festival to which the boy, now grown up, brings his professor. This intellectual in rimless spectacles, straw hat, and kimono is portrayed as an effete, Westernized Japanese; here Inagaki reflects the suspicion of intellectuals always current during fascist periods. Unlike the professor, whom the boy now seems to favor, Matsu is, despite his shortcomings, a true Japanese. He is the only one who remembers and can keep alive the old traditions; only he knows how to beat the Gion drum properly. Dropping his kimono off his shoulders, he stands in the sun before the drum. Inagaki swish-pans from drum to Matsu, as he readies himself to manifest the authentic Japanese spirit. The closeness of the Japanese to their ancient traditions, which in themselves were supposed to have rendered the Japanese superior to the enemy, could not but have pleased the Army in 1943.

The Anti-war Film
in Japan

The Japanese people shall be afforded opportunity and encouraged to become familiar with the history, institutions, culture, and the accomplishments of the United States and the other democracies.
"Basic Initial Post-Surrender Directive"[1]

The flourishing of the "pacifist" film in postwar Japan must be seen in the context of the role of the American Occupation, which strongly determined the themes that could be portrayed in films during its tenure in Japan. Immediately after the end of the war, the office of General MacArthur (SCAP) handed down to the Japanese film industry a list of prohibited subjects: These included

> anything infused with militarism, revenge, nationalism, or anti-foreignism; distortion of history; approval of religious or racial discrimination; favoring or approving feudal loyalty or treating human life lightly; direct or indirect approval of suicide; approval of the oppression or degradation of wives; admiration of cruelty or unjust violence; anti-democratic opinion; exploitation of children; and opposition to the Potsdam Declaration or any SCAP order.[2]

Such demands belong to the early days of the Occupation, when the first concern of the United States was to add to Japanese social life a democratic façade similar to that of the Occupier, the better to encourage Japan to join the international community through a shared ideology. Some of the more naïve technicians of the Occupation at the beginning sincerely believed in their mission to rescue Japan from feudalism and were inspired by an idealism stemming from history lessons they had once absorbed about the American way of life. As purveyors of the democratic spirit in this far-off land, they zealously encouraged among the Japanese freedoms, such as the desirability of the oppressed to struggle for their rights, that had long since met official opposition within the United States itself. By 1947, the "cold warriors" in Washington realized their mistake. Faced by the threat that the Chinese Revolution might spread to other areas of Asia, they placed the need to maintain Japan

[1] *Political Reorientation of Japan, Report of the Government Section, Supreme Commander for the Allied Powers*, cited in Livingston, Moore, and Oldfather, eds., *The Japan Reader*, 1:11.

[2] Cited in Anderson and Richie, *Japanese Film: Art and Industry*, p. 160.

as a bulwark of capitalism and American interests in the Far East ahead of advocating an anti-feudal democratization within Japan.

But in 1945 the dictates of SCAP regarding what themes ought to be stressed in Japanese films called for radical change. They asked the film industry to encourage the unhampered growth of independent trade unions and the introduction of truly representative government. Films were to approve the valuing of the individual and his unique and separate opinions. Japanese directors were to stress how all Japanese

> were endeavoring to construct a peaceful nation; how soldiers and repatriates were being rehabilitated into civilian life; how the Japanese in industry and farming were resolving the problems of postwar life; how labor unions were peacefully organized; how the hitherto bureaucratic government was cast off and true governmental responsibility adopted; how the free discussion of government problems was encouraged; how every human being and every class of society was respected; and how historical personages, too, struggled for government representation of the people and for freedom.[3]

This list reflects more wish-fulfillment than reality. For while many films were dutifully made incorporating these subjects, in many instances they were poor films, half-hearted in their exposition of themes that were not part of the director's personal philosophy. Films, of course, could not accomplish such aims in any event, even if the filmmakers strongly believed in them, for movies reflect existing social attitudes as much as they shape them. In reality, trade unions independent of management have not flourished in postwar Japan, and the efforts of the unions for an independent voice were stifled by MacArthur himself, beginning on February 1, 1947 when he banned the general strike set for that day. The bureaucratic government has never been truly cast off, as the hegemony of the Liberal-Democrats, the conservative ruling party, has made all too clear. Japan remains as racist as ever with regard to such oppressed groups as the Koreans and *burakumin*.

But if the American Occupation suddenly changed its mind about the desirability of such freedoms for the Japanese as the Cold War approached and it was feared that the growing discontent and labor activity might lead to a real dismantling of the old authoritarian system in favor of social revolution, film directors and intellectuals nevertheless responded with relief to the absence of overt repression for the first time in more than a decade. Some of their efforts were perfunctory; others, like Kobayashi's anti-war epic, *The Human Condition*, masterpieces of film art. Kurosawa, with Kajiro Yamamoto and Hideo Sekigawa, made a pro-labor potboiler called *Those Who Make Tomorrow* (*Asu o Tsukuro Hitobito*, 1946) about the conversion of a white-collar employee by his radical daughters to the workers' cause,[4] clearly a propaganda effort. Tadashi Imai directed *An Enemy of the People* (*Minshu no Teki*, 1946), which he himself has called

---

[3] *Ibid.*, p. 161.
[4] See Richie, *Films of Akira Kurosawa*, p. 28.

"not much of a movie."[5] Its theme contrasted the lives of workers before the war, when they were severely mistreated, with afterwards, when they "stand up for themselves and organize a union."[6] It was clearly another policy film incorporating one of the subjects encouraged by the C. I. & E., the Civil Information and Education Section of the Occupation.

But almost as soon as the Americans departed in 1952, a host of unique and excellent films about the period leading up to and through the war began to emerge. It was as if floodgates had been opened and the best of Japan's intellectual and artistic energies were now being devoted to film. The medium was enlisted by Japan's finest directors to examine their own recent history, just as their films up to the war had repeatedly turned to the last days of Edo and the Tokugawa shogunate in a similar effort.

The most popular and moving film made in Japan about the period leading up to the war was Keisuke Kinoshita's *Twenty-four Eyes* (*Nijushi no Hitomi*, 1954). The growth of militarism and political repression through the thirties in Japan are examined from the point of view of a primary schoolteacher named Miss Oishi (Hideko Takamine). Helplessly and in silent protest, she watches as her innocent first graders of 1928 are transformed into chauvinist patriots ready to die for the Emperor.

To the residents of the primitive fishing village of Sadojima on the Inland Sea where she begins her first teaching job, Miss Oishi is quite a radical and the subject of endless gossip. Unlike her traditional predecessor, always in kimono, she wears Western clothes and rides a bicycle to school. One of the local housewives accuses her of "acting like a man." She is a person who thinks for herself, one who seems likely to be troublesome to the authorities once they appropriate Japan's educational system to perpetuate the ideology upon which the war would be based.

But as the film progresses, Kinoshita oversimplifies its political dimension by making Miss Oishi abandon her protest against Japanese imperialism to become a simple pacifist who hates war because it kills people. As soon as this happens, nearly midway through an almost three-hour-long film, *Twenty-four Eyes* begins to degenerate into sentimentality. By the end, when the war is over and Miss Oishi attends a reunion with her seven surviving students (there were originally twelve, thus the "twenty-four eyes" of the title), the director is wringing out every last drop of feeling from his audience and the film becomes almost unwatchable. The characters cry, the audience cries, and the film finally loses all connection with the particularities of the thirties and forties in Japan to become a lamentation on all human suffering.

Yet, in the early part of the film, Kinoshita handles with some deftness the slow tightening of repression in the schools during the thirties. Miss Oishi asks one of her pupils where the Emperor is and he replies, "the Emperor is in the cupboard." Gently Miss Oishi undermines the cult of the sanctity of the Emperor, which included the sanctity attached to the

---

[5] Joan Mellen, "Interview with Tadashi Imai," *Voices from the Japanese Cinema*, p. 106.
[6] *Ibid.*

Twenty-four Eyes: Miss Oishi defies the prevailing attitudes of the Japanese government in the thirties by treating each student as if he were a uniquely valuable individual.

Emperor's portrait, by pointing out that it is only a picture which happens not to be hanging on the wall because a proper place is lacking. But the Emperor himself is not omnipresent, watching them all from rural schoolhouse closets.

Miss Oishi also defies the prevailing attitudes of the Japanese government in the thirties by treating each student as if he were a uniquely valuable individual, as the Occupation had demanded. But Kinoshita's filmmaking here is so fine that it renders him immune to the charge that he is borrowing his ideas from the American Occupation, an accusation Japanese critics were fond of making when, in the fifties, directors showed individuals rebelling or when they introduced the subject of "democracy." Not only does Miss Oishi insist on calling each child by his nickname, but she associates the creative work of each with his separate personality. At home, in close-up, she turns over their lessons in calligraphy, with Kinoshita cutting to the face of each appropriate child, including on the sound track the child's voice as he or she responded to Miss Oishi's first roll call. "There were twenty-four eyes looking at me," she tells her mother, "I'll never forget them." And because the children in her class are valued as unique individuals, they will never forget her either.

As the thirties continue, one of the teachers is accused of being a "red" for having a friend who tried to spread anti-war ideas. Miss Oishi stands up and announces that she was impressed by their pamphlet, which she used in a classroom lesson. She is ordered to be "patriotic," and the principal burns the offending booklet. In the next scene, undaunted, Miss Oishi teaches her class the meaning of "communist," "capitalist," and "laborer" without the aid of the book. Finally she is absolutely forbidden to use such words as "proletariat" and "capitalist" in class.

In this rural backwater of the Inland Sea, hardly the Tokyo of Kurosawa's *No Regrets for Our Youth* where effective protest could temporarily be mounted against the clique of militarists, Miss Oishi cannot help but be politically impotent. And, as in *The Whole Family Works*, poverty comes to these people simultaneously with repression and the war. Just as Miss Oishi can do nothing to save pupils like the eleven-year-old Matsue sold by her father into servitude, she can do nothing about the growing hysteria and chauvinism which reached even so isolated a place.

Neither her pupils nor her own children are able to absorb Miss Oishi's pacifist ideas as Kinoshita brilliantly illustrates the weight in Japan, at this time as at others, of conformity. The power of organizational identity is so strong that the boys in her class call Miss Oishi a "coward" when she tells them it is better to be a fisherman than a soldier. They disagree, perhaps with some justification, because rural poverty provided the government with recruits for whom army life was better than the near-starvation at home. The poverty of the masses served the Imperial cause much better than a national prosperity would have. In a clear adoption of Occupation policy regarding the liberation of women, one of Miss Oishi's girl students writes a composition about the need for women to have regular jobs and take care of themselves—a pressing subject, given the wartime need for women to survive without their men, as well as the postwar urgency in Japan for women to assume responsibility for their own lives.

Once she is reprimanded for her subversive classroom approach, the high-spirited Miss Oishi is suddenly defeated. She begins to behave in all areas of her life as she never before has done—like a traditional Japanese woman. One of her pupils wishes to enter a conservatory and study music. The girl's mother protests, on the selfish ground that her daughter's studying music will not help the family in their restaurant business. The girl, sensing defeat, hangs her head. And Miss Oishi sits by, interjecting only, "I'm ashamed I can't say any more now." Previously the champion of her students, always placing a high value on personal fulfillment, she refuses to intervene even in areas not directly related to politics.

Kinoshita thus creates an inconsistent character. The radical of the early scenes at home never even articulates to her mother or to her husband what we have seen experience has taught her: that Japan's youth is used for selfish ends both by parents and society, and never valued for itself. Unable to exalt loyalty and patriotism in the classroom, Miss Oishi resigns from teaching until after the war. Japan's entire educational system had been mobilized in the service of the imperialists, and there could be no place even for a Miss Oishi who repeatedly says that she opposes the war only because it kills people. The China War is followed by the Axis alliance. None of the boys in her class has the slightest doubt about the value of becoming a soldier. This, too, is realistic because no matter how valuable the example Miss Oishi may have set, the pressures of the society at large are so strong as to make resistance in the very young unthinkable.

Yet it remains incongruous that, even as a mother, Miss Oishi is so totally ineffective in teaching her children that the war was wrong. At home Miss Oishi's sons play at war. And after the war, when her husband has been killed, her children are sorry that they were too young to have died for their country. They reprimand their mother for not crying because Japan lost the war and, like her pupils, they call her a coward.

The danger of making Miss Oishi so ineffectual, realistic as this may be for Shodo Island, is that Kinoshita has thus discounted the voices of those repressed during the 1930s who were capable of articulate political dissent. There were such people. But their courage, despite Kinoshita's false implications, cannot be symbolized in the lonely figure of the pacifist Miss Oishi. These dissenters were, until they were silenced, far more politically coherent and interested in tracing the war to its roots in the culture than Miss Oishi, who never for a moment challenges or disobeys the authorities when they reprimand her for the mild liberties she does take. It is as if Kinoshita were saying that no Japanese effectively could or did oppose the military clique throughout the thirties—a means of justifying, perhaps, those who remained silent. Fearing some association of this film with ideas of a leftist character which circulated in the thirties—and right after the war—Kinoshita safely chooses to define dissent solely in terms of a teacher's unobjectionable opposition to killing. To avoid the charge that he is over-simplifying, he places her, not in Tokyo but, as in the original novel by Sakae Tsuboi upon which the film is based, in a rural fishing village, the birthplace of author Tsuboi, where political ferment could not exist.

This political oversimplification is reflected in the aesthetic weakness of *Twenty-four Eyes*, particularly in its saccharine sentimentality. The background music varies between "Annie Laurie," "There's No Place Like Home" (which Ichikawa would use with much more effectiveness in *The Harp of Burma*), "Auld Lang Syne," and "What a Friend We Have in Jesus," interspersed with Japanese folk songs sung by the children. The atmosphere engendered is one of inevitable suffering. The plot deteriorates at points as well. After the war Miss Oishi's daughter suddenly falls from a persimmon tree and dies. Kinoshita wishes to indicate the famine engulfing Japan after the war, so that a child would have to resort to climbing trees for food. But the heavy-handed incident seems to give us more pain for its own sake, more tears when we are already sated. It is no wonder that after the war, when she returns to teaching (and in a rare moment of humor for this part of the film), Kinoshita has Miss Oishi's new pupils give her the nickname "Crybaby Sensei," a detail from the original novel.

At the reunion party of her first class Miss Oishi is given a new bicycle, symbolic of her radical youth thwarted so long ago. The lives of all Japanese have been blighted by the war, and, although she can only be in her forties, Miss Oishi is now an old woman. Hope for the future, says

Kinoshita, may be found in the words "Peaceful Japan," written on Miss Oishi's post-1945 blackboard.

In many ways *Twenty-four Eyes* is a deeply moving paean to the suffering brought upon the Japanese people by the war. Where it fails is in sustaining and developing the image of the radical young teacher in foreign clothes pedaling away on her bicycle, an indomitable spirit from whom we might have expected a greater understanding of the political realities of the 1930s in Japan. For Miss Oishi's ideas were once focused enough to include even the demystification of the cult of the Emperor. Heavy, heart-rending sentimentality engulfing his film—and the audience— in unquenchable tears and preventing any application of its lessons to the neo-feudal present is the price Kinoshita pays for having so diluted the views of those who opposed Japan's imperial adventures.

Another typical example of a postwar film attacking the repressive 1930s was Kimisaburo Yoshimura's *Cape Ashizuri* (*Ashizuri Misaki*, 1954), scripted by Kaneto Shindo. The same director who had earlier exalted Tank Commander Nishizumi here reflects with complete disapproval on the barbarous authoritarianism of pre-war Japan. The poignancy of this film renders any charge of hypocrisy against Yoshimura quite beside the point. It is true that some of Japan's best directors, like Imai, Kinoshita, and Kurosawa, made films during the war rendering some service to the war effort. Yet the enormous body of profoundly dissident films coming after the war, made by many of the same people, forces us by their magnitude to view as almost irrelevant the fact that they made wartime semi-propaganda films. None of them seem to have been as scandalous as *Hitlerjunge Quex*, or *Triumph of the Will*, or *Der ewige Jude*, perhaps because Japan had no need to resort to fascism. To these examples of virulent propaganda, films like *Mud and Soldiers*, *The Most Beautiful* and the disarming *Tank Commander Nishizumi* bear no resemblance.

The February 26, 1936 officers' coup was the most dramatic event of the pre-war years, and has been the subject of several films focusing on Japan in the 1930s. Ikki Kita's 1919 *Outline Plan for the Reorganization of Japan* (*Nihon kaizo hoan taiko*),[7] which was immediately banned by the government but continued to exert wide influence, was the most important "fascist" document of the pre-war period. In it Kita, a radical right-wing nationalist, openly advocated a coup d'état against the existing government and the proclamation of martial law to rid the Emperor of the weak bureaucrats by whom he had been surrounded. The Constitution was to be suspended, and with it all the rights and freedoms it awarded the people. The Parliament (Diet) was to be dissolved in this attempt to restore Japan to her true identity and to re-create the spirit of the Meiji Restoration which, according to Kita, had since been lost. The peerage system was to be abolished as, like Hitler and the German National Socialists, Kita attempted to win the support of the working class and the peasantry by pretending that his program was in their interest. Like Hitler,

---

[7] See *Sources of Japanese Tradition* (New York: Columbia University Press, 1970), II: 268–277.

Kita used anti-capitalist rhetoric, promising an emasculation of the evil *zaibatsu* (giant corporations) and a new union of the Emperor with the people. The prerogatives of the patriarchy were reasserted, as they later would be in Germany. Women would be denied the right to participate in politics because they had not yet "awakened," and, in any case, submitting women to verbal warfare would do violence to their natures. The Emperor's wealth would be reduced and he would return his real estate and stocks to "the nation," in keeping with Kita's ideal of a "purification of the Imperial Court." A council of advisers, presumably chosen from the military (since the plan also called for territorial expansion abroad), would replace the Diet.

Inspired by the ideas of Kita, on February 26, 1936 the *Kodo ha* (Imperial Way Faction) of army officers, about 1,500 strong, attempted such a coup d'état. They began by assassinating as many public officials as they could, murdering, among others, two former Premiers, Saito and Takahashi. The brother-in-law of Prime Minister Okada was murdered in his place, in a case of mistaken identity. Then the young officers, none of whom possessed a rank above captain, set up an occupied zone in the center of Tokyo and awaited further support in the form of the Emperor's endorsement of their action. They declared that whatever they had done was an expression of their duty to the Emperor, whom they supported.

The response of the Emperor, as well as of the government, was to call out the Army and Navy and immediately suppress the rebels. "Whatever their excuses," Hirohito is reported to have said, "I am displeased. They have put a blot on the nation. I call on you, War Minister [Kawashima] to suppress them quickly."[8] After four days the young officers surrendered, never having been openly supported by the two generals, Mazaki and Araki, who had encouraged them from behind the scenes. Thirteen were executed at once, and in secrecy. The two generals were put on reserve with the stipulation that hereafter the War Minister would always be chosen from officers on the *active* list. A year later Kita was arrested and executed as well. Ironically the effect of the February 26th incident was to strengthen the power of the Army, which now no longer had to argue explicitly that, given the real danger of such outbreaks of disorder, its power should be increased, its forces strengthened. The military became the most powerful force in the country at the expense of, rather than led by, Kita and the young officers who espoused his ideas. The Emperor had no need of Kita, nor Japan of overt fascism, because the power of the military, like that of the sanctified Emperor himself, had already been assured.

This traumatic event, epitomizing the tensions in Japan during the thirties, has inspired directors in their search for which elements of the national identity contributed to and made possible the events of the war period. One of the most disturbing of these films is Yoshishige Yoshida's *Coup d'État* (*Kaigenrei*, 1973). Yoshida wished to avoid the visual triviality of presenting the officers' coup, as Hiromichi Horikawa does in *The*

---

[8] Cited in David Bergamini, *Japan's Imperial Conspiracy* (New York: Pocket Books, 1972), p. 674.

Militarist (*Gunbatsu*, 1970), as a prelude to a stereotypic account of the life of General Tojo or some other militarist upon whom all blame for the war could then be heaped. Horikawa portrays the cutting down of former ministers and government officials in the February 26th incident as a Tokugawa-esque bloodbath, with surreal angles and blood dripping into the snow. It is a picturesque rendition, reminiscent of nothing so much as the assassination of Premier Ii in Okamoto's *Samurai Assassin*. Later in *The Militarist*, in another cliche, we observe the mutineers at the point of death, shouting "long live the Emperor," while in voice-over a narrator finds it necessary to inform us of the collapse of the coup d'état. Spectacle substitutes for political depth, making the February 26th plot seem more like a ballet than an important event in Japanese history.

Adapting a revolutionary approach to the narrative film like his contemporary Nagisa Oshima, Yoshida refuses to tell the story of Kita through the linearity that has functioned in Japanese cinema as a thinly veiled substitute for the *benshi*, the live commentator who explained the plot to silent-film audiences in Japan. During the silent era, the *benshi*, each with the embellishments reflecting his own personal style, would duplicate in words the action of the film. The successor to the *benshi* has been the traditional, didactic historical film, full of explanations conveyed through subtitles or voice-over narration. This is the style employed by Horikawa and other directors of the pedestrian historical film. The audience, spoon-fed, is prevented from actively participating in the experience of the film.

Breaking with this tradition was important to Yoshida because he wished to offer a new look at Ikki Kita and to organize the story of the officers' coup in part around the psychological imperatives flowing from Kita's personality. In *Coup d'État* flashback becomes indecipherable from the present, dream and reality merge in the manner of the French new wave. Yoshida refuses to be didactic in the manner of a propagandistic war film placidly chronicling the march of events, which are presented as unambiguous, their meaning immediately decipherable to all. For Yoshida the truths of history cannot be so easily explained; Kita manifested a nuanced personality, sometimes psychopathic, at other times bold and appealing, as he challenged the Emperor to unite himself directly with his Japanese subjects.

Before we are introduced to Kita, we must bear witness to an act that was a direct consequence of his teachings: the murder of the head of the Yasuda family, one of the largest of the *zaibatsu*. Before he stabs this old man wearing his fragile *yukata* (summer kimono), the murderer counts slowly from one to ten, sanctifying the action by increasing the danger to himself and adding what he believes to be a spiritual dimension to the bare bones of a blatant terrorist assassination. Only then are we introduced to Kita himself, who seems to be an extremely religious man, constantly praying before a Buddhist altar.

At first, Kita's religiosity seems to be a function of his insecurity, psychological no less than political. It is as if, by so diligently observing religious practices, he might escape from the violence surging beneath a

Coup d'État: Yoshida is interested in the psychology of the fascist and in how fascist-like values entered the fabric of Japanese society.

seemingly calm and impassive exterior. But the endless Buddhist rituals in which Yoshida's Kita participates also appear to be an expression of his sincerity, the devotions of a man who seems distant from sordid political ambitions. We meet, not a wild-eyed fascist, but a traditional man dressed in a kimono.

Then Yoshida upsets our expectations. Kita admits that his devotions are part of an image he is consciously creating for himself. "It is important to me," he says, "that they know I do Buddhist rituals"—"they" referring to those close to the Emperor, whom he indeed expects to liberate from the decadent bureaucracy. He has sent a gift of Buddhist prayer books to the Emperor in an unmistakable declaration of his belief that this godhead has dangerously distanced himself from the religious purity expected of an anointed leader. In acknowledgment the Emperor sends Kita a blank sheet of paper, an indication that his reprimand has fallen on deaf ears. But Kita interprets this "thank you" note as the Emperor's having accepted his challenge "smiling." Yoshida's Kita is a clever, manipulative man whose every action turns out to have been calculated, a man who responded to the moral crisis of Japan's rise as a spiritually barren superpower with a point of view that transcended mere crypto-fascism.

Yoshida's Kita believes that those who stand for upheaval are as much a part of the revolution as those who do the fighting. He assumes, by his own admission, responsibility for the officers' coup. Even the assassin of Yasuda in the first scene has left a will directing that his possessions be delivered to Kita, a will that also contains a direct quotation from one of Kita's works. Thus the film does not suggest that Kita's execution for responsibility for the officers' coup was unjust because it was based only on the influence of his writings and because he himself did not personally participate in the killing. The film is not an allegory about the question of the constitutionality of people being held responsible for ideas that lead others to commit acts of violence. Nor is it an attack on the present Japanese Subversive Activities Prevention Law, which unjustly permits such punishment in Japan today.

Yoshida is more interested in the psychology of the fascist and in how fascist-like values entered the fabric of Japanese society. Kita is not presented as an isolated fanatic but as the product of an environment in which all children are trained to respond to the world with a self-denial that can lead only to deformation of the personality, to varieties of fascism. Kita objects to his adopted son Taiki's killing insects, not on humane grounds, but because he believes that such gratuitous cruelty indicates fear. Fear is to be purged from Japanese youth, who are punished when they express any sign of weakness, any emotion that should be seen as normal.

Kita dreams that he is the Emperor, and then cuts his hand with a razor to punish himself for the arrogance and megalomania of such a dream. Even for the fantasies of the unconscious the Japanese are flagellated, and Kita, the most rigorous censor of his own impulses, punishes himself more harshly than would the sternest army disciplinarian. It should be no wonder that such stringency would lead to madness. When we were little, Kita tells his wife, and we were afraid, we were punished that we might be made strong. For Yoshida, herein lie the seeds of fascism and a fascist culture.

Sadism, masochism, and self-hatred are the emotions that Yoshida suggests have led to Kita's manifesto. So unable is Kita to accept himself as a man, possessing all the human frailties, that he even refuses to allow his wife to have children; he is repulsed by the thought of having others around who look like him. The police are mirror images of Kita, their ruthlessness the legacy of the same fear of weakness with which he is obsessed. They will gain the opportunity to institute martial law with the coup of the young officers, and it is they who recognize Kita's plan as "masochism," the "fantasy of a war veteran." Applying severe discipline toward oneself and toward one's allies is Kita's unconscious justification of the coming assassinations of the statesmen whom his manifesto accuses of having separated the Japanese people from their Emperor.

With a high-angle, downward-looking shot, reflecting the director's distaste for the police in their storm-trooper boots banging on the wooden floors of the house, Ikki Kita is arrested. His close contact with the conspirators and participants in the coup has been revealed to the police by a cowardly young officer who joined the officers' coup but had been afraid to set off the bomb sabotaging an electric plant, as he had been instructed. Kita has sympathized with him, and the betrayal is a result of the man's perverse inability to live with the fact that Kita did *not* doubt him. This inconsistency in Kita's generally unyielding, pitiless demeanor, this single moment of compassion, costs him his life.

Yoshida implies that the smallest emergence of a humane response undermined military fanaticism, built as it was on sheer acts of will, the type of determination reflected in the first assassin's counting to ten before killing Zenjiro Yasuda in the opening sequence. One of the arresting officers speaks to Kita of his betrayer: "He wasn't a spy, but your trust made him want to be. Perhaps he is your truest disciple." The movement inspired by Kita could not allow for the slightest degree of trust, compassion, or human feeling. When these emotions surface, the entire movement falters.

Coup d'État closes on Kita's execution. He is taunted by his executioners with the statement that the Emperor, untouchable by such right-wing politicians as himself, has dismissed him out of mercy as merely a "tiny schemer." Fascist movements may come and go, Yoshida implies, but the sanctity of the Emperor and his power over the Japanese people, of which Kita ironically wished to make a further fetish, remains unchanged. Kita sees a vision of a line of young officers in white, his disciples. They are those who died for his ideas. Some are on crutches, some stand tall. All are revealed as vulnerable before an authority that indeed makes a would-be fascist like Kita seem a "tiny schemer."

That the threat to the Japanese people lay finally not with Ikki Kita, but with those who defeated him, is expressed by Yoshida in the shot composition of the death scene. In one shot Kita, standing in a hole, occupies only the bottom third of the screen. He submits willingly to being tied to the cross behind him. The young officers who had made the coup died shouting "long live the Emperor," but he will not. "I make a point of not joking when I am about to die," says Kita; indeed it is a bitter jest that he, whose views called for protection and strengthening of the Emperor's power, should die at the orders of this same Emperor, who is using Kita's execution for that precise purpose: consolation of his own authority.

The last shot shows Kita fatally wounded in the head, blood soaking through his blindfold and mercilessly dripping down onto his face. He appears small, pathetic, vulnerable, only a single human being, after all. The enemy of Japan in the thirties, finally, was not this one man, nor those who followed him, but the entire structure of the Japanese state, the values by which it educated its children, and its cult of the sanctity of the Emperor. Against such power, Ikki Kita, who had vomited at the smell of the bloodstained clothes of Yasuda's assassin—clothes sent to him because his manifesto inspired the act—was no threat to Japan at all.

Imai's *Until the Day We Meet Again* (*Mata Au Hi Made*, 1950), followed the postwar Comintern line implicitly seeing the wartime enemy, the Americans, as liberators of the Japanese from fascism. The "blame" in this film is thus always placed on Japanese feudalism, rather than on the brutalities against civilian Japanese or policies of the enemy. In the case of *Until the Day We Meet Again* this can also be explained by the fact that it was made during the American Occupation and under the watchful eye of its C.I. & E. But Communist Party policy was so closely allied with the views of the American Occupation that it provided Imai with no problems. Stalin's position after Potsdam allowed party members like Imai honestly to believe that, as Imai has recently said, "America created democracy in Japan . . . like it or not, history proves that American military power was the greatest force involved in liberating us from fascism and liberating the entire era from fascism."[9]

In *Until the Day We Meet Again*, a young couple, Saburo and Keiko, fall in love. It is 1944 and he is called to the front. On the day he leaves, she is killed in an air raid and they never have the opportunity even to bid each other farewell. Imai's point in telling this story is that the young couple had a *right* not to have been destroyed by the war.

In contrast to Saburo and Keiko, who stand for freedom and personal happiness, are Saburo's father, a judge, and his brother, a soldier. The father has been so dehumanized by his obeisance to authority that he refuses to take off from work even when he learns that his soldier son has been injured in a railyard accident. This son's personality had undergone a complete transformation when he entered the army, turning him into a rigid disciplinarian, scorning weakness and ever mindful of everyone's "duty." Saburo, expressing the C.I. & E.'s urgings of Japan's directors to exalt individual judgment, challenges the absolute obedience demanded during Japan's imperial period and argues that no one should fight without considering the rights and wrongs of the war. His brother, who uses violence to win the argument when logic fails him, knocks Saburo down and replies that you can't think and fight at the same time, the caricature of this reply turning the soldier into a straw man whose point of view Imai can easily dispose of. "Think about the soldiers who are fighting for you," says Saburo's brother, "Are you a Japanese? . . . You should obey people who are older and know more."

The Occupation also wished the Japanese director to show that the people could rehabilitate themselves and that even the staunchest militarists could be reformed. Thus this brother, lying in his hospital bed after his railyard accident, undergoes another transformation. Forgetting his militarism, in a close-up lending his words the utmost sincerity, he tells Saburo that he wants only for him to be "happy."

Only one work fully treated Japan's part in the Second World War with

9 Mellen, "Interview with Tadashi Imai," p. 101.

Until the Day We Meet Again: Saburo, expressing the C.I. & E.'s urging of Japan's directors to exalt individual judgment, challenges the absolute obedience demanded during Japan's imperial period.

an honesty that refused to obfuscate. Even fine films like Kon Ichikawa's *The Harp of Burma* (*Biruma no Tategoto,* 1956) propagandistically tried to reverse the image of Japanese cruelty, universal throughout Southeast Asia, by humanizing the Japanese soldier. Masaki Kobayashi's three-part *The Human Condition* (*Ningen no Joken,* 1958–1961) alone looks at the Second World War without illusions, not seeking to protect myths rendered obsolete by the war, and exposing every truth of which the director had been made aware. *The Human Condition,* its three parts easily seen as one aesthetic entity, is one of the most brilliant historical films ever made. It begins with an attack on the inhuman practices within the Japanese army and ends with a bitter denunciation of Stalinism from the point of view of the socialist hero, Kaji (Tatsuya Nakadai in his greatest role), a Japanese soldier who has been captured by the Russians and placed in a prisoner-of-war camp. At the end of Part Three Kaji dies, his death a symbolic result of his having been betrayed, first by

Japan but equally, and causing a greater disillusionment which deprives him of the will to survive, by the inheritors of the Russian revolution. The Soviets are revealed as hypocrites treating the individual with as much contempt as did the Japanese militarists. His future rendered empty and without purpose by this betrayal of the ideal he once believed would lead to the creation of a just society in Japan after the war, Kaji dies in the snow somewhere in Soviet Asia, a victim of both fascism and "Communism."

In each film Kobayashi suggests the impossibility of an individual alone succeeding in altering the values of an entire system. Kaji tries to be a fair and just person within organizations based upon the exploitation of others and finds, of course, that he cannot. Part One, *No Greater Love*, asks whether a slave labor camp can ever be run humanely, Kaji's first impossible ideal. The setting is a Chinese prisoner-of-war camp run by the Japanese in Southern Manchuria in 1943. Actually, it is a *slave* labor camp, in which the prisoners are not captured Chinese soldiers but kidnapped civilians. Kaji agrees to fulfill his military obligation in this camp to test his theory that men, even those defined as "the enemy," can be treated with respect "in the colonies." This assignment is to exempt him from military service at the front. *No Greater Love* exposes the contradiction of an idealist coming to improve working conditions

The Human Condition, Part One—No Greater Love: Kaji's being a Japanese means that he must become an inevitable participant in the brutalization of these Chinese, whatever his personal views may be.

in a place where the first motive of the Japanese is profit to be derived from Chinese labor. For these less than voluntary workers to be forced to work hard enough, the Chinese must be treated with the utmost cruelty. Those who attempt to escape are tortured. From the point of view of the Army, which oversees the project and which is concerned not only with profit but with the morale of the Japanese soldiers, all the Chinese can die so long as no one escapes.

In one of the film's most powerful scenes, cattle cars filled with Chinese arrive, the image reminiscent of films like Gillo Pontecorvo's *Kapo*, which exposed the brutality of the Nazis toward the Jews. The Chinese prisoners emerge: bandaged, gaunt, and starving. Escaping from the inhuman confinement, they rush to the waiting food carts, and Kaji must seize his whip to ward off an incipient riot, since the Chinese are in no condition to eat the raw lentils that have been brought as their fare. His being a Japanese means that he must become an inevitable participant in the brutalization of these Chinese, whatever his personal views may be. When Kaji suggests that the weakened Chinese be allowed a month off without working, this view is interpreted by his military superiors as a criticism of their methods, as an act of insubordination. A dog is thrown against the electrified barbed wire fence to demonstrate to the Chinese what will happen if they attempt to escape. Instead of being granted time off, the Chinese are told that production must increase by twenty percent. Outlined against the sky, the silhouetted figures march to work. When the foreman murders one of them, it is reported as an accident.

In the midst of such degradation, Kaji tries to create a moral oasis through his relationship with his wife, Michiko. While by day the Chinese are starved and beaten, Kaji returns every night to his wife in their little cottage complete with curtains, tablecloths, and freshly laid eggs, the accouterments of a civilization made possible by the slave labor of the Chinese. As time progresses, Kaji and his wife no longer get along so well, as if no happiness could be built upon a denial of the humanity of others. She accuses him of striking a Chinese boy so as not to lose face, and later, when he wishes to help some of the Chinese to escape, she tries to stop him, fearful that he will be killed. His revolutionary desires are immediately at war with safeguarding his personal happiness. Kaji argues that should he not act on behalf of the Chinese, he would "no longer be a man." Michiko's reply is that by caring for the Chinese, he is sacrificing her: "Are my words those of a stray dog?"

Thus do the moral issues crystallize. The leader of the Chinese prisoners, speaking for Kobayashi, believes that man can be strong only when he discovers the source of his unhappiness. Having learned the cause of his pain, he can then devote his life to struggling against it. Kaji concludes that the use of force is justifiable only when it is used to overcome tyranny. But this does not resolve his personal dilemma. He asks the Chinese to trust him, but they neither can nor should. Despite his personal sympathy for their plight, he is still a Japanese. He can give away his flour rations, a small act of liberality that does not cost him very much, but he cannot endorse their escape plan.

Kaji has not yet understood how history sometimes narrows one's choices. It is bitterly traumatic for him when he comes to realize that he has become personally responsible for what the Japanese nation does, that there is no such thing as a "good German," a "good Japanese." "It's not my fault that I'm Japanese," says Kaji at last, "yet my worst fault is that I am."

The escape plan fails, and in the face of *Kempetai* executions Kaji can only plead to the beleaguered Chinese, "I have no authority," as indeed, however noble his motives, he has no power within an unjust and authoritarian system. The Chinese leader tells Kaji that his life is a contradiction between himself and his work; it is a contradiction he will still not have resolved by the end of Part Three.

The execution of the rebels proceeds, the blade of the executioner's sword dampened so that the victim's fat will not stick to it. Sadistically, the authorities force Kaji to serve as the official witness. The camera angles create a dizzying effect, turning the action on its side, as if Kaji's world were at last and finally being turned upside down. The executioner fails to cut off one head because he had hesitated, momentarily recognizing his victim as a human being, an obvious piece of irony but effective in this macabre context nonetheless.

Inevitably, Kaji himself is arrested as an enemy sympathizer. His crimes include the possession of books written by "foreign barbarians." Only the outcry of the Chinese on his behalf saves him from execution, the authorities fearing a full-scale rebellion which they might not be able to suppress. And at the end Kaji is given what will ultimately become a greater punishment than death. He is called up to active military service, where his attempts to retain his humanity will be even more unsuccessful.

Part Two, *A Soldier's Prayer*, searingly exposes life in the Japanese army, where physical weakness is despised and special punishments are reserved for any one who challenges authority. Kaji and his friend Shinjo are called "filthy Reds" for their socialist beliefs and are ostracized by the others. Kaji is assigned latrine duty, while Shinjo, a self-avowed Marxist, is given duty around the clock without any possibility of sleep. But Shinjo hopes to escape to the "land of freedom," the Soviet Union. Side by side, Kobayashi works his two motifs: the flagrant, mindless degeneracy of the Japanese Army and the illusory idea that Stalin's state represented a humanitarian social advance for man and a refuge against authoritarianism.

Kaji has been separated from his wife, Michiko, but in the most poignant scene of Part Two she comes to the camp and they are permitted to spend one night together. It is dusk, and the sharp contrasts of light and dark seem to suggest a momentary clarification of all issues. What they have together is good. Everything else—the onrush of history, Kaji's role as a Japanese soldier, Kaji's desire for a true democracy, which will prove to be only a dream—is uncertain. Before she leaves, Kaji asks

The Human Condition, Part Two—A Soldier's Prayer: Kaji and his friend Shinjo are called "filthy Reds" for their socialist beliefs and are ostracized by the others.

Michiko to strip and stand by the window so that he can remember how she looked, a scene photographed in the nude and cut by the Japanese censor. Michiko cries, "I have nothing to offer you. Nothing. Please take me." Despite the cuts, the scene stands out as sharply three-dimensional, as if the camera had rendered Michiko's figure in full light rather than in shadow.

The army is attacked in this film primarily through the sadistic treatment of a soldier named Obara, who wears glasses. For his fellow soldiers, the physically delicate Obara suggests the weakness within themselves that they both fear and despise. By his superiors, Obara is condemned for not assuming the role at home of the tyrannical patriarch, and not passing on to his wife enough "resolution" so that she will not quarrel with his mother in his absence. "Such effeminate ideas," he is told, "are more dangerous than Communism." The feudal mentality of the army is expressed as, with an officer standing over him, Obara is forced to write to his wife demanding that she depart from his house, a very harsh punishment for a pre-war woman since remarriage was extremely unlikely.

Kaji tries to help Obara survive the long marches to which the men are subjected, but because inhumanity has been built into the system, he cannot. Waiting for Obara to catch up with the others, Kaji risks punishment for his own failure to perform the rigorous physical training. His masculinity repeatedly questioned by his fellow soldiers, Obara is asked whether he has anything "between your legs." And, in a scene epitomizing the homosexual sadism suffusing army life, he is made to act the part of a prostitute for sex-starved, vicious men. Humiliated, he enters the latrine with his gun. Three times it fails to go off. When he gives up the idea of suicide, because "one can die any time," the gun goes off and he has "inadvertently" killed himself.

Kaji demands discipline for those who tortured Obara. It is part of his nature always to seek moral responsibility. But he is asking for redress from the Japanese Army, an institution that draws its *raison d'être* from the maintenance of fixed hierarchies, absolute obedience, and extreme physical discipline. Justice and humanity would render such an institution extinct. Shinjo deserts, attempting to reach the Soviet Union, but Kaji refuses to go with him. He remains committed to Japan and the Japanese, to righting the wrongs on his own side. "Prettier flowers on the other side doesn't make it right," says Kaji. Desertion implies that one is relinquishing responsibility for his own country, and this is something that Kaji could never do. Kaji's heroism lies in his refusal to abandon either Japan or his humanity; he was a figure beloved by Japanese film audiences, who wrote letters to Kobayashi begging that he not be allowed to die in Part Three.[10] Kaji, who so adamantly refused to yield to authoritarian tyranny, could not help but appeal to Japanese people still, in the late fifties, struggling within a neo-feudal society.

Near the end of *A Soldier's Prayer* Kaji is given the assignment of protecting new recruits from the sadism of the veterans, who can enjoy their higher place in the hierarchy only by humiliating the weak, younger men. Kaji has tried to isolate and train the recruits by himself, separating the veterans from their victims. Furious at this thwarting of their sadistic drives, the veterans attack Kaji, one of them actually stuffing a slipper down his throat. There is no way to evade the violence endemic to life in the Japanese Army. If the recruits are to be protected, Kaji must himself take the beatings destined for them. Kaji's very life is saved only because his new assignment takes him out into the fields to dig trenches in preparation for the coming attack by the Russians.

When the fighting begins, the Japanese are revealed to be insufficiently armed. Conflicting orders create confusion everywhere. The officers are more concerned with their own prerogatives, with each assuming the powers appropriate to his rank and status, than with saving the lives of the men. Long traveling shots expose the vulnerability of the Japanese soldiers as they frantically begin to dig anti-tank trenches. Kaji, a superior individual because, contrary to the traditional Japanese way, he has never respected power and hierarchy for their own sake, is alone capable of individual judgment. He tells the officerless men that they must think for themselves, make their own decisions in the struggle to survive the Russian attack. But individual judgment is something army life has rendered them incapable of. As a result of the army's insistence upon absolute obedience, to the exclusion of developing the reasoning power and leadership potential in each man, most of them will die.

Kobayashi reveals that the army did little to protect the ordinary recruit, a theme in direct contradiction of the army benevolence and paternalism manifested in *Mud and Soldiers* and *Five Scouts*. The camera tracks at a low angle between the foxholes as the recruits, armed only with small rifles, stand up to the Russian tanks. At times the camera seems to be under the tanks with the men. At a surreal moment Kobayashi focuses on a bloody severed arm abandoned on the rocky terrain. The Russian tanks, in a foreshadowing of the Russian inhumanity of Part Three, aim directly for Japanese bodies, dead or alive, rolling over them and even rolling over the hole in which Kaji crouches.

At the end, it is dusk on an abandoned landscape that suggests an image of the end of the world. Kaji and only two others have survived, through will and the naked instinct of self-preservation alone. But they have also survived because, violating the dictates of the army, they have recognized the futility of fighting to the death in this situation. Russian foot soldiers arrive to pick among the bodies to make sure there are no survivors. Kaji must murder a fellow Japanese who attacks him in a fit of madness, the man having become deranged through witnessing the terrible massacre —an event that would, of course, be unthinkable in any film made during the war. Running into the dusk and out onto the bleak horizon, Kaji reiterates his determination: "I will stay alive!"

The title of Part Three, *The Road to Eternity*, is ironic because the only eternity Kaji will find lies in oblivion and not in the socialism that has fortified him and men like Shinjo with the hope that a better society could be constructed out of the ruins of the old. The Russians are fat and smug. But the full revelation of Soviet hypocrisy is left for the end of the film, when a weakened Kaji, captured at last, is finally relieved of any belief whatsoever that the Soviet Union represents a more just social order than the feudal Japan he has known. The future of Japan becomes a dominant theme. With the war drawing to an end, Kaji understands that the Japan he knew is dead. The task of the Japanese now is to create a society based upon democratic principles that value the individual, a society that exists only to fulfill the needs of its members.

"The people are mostly like myself," says Kaji, "helpless." Kaji's death at the end symbolizes Japan's failure to have become truly democratic since the war. This failure is blamed by Kobayashi on the Russians, who have set no example of a free society despite their claims to be the inheritors of the Bolshevik Revolution. Perhaps too easily, Kobayashi associates socialism with the model offered by the Soviet Union. He never allows Kaji to reflect that, while the Soviet Union has obviously betrayed the ideas of Marx and Lenin, a socialist state could still exist independently of the Soviet example and free of its influence. But, given the close ties between the Japanese Communist Party and the Soviet Union throughout the postwar period, and the absence of independent and organized alternative leftist forces in Japan, Kobayashi's association of socialism with the Soviet Union is perfectly credible.

As Kaji and his little band of survivors make their way through the countryside, Kobayashi, revising the picture offered in *Tank Commander Nishizumi*, illustrates how deeply hated were the Japanese by the other peoples of Asia. The local populace in the area blames Kaji, simply because he is a Japanese, for the terrible pillaging done by those who preceded him, reiterating the central motif of Part One when Kaji asked the Chinese in the slave labor camp to value him for himself and ignore the fact that he was a Japanese. And at the end of *The Road to Eternity*, with absolute logic, Chinese peasants spit upon and refuse food to the starving Kaji, who to them is one more despised Japanese.

The Russians prove themselves to be no less cruel than the hated Japanese, despite the mythology attached to the Red Army as liberators. Russian soldiers everywhere abduct and rape civilian women. When their needs have been satisfied, they toss their victims from the trucks out onto the open road, unconcerned whether they live or die. Kaji is appalled: "The Red Army wouldn't. . . ." His new friend, Tange, another socialist, like so many before and since, justifies Soviet atrocities on the ground that the crimes of a few prove nothing.

But Kaji is too honest, and has suffered too much, to be convinced by this spurious reasoning. "Minor facts ignored by history," he says—in a heavy-handed use of voice-over, indicating a lapse in technique but saved by the hero's passion—"can be fatal to the individual." Kobayashi has his hero stand for morality and humanism at the service of no system or ideology. His is a purity that the world of his time cannot permit to survive. Tange, as a Stalinist, repeats the party line: "Russia wants nothing . . . her aim has always been the liberation of China," a lie which the behavior of the Russian troops exposes without the need of verbal refutation. Kobayashi could well have pointed out what these ironies indicate he understood all too well: that Stalin's making Chiang Kai-shek a member of the Third International in 1926, only to have Chiang bar all Communists from positions in the Kuomintang, historically belies the propaganda of Russia's supposedly altruistic concern for the liberation of the Chinese. Kaji's total disillusionment with the Soviet Union will finally and unequivocally occur at the prisoner-of-war camp for captured Japanese soldiers run by the Russians. The unity of form and content characterizing *The Human Condition* is nowhere better expressed than in the fact that this will be a slave labor camp, exactly like that operated by the Japanese in Part One.

As a prisoner of the Russians, Kaji is treated as horribly as the Japanese had treated the Chinese slaves in *No Greater Love*. Called "dogs," by the Russians, the Japanese are reduced to slave labor in the freezing Siberian winter with neither proper clothes nor shelter. A sinister quisling Japanese interpreter deliberately mistranslates the words of the captured Japanese so that Kaji cannot communicate at all with the Russians.

The Human Condition, Part Three—The Road to Eternity: Kaji is granted a full understanding of what the Russians actually represent: naked authoritarian tyranny, hierarchies elevating a privileged few, hostility toward the individual, qualities exactly like those of the feudal Japanese leadership.

Protesting against the harsh conditions, he is repeatedly punished as a "troublemaker." The officer in command, a racist as are all the Russians, calls Kaji a "fascist samurai." Meanwhile, "Kapo" equivalents receive officers' rations so long as labor norms and quotas are met, no matter that the men must stagger under superhuman loads. Kaji is even reprimanded for clothing himself in discarded burlap sacks to keep warm; the representatives of the "Workers' State" berate him for stealing this "property," an irony bitter if obvious. Dressed in his burlap, Kaji has ceased to be a Japanese soldier. Yet he is no longer in possession of alternative values because, irony of ironies, it is precisely his faith in socialist principles that makes him even more suspect to the Russians than it did to the Japanese militarists.

With a huge portrait of Stalin behind him, the Russian commander accuses Kaji of being an "exploiter of labor," and assigns him the onerous task of pulling up railroad tracks in the freezing cold. Kaji's crime has been the request for an aspirin for a sick comrade. Brought before the authorities, Kaji, the most humane of men, is accused of "war crimes" because he is forced to admit that during the course of the war he had indeed attacked both Russians and Chinese. The interpreter continues to mistranslate Kaji's words, but it becomes overwhelmingly clear that the Russians are deliberately incapable of seeing Kaji as an individual, just as, it is implied, they treat their own more outspoken subjects with suspicion and alarm.

Kaji's final defeat is thus at the hands of the Russians. Kobayashi repeatedly cuts to a close-up of the poster of Stalin, whose policies, this film shows, have made a travesty of socialism. Kaji is granted a full understanding of what the Russians actually represent: naked authoritarian tyranny, hierarchies elevating a privileged few, hostility towards the individual—qualities exactly like those of the feudal Japanese leadership. Kaji knows that most of the prisoners are not "class enemies" of the workers, but working-class Japanese who are themselves the victims of exploitation, of having been used in this war by their superiors. Nor is Kaji seduced by Tange's further defense of the Russians on the ground that their strategy calls for the pursuit of their own interests first, a euphemism for Stalin's policy of "socialism in one country," an argument which Kobayashi, concerned about the renewal of his own society, quite rightly holds in contempt.

Kobayashi has said that had he been an officer rather than a rank-and-file soldier during the Second World War, he could not have made this film.[11] Kaji clearly reflects Kobayashi's own struggle, and his own crisis of belief. The lack of distance between Kobayashi and Kaji is one of the film's great strengths, as well as the source of its greatest weakness. It causes Kobayashi to continue with some scenes far too long, especially with the scene of Kaji's death. But the identification between director and character adds emotional resonance to Kaji's death, for his defeat expresses everything Kobayashi himself had obviously experienced in relation to Japan and the Japanese army, to Soviet socialism, and to the postwar prospects for justice everywhere.

After *The Human Condition*, the two most important Japanese films about the Second World War were Kon Ichikawa's *The Harp of Burma* and *Fires on the Plain* (*Nobi*, 1959). In making two such different films on the same subject—the horrors of war experienced by besieged and abandoned Japanese soldiers—Ichikawa reveals his own lack of a consistent point of view or personal commitment. Ichikawa's anti-war films are the opposite of Kobayashi's, whose films may be more didactic but reveal a much more coherent and persuasive understanding of history.

Ichikawa's anti-war works are far less intellectually serious than *The Human Condition*. They take their coloration from the novels from which they are adapted and from the personalities of both Ichikawa and his screenwriter wife, Natto Wada. Ichikawa has always willfully insisted that the ideas expressed in his films are of no particular consequence. We are apt, therefore, to discover among his works, ostensibly dealing with the same subject, inconsistencies of philosophy. Ichikawa's uneasiness with value judgments has led to his fondness for making films about athletic events such as *Tokyo Olympiad* (1965), *Youth*, and a

[11] "Interview with Masaki Kobayashi," p. 138.

segment of the international production about the Munich Olympic games, *Visions of Eight* (1972). As Ichikawa says at the end of *Youth*, seemingly speaking of high-school baseball tournaments but actually revealing as well his aesthetic credo, "the thing is the game itself, not who wins." What his films "say" is of less concern to Ichikawa than the way it is said, a philosophy that has sometimes led him to make films, like *Youth* itself, magnificent in their technique, but shallow and devoid of any serious content. Thus we can find among Ichikawa's *oeuvre* the lyrical *Harp of Burma*, a sentimental if often beautiful whitewash of the Japanese presence in Southeast Asia, and the fiercely expressionistic *Fires on the Plain*, a film unrelenting in its criticism of the Japanese army and bitter in its denunciation of official imperviousness toward the sick and wounded during the last days of the war.

If one can ignore its representation of Japanese soldiers and officers as sweet and gentle victims of a war with which they have no real connection, *The Harp of Burma* is a moving pacifist statement. Through a simple and sympathetic look at what it means to be a Japanese, Ichikawa succeeds in retrieving for the audience a renewed sense of their national identity. His aim is to destroy myths about the lack of concern for all human life during the war.

The hero, a soldier named Mizushima, is appalled by the waste of war, by the bodies of his dead comrades dotting the Burmese landscape. Mizushima's spiritual odyssey begins when, after the official end of the war, he is assigned to convince a group of soldiers, who continue to hold out, to surrender to the British. Although the officer asks his men to vote on whether or not they should surrender, he has already indicated his own view that, having pledged themselves to die fighting on behalf of the Emperor, they should continue to struggle to the end. And indeed the men immediately return with the decision to resume fighting. The desire for approval from their superior (and, by indirection, from their ultimate superior, the Emperor), and the need to sustain harmony as a means to this end, lead to the sacrifice, in this scene, of common sense, individual judgment, and the lives of all these men, who are promptly killed by the British.

Yet, wrong-headed as they might have been, these Japanese soldiers manifest a sense of unity with those who died by their side. They have argued that to surrender would be "an insult to the men who perished and an abandonment of the souls of their dead comrades." From this feeling of kinship with the Japanese dead, Mizushima discovers his own salvation. He decides to become a Buddhist priest, remaining in Burma where he can pray for and comfort the scores of Japanese dead unburied and unmourned in a foreign land. For the Japanese, this is one of the most ignominious of deaths. As the men in *Mud and Soldiers* also revealed, the greatest horror of war was not death itself but that one's bones should lie abandoned in a foreign country. After his troop is repatriated to Japan, Mizushima remains behind to bury the Japanese dead and pray for their souls, that they may not remain forgotten in Burma.

So lonely a choice is especially poignant for the Japanese because of each man's strong love for the group to which he belongs and all its members, a love that extends to "Japan" itself. This group solidarity is affectionately portrayed by Ichikawa as the most human and the most typically Japanese response to such a situation.

The members of Mizushima's group feel intense loyalty toward each other and are forever singing in unison. This singing reflects a solidarity among the Japanese that makes bearable these last difficult days which they must spend in a British prisoner-of-war camp. As they sing, they are accompanied by Mizushima, who has learned—almost through some psychic power since he has had no musical education—expertly to play the Burmese harp:

> Autumn nights grow darker
> Under foreign skies.
> Wretched is the wanderer
> Suffering all alone.
> His thoughts go back home,
> Longing for his parents,
> Seen only in his dreams.

The Japanese soldiers long, not for wives or sweethearts, but for their parents and for Japan, the antithesis of "foreign skies." The worst punishment they can imagine—and one that Mizushima will voluntarily assume—is being isolated, cut off from the group, from Japan, and from one's parents, for the group alone can grant the individual identity and purpose. In such a culture Mizushima's decision is especially difficult. His comrades identify with the pain he is certain to experience once they have departed. They go to great lengths to convince him to return to Japan with them; they even teach a parrot to say, "Mizushima! Come with us back to Japan!" and then have this bird delivered to him.

But Mizushima has decided to sacrifice loyalty to a single group for devotion to a larger entity, the group of Japanese dead who have lost their lives in this senseless war. His decision becomes an affirmation of the most traditional sense of what it means to be a Japanese. Mizushima will unite himself with the family of ancestors comprised by these dead.

The point of view of *The Harp of Burma* is thus as traditional as Buddhism itself. Mizushima merges his essence with that of all Japan, and has no need to return to its geographical shores. Ichikawa expands this theme to include the unification of all men regardless of their nationalities, through the trauma of war. Three cultures are represented in *The Harp of Burma*, three languages spoken: Japanese, Burmese, and English.

At first, and quite naturally, given the circumstances, these groups respond to each other only with suspicion and ill will. Fearing the British, and fearing, too, that in any skirmish the ammunition dump will be blown up, causing death to all, the Japanese affect unconcern when their adversaries appear, clapping their hands and singing "There's No Place Like Home," since fighting by now is out of the question. From the darkness the British sing the song back at them—in English (and in the accomplished voices of a professional chorus that lends a note of unreality to the scene). Mizushima adds the music of the third culture, accompanying them all on the Burmese harp.

Earlier in the film when, on a scouting mission, Mizushima had been disguised in Burmese dress, his comrades had laughed and told him that he looked so much like a Burmese that perhaps he should remain in Burma —unaware, of course, of how ironic these words would later seem. The shared humanity of the three nationalities is also expressed through the camaraderie developed between Mizushima's group and an old Burmese woman who "trades" with the interned Japanese soldiers and helps them to communicate with Mizushima. She bears no grudge against the Japanese, speaking Japanese in an Osaka dialect herself. Part of her role in the film is to dispel the notion that the native peoples of Asia despised the Japanese, as Kobayashi and other more honest directors would maintain.

Ichikawa also seeks to undercut the image of the Japanese soldier as rapist and plunderer through his characterization of the captain of the group, played by Rentaro Mikuni. The captain is kind and benevolent, encouraging the men to maintain their dignity when they are captured, and promising—again with unconscious irony—to leave no one behind if they are lucky enough to be able to return to Japan. To dispel the "myth" that during the war the Japanese were fanatical in their determination to fight to the death, regardless of the odds against them—that they were mindless *kamikazes* in their service to the Emperor—this captain is pained by the thought that more Japanese should die. It is he who encourages Mizushima to accept the assignment of convincing the hold-outs to surrender. And it is he alone who understands, presumably through some spiritual sentience granted the higher members of the hierarchy, what he calls Mizushima's "great decision."

Ichikawa does not succumb to the temptation of caricaturing the British, as Tadashi Imai would the Americans in his 1972 *Eternal Cause* (*Kaigun Tokubetsu Nenshohei*). They are not attractive or humane, although the British commander does wish Mizushima luck in his attempt to save the hold-outs; he is not especially desirous of inflicting greater casualties out of a lust for revenge. Nor are the British soldiers particularly perceptive. In the scene in which the Japanese frantically sing in their last effort to lure Mizushima back among them, the British racists remark on how the Japanese love to sing. Nevertheless, the British are not portrayed in this film as stereotyped brutes.

The deepest beauty of *The Harp of Burma* derives from the character of Mizushima, who scarcely utters a word throughout. We see him chase away the vultures, shielding his face from the stench as he begins to bury the Japanese dead. With no one to observe him, he salutes a dead comrade who died holding a photograph, presumably of himself with a child.

In his magnificent last confrontation with the troop, Mizushima faces his former comrades from behind the barbed wire of their camp on the night before their departure. At first they cheer wildly, believing that he has returned and will go home with them after all. On his Burmese harp he plays, tenderly and gently, "There's No Place Like Home." Without words he affirms that he has not ceased to love either them or Japan. Rather, he has a higher duty. A tear steals down his cheek. Then he is gone. This may be the most moving scene in the history of the Japanese film.

In a letter read to the others by the captain on the ship carrying them back to Japan, Mizushima explains that, much as he longs to see his parents, he cannot leave the bones of the Japanese dead scattered at random. He expresses a philosophy close to the Japanese *mono no aware* which implies that human suffering is inevitable and must be accepted without question, a point of view Kobayashi would be incapable of. "The why of tragedy is not for humans to know," Mizushima writes, "we can only relieve suffering." For Ichikawa, this is the most noble expression of what it means to be human. The others speak of what they will do once

The Harp of Burma: Mizushima, who will probably never see Japan again, is the truest Japanese of all because he is uniting himself with all the living and all the dead.

they return to Japan. Their ambitions, compared with the self-appointed mission of Mizushima, are selfish and silly. One will rush to the Ginza, another to the movies, another will "eat a lot." Somebody sums it all up: "Everybody has his own life to live." Already, on the ship, their thoughts turn away from Mizushima toward the self-indulgent lives they will lead as soon as they return to Japan.

Mizushima, who will probably never see Japan again, is the truest Japanese of all because he is uniting himself with all the living and all the dead. Dark shadows of dusk pass over the parrot Mizushima has sent them— a twin of the parrot they had sent him—with his reply to their message: "I can't go back with you." The captain is deep in thought as the sun sets. And the last shot of the film belongs to Mizushima, marching forward in determination over the barren, "blood red" Burmese soil. His suffering will redeem them all.

In *Fires on the Plain*, set on the Leyte-Philippine front in 1945, the mood is one of hysteria. Food has run out for the Japanese forces. No one is accepted at the field hospitals unless he possesses five days' worth of rations. The men are ordered by their commanders that, should the hospital refuse to take them, they are to commit suicide. There is no kind captain played by Rentaro Mikuni who would advise them to surrender rather than die senselessly.

But in *Fires on the Plain* the enemy is portrayed as so barbaric that surrender is out of the question anyway. Prisoners of war are not taken, and inflamed native guerrillas everywhere await their prey—the vulnerable, starving remnants of the Japanese Imperial Army. At the climax of the film the hero, Private Tamura, discovers rampant cannibalism among the few surviving Japanese. Although in the original novel Tamura survives to return to Japan, where he enters a mental institution, Ichikawa chooses to allow him to die. Tamura's death is seen by the director as his salvation, an alternative to living on by cannibalistically devouring the remains of his fellow soldiers. His final rest is awarded him through Ichikawa's own humanity, a respite the director could not bring himself to deny his long-suffering character.[12]

Throughout the film Ichikawa unrelentingly imposes images exposing the grotesque barbarism of war. With a splash of blood, a starving Tamura bayonets a dog. Piles of dead Japanese include a hand sticking up into the air from amidst the skulls and bones. Tamura is horrified to discover they are "Japanese!" A tear runs down his cheek as one of the soldiers greedily stuffs stolen salt into his mouth. The Japanese are strafed by American planes, harassed by guerrillas, and, in their tattered boots, unable to walk. It is in this context that cannibalism asserts itself.

Far from singing to the Japanese as the British did in *The Harp of Burma*, the Americans in *Fires on the Plain* are ruthless, "fat as pigs." They call their victims "Jap bastards" and murder them in cold blood out of pleasure as well as to avoid the inconvenience of taking prisoners. The

12 Joan Mellen, "Interview with Kon Ichikawa," *Voices from the Japanese Cinema*, p. 125.

Fires on the Plain: The real horror is not the eating of human flesh—which the camera portrays as an aberration of the desperate—but the atrocity of war itself.

search of the Red Cross for survivors on Leyte is shown to be perfunctory. When one man does surrender, a native immediately shoots him down. The open sky is enormous, the plains barren and full of peril, offering no place to hide. To survive, Tamura eats dirt, grass, and leeches.

With a deep tilt Ichikawa draws our attention to a severed human hand which, grotesque as it is, nonetheless becomes a temptation to the starving men. Tamura, already out of his mind, tries to hold out: "I won't, couldn't eat human flesh." His companion, Nagamatsu, is less scrupulous, stuffing some "monkey meat" into Tamura's mouth. Tamura spits it out: "I can't eat it. My gums are soft. My teeth fell out." His next question is, "Who was it?" Ichikawa maintains a distance that refuses to permit his film any easy *voyeurism* or enjoyment of horror for its own sake. The cannibalism is seen as one more element in a war that has already produced a plenitude of horrors.

At the end, Nagamatsu, after killing one of these "monkeys" with a grenade, proceeds to do the necessary butchering with his sword. Blood sticks to his beard and spatters over his body. Crazed, horrified, more in an act of unconscious humanity than moral judgment, Tamura kills him. Then he begins to walk toward the fires on the plain set by the enemy. He knows he will be killed but, just as he could not help but kill Nagamatsu, he cannot restrain the impulse to "see people who are living normal lives," to re-enter a human community.

Shells explode all around him and he falls. Ichikawa's usual moral distance is particularly effective because he wishes to challenge our expectations.

In a film daring in its depiction of cannibalism, he argues that the real horror is not the eating of human flesh—which the camera portrays as an aberration of the desperate—but the atrocity of war itself.

The interest in examining what the Second World War was really like for the Japanese soldier continued through the 1960s and even into the 1970s. But the demise of the serious anti-war film had long been apparent. With the war part of the distant past, and Japan once again a superpower, any re-experience of the war seemed, from the mid-sixties on, to have become gratuitous, even from the point of view of directors critical of the direction Japan had taken. Only during the transitional stage to economic recovery, in the fifties, when, perhaps, there was a chance that the new society might not be so wholly constructed upon the values of the old, could meaningful films about the war be made. Although the resurrection of a neo-feudal social order should have been foreseen in MacArthur's reconstitution of the *zaibatsu* and retention of the Emperor, the period of transition to superpower produced such monumental works as *The Human Condition*. By the mid-sixties, with the defeat of the anti-war movement— and despite such exceptions as *Under the Flag of the Rising Sun* (*Gunki Hatameku Motoni*, 1972) still later—such assessments of the war were reduced to criticisms of the army alone, as if it were a free-floating entity and not under the command of the Emperor and the government. The simplistic approach of some of the later anti-war films reflects their directors' loss of faith in the possibility that the structure of Japanese society could be so altered as to prevent another such occurrence.

Worse yet, under the guise of the anti-war film, apologia for Japan's ruling group, which had engineered its imperial adventures, began to appear. Kihachi Okamoto's *The Emperor and a General*, literally rendered as *Japan's Longest Day* (*Nihon No Ichiban Nagai Hi*, 1967), presents the unappealing phenomenon of the anti-war film serving as propaganda for the moral, political, and economic rehabilitation of the ruling class which presided over Japan during the war years.

The focus of *The Emperor and a General* is an actual abortive rising of fanatical young army officers in the early morning hours of August 15, 1945, before the Emperor's pre-recorded message of surrender could be broadcast to the Japanese people. As history reveals, this rising was suppressed. Not so subtly, the film seeks to place the blame for the entire war on a handful of over-zealous young officers. Where, as it must, the film indicates that higher-ups like War Minister Anami (Toshiro Mifune) supported the war, it suggests that such men were innocent of beginning the hostilities. Nor are they responsible for the defeat, or for the overwhelming suffering visited upon the Japanese people. They are guiltless because they had been misinformed about Japan's material capacity to conduct the Second World War. These are humane men who love Japan and her people. To the entire populace they would justify their motives in a manner parallel to that of the English poet Richard Lovelace's "To Lucasta, Going to the Wars": "I could not love thee, dear, so much/Loved I not honor more."

Okamoto's grandiose apologia absolves from guilt for Japan's misery everyone from the Emperor to the Prime Minister to the Ministers of the Army and Navy. When the action of the film begins, atomic bombs have already been dropped on Hiroshima and Nagasaki. Still photographs record the devastation. Yet War Minister Anami continues to oppose surrender unless the Emperor is permitted to remain on his throne, the Occupation rendered negligible and barred from designating war criminals, and the Japanese permitted to disarm themselves. In his heart he favors a last-ditch fight on Japan's mainland. But his motive is solely the preservation of his country's honor and no one would blame him for wanting to spare the Japanese the humiliation of a protracted American Occupation.

Japan is saved from such a foolhardy course, which would have cost so many lives, by her benevolent Emperor. *The Emperor and a General* exalts, absolves, and further glorifies the already sanctified Hirohito. It is the compassionate Hirohito—from whom, even as he is played by actor Koshiro Matsumoto, the camera keeps a respectful distance—who insists upon sur-

The Emperor and a General: The *seppuku* of Anami, like the cult of the sanctity of the Emperor, another feudal vestige, is fully endorsed by the director as appropriate and redolent of dignity.

render. Usually we are allowed to view only the back of Matsumoto's head, or his white-gloved hand, as if, as late as 1967, Okamoto through his very camera work were sustaining the cult of Emperor worship. This utterly kindly man now says, "Prolonging the war will end the Japanese race. End the war!" Later, wiping away a tear, an act which inspires the sobs of his ministers, the Emperor says, "I cannot watch my subjects bear more hardships. I am prepared to do anything . . . go anywhere." And he orders the surrender.

One cannot help but wonder how such a fine, noble man could have condoned the war in the first place, or how any of the noble innocents we witness at their deliberations could have sent one-quarter of all Japanese males into combat, as they did. "Kill me if you have any complaints," says the heroic War Minister Anami (the General of the film's title) to his staff, ordering them to comply with the Emperor's decision. Later he will commit *seppuku* for his part in the war by first cutting himself across the belly and then—forsaking the usual beheading by a second, and out-samurai-ing the samurai—slashing open his jugular vein. Blood splashes as Okamoto, even in depicting the last day of the war, cannot forgo his usual bloodthirsty *mise-en-scène*.

The *seppuku* of Anami, like the cult of the sanctity of the Emperor, another feudal vestige, is fully endorsed by the director as appropriate and redolent of dignity. The good-hearted War Minister, whose superior moral character is manifest despite his early refusals to surrender, prevents any of his officers from dying with him, as they are eager to do. He urges them instead to build the new Japan. Nor does he take part in the attempted coup by the wildest of his officers, who run rampant in the Imperial Palace for a few hours, searching for the record of the Emperor's broadcast of defeat, before they are subdued. Sober-minded, older officers, out of a suddenly discovered compassion for the Japanese people, accept the defeat with grace and disarm the unruly ones.

There is, in addition, a profound sense in which *The Emperor and a General* is not about the Second World War at all. Rather, its truest concern is with endorsing and praising the Japanese system of rule, with showing that the Japanese government has always operated along democratic lines, even during the most trying moments of the war. From the beginning of this two-and-one-half-hour film, we are shown repeated cabinet and council meetings, initiating us into how well this government has always worked. The terms of the surrender are in question as Okamoto works his paean to the Japanese principle of consensus, by which unanimity on an issue is reached through compromise and endless discussion. The surrender terms take time to define, time that allows the fanatics to organize and rise up, because true consensus can be accomplished only after long debate. In the Japanese version of "democracy" there is no guarantee of the right of a minority to a dissenting view; unanimity takes longer to achieve and thus the delay ensues. But it is worth the wait because, Okamoto implies, this is how democracy works.

The key moment in the film comes in one of these debates when a dispute arises between War Minister Anami and the Minister of the Navy (So Yamamura). (Okamoto uses an all-star cast, with even Tatsuya Nakadai as narrator, only to waste it with an utterly pedestrian style). The problem is ending the war on "honorable terms" so that it could not be said that those who perished did so for a lost cause. The immediate conflict centers on the use of the word "adverse." The Minister of the Navy, wishing for a quick surrender and a ready admission by Japan of being in the wrong, favors the use of the word. Anami, a partisan of the "lost cause" argument, opposes it. A stalemate results. The Minister of the Navy retreats to the men's room, looking anguished. Then back he comes to the council room, agreeing to the change. Like a good Japanese, he is willing to sacrifice principle for the sake of a greater good, in this case the immediate end of the war on no matter what terms. Planes are still taking off, piloted by zealots ready for more combat. Compromise serves the more important end. And we have witnessed Japanese democracy at work.

Okamoto argues that the Japanese may have been misguided in their war effort, but they were never fascists or even dictatorial militarists. At heart they were always democrats working within a democratic system. There is nothing in the war period, Okamoto tells his audience, of which they need be ashamed. The atrocities of the Japanese invasion of China are, of course, never mentioned. And as if enough time had passed for the truth to be safely discarded by 1967, a Japanese director could thus dissemble about the facts concerning one of the most important historical events of the century, for the sake of bolstering the egos of the Japanese. As Prime Minister Suzuki (Chishu Ryu) is made to say with tears in his eyes: "Everything we did was for love of our country." Could such a man be a war criminal? Clearly not.

Anami presents him with the gift of a box of cigars and the Prime Minister, instantly, delicately, understands that this means farewell, that Anami is off to his *seppuku*. The ceremonious offering of the gift heralds the first stage in the War Minister's progress toward self-immolation. These are men capable of refinement of feeling, mutual respect, even exquisiteness of sensibility. Their fervent wish, as Anami puts it, is that the young live on to see that such a mistake never happens again. These leaders were never fanatics. In fact, only a few if any were to blame, perhaps only the zealots who, by the time the Emperor's broadcast is played on the radio, have died by their own hands. The barrage of statistics we are offered in voice-over is to convince us further that, after all, we should not blame the Japanese for the war, nor should they blame themselves, because it is they who suffered most: fifteen million homeless, three million dead, of which one million were civilians. The film ends on a "prayer" that "such a day will never visit Japan again."

As the war retreats into the past, filmmakers like Okamoto enlist themselves in rewriting and distorting history. The intention, however, falls short because it seems plainly incredible that such magnanimous men as Okamoto have shown us could have permitted even a single moment of combat. As sheer propaganda, *The Emperor and a General* far exceeds any of the Yamamoto films, such as *The War at Sea from Hawaii to Malaya*, which confine themselves to a description of the emotions engendered as the Japanese were being urged to die for their country. More insidiously, Okamoto attempts to rehabilitate the repressive militarists of the thirties into noble devotees of democracy. It is a shameless film.

The Devastated Homeland

Nobody cried "hurrah for the Emperor" when we died. We all hated him because we knew he cheated us. We all thought of killing him when we got back to Japan. I came home and found out why Japan had achieved this development. It was for money, wasn't it? The Emperor must've started the war because he wanted money, too. . . .

> Matsuyoshi Fujita in Shohei Imamura's
> *Matsu the Untamed Comes Home*

The devastation visited upon Japan in the last days of the war was so severe that it dwarfs the two atomic bombings at Hiroshima and Nagasaki. In one incendiary bombing of Tokyo, in March of 1945, in which a napalm-like substance was used, 197,000 people were reported dead or missing, more than the 130,000 dead at Hiroshima.[1] Fifty percent of the housing in sixty-six cities and towns was destroyed.[2]

In 1953 Kaneto Shindo produced for the Japan Teachers Union[3] *Children of the Atom Bomb (Genbaku no Ko)*. Its sole theme is the horror of the bombing, and it offers no political understanding or exploration of the motives of the American government in dropping the bomb. Instead, *Children of the Atom Bomb* is content simply to evoke the bombing and its consequences, as seen through the eyes of a Hiroshima-born teacher returning to her birthplace for a summer vacation. There she searches for her former pupils, each of whom is now an atomic bomb victim.

Shindo's refusal to take any stand regarding the propriety of dropping a nuclear weapon on the civilian population of Japan is revealed early in the film. After the teacher says a prayer for her parents, who died in the bombing, a flashback reveals her as a schoolgirl listening to a radio report of a Japanese victory in China. The implication is that Japan, who is guilty of

---

[1] Cited in Robert Guillain, *Le Peuple Japonais et la Guerre*, in *The Japan Reader*, 1: 483.

[2] *The Japan Reader*, 1:475.

[3] At the time this union, the Nikkyoso, was extremely militant, its 1951 Code of Ethics revealing a vision of a real liberation of Japanese society from the feudal militarism of its recent past: "Upon our shoulders have been laid the historical tasks of protecting peace . . . and realizing a society free from exploitation, poverty and unemployment. . . . The youth of the country must be raised and educated to become capable workers who will give themselves . . . to the accomplishment of these tasks. . . . Teachers shall live and work with the youth. . . . Each teacher shall make an intensive critical examination of himself and shall study and make efforts to prepare himself for his new role in education. . . ." Cited in Halliday, *Japanese Capitalism*, p. 250.

Children of the Atom Bomb: Its sole theme is the horror of
the bombing, and it offers no political understanding or exploration of the motives of the American government in
dropping the bomb.

her own share of wartime atrocities, bears equal responsibility for what
happened at Hiroshima. The atomic bomb, treated as a consequence of
war in general, becomes no different from any other form of combat. By
paralleling the atomic bombing of Hiroshima with the Japanese invasion
of China, Shindo suggests that the two events are perhaps different in
degree, but not in kind.

The finest Japanese film on atomic war was Akira Kurosawa's 1955
Record of a Living Being. The central character is Mr. Nakajima, the
owner of a factory, who becomes obsessed during the mid-1950s with
genuine dread of an impending new atomic attack on Japan. Determined
to sell all the family possessions, including his factory, and migrate to
Brazil, he is thwarted by his children, who convince his wife to help them
escape this fate by having Nakajima declared mentally incompetent. In

despair, and as a means of coercing them to make this move with him, Nakajima (Toshiro Mifune) burns down the factory. In the end he is confined to a mental hospital where he confuses sunlight streaming into his cell with the burning of the earth, the result, in his now truly disordered mind, of another bomb having been dropped as expected.

It should be noted that *Record of a Living Being* was made in the midst of hydrogen bomb tests at Bikini and elsewhere. Fear of radioactive fallout was especially acute in Japan. And a conversation with his friend, composer Fumio Hayasaka, then fatally ill, on the subject of the Bikini experiments led Kurosawa to his decision to "make a satire on the H-bomb."[4]

Over the credits, with visuals of teeming Tokyo streets, Kurosawa and Hayasaka add an ominous-sounding music, as if it were the whistle of a spirit presaging the end of the world, which the people, bustling along, have failed in their self-absorption to recognize. This music and its accompanying imagery suggest the validity of Nakajima's concern about a new atomic attack, the threat of which only the most sensitive and genuinely benevolent among us perceive. Everyone else is preoccupied with the selfish details of his personal life, having long since forgotten the suffering of the people of Hiroshima. Nakajima is a better person because he alone remembers this slaughter of the innocents and wishes to protect his family from a similar fate. Nakajima is also made a sympathetic figure by the introduction into the film of a dentist named Harada (Takashi Shimura), who is one of the three mediators at the Domestic Relations Court where Nakajima is hauled by his angry sons.

Harada, whose job it is to determine whether Nakajima's obsession with the atomic bomb is proof that he has lost his mind, represents common sense and the truth as every right-minded Japanese would see it. He refuses to dismiss Nakajima's obsession as the delusion of a madman. "Aren't we worried about H-Bombs ourselves? It's a feeling all of us Japanese have more or less . . . the very sight of him strikes home to our hearts." Harada speaks for Kurosawa and for the film. Through the absurdity of having a single Japanese—and, by extension, all Japanese—selling his possessions and leaving his country for good, Kurosawa tries to direct his audience not to forget what happened at Hiroshima and Nagasaki. In this spirit Harada reads a book called *The Ash of Death* about the effects of the atomic bomb, and remarks that "if the birds and animals were to read it, they'd flee from Japan."

If the idea of buying a farm and moving to Brazil seems insane as a solution to the problem of nuclear war, it is not for the reasons expressed by Nakajima's selfish, quarrelsome family, who wish only not to sacrifice the conveniences of living in Japan in exchange for a South American rural backwater.. The most magnificent moment in the film, and one of the most brilliant scenes in the history of Japanese cinema, comes on the morning after Nakajima has burned down his factory. Panning horizontally and vertically, Kurosawa surveys the ruins. In overhead shots we observe that the factory workers, who had been Nakajima's employees, have

---

[4] Quoted in Richie, *Films of Akira Kurosawa*, p. 109.

gathered around his house. Two bicker among themselves as to the cause of the fire. One even begs Nakajima to forgive *him*, assuming a responsibility for this disaster that is clearly not his.

Nakajima kneels and admits that he set the fire himself. And the workers immediately reply with the most logical of answers, exposing the flaw in his plan that Nakajima had failed to perceive: "You don't mind if we starve? Can we go to the dogs?" Groveling in the mud, Nakajima at once realizes his mistake. For his plan to have made sense, to have been truly humane, everyone connected with him—and, ultimately, all of Japan— had to be saved from atomic attack, not only his own extended family. And so, because he is a good man, he must beg the forgiveness of those whom, in his selfishness, he would have left behind to perish, and whom he has now rendered unemployed: "My error. Forgive me. I'll find a way to take you all. I was wrong to think only of ourselves. We must all survive."

This further confirmation of his sincerity coincides with Nakajima's descent into real insanity, for of course he could not take all Japanese to South America. Yet if his fears are well-founded, all Japanese would have to abandon Japan if they were to survive. Nakajima's scheme is also "insane" because his plan not only failed to see that, were Japan in danger of nuclear attack, he should be concerned with all Japanese, but also that not only Japan is in such peril. Other nations may also become the victims of such a disaster. As Nakajima's parasitic son-in-law points out, "No place on earth is safe."

The style of *Record of a Living Being* becomes uneven in the last part of the film once Kurosawa abruptly abandons Nakajima to express a larger point of view, one beyond that of his good-natured but intellectually limited character. There is no one to take Nakajima's place at the center of the film once his vision has been exposed as inadequate, and the spectator is left disoriented. In prison, where Nakajima is temporarily locked up after he has burned down his factory, another point of view is offered by two fellow prisoners who now briefly reiterate the error of which the well-meaning Nakajima has been guilty: "H-Bombs, eh! . . . why don't you move out of the earth?" Yet they also remark, "let the Prime Minister do the worrying," arguing that such things are not our responsibility, and thus returning us to sympathy with Nakajima, who understood that we must not leave the question of our survival in the hands of others.

Nakajima is the typical Kurosawa hero, too great a man not to insist on doing something about his fate. "I hate to be killed," Nakajima had said in his understated way. It is not a question of cowardice that leads him to choose migration; this is why *I Live in Fear*, sometimes used as the English title for this film, is a mistake. "I have no fear at all," Nakajima remarks at one point. He experienced fear only, as he tells Harada, after the case had been decided against him. Then he began to feel "helpless . . . as I think of it, it gives me the jitters . . . this is a living inferno." As patriarch and head of his family, he was even willing to forgo this supremacy if it meant saving his family from extinction. In one scene he gets down on his hands and knees and begs them all to go with him to Brazil, because, he

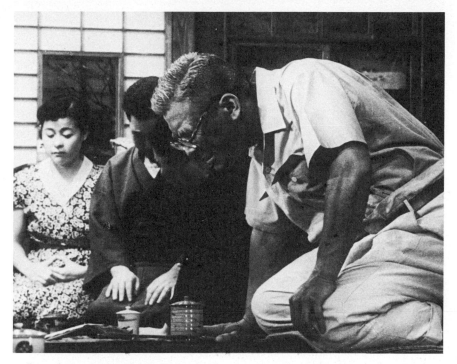

Record of a Living Being: Through the absurdity of a single Japanese—and by extension all Japanese—selling his possessions and leaving his country for good, Kurosawa tries to direct the audience not to forget what happened at Hiroshima and Nagasaki.

pleads, pointing to the baby of his youngest mistress, "I can't let an H-Bomb get him."

Nakajima is "insane" because his vision isn't large enough, not because it is too grand. The implication which Kurosawa does not develop, creating the most serious weakness of the film, is that the actions of any single individual alone cannot solve the problem of the ever-present threat of nuclear war. Yet, if we are all to be saved, a strategy replacing Nakajima's faulty vision must be envisioned by someone. By default, the film is left to express only the limited view conveyed in those first shots over the credits; we are too absorbed in the routines of our personal lives to be anything more than apathetic. Our imaginations are too circumscribed by our own greed for us to care enough to do something toward preventing a nuclear war. Kurosawa falls short of counterposing to Nakajima's quixotic plan a more effective means of approaching the threat of nuclear war. Lacking this dimension, the film seems incomplete, as if something remains to be said.

Visiting Nakajima in the mental hospital where he has been permanently confined, dentist Harada feels guilt over having precipitated Nakajima's breakdown. And in deep focus, while the truly insane cavort behind him, Nakajima's doctor, inspired by his case, wonders whether he himself is a sane man: "Or am I the lunatic?" The theme of the double—the interchangeability of our identities—was introduced earlier in the film in a wipe from Nakajima at court in close shot to Harada in his undershirt at home, still pondering the case. The imagery is like the double reflection of kidnapper and victim at the end of *High and Low* (*Tengoku to Jigoku*, 1963): one could be the other. The introduction of the image of duality is another means Kurosawa employs in *Record of a Living Being* to force us to question premises we have always taken for granted and to consider their opposite. We—who do nothing about the threat of nuclear war—are the lunatics. Nakajima—who did as much as a single man can do—is the visionary.

The point of view of *Record of a Living Being* shifts further away from Nakajima in the last scene because he has now become truly psychotic. Again the film takes on a lopsided effect, although by this means Kurosawa is able to introduce another facet to his theme: only men who are indeed mad can be complacent about their safety. Now insane, Nakajima believes the danger of nuclear attack no longer exists. In the asylum he believes he has found a place where the bomb can be escaped. "Here you're completely safe. Be assured. By the way, what happened to the earth? Still many men there? They'd better escape soon. They'd better wake up. This planet is safe."

Here Kurosawa leaves the theme of nuclear attack. Instead of suggesting a more profound direction than that taken by his hero with his 8mm films of farms in Brazil, he concludes with a rather flat challenge to our sanity. Given the magnitude of the subject, the ending of *Record of a Living Being* offers an insufficient perspective.

The literal ending of the film also attempts to provide a moment of uplift which tries to do through symbol what the film has finally failed to achieve. The humanitarian ending seems as false and gratuitous as the woodcutter's restoring the priest's faith in humanity by offering to adopt a suddenly abandoned baby at the end of *Rashomon*. Harada, coming from his visit with Nakajima, descends the hospital stairs. Passing him on her way up, providing a nice conflict of motion within the shot, is Nakajima's young mistress with her baby. Only she had been unselfish enough to be willing to go to Brazil because Nakajima had set so much stock in this dream; now it is she who cares enough about him to visit. The baby "ascending" the stairs seems a rather facile means of suggesting an equally trite idea: that hope resides in the future with the young. This suggestion that human kindness is all leaves the film with a very weak ending. It implies a view that the film seemed to derive its *raison d'être* by challenging: that no one can—and hence should not try to—do anything about nuclear bombs, and that small acts of human kindness remain our only source of redemption. By further implication, the ending even suggests that to try to escape nuclear attack will lead one only to the asylum doors. Yet, despite these weaknesses, the film itself, like Nakajima's own noble effort, contains so much that is fine—and grandiloquent—that Kurosawa's failure to perceive exactly how to resolve his subject can never wholly diminish its power.

Given the continued American military presence in Japan into the 1970s, it should not be surprising that some of the most powerful of the post-war films were satires condemning the injustices of the victors toward the defeated Japanese. In *The Idiot*, concerned as he is with fidelity to Dostoevski's novel, Kurosawa nevertheless introduces the theme of the trauma to Japan's young soldiers of the horrifying last days of the war. The hero, Kameda (Masayuki Mori), Dostoevski's Mishkin, has a nightmare on the crowded ship returning to Japan early in the film. As the camera slinks down the stairs along and past the sleeping bodies jammed together like sardines, Kameda dreams that he is about to be shot by the Americans as a war criminal.

Only at the last possible moment do the authorities discover that they have the wrong man. Later, Kameda describes his having almost been killed by the victorious Americans as one of the defining experiences of his life. Because he is inherently a good man, it taught him not to value his own existence but to cherish that of others. "The world suddenly seemed dear to me," he says. "I wondered why I hadn't been kinder." And, accompanied by a choral soundtrack, he adds, "I felt as if I were going mad."

Kurosawa attributes the compassion toward others of his Japanese Mishkin to his coming this close to senseless death during the war. His "idiocy," manifested as an emotional vulnerability, seems much more unacceptable in the Japanese than in the Russian context. But Kurosawa renders credible such apparent weakness in a Japanese male, who generally conceals his feelings by presenting to the world the facade of a fearless samurai, by tracing it back to Kameda's having survived the purgations of the war.

One of the most powerful treatments of the subject of the war criminal was Masaki Kobayashi's *The Thick-Walled Room*. It was made in protest against the cruel treatment of Japanese soldiers and low-ranking officers after the end of the war, and particularly against the hastily arranged war crimes trials in which it was enough for one or two native "witnesses" to point him out for a Japanese to be condemned to a long prison sentence.

Kobayashi's heroes are Japanese conscripts, the rank and file of the army who are unjustly designated as "B" and "C" ranking war criminals, although their actions were always at the behest of a commanding officer, himself not always so punished. ("A" category war criminals were those condemned at the Tokyo trials and were people in positions similar to that of Adolph Eichmann in Germany). Kobayashi's interest, however, is not so much in blaming the American army for carelessly ruining the lives of men who had already suffered so much. *The Thick-Walled Room* goes much further, condemning the entire system which during the war permitted these conscripts to be so used by their superiors, only to punish them later for the obedience and loyalty that the Japanese army had taught them was the highest good.

Although the Americans who guard and abuse the "criminals" in this film had officially departed with the Occupation the preceding year, 1952, the Shochiku company, for whom Kobayashi made the film, was asked by the Japanese government "voluntarily" to withhold it from distribu-

The Thick-Walled Room: Kobayashi becomes a partisan of neither side, the Japanese nor the American.

tion so as not to offend the United States. Kobayashi was requested to cut and alter the film, removing his unflattering portrayals of the Americans. His protests and attempts to convince them otherwise were in vain. Finally he chose to shelve the firm entirely and to wait for a more auspicious moment when it could be shown intact. *The Thick-Walled Room* was finally released in 1956.

In one of the most interesting political films to emerge in the postwar period, Kobayashi, as in *The Human Condition,* becomes a partisan of neither side, the Japanese nor the American. The imprisoned Japanese soldiers are not portrayed as innocents who never committed crimes of war. Some had, in fact, murdered native civilians, for which they are punished by lifelong nightmares, as well as by incarceration. But all these barbarous acts, Kobayashi insists, were done under orders.

The Americans, while they are not wholly condemned, are most often represented in this film as callow and merciless. At the Sugami Camp, a prison housing these "war criminals," they poke the men with rifles, singing "My Darling Clementine." They punish the men with hard labor for the crime of reading a newspaper and are shown to be the corrupters of Japanese women who wait for them at night beyond the barbed wire.

In a flashback to a war crimes trial held in Indonesia, the Americans herd the Japanese like cattle, while the natives gleefully run, carrying spears and sticks, to participate in the makeshift executions. One MP cruelly and gratuitously grabs away a rag doll one of the Japanese soldiers had been clutching for comfort. In the most powerful moment of the sequence, three Japanese are killed at once, in a shot composed so as to remind us of the image of Christ and the two thieves. The Americans, as if always in need of some victim, some scapegoat, then turn on the natives and abuse them. Kobayashi's point is that if the Japanese mistreated the local population in the Pacific theater, the Americans did the same, and that all men behave in the same way during war.

Kobayashi's bitterest satire is directed toward the Japanese officer class, toward those who rule and force others to implement the decisions they make solely to perpetuate their power. When someone in the film says, "if you really understand, you can't be a good officer," the point applies to both sides. Anderson and Richie suggest that Kobayashi compromised his integrity by one-sidedly attacking the Americans, particularly in one war crimes trial run by the United States in which the judge and prosecutor are shown to be the same person, implying a widespread model.[5] But the scene is so brief as to absolve Kobayashi of even the implication that this one incident represents the behavior of the Americans on all occasions. And it is more than compensated for by the crematorium scene, in which the Americans are humanized and shown to be compassionate. An American soldier says "*Arigato*" to a girl offering winter flowers for the dead. Such moments serve to express Kobayashi's feeling that men are corrupted by the system they serve, and that human nature, when left to express itself beyond political exigencies, may present a very different picture.

The criticism that Kobayashi is guilty in this film of unmediated anti-Americanism is undermined as well by the fact that he is equally critical of the official Japanese side. The war criminals believe, correctly as it turns out, that the end of the American Occupation and the transfer of power to the Japanese will not ensure their release. And Kobayashi is totally sympathetic with their view that those who didn't oppose the war, and those who started and sustained it, such as the heads of the giant corporations, are much more responsible for any atrocities committed than they. Like the Americans, the Japanese army mistreats its prisoners. In flashback we witness an American being beaten by his Japanese captors, only to be dragged out, scarred and bleeding, to die, as the traveling camera passes along a line of appalled American prisoners of war.

One of the Japanese "war criminals" believes he is in prison because he is a Korean, and that only during the war, when he was risking his life, was he considered by the government to be a "Japanese citizen." The film becomes a microcosm of all the injustices permeating Japanese society. The more insistently Kobayashi reveals that it was official power that was truly responsible for the war, the more sympathetic becomes his treatment of the men confined to their "thick-walled room." These war criminals are shown to be deeply distraught over the violent acts they were ordered to commit against the native populations of the Pacific Islands. One dreams

---

[5] *Japanese Film: Art and Industry*, p. 221.

that he is reaching for some flowers, only to have them wither at his touch, so disgraced and degenerate does he feel himself to be. Kobayashi's view is that such remorse and suffering should be punishment enough for these hapless men.

The most sustained characterization is that of the bearded Yamashita. Led by his troop commander, Hamada, Yamashita and his fellow soldiers are shown in flashback trekking through the swampy Indonesian jungles. At intervals the group is strafed by American planes. And in the midst of this wilderness they are succored and fed by a friendly native, a sweet man who, when they are gone, washes the dishes in a stream, singing as he works. Yamashita's figure appears reflected in the stream. He has been sent back by Hamada to kill the native, who is now a danger to them because he has seen their faces. Yamashita shoots him down in cold blood, to be forever haunted by the memory of this senseless murder.

Captured as a war criminal, Yamashita had been tortured and beaten, awakening in the morning to find himself lying in a pile of mud. At his trial he appears more dead than alive. We witness his superior, Hamada, lying and testifying that there had been no reason for the native to have been killed. As a result of this testimony, and taking the word of one witness, Hamada, who is himself more to blame for the murder, the Americans sentence Yamashita to life imprisonment.

The injustice visited upon men like Yamashita affects their families as well. His mother cannot visit him in prison because she will lose her ration privileges if the Americans see that she can afford a train ticket, so scrutinized and harassed are the civilian Japanese by their occupiers. Meanwhile, Hamada, now free and a neighbor, plots to evict Yamashita's mother from her land or to seize the land in exchange for jobs at his factory which he would offer to other members of this impoverished family. Beset by these consequences of her son's wartime experiences in Indonesia, Yamashita's mother attempts suicide.

In response to this family crisis, Yamashita is given a one-day leave from the prison. On the streets he is shocked to find wounded former soldiers playing musical instruments or begging for money, as Kobayashi condemns Japanese indifference to those who had willingly gone off to sacrifice their lives for the fatherland. By the time Yamashita arrives home, his mother has died. In a flashback we hear the voice of a woman crying, "Who killed my son? Who killed my son?" He has lost a mother, just as the mother of his victim had lost a son. At this moment the image of his victim's mother rushes into Yamashita's consciousness, she who had beaten him with a stick and caused him to cry. The overlap of his sobs in the past coincides with his sorrow at the funeral of his own mother.

Yamashita decides to kill Hamada in revenge. At Hamada's house he finds his enemy in bed with his baby, simultaneously the loving father and the betraying comrade. Facing Hamada, Yamashita grabs for his neck. In an extreme close-up he sees in a brilliant short intercut, not the face of Hamada, but that of the native he had killed in Indonesia. Yamashita will not kill Hamada because "killing is inhuman, whether or not the victim deserves it," the pacifist point of view toward which the film leans.

Choral music presides at the end as Yamashita and the others are locked once more into their cells at the Sugami prison. The suffering of these "B" and "C" war criminals will continue as long as the society proceeds on its unregenerate course in which, as someone says, "anyone for peace is called a Communist." McCarthyism reigns in Japan as it does in the United States in the 1950s. With official Japan as corrupt as it is, mercy is out of the question for these men. Kobayashi does not spoil his film—or distort history—by suggesting any hope for these Japanese war veterans who are among Japan's most ill-used victims.

A brilliant protest against the continuing American military occupation of Japan was Shohei Imamura's *Pigs and Battleships.* Its hero, a youth named Kinta, has his life destroyed within the semi-gangster milieu spawned by the American base at Yokosuka. Kinta and his fellow would-be mobsters live off the black market graft nurtured by the base and, in symbolism that never suffers for its obviousness, raise hogs to be fed on the garbage of the American base, just as the Japanese have been force-fed the garbage of American culture since the war.

The Americans are, of course, the "pigs" of the title, for they truly behave like pigs toward the Japanese men and women in this film. But the pigs are also these Japanese *yakuza* themselves, since not only do the Americans abuse them and treat them as something less than human beings, but they themselves have been tempted by the greed and the example set by the occupiers. If the Americans are amoral, their petty *yakuza* imitators who would live off the leavings of their profligate wealth are equally so.

With much more subtlety than Kobayashi, Imamura mourns the weakening of Japanese culture by its miscegenation with American values, the inevitable result of the American presence in Japan. On Kinta's jacket—in English—is written "Japan." When he says "I love you" to his girlfriend Haru, it is also in English, as if his deepest self has been penetrated and distorted by the American succubus. In many of the shot compositions in the background, overshadowing the lives of Kinta and Haru, Imamura presents gargantuan images of the bay full of American ships. They express the temptation of ill-gotten wealth tantalizing boys like Kinta, and to be achieved only through symbiotic ill-doings with the Americans.

Imamura sometimes presents his own point of view through the character of Haru (Jitsuko Yoshimura). Constantly she urges Kinta to free himself from the corrupt black market environment spawned by the Americans at Yokosuka and become a blue-collar worker at a factory in Kawasaki. She even threatens to "play around with the G.I.'s" if he doesn't agree to the move. But the temptations presented by the Americans are too strong for directionless youths like Kinta to resist. For these temptations and the materialistic values brought to Japan by the

American army have permeated Japanese culture down to the education system. Japanese children are indoctrinated into believing that Western culture is superior to theirs. Imamura has Haru's nephew study a post-war schoolbook from which he reads aloud: "The reason Japan developed so fast was that it adopted Western culture so effectively," a view prevalent among Cold-War-oriented American academics in Japanese studies, the "modernization" school, and accepted in Japan by Japanese eager to curry favor with the powerful.

Imamura's feeling is that the contribution of American culture to Japanese life is summed up by Yokosuka and its environs. At the end of *Pigs and Battleships* Kinta is to die a tragi-comic death amidst a herd of hogs running free. Haru, however, despite the temptations offered by the big new American battleship arriving at the port and stimulating a crowd of women to come and say "hello" to the Yankees, wipes off her lipstick and leaves for Kawasaki, where she and Kinta were to have begun their new life together.

Everywhere Imamura's imagery challenges the right of the Americans to remain in Japan. Early in the film, as a girl is rounded up in a paddy wagon after a raid on the red light district, she vows to become a ghost and return to plague the Americans. The "Star-Spangled Banner" is played over a pan of Yokosuka harbor, an assertion that Japan has become little more than an American possession. Imamura's credits at the beginning of the film take up only one-third of the screen, the remaining two-thirds filled with battleships and trucks full of hogs on their way to the naval base, as if the Japanese were being crowded out of their own country. Slums surround the American base and gangsters flourish. If the black market is a temptation to the male youths, the omnipresent houses of prostitution to service the sailors offer the promise of instant wealth to impoverished young Japanese women like Haru. Some even dream of going to America. Upset with Kinta, in one scene Haru does solicit among the American sailors, only to have three of them rape her. Afterwards, in homosexual glee, ignoring the woman who was never of more than sadistic interest to them, the three take a shower together, singing "I've Been Working on the Railroad" at the top of their lungs. When Haru tries to take some money for her pains, they beat her mercilessly, fearing no recriminations from the military authorities.

Toward the would-be gangsters with their joint Japan–United States pig farm, Imamura is ironic. No matter how illegal their actions, for sheer depravity they could never equal the American military. In one scene Imamura has them decide to adopt "democratic methods" for their organization; in another they greedily devour a roast pig only to discover a tooth in it and find they had eaten a pig to which a corpse had been fed as a means of disposing of the body.

Yet no matter how ruthless their own behavior, they remain vulnerable and easy prey for the Americans. The chief among these gangsters (Tetsuro Tamba) attempts suicide when he learns—from X-rays that turn out not to have been his own—that he has stomach cancer. Inept

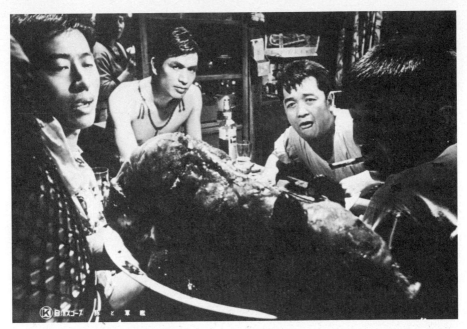

Pigs and Battleships: Toward the would-be gangsters with their joint Japan—
United States pig farm, Imamura is ironic. No matter how illegal their actions,
they could never equal the American military for sheer depravity.

and ridiculous, they are soon to be taken over by truly professional
gangsters moving into the area. Before long a sleek Nisei appears, to
cash in on the lucrative Yokosuka operation, calling the Tamba-style
amateurs ineffective *yakuza,* "pigs."

Pigs and Battleships, with its lack of any hero with whom we could
identify, is an angry film. Imamura is bitter and outraged at the Japanese
for so catering to the Americans for money alone, and for admiring the
supposedly superior strength of their enemy, allowing themselves all the
while to be brutalized and degraded. As Phantom jets blaze in the skies,
a reflection of the "nuclear umbrella" for which Japan has mortgaged
the culture of its people, we hear Japanese spectators murmur admiringly,
"Americans are so great. Different from our Self-Defense Army." They
wave both Japanese and American flags. And when they are not fawning
on the Americans, they are playing the "March of the Battleships,"
longing for their own days of military glory, now forever past. Imamura
thus directs his satire at his own people, rejecting the facile rhetoric of
anti-Americanism and refusing to blame the Americans alone for the
debasement of Japanese culture. For this to have occurred, the Japanese
themselves must have acquiesced in their own enslavement; it was for
them to remember who they are. Imamura mourns that the Japanese so
doubt their culture, simply because they lost the war, that they immediately exchange their uniquely Japanese ways for the bastardized
American culture thrust upon them by the Occupation.

Imamura's savage farce reaches its culmination in a brilliant ending.

One night, all the hogs are loaded in trucks. It is to be Kinta's last gang operation, after which, he has promised, he will accompany Haru to Kawasaki. But the gang has turned against Kinta, hoggishly desiring to keep all the hogs for themselves. Tamba, Kinta's protector, didn't bother to prevent this betrayal since, based on that wrong X-ray, he believed that he was dying anyway.

Kinta grabs a machine gun and fights it out with his former friends, while the Japanese police give them only a traffic ticket—despite the bedlam that has broken loose—because they have been bribed by the Americans and are themselves in on the sale of the hogs. In the fray the hogs get loose and descend from the trucks into the streets. The American "pigs" have set the Japanese "pigs" against each other and Kinta is fatally shot. The real pigs now chase the horrified gangsters to the end of the road, while all the while they call each other "pigs." The gangsters trip and fall in their haste and the pigs trample and crush them, just as these *yakuza* have been no match for the Americans. In a filthy bathroom, a thirsty, wounded, expiring Kinta tries to drag himself to a water hose. With the camera overhead emphasizing the squalor of his last moments, he falls dead, his head leaning over the toilet.

In the rescue operation that follows, some of the stretchers bear the bodies of men, some those of pigs, making no distinction between them, as the Japanese have been rendered pigs by pigs. Finally locating the body of Kinta, no one having had the decency even to close the dead man's eyes, Haru can only yell "fool" at the top of her lungs. With artificial light spotlighting her face, Imamura uses her as a voice of conscience needed to awaken the Japanese from the corruption to which they have been assenting. In her departure from Yokosuka, Haru suggests that it is better to be a low-paid factory worker than a *yakuza* made rich by dealings with the Americans. Imamura's position with respect to the continuing American military presence in Japan couldn't be clearer. If the Japanese were to be true to themselves, they would scorn and shun the Americans. And the Japanese are ever in danger, not only culturally, but in terms of their very lives, the longer they tolerate the existence of the Yokosukas within their borders.

Much less politically explicit were those films, sometimes documentary in style, portraying the devastation of the war as it affected the lives of ordinary Japanese. The widespread unemployment, near-starvation, and homelessness caused by the American bombings of Japan's cities in 1945 undermined the institution of the family much more than any Occupation edicts about democratization. Some believed that Japan's defeat in the service of the ultimate principle of feudalism—loyalty to the Emperor—led to the undermining, especially in the young, of many of the traditional obediences that, like the war, may have been unhealthy and inappropriate all along. To some extent, new freedoms entered the culture with an educational system that no longer inculcated doctrines of absolute submission to authority. It became possible, at least in theory, for women to engage in politics, business, and aspects of social life that had hitherto been closed to them. These were uncertain times, when people were not sure how far these new freedoms should be extended. Many, like director Yasujiro Ozu, mourned their presence altogether.

But such epochs, when it seems at last as if the entire social order is being transformed, are immensely valuable and rich to the artist. Japanese films during the ten years following the war gained an immediacy and relevance by focusing on the very problems being debated in the society at large, problems as yet unresolved. An extraordinary number of superb works were made at this time, comprising, perhaps, the finest single group of films ever made in Japan.

Pigs and Battleships: In the rescue operation some of the stretchers bear the bodies of men, some those of pigs, making no distinction between them, as the Japanese have been rendered pigs by pigs.

Most of these films speak against war because of the havoc it wreaks on the lives of ordinary citizens. Their directors are more concerned with the phenomenon of the passing of the traditional way of life than with the particular issues on behalf of which the war was fought and lost. In A Hen in the Wind (Kaze No Naka No Mendori, 1948), Ozu brilliantly and honestly confronts the postwar moment. A wife (Kinuyo Tanaka) whose soldier husband (Shuji Sano), a prisoner of war, is long in being repatriated, has no recourse but to turn to a single night of prostitution as a means of financing her son's hospital bills. The husband returns. When his wife admits to him that she sold her body, he reacts violently. And even when, intellectually, he realizes that, as a woman with no means, she had no choice but to sell herself, his feelings toward her remain those of shame, loathing, and revulsion.

Running parallel with this "home drama" of husband and "unfaithful" wife, Ozu simultaneously tells another story, an allegory of the fate of traditional Japanese values in the postwar period. Returning from the front, Japanese soldiers are confronted by a tawdry, Westernized Japan which has prostituted itself to the culture of the Occupation. Just beyond the office where the hero returns to work, there is now a sleazy cabaret where men and women dance cheek-to-cheek in Western style to cheap jazz, a music made similar by Ozu to the canned music at the house of prostitution where the wife spent that one fateful night.

There the husband goes, in anguish and distrust, to discover whether his wife had indeed spent only one night under this roof, as she claims. In a fine and subtle interjection of "comment," Ozu shows us the husband at this brothel, but never his wife. We don't see her there precisely because Ozu wishes to argue that, spiritually, in her deepest self, she never was there, just as a real and authentic Japan can and will continue to exist as long as it retains its determination to resist, as best it can, the Occupation's despoliation of the culture.

Ozu's aim is to reconcile the Japanese to their culturally decimated homeland, just as the husband must come to terms with the fact of his wife's "impurity." She prostituted herself to protect what was good in Japanese life, symbolized by the child, Hiro, named, not coincidentally, for the Emperor. Ozu is thus telling the Japanese to submit to the new society for the sake of a greater good, something precious within Japanese life which, he is confident, will remain unsullied by the Occupation.

More clearly than most postwar directors, Ozu shows the cultural dilemma facing the Japanese. On his visit to the brothel the husband is offered a twenty-one-year-old prostitute, whose favors he refuses. The two glance out the window at a grade school next door. Wafting across come the sweet voices of singing children. She herself once went to that school. Now she—Japan—once innocent, must sell herself. The girl's justification is that the war has made her the sole support of her family, an excuse as valid as that offered by the man's own wife for performing the same act.

This scene in the brothel in A Hen in the Wind represents one of the most acute moments of social consciousness in Ozu's films. It is exceeded only, perhaps, by the last shots of another postwar Ozu work, *Record of a Tenement Gentleman* (*Nagaya Shinshi Roku*, 1947). Amid the wreckage of a devastated Japan, Ozu focuses on a crowd of orphans in Ueno Park clothed in rags. Smoking, they are motionless, only now and then intently scratching their lice-ridden bodies. These orphans are sitting under a statue of Saigo Takamori with which Ozu, in a full shot, had introduced the scene.

In the 1870s Saigo was a fierce advocate of imperial adventures for Japan in Southeast Asia. His statue must now face the victims of his grandiose scheme for the conquest of Korea, a plan rejected in his own time only to be made a vital part of national policy in the imperial war he did not live to see. Ozu has someone remark that there must be a million such children in postwar Japan. And under the statue of Saigo some of these homeless children hover, the legacy of such militarist policies as his. It is the most politically meaningful image in the entire Ozu canon, inspired as it is by his horror of the new Japan to which his young men had to return from the war.

The theme is fully realized, however, only in *A Hen in the Wind*, which Ozu has called a "bad failure"[6] without explaining why. One reason may well be the shifting of the film's point of view from that of the wife, to, upon his return, that of the husband. In the first half of the film we see only the wife and, of course, we sympathize totally with her as she worries over her ailing child. Like the boy in Ozu's silent *Passing Fancy*, he has succumbed to colitis as a result of the overindulgence of an insecure parent. We watch her selling her kimonos, worrying over not having enough to eat, not having enough money even to buy rations. But once the husband returns from the war, Ozu wishes to expand his theme to view the moral consequences of the entire postwar culture, and the film seems structurally to break in half.

The second part of the film, recording the husband's anguish, is easily the more subtle and complex. As in *There Was a Father*, the moral questions at issue are resolved in a somewhat didactic scene in which a temporarily erring character, in this case the husband, is led back to his duty. The "*sensei*" in *A Hen in the Wind*, as so often in Ozu, is played by Chishu Ryu, the director's surrogate, who here plays the small role of the husband's boss.

The boss points out to the husband that if he can forgive the twenty-one-year-old prostitute and help her to find a more respectable job, why can't he forgive his own wife? The husband, in all honesty, replies that his feelings won't permit him to change. His boss then advises him, as Ozu implicitly advises all older Japanese appalled by the postwar confusion, to change his feelings through "will power" and "do it fast."

Thus, reluctantly, Ozu urges the Japanese to accept the decimation of the traditional culture, which is perhaps why, despite Ozu's horror at the Westernization of Japan, this film could never have displeased SCAP and the Occupation censors. The husband must forgive his wife, just as in their

[6] "Ozu on Ozu," *Kinema Jumpo*, June 1958. Translated by Leonard Schrader.

An Autumn Afternoon: Ryu, at the thought of the blue-eyed ones in New York plunking samisens, remarks that it might not have been such a bad thing, after all, for Japan to have lost the war.

office in the Time/Life International Building, he and his fellow workers must live with the cabaret music blaring just beyond their desks. At such a time more than ever strength of will is demanded of the Japanese people that they might accept the new society. The jazz of the cabaret, representing the new culture, makes the husband sad. His boss, offering him more *sake* if he needs it, advises him to "make it sound happy" through an effort of will. As always, Ozu concludes that we must accept the powers that be, make a virtue of necessity. It is a moment he will repeat over and over, the last time in his final film, *An Autumn Afternoon* (*Samma no Aji*, 1962), when Ryu, at the thought of the blue-eyed ones in New York plunking samisens, remarks that it might not have been such a bad thing, after all, for Japan to have lost the war.

But it is not easy to accept the profaning of something sacred, as traditional Japanese like Ozu and the husband of *A Hen in the Wind* believe their culture to be. When the husband returns after two days' absence, his wife, true to the Japanese manner of attempting to deal with an unresolvable problem by ignoring it, welcomes him home as if nothing has happened. Furious, he pushes her away. When she persists in seeking a reconciliation, he pushes her even harder, sending her sprawling down the steep flight of stairs leading to their tiny apartment. With a fierce clatter, her head bumping on every step, she falls to the bottom, unconscious. It is the moment of the greatest violence in all of Ozu's films, expressive of the director's own anger at what the war and the Occupation have made of

Japan. It is especially horrifying because we feel that in some sense the director half sides with the husband, sadistically punishing this woman for not somehow, however impossibly, being stronger.

Her husband does not help her up, but retreats upstairs, leaving her to hobble up as best she might. He places himself with his back to the door. She begs his forgiveness, all she can do, entreating him to "do anything you like . . . I can take anything." Ozu does not overtly condemn the brutal act of violence because only with such an extreme physical action can the husband achieve the catharsis necessary to accept his wife's prostitution. He had told his boss that as soon as he heard of her "fall," he felt always "like shouting." His pent-up anger required a dramatic form of release, and Ozu thus does not blame him for a cruelty he cannot help, any more than the wife could help what she did. No one is to blame. Although this time Ozu doesn't explicitly introduce the phrase "it can't be helped," he might well have.

The couple are now free to agree to love and trust each other more. In an embrace rare for an Ozu film, but suitable following the equally rare violence, Tanaka's arms meet behind her husband's back. Her hands are clasped together as they had been in the earlier scene when she prayed for her son's recovery. The clasped hands bespeak not only a prayer that things will at last take a turn for the better, but also her own will to go on, her thankfulness at having been given the chance.

In the final shot of *A Hen in the Wind*, the title suggesting a woman, Japan, no longer stable and secure, a dog walks toward the camera. It is the dog the wife had yearned for in her youth before the war, when she dreamt of living in a house surrounded by grass and having a terrier or an Airedale. The war has forced the Japanese to modify their ambitions, yet, with the brief appearance of the dog of his heroine's dreams, Ozu suggests that better days may lie ahead. But first the Japanese must learn not to struggle recklessly and impotently against the fait accompli of their transformed culture. In acceptance alone may be found peace, harmony, and the only means of preserving those pure values which, finally, even the crassest of Occupations can never touch.

"All are lost in this postwar darkness," says a title before the credits in Keisuke Kinoshita's *A Japanese Tragedy* (*Nihon no Higeki*, 1953). The newsreel footage which opens this film begins with the Imperial decision to terminate the war and includes war crimes trials, the news that the Emperor is not to be tried (the very presence of this piece of information suggesting Kinoshita's view that he should have been), and the creation of a new constitution (1946). Eight years later, Kinoshita goes on in his titles, corruption and poverty remain. Personal tragedy engulfs the Japanese people; crime has become a daily occurrence. The story he will tell, says Kinoshita, "contains the seeds of a tragedy that may someday envelop all of Japan."

A Japanese Tragedy, modeled rather closely on Theodore Dreiser's *An American Tragedy*, is about a woman who has raised her children alone during the trying years of the war and the Occupation. For their survival, she has engaged in every kind of humiliating behavior from black market hoarding to prostitution. When the film opens, she is working as a maid at an inn, her youth having long passed. Her grown son now informs her that he wishes to be adopted by a wealthy doctor and his wife who lost their own son in the war.

Materialism pervades the new Japan of A *Japanese Tragedy*; the mother herself dabbles in the stock market. Everyone speaks only about money and the comforts it brings, a sign for Kinoshita of the degeneration of the Japanese character as a result of the war experience. The excessive materialism of the son and daughter, who care only about wealth and status, is placed in the context of the corruption of the entire society, which Kinoshita underlines by including shots of newspaper clippings describing big corporation executives caught in fraudulent activities.

Intercut as well throughout the film are scenes of the war years, expressing the suffering experienced by the Japanese people. The mother hides rice from her neighbors, and her children are humiliated at school by their classmates, who ridicule them because their mother engages in illegal activities. Not blaming her, Kinoshita has a student comment that all the rice *everyone* eats comes from the black market. Teachers at this school are accused by their students of having lied by telling them that the war was just. These experiences have been indelibly printed on the minds of the woman's son and daughter. Having realized that everything for which the Japanese once stood is now being rejected as erroneous and of little value, they have been left without anything in which to believe. As a result they have become hard and without feeling. The postwar confusion has rendered them inhuman.

Kinoshita's sympathies, however, are much more with the mother than with the children so eager to seize the new freedoms which the end of the war is granting to the Japanese. Filial love has disappeared, and yet this mother, whom her children once discovered in her capacity as a prostitute, still deserves their love. But they are no longer capable of the emotion. She tells the cook at the inn where she works to love his mother, and the singing troubador who frequents the place to do the same. Having been deformed by the environment, her own children hate her so much that when they tell her about her son Seiichi's prospective adoption, and she is visibly upset, they refuse even to walk her back to the inn. The daughter brutally admonishes her for making a scene. The son doesn't react at all to her distress.

The mother's last meeting with her son follows. Seiichi is shown in the luxurious mansion of his new father, reveling in the fine appointments. It is only in this scene, and amidst a flood of accusations, that he calls her "mother." His argument is that he will do whatever becomes necessary to succeed, allowing no scruples to come between him and his ambitions. "You know about men and sake," he tells his mother. "You're stupid. I know how to live in today's Japan." As indeed he does. He is the man of Japan's future, a self-centered materialist concerned only with his own prosperity and unmindful of any pain he causes. Worn out by the struggle, and having at last seen her children as they really are, the mother consents to the adoption. In "gratitude," ironically since she is now legally about to lose this right forever, her son calls her "mother" a second time.

It is at this point in her travail that the mother finds herself on a railway platform. She is at a crossroads in her life, as all of Japanese society after the war found itself at a moral crossroads. We watch as, in deep focus, a train appears in the distance. It turns the corner and we now know what choice she has made. She drops her bag, her shoes fly off, and she falls in front of the train. One sandal left behind, redolent of her vulnerability, is all that remains in a full shot which Kinoshita allows only a very short take.

In a coda she is mourned by the troubador and the chef whom she had urged to love their mothers. Her own children's reaction to her death is not filmed by Kinoshita, as indeed this is totally unnecessary, given the indifference we know they feel. For Kinoshita, the Japanese people as a result of the war have lost all that was precious in their heritage. Throughout the centuries, the love of children for parents, filial piety, and loyalty symbolized the humanity of the Japanese. These have now disappeared. Remaining are greed, disrespect, and selfishness. Ahead is a future of pain, given the utter deterioration of the culture's moral fabric.

A *Japanese Tragedy:* Throughout the centuries the love of children for parents, filial piety, and loyalty symbolized the humanity of the Japanese. These have now disappeared.

With Ozu and Kinoshita, Kon Ichikawa is equally dismayed over the moral chaos afflicting Japan after the war. Like Ozu, Ichikawa in *Mr. Poo* (*Pu-San*, 1953) focuses on the vulgarization of the Japanese character that has ensued, a hardening especially apparent in the Japanese woman, who has lost her natural grace and generosity of spirit. In the background of *Mr. Poo* loom *yakuza*, gangsters controlling every facet of the postwar society, including the educational system.

Unemployment reigns. In shame, fired workers must sell toy harmonicas on the street. Food is precious and scarce. Meanwhile, a full-fledged Japanese army reconstitutes itself in the wake of the Occupation, having been awarded the blessing of the SCAP, General MacArthur. In *A Japanese Tragedy* Kinoshita had also focused on this astounding and seminal event in a shot of a newspaper headline ordering expansion of the police to disperse the growing crowds of demonstrators dissatisfied with their government and the injustice permeating the new society.

That a new Japanese militarism is clearly on the horizon is one of the central themes of *Mr. Poo*, presciently depicted in its full force by Ichikawa and screenwriter Natto Wada. The American-authored New Constitution of 1946 had forbidden Japan from rearming under any circumstances, but no matter. In a world seen by Ichikawa as set squarely on its head, such incongruities can only be reported sardonically, prime material for this black humorist in one of his best films.

The title "Mr. Poo" refers to a character created by a satirical cartoonist, but he is only Ichikawa's starting point. The actual hero is a befuddled mathematics teacher named Mr. Noro, who works at a school catering to students who have failed at their university entrance examinations and are furiously cramming so that they may pass the next time. Noro's life chronicles the fate of a typical Japanese just after the Occupation. Participating, at the urging of one of his students, in a mass demonstration, for which the essentially cynical Ichikawa manifests no sympathy whatsoever, Noro finds his photograph in the next day's newspaper. At once he loses his teaching job, despite the fact that he is not, nor ever has been, a Communist Party member. The "red purges" are aimed at any dissenter, however small his voice. Unable to find work as a teacher, Noro winds up as a factory worker lucky to get a job packing clips for machine guns as postwar Japan devotes itself in full measure to rearmament.

Mr. Poo is framed by two automobile accidents in which trucks almost demolish the pedestrian Noro, just as the new rush to militarization is running roughshod over the sensibilities of the Japanese people. In the pre-dawn scene at the end, Noro is on the deserted Tokyo streets because the machine gun factory, in its haste to arm Japan, begins its daily operations at 7 A.M. Noro is again almost run over, this time by a convoy of military trucks speeding to an undisclosed destination, as Japan's new army is likely to do someday.

Noro is a widower, an old-fashioned, highly sympathetic Japanese. In the face of the postwar confusion, he is an innocent bystander. Through circumstance, he is an acquaintance of an ex-colonel named Gotsu, once a purged war criminal who made a fortune on a best-seller about his experiences in the Japanese army. He cried when he wrote it, or so he confides to his drinking companions. Now a Diet member, un-purged Gotsu, midway through *Mr. Poo*, is arrested, this time for bribery, only to write a second book, this one about his prison experiences. The new book is advertised on every pillar and post in the early morning Tokyo streets passed by Noro in the last scene as he makes his way toward the factory where he will offer his small, unwilling contribution to the remilitarization. It is a clever, witty, structural link between the beginning of the film when Gotsu cavorted in his favorite bar while Noro was being run down by a truck, and the end, where Gotsu is resurgent while Noro, the ordinary man who will never enjoy any of the benefits of the coming postwar prosperity, must again evade hostile traffic.

As usual, Ichikawa satirizes one and all. In the same bar where Gotsu brags about how his book about the Japanese army brought tears to his readers (as well as to himself), a Communist Party member reprimands a composer for not having enough of "the people" in his music. Ichikawa mocks the cliché and deepens his satire by suggesting that it may well be the sole contribution of the Communist Party to aesthetic theory. This party member then takes a cab home, his personal life and the comforts he enjoys standing in direct contradiction to the Marxist philosophy he spouts during evenings in Tokyo bars. Ichikawa leaves him and he is not to reappear in the film, his contribution to postwar recovery having already been fully assessed by a disdainful director.

The widowed Noro longs fondly for Kanko, daughter of the family with whom he boards. The new postwar woman, her values awry, Kanko cannot appreciate the kindly, tender Noro at all. Ichikawa markedly contrasts her with the sweet nurse who treated Noro for the sprained hand he suffered during his first accident. This nurse retains a manner reminiscent of the old Japan, now lost forever. Her every action bespeaks compassion, even at the end when she meets the penniless Noro in a flower shop and immediately insists upon lending him the money for a hyacinth he would offer the unfeeling Kanko. She, a spoiled, willful, stubborn woman, stages a suicide when her mother opposes her choice in marriage.

The loss of the old manners, once the treasure of the Japanese, is mourned by Ichikawa. Packed trains make dignity impossible. Noro's male students yell like wild banshees when his sprained hand makes his handwriting difficult to read. A student nephew of Colonel Gotsu in Noro's class offers to write on the blackboard for Noro, only to charge him one hundred yen for this favor, which is reduced to eighty, a bargain rate.

As in A *Japanese Tragedy*, materialist values have swept the society, especially the young. Ichikawa shares with Kinoshita the view that the young have been more deeply corrupted than their elders, their natures so calloused by the social trauma of this transitional period after Japan's defeat that they can scarcely feel any generous emotions at all. Kanko, a teller in a bank, finds pleasure in handling new money in a comic sequence full of superimpositions. Far surpassing Kinoshita in his understanding,

Ichikawa places the real blame on the resurgence of war criminals like Colonel Gotsu, now once again in full command of the society. By not finally and fully purging such people from the national life, Japan has left the door open to deceit and depravity on every level of society, from the upper echelons of government and big business to small schools like that in which Noro teaches.

And Mr. Noro? Like a traditional Japanese, he does not complain. When the *yakuza*-surrounded boss of his school has him work night and day without giving him the raise being awarded to all the other teachers, Noro replies, "I understand perfectly." He is subservient to his superiors, as he had been instructed to be in pre-war Japan. No matter, he will be fired anyway, as Ichikawa, scorning such submissiveness, reveals that the appeasement of injustice only results in its growing stronger.

As a traditional Japanese, Noro is confounded by the new, raging political discussions among his students. The would-be reactionary is against the celebration of "Foundation Day," a nationalistic holiday, because in recent observances of this occasion "sincerity" has been absent. The Mishimas are already on the scene. His opponent in this argument, in the full flush of postwar exuberance, would redefine "Foundation Day" as when the laborers overthrow the capitalists, hardly its original significa-tion. No one knows what he's talking about and apolitical Noro, an Ichi-kawa surrogate at this moment, walks away in confusion.

Ichikawa, like Kinoshita and Ozu, portrays the postwar epoch as lacking any abiding values or meaning that could see these people through toward the construction of a society expressive of all that had been valuable in their culture and ·yet free at last of feudal oppression. Instead, Marxist ideologies are debated with fury, but with neither conviction nor relevance. Demonstrations rage in full force, with Ichikawa intercutting newsreels with his own enactment so cleverly that it becomes difficult to distinguish between them.

Caught in the middle of the mass demonstration which will prove to be his downfall, Noro has his head bloodied and is arrested as well. Later, at the police station, he observes a young demonstrator being retrieved by his mother, a nice touch, for Japanese men do indeed stay "Mama's boys" so long. The demonstrator, no dissident, whines, "I want to go home. I don't like Tokyo. I'll be a farmer." So much for the view that the enor-mous postwar demonstrations represented any form of renewal for Japan, any sign of hope, any significant protest against either the cultural degen-eration or the remilitarization of Japan.

Despair is thus at the heart of Ichikawa's very funny, essentially nihilist *Mr. Poo*. Insanity is the order of the day. A tuberculosis patient with a chance at a job begs a young doctor to write him a false health certificate. The doctor, unperturbed by the possibility that the man may infect his fellow workers, urges him to work hard and qualify for sick leave. "A war would finish everything," the doctor muses. It is a very funny remark, an example of the black humor in which this film abounds. The young nurse who befriends Mr. Noro is called "innocent and pure" by this young doctor. But he goes on to remark that she is not to his liking: "too much so makes one unattractive." These are the new values now being accepted so willingly by the Japanese.

The doctor would, if he knew her, prefer the manipulative Kanko. Ichikawa is depicting a society learning to be far more at home with hypocrites like Colonel Gotsu, who yells at his chauffeur for not bowing deeply enough and who retains feudal attitudes. The young follow suit. Noro's students cannot look him in the eye once he is fired. Meanwhile movie theater audiences, Kanko the most rapt among them, watch newsreels of hydrogen bomb tests with eagerness and not a shadow of discomfort. Such is the new Japan, its citizens bewilderedly eating cabbage (as Noro does) because they have been told that their diet lacks "animal protein." Noro, our Everyman, is given this irrelevant advice when he comes for attention to his sprained hand. Instead, he is offered cliché'd panaceas which have been made substitutes for true reconstruction in this difficult hour.

Noro wants only to survive and to be himself, to enjoy his simple pleasures, like cooking his own soup. Instead, he loses a girl who traditionally would have appreciated him and been willing to share his life. Such girls, a director like Ozu would stubbornly insist in a film like *Early Summer* (*Bakushu*, 1951), still do exist, although Ozu would be the first to agree on how rare they have become.

But such a companion is not in store for Ichikawa's Noro, consigned to his machine gun factory. He leaves us as a tiny figure walking into the dawn in the last shot of *Mr. Poo*. It is for the innocent Noros that Ichikawa and Wada, despite all the comic moments in this hilarious film, retain their deepest and most abiding sympathy.

Mikio Naruse in *Floating Clouds* (*Ukigumo*, 1955) locates the immorality of postwar Japan in terms of the renewed exploitation of women. His theme, akin to that of Ichikawa in *Mr. Poo*, is that the traumas of the war have brought no new justice to Japan but have served only to exacerbate the feudal exploitation characteristic of the past. Unlike Kinoshita, Naruse is incapable of idealizing feudal injustice. The hero, Kengo Tomioka (Masayuki Mori), and the heroine, Yukiko Koda (Hideko Takamine), were lovers during the war when he was a soldier at the front and she a nurse. Repatriated in November of 1946 from Indochina, Yukiko attempts to revive their relationship. Alone and starving, like the characters in the Imai and Kinoshita films describing the hardships of the immediate postwar period, Yukiko seeks the help of her former lover. Tomioka, whose wife has kept house during his absence, may be more prosperous than she, but he is too selfish, weak, and unfaithful to respond to her plight.

Based as it is on a novel by Fumiko Hayashi, who expressed strongly and bitterly the demeaning of Japanese women like herself, the sympathies of *Floating Clouds* are totally with Yukiko, struggling to survive in postwar Japan. Straight cuts between her love affair with Tomioka in Indochina and the present indicate that for Yukiko there is no emotional hiatus between what happened then and her feelings for Tomioka in Japan now. At one point Naruse cuts on a kiss beginning in Indochina and ending in the present. But Tomioka lacks Yukiko's constancy. He is a user of women, a selfish man expecting always to be pampered and indulged. All the women with whom he is associated die in the course of the film, his wife of tuberculosis, a mistress murdered by an irate husband, and Yukiko also of tuberculosis. Tomioka is incapable of feeling compassion for any of them, forever thinking only of himself and how quickly he may satisfy his needs of the moment.

When the film opens, the war has just ended. In Tokyo homeless people stand eating their meager fare in the streets. Yukiko calls herself a helpless repatriate and envies men who are finding it easier to survive, as they always have in Japanese society. Tomioka tells her to forget the past and tries to buy her off with money, since her presence is proving to be an embarrassment to him. In response, unable to afford the luxury of pride, she offers herself to him sexually, the way Japanese women have always prostrated themselves before unworthy men. "Do what you want with me," says Yukiko. But Tomioka, a representative of the selfish ethos that will overwhelm Japan after the war, refuses her outright. "Everything has changed now," he tells this lonely, impoverished woman. He uses the postwar chaos, as do Kinoshita's second generation characters in A *Japanese Tragedy*, as an excuse for his unmediated pursuit of self-interest.

Jobless, Yukiko sells her brother-in-law's bedding to buy an overcoat to see her through the winter. Reality for Yukiko is now so bleak that she lives in a fantasy world where she dreams of the love she and Tomioka

Floating Clouds: Naruse suggests that having failed the Japanese woman in the postwar environment, the Japanese male has lost his integrity.

shared in Indochina. She is a victim of these memories. Hostesses are required to service the sexual needs of the American soldiers brought to Japan by the Occupation, and in this capacity Yukiko locates her only opportunity to support herself. When an American approaches her on the street inquiring as to whether she is "alone," she accepts him and turns to prostitution as a means of surviving.

In this way, Yukiko ceases to starve. But the price of her survival is a vulgarization of her very person and character which deeply upsets both Hayashi and Naruse. Yukiko now smokes, wears dark red lipstick, cheap earrings and an embroidered Hong Kong sweater. In her room a radio blares out "Jingle Bells." She has now become bitter, unable to discern any difference between Tomioka and the G.I.'s whom she entertains. "He fools around the way you did in Indochina," she tells Tomioka during one of their rare meetings, referring to one of the men with whom she sleeps.

Naruse suggests that, having failed the Japanese woman in this postwar environment, the Japanese male has lost his integrity. He has become no better than the exploiting Americans. Yukiko reinforces this parallel when Tomioka, having nothing better to do, asks to stay the night. "Isn't that what you came for?" she demands. It is the same thing all her male visitors want, and she is not unjust in calling him a "parasite." Tomioka calls her a "strong, independent woman," what she has had to become because he has failed her so completely.

The sufferings at the end of the war have been met by Yukiko with a strength that life seems to grant only to the oppressed. Women, in one sense, have been better able to survive with their integrity intact because, having always been enslaved within Japanese society, they possess the resources to get along. The men who have been their exploiters have grown spiritually weak and stand helpless before the furious competitiveness of the new Japan. Tomioka's fortunes fall while Yukiko's rise. In the streets outside Yukiko's room, another oppressed group, the workers, sing the "Internationale," reflecting author Fumiko Hayashi's own proletarian sentiments, which allow her to parallel the enslavement of the working class with that of women.

Yet Naruse and Hayashi are not so unrealistic as to present Yukiko as a superwoman who can withstand any and all hardship. Her economic conditions improve, but her consciousness does not develop sufficiently for Yukiko to understand her condition. For Hayashi, the Japanese woman has been too deeply enslaved for her as yet to understand her own oppression for what it is. No matter how much Tomioka abuses her, Yukiko cannot forget him. She remains a woman who, despite her bitter experiences, cannot conceive of life without a man. In particular, she cannot forget their romantic interlude in Indochina and tells Tomioka to come and see her any time he remembers what they once had together.

Meanwhile, Tomioka views her as he would a stranger, and is further alienated by her increasing maturity. Critically, he observes that she is showing signs of age; she is no longer the twenty-two-year-old with whom he dallied during the war, unmindful of the future and his waiting wife. Once Yukiko's physical appearance no longer pleases him, Tomioka takes a new mistress named Osei at the very inn where he and Yukiko have come to spend a few days together. In the background of many of the shots, trains pass. Japan, and Yukiko with it, is rushing into a future filled with the symbols of technological progress. These Naruse presents in sharp contrast to the absence of moral progress or self-knowledge among his characters, of which the primary symbol remains the continuing exploitation of women.

Like so many postwar Japanese finding their lives empty and without spiritual value, Yukiko joins a new religious sect, parallel to the neo-Buddhist Soka Gakkai which Imamura's heroine in *The Insect Woman* (*Nippon Konchuki*, 1963) also joins out of loneliness and despair. Yukiko becomes the treasurer of the "Congregation of the Believers in the Sun," which draws members with its promise that "sun-worshippers are not mortal." This sect is shown to be obviously fraudulent, but the needs of the Japanese people for some sustaining philosophy during this period are shown to be so great that the coffers of the organization are soon full. Yukiko decides to rob the Congregation of 300,000 yen with which to go off with Tomioka, still a slave to the passion that was nurtured during the war.

At the end, without financial resources of any kind, Tomioka takes a job as a forest ranger in Yakushima province. He has been reduced to complete poverty. Now fatally ill, Yukiko insists upon accompanying him, although in Yakushima it rains every day. So weak has she become that she must even be removed from the ship on a stretcher. But, incapable to the end of leaving her selfish lover, Yukiko must die in his presence.

In a rather strange ending we watch Tomioka applying lipstick to Yukiko's corpse, as if to return her to what she once was when he loved her. Naruse dissolves to a scene of the two together in Indochina, with her as the pursuer rushing after him into a forest, just as she had insisted upon coming with him now. The dissolve and flashback, which could only be from Tomioka's point of view, are somehow inconsistent with the man's character since they suggest a feeling for Yukiko that he has long since lost. And he has seemed to be a man completely incapable of fond memories.

But Naruse refuses to allow Yukiko to die without affecting Tomioka. He suggests that Tomioka's very emptiness has resulted in this memory's assuming a primary place in his consciousness. This last unrealistically placed flashback may well be simply a mode of poetic justice imposed by the director on his selfish character. However desirous Tomioka has been of forgetting Yukiko and the past, Naruse, accomplishing Yukiko's own revenge, will not permit him to do so. His unconscious mind betrays him by refusing to allow him to be as callous as he has chosen to be.

Naruse ends with no more hope for a morally embattled postwar Japan than either Imai, Ichikawa, or Kinoshita was able to muster. His lovers share barely a moment of happiness once the war ends. And the emotional emptiness of Tomioka is that of Japan itself, weak and uncertain of its direction, a theme that recurs over and over in these films chronicling the postwar period.

In contrast, however, are some of Kurosawa's postwar films which end on a moment of uplift and hope. Yet he too cannot fail to see Japanese culture as having been fatally damaged by the war. *Drunken Angel* (*Yoidore Tenshi*, 1948) proposes a very limited alternative to Japan's postwar spiritual inertia in the form of a very flawed, alcoholic doctor who tends to slum patients, as if the society were in desperate need of better health, the war having inflicted disease on the community at large. The swamp outside the "drunken angel's" office suggests the breeding of disease, at this transitional moment in Japan's history, by a set of gangsters who stalk the neighborhood like carpetbaggers in the American South, come to make their fortunes out of the disarray left by the war. Toshiro Mifune plays one of these gangsters, Matsunaga, who suffers from tuberculosis. The doctor tries to help him, but fails.

Like all Japanese films, *Drunken Angel* tends toward allegory. The fate of the society is its real theme; the question the film finally asks is not, will Matsunaga be saved by the doctor? but, what will happen to Japan and can the culture itself be restored? The young Matsunaga represents Japanese youth emerging from the war, wounded yet full of energy and courage. The doctor believes there is hope for him because he "hates disease," just as there is hope for Japan, a country full of physical vitality, its people capable of the spiritual renewal which yet seems so increasingly elusive for them.

The postwar setting of *Drunken Angel* is dominated by the night club Matsunaga frequents. Women in the guise of Western prostitutes sing American pop tunes and dance the Lindy Hop, both treated as symbols of corruption. Under its postwar burdens Kurosawa finds that Japan—as represented by Matsunaga—"[does]n't want to be saved, particularly." "We all die anyway," Matsunaga says, out of the postwar mood of ennui and despair that afflicts all of Japan.

It is this mood that makes Matsunaga susceptible to the chief gangster, Okada. It causes him to throw the flower, which was a symbol of his willingness to engage in the difficult struggle to get well, into the filthy swamp. Finally, the doctor cannot save Matsunaga because the problem is bigger than the individual. It involves the corruption of the entire society. "Your lung's like this place," the doctor tells him, pointing to the swamp. At this moment someone dumps in a wheelbarrow full of garbage. "There are a lot of rotten people around you," the doctor says, "there's no hope for you unless you break away from them." Japan, too, has been besieged by *yakuza* so numerous that the people have no hope of breaking free from their grasp.

But, as in his great masterpiece *Ikiru*, Kurosawa refuses to blame the degeneration of Japan on the corrupting American and Western influence alone. Matsunaga dies and Japan remains unregenerate because, Kurosawa insists, even after the war Japan retained feudal norms at the heart of social life. Matsunaga decides that he must "settle it" with Okada by himself because "he'll lose face" should the doctor go to the police with his story. He can conceive of no means of protecting himself other than a feudal code of honor reflective of the same mentality that drove Japan into the war in the first place. People like Matsunaga continue to resurrect the same samurai-derived notions as if they had learned nothing from the repression and militarism of the 1930s and 1940s. *Drunken Angel* rejects the bravado of the yet to be invented *yakuza* film, as it rejects the ruthless code of *bushido* which the *yakuza* film will elevate as the justification for its nihilistic violence.

"The Japanese like to punish themsleves with petty sacrifices," says the doctor, appalled that Okada's former girlfriend, who is now his assistant, and whom Okada had brutalized, would return to the gangster to "avoid trouble." Throughout the film Kurosawa insists that the Japanese after the war had to find a new image of themselves if they were to build a healthy society. Instead, Matsunaga does the opposite. He drags himself from his sickbed to "save his reputation," in danger because Okada has reassigned his territory. And, weakened by his illness, he dies in the encounter.

All the doctor can do after this defeat is to throw a rock into the swamp in frustration. For Kurosawa, in the postwar period Japan finally has lacked the perception to conceive of a new identity for itself commensurate with placing a strong value on the needs of the individual human being. Instead, as if on a perpetual treadmill, the Japanese have insisted upon honoring the forms establishing hierarchy that have dominated relationships between people in the centuries leading up to the war.

In postwar Japan Kurosawa discovers the regaining of humanity through service. As in the case of his great samurai Kambei (*Seven Samurai*), it is for the good and strong to set the example of selflessness. Social regeneration is only conceivable in terms of their individual acts. The opportunity for sacrifice of the self comes to all the Kurosawa *Übermenschen*, from Yuki in *No Regrets for Our Youth* to Yasumoto, the young disciple in *Red Beard*. In Kurosawa's films made in the forties and fifties, it is the aftermath of the war that demands such sweeping and total renunciation.

Kurosawa's most powerful portrayal of postwar Japan comes in *Ikiru*. Its hero is sixty-year-old Watanabe (Takashi Shimura), a middle-rank official in a Tokyo ward office. Discovering that he has terminal stomach cancer, Watanabe seeks before his death to perform one single meaningful act—which would be the first of his life.

Immediately Kurosawa exposes as fraudulent the notion that the Occupation has brought meaningful social change to Japan. A group of women, petitioning the "Citizens' Section" at City Hall that a polluted swamp in their neighborhood be drained since it is a hazard to their children, are shunted from bureau to bureau as Kurosawa savagely satirizes the claims of the government to concern for social welfare. Finally, one woman remarks, "There's no democracy here," an obvious dig in 1952, the year of its departure from Japan, at the Occupation with its claim to having "democratized" Japan. Although bureaucracy, of course, was not new to Japan with the postwar period, the confusions of the war and the Occupation exacerbated its inefficiency and also exposed its essential contempt for the needs of the people. The spirit of ferment and dissent in this period also allowed Kurosawa to make a film on a theme that would not have been tolerated in pre-war Japan.

Returning home after he has discovered, despite the hypocritical lies of his doctor, that he has less than a year to live, Watanabe sits in his darkened house, alone. A slow dolly in from outside indicates the return of his son and daughter-in-law, she humming, off camera, the American pop tune "Too Young." This song at once introduces the theme of the loss of character and dignity brought by the Occupation and the Americanization of the culture. The daughter-in-law, a selfish, greedy young woman, eying the darkened house, asks, "Is it a black-out?" as if at this postwar moment the war years have not yet been forgotten, their memory, as in *A Japanese Tragedy*, itself contributing to the amorality of the people. A moment later she expresses the wish that they did not live in a Japanese-style house at all.

The dissatisfaction with things Japanese and preference for a Western style of life are, for Kurosawa, a sign of cultural decay. Playing "Too Young" on her record player, the daughter-in-law remarks to her husband, apropos her desire to live as she chooses without regard for the wishes of her father-in-law, Watanabe, "We must think about ourselves, what about us?" Her admiration for things American and her selfishness are results of the same corrupting influence.

The Americanization of Japan is further condemned by Kurosawa in the Nighttown sequence in which a self-styled Mephistopheles takes the dying Watanabe out for an evening of "enjoyment." Women dance Western style, strippers perform, and the complete Americanization of Japanese leisure-time activities is broken only by Watanabe's sitting down, facing the camera and singing an old and very well known Japanese ditty, "Life Is So Short." He is still a Japanese, and in his retention of his own culture there remains hope that he will be able to perform a good and compassionate act before his death. Watanabe vomits in disgust at the end of his foray on the town, as "Music-Mambo, Take it Away" blares in the background. The equation of sickness with Westernization permeates the Nighttown sequence.

In Watanabe's brief "affair" with the young co-worker with whom he seeks solace as a second means of discovering at last how "to live" (which is how the title "*Ikiru*" translates), Kurosawa again introduces images suggesting the unwholesome miscegenation of cultures. The girl in her torn stockings knows that only shops specializing in foreign goods carry the treasured Western stockings Watanabe buys and she so covets. Quitting her boring job at the Citizens' Section, she is employed by a factory making toy mechanical animals for the children of Japan. These are Western-style objects, but they will serve to give Watanabe the clue to how he can locate some meaning in his existence before his death.

Ikiru: The Americanization of Japan is further condemned by
Kurosawa in the Nighttown sequence in which a self-styled
Mephistopheles takes the dying Watanabe out for an eve-
ning of "enjoyment."

The epiphany that will release him from the tedium of an aimless
existence—one obedient to the demand for subservience insisted upon
for anyone who works within the bureaucracy—occurs in a tearoom. The
girl speaks of how much she enjoys making these toy animals; she believes
she is doing something for "the children of Japan." In deep focus behind
Watanabe and the girl a group of Japanese youngsters are celebrating a
birthday party. As they begin to sing "Happy Birthday," in English, and
the birthday girl ascends the stairs to the room, Watanabe descends beside her. The conflict of motion within the shot is half ironic since it
is he, moving downward, who has at last reached a kind of transcendence.
A thought has grown in Watanabe's mind as a result of the girl's effusive
statement about why she enjoys making toy animals. It is underlined for
us by its juxtaposition with the singing of "Happy Birthday."

In the next sequence Watanabe is at last ready to "do something."
And as he decides to arrange for the drainage of the swamp and the

building of a playground for the neighborhood children on the site, we hear the faint sounds of "Happy Birthday" on the sound track behind him. It is as if once the Japanese begin to think and act for themselves, they have nothing to fear from the Westernization of their culture. Just as the girl is right in arguing that Watanabe's son is not to blame for his father's having become a "mummy," not remarrying but devoting his whole life to his job, Kurosawa argues that injustice in postwar Japan cannot be blamed solely on the infiltration of Western culture. You, the girl argued, by inference referring as well to the feudalism still permeating Japanese institutions, are to blame if your life is empty and without purpose.

Kurosawa thus refuses to place the responsibility for Japanese failings on the invasion of the foreigners and the Occupation. Part II of the film, all in flashback, chronicling how Watanabe indeed built the playground, is a satire on traditional Japanese attitudes, a satire begun in *Drunken Angel* and completed here.

The subordination of the individual to the group, upon which all Japanese bureaucracies, governmental and private, are structured, is seen by Kurosawa as preventing humane responses to the needs of those whom these bureaucracies were supposedly constituted to serve. Watanabe is Chief of the "Citizens' Section" of the government, yet in the first sequence neither he nor any of his underlings shows the slightest concern for the women petitioners seeking to rid their neighborhood of the disease-breeding swamp.

Ikiru: The subordination of the individual to the group, upon which all Japanese bureaucracies, governmental and private, are structured, is seen by Kurosawa as preventing humane responses.

What counts in this bureaucracy is precedent, behavior safe because it is exactly like that which came before. Rewards to employees are made on the basis of such questionable virtues as seniority and "attendance," the latter a virtue in which Watanabe has particularly excelled. That these officials deem it dangerous in the extreme to violate the status quo, thus jeopardizing their secure positions, ensures that none of the people's petitions can be taken seriously. For petitioners, by definition, always come in search of change.

The deputy mayor, a despicable man who tries to take all the credit for building the playground, speaks the truth at Watanabe's funeral when he says that "anyone who knows the organization knows he [Watanabe] could not have made the park by himself." Individual judgment is taboo, since any unique act would involve an implicit challenge to one's superior, a suggestion that the latter has been lacking in his own duty. Watanabe does build the playground by himself. But to do so he must violate many of the norms that define how a man in his position ought to behave. In order to become a human being, he must cease to be a Japanese bureaucrat.

To achieve this end, Watanabe must humble himself before minor officials. Even inappropriate humility is frowned upon by this hierarchy since, like inappropriate self-assertion, of which Watanabe will also be guilty, it poses an implicit challenge to the whole structure of superior-inferior upon which rests, as Chie Nakane has pointed out, all of Japanese society, with its vertical social organization. By stepping out of his place, Watanabe would suggest the inefficacy of the entire system. And he would incur the certain anger of those in the higher ranks. All the while it is clear that Watanabe risks challenging the premises and prerogatives of the government bureaucracy because he has nothing to lose. Only the immediacy of his death gives him the courage to be revolutionary.

Watanabe breaks with proper Japanese etiquette by aggressively pursuing the playground project. He even conducts what amounts almost to a sit-in at the office of the recalcitrant deputy mayor. Interrupting a conversation about the sad state of present-day geisha, Watanabe asks the deputy mayor to "reconsider" his refusal, something no inferior should ever dare demand of a superior in the Japanese hierarchy. For a loss of face must inevitably result from going back upon one's word. In the scene in the deputy mayor's office Watanabe's outrageous violation of all propriety is underlined by Kurosawa in a long take with no sound. Watanabe's silent refusal to depart constitutes an aggressive act. At such a moment, when a man so flagrantly casts all caution to the winds, words from any quarter would be superfluous.

Moral force makes possible physical courage, as Watanabe willingly endures the abuses of the *yakuza* who are involved in all government projects from behind the scene, and in whose interest the building of playgrounds for children occupies no place. Watanabe puts up with their familiarity and insolence because he hasn't the time for false pride, nor, the film implies, do any of us. Paradoxically, however, Watanabe's new-found revolutionary fervor allows him more time for himself than he ever had in his life. Sensing his increasingly imminent end, he can admire a sunset for the first time in thirty years. Unlike so many Japanese, who argue that there is greater courage in conformity and adherence to the needs of the group, Kurosawa insists that it is only rebellion that makes a man human, given society as we know it. It is this insight which makes us think of him as "Western."

At the end, after Watanabe's death, hierarchy reasserts itself. As in *Drunken Angel, The Quiet Duel* (*Shizukanaru Ketto*, 1949), and *Record of a Living Being*, Kurosawa recognizes that the acts of the solitary heroic individual do not change the world. Although at Watanabe's funeral his co-workers, inspired by his example, had vowed to change (albeit a vow made under the influence of alcohol), they revert immediately to their old pattern. Each bureaucrat remains mindful first of the wishes of his superior. All those in the highest positions choose to perpetuate their power at all costs, and they continue to fear above all the slightest tremor that would necessitate behavior not based upon precedent—for Kurosawa, a highly feudal approach.

In the last sequence Kimura, the one colleague who had truly valued Watanabe, rises out of his chair in protest as a new problem comes to their bureau only to be shunted to another office. His chair falls back, he picks it up and the camera tilts down with him as if he were being submerged. By the time the shot is completed, he is hidden by the stacks of paper piled high on his desk. Descending back into his chair, he is defeated by the weight of the bureaucracy.

Unlike Watanabe's, Kimura's rebellion is brief indeed. Kimura may admire what Watanabe had done, but he cannot emulate it, although he, like all of us, is equally under a death sentence. A typical Japanese, he reverts to his place. And, for Kurosawa, Japan re-emerges out of the postwar moment with the oppressiveness of its feudal past intact.

One of the most powerful and brilliant films dealing with the effects of the Second World War and its aftermath would not be made until 1970. This was Shohei Imamura's *History of Postwar Japan as Told by a Bar Hostess* (*Nippon Sengoshi—Madam Onboro no Seikatsu*). Using the documentary approach of the *cinéma vérité* interview, the film consists of Imamura himself questioning an actual bar hostess, named Etsuko Akaza, who had bought the "Onboro" bar in Yokosuka, the setting as well of *Pigs and Battleships*. While "Madame Onboro" traces the history of her life from the end of the war to the present, Imamura intercuts actual newsreel footage of the tumultuous political events of the postwar period beginning with the arrival of General MacArthur in 1945.

Sometimes the newsreels ironically contradict what Mme. Onboro tells us. As a bar hostess servicing the American base at Yokosuka, she has made her peace with the Americans, while Imamura, through his choice of newsreel footage, is violently anti-American. Imamura sees the Occupation and the years of the Japan-American Security Treaty (AMPO) as having been, in their own way, of almost equal destructiveness to

Japan as the war itself. Mme. Onboro, to whom Imamura never had the opportunity of showing the final cut of the film, remains unaware of how, through the newsreels, Imamura is contrasting her praise of the Americans with the very harsh realities of Korea and Vietnam. While we watch demonstrators trying to close down the American base at Yokosuka, we hear Mme. Onboro opposing this action for reasons of self-interest alone. If the base were closed, she would lose the business of the American sailors.

At other times, Mme. Onboro's suffering after the war makes her an effective critic of the postwar period and the newsreels confirm her point of view. The energy and vitality of Etsuko Akaza, directed as they are solely to her own struggle for survival, correspond to the enormous outpouring of protest in the mass demonstrations occurring in these years from 1945 to 1970. In a way, the resilient Etsuko becomes a symbol of the strength and energy of the Japanese people after the war as they sought at last to have a hand in shaping their society.

By the end of the film Etsuko has become a representative of "Japan," and her attitudes express how Japan has coped with the Occupation and its aftermath as both victim and willing participant in its own victimization. In the real-life conclusion, Mme. Onboro journeys to America where she will marry a sailor half her age. But if Mme. Onboro chooses to build a life with one of those who have been the engineers of her country's subjugation, her choice is the result of Japanese intolerance toward members of the outcast group, the *Eta* or *burakumin*, to which she belongs. As a victim of Japanese racism, she has suffered more from her own people than from her contact with the Americans.

Sometimes Imamura himself appears in a shot, as at the beginning when he invites Etsuko to take part in the film. Often we hear his voice. But even in so strongly political a film, Imamura refuses to urge his own judgments upon us, either to praise or to blame Mme. Onboro. The ironies are all expressed cinematically, entirely through the juxtaposition of the documentary materials with the commentary provided by his character. Mme. Onboro is an outspoken partisan of American men. "They were all kind and gentlemanly," she says, while on the newsreels we watch MacArthur exiting from a plane. "They brought soap and chocolate," she tells us, offering this further evidence of the kindness of American men. "There was nothing to worry about. People calmed down." Her view is both truthful in terms of her own experience, and false in the context of the larger realities of the American involvement in Asia, which Imamura also includes in the film. For Mme. Onboro, who has had two ne'er-do-well Japanese husbands who beat and abused her, American men are infinitely more desirable, the American atrocities from Hiroshima to Mylai, included by Imamura through his newsreels, notwithstanding.

Like Kurosawa, Imamura lays a good share of the blame for the valueless society Japan has become at the door of the Japanese themselves. Etsuko Akaza's family were slaughterers and therefore automatically members of the *Eta* class. As a group akin to India's "untouchables," they remain, well into the twentieth century, so abused and segregated that they can marry only others of the same caste. Before the credits, in documentary footage taken in a slaughterhouse, a cow is led away, hit over the head and lifted up on a chain while blood pours onto the floor. While the slaughtering proceeds, shots of Vietnamese prisoners of war are intercut, as if Imamura were suggesting that the impulse that makes it possible to torture animals finds similar expression in such places as Vietnam. This juxtaposition, condemning cruelty to animals, serves not to endorse Japanese discrimination against the *Eta* for their profession, but to suggest that a violence endemic to Japanese society accounts for Japan's violent acts against her Asian neighbors. The analogy seems confusing because it comes in the midst of what seems to be an account of Etsuko's particular past.

We learn that Etsuko's mother had told her that she could never "wipe out [her] background." At that moment she had quit school, in recognition of the fact that she would always be an outcast. And Etsuko herself attributes her later prostitution to her knowledge that "no well-brought-up guy would take me." She had gone to live with a neighborhood policeman who had protected her family in the black market sale of meat.

Imamura reminds her of the moment when the voice of the Emperor was heard by the Japanese people for the first time, in his radio broadcast announcing the end of the war. In the newsreel recording this moment, Imamura points out to her that people are crying, but Etsuko contradicts what the images seem to assert. "The people did not cry," she insists with a common sense born of experience, they were "relieved." They worried mainly about what would happen next. Even newsreels can mythologize, and Mme. Onboro's role for Imamura becomes in part to demystify the war years and to express how the Japanese really felt about the defeat and the war's aftermath.

At times, Mme. Onboro stands for the best and strongest aspects of the Japanese sensibility. Etsuko had her first menstrual period when she was fifteen, the same year the war ended, as if in her own person she was "Japan," coming to maturity at the same moment that her country gained the opportunity to enter a new phase of its development. Etsuko's having sacrificed her virginity for economic survival is juxtaposed with images describing how other Japanese endured the same postwar miseries: homeless people sleeping on subways, crowded trains, breadlines. In editing that draws its inspiration from Eisenstein's *Strike*, Imamura cuts back to the slaughterhouse where the carcasses are now hung up. Etsuko was a victim, not only of the war but of traditional Japan, not only of the racism against the *Eta* but of false and destructive attitudes toward themselves and their children assimilated by the *Eta* as a result of their being Japanese. Although the policeman, Shimura, beat Etsuko, her parents begged her to remain with him, arguing that he would improve once she had a child. As tradition-bound Japanese, shrinking from the loss of face consequent upon divorce—a sign that one has failed in a commitment of great importance—they had encouraged her to stay with this man even after his abusiveness included not only philandering but physical violence. Etsuko is healthier than her parents because she is less bound to empty traditions than they, because she refuses to suffer unnecessarily.

Although she was a member of an oppressed group, the political struggles of the postwar years did not interest Etsuko at all. Her indifference was typically that of so many Japanese, who have assimilated a Buddhist sense that there is nothing one can do about the injustice of this world. A relative had become a Communist, but during the May Day demonstrations of 1952 she herself had spent the afternoon in Shinjuku seeing *Gone with the Wind*. Meanwhile, the newsreels show us huge crowds chanting "give us rice" and marching to the Diet, only to be stopped by the police and an order of General MacArthur. Imamura had effectively marked the date of the turning point of the Occupation toward reinstatement of the *zaibatsu* and a "police reserve" ("it is an army, but only to protect peace") with a shot of MacArthur's famous written edict of January 31, 1947, forbidding the general strike scheduled for the next day.

Newsreels of the Red Purges inform us, in titles, of twenty-four cabinet ministers and 10,000 government workers having been dismissed. These events, Imamura reveals, coincided with American bombings in Korea. Another title reads "gold," and we see people panning for gold in Korea, the juxtaposition suggesting Imamura's analysis of why the Americans were in Korea in the first place. With the onset of the Cold War, the Occupation authorities became increasingly belligerent toward left-wing opinion of any kind within Japan. Later, while we see police throwing tear gas into Waseda University, Mme. Onboro is telling us, absurdly, of how she asserted her independence from her husband by having an affair with a student. Her discussion of this affair is humorously followed by the title announcing the end of the Occupation: "Japan Gains Independence."

Yet, as a free spirit, Mme. Onboro transcended her own apathy. In her Yokosuka bar she was democratic. "We welcomed all kinds and all races," she tells Imamura with pride. "Other places catered to Japanese. But we took in anybody." Although, out of the moral disorientation of the postwar period, Japanese in droves were joining the neo-Buddhist Soka Gakkai sect with its emphasis on will power and positive thinking as solutions to the problems facing the Japanese in this troubled time, Mme. Onboro muses that she refused to join. "It didn't seem to help anybody much." Later, she did become a member and money was extorted from her. But, no fool, she managed to use the organization to secure her divorce from the policeman Shimura. Meanwhile the newsreels show a huge mob of Soka Gakkai worshippers, cattle-like in prayer.

Mme. Onboro is most engaging in her comments about the role of the Emperor and his family in Japan. She tells Imamura that when Americans had asked her whether the Emperor's family were gods, she had replied,

"They're just decorative people." The newsreels show the wedding of the Crown Prince and Princess Michiko and reveal a malcontent throwing a stone at the Imperial carriage. Toward this extreme action, and despite her generally apolitical point of view, Mme. Onboro is sympathetic: "He was probably angry at how much was spent on the ceremony." Instead of building the new Imperial Palace, she suggests, they would have done better to construct an orphanage.

The scenes at Yokosuka distance us from Mme. Onboro, who has cast her lot with American men. A zoom in on American ships in Yokosuka harbor sets the scene. Girls, we learn from the narration, were sleeping with between thirty and forty men a day. An American plane flies threateningly low, as people protest against the continuing presence of the American military in Japan.

It is at this critical time that Etsuko opened her "Onboro" bar in Yokosuka. A girl student has died in the demonstrations against the renewal of the security treaty with the United States, an event recorded in so many postwar films, from Hani's *A Full Life* (*Mitasareta Seikatsu*, 1962) to Oshima's *Night and Fog in Japan*. Mme. Onboro, failing to understand the political importance of the demonstrations, believes that this death was a waste, and that the girl should not have demonstrated. The huge demonstrations against the impending visit by Eisenhower to Japan make it impossible for the helicopter of his representative, Hagerty, to land. Three hundred thousand march to the Diet. A

The History of Postwar Japan As Told by a Bar Hostess: Absurdly, in the midst of these tumultuous events for her country, inspired by the relationship between Japan and the United States, Mme. Onboro finds solace in the arms of a series of American lovers.

The History of Postwar Japan as Told by a Bar Hostess:
The presence of the American military has shaped Mme.
Onboro's life, as it did the lives of so many Japanese in
her time.

terrorist named Yamaguchi assassinates a left-wing leader named Asanuma
in the Diet. And, absurdly, in the midst of these tumultuous times for
her country inspired by the relationship between Japan and the United
States, Mme. Onboro finds solace in the arms of a series of American
lovers.

In 1963 she is with an American sailor when John F. Kennedy is
assassinated. She tells Imamura that this lover "wasn't so shocked" at
the news, a clever interpolation by Imamura, although it must have
been inadvertent because only much later would Pentagon and Central
Intelligence Agency involvement in the assassination be suggested.

While she is with another American lover, the Japanese people protest
against the presence in Japan of the nuclear-powered submarine *Enterprise,* and shout "Yankee Go Home." One of her lovers, Chuck, was even
on the *Pueblo* when it was captured by the North Koreans and she recognizes him as the "fat one" in Imamura's newsreel. Imamura also shows her
footage of American atrocities in Vietnam, which she refuses to believe
because, she says, she did not see them with her own eyes. She thus exhibits

both the strengths and the weaknesses of Japanese pragmatism, its clear-sightedness as well as its propensity for moral indifference. The piles of Vietnamese corpses inspire Mme. Onboro to respond only that those who start the wars are the bad ones, a position at least in part the result of her taking so many lovers among the lower ranks of the American military.

Etsuko bears a "half-breed," the child of a foreigner, an act which appalls her *burakumin* parents, racists themselves. Newsreels picture the discrimination in Japan against these racially mixed children. Yet, with her characteristic grit, Onboro refuses to have the abortion insisted upon by her father, who still—as the Japanese patriarch—believes he has a right to determine her life choices. Precisely because discrimination against her as a *burakumin* has haunted Mme. Onboro all her life, causing her to fear the arrival in Yokosuka of anyone from her home town who might make this truth known, she has no qualms about bearing a "mixed blood" child. Her act is one of defiance against the Japanese racism that had been so cruelly directed toward her in her youth. Finally, Imamura accompanies her to Haneda Airport where a Japan Air Lines flight will take her to America. The presence of the American military has shaped her life, as it did the lives of so many Japanese in her time, even of those who remain unaware of it.

Mme. Onboro's last full interview with Imamura occurred with the enormous ships in Yokosuka harbor passing behind her and with guns going off periodically. Her parting words to Imamura were that if her American husband goes out with other women, she will not divorce him until she has her American citizenship and can open a new bar in San Diego. She bows to Imamura and boards the plane with her baby and her sailor.

Toward postwar Japan, Imamura is both mocking and despairing. He admires that resilient survivor of those years, Mme. Onboro, yet mourns a Japan which so fails its oppressed (she suffers doubly as a *burakumin* and as a woman) that they fall into the hands of the Americans who, in the wake of the war, have brought nothing but heartache to Japan. With the eye of the anthropologist, as always, Imamura relocates the strength of the Japanese people through Mme. Onboro. Her primitive attitudes may sometimes be appalling, as when she admits that she always disliked her older daughter because she reminded her of the girl's father, the policeman Shimura. Yet in her personality there is, as well, tenacity, a demand for freedom, and an admirable determination to make up her own mind about things. Her sense of values in some deepest sense has not been corrupted by her running a bar for foreigners, for her earthy nature has prevented her from becoming a sycophant of privilege and position; she had become involved only with rank-and-file sailors rather than officers who would try to control her. Although she is a *burakumin*, she never pities herself as a victim, but wants only to make her own way through her own efforts.

Thus does "Mme. Onboro" go to America to begin her new life. Despite her bad Japanese husbands and sometimes irresponsible and unsatisfy-

ing American lovers, except for the last, the twenty-three-year-old Harry,
she has survived in good spirits, confident of the future, undaunted by
obstacles that may come her way. For Imamura, she embodies all that is
best, if sometimes also what is worst, about Japan and the Japanese.

Almost as a coda to *The History of Postwar Japan* are television documentaries Imamura made about unreturned Japanese soldiers. For various
reasons, instead of returning to Japan after the war ended, these men made
new lives in other countries of Southeast Asia. Labelling them Japan's
"deserted people," Imamura suggests that Japan, once having made use of
such men, has now abandoned them to lives of anonymity and loneliness
in these outposts of progress.

In *Matsu the Untamed Comes Home* (*Muho Matsu Kokyo Ni Kaeru*,
1974) Imamura arranged for a former Japanese soldier, resident in Thailand, to return to his Nagasaki home after an absence from Japan of thirty-
three years. From the moment Matsuyoshi descends from his plane at
Haneda to his return to Thailand at the end of the film, Imamura follows
him with his camera. Imamura's interest again is in viewing Japan from
the eyes of such "deserted people," who were willing to give their lives for
their country during the war only later to be mistreated and scorned as an
embarrassment to the State in these times of prosperity.

Perhaps the most brilliant and feeling of Imamura's fine documentaries
is *Karayuki-san* (1973),[7] the story of another of Japan's deserted people, a
prostitute kidnapped to Malaysia in her youth. At the age of seventy-three
she remains in Malaysia, unrepatriated and alone. Like Mme. Onboro,
Karayuki-san is cheerful, never complaining about what must have been an
unspeakable life. Her only need is of one *yukata* in which to be buried.
Late in the film she and Imamura visit a cemetery reserved for women
like herself. She tells him that she "was very unlucky. This was my destiny.
If I had a lot of money I wouldn't have been deceived." Imamura presses
her and suggests what seems to be an outrageous idea: that she might, in
part, have been responsible for her fate.

But she agrees. She had been "thoughtless." She had given up. In voice-
over Imamura comments: "There were 10,000 such women who left Japan,
cooperated with the war, and were then rejected." Karayuki-san is then
a sacrifice to Japan's prosperity. At the end, with Imamura's help, she
returns to Japan as a guest of the Chief of the Burakumin League, since,
like Mme. Onboro, in Japan she had been a member of the *Eta* caste.

Midway through the film Imamura visits Karayuki-san's home village
near Hiroshima by himself and shows her picture to the villagers there.
They don't remember her, further evidence that Japan has indeed abandoned her. She had left school after the fourth grade to work in a textile
factory, since her family, as *burakumin*, had found it difficult to make ends
meet. One of her brothers, a merchant, was physically handicapped and his
customers demanded that he hand them his merchandise with chopsticks
so as not to touch him. Discrimination, in multitudinous varieties, plagues

---

[7] "Karayuki-san" is the generic name for Japanese women sold into prostitution in
various parts of Southeast Asia during the early part of the twentieth century.

Japanese society, including that against the disabled and deformed. In voice-over Imamura makes a rare value judgment: "The discrimination hurt me."

On Malaysia, Imamura and Karayuki-san tour the prostitute quarter where, fifty-four years earlier, she had arrived as the prisoner of a slave trader. Playfully he tells her that, bald and toothless as she now is, she must once have been pretty. And she replies, good-humoredly and with some irony, "No, I was just like this when I was young." Imamura leads Karayuki-san to re-create the moment when she had been brought to Malaysia: "I cried and he [the "master"] didn't let us go, so I just gave up." The sound of a horse clopping along on the sound track recalls that day, long ago, when she had been taken in a horse-drawn cart through the streets of Singapore.

Now, although she is a sad figure in her old, brown-print dress with her cheap leather handbag, Karayuki-san, guided by Imamura, becomes a figure of dignity. That she has the opportunity to tell what happened to her lends significance to her shabby life. And this is enhanced by the seriousness with which Imamura takes her. Imamura's making a film about Karayuki-san and others like her, which no one else has done, becomes the most meaningful event of her life.

Together they visit 20 Melay Street, the site of the brothel where she had been taken by the "master" who would not even permit her to write letters to Japan. Rather, like the slave trader he was, he would write letters for her without allowing her to read what he wrote. Panning the place with

Karayuki-san: The story of Karayuki-san is immensely sad, for she has been exploited as a woman and as a Japanese and as a *burakumin* or *Eta.*

a hand-held camera, Imamura reveals the slum where Karayuki-san had once been a slave. And he locates her experience within the context of Japan's historical role in Southeast Asia.

Chinese industry had made progress competing with Japanese traders in the first decades of the twentieth century. She had been a piece of "Japanese merchandise" attacked by the Chinese, a target of their anger against the Japanese. Karayuki-san thus became a victim of conflicting economic forces, as badly used by Japan's enemies as by the Japanese themselves. During the war she had been placed in a concentration camp hospital in India, since Japanese could not be trusted. She and the other women like her had not cared whether Japan won or lost because she would receive no benefits either way. When she says she still misses Japan, Imamura gently asks: "Did Japan do anything for you?" and she must reply: "No, nothing."

The story of Karayuki-san is immensely sad, for she has been exploited as a woman and as a Japanese and as a *burakumin* or *Eta*. When she had been allowed to write to Japan, her elder sister had asked her to send money. Like so many Japanese prostitutes, she had been exploited by her own family as well. Yet, in her loneliness, upon hearing of the death of her brother, she had dreamt of how he had combed her hair when she went to school, as if he had come to Malaysia to visit her. The shadows of such memories are all that remain. Number 20 Melay Street is now occupied by contemporary prostitutes, one of whom smiles up at Imamura, a potential customer.

Imamura discovers, through his travels in the countries of Southeast Asia chronicled in these documentaries, that the war must be seen in the context of Japan's history of appropriating the wealth of its weaker neighbors for much-needed natural resources and using them as markets. While this was the original motive for the war, thirty years after Hiroshima it remains the governing force behind Japan's relations with these countries. Imamura finds that the prosperity of modern Japan has been built upon the sacrifice of individuals like Karayuki-san, used and then abandoned by the State.

The Japanese, says Imamura in his documentaries, must be defined by the price their wealth has exacted from such "unknown" people. The Imperial army may no longer be marching through Southeast Asia under its old banners, but the behavior of those who rule remains the same as it was during the war, as Matsuyoshi so eloquently puts it for all his simplicity and inarticulateness: "I think Japanese people are all insane with greed." Nor do any of Imamura's documentaries suggest that he is wrong in his analysis of where the responsibility lies. Matsuyoshi, speaking for Imamura, can only confirm the director in his distress: "I came home and found why Japan had achieved this development. It was for money, wasn't it? The Emperor must've started the war because he wanted money, too."

PART

4

WOMAN IN JAPAN

The Husbandless Patriarchy

In keeping with her real-life position in the society, rarely is a woman, whether as wife or lover, portrayed in the Japanese film as an independent human being. Almost never does she command respect as a person separate from a man. The very concept of a relationship between two equally valuable human beings seems foreign to her universe. Whether set before or after the Meiji Restoration, before or after the Second World War, most women in Japanese films differ very little from Shinoda's Osan in *Double Suicide*, ready to pawn her clothes, and her honor, so that her husband, the merchant Jihei, might redeem his courtesan, Koharu. In the very fiber of her being, Osan lives as if she has no rights of her own. Shinoda adds no irony when Osan becomes offended that Jihei should even ask forgiveness for his infidelity: "A wife's duty is to forgive and give everything."

In this story, set in 1690, but still applicable in so many ways today, both wife and whore try to maintain a love relationship in a society demanding at every turn that the individual always seek first to fulfill preconceived social obligations (*giri*). Only when these duties do not come into play can a woman pursue *ninjo* (personal inclination). But in a social order in which rules predominate even in sexual relationships, *ninjo* comes to be only a choice between different, conflicting *giri*. And because she is a member of the caste at the lowest position in the social hierarchy, the rules governing the life of the Japanese woman are stringent indeed.

Jihei has fallen in love with the prostitute Koharu. Disgrace falls on his wife Osan, however, not because he is unfaithful, since such behavior was more the rule than the exception, but because he loves his mistress so much that he neglects his business and even plots to disrupt his home by redeeming her. Koharu, enslaved in a brothel, can only be set free by paying a great deal of money, which a fat, vulgar merchant named Takei is only too eager to provide. Choice plays little part in her life. "I didn't willingly become a courtesan," Koharu laments, "a woman like any woman, why me?"

But Osan, the wife, is equally a slave, first to her father and later to her husband. When Jihei becomes impatient and abuses her, she has no recourse but to plead, "what have I done that you should treat me like this?" Any courtesy she is granted can come only from the indulgence of her husband, never from her right to respect. A fate worse than Jihei's sexual neglect is that Jihei's dissipation may cause Osan's father to claim her back. If this happens, she must return to her original home without her children, who, by law, belong to the house of her husband. And as Osan's own mother scornfully reminds her, the responsibility for the failed marriage would rest with her: "It's a woman's fault if a man wanders."

Thus are all the characters in *Double Suicide* hopelessly tormented by conflicting *giri*. Jihei owes *giri* to Osan, who will be disgraced if her father takes her back. He feels as deep an obligation to Koharu, whom he cannot allow to fall into the hands of Takei, for she has threatened to commit suicide if Takei buys her. Osan owes *giri* both to Jihei as her husband and to Koharu as another woman, a member of the same suffering caste. "We must save her," Osan says, "as a woman, I can't let her do it [submit to Takei]." Koharu owes *giri* not only to Osan and Jihei, since Osan has written Koharu a pleading letter begging her not to let Jihei die, but also to her own mother, who would starve as a beggar were Koharu, her sole support, to die. Her *giri* to Jihei is such that she cannot accept Takei, since Jihei has threatened to commit suicide himself if she does. Yet if she remains loyal to Jihei, who lacks the money to redeem her, she will probably be forced to commit double suicide with him. And thus she would be violating her *giri* to Osan, left a widow in a culture where remarriage for a woman was considered "dirty." When Koharu and Jihei finally do commit double suicide, they deliberately arrange for their bodies to be found in different places because, otherwise, Koharu fears she could not face Osan in the next world. Both man and woman cut their hair, as if they were assuming the roles of priest and nun, thus severing family obligations, and symbolically the very passion which brought them to this impasse.

The dichotomy between wife and whore described so accurately in *Double Suicide* persists in contemporary, patriarchal Japan with its concomitant belief that there are "two kinds" of female, the "wife" and the "loose woman." The double standard graphically exposed in *Double Suicide* ensures that love as pleasure and—in this limited sense, at least— the valuing of the woman for herself are granted only to the loose woman. Koharu is made infinitely more attractive than Osan with her blackened teeth (the mark of the married woman during samurai times), although both are played by the same actress, Shima Iwashita. The wife as keeper of the hearth and nurturer of the children, as preserver of the family name, is of no interest as an object of passion; in one scene we watch Osan ready herself for sex in the mistaken belief that Jihei has given up Koharu, only to observe her husband, his body drawn up in a knot, sobbing violently in his bed. In such a system it would have been, and is, dangerous to view the wife as a lover, since this might interfere with her social functions as a wife, which must come first, just as a woman's functioning as a self-supporting, creative individual might at moments come into conflict with her role as either wife or lover.

Takeo Doi has argued that *amae*, the desire for passive, dependent love originating in the overindulgence of Japanese mothers, particularly toward their male children, governs the relations between the sexes in Japan, as it does all human relationships there.[1] But if *amae* is defined as the mutual recognition of each other's need for indulgence, what we find in the Japanese film is that even such an infantile definition of "love" emerges primarily in relationships between lovers, rather than in those between husband and wife. There is a mutuality in the suffering of Jihei and Koharu that is never shared by Jihei and Osan. And the last moments of their lives are spent together.

Of course, *amae*, even between lovers, is impossible as the governing emotion between two equal human beings. Implied in this quest of each to be the passive love object of the other is that both reject the role of adult. Neither wishes to be the provider of the indulgence. *Amae* in this context also means a rejection of the lover's "otherness," which is why equality in the relations between Japanese men and women, even when they are not burdened with the freedom-denying roles of "husband" and "wife," is almost impossible. Only acceptance of someone else's "otherness" allows respect and equality. Doi fails to emphasize that, in the relations between Japanese men and women, *amae* in practice is rarely if ever accorded to the women, always to the men. In the previously discussed *Floating Clouds*,[2] although Yukiko needs more support and affection from her lover than he does from her, it is *he* who seeks *amae* in Doi's sense and she who is always ready to offer it to him. It is difficult, in fact, to perceive how he offers her the slightest indulgence or consideration, to director Naruse's great distress.

Doi's *amaeru* can be seen as a legacy of feudalism which subsumed the individual within a hierarchically ordered collective. While he lacked a separate identity, he was also free of the burdens of decision-making and the risks, if the privileges as well, of moral responsibility. Placing everyone within a collective, Doi has found, has had the psychic effect in the Japanese individual, man or woman, of encouraging a much more exaggerated need than that found in Western culture to return to the womb. Not having been expected to shoulder moral responsibility has led to an ever-present desire in this individual constantly to flee from the demands of adulthood. Thus does Shinoda's Jihei seem weak and unmanly, timid and full of anxiety.

For Doi, the degree of the inner desire to *amaeru* can be measured by how profoundly the individual possesses *jibun* (an awareness of self), a quality neither Chikamatsu nor Shinoda would allow to their merchants. Those who have *jibun* are capable of controlling the desire for *amae* (the noun), "while a man who is at the mercy of *amae* has no *jibun*."[3]

---

[1] *The Anatomy of Dependence* (Tokyo: Kodansha International, 1973).
[2] See pages 225–29.
[3] Doi, *Anatomy of Dependence*, p. 19.

The minimizing of personality in Japan, what Inazo Nitobe has called "depersonalization" caused by the continuation of feudal structures in the culture,[4] has permitted the flourishing of *amae*. It is a childish need because, in its claim upon the indulgence of another person, it ignores that other's similar needs as a separate human being. There is a basic inequality, and even callousness, built into the emotion of *amae*, for to ask *amaeru* of another is to deny the possibility of his asking it of you. As Doi shows, in the parent-child relationship *amae* is, of course, natural and fitting; the nurturer gently initiates the fledgling in the ways of the world, a process that demands indulgence. It might be argued that there is recognition of the individual in *amae* because it presupposes, on the part of both the person indulged and the person doing the indulging, mutual acceptance of each other. Once one is granted *amae*, that person is loved for himself, his strengths appreciated, his weaknesses tolerated. Such a view accepts the plurality of personality. But the psychological democratization of an *amae* relationship in practice is afforded to only one of the two participants.

It is also true that this need of *amaeru* produces a constant potential of conflict between two people, unless one succumbs with grace to the predominance of the other, as Osan does for Jihei, as women continually do for men. Thus, as Doi points out, uncontrolled *amae* has produced "little emperors . . . here, there, everywhere."[5] The real Emperor becomes the embodiment of satisfied *amae*.[6] Doi's conclusion is that "the aim from now on, surely, must be to overcome *amae* . . . to discover, in other words, the other person."[7]

The total subordination of the needs of the woman to those of the man is not quite as true in Kaneto Shindo's *Story of a Beloved Wife* (*Aisai Monogatari*, 1951) as it was in Shinoda's *Double Suicide*. But in this idealization of an Osan-style wife, albeit set in modern times, during the Second World War, it is again the man who is always in need of *amae*. By the end of the film the woman has died, as if of exhaustion and devotion to the man. Although her consciousness would not permit her to understand this, she was perhaps the one whose needs were the greater, a point of view, however, inaccessible to this male director.

The wife in this autobiographical first film has, in fact, no conception of needs of her own as distinct from those of her husband. Like director Shindo, the husband is a scenario writer, his problem that of convincing a much-admired director (a thinly disguised characterization of Kenji

[4] *Japanese Traits and Foreign Influences* (London: Kegan Paul, Trench & Trubner, 1927), pp. 25–26.

[5] Doi, *Anatomy of Dependence*, p. 61. It is interesting that director Kurosawa himself, despite the frequently anti-feudal content of his films, has been regarded in Japan as the "*Tenno*" (Emperor) of Toho, presumably not only for his dictatorial manner on the set, but also, as Yoichi Matsue, his producer for *Dodes'ka-den* and *Dersu Uzala*, has remarked to me, because of his childlike and frequent need to be indulged.

[6] *Ibid.*, p. 63.

[7] *Ibid.*, p. 84.

The Story of a Beloved Wife: The wife has, in fact, no conception of needs of her own as distinct from those of her husband.

Mizoguchi, for whom Shindo had worked before beginning on his own) to accept his work. Always in the background is the encouraging wife.

The most interesting women in the Japanese film are creations of those directors who bitterly oppose and rebel against this traditional role for women. There are no examples in the Japanese film of a woman who has carved out a meaningful role for herself as an individual, and who is also valued as such by a man, because a women's revolution is not yet at hand in Japan. One exception is Susumu Hani's *Bride of the Andes (Andes no Hanayome,* 1966), whose heroine could be valued for herself, however, only in Peru, thousands of miles from Japan.

Mizoguchi: *Woman as Slave*

Comparing today with the Nara (710–794) and Genroku (1688–1703) periods, I don't find much difference: women have always been treated like slaves.

I've always felt that communism solves the problems of class, but overlooks the problems of man and woman which still remain afterwards. So I'm especially interested in the problems between men and women.

Kenji Mizoguchi[1]

Those directors protesting against the oppression of the Japanese woman believe that even the failed rebellion is worth the effort. The finest films of Mizoguchi, who of the older directors best understood how the Japanese patriarchy demeans women, are those in which his women fight the hardest against their fate. The men in Mizoguchi's films are always weaker than the women, not because he was unable to characterize men, but because their childishness is meant to be an analogue to moral emptiness. The assertions of women in a patriarchy where they have no power, where they can be summoned as concubines to a daimyo—or sold by parents to a whorehouse—are acts more worthy of representation than those of a *bushi* participating in his daily willful abuse of the weak.

Mizoguchi's films reveal that it is absurd to speak about the relations between men and women in the context of the social role of the Japanese woman as long as she remains victim of the Confucian obediences to father, husband and son. The implicit argument behind his portrayal of the relations between men and women is that women are forced to sacrifice themselves simply by existing. Revolution against one's condition as a slave, which also demands sacrifices, is then infinitely preferable to passive submission to an enslaving fate. Osan, in his *Story from Chikamatsu*, riding off to her crucifixion (the punishment for a woman's adultery during the Tokugawa period), achieves a level of humanity she could never have enjoyed as the acquiescent wife of the merchant Ishun. In *White Threads of the Waterfall* (*Taki no Shiraito*, 1933) Mizoguchi bitterly satirizes the utter hostility of Meiji society toward women who, day after day, were sacrificing themselves to its prosperity. He scorns the entire Meiji concept of success. The society in which Kinya, the young man the heroine Taki puts through school, rises to prominence is un-

[1] Matsuo Kishi, "A Talk With Mizoguchi," *Kinema Jumpo*, April 1952. Translated by Leonard Schrader.

White Threads of the Waterfall: Mizoguchi bitterly satirizes
the utter hostility of Meiji society toward women who, day
after day, were sacrificing themselves to its prosperity.

worthy of Taki's sacrifice because it is incapable of showing her mercy.
Reduced to whoredom and then murder by the superhuman task she
has undertaken, Taki finally has no recourse but suicide. Through his
treatment of women Mizoguchi very early makes the same point directors
like Imamura would later make for Koreans, *burakumin*, pollution victims,
and others whose lives have been sacrificed to Japan's postwar development. Japan emerges strong after the Restoration, according to Mizoguchi,
only by using and then discarding those who mistakenly sacrifice themselves in the belief that to be successful in the new society and to dedicate
oneself to its economic growth is worth any effort.

In 1936 Mizoguchi made his most brilliant pre-war film, *Osaka Elegy*
(*Naniwa Ilika*), shot in twenty days and banned after 1940 for "decadent
tendencies," a euphemism barely concealing the military government's
fear of the radicalism of Mizoguchi's satire of the ruthless, all-pervasive
Osaka capitalism. In this film the mature Mizoguchi style emerges for

the first time as he creates, entirely through visual means, a balance between the fate of the heroine Ayako and the corrupt, degenerate values of Osaka. The plot concerns the seduction of Ayako, a switchboard operator, by her boss. In the background, however, is an equally important theme: the destruction of the individual by the greed of a boundless laissez-faire capitalism and its hostility toward anyone too weak to compete in the jungle of Social Darwinism that was Osaka—and Japan. Rhetoric about the dawning of an era of "freedom" fills the air, and Ayako even reads an article about "women's liberation." Mizoguchi reveals both to be a sham in this Osaka where money rules all and "freedom" is the province only of the businessmen frantically attempting to build mini-, if not authentic, *zaibatsu*.

Ayako is corrupted (she becomes a prostitute) not only by her boss but also by her family's need for money, the symbol of Osaka. As a woman, her role is to sacrifice herself to the needs of her family. The twentieth century has brought no amelioration of the traditional function of the Japanese woman. At first, Ayako tries to borrow from a weak and spineless fiancé, a typical Osaka company-man-to-be. He refuses her. Behind them in the shot is a construction site, bespeaking the rapid progress that is Osaka's *raison d'être*. At home, money is the main topic of conversation; Ayako's brother, having lost all connection with the traditional Japanese value of austerity, is obsessed by greed, a passion difficult to satisfy in the fiercely competitve society of the thirties.

Beset by the prevailing family pressure for her to help them, Ayako accepts the liaison with her boss and is transformed into a *"moga"* or modern girl. Her entire personality undergoes a change, as Mizoguchi portrays the psychic price a woman must inevitably pay for selling herself. Ayako now smokes, listens to Western music, and files her fingernails à la Mae West. Temporarily, the camera assumes the point of view of her boss climbing the stairs, ending outside the curtained window of the room where Ayako awaits him. Later, Ayako and her boss attend a performance of *Double Suicide* at the Bunraku Puppet Theater, where the traditions of the play and the strong passion of Jihei and Koharu for each other contrast with the loveless relationship between Ayako and her lover, and with the deflated mock-heroics of life in the present. The boss's wife discovers them, and intercut with a tumultuous Bunraku scene is her expression of rage, an indecorous fury which, by its very disruptiveness, provides a further judgment on the destructiveness of Ayako's affair.

Ayako nevertheless pursues this relationship with her boss because of unrelenting family pressures. Brother and sister conspire against her, a sister pleading that the older brother needs money while the camera tracks behind Ayako's back until she is left standing, alone and frightened, on subway stairs. A shot of the empty stairs after she has gone is followed by a low-angle shot of the tall buildings and speeding cars of Osaka, the city that will overwhelm her. In a fine, three-layered, deep-focus shot Mizoguchi reveals three family members occupying different levels of being, the need for money having so alienated them that, although they are in the same room, it is as if they occupy wholly separate universes. The indolent older brother lies in bed, drinking tea, in the left foreground of the shot. The father is in the background, the period of his influence, having ceased. Ayako is in the right foreground, now the only means by which the family can still compete in the struggle for financial survival in the new Japan.

In the climactic scene Ayako blames her callow and weak boyfriend for not having given her the money so that she need not have sold herself to her boss. Mizoguchi accepts this assessment. In the society of her time Ayako has had no choice but to become a *"moga."* A second lover, finding her with this cowardly fiancé, demands the return of the money he had given Ayako. Bravely, she suggests that she and her boyfriend work hard to pay him back. Encouraged by the possibility that she can do something about her fate, she begins to whistle. Disconsolate, her fiancé looks on. A moment later, Ayako is being arrested for having stolen the money, the camera tracking back and forth from her to the boyfriend, who is accused of using her to get money for himself. His wish not to become involved has resulted only in his being implicated, the thing he feared most.

At the end, Ayako returns home from the police station, still cheerful and glad to see her family: "It's a long time since we've eaten together." But rather than with welcome, she is greeted only with recriminations. Even her younger sister whines that she will no longer go to school, so humiliated is she by the "disgrace." Ayako walks out alone and stands on a bridge, while debris floats to the surface of the water below, as aimless as herself. The doctor of her boss passes by, but he, as a representative of this society, has no answer to her question: "What can you do for a woman who has turned into something like this?" Like the society which condemned Taki, Ayako's Osaka treats her as human debris. The doctor walks one way, Ayako the other. Prostitution is her final fate.

In the last shot of *Osaka Elegy* Ayako walks full into the camera in the film's only close-up; it suggests her heroism but also a hopelessness shared by the director, as overwhelmed as she by the values of this Osaka. Except for this last shot, Ayako has always been portrayed in relation to others, reflecting Mizoguchi's judgment that her "choices" have all been the result of pressures from without. Through his shot compositions in which Ayako has always been seen with boss, father, brother, or boyfriend, Mizoguchi has revealed, paradoxically, her profound isolation and total inability to locate an avenue for resistance, let alone rebellion.

Throughout his career Mizoguchi saw in his country of the double standard the prostitute as symbol of the oppressed Japanese woman. His married women sell themselves as well, and he certainly would have lamented the fate of Ozu's independent-minded Noriko in *Early Summer.* At twenty-eight Noriko, who has said that she would prefer to remain single, finally yields to family pressure and marries a neighboring widower about to take up work in cold, rural Akita. A theoretical opponent of marriage, Noriko consents to marry this man, whom she clearly does not love, because she is needed and can build a life with him. He is acceptable primarily because he was the best friend of her younger brother who died in the war, as well as being a colleague of her elder brother who is a doctor; a family bond already exists between them. Passion between these two seems inconceivable; Noriko herself seems to choose this man precisely because she, disliking what she clearly recognizes as the serfdom of marriage, will be more secure in an arrangement between friends rather than lovers.

Mizoguchi, however, would have viewed Noriko's decision as a sacrifice and would have challenged the association between marriage and service as if these terms were identical. Ozu accepts as natural a dutiful marriage based upon a mild feeling of companionship between two people. Mizoguchi always views the relations between men and women as invariably involving the man's using the woman as an object to satisfy his needs—a practice he deems absolutely indefensible. He would liberate the Japanese woman from the duplicitous contract wherein, in exchange for sacrificing her abilities and her very identity, she gains "control" of a household. Taken as a whole, Mizoguchi's body of films about women subtly equates the traditional wife with the prostitute. Each sacrifices all that she has, all that she is. The life of the Japanese woman, for Mizoguchi, is symbolized by a prostitution of the spirit.

Mizoguchi depicted a group of prostitutes in his last film, *Red-Light District (Akasen Chitai,* 1956), mistakenly translated in the American ver-

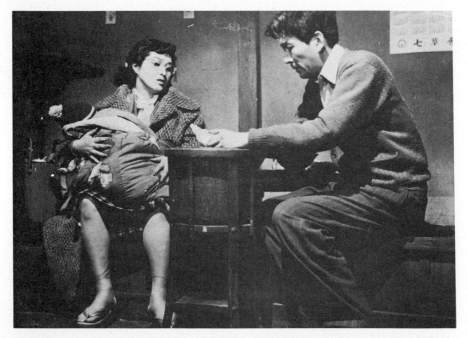

Street of Shame: The "heroine" is the prostitute, represented by five very different women, all of whom are portrayed as valuable human beings.

sion as *Street of Shame*, with inappropriate pejorative and moralistic connotations. The setting is a seedy, desperate, run-down Yoshiwara (prostitute quarter) at the moment in 1956 when prostitution is about to be
outlawed in Japan. The "heroine" is the prostitute, represented by five very
different women, all of whom are portrayed as valuable human beings
whose suffering would only be exacerbated by the outlawing of their
"profession."

In the last scene, the young maid of the house is about to lose her virginity. Her mother's frequent demands for money, after a mining accident suffered by the father, have left her no choice. As she passively
succumbs, her face is powdered. "Discard it with good grace," advises a
rebellious Mizoguchi heroine, offering a tidbit to sweeten the pain. When
this child ventures a glance outside, the street is filled with soliciting
women. A whistling, eerie music merges with their cries. Barely able to
speak, she hides behind a post in a brief, temporary respite. The final slow
fade spares us and Mizoguchi the agonies of viewing her final fall.

In *A Picture of Madame Yuki* (*Yuki Fujin Ezu*, 1950) Mizoguchi offers
an analysis of the psychology of a woman he could not achieve in films like
Utamaro And His Five Women, *Women of the Night* (*Yoru no Onna-
tachi*, 1948), or *Red-Light District*—films primarily concerned with a
group of women within a social context that was of equal concern to the
director. Mizoguchi made *Madame Yuki* for Shintoho Takimura Productions on the condition that the producer Takimura would then permit him
to do a film based on the stories of Saikaku. *The Life of Oharu* (*Saikaku
Ichidai Onna*) was indeed made in 1952, but for another company, Daiei.

Mizoguchi's theme in *Madame Yuki* is the prostitution of the wife, a
role often no less redolent of degradation than that of the whore. Yuki
(Michiyo Kogure) is a woman of great beauty, her room filled with the
aura of incense and mystery. Yet she remains enslaved to a vulgar, loutish
husband. Yuki is forever prey to this man's sensuality. Even when he brings
home his cabaret-singer mistress, whose dark lipstick bespeaks her vulgarity,
Yuki can still yield to him. A *koto* player who is a neighbor (Ken Uehara)
admires Yuki but, passive and unmanly as he is, Yuki cannot view him as
man enough to free her of her husband. Instead, he hovers in the background of her life. Yuki does go so far as actively to consider divorce, but
she always succumbs to her husband's advances. In one scene the maid,
surprised, comes in upon the husband reposing in Yuki's room. Yuki's
fallen kimono lies in view, a symbol of the collapse of her will to resist him,
as is her obi buckle with a Noh mask imprinted on it. "A devil lives inside
woman," says Yuki. It is the same devil tormenting Luis Buñuel's *Belle du
Jour*, a woman who could be aroused only by the perverse, and never by
her gentle, considerate husband.

At the end, Yuki kills herself, lacking the strength to overcome the
indecision and humiliation which are the alternatives to a frightening
struggle for freedom. Uehara tells her that to be saved she must solve the
problem for herself, something a Japanese woman of gentility who has
been conditioned to passivity simply cannot do. Uehara plays modern

A Picture of Madame Yuki: To be saved, she must solve the
problem for herself, something a Japanese woman of gentility
who has been conditioned to passivity simply cannot do.

music on the piano, as if Mizoguchi were saying that we must find the
means to cope with the postwar world as it is, instead of living among
idle dreams.

But Yuki is a woman whose personality has been shaped by centuries
of conditioning which taught the Japanese girl from childhood on that
she must accept the conditions of her life. Although Mizoguchi sees the
need for the Japanese woman to change radically, he is also very aware
of how difficult this will be. Speaking for the director, Uehara becomes
impatient with Yuki's passivity: "You never try to struggle against your
suffering. You're a human being. You must have the confidence to live
as a human being. Become strong!" Yet Mizoguchi also believes in the
truth of Yuki's reply: "You tell me to do what I cannot."

Yuki disappears. Her clothes once more lie discarded on the floor. The
camera tracks with the husband as he searches for her. But she is already
in the misty woods, small against the landscape. When Yuki's body is

found (she has drowned herself), the maid who had admired her so much throws Yuki's obi and the buckle with the Noh mask into the lake in anger. "You coward, you coward," she screams as Mizoguchi dollies *down* for his final shot, to the lake waters rippling and moving. The maid speaks for the angry Mizoguchi, as if he had been finally betrayed by a character so unworthy of his passionate anger over the oppression of the Japanese woman. The heroine of *The Life of Oharu* will not so disappoint him.

After *A Story from Chikamatsu*, *The Life of Oharu* is Mizoguchi's greatest film. It opens as an aged prostitute recalls for her friends the history of her life, a story that embodies the fate of all women in feudal Japan. Huddled in the cold beside a fire under a bridge are Oharu and her fellow prostitutes, all well past fifty and suffering hard times. A priest unfeelingly objects to their illegal lighting of a fire in the vicinity of the temple, while in the background we hear monks chanting Zen sutras, of little solace or relevance to these abandoned women.

Organized religion emerges in this film as one of the most sinister oppressors of the Japanese woman. As the camera tracks, following the wizened Oharu moving away from the scene, the chanting grows louder and louder. The camera increases its motion, as if in competition with the chanting voices. By contrasting camera movement with sound, Mizoguchi seems to be presenting two forces at eternal war: suffering women and institutionalized religion, which turns a deaf ear to their cries of pain.

Oharu enters a Buddhist Temple of the Rakans, filled with statues of life-sized monks, each with a unique and individualized visage. Mizoguchi pans these figures until Oharu's eyes focus on one face, which dissolves to that of the actor Toshiro Mifune, meant to remind Oharu of the first man who loved her. A flashback now removes us to 1686, when Oharu's story properly begins, and she is a very young woman attached to the court. The irony is that once we enter the flashback, the young man who loves Oharu, a page at the Old Imperial Palace, is not played by Mifune at all. Many years later she remembers him as a man much more handsome, vital, and energetic than he really was, one of the tricks life plays on lonely women. Her error is recorded by the camera without comment and in the understated manner that has made Mizoguchi one of the greatest directors in the history of world cinema.

Another dissolve takes us to the court, where Oharu's troubles begin when she accepts the advances of this man of lower rank than herself. Obedient to the norms upholding a rigid class structure, she is at first outraged when he sends her a poem declaring his love. In order to meet her at all, so bound by convention are those chosen to serve at court, he must use deception and pretend to be delivering a message from their superior.

"Who would read a letter from a mere page?" says Oharu when they meet in the graveyard. Katsunosuke's reply teaches her the meaning of life as Mizoguchi would have us see it. There are values that transcend those defined as *giri* or obligation by the class society. "I'm loyal and sincere," says this page, Katsunosuke, "you can despise my low rank, but you

The Temple of the Rakans in Tokyo.

can't ignore my devotion." He asks who among the nobility would care enough to marry Oharu and make her happy: "a woman can be happy only if she marries for true love."

Within the context of the feudal society of the time, this is an outrageous, revolutionary idea, one that requires the breaking of laws, the punishment for which is death for the rebel. The class boundaries of Japanese society as a whole would have to be broken were marriage to be based upon love. For no matter how much Oharu and Katsunosuke care for each other, neither the Imperial Court nor her father would ever permit them to marry.

Still in the graveyard, Oharu embraces Katsunosuke, with Mizoguchi employing a variation on his famous one-shot, one-scene technique, in which an entire scene is conveyed in one shot with no cuts to vary the angle or change the point of view. Mizoguchi employs this technique at the most intense psychological moments in his films, even at times photographing a scene for five minutes from a single point of view. "During the course of filming a scene, if an increasing psychological sympathy begins to develop," he has said, "I cannot cut into this without regret. I try rather to intensify and prolong the scene as long as possible."[2] This take

[2] Kenji Mizoguchi, "Three Statements," reprinted in Peter Morris, *Mizoguchi Kenji*, p. 10.

between Oharu and Katsunosuke in the graveyard is very long, a sign that Katsunosuke's words have been experienced by Oharu as truth.

As she falls to the ground in passion, amidst the dying autumn leaves, Katsunosuke lifts and carries her out of the frame. The camera, remaining, tilts down ever so slightly to reveal two graves side by side, a foreshadowing of the fate of this forbidden love. Another long take focuses on the scene now empty of human beings, the length of the shot expressing the power of an environment that cares nothing for the feelings of people. The long take which Mizoguchi uses so frequently often asserts a problem admitting of no easy resolution. It is the cinematic opposite of rapid cutting which suggests change, hope, progress, and development, and which characterizes the film style of Kurosawa. The long take, in Mizoguchi's hands, bespeaks the recalcitrance of the outside world, the difficulty of change, the spuriousness of optimism.

At the inn where they have gone to be alone, the police burst in upon Oharu, the daughter of a samurai, and Katsunosuke, a mere retainer. A rapid fade-in and fade-out at once removes us to a long shot in which Oharu is being sentenced for her crime. Her parents are simultaneously punished; she is an extension of them and not a separate individual, the very term an anachronism in feudal Japan. According to Tokugawa justice, the parents are as guilty as she.

As we view the scene in long shot, Oharu's "crime" is read out loud. She is guilty of misconduct with a person of low rank. To emphasize their powerlessness, Mizoguchi stubbornly reveals only the backs of their heads as she and her parents are told that they are to be exiled from Kyoto. They bow in obedience. To debate the question would constitute a further crime.

A dissolve within the scene to the crowd waiting outside is employed not to indicate the passage of time (the more frequent use of this technique), but to express the shame of this family before those who know them, as much a part of the punishment as the exile itself. The camera remains at a very low angle as Oharu and her parents cross a bridge into the next phase of their lives. From under the bridge, in extreme long shot, Mizoguchi shoots three tiny figures on the horizon. They are indeed insignificant. Before the fade ending the sequence, on a sloping horizon remain one bare tree and three tiny silhouettes. The shot composition itself contains a protest against feudalism.

In exile, Oharu is upbraided by her father for destroying family honor and causing them to live in shame. She replies with the truth she has by now fully assimilated: "Why is it immoral if a man and woman love each other?" But the high angle looking down at Oharu is from the point of view of her father, and reinforces only her powerlessness, despite her growing awareness.

Oharu and her family suffer the pain of exile. But Katsunosuke, a male, and an inferior who violated the laws governing rank, must be executed. He sends Oharu a message she will find it very difficult to fulfill: "Please find a good man. Be sure to marry only where there is mutual love." He hopes for a time when there will be no such thing as social rank and people can marry for love. The steel of the sword raised over his head glints in the sun. We are permitted to see the sword in close-up, but not the death blow, because Mizoguchi wishes us to remember Katsunosuke in his strength. Unlike Kurosawa, Mizoguchi, in a much more traditionally Japanese approach to characterization, rarely uses facial expressions to reveal personality. A kimono obscures Oharu's face when she learns of Katsunosuke's death. Her emotions are revealed, instead, in the next action she takes. She makes an unsuccessful attempt at suicide.

Oharu now begins her descent, a plunge unapparent because there is first a seeming rise in her fortunes. The retainer of Lord Matsudaira arrives in town bearing a scroll painting of the ideal woman whose likeness is to be approximated by the concubine he will select for his Lord. Lady Matsudaira is barren and the clan will be ruined unless a woman is found to bear Matsudaira a child.

Mizoguchi satirizes the prevailing standards of beauty. The ears of this paradigm must not stand out; her feet can be only twenty-one or twenty-two centimeters long; she must have neither odor nor moles. The camera tracks down the line of assembled beauties, as if they were cattle at auction, while the fat retainer, ruler in hand, examines them for imperfections. A deep-focus shot reveals the whole line reaching back into oblivion, as if all women in Japan were every day being subjected to the inhumanity of such scrutiny, reduced to sexual objects. None pleases him until he discovers Oharu at dancing school. Somehow she had escaped the public inspection, a further hint of her rebellious nature and unwillingness to be humiliated. Before she can say a word, Matsudaira's retainer rushes in on the scene and announces to all, "I'll buy her!"

Oharu's parents, particularly her father, are delighted by the opportunity to sell their daughter. The father promises no longer to curse her for their exile. But Oharu's rebellion continues. She now announces that she doesn't wish to be a concubine: "Katsunosuke won't permit me to." But physical violence will be employed against any woman who defies the wishes of her superiors—lord, father, or husband. Oharu's father throws her brutally to the ground. In the next sequence she is in a sedan, arriving at Edo to become Matsudaira's concubine.

Lady Matsudaira, whom Oharu very much resembles, is told to subordinate her own feelings "for the sake of the clan." Women are set against each other in a society where each day marks a struggle for survival. In deep focus, a performance of the Bunraku at court finds the puppets acting out Oharu's arrival and the jealousy it engenders. The play is a means by which those sympathetic to Lady Matsudaira are to be reconciled to the change in her circumstances. With such subtlety, harmony is enforced without public dissension and malcontents are silently ordered to conform.

When Oharu bears a son, she is told that she has not "borne" a child, but that she has been "caused to bear" one. The child is immediately removed to be nursed by someone else, and, of course, belongs—as did all

The Life of Oharu: Oharu next is sold as a courtesan to the Shimabara whore-house, where her rebelliousness, ever endorsed by Mizoguchi, expresses itself.

male children at the time, regardless of class—to the father and his family. While Oharu's father is profligately buying silk in the hope of becoming a merchant, she is banished because Lord Matsudaira loved her so much that he was expending all his energy on their relationship. In the clan system, even the powers of an individual lord are limited. Oharu, as a woman, cannot please whether she is deemed adequate or inadequate. She is given five ryo for her trouble, an incredibly paltry sum, but a measure of a woman's worth. In anger, her father hurls her against the sedan in which she arrives home.

Oharu is next sold as a courtesan to the Shimabara whorehouse, where her rebelliousness, ever endorsed by Mizoguchi, expresses itself as she flings the money of an arrogant customer back into his face. "I'm not a beggar," she proudly asserts, a forehadowing of her final fate. "But you arc no different from a fish," she is told, "we can prepare and dispose of you as we wish." As her merchant customer is unmasked as a counterfeiter, Oharu stands in one of the finest deep-focus shots in the film, a small, lonely figure on a balcony observing the chaos of the man's apprehension in the courtyard below. She is almost unnoticed by us, just as her rebellion is temporarily overlooked by her superiors in the urgency of the moment.

Rapidly descending the social scale, Oharu becomes servant to a merchant. As soon as the man discovers that she has been at Shimabara, he attempts to seduce her. The religious satire enters the film once more as the merchant begins his approach to Oharu while pretending to be engaged in Buddhist prayers. Meanwhile, his jealous wife torments Oharu, who

The Life of Oharu: The only kindness shown Oharu in her long travail is by the old prostitutes of the first sequence; as the most demeaned of women, they have known the same pain.

achieves her revenge by sending a cat late at night to pluck off the woman's wig to which Oharu, as the woman's hairdresser, has applied an appropriate odor. Thus is the wife's baldness revealed to her husband, a revelation that she has feared would ensure his leaving her. Women who might be natural allies destroy each other, while men are aided in the oppression of women by the competition among them for men, their only means of survival.

Only once does Oharu marry. Her husband is a fan-maker who is devoted to her. In a rather crude manipulation of plot, Mizoguchi has him attacked by thieves and murdered. In his final moment he is shown holding an obi, a gift destined for Oharu. Although he loved her for herself, the world

The Life of Oharu: Women who might be natural allies must destroy each other, while men are aided in the oppression of women by the competition among women for men, their only means of survival.

separated them anyway. Oharu becomes a nun, but when the merchant of the bald wife pursues her at the temple and she rebels, she is condemned by the head nun for licentiousness in a brilliant satire on the hypocrisy of religious orders.

The merchant arrives at the temple, demanding the cloth she has not yet paid for. Oharu insists that she has already converted it into a kimono and begins stripping herself as if to return the goods. The nun, viewing the kimono on the floor (an image of sexual relations, as in A *Portrait of Madame Yuki*) and the naked Oharu, immediately casts her out. But the nun is angry, not because of Oharu's violation of the rules of the Buddhist order, but because she herself has been sexually aroused. "Do you provide me with a visual demonstration, hoping I would join you?" she demands of Oharu, indicating a barely concealed desire to do just that: "I can't be tempted by a whore like you." Oharu is now punished for the nun's own repressed feelings. Religious orders offer no refuge for the oppressed but, rather, cooperate in their oppression.

The only kindness shown Oharu in her long travail is by the old prostitutes of the first sequence; as the most demeaned of women, they have known the same pain. And they have learned that "whatever we do, it doesn't make any difference to the world." Oharu joins them and, unfortunately, is selected by a pilgrim in Mizoguchi's final thrust at organized religion for its failure to offer compassion to the suffering. This pilgrim drags Oharu into the light, where he uses her as a means of convincing his followers to renounce the evil of sexual intercourse. "Take a good look at this witch," he leers, "do you still want to lie down with a woman?" Oharu becomes an example of the sinner. In bitterness she protests, "you'll always be able to remember you came face to face with a real witch!" But her rebellion now falls short because she has no choice; she must retrieve from the floor the coins they have thrown her way.

Religious hypocrisy is paralleled by that of the political structure. The Matsudaira clan would accept her back, except that, by becoming a courtesan, she has not kept her loyalty to those pompous and cruel "descendants of Ieyasu Tokugawa," as they term themselves. Mizoguchi now offers his full contempt for class superiority, and for those who claim to be valuable on the ground of family connection. In her last rebellion, Oharu breaks free of the clan elders to have one look at her stuffed-shirt of a son. As he passes with his entourage, his face bespeaks what he is—an adolescent, callow and empty, a scion of those who have long ceased to have any claim to humane emotion, an emblem of a dying aristocracy.

In the last sequence, an aged Oharu, now a beggar, seeks alms. In a house where a woman holds a baby, she is treated kindly; at another, a man waves her away, a symbol of his sex's treatment of women. Oharu looks toward a pagoda in the distance; raising her eyes in prayer, she walks out of the frame. And the camera is left in this last shot to focus on the pagoda, as if Mizoguchi were blaming it for her suffering. Only Yuki, a woman of modern Japan, but never Oharu, is told by the director that she ought to have shown greater strength. In this, perhaps the finest film ever made in any country about the oppression of women, the director, shunning didactic moralizing, can only echo her pain.

One "mistake," even when it is based purely on a misunderstanding, can ruin a woman forever, a fact equally true for Ayako of the 1930s in *Osaka Elegy* and Osan of Mizoguchi's *A Story from Chikamatsu* in Tokugawa Japan. At first Osan is only grateful to Mohei, her husband's worker, for standing by her. She neither loves nor desires him. Rather, they are brought together only by the circumstance of having to flee through mud and swamps, fugitives like runaway slaves in the American South. Should they be caught, the punishment would be crucifixion, with no one stopping to inquire whether or not they had in fact been lovers. Osan "belongs" to her husband as a serf would to a feudal lord. Only extremes of social chaos, brought on by the merchant's rapid ascent to power, have led her to such impropriety, to what she calls so "strange" a fate.

From choosing death through suicide on ironically calm Lake Biwa, Osan moves, for the sake of an authentic love, to a willingness to defy the society's highest laws defining a woman's behavior. In four cuts Mizoguchi develops her emotions. Lake Biwa appears with a solitary temple in long shot against the sky. The boat from which Osan and Mohei plan to drown themselves then rows into the frame, still in long shot. A dissolve next brings the edge of the boat close to us but in very shallow focus. A closer shot reveals Mohei tying Osan's legs together, readying her for the suicide.

Mizoguchi then turns to his characteristic one-shot, one-scene technique. The long take in the beautiful Lake Biwa scene begins as Mohei declares his love for Osan. The rowboat in which the two have been drifting is now anchored firmly in the center of the shot. When Osan's feelings become impossible to contain and she announces to Mohei "your confession [that he loves her] has made me change my mind. I don't want to die," both are standing in the precariously rocking boat. It is a moment of extreme transcendence, perhaps the first in Osan's life in which she has expressed what she feels as a unique, separate human being. She grabs Mohei and the boat begins to move, the camera remaining static, as if fully endorsing Osan's choice of *ninjo*, or, rather, of a higher *giri*, a duty to the growing love between herself and Mohei. Mizoguchi at last need not intervene. He dissolves to the empty boat on the lake, now interpolating a very short take. His woman has achieved her humanity, defined always for Mizoguchi in terms of an act of rebellion against feudal norms.

But the rebellion of one individual does not a revolution make. The moment of Osan's greatest happiness is rapidly followed by a descent leading to her crucifixion. Mohei, knowing that this is the fate awaiting them, would send her back to "the Master." It is she who becomes the stronger of the two, insisting that she cannot live without Mohei. The first taste of freedom strengthens one's character. It transforms us from passive acceptance to active insistence upon controlling our own destinies. And it is at such triumphant moments in their development that Mizoguchi loves his women best.

Class differences recede, as if a liberation for women in Japan would

A Story from Chikamatsu: From choosing death by suicide on ironically calm Lake Biwa, Osan moves, for the sake of an authentic love, to a willingness to defy the society's highest laws defining a woman's behavior.

mean a simultaneous social emancipation for all. "You're no longer my servant," Osan tells Mohei, "you're my beloved husband, my master." That she calls Mohei, the man she has chosen, her "master" in no way invalidates Osan's achievement. Choosing whom to love, in the context of the life of a woman under feudalism, constitutes the highest degree of revolutionary struggle.

The world, of course, conspires against Mohei and Osan. It could not do otherwise. Her brother, outraged at her persistent refusal to return to Ishun, says that Osan should be "cut to pieces." It is he who turns her in to the police at the house of her mother, where Mohei, inspired by Osan's own resilience, had claimed her. Their destinies are finally resolved in a last one-shot, one-scene in which a slowly panning camera reveals to us Osan and Mohei tied together, riding off to be crucified. Osan looks serene, Mohei cheerful. The camera remains still as they ride off into long shot, as if satisfied at having told a story so full of nobility. Each camera set-up has seemed determined by Osan's movements on her path to liberation, as if guided by the magnificence of a Japanese wife triumphantly escaping her bondage. Death is a small enough price to pay for spiritual transcendence. It has awaited all revolutionaries. Mizoguchi would urge us, finally, that it need not be feared.

As a coda to his films about the oppression of women, Mizoguchi made his first color film, *The Princess Yang Kwei Fei* (*Yokihi*), in 1955, the year before his death. The story is not properly that of a woman, but of the Emperor Hui Sung, who falls in love with a scullery maid named Kwei Fei, and then loses her in an execution necessitated by political upheaval over which he has no control. It is a testament to the undying love aroused by Kwei Fei and of the capacity for such love in a man. *The Princess Yang* is thus a paean to the feelings between men and women that should be possible, but which the world rarely permits. It is a much weaker film than A *Story from Chikamatsu*, which immediately preceded it, perhaps because Mizoguchi is at his best when he is absorbed in a struggle against oppression. In *The Princess Yang*, when forces separate the lovers, rebellion is assumed to be impossible, despite the man's being an Emperor!

The Emperor finally comes to the close of his troubled life. He calls the dead Kwei Fei's name, and in a metaphysical moment that becomes Mizoguchi's argument for a Buddhist-oriented renunciation of the possibility of happiness in this world, she replies, having waited faithfully in the next world for his arrival: "I've come to take you. I have been waiting for this moment for years. Give me your hand. Let me guide you . . . no one will ever disturb us this time." At last Kwei Fei can offer the Emperor a "happiness that has no ending." Together they join in uproarious, joyous, cosmic laughter, as curtains blow in the now empty room, a sign of the presence of the supernatural. It is Mizoguchi meeting the moment of his own death, and welcoming his departure from a world that has offered only grief to woman—and to man as well. Rebellion has achieved little; death and the unchangeable offer the final and only relief.

If in *The Life of Oharu* Mizoguchi lived inside his heroine, a Flaubert to his personal Madame Bovary, in *The Princess Yang Kwei Fei* his is the point of view of the besieged, imprisoned Emperor. At the end of a long and distinguished career in which he directed more than eighty films (the exact number is unknown), Mizoguchi experiences a sense of exhaustion. Instead of rebellion against feudal norms, he now prefers communication with a world beyond the tawdry, blemished land of the living. It would remain for younger directors like Susumu Hani to take up with renewed vigor the theme of the oppression of the Japanese woman.

The Two Naruses

. . . the people won't turn out for stories about a strong, independent woman. The audience prefers and is pleased only with stories about a weak woman's torment and abuse. But I shared none of their feelings that untraditional women are unattractive, that strong-hearted women are despicable and disgusting.

Mikio Naruse[1]

The sense of resignation accumulates like grime on my skin.

Mikio Naruse[2]

Of somewhat lesser rank than Ozu, Mizoguchi, or Kurosawa, Mikio Naruse is nevertheless one of the most interesting Japanese directors. He lacks the style of either a Mizoguchi or a Kurosawa and lacks the assurance of an Ozu. Yet there is a deeply felt quality to his films, an openness to the oppressiveness of Japanese culture more appealing than the closed world of Ozu, his friend and contemporary. After Mizoguchi, of the older directors Naruse shows the greatest concern with the plight of the Japanese woman.

Yet in the large number of films he made about the exploitation of the Japanese woman, two Naruses emerge: one Naruse who urged her to conform, and another later and more interesting Naruse who saw the need and inevitability of her rebellion against the social place and range of personal expression allotted to her in neo-feudal Japan. Naruse's reactionary films about the Japanese woman were made early in his career. A typical example was *Wife! Be Like a Rose!* (*Tsuma yo Bara no yo Ni*, 1935).

The story is of a man who has two wives. One is a poet to whom he is legally married, the other, a rural housewife with whom he has lived for years and who has borne him two children. The grown daughter of his legal marriage now insists that her father come home and properly resume his life with her and her mother. But the poetess, a "mod," liberated woman of her day, turns out to be an unfeeling and nagging wife, objecting even to the amount of sake (that palliative of the Japanese male) he drinks. And he, in turn, cannot wait to rush back to the country and the arms of the self-sacrificing *hausfrau* waiting for him there, "like a rose." The poetess, Etsuko, may weep at having lost

[1] *Kinema Jumpo*, December 1960. Translated by Leonard Schrader.
[2] Interview with Matsuo Kishi, from Kishi's *Collected Film Writings* (Tokyo: Ikeda Shoten, 1955). Translated by Leonard Schrader.

Wife! Be Like a Rose! The independent, creative woman is tainted by what for Naruse is a perverse psychology; she likes her husband only when they are not together.

him but the daughter, Kimiko, now truly understands her father and endorses his choice.

The independent, creative woman is thus tainted by what, for Naruse, is a perverse psychology; she likes her husband only when they are not together. Far from showing any admiration for her achievements as an artist, Naruse ridicules Etsuko for having been able to write about emotions but being unable to create a harmonious family life with a man. Naruse also criticizes her for pouring emotional energy into her work that would have been far more appropriately spent in attending to the needs of her husband. Etsuko is characterized as proud and selfish, as well as petty, and we are even treated to the sight of her, childlike, lusting after a new kimono, which she can ill afford, for her student's wedding. Luckily, her daughter Kimiko knows better. She, unlike her mother, is willing to don an apron and fry the dinner cutlets. That Kimiko thus knows so well how to be a woman assures us that she, unlike Etsuko, will make a good wife.

The second wife, Yuki, whom Naruse presents totally without irony, was once a geisha. She is now a hairdresser, and the measure of Naruse's democratic sensibility in this film is that he can permit a former geisha to achieve the highest value as a Japanese woman. Thus, she encourages her man to visit his legal wife and daughter, and she even tells her own children to call Kimiko, who comes to visit them, "father's precious person." Unbeknown to her husband, she sends Etsuko and Kimiko support money that would have permitted her own daughter an education.

The money Yuki had saved for her daughter's wedding also is given to Kimiko. The truly good wife assumes the responsibilities of her man as if they were her own. She accepts poverty and is even reconciled to the fact that one day she may have to let this man go. Naruse rewards her. Far from abandoning this paragon, her husband, at the end of the film, will flee from Etsuko gratefully to Yuki's waiting arms.

When her husband visits her, Naruse has Etsuko behave in an irrational, contrary manner. She insists on taking a taxi when he prefers to walk and, in general, commits the sin of asserting her own preferences, demanding that they go to the theater, where he falls asleep. Finally he decides to leave, but she is not even present, having, inexplicably, retired to her room to write a poem. Interests of her own, let alone a profession, are shown to conflict irreconcilably with a woman's duties as a wife. The daughter Kimiko, Naruse's surrogate, is now totally in favor of her father's leaving her mother for Yuki. As Etsuko cries, Naruse dollies in to Kimiko watching her coldly, never again to be deceived regarding how women should behave. The music of the ending is the tune sung earlier by the father's son and Yuki, a symbol of the happiness of his peaceful existence with a wife who is truly "like a rose."

Repast: Happiness for this woman will be in serving as a support for her struggling husband.

Although *Repast* (*Meshi*, 1951) is based upon a story by Fumiko Hayashi, a woman writer deeply committed to the struggle against the enslavement of her Japanese sisters, and the inspiration for many of Naruse's best films about women, the novel had been unfinished at the time of Hayashi's death. The production was supervised by that arch-conservative of Japanese male writers, the (1968) Nobel Prize winner Yasunari Kawabata. And it is perhaps to Kawabata that we may attribute the compromises imposed on the heroine, a discontented house-wife.

In urban Osaka, after five years of marriage, a wife (Setsuko Hara in a very fine performance) finds that her hopes and dreams of an inter-esting and fulfilling life have disappeared. The daily round of chores drains her of all energy. Her domestic life with her colorless husband (Ken Uehara, with no trace of his depiction of the dashing Tank Com-mander Nishizumi) lacks all joy. An unfeeling, insensitive man, he reads the newspaper at the breakfast table and, unmindful of the un-happiness and deprivation afflicting his wife, treats himself extravagantly to brown-and-white summer shoes.

To escape an arranged marriage, the husband's young and pretty niece comes to pay the couple a visit, and husband and niece begin a flirtation that heightens our sense of the oppression of the wife. In a successful use of parallel montage, Naruse has uncle and niece tour Osaka while the wife scrubs clothes on a washboard. The two parade through Osaka Castle as Naruse cuts to her finishing the laundry only to begin scrubbing the tatami mats.

Returning home from a class reunion, the first time she has been out of the house for months, and where she has been humiliated by having to wear a suit she owned before she was married, Hara finds uncle and niece alone upstairs in a compromising situation. He is ministering to her "nose bleed." The wife at last rebels: "What were you doing upstairs? Every time you see my face, you only say you're hungry."

Off she goes to Tokyo to think things over. But foreshadowing this wife's final capitulation to domesticity has been Naruse's depiction of the husband, not as a true villain but as merely careless and unthinking. In a sympathetic shot we see him after her departure, eating, lonely and abandoned, at his office desk, something, presumably, no man should be forced to do, let alone a married man. The house is filthy, another im-plicit criticism of the absconding wife. "Repast" also means "rest" or "respite," all the film finally suggests this couple needs. By no means does Naruse call for a revolutionary upheaval of their lives or even for a sharing of the dreary household chores.

For a while the wife plans to make a new life for herself in Tokyo. But there she discovers widespread unemployment and a friend who is reduced to opening a street stall. Hara's unsympathetic mother tells her to go back, or her husband will soon find someone else. Her opportunities include a liaison with an interested cousin, which Hara rejects because she is still a wife and will always be one in the traditional Japanese sense. "Did you think I was that kind of woman?" she virtuously rebukes him. Having once assumed the role of wife, she can never transcend it. Halfway between marriage and liberty, she is not free, but disoriented, and a measure of her weakness is that she has become so sloppy that her mother must hang up her discarded kimonos. When her brother-in-law accuses her of being a parasite, Naruse goes along, not with the harshness of this judgment, but with its substance. Without marriage a woman becomes dependent, careless and lazy, lacking any place in the world.

On the night of a festival, with drums beating in the background— a lame attempt by Naruse to herald his arrival—the husband appears in Tokyo. Together they drink and share a meal. What they have in common are the small things of life, such as where he left the cat when he made this trip. They leave for home together, she tearing up a letter she had written breaking with him. She asks if he knows what was in the letter, and with characteristic Japanese *enryo*—the formal, almost ceremonial behavior between people very close to each other, and by which harmonious relations are maintained—comes back his reply: "I'm

The Flavor of Green Tea over Rice: The pleasure of being with her women friends far exceeds the unendurable tedium of the moments Taeko must spend with her plodding, taciturn husband.

sleepy." For sake of the peace required for them to live together, it is best that he not know.

In voice-over, the wife makes a virtue of necessity. She sees herself drifting in the waters of life and yet somehow remaining afloat. "My happiness," she tells us and herself, "is seeking happiness with him." She recognizes that he, too, is discontented, tired of life, yet refusing to give up. The life of the salaried man is far from one of fulfillment. Happiness for this woman will be in serving as a support for her struggling husband. The last shot of the film is of a street filled with women washing clothes, the mundane nature of the chore belying the serious part they are playing in maintaining harmony and order.

The following year Ozu made a remarkably similar film about a discontented wife, *The Flavor of Green Tea over Rice* (*Ochazuke*, 1952). As in Naruse's *Repast*, food, that symbol of domestic consanguinity, appears in the title. It is instructive to view how close to Ozu, and yet already how distant, Naruse was at this stage of his career in his treatment of the Japanese woman. In the Ozu film we find a wife, refined and fastidious, yet willful in her desire to have her own way. At the end she is reconciled to her seemingly crude but actually "pure" husband over a "repast" of uniquely Japanese ingredients: green tea poured over rice (*ochazuke*).

Naruse, a man of more ambiguous and complex sensibility than Ozu, had a far different attitude toward that supposedly typical Japanese dish, green tea poured over white rice. For Naruse to call such a dish an expression of the Japanese character, as Ozu implies, amounts to an oversimplification of the much richer and more nuanced experience of many Japanese people, including, for example, artists like himself:

> Provincialism prevails. Aside from a sparse scattering of the rich, our islands are jam-packed with the poor. Our aesthetics reflect this poverty: nothing rich or spicy. Plain tastes like green-tea-over-rice are regarded as authentic Japanese-ness by literature and all the arts. Since the Japanese people are like this, a filmmaker must be resigned to the limitations of this way of life.[3]

Ozu would, if he could, return the Japanese to a simplicity of experience typified by *ochazuke*; Naruse would convince his countrymen that their actual lives are far more complex than this supposed symbol of the authentic Japanese experience would imply.

In *The Flavor of Green Tea over Rice* Ozu's tone is light and comic, implying from the start the final reconciliation of husband and wife. *Repast*, however, is much more somber, steeped as it is in the tedium of the *shomin-geki*, or drama of lower-middle-class life, where the renunciation of one's personal desires remains always painful to accept. Yet the plot similarities are numerous.

Cleverer, and with greater options than Naruse's wife because she is of a higher economic status, Ozu's Taeko begins at once by fleeing from her

[3] Matsuo Kishi, "A Talk with Naruse" (1952), cited in Kishi's *Collected Film Writings*. Translated by Leonard Schrader.

husband for temporary "respite," concocting a lie so that she can enjoy herself at a hot springs resort. To her friends she calls her husband the "thick-headed" one, and expresses regret that she has married him. The pleasure of being with her women friends far exceeds the unendurable tedium of the moments she must spend with her plodding, taciturn husband, an experience of Naruse's heroine as well. Segregation of the sexes abounds in social situations in Japan, and in both films men mix together socially without their wives, and women relax only with their own friends. In both films relaxation and genuine pleasure are possible only when those of the same sex meet. Sometimes at these gatherings, so frequent in Ozu's films, old school or war songs are sung; only at such times can people really be themselves. Both Naruse and Ozu take as their premise a war between the sexes that puts men and women ever on their guard when they are together. And, of course, both are faithfully describing the Japanese reality.

Nothing about her husband pleases Ozu's Taeko, who is much more outspoken than the wife in Naruse's *Repast*. She wishes that he were more intelligent, although occasionally she finds his stupidity convenient. By the end of the film Ozu will argue that the husband has in fact been exercising considerable *enryo*, or self-restraint, for the sake of allowing his wife room to fulfill her own needs, and that he has been far from thick-headed. But at the beginning Taeko is so bored that she even wishes he would go somewhere far away—which, to her later distress, he will. As he sits peacefully eating his dinner, she finds fault with his table manners and refuses to eat with him. Pursuing him upstairs, she tells him she despises his choice of cigarette brand and objects to his traveling third-class on trains. At the age of forty or thereabouts, she looks forward to a very bleak future with a man who so little suits her.

Just as Naruse introduced a subplot involving the next, supposedly more liberated generation, Ozu presents us with Taeko's niece, Setsuko, although without Naruse's sexual connotations and threat to the wife. Ozu's Setsuko, as a modern girl, does not flirt with her aunt's husband but simply objects to *o-miai*, the system of arranged marriages which she calls "feudal." She will have only a man she loves, and flees from an *o-miai* introduction at the *Kabuki-za* (theater) where her aunt sits chaperoning a pallid, humorless young man.

But while recognizing that times are changing, Ozu only seemingly adjusts his expectations of his characters. He applauds Setsuko for refusing this *o-miai*, not because he objects to the institution as such but because he knows that disharmony will result from her choosing the wrong young man. At the end, the young man she does "choose" is most acceptable to all. He has business relations with her uncle, and, having passed his examinations, he fulfills the film's central idea that "reliability" is the quality most to be sought in a husband. The man Setsuko will marry, Noburo, would have been the subject of an ideal *o-miai*; only a mistake, and not a fault in the institution, temporarily produced the wrong partner. Despite the adjustment of forms that allows the young couple to "date," the old values remain intact. The good and proper young woman, regardless of her generation, finally wants not independence, implicitly defined by Ozu as anarchy, but exactly what her elders have always defined as best.

The turning point of *The Flavor of Green Tea over Rice* approaches as Taeko is blamed by her own friends for her fastidiousness. Unlike the situation in the Naruse film, the wife's side is finally given very little credibility. As a schoolgirl, Taeko had refused to leave the house if her hair were not properly combed; she wore "long skirts" every day. Now she is a danger to the harmony of the community because she still demands what no adult can have—everything her own way. Where Naruse blamed the wife's unhappiness in part on social conditions, on the emptiness of her daily life and the absence of interesting options for the woman outside the home, Ozu, more conservative, suggests that it is in the nature of things not only for the wife, but for all people, sometimes to be thwarted in their desires. Only a spoiled child could believe otherwise.

Like Naruse's wife, Taeko flees "to have my way for a while." About to be sent, at short notice, on a business trip to Uruguay, her husband tries to call her back by telegram, but she stubbornly refuses to answer and arrives only when he is gone. Yet *The Flavor of Green Tea over Rice* is a comedy and order remains ever accessible. The husband's plane develops engine trouble, and he returns to find his wife properly chastened. They share a meal of green tea over rice, fixing it together in their kitchen, a place where only the maid has hitherto ventured. Taeko apologizes, having learned the true worth of what her husband represents: "the intimate and the primitive, not starchy but easy." Such harmony is symbolized by his favorite dish, green tea over rice, uniquely Japanese in being "simple and unpretentious. It's how a married life should be."

Grand passion is seen as an impossible dream and undesirable anyway, an implication of both films. What counts is mutual understanding beyond language. The husband had known of Taeko's lies about why she went to the hot springs, but had chosen to exercise *enryo*; he had been far wiser than she imagined. And, by the end of *The Flavor of Green Tea over Rice*, Taeko has, in fact, truly fallen in love with her husband, becoming fascinated "even by his most loathsome points." She laughs at herself and her niece laughs even more at this romanticism of the older generation.

There are, of course, differences as well as similarities in the endings of *Repast* and *The Flavor of Green Tea over Rice*. While in both the estranged couple share a meal together, in the Ozu film the husband and wife achieve a much greater harmony. And Ozu's Taeko even experiences a sexual awakening in her relationship with her husband. Naruse, at the end, has his wife alone with her thoughts, staring out of a train window and expecting her fulfillment to come only from serving as a support to a man. She knows she will have to be more accommodating than her husband, more self-sacrificing. Far from falling in love with this man anew, she has a very clear-sighted view of a future that will be devoid of such love. Ozu, seeming to reject the necessity of passion in marriage, delightfully (if propagandistically) suggests that through a yielding of the ego, passionate love will suddenly materialize when it is least expected. Naruse by far the better psychologist, could never suggest something so preposterous, and the ending of *Repast* is accordingly deeply sad. In his insight into the silent, forced submission to circumstance of the Japanese wife, Naruse shows a sympathy with the trials of the Japanese woman of which Ozu was incapable.

And yet, one year after *Repast*, in *Mother* (*Okasan*, 1952) Naruse could almost obscenely idealize the Japanese woman as housewife. As its title makes obvious, *Mother* belongs to the genre of the *haha-mono*, or "mother-picture," glorifying the role of housewife and "Mama-san." It is perhaps a measure of Naruse's continued uneasiness toward the situation of women at this stage of his career that he could make so stereotypic a genre picture, with even the further romantic variation on the usual *haha-mono* that in this film the mother is appreciated and not abused by the children who are her *raison d'être*. The last lines of the film, narrated in voice-over by her eldest daughter (Naruse's surrogate), make this clear: "Mother, whom I love very much! Are you happy? Stay with us forever!" The sentimentality of the *haha-mono* is amply fulfilled. This genre, however, flourished primarily *before* the war. *Mother* is a postwar film, indicating how much later than Mizoguchi's, for example, was Naruse's development as an artist concerned with liberating the Japanese woman from her traditional role. With the society so deeply in flux in the postwar period, it seems incongruous to glorify the mother as a woman who never once desires a life of her own and yet this is exactly what Naruse does. It would be difficult to mention a Japanese film more vociferous in its endorsement of the traditional, Confucian expectations of the Japanese woman. It is almost as if Naruse felt he had to make *Mother* as advance penance for the revolutionary treatment of the oppression of women to come in his later films.

In 1954, with his adaptation of Kawabata's *The Sound of the Mountain* (*Yama no Oto*), Naruse turned to the *tsuma-mono* or "wife-picture" which, as Anderson and Richie point out, was a postwar genre generally concerned with the struggles of a wife for her identity.[4] Yet this transitional picture in Naruse's career far transcends the genre of the *tsuma-mono*. The director's sympathy for the Japanese woman seems at last to be approaching a genuine understanding of the paucity of options open to her in a neo-feudal society.

At the heart of the film is Naruse's belief that the Japanese woman educated before the war is destined to suffer because of an upbringing that has taught her only self-sacrifice. Only in self-abnegation is she comfortable with herself, for her identity is psychologically indistinguishable from the cultural norms assimilated for centuries by Japanese women from girlhood on. The dictates of her very psyche have incapacitated the Japanese woman for struggle against an unjust fate.

A more mature Naruse emerged in *Untamed* (*Arakure*, 1957), his first complex treatment of the plight of the Japanese woman. In the films about

---

[4] See *Japanese Film: Art and Industry*, pp. 319–320.

The Sound of the Mountain: The Japanese woman educated before the war is destined to suffer because of an
upbringing that has taught her only self-sacrifice.

the Japanese woman who has no choice but to rebel against her exploitation, Naruse replaces the passive if sentient Setsuko Hara with Hideko
Takamine playing the besieged heroine. Revolutionary discontent seems
etched on her face—along with a latent determination and resiliency
unexpected in a sex taught that life's rewards lie in being pliant.

Untamed opens in the 1920s, the Taisho era. Its genre, that of the
saga, is one Naruse perfected in his late films about women. But in the
Japanese context the story of a woman, and especially a pre-war woman,
who refuses her fate far transcends soap opera, no matter how clichéd some
of Naruse's filmic conventions seem today to Western eyes. The Japanese
woman before the war who would live economically independent of a man
—and who insists upon being treated as his emotional equal—might, in
this neo-feudal context, best be compared in the West with a Spartacus
or a Nat Turner.

In *Untamed* Naruse slowly and cumulatively explores the options open

to the Japanese woman. Takamine, as Oshima, begins as the new bride of
a man whose previous wife has fled his domain, paltry as it is: a grocery
store he had expected her to manage. If the first wife was sickly, the second,
Oshima, has been selected because, coming from a peasant background,
she bears the promise of being hard-working. Yet this weak and despicable
male, who would seem a caricature were he not manifesting so true-to-life
an attitude of the male in the Japanese patriarchy, gets more than he
bargains for. From her childhood on, Oshima has borne a scar from a hot
iron for having disobeyed her mother, a hint of the strong nature that will
not permit her to spend her adult life in servitude. Skirting the issue of
how this particular woman achieved the strength to defy authority and
risk surviving by her own efforts, Naruse suggests almost that she was born
that way, as willful and strong a child as she will be a woman. From her
first husband, *she* fled on their wedding night, inspiring her mother to
advise the new husband that Oshima must be scolded and made to work
hard. The subordination of women in Japan could not have lasted so long
were it not for women themselves proving to be the most stalwart collabora-
tors in the exploitation of their own sex.

In this new marriage the man is intensely critical, objecting to how
much make-up Oshima wears and criticizing her even when, in his opinion,
her sash is tied too low. And, of course, he is unfaithful. Naruse's style
is that of the chronicler, his editing workmanlike but undramatic, his shot
compositions adequate but nowhere approaching the visualization of

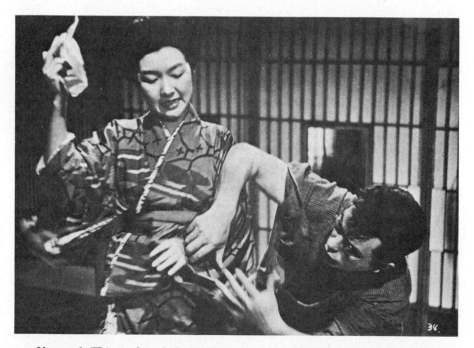

Untamed: This weak and despicable male, who would seem a caricature were
he not manifesting so true-to-life an attitude of the male in the Japanese
patriarchy, gets more than he bargains for.

woman's servitude we find in Mizoguchi. Instead, Naruse relies on full, close shots of Takamine as she is struck by each new blow of her husband's arrogance. Each episode of her oppression is punctuated by the unambiguous determinism of the fade.

As in Japanese society as a whole, Oshima's husband enjoys absolute power over her. He can always send her away, divorcing her by decree. And when Oshima loses a baby her husband had maliciously denied was his, he does just that. Her foster parents refuse to take her back, as if once their part in raising her had ceased, they lost all feeling for her. At a mountain inn she becomes a housemaid, there to work off the debts of a brother. As a lifelong member of her natural family, although she had been adopted, it falls to her as a woman, the lowliest of family members, to assume this responsibility. If the Japanese woman has any rights, Naruse implies, it is to assume the obligation to labor for others.

Oshima learns to support herself by sewing, working first in a factory owned by a man named Onoda (Daisuke Kato) where they have never seen a woman tailor before. Each momentous step she takes makes the next easier, as if Naruse were saying that once a woman sets herself on the path to liberation, she will succeed in avenues neither she nor the society ever thought possible for a woman. It is only after many small rebellions, which strengthen her will, that Oshima can take the step of opening her own tailor shop.

The entrepreneurial impulse as a means to liberation is as revolutionary for this Japanese woman as it was for Europe's striving middle class during the Renaissance. It is a means to self-determination and recognition for a group previously ineligible for human rights. It is thus a revolutionary leap when Oshima stops working for others in the lowliest of capacities and begins to work for herself. When an old friend, disheveled and worn, meets her on the street, she tells Oshima that she looks lovelier now than she did in her first youth. Hardship may have toughened this woman, but it has left her resilient. Surviving by her own efforts has suffused her with self-respect and a new vitality.

Naruse is too honest a psychologist not to recognize that Oshima's personality will be affected by her struggle. Her tyrannical impatience with the weaknesses of others is manifested in her intolerance toward Onoda, now her partner, whom she accuses of not working hard enough. Her struggle has exacted a never-ending vigilance from Oshima for fear that she might lose all she has gained. Irrationally, it leads her to berate Onoda for not staying up and working all night during rush times as she does, for not caring about the work as much as she. At times the precariousness of her success causes Oshima momentarily even to lose all control over herself; in one scene she sprays Onoda with a hose to "wake him up." But even hard work will not ensure success to the powerless, and the shop fails.

Undaunted, Oshima rents a Singer sewing machine for a month without charge, accepting the stipulation that afterwards she will pay it off in installments. In full shot Naruse focuses on the sewing machine, her means to freedom, just as the machines of the Industrial Revolution were to be the hoped-for instruments of the liberation of the masses in the nine-teenth century in Europe. With the cunning of those who cannot afford to take survival for granted, Oshima reasons that if she fails to make any profits within a month, she will say the machine didn't work and try the same thing with another.

The new shop that does succeed is predictably called the "Onoda" Tailor Shop, using the man's name and not the woman's. Oshima and Onoda now, quite ridiculously, wear Western clothes, looking like replicas of Queen Victoria and Prince Albert. Despite the economic success which is the result of her efforts and not his, the culture continues to view Oshima in the same terms in which it has always viewed women. Onoda's father, living parasitically off the two, says that she is "not a woman," not feminine, because she is out all day soliciting customers. She, in turn, refuses to treat and serve the old man as a guest, as would a traditional wife. For this offense to the patriarchy, Onoda slaps her across the face.

The music is sprightly as Oshima rides her bicycle looking for customers. She is happiest when she is alone. With Onoda, all is conflict. He com-plains that she is "like a man"; he wants her to study flower arranging! When she refuses, in a reversal of roles revealing a prescient Naruse, Onoda himself takes lessons, only to begin a flirtation with the flower-arranging teacher.

A young tailor named Kimura (Tatsuya Nakadai) begins to work at the shop with fresh ideas and criticisms of Oshima's old-fashioned tailoring patterns. It is with him that, once again, she will reshape her life. The years have kept her young. In this portrayal of the love between an older woman and a younger man, Naruse transcends the work of con-temporary directors, including Bernardo Bertolucci, who can accept only the idea of an older man's falling in love with a younger woman, but not the reverse. Kimura admires Oshima's strength and the beauty that has resulted from her having lived life deeply and fully.

At the end, with Kimura's help as her cutter, Oshima will become inde-pendent once more. Out into the rain she proudly marches to Naruse's uplifting music. Under her new umbrella she walks along facing the future, as unafraid as ever. In long shot we finally lose sight of her, if not of her spirit. She is all that the Japanese woman—and all women—can be. She has never flinched from paying the price of her freedom, including facing the indignation of women less courageous than she. The film is carried by Naruse's characterization of an "untamed" woman and by Takamine's performance, an embodiment of the unwillingness of all oppressed people to be dehumanized. That this woman rises above the role declared for the Japanese woman becomes a testament to the humanity of us all.

Less epic, but with an equally rich psychology, was Naruse's other great film about the oppression of women, *When a Woman Ascends the Stairs* (*Onna ga Kaidan o Agaru Toki*, 1960). The heroine, again played by Takamine, is a "Mama-san," a bar proprietress whose work is to entertain men for money. The degradation of her life belies the popular chauvinist myth in Japan that the prevalence of so many "Mama-sans" in the home, as in the world, constitutes a "matriarchy." Takamine's function, and that of the 15,000 Ginza hostesses like her,[5] expresses for Naruse the servitude of all Japanese women.

The Mama-san of this film is proud, refusing to descend to the level of a prostitute begging men to patronize her establishment. The problems of such women—which are those of all women, but intensified—include growing old and the temptation of suicide, to which, early in the film, a hostess at the "Bluebird" bar succumbs. Naruse uses the Mama-san's voice-overs to describe the lives of such women, beset by debts and creditors and having to maintain body and wardrobe with as much vigilance as the geisha, if with fewer financial resources. Thus does Takamine confide to us the trials of her day: "Then it gets dark. I hate to climb the stairs. But once I'm up, I trust to luck."

Intense competition turns the hostesses at the various bars against each other as they struggle to lure customers, mostly higher-ranking corporation executives, whose numbers are small in ratio to the proliferating number of bars and hostesses. Younger bar girls like Junko, who lures away Takamine's bartender (Tatsuya Nakadai) to open up her own place, are always a threat. For this is one of the few "professions" that have been open to the enterprising Japanese woman. Survival in it takes grit and an easiness of scruples. Takamine will ultimately fail to ensure herself financial security because she is too virtuous to accept a regular patron; it seems too "dirty." She won't wear a brightly-colored kimono, choosing to dress in accordance with *shibui*, the lower-keyed colors commensurate with her age. She is already thirty, no longer, by the standards of the patriarchy, a young woman. A ubiquitous, whining mother and brother, as is the case with so many Japanese women who must sell themselves, forever extort money from her.

Sometimes Naruse cannot resist irony as he dramatizes the fate of these powerless women with whom he sympathizes so deeply. An old man offers Takamine money to open her own place in exchange for an "understanding." "Time you quit working for others" is his inducement. For the most part Naruse explores, with the same degree of silent suffering endured by his heroines, this tawdry world where toilets are shared between bars squashed into tiny quarters, and where men use and discard women under a guise of cordiality.

For Takamine, the accumulating years only make these unctuous men she must entertain all the more repulsive. The camera tracks with her as, over and over, she ascends the stairs to her bar. Naruse offers a close-up of her feet which must bear her nightly to the scene of her psychic defilement. One man (Daisuke Kato) who seems kindly and says he loves her— he brings her "Black Narcissus" perfume and actually proposes marriage— turns out to be married and just another philanderer. This is the kind of man women of her class attract. His seeming generosity and kindness are but one more variant on the psychological mask men use to permit them

[5] At present there are estimated to be about 500,000 such bar hostesses.

full exploitation of these vulnerable, lonely women whom only the most threatened men in male-oriented Japan would dare term "matriarchs."

Exhausted by the struggle and by this disappointment, Mama-san throws herself into the arms of an executive named Fujisaki (Masayuki Mori as another of the morally weak Naruse men). And she finally yields to an affair typical for a woman of her kind. She even allows herself to fall in love with this man, confusing the paltry physical affection he offers with memories of her husband who had died years before, that death which necessitated her becoming a bar hostess in the first place. On the night they are together, with Naruse's psychology at its best, she dreams of her dead husband returning and bearing gifts appropriate to the time they shared together, the early postwar years when food was scarce: potatoes, onions, and radishes.

Fujisaki, a dutiful company man, an automaton compared to this woman so much more capable of genuine affection as well as moral dis-

When a Woman Ascends the Stairs: The spiritual motion of her climb is indeed a descent, in contrast to her having just ascended the stairs.

crimination, is transferred to Osaka. He gives her stocks and money, but, typically, he won't break up his home. Her pride intact, Mama-san goes to the train station from which he is departing to return his stocks, which she finally refuses to accept. Beside him sits a wife whom Naruse has made homely and unappealing, perhaps unwisely, since this choice suggests an implicit justification for the husband's adultery. The stereotype of the ugly wife waiting at home is actually quite unrealistic in the Japanese scene, where company men with quite attractive wives nevertheless wander nightly to the hostess bars.

The last scene finds Takamine once more ascending the stairs to her bar, determined to "become strong." The camera dollies in to her as she bows to the assembled women, as if her ambiguous half-smile were meant for us all, we who tolerate the exploitation of such women, not to mention those in the audience who actually enjoy their favors. It is the first full close-up of Takamine in the film and it comes at a seeming moment of defeat. Yet, simultaneously, such a close-up indicates Naruse's sense of her value. The spiritual motion of her climb is indeed a descent, in contrast to her having just ascended the stairs. But her defeat is only partial, for she retains her capacity for survival as well as her superiority as a human being to the men who have tried to degrade her.

After the weak *The Other Woman* (*Tsuma to Shite Onna to Shite*, 1962) Naruse's adaptation of Fumiko Hayashi's autobiography, *A Wandering Life* (*Horoki*, 1962)[6] again reveals this director approaching the height of his powers, as if restored by bringing to the screen the life story of Hayashi, the writer who had so frequently inspired him. A hint of Naruse's personal attachment to Hayashi is revealed in such small incidents as the pilgrimage he and his staff planned to make to her grave after the shooting of *Wife* (*Tsuma*, 1953).[7] *A Wandering Life* would be the last of Naruse's six Hayashi adaptations, which included *Repast*, *Lightning*, *Wife*, *Late Chrysanthemums* (*Bangiku*, 1954), and *Floating Clouds*.

A Wandering Life allows Naruse to introduce to his spectrum another and most rare type of Japanese woman, the artist. Hayashi's story is not only that of a rebellious woman of peasant origins seeking independence, but also of such a woman becoming a respected literary figure. It is a monumental film, although, because it is set in our own century, it lacks the historical dimensions of Mizoguchi's *The Life of Oharu*. But if Oharu's struggle can

[6] Adaptations by other directors of Hayashi's work lack the psychological density of Naruse's *Floating Clouds*, *Lightning* (*Inazuma*, 1952), or *A Wandering Life*. One of the best known of these is Yasuki Chiba's *Downtown* (*Shitamachi*, 1957) about a love affair between a war widow selling tea for a living and a workingman struggling for survival in postwar Tokyo. The woman (Isuzu Yamada), straining to withstand the temptation to end her poverty by succumbing to prostitution, finds respite with this man (Toshiro Mifune), who shows kindness to her bewildered, lonely son and desire for her. In a sentimental ending the woman learns of the man's death in an accident with his truck the night before, leaving her as helpless as she was at the beginning of the film when she had asked him if he wished to buy her tea. Dust from passing trucks is thrown on her and the boy as they trudge along the road, two helpless people for whom the man's love was a moment of temporary joy in otherwise dreary, deprived lives.

[7] "Interview with Akira Iizawa," *Kinema Jumpo*, May 1953.

readily attract sympathizers who mourn the oppression of women in Japan's feudal past, Hayashi's, much closer to the situation of the Japanese woman today, inspires anxiety and discomfort, a measure of Naruse's success in capturing the psychological bondage plaguing his heroine.

Naruse opens Hayashi's story in 1915 (the real-life author had been born in 1904). As a little girl, she watches as her stepfather, a peddler, is arrested for cheating his customers. Like Mama-san in *When a Woman Ascends the Stairs*, Fumiko, also played by Hideko Takamine, records her thoughts for us in voice-over, a successful device for capturing the heroine's sense of loneliness and alienation. In 1923, the year of the great Kanto earthquake, she and her mother (Kinuyo Tanaka, Mizoguchi's Oharu), bearing heavy packs, are desolate peddlers of underwear. Times are bad, and Hayashi's mother must suffer under the further burden of her daughter's being a "strange girl."

Fumiko's problem will be that she is "unlucky in love." (The real-life Hayashi had moved to Tokyo with a student, only to be deserted upon his graduation. After an extraordinary two initial failures in matrimony at a time when, even as now, divorce was considered a disgrace, especially for the woman, Hayashi married a young painter in 1926.)[8] In the film Fumiko recognizes that, as in the case with Buñuel's *Belle du Jour* and the heroine of Naruse's *Untamed*, only cruel and domineering men seem attractive to her. Yet she is powerless to alter her responses.

Takamine enacts Hayashi as a woman lacking all confidence, one whose self-hatred finds expression in her choosing men who abuse her, a pattern she retains even after she is acknowledged as a successful writer. Because he evokes no magic, she will not admit into her life a kindly widower (Daisuke Kato). The drooping, discouraged, self-abnegatory posture Takamine maintains throughout the film successfully conveys Hayashi's low opinion of herself, the result of the number of life's punishments she has been forced to bear, as well as of a socialization approving only qualities in women that she would always lack.

Describing herself as a "country girl in town," she stands as one among many on long employment lines. From her childhood on, Fumiko knows that the first step toward independence for a woman must always involve financial self-sufficiency. But to get such work, a Japanese woman of her time had to face constant humiliation from male employers. One prospective employer she pursues, as she herself puts it, "like a dog." She lands a job keeping accounts, but doesn't believe enough in herself to complete her tasks: "If I did all these figures, I'd be insane by nightfall." And indeed that night a telegram informs her of the termination of her employment. Meanwhile, her sick mother, herself a victim of unjust conditions, writes to ask for money. Her mother is unable to earn her own living because these supposedly ruling "matriarchs" were neither educated, encouraged, nor accepted as wage earners, a

    [8] *Synopses of Contemporary Japanese Literature* (Tokyo: Kokusai Bunka Shinkokai, 1970), 2: 147.

conspiracy against women at the heart of their historical enslavement. She has no choice but to exploit her daughter.

A hostess at a bar, Hayashi yet manages to write poetry and to read Heine, Whitman, and Pushkin. She is invited to contribute to anthologies. And her only personal happiness becomes sublimating desire to her art, as in one poem she writes, "I am in love with the Buddha/When I kiss him on his cold lips."

Throughout the film parades a stream of unworthy men. These include an actor who makes Fumiko support him, only to bring another woman to their home. What is amazing is that Hayashi can continue to write her poetry under such emotional stress, poems with such titles as "The Workingwoman's Song," and works describing "shawls thin as a stream worn by girls on the street," for Hayashi belonged to the school of proletarian writers of the 1920s and 1930s in Japan.

Pouring her life into her art transforms Fumiko Hayashi into a lovely woman. She always looks beautiful when sitting at her desk writing, and hapless when she must face the world. As with women today, knowing about her weakness for men who treat her badly and how it causes her so much pain is not enough to break the emotional pattern governing her life. Masochistically, she continues to permit men to beat and abuse her. This, in fact, only makes her want them more.

Married to a fellow writer, she yields to his demand that she go out and mail his manuscripts to publishers. When these manuscripts fail to

©TOHO Co. 1962 放浪記

A Wandering Life: As with women today, knowing about her weakness for men who treat her badly and the pain it causes her is not enough to break the emotional pattern governing her life.

A Wandering Life: "I will write," she says, as if to convince herself; "a wandering
life is not all of my life."

sell, he beats her out of frustration. Constantly she is ordered to fetch
cigarettes and food, and in one scene he throws over an entire dinner. If
she came to marry again, Fumiko tells herself in a lucid moment, she
would choose a carpenter or a rickshaw man. Her husband is unfaithful
and demeans her writing, and yet she can only blame herself because
she chose him for his good looks. Finally, she gains the strength to leave,
although being alone means she must return to her job as a bar hostess.
Later, a painter whom she loves helps her to avoid arrest, but by this time
she has sunk to prostitution as a means of survival. And yet, like the best
of the Naruse heroines, Fumiko has the courage, as Hayashi put it in
the original novel, to "dare to live" and to "immerse myself in myself."[9] "I
will write," she says, as if to convince herself; "a wandering life is not all of
my life."

The last sequence finds Fumiko an old woman in 1951, the actual
year of Hayashi's death. She is, by now, enormously prosperous. The
ubiquitous widower Kato visits her and her mother, who live together in
a spacious and grand house. The poor who come begging to her door, she
turns away, sending them out to work because experience has taught
her that people must help themselves. She conveniently ignores the
widower's having helped her, as well as the aid of the painter who is
now her husband. Life has made her hard. And Naruse, typically, lapses
into vagueness.

The ending of the film is saved, however, by one dissolve to a dream

[9] *Introduction to Contemporary Japanese Literature* (Tokyo: Kokusai Bunka
Shinkokai, 1939), p. 197.

the elderly Hayashi has of herself as a child, with her parents carrying packs on their backs. In her unconscious mind they will always be striving peddlers. Whatever success we attain, we carry with us the pain of where and what we have been. Naruse is too clever to end on a note of triumph, Hayashi's having "made it." The success that has come to her in these last years cannot begin to compensate for the pain of a lifetime. What counts, however, is her having struggled so unrelentingly to become, for her time as for ours, that rarest of Japanese women, the recognized artist.

Restricted by a lethargic sense that the world is unchangeable for the better, Naruse does not go beyond chronicling how the Japanese woman has been exploited. The would-be independent woman (*Untamed, When a Woman Ascends the Stairs, A Wandering Life*) is subjected to an unending stream of indignities and abuse. Psychologically, she does not bear up well under the strain of having deprived herself of the rewards of the compliant woman. The wife, Naruse shows in *The Other Woman*, at least retains home and hearth, if not that spurious fulfillment Chie Nakane condescendingly assigns to the Japanese "mistress of the household."[10] By implication Naruse doubts whether, for the intellectually vibrant Japanese woman, happiness with a man is possible at this moment in history, so feudal are male needs and expectations. No revolutionary, Naruse neither predicts nor welcomes the kind of upheaval that would make possible true equality for women in Japan. But he is too honest not to admit its dire necessity.

[10] "Women: A Cross-cultural Perspective," *PHP* (Tokyo), February 1975, p. 10.

Tadashi Imai: *Woman Under Feudalism*

> ... to me the most important thing for women to
> overcome is the old definition of who they are.
> Tadashi Imai[1]

Any director in opposition to authoritarianism in Japan could not help
but focus on the plight of the Japanese woman. Imai, with his left-wing
sympathies, systematically, if with less subtlety and psychological insight
than Naruse, sees the exploitation of the Japanese woman as an inevitable
and direct consequence of feudal injustice. Imai's portraits of women never
degenerate into rhetorical feminism because at the heart of his understanding is the recognition that women were not the only group oppressed
by feudalism. Imai's women are brutalized not merely because they are
women and, in a patriarchy, women are treated as objects. Rather, Imai
traces the exploitation of the Japanese woman to its source in the very
existence of a feudal hierarchy on which women occupied the lowest rung.
Feudal morality decreed that woman ever sacrifice her psychological and
spiritual needs for the sake of those to whom a social order based rigidly
upon rank and status had granted higher value. Imai's women, in three of
the best and most typical films he made about the suffering of this caste
under feudalism—*Muddy Waters* (*Nigorie*, 1953), *Night Drum* (*Yoru no
Tsuzumi*, 1958) and the weaker *A Woman Named En* (*En to u Onna*,
1971)—thus suffer a shame from which they have no recourse. It is the
inevitable shame of those who must live under the constant tension of
having been designated inferior human beings by a seemingly insurmount-
able and unidentifiable force. For Imai, shame is the psychological fate of
the Japanese woman, the humiliation of one whose very existence continues
only under sufferance.

Night Drum, perhaps Imai's best film, is a powerful depiction of the
abuse of women under feudalism. The setting is the eighteenth century,
the height of Tokugawa power. A woman named Tane (Ineko Arima),
wife to a samurai retainer, commits a single act of adultery during the
alternate year when her husband is forced by the shogun to reside in
Edo. He, Hikokuro (Rentaro Mikuni), is so sturdy a samurai and so
honorable, so scrupulous with clan funds, that he won't even allow his

[1] Joan Mellen, "Interview with Tadashi Imai," *Voices from the Japanese Cinema,*
p. 110.

men *sake* on the long journey home. There rumors await him of his wife's infidelity with the drum teacher from Kyoto, Miyaji (Masayuki Mori), who has been instructing their adopted son, Tane's younger brother.

On the surface, Hikokuro and Tane seem to accept with good grace the limitations on their relationship exacted by Tokugawa power politics which forced clan samurai to reside every other year in the capital, Edo (Tokyo) as a means of ensuring against uprisings and plots. "I come back each time to a new honeymoon," Hikokuro laughs, "is that the purpose of the law?" The couple seems to have made a virtue of necessity and the long separations have not weakened their love for each other. Yet it is only director Imai, and not Hikokuro, who is conscious of the physical punishment such separations inflicted upon samurai women. For, as one of the samurai brags, he left a courtesan who cried upon his departure from Edo. Samurai residence in the capital did not mean that the men lacked female companionship. Tane's adultery is placed in the context of a double standard in which women, but not men, were expected to remain celibate for a year at a time.

Assuming the rumors to be true, the family council meets, fearing that Tane's adultery has discredited them and weakened their political position within the clan, giving the feudal daimyo carte blanche to destroy them. It is their obeisance to the dictates of the feudal hierarchy, and their hysteria over the possibility (it remains only that) that they may have their property confiscated, that make for Tane's downfall. Loans which the family is negotiating from the clan may be jeopardized. Before such transactions and clan politics, the life of one woman seems a paltry thing. All members of the family, men and women alike, are unrelentingly determined that Tane be punished according to the full measure of the law. And death, of course, was the only appropriate means by which she could obliterate her sin. Against this reasoning, anguished though he may be because he loves her, Hikokuro does not struggle.

Up to the moment of her fall, Tane has been a model wife, praying every day for her husband's safe return, lonely but accepting of her circumstances. On the day she makes love to the drum teacher, she is at first approached by another would-be seducer whom she succeeds in warding off. He taunts her with the rumor that her husband has another woman in Edo. Lying, he "informs" her that Hikokuro has been ordered to spend another year in the capital.

Tane's confidence is at once undermined. Her frustrations, which hitherto were susceptible to repression—or sublimation—now surface. To this is added her drinking a great deal of *sake,* for it is Peach Festival Day. The attack by this crude, self-serving former suitor, climaxed by his actually threatening her with his sword, exposes the vulnerability to sexual assault of these abandoned samurai women, no matter that the punishment, even for being an unwilling victim of rape, was death. It is this man, from whom she manages to escape, who finally does cause Tane's

death by exposing, out of pique, her adultery with the drummer, which
shortly follows her rejection of him.

Tane's interview with the drummer, Miyaji, begins with her begging
him to say nothing of having inadvertently rescued her from a seducer
by happening along. They drink *sake*, sharing the same cup, as if it were,
she says, "a lovers' pledge to seal your lips." With the festival drums
beating in the background, Imai's means of objectifying Tane's growing
sexual desire, they embrace.

Hikokuro may love her, but once Tane admits to the truth, he can
envision no alternative to her suicide. A member of a feudal structure,
he only knows how to live by the rules. Tane ties her own legs together.
When, in a surreal angle shot, she is unable to plunge the knife into
her chest, Hikokuro does it for her, swiftly and expertly so that she might
avoid additional suffering.

But the story is not yet over. The last sequence forms a coda to
the action, an expression of the unspeakable toll taken of Japanese *men*
by the feudal oppression of women. His hair grown out, his eyes wild
with pain and confusion, Hikokuro arrives in Kyoto at the time of the

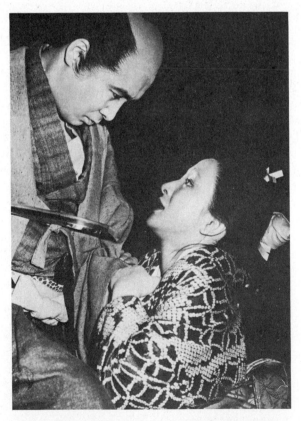

Night Drum: The attack by this crude, self-serving
former suitor exposes the vulnerability to sexual
assault of these abandoned samurai women.

Gion Festival. The wildly beating drums recall those on Peach Festival night when the adultery took place. A shell of a man, Hikokuro runs through Miyaji with his sword, ending up almost with his head on his victim's shoulder in a grotesque mockery of an embrace.

The murder occurs in full sight of the festival crowd. Yet it is carried out with complete impunity, since the vendetta had been registered with the authorities and such revenges were sanctioned by law. The camera dollies in to Hikokuro observing what he has done. He drops his sword— pained, empty, anguished, and fully aware now of the pointlessness of his having killed both Tane and her "lover."

The system that cruelly and absurdly took Tane's life also robs its men of their sanity. Their perpetuating such crimes on their women does not ensure the survival of the patriarchy, despite its insistence upon absolute certainty that the sons to whom these samurai would pass down their power were, in fact, theirs. For such a system finally destroys all of its own, including, and most particularly, its men, who have become dehumanized and, hence, weak. Imai's final point is that the oppression of women under feudalism guaranteed not the maintaining of feudal power but the certainty of its collapse from within.

Imai's treatment of women is always conjoined to an attack on the social structure which has institutionalized their servitude. His understanding of the Japanese woman, more akin to Mizoguchi's than to Naruse's, is founded on the perception that her situation will not truly improve unless a more equitable social system is constructed whose functioning does not depend upon woman's inferior status. Imai argues, most persuasively in *Night Drum* but in all his best work, that men, by oppressing women, have themselves become equally oppressed and emasculated. In the sense that it is directed to a patriarchy still in power and which stands most to gain by the continuance of the status quo, his is, of course, a futile plea. It is certainly one that has, as yet, gone unheard.

Hani's Awakened Women

> Only now are we beginning to have a society which
> is almost ready to accept women as complete human
> beings.
>
> Sachiko Hidari[1]

Susumu Hani has attempted for today's Japanese woman what Mizoguchi did for her sisters who lacked freedoms inconceivable in Japan until
after the Second World War. To the idea that Japanese women are fulfilled within their roles as wives and mothers, and to the myth that the
Japanese woman is free because she is the true ruler of her household,
a "matriarch," Hani would counterpose the latent discontent of such
women. It is Hani who has best understood that to be cast in the role
of manipulator, mediating one's desires through another person with
greater power, is itself a mode of enslavement.

More than any director, Hani has challenged the idea that the Second
World War represented a significant change in the status of the Japanese
woman, that when at last, through General MacArthur, she was granted
suffrage and coeducation with men, a new woman was born out of the
ruins of Japan's defeat. Hani's are all women of postwar Japan. The
Confucian obediences would seem to affect them not at all. Meddlesome
mothers-in-law are kept at a respectable distance, as are other supplicating
relations. Divorce is a real option for this woman, as is remarriage if she
desires it. The professions now appear to be open to the Japanese woman,
whose struggle for her liberation seems remarkably similar to that of her
Western counterpart. All, however, is not as it seems. The struggle of
Hani's women for unique and separate identities proves to be as difficult
as that suffered by Naruse's Oshima in *Untamed*. All of Hani's women begin in his films as deeply enslaved to the traditional definition of the
Japanese woman as the pre-war or even the feudal woman. The only
difference may be that the psychic chains binding her are externally less
visible.

By the time he did *A Full Life*, his first film about the Japanese woman,
Hani had already developed his semi-documentary style. The innovations
Hani brought to the Japanese film parallel those of the simultaneous
French New Wave: the hand-held camera extensively employed, non-
professional actors (although the heroine of *A Full Life* is a star, Ineko

---

[1] Joan Mellen, "Interview with Sachiko Hidari," *Voices from the Japanese Cinema*,
p. 202.

Arima, many of the supporting players are amateurs), a plotless, seemingly structureless story, and the use of asynchronous sound frequently in counterpoint to the meaning of the visuals.

All these techniques become perfect stylistic equivalents for the tentative quest of the heroine, Junko, for a "full life." The seemingly random camera work expresses her indecisiveness and lack of confidence as, at the beginning of the film, she decides to leave her husband and return to a career in the acting profession which she had sacrificed when she married. Although A *Full Life* is not Hani's strongest film on the subject of a woman's quest for a meaningful life—*She and He* (*Kanojo to Kare*, 1963) is a much more fully realized work of art—it is perhaps the most revolutionary film made up to that time in Japan about a contemporary woman's quest for independence.

The events of the film are filtered through the eyes of Junko, who comments in voice-over on the life of a woman in a city controlled by men, with even store windows designed to attach her to a household, consuming the products that keep prosperous postwar Japan affluent. Junko calls them "man-made snares." The camera tracks with her along the street. But the lures of consumerism will not be enough to keep this woman tied to the middle-class boredom of being wife to a man who lives only for himself, and who, when the film opens, has disappeared for four days without warning. In voice-over Junko remembers how he had promised to make her happy if only she would lean on him; she has bartered her freedom for the spurious security of having a "daddy," who turns out, of course, not to be a "daddy" at all but an irresponsible and selfish man. Sexual surrender to such a man was fraught with danger, although Junko had not understood this: "Easy to let myself go. But how can I get myself back, once I've done it?" Like women everywhere, she has used sex as a means of postponing the forging of a separate identity.

With neither savings nor a job, Junko decides to leave this husband so preoccupied with his own success. In response to her demand for more freedom, with which she greets him upon his return, he makes love to her as, on the sound track, trains and cars roar, belying the idea of marriage as refuge and sanctuary. When her moment of rebellion comes, still a woman not yet in possession of herself, Junko *asks the permission* of her husband to move out, as if she were still a slave needing the sanction of the master, even for the action that would finally deny him his power over her. Like Western women, the wife has been kept so financially dependent that Junko now finds that nothing is hers: "I never asked him for a pair of gloves or a handbag . . . but now that we're parting, ownership becomes important."

Instead of finding a job as an actress, which seems too difficult, Junko settles for work at kennel club shows. There she sweats and her hands perpetually smell of the dogs. Her independence has predictably reduced her to a proletarian style of life, to a tiny, dilapidated room with only a little curtain to shield her from a sea of neighbors. It is the fear of such poverty that keeps so many wives everywhere bound to loveless marriages.

Yet Junko has not become bitter. She still longs for a man and for love, although she has learned that first "we must love ourselves." She knows that the kind of love offered by the typical Japanese husband is not enough. That a revolution against the prerogatives of the Japanese male will not be easy is expressed by Hani in a surprise visit by Junko's husband, who promptly removes his jacket, shirt, and tie and loosens his pants. His pity and seeming concern that Junko is "worn out" are preludes to the inevitable sexual assault, pathetically disguised by a cheap evocation of "how happy we used to be." In the tiny apartment Junko cannot escape his caresses. The very Japanese environment, overcrowded and unsecluded, placing no value on privacy, conspires to ensure men power over women. Psychologically—and Hani is one of the best psychologists in the Japanese film—such defeats can only lessen one's will to rebel. Thus Junko's courage becomes all the more remarkable. Later, in a theater acting a part in which a woman begs a man not to leave her, she finds it almost unbearable even to remember the lines and must repeat them over and over again.

Hani conjoins Junko's struggle with the student movement of the opening days of the 1960s, the Zengakuren demonstrations seeking an end to Japan's Security Treaty with the United States (AMPO). Each requires a transformation of Japanese society, and Junko finds some degree of personal fulfillment in allying herself with a larger, organized cause parallel to her own. The Japan that would shelter itself under a "nuclear umbrella" provided by the United States, while remilitarized "Self-Defense" units disperse civil unrest at home, is the same Japan that keeps its women in neo-feudal bondage. Only when she becomes a political activist with beliefs of her own can Junko satisfactorily begin a relationship with another man.

In one fine scene she is on the street soliciting signatures for an anti-Security Pact petition. The camera dollies in to her face as she spies her husband walking by with a very young woman. Immediately Junko grabs a megaphone, shouting, "Please sign for the peace of Japan," her zeal a means of repressing her pain. Yet she has at last found an alternative to the sexual enslavement offered by her husband. She has committed herself to something beyond the narrow confines of the nuclear family. We view Junko in a restaurant with her new man. As he proposes marriage, we hear the sounds of demonstrators singing in the background, a matching of image and sound symbolic of the conflict between public and private desires which is always part of the complexity of a "full life." When she participates in the demonstrations, Junko misses this man. Yet she also knows that a life centered only around a relationship with a man is unsatisfying, too.

The Zengakuren demonstrations end with a girl's death and the failure to abrogate the treaty. The intellectuals and artists who took part are blacklisted. Junko sits sewing a shirt, having entered a "new life," but this time with the confidence of being able to "face anything now." Hani leaves her occupied with this domestic task, an inevitable setback to her struggle for liberation analogous to the crushing of the student movement. But by no means is she defeated. For the first time in the film, she smiles.

In *She and He* Hani turns to a much more traditional middle-class husband and wife, typical consumers in prosperous postwar Japan. Unlike Junko, who had been part of the avant garde before her marriage, the wife Naoko (Sachiko Hidari) in *She and He* is far less intellectual or conscious of the limitations of marriage when the film opens. Through this ordinary woman Hani wishes to expose how Confucian relationships are still demanded of the Japanese wife in the 1960s.

Naoko is treated by her husband, Eiichi, like a child. A fire in the lot outside their high-rise apartment complex inspires her to offer help. He refuses to permit her to go because she might "get hurt." Like Junko, Naoko has assimilated the role society expects of her, so that employment of authoritarian force to guarantee her submission is entirely unnecessary. She feels obliged to ask Eiichi's permission to go.

Hani accounts for Naoko's struggle for independence by giving her a childhood in Manchuria. She has experienced more of the dark side of life than the middle-class housewives who rebuff her. Having suffered herself, she wishes to offer solace to a ragpicker and his blind, adopted little girl, who have taken up residence in that lot adjacent to their building, especially since she has discovered he is a former classmate of her husband's.

The ragpicker, Ikona, will be an immediate antagonist for Eiichi because he has consciously and deliberately rejected the option of becoming a "salary man." Naoko, alone of all the residents, feels compassion for the poor and homeless living on the periphery of a prosperous social order. And Hani implicitly defines "middle-class" as assent to a social structure that both discriminates against those who will not live by the rules, like this ragpicker Ikona, and oppresses women.

Eiichi, proprietorial, warns Ikona not to "misuse my wife's kindness." Ikona's existence troubles their lives, offering a silent reproof to their privatism. Only with Ikona, however, can Naoko discuss the pain of her childhood. For Hani, Ikona is a more authentic human being than Eiichi because he will not accept a life immune to the pain of others, an insulated life. He rejects the job at the Water Sanitation Association, procured for him by Eiichi out of duty and a sense of shame that a classmate of his should descend to such proletarian depths.

In the course of becoming an adult human being, Naoko rejects the middle-class values of her husband and neighbors. She assumes an identity separate from that of her husband, one as incongruous to this setting as Ikona's great black dog Kuma, overwhelming the neat little modern apartment of Naoko and Eiichi. The change in Naoko is reflected even in her physical appearance, in the new hair style which embarrasses her husband because it makes her seem "mature." In Naoko, the Japanese woman emerges from centuries of enforced childhood.

But, finally, Eiichi will not tolerate his wife's attempt to reach beyond the closed circle of their relationship. While he is away on a business trip, she nurses, in the sanctuary of their apartment, the blind child Hanako, who has pneumonia. With a zoom back from outside, as if to allow the audience to flee from the storm of his anger, Eiichi closes the window with a bang as he discovers this invasion of his private life. "What are they to you?" he sputters from between clenched teeth. And, cheaply, he condemns Naoko for not knowing what she wants. She replies, honestly and with dignity, enjoying all of Hani's sympathy: "I was trying to find out. I want to know." Eiichi's reply is that of a frightened husband whose wife's fulfillment and her achievement of a separate identity are threats to his very existence: "I'm an ordinary man. I want an ordinary life."

As a woman and a free human being, Naoko would define herself in terms of a much larger group than that of the nuclear family. She would identify with the whole of suffering humanity. Eiichi, out of the narrowness of wishing to isolate her within the confines of their high-rise apartment tower, would, by so doing, deprive her of a unique identity. The good patriarch, if something less than the good husband, he needs her to be a typical middle-class housewife, spending her days lavishing enslaving and seductive affection on her sons as a "Mama-san," preparing

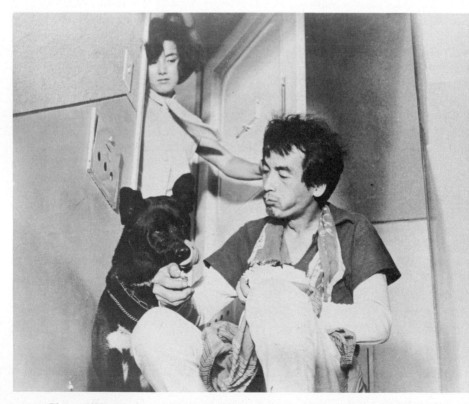

She and He: Naoko would, as a woman and a free human being, define herself in terms of a much larger group than that of the nuclear family.

them, in their turn, to be at once infantile and all-demanding tyrants as husbands. Later, they would expect from their wives the same smothering indulgence originally granted them by their frustrated mother. Naoko would be expected to wait until midnight when her husband, having spent the evening in companionship with men like himself, with whom he feels far more comfortable than with his wife, wends his way home from his favorite hostess bar.

The last scene of *She and He*, like the first, finds Naoko in bed beside Eiichi. She lies awake, her eyes bright and looking off into a distance that may yet be too far away for her to explore. The man sleeping beside her may offer all the comforts of life in modern Japan—an apartment full of appliances, presided over by a gigantic color television set. The final prize he holds out as a reward for her subservience is a baby. Naoko may indeed capitulate, since she is so dependent upon her husband, even for the "pocket money" he doles out to her as to a child. But the moment of discontent, the first harbinger of change, has also descended upon her. It is an awesome burden, but one which, Hani says, must be assumed.

Hani's heroine in *Bride of the Andes* is a mail-order bride. Played, as was Naoko, by Sachiko Hidari, she journeys to Peru with her son Takeshi, there to marry an archaeologist whom she has yet to meet. She has agreed to come to this Quechua Indian village because the man, Taro Ueda, seemed from his description to be someone on whom she could "lean," so intolerable and precarious has been her life in Japan as a widow. Hani omits her prior life from depiction, taking it for granted that the audience is well aware of the trials confronting the woman who must live in Japan without the financial and social protection of a man. His concern, once again, is to define "liberation" for the Japanese woman.

Hani's films set outside Japan must be seen in the context of a history of fierce xenophobia which has been part of Japanese culture for centuries. It came to the fore particularly at the moment of Commodore Perry's invasion of Japan in 1853. *Ronin* swore to kill foreigners at any and every opportunity. A man named Izumi Maki, expressing the mood of the time, wrote: "If this country is taken over by the foreigners, there will be no use in living and no other way for my whole family than to die."[2] This hysterical fear of foreign domination, which culturally became a hatred of foreigners, continued into the twentieth century and emerges frequently in Japanese culture, as for example in Junichiro Tanizaki's 1928 novel *Some Prefer Nettles*, whose message is that to accept foreign ways is to court unhappiness; a Japanese can find peace only by being as intensely Japanese as the times permit. More recently, Hani's contemporary and fellow film-maker, Nagisa Oshima, has found it necessary to distinguish himself from Hani, with an implication of superiority, on the ground that *he* could never make a film outside Japan.[3] (Hani had made *Bride of the Andes* in Peru,

<hr />

[2] "Bakumatsu Shishi no Tegami" (Letters from a Patriot in the Last Days of the Shogunate), Livingston, Moore, Oldfather, eds., *The Japan Reader*, 1: 85.
[3] "The Japan and Japanese in Myself," *Tokyo Shimbun*, January 18, 1971.

The Song of Bwana Toshi [*Buana Toshi no Uta*, 1965] in Kenya, and *Miyo* [1971] in Italy.)

Unlike Oshima, who despite his abiding criticisms of the entire structure of Japanese society can contradict his own social analysis by assuming the stance of a nationalist and xenophobe, Hani believes that one avenue for the liberation of the Japanese from a neo-feudal social order may lie precisely through communication with other cultures. If Naoko in *She and He* could find no outlet for her impulses of compassion, the woman in *Bride of the Andes* locates a means of expressing similar needs among the Indians of South America, free of the insularity of the Japanese archipelago. And when she achieves the satisfaction of having successfully expressed her deepest impulses, her relationship with her husband enters a new stage. As undemonstrative as a Japanese man can be, Ueda says only, when he realizes that he loves her, "I'm glad I met you." But these words, so long in coming, bespeak genuine affection. At this moment, registering its significance, she expresses the wish to bear his child.

Hani finds it difficult to discuss the liberation of the Japanese woman without simultaneously indicating how authoritarian Japanese culture oppresses other powerless people. He refuses his women private solutions to their struggles for freedom because he has defined human liberation in general as a commitment to those in need. His men, like Eiichi in *She and He*, are in greater spiritual bondage than his women because, in their selfish pursuit of success within the neo-feudal hierarchy, they show little concern for anyone outside their own family.

Hani's women are more fortunate in beginning from positions of greater enslavement. Because it is revolutionary, requiring a transcendence of the entire culture with its egocentric ethos, their struggle leads them to experiences in which, as if in Zen *satori*, the self withers away. Each of Hani's women discovers her identity only when she has ceased to care about what makes her different from others—Junko in the Zengakuren demonstrations, Naoko with the indigent ragpicker and his child, the bride of the Andes when she is concerned with preserving and nurturing the Indian village.

Like Mizoguchi's, Hani's women are stronger than his men because of this capacity to live on behalf of others. It is a far cry from the traditional resignation and self-sacrifice expected of the Japanese woman because it is freely chosen and is possible only when feudal restraints are removed. It involves an expression of self in explicit defiance of the Confucian definition of a woman's role. But that Junko, at the close of *A Full Life*, is once more safe with a man, that Naoko's struggle remains unresolved, and that the bride must travel to Peru in order to live as a free woman, these endings suggest Hani's realistic caution that such liberation at present remains the exception rather than the rule in contemporary Japan.

Shohei Imamura:
Woman as Survivor

Wherever you go, you find
strong women like this.
Shohei Imamura[1]

A far more eccentric image of the modern Japanese woman emerges in the films of Shohei Imamura. Unlike Hani's, Imamura's women are not consciously in revolt against their traditional place. They are also much more unpredictable, less rational, physically stronger, and more tenacious. Imamura's interest is in the Japanese woman of peasant origins, in whom he locates the greatest potential for independence of spirit and strength of character. These are women who have always enjoyed a freedom of sexual expression denied to their middle-class sisters. As rural workers, farmers, or even as cultivators of silkworms, they have also achieved the financial self-sufficiency that is a requisite for the freedom of any woman. The experience of the peasant woman is thus far richer than that of a confined housewife like Naoko in *She and He*. Living on the verge of mere subsistence, the importance of her role in the family and the village has manifested itself in the richness of personality the peasant woman has been permitted to develop.

Imamura suggests that the source of the liberation of such women lies in the inexhaustibility of their natures. When they are frustrated and enslaved by those feudal restraints placed on every Japanese woman at one time or another—when they move to the cities, for example—remedy lies, not in the kind of approved social action taken by Hani's women, but in a return to their original equilibrium. Only when they are removed from the conventions of a narrowing, urban existence can the strange raw edges of the characters of these women re-emerge and once again find unabated expression. Much more pessimistic than Hani about the outcome of any individual's strife with the norms of neo-feudal Japanese culture, Imamura looks to his uneducated, vital, primitive women to summon the energy for their survival out of the resources of their very strong personalities and indomitable wills.

Imamura's approach to the Japanese woman—and to all Japanese—is that of a cultural anthropologist studying not the ethnography of primitive

---

[1] Conversations with the author, Tokyo, November 1974.

The Insect Woman: Is Tome a rebel? Is she blasphemous? Her actions are determined by the logic of her character rather than by restraints imposed from without.

islanders but that of his own people. The title of his film known abroad as *The Pornographer* (*Jinrui Gaku Nyumon*, 1966) translates in fact as *An Introduction to Anthropology*. Imamura's interest as a scientist is to discover through his art a primal Japanese culture still existing in a pure state in rural areas where industrialization has not yet had the opportunity to penetrate.

In Tome of *The Insect Woman*, in Toriko of *Kuragejima: Tales from a Southern Island*, and in the half-urbanized heroine Sadako of *Intentions of Murder*, Imamura would locate the strength of being a Japanese. He describes Tome in the film as a person "living by instinct, with no sense of right and wrong," like an insect. But Imamura comes to praise and not to blame her for this primitivism; he would challenge the value judgments we would automatically apply to such an amoral woman. Imamura suggests to his Japanese audience that to understand itself it might be wise to abandon a rationalism imported from the West and uncongenial to Japanese culture.[2] In the portraits of his strong women, part of Imamura's theme is that what ensures their survival might seem, to eyes distorted by modernization, to be mere irrationality. Nevertheless, an almost mystical anti-logic characterizing the Japanese woman is also at the root of her capacity to endure.

Tome's mother's husband (who is not her biological father) is retarded but, in keeping with his challenge to the supposed humanism of Western

[2] Conversations with the author.

rationalism, Imamura deliberately endows his "insane" characters with a sanctity he believes they once enjoyed in ancient Japanese culture. In the past they were respected as being in touch with a world beyond this visible universe, and for this gift they were honored. Toriko, the wild, incestuous girl of *Kuragejima,* is also retarded, but she lives among the "sane" in un-selfconscious symbiosis. In *The Insect Woman* Tome's foster father is the only person capable of showing her, and later her daughter, Nobuko, any kindness. As a child, Tome innocently asks him if they're "man and wife," since they sleep together; incest was not yet a taboo or a "sin" in the original homogeneous Japanese culture where all, in some sense, are related by blood. The other villagers, unlike the child Tome and the retarded man, are already "civilized." They see shame in Tome's closeness with her foster father, a measure, for Imamura, of their distance from an authenticity that was once universal to the culture. Imamura implicitly argues that inbreeding has not produced a nation of idiots—a challenge to the entire logic of the incest taboo, which he sees as alien to Japan. If the rural people have been corrupted by shame at the suggestion of incest, it is a measure of their alienation from being Japanese rather than a sign of Tome's or her foster father's depravity.

Just as rural Japan has steadily given way to "civilization," Tome begins her odyssey of survival in 1942 by going to work in an urban factory to aid in the war effort. Her struggle to support herself and her daughter Nobuko leads her to all levels of experience offered in postwar Japan, to all the means through which it defeats its women. When she bears Nobuko, the product of rape, in 1943, the women who deliver the baby debate whether to "let it live or give it back." Tome, the supposedly animal-like, inhuman "insect woman," wants the child to live. "Pa," who sucks Tome's breasts to relieve her pain, since the baby does not take enough of her milk, assumes the care of Nobuko when Tome returns to the factory.

Is Tome a rebel? Is she blasphemous? Her actions are determined by the logic of her character rather than by restraints imposed from without. In this self-containment lies her heroism, regardless of the depths to which she will descend. While the Emperor makes his famous radio broadcast announcing Japan's defeat, Tome is having her breast fondled by a lover. The fate of this patriarchal nation which has so doggedly pursued and discriminated against women is of no concern to her. When the man tells her that Japan has lost the war, Tome calls it a lie. What has permitted her survival is that ideas imposed from without, even "objective" truths such as Japan's losing the war, are of no moment to her. And, in her seeming stupidity, she can lead a pure life.

Tome becomes a passionate union advocate when she is personally abused at the factory; she is "stupidly" uncompromising in her demands on management, despite the danger of being fired in the Red Purge. In 1950 Tome becomes a maid to a woman living with an American, offering Imamura an opportunity to express the alien nature of the foreigner as seen through Tome's (and his own) eyes. The hairs standing up on the American's skin suggest an image of repulsion. "He's too big," says Tome

The Insect Woman: Imamura stands further back from his characters than any director of his generation. Never would he judge a Tome; life will provide its own punishments.

with characteristic bluntness. Nor does Imamura spare us the sight of Tome lying in bed at night, wracked by sexual frustration. It is a sign of her strength that, despite her harsh experiences, she has not been deadened to feeling, that, like those of an "insect," her instincts remain intact.

If Tome does finally descend to the level of an unfeeling insect, her fall occurs not in rural Yamagata, where one might think people live without values, but in the new Japan, where ruthless competition has become the norm. If Tome's ignorance is "monumental" and her naivete "vulgar," as Japanese critic Tadao Sato emphasizes in his "Feminist Tradition in Japanese Film,"[3] it is not primarily for the purpose of comedy, as Sato, misunderstanding the value Imamura places on Tome, would have us believe. Through her openness and an innocence retained despite the life she must lead, Tome reveals a healthy capacity to express verbally what others conceal with skillful subterfuge and considerable hypocrisy. "Can I call you Daddy?" she asks her oily patron, "'cause I don't have a real father." There is strength precisely in Tome's seemingly naïve compulsion to say not only what she feels but what she is.

As a madam herself, Tome is cruel to her "girls," as exploitative of them as her own madam had been of her. In a quarrel she disfigures her maid, Hanako, with boiling water, and then refuses to pay for the plastic surgery required. As soon as Tome achieves power over others, she becomes like a savage. This hardness is the price life exacts for her hard struggle. And

[3] Translated by Peter High.

Imamura stands further back from his characters than any director of his generation. Never would he judge a Tome; life will provide its own punishments. The disfigured Hanako steals Tome's money and her establishment. At the police station, in an expression of impotence, Tome strikes at her frantically without actually making contact, in a series of freeze frames that only underline her powerlessness.

Tome's daughter Nobuko, however, is even more resilient than she. A rambunctious country girl (Jitsuko Yoshimura, as sensual as she was in *Onibaba*), Nobuko hates Tokyo and plans to join a research farm, there to live out her years instinctually, to be as natural a woman as Tome's old granny who, at ninety-one, is "healthy as the devil." Tome herself is now middle-aged and poor, having been abandoned by her *yakuza* patron after she was sent to prison, framed for participating in one of his jobs. Nobuko becomes this same man's mistress as a means of obtaining the 200,000 yen she requires as her investment in the communal farm. It turns out to be the same 200,000 the man originally stole from her mother. However, Nobuko manages to steal much more before, in a neat double-cross, she returns to the farm for good. The *yakuza* enlists Tome, now entirely down-and-out, to inform Nobuko's boyfriend about their affair, as a means of forcing her back to Tokyo.

On this mission, Tome sets out for the country, having run out of a place on earth for herself. She trips on the now unfamiliar rocks and breaks her shoe. She calls the countryside "terrible," tripping once more as Imamura freezes the frame and ends the film. It is an open ending because we are not sure whether she will tell Nobuko's young man about the patron—or, indeed, whether it would matter to him.

A troubled person in a troubled world, Tome is left with nothing in her life of grace or of peace. The one flashback to which her mind recurrently returns for comfort reveals her foster father sucking a boil from which she had been suffering when they had lived together in what seems like so long ago. This image was also intercut by Imamura when, weary and alone, Tome was released from prison. It reveals the simple longing of a simple woman for uncomplicated human contact devoid of manipulation. Such unhypocritical, close involvement with another human being has been absent from her life since she first journeyed to Tokyo. The repeated image expresses not only the kind of affection longed for by Tome but an indictment of contemporary Japan, where such expressiveness seems out of place and slightly obscene.

A woman on the periphery of prosperous Japan, enjoying none of the privileges of Hani's middle-class women, Tome in her very survival remains remarkable. She is, as played by Sachiko Hidari in her finest role, neither beautiful nor noble, values that are inapplicable and of no concern to Imamura. That he should have made a film exploring the strengths of such a woman at all constitutes the director's highest tribute.

In *Intentions of Murder* a wife named Sadako is married to a nagging, emasculated, bullying weakling of a man, a clerk in a library who in his spare time secretly engages in a ten-year-old affair with a fellow librarian.

Intentions of Murder: The rape has released the impulses of Sadako's
deepest nature. It frees her of her servitude..

Sadako, bovine and seemingly uncomprehending of everything around her,
an "insect" like Tome, is more a servant to him than a wife, and was, in
fact, the maid to his family before the marriage.

While her husband is attending a conference in Tokyo, she is raped.
Sadako's subsequent reactions to this experience reveal that the rape has
released the impulses of her deepest nature. It frees Sadako of her servitude and returns her to a primal sense of peace with herself. It transforms
her into a woman in touch with the sources of life itself. Simultaneously,
it allows her to demand civil rights from a husband who would, forever if
he could, treat her more as a serf than as an equal.

During the first rape (there will be two by the same man), the attacker
uses physical violence. In startling imagery which, in anyone else's hands,

might seem like cliché, Imamura projects an image of a train rushing as if to overwhelm the camera as a means of suggesting the consummation of the rape. But afterwards the man kisses her on the mouth with genuine affection, and she is deeply aroused. Imamura cuts to a flashback of Sadako's girlhood in the country, where she helped in the cultivation of silkworms and sensually allowed the worms to crawl along her leg. Only in her rural youth was Sadako erotically free. Only then were her impulses not yet thwarted by the narrow confines of city life and a husband who does not value her.

The screen begins to turn 360 degrees as Sadako awakens to the reality of a room where a violent act has occurred. A lamp has been knocked over, a screen broken, a knife left behind. But what seems to involve only trauma will turn out to provide the source of liberation. What we, through Western-influenced eyes, might judge as horror may, instead, lead to freedom. For Sadako has somnambulistically been assenting to something less than a full life. Being raped, as a symbol of being chosen, will, paradoxically, lead her once more to value herself and demand her prerogatives as a woman and as a wife.

At first, her reactions involve accepted and approved responses to the rape. In voice-over Sadako whispers, "I must die," as Tokugawa samurai women, raped, had no choice but suicide even if they had been assaulted against their will. But Sadako is clearly no samurai woman, but a modern, working-class, sturdy individual who knows enough—or will learn it through her experience with this tubercular rapist, in reality so much weaker than she—to hold her own feelings sacred. The strictures internalized by middle- and upper-class women cannot touch her very deeply. Yet, tied to an unpleasant husband whose advances she can only endure, but one who holds absolute power over her, she is a woman with few options. What will save her is the understanding of how strong her nature as a woman really is. In a flashback to her girlhood we see Sadako, who was an illegitimate child, as a young woman who had always liked sex. Condemned by other women for this lasciviousness, it is yet something which Imamura suggests she would do better to be proud of, for, awakened, it will lead her to an understanding of powers and rights she never knew were hers.

In slow motion Imamura cuts to Sadako about to run in front of a train. Calling out her son Masau's name, she cannot kill herself. Like all Japanese women, she is caught between duty and self. The true Japanese spirit will survive within her, however, because, like Tome, she has lived too far from the mainstream of this class society to be truly subject to its rules. Meanwhile, when her husband returns from Tokyo, she is able to make love to him, as if the rapist had literally revived her. At the library her husband catalogues Marcuse's *Eros and Civilization*, but it is Sadako who is the testament to the book's validity. Only in an uneducated woman with no access to "civilization" can Eros still flourish triumphant.

The rapist lurking outside, awaiting his opportunity, attacks Sadako again. But he is now clearly not a threatening force but a pathetic, tubercular young man in love with his victim. The camera is in close on their awkward lovemaking, as if under her very foot when he grabs it, lending a mood of the absurd to the act of love which Imamura seeks to demystify as precisely something not to be approached with solemnity and high seriousness.

Unable to make sense of her situation, a now pregnant Sadako develops "intentions of murder" toward the rapist who loves her. In a moment of calm, he invites her to go away with him and then, abruptly changing his tone, threatens to kill her if she refuses. They are all people on the verge of violence, people of limited resources and, in modern Japan, limited capacities to survive. The rapist himself is the son of a prostitute; he had watched his mother kill one of her children. There is no one in the world in whom Sakado can confide. Like Tome, she has only her instincts to guide her.

In part, the rapist becomes Imamura's surrogate, the only one in the film who loves Sadako and is capable of valuing her for herself: "You're a woman just exactly as I thought," he says. And indeed Imamura means for us to see her as deserving of sympathy, despite her sloppy, unattractive exterior and her lack of consciousness, because she has been so abused by her family as a human being unentitled to basic human rights. Her own son has been registered as the legal child of his grandparents. To gain the right to her own child, she would have to go to court where, inarticulate and powerless as she is, she would probably lose to the strong tradition decreeing that children belong to the family of their father and that men may register women as their legal wives only when and if they so choose. Now her husband decides to move to the country where Sadako fears she will be treated like a servant once again. Meanwhile, the husband's librarian mistress, absurdly wanting Sadako's unappetizing husband to marry *her*, dogs Sadako's steps in search of evidence of an infidelity that will allow the total usurpation of Sadako's place.

The rapist, wholly sincere, confides his love to Sadako while she, resisting, reveals to us that she cares very little for him at all: "I'm not sympathetic to him . . . I don't have to listen to him." Their relationship is only a physical one, based upon a passion that will not be denied. As such, it is simultaneously touching and ludicrous. Seeming to accept the rapist's demand that she run away with him, Sadako boards a train with him for the countryside, carrying with her a thermos filled with a poisoned drink. She has determined to free herself from the danger of involvement with him by murder. It seems to Sadako to be a logical and correct course of action.

With Imamura's precariously hand-held camera recording her furtive, animal-like motions, the librarian follows the two. At the crucial moment, Sadako allows all the poison to spill out. She is unable to kill this helpless young man. And while they are making love in an icy tunnel, the man dies anyway of a heart attack. Back in town, the librarian, overreaching herself in frantically snapping more pictures of the Sadako she has at last caught at adultery, is hit by a truck, her body flying up into the air. It is as if she had no claim to be human, an example of poetic justice with all the vengeance of Imamura's black sense of humor. But the camera with the films incriminating Sadako survives.

Yet when her husband confronts her with the pictures, unmistakable evidence of her adultery, Sadako denies it all. Imamura sees not stupidity but strength in her refusal to acknowledge evidence against her recorded in so alienating an object as a photograph, just as Madame Onboro in *A History of Postwar Japan* refused to believe in the American atrocities at Mylai because she had not witnessed them with her own eyes. Sadako pits the illogic of her strong will against science and wins. She substitutes her stubborn self-definition of reality and defeats her dumbfounded husband through tenacity alone.

Being reawakened by the rapist to her nature as a woman gives Sadako the strength to insist upon her rights. At this point she has enough power over her husband to demand that if he expects her to move to the country, he must alter their child's legal registration, making him her son at last. In the final scene Sadako is at peace with herself amidst a crowd of laughing country women. She puts a silkworm on her shoulder. As she feeds it mulberry leaves, it crawls over her body. In a very slow tilt up, the credits appear. On her face is recorded an ecstasy new for the character. It is as if Sadako were at last restored to herself, a sensual woman in an environment where she can express that sensuality. Imamura's belief in the basic irrationality of human existence is nowhere better expressed than in the fact that it took a brutal rape to release this woman's strength.

And the Japanese woman today? Directors like Hani and Imamura imply that she must struggle for her rights without the aid of Japanese men, who are too comfortable within the patriarchy which exists to service their needs. Of the men in all these films lamenting the oppression of the Japanese woman, it was only Oharu's first lover, executed for this outrageous view, who felt unthreatened enough to tell a woman that she should live as she feels. Not by any means, however, are all the male directors (and there aren't presently any commercial women directors) who criticize Japanese feudalism in sympathy with the Japanese woman in her bondage. Some directors known for their progressive views may even continue to make paeans to the supportive wife, like Kaneto Shindo in his sickeningly sentimental *Story of a Beloved Wife*, or testaments to the multifarious sexuality of the whore, like Kazuo Kuroki in *Assassination of Ryoma*.

To "esteem" woman is only to keep her enslaved so much the longer. This is the "feminism" endorsed by such Japanese critics as Tadao Sato,[4] who condescend to the Japanese woman while pretending to sympathize with her. Critics who lack Mizoguchi's appreciation of the need for Japanese women to alter their condition cannot help but misunderstand his films. And unlike a critic like Sato, Mizoguchi could never patronize the

---

[4] *Theoretical History of Japanese Film*, translated by Peter High. Also in personal conversation with the author in New York, April 1975.

Japanese woman by placing her on a pedestal as an object awaiting the esteem of a man.

It seems likely that Hani's message is the prescient one. The majority of Japanese women may one day soon recognize that not fighting for one's rights as an individual capable of creative work outside the home, and as a leader in the society, is to deny one's humanity. One recalls the row of women furiously applauding Isuzu Yamada playing Nora of Ibsen's *A Doll's House* for the first time in Japan in Kinugasa's *Actress* (*Joyu*, 1947). And one is reminded that discontent already marks the first stage of a revolution.

PART

5

THE FAMILY UNDER SIEGE

Filial piety in Japan dates from the Chinese *Hsiao King* and has always involved much more than reverence of one's parents or ancestors. As the basis of the entire ethical system, it extended absolute obedience to authorities ranging from members of one's immediate household to the entire world at large. "He who loves his parents," reads the *Hsiao King,* "will not risk to incur others' hatred and he who reveres his parents will not risk others' contempt."[1] According to this tradition, such filial piety, beginning with service to one's parents, "proceeds to the service of the ruler; [and] ends with the perfection of one's character."[2]

The family as an institution in Japan thus always worked to maintain the existing government in power. Family members were trained to submit to those above them, the father at the apex, facilitating the same submission to the State, whoever happened to be in power, Tokugawa shogun or Meiji Emperor. Within the family presided over by a patriarch —the surrogate for Emperor or shogun—sons, themselves future patriarchs, occupied much higher positions than daughters, wives or mothers. The power relationships within the family were those that members would face within the society itself. The submission to hierarchy at home would be duplicated, for example, in the salaried man's same acquiescence to a fixed place within the corporation he would join; there he would discover a hierarchical structure similar to that of the individual household.

The Meiji Restoration did little to weaken the power of the Japanese family. As previously stated, early reforms gave way in 1898 to restoration of the right of eldest sons to the exclusive privilege of inheriting all the family property. Only the head of the family could make marriage or adoption plans; only in his care was the ancestral spirit of the family maintained. And only if there were no male heirs, could a woman inherit property. An account of how the family functioned in the household of a Meiji official indicates the suppression of spontaneity and self-confidence of lower-ranking family members that was the inevitable legacy of such a system:

No matter how small the house in those days, every person's room was strictly fixed, just as in a great daimyo's mansion. When the lady of the

1 Quoted in Nitobe, *Japanese Traits and Foreign Influences*, pp. 74–75.
2 *Ibid.*

house went into her husband's room, she conducted herself with the same formality as if she were calling at another house, and the same was true of children. In fact, if children were not summoned by their father, they did not go into his room. When they were summoned, of course, it was usually to be scolded, and often after they were grown they still dreaded to be called to their father's room for fear that they would just be regaled with some complaint or other.[3]

Toward the patriarch, affection was always understood in terms of order, while the woman's natural impulses toward love were directed much more to her children than to her husband. As if training them for their lives ahead as Japanese citizens, the patriarch by his very posture demanded of his children self-effacement and conformity. Self-assertion was regarded as an unpleasant form of egotism, to be purged from the unruly at all costs.

The burgeoning economic life under Meiji evoked fierce impulses, however, that could not always be contained at home. With Japan's emergence as an industrial, capitalist power, the authority of the family could not help but be weakened. Because of the introduction of a socio-political system based upon free enterprise, Meiji Japan could not help but raise the question of the rights of an individual who was now to become an entrepreneur, with the privileges and responsibilities of that role, regardless of his prior status in the social hierarchy. The word *minken*, denoting "popular rights," entered the Japanese language at this time; the newly coined general word for "rights," *kenri* (from *ken* for "power" or "influence" and *ri* for "interest"), reflected as well an individualism within the economic texture of the society that inevitably overflowed into the social institutions of the culture as well. That a single individual was owed something even approaching "inalienable rights" of course conflicted at once with the traditional notion of the family, in which the collective, but not any single person, enjoyed "rights" and, in return, assumed responsibility for the actions of any of its members.

The strain of this contradiction began to manifest itself long before the Second World War, as Junichiro Tanazaki reveals in his great novel *The Makioka Sisters*. The father has left no money to any individual daughters, leaving the new head of the family with absolute control over the lives of its women. One daughter, significantly the youngest, Taeko, tries to support herself as an artist, opening her own studio. She smokes and is seen with "the Okubata boy walking by the river," as daring an instance of defiance as being discovered in the act of sexual intercourse might have been to her counterpart in the West at the time. Taeko, in the new Japan, must create her own life—economics makes this necessary—yet she is hindered because her every action still affects the marriage prospects of her sisters. The family system, weakened, created a harsher state of existence for its members than when it was intact and everyone knew his place, when the sacrifice of originality for amenability and

[3] Shibusawa, ed., *Japanese Life and Culture in the Meiji Era*, pp. 122–123.

harmony automatically produced the rewards of protection and emotional security.

Of all Japanese directors, no one laments the disintegration of the old family system more than Yasujiro Ozu, and no one chronicles its demise with more deeply felt pain and bewilderment.

Ozu: *The Family Upheld*

I'm considerably more sympathetic with the older generation.
Feudalism hasn't really disappeared from the Japanese heart.
Yasujiro Ozu[1]

Before the War, Ozu was equivocal in his approach to the Japanese family. Perhaps because he did not foresee how deeply its foundations would be shaken by Japan's defeat, he permitted his work to reflect an ambivalence about the salutary effects of its function. In the silent *I Was Born, but . . .* Ozu appears not as a partisan of the institution, as he would later become, but merely as a realistic social commentator on the manner in which the Japanese family functions to socialize the young into an acceptance of the status quo. Appalled by the sight to which they are treated of their father as a toadying subordinate to his boss, the two boy heroes, aged eight and ten, challenge the authority of their parents. They see little value in the advice they have been given to study hard at school if the outcome of their toil will involve them merely in becoming subservient, like their father, to bosses of less talent than themselves. They are angry at their parents for initiating them into a world where rank in the hierarchy has been achieved through money and position rather than merit.

The blind obedience of their father to his overbearing superior sickens the two boys and they find it impossible any longer to respect him. And thus do they upset the entire equilibrium of the family. Knowing they are right, the father finds it difficult indeed to instruct them, as his role as father decrees, in the acquiescence to authority necessary for the day when they must become subordinates to those inferior to themselves in strength and achievement, such as the boss's empty-headed son of their own age, ridiculous in his Little Lord Fauntleroy suit. The action they take against this outrageous state of affairs is a hunger strike. Its defeat is as inevitable as the continuance of the hierarchy itself, which Ozu at this early point sees as not only immutable but also as clearly unjust.

Each day the father visits the boss at his home in the hope of getting ahead. His submissiveness is contrasted from the beginning with the brashness of his sons, who have not yet fully appreciated where power lies. The rich man's son has, through bribes, enlisted the local bully on his

[1] Both statements are from Akira Iwasaki and Shinbi Iida, "A Talk with Ozu," *Kinema Jumpo*, June 1958. Translated by Leonard Schrader.

side, for he is physically weak as well as feeble in character. This ploy fails because our heroes are so much cleverer. Ozu uses a widely traveling camera; *I Was Born, but* . . . was made before he developed his typical static style. He reserves most of his traveling shots for the exploits of the two boys, the camera paralleling their energy and moral buoyancy which will not easily tolerate injustice.

As a traditional patriarch, the father demands that his two sons religiously obey the rules of the world outside. These include getting an "E" for excellence at school. A reaction shot, as one boy flashes a quick glance at the other, indicates their immediate unwillingness to accept such an order; that its value is spurious is taken for granted. What is unique for this early work is that Ozu's own point of view is clearly that of the younger generation. To make his point the father brags that *he* had always gotten an "E" in arithmetic. His loss of prestige in their eyes will be socially dangerous precisely because it will weaken the father's power to see to it that they subsume their youthful vitality to the norms of Japanese society. The action is set in the 1930s, and with nary a reference to history or politics, Ozu remains well aware throughout that there is no place in this culture for the rebel or the dissenter. Knowing this, Ozu ensures, if with great reluctance, that his heroes accept the father's ideas by the end of the film.

In a marvelous use of matched cutting Ozu moves from a traveling shot at the school where, subject to extreme discipline, the boys march in military style, to a continuation of the same shot down the desks of conforming office workers at their father's company, similarly regimented. The school prepares the boys for the discipline demanded by the authoritarian-structured society they will enter in their manhood, where everybody must behave identically. The matched traveling shot likewise suggests the inevitability of the sons' assuming adult lives just like that of their father, foreshadowing the film's resolution.

Later in the same sequence, Ozu again uses the matched traveling shot, this time cutting from the office back to the schoolboys writing at their desks. Ozu sees discord and rebellion as natural in so rigid a society. His acknowledgment of the logical unwillingness of the two young heroes to conform is expressed in the traveling shot's now continuing in the meadow where, as truants, having fled from the school, they are practicing forgery of the coveted "E" expected by their father. Their mother, less corrupted by the demands of the society because she remains at home, if also less aware of what life is really like, will be fooled by the forgery, just as she, while seeming to be well aware that it is all but impossible that they not become company men like their father, nevertheless quixotically tells her sons at the end, "*you* become somebody!"

When their teacher arrives to complain about the truant sons, Ozu assumes the angle that would become his trademark. The camera is stationed three feet from the floor, as if it were itself a traditional Japanese, seated with everyone else on the tatamis. In this scene the low angle is associated with the father's traditionally Japanese response, his shame at the disgrace brought upon the family by the rebellious boys. The typical Ozu angle does not here carry the wider perception of the director. The father tells the sons that they must go to school to "become somebody." Yet the film makes clear that, no matter how the sons excel at school, they will never become more than subordinates to a self-important, pompous boss like the one who bullies their father. Tatami-angle notwithstanding, the film is ironic toward the father who would socialize his sons with claims that they can be what even these eight- and ten-year-olds perceive is impossible. The father's advice on how to defeat the neighborhood bully is also clearly wrong. He tells them to "ignore him," when they know that only an unequivocal defeat will rid them of their tormentor. Equally, the world into which this father would initiate his sons is painfully inadequate, although he has refrained from telling them so, and they are perhaps as angry at this hypocrisy as they are at having to live in an unjust world.

The quarrel among the neighborhood boys hinges on whose father is "greatest," and on this issue our heroes must meet defeat. The delivery boy won't beat up the rich man's son, although he will aid them in thwarting the bully, because the boss's family buys more than theirs. At an evening party at the boss's home, their father actually bows to Taro, the boss's *son*. Worse, in the home movies which are shown and which they must watch, their father makes a fool of himself on camera to please the boss. In the film within the film he acts the clown, putting out his tongue and crossing his eyes, to the embarrassment and chagrin of his sons.

The boys storm home, immediately creating a tantrum to hide from themselves, as long as they can, their essential impotence. Still indulged as Japanese children of eight and ten, they can openly confront their father for his hypocrisy: "You tell us to become somebody, but you're not. Why do you have to bow to Taro's father? Why don't you become a director?"

When their father responds that the boss pays his salary so that the family can eat, the sons begin a hunger strike, a simultaneously logical and touchingly absurd tactic. It is a protest against all the injustice of the world, and particularly against the equation of wealth with power. The boys, enjoying the freedoms accorded the Japanese child during the few short years before full conformity is demanded, call their father "a nobody, a nothing," and toss books and toys everywhere. The younger child even kicks his father. If ability means nothing, they argue, why go to school at all? "I'm stronger than Taro and get better grades," one shouts, "If I have to work for him when I grow up, I won't go to school." With a swipe of a cleaver, the children cut a hole in a sack of rice and feel temporarily relieved as the grains begin to run out all over the floor.

Reaching for his own palliative, a bottle of Hennessy cognac, the father acknowledges the truth of everything his sons have been saying, and Ozu at this moment shifts his own point of view to that of the patriarch. "It's a problem they'll have to live with for the rest of their lives," the father admits. He knows the life he leads is a "sorry" one and hopes for better things for his sons, that they will at least escape being "employees." There is even a certain heroism in his putting up a brave front for his sons and not wallowing in self-pity over his own meaningless and wasted life. As genuine pathos suffuses the film, the mother offers the children rice balls, a delicacy, as she tells them: "You grow up and become greater than father, why don't you? I'd worry if you didn't become somebody." The director beams beneficently just off-camera, now himself a parent reconciling the children to their fate as Japanese.

In an unfeeling world, Ozu offers the family as a refuge and sanctuary, kindly and gently preparing us for the humiliations of the life ahead. The breakfast eggs are uncovered. Things at home remain good, and family warmth alone makes it possible for the sons to accept what they and their father must be. In acknowledgment of this fact, they encourage their father to say "good-morning" to his boss when he hesitates, unwilling to sacrifice any more of their good opinion. Relieved that they are reconciled to things as they are, that he has thus so well fulfilled his role as father, he enters the boss's car for the morning journey to the office. When cowardly Taro, having suffered their blows, acknowledges that their father is "greater," he is corrected. Our heroes know better.

On this morning of reconciliations, the boys even bow to the teacher. Truancy is forever out of the question; rebellion has finally been rendered absolutely pointless. *I Was Born, but . . .* closes on a long shot filled with undifferentiated figures of boys in their school uniforms, too far away from us to be individualized. They merge together, as our heroes have learned to submerge their intelligence and their own superior values to life as it must be lived.

Made a year after *I Was Born, but . . .*, *Passing Fancy* is also about the primal relationship between a father and son, the mother having abandoned the household years before. The setting is not lower-middle-class, but firmly proletarian. The theme of reconciliation to life as it is remains the same.

Having been taunted by his friends because his illiterate father, Kihachi, infatuated with a young woman, Harue, now no longer goes to work but spends his days mooning over her at the local restaurant where she works, Tomio, the son, throws his school uniform and books into a heap in the corner of their shabby room. Formerly a good student, he now finds study pointless. Life has dealt him too weak a hand for merit to matter. In frustration he tears all the leaves off a bonsai plant.

Faced with his father's anger, Tomio compares himself with George Washington chopping down the cherry tree, a story his uneducated father has never heard of. He calls his father a fool: "You don't go to the factory. You're on booze . . . you can't even read the paper. What a fool!" By the end of the sequence, he has struck his father around the head over and over again, his only means of dealing with the inadequacy of life. Then Tomio bursts out crying; he is the one most hurt. He returns to his desk to study, all he knows how to do, all he *can* do. And he flings himself into his father's arms because if love and family feeling are not enough, without them life would be unbearable indeed.

To compensate for his established inadequacy as a father, the next morning Kihachi gives Tomio fifty sen, an enormous amount of money for a child, which Tomio spends to make himself so sick on every kind of junk food imaginable—from toffee to watermelon—that he is placed in the hospital. The money for the hospital bills must now be raised, affording Ozu the opportunity to emphasize the warm hearts and kindness of the poor toward each other. Harue is willing even to become a prostitute to repay her "uncle's" kindness, the always-available option for a young Japanese woman in a country where adultery has been institutionalized. Jiro, the father's young worker friend, finally borrows the money from the barber. Ozu has laid the foundation for one of the most superb endings of any of his films.

For one of the men—whether Jiro, now in love with Harue, or Kihachi —must hire himself out as a laborer in remote Hokkaido to repay this debt to the barber. Kihachi cannot permit the willing Jiro to go, since it was his son who was sick. He chooses to make the sacrifice himself. "Children can grow up without parents," he asserts, as wrong about this as he has been about everything. The barber, moved by Kihachi's sincerity, is willing to forgive the debt, but Kihachi is too proud to accept this extraordinarily generous offer and boards the ship for Hokkaido.

Among his fellow laborers, Kihachi defines himself in terms of his fatherhood, innocently telling these seasoned, sophisticated men Tomio's silly jokes, including the ubiquitous, "Why are there five fingers on the hand?" —"So that it can fit into a glove." As the boat glides along in a rural sequence unusual for Ozu, Kihachi in his ignorance asks if they are passing "America." They have barely left Tokyo.

Having told these jokes and bragged about his son, Kihachi has been restored to his true and only meaningful identity—that of being a father. He removes his pants, jumps off the boat and begins to swim, returning to his son. In the water he repeats another of Tomio's jokes: "Why is sea water salty?" "Because salted salmon live there." Laughing happily to himself, Kihachi also repeats the irritated answer he had given to all of Tomio's riddles: "Very funny!" He swims to shore.

It is a sequence rare in Ozu, involving a human being immersed in the elements and there achieving peace with himself, Kihachi's swimming is filmed as a natural and beautiful act, expressive of an emotional resonance Ozu attaches to the return to his son. The endings of Ozu's films are most often passive. Yet here the resignation of the earlier scene, in which the son had to accept his father for what he was, is transformed into an active gesture. Kihachi takes his fate into his own hands; a physically exertive action, also rare for Ozu, accompanies his decision not to break up the family, the only meaningful thing is his otherwise dreary life. The last shot, of towering cypresses, is Ozu's means of reassuring us that order has at last been restored.

From early on, the family remains for Ozu the last place where people can be themselves, can safely express their protests against the harshness of the world, and can even develop and retain their identities. Long before the war, Ozu finds the family undermined by urban life and the industrial waste attendant upon modernization. In the pre-war films Ozu remains aware of social injustice and, as a result, often focuses on lower-middle-class or even working-class families. In the later films, where his families are of the highly privileged upper-middle class, he seems much less disturbed by social confusion.

The family of *The Only Son* (*Hitori Musuko*, 1936) is much poorer than that of *I Was Born, but . . .* , although the gentility of the son raises it above that of *Passing Fancy*. Ozu remains interested in the tensions caused by the struggle for success within a rigidly stratified Japanese society. The family is again a bulwark against the cruelties of the world, but in 1936 Ozu still allows himself to feel the pain of failure and economic defeat, themes he will banish from his "home dramas" of the fifties and sixties.

After the War, Ozu begins to take the corruption of society for granted, confining his distress to intercut images of filthy smokestacks, towering office buildings, or the roar of traffic on Tokyo streets. Much more emphatically and moralistically, he opposes the disintegration of the family, seeing this institution as a last refuge against a social harshness which has become as much a part of the natural order as growing old and dying. Ozu's implicit hope, in all the films he made after the War, was that traditional Japanese values could be continued within the context of the family, despite the social degradation outside. Filial piety becomes a requisite for an individual's respect for himself. The more traditional values seem to be disappearing from Japanese reality in the postwar confusion, the more does Ozu assert their meaning and necessity. Because the world has become so unamenable to the old Japanese ways, Ozu upholds as an ideal the one bulwark he can find against total moral anarchy: harmony within the family.

This highly romantic, quixotic notion is mediated by Ozu's full awareness of how rarely the world allows the family to remain an isolated bastion. However staunchly we may be devoted to the continuance of traditional values, as was Noriko, the one good child, even if only a daughter-in-law, in *Tokyo Story*, we may, in spite of ourselves, fail to live up to what we know to be right and good. The world will not permit the family to remain uninfluenced by its currents. Yet there is heroism to be achieved in the effort to prevent the new values from changing us. Despite its placid exterior, the typical Ozu film is thus full of conflict and tension as his "good people," whose superiority is as much a given as that of Lady Murasaki's denizens of Heian-Kyo, struggle to hold on to the values epitomized by the harmonious family, values they are ever in danger of losing.

What Ozu does not seem to understand, however, is the full significance of the traditional family. The family has always served to preserve the status quo and established values, training its members in conformity and acquiescence to the prior claims of authority. Thus, paradoxically, it is the traditional family itself that prepares people to give in to the new status quo. The rampant social decay attendant upon merchant industrialism has undermined tradition, old manners, and fixed ways. But if the family came out of that past, its very discipline is the means of inducing acceptance of the present. The filial piety invoked by Ozu works, in fact, to immobilize opposition to the present precisely as it did in the past. This is the family's real dilemma, the contradiction that has rendered it unwittingly the final instrument of its own dissolution.

Such nuances, however, usually do not surface in Ozu's films. Most often, Ozu contents himself with the device of moral contrast, pitting the abuse of the individual in a bureaucratized world against the return to old ways, now themselves full of strain and evoking restlessness, but still superior to an aimless, egocentric way of life without family commitments. *Early Spring (Soshun*, 1956) describes a universal discontent among the Japanese. It is felt by all the salaried men in the film whose futures seem both unfulfilling and insecure, since they may be transferred by the company to the provinces at any time. This discontent is epitomized in the faltering marriage of the central characters. The husband escapes from the tedium of his life in a love affair, leaving his wife to sit at home alone, fanning herself. Finally she flees, only to be advised by her mother to return, a piece of advice approved by the director. Precisely because the life of the salaried man is so dehumanizing, a stable family life is all the more needed by both husband and wife. The hero, who had been enjoying himself with mistress and friends, is urged to be kinder to his wife.

The renewal of their relationship will be possible, however, only outside of Tokyo, symbol of the dissolution that has torn this little family asunder. The husband's transfer allows them the opportunity to renew feelings weakened by the environment of sleazy bars, gigantic glass office buildings compartmentalizing men into robots, packed trains, and streets filled with black smoke spewed out as factory waste. Ozu associates, quite brilliantly, the man's abuse of his wife, such as his mindless anger at dinner's not being ready and his infidelity, with alienation at the workplace. A close-up of smokestacks and smoke comprises the last shot of *Early Spring,* Ozu's silent accusation of modernized Japan for its assaults upon the values that had previously allowed the Japanese to live in harmony and mutual respect.

The darkest and strongest of Ozu's films about the disintegration of the family is *Tokyo Twilight (Tokyo Boshoku*, 1957), which directly followed *Early Spring*. It is as if Ozu felt that he had not yet adequately treated the mood of discontent and alienation which the Japanese family was proving so incapable of combatting. In *Tokyo Twilight*, more richly complex than *Early Spring* because it treats two generations, the family is in complete disarray. The mother had left the father, running away with another man many years before. She had abandoned him with two young daughters to raise, an event that has so traumatized them all as to make the daughters, each in her own way, incapable of constructing meaningful lives of their own.

The younger, Akiko (Ineko Arima), who suffered more from the loss of her mother, has an abortion and commits suicide at the end of the film. The elder, Takako (Setsuko Hara), hardened by the strain, is brutally unfeeling toward the mother (Isuzu Yamada), who reappears in Tokyo after an absence of many years. But Takako herself is the victim of an unhappy arranged marriage from which Ozu, in despair over all this chaos, will allow her no escape. Not once does he suggest that the rigidity and closed authoritarian discipline of the Japanese family may have contributed to the discontent and flight of the wife. Ozu seems equally unaware that, by being so inflexible, the family has prevented young people like Akiko from forging values more in keeping with the new postwar era, values that would not lead to self-destruction and moral and physical promiscuity. He remains unaware that the family, with its absolute norms implicitly endorsing conformity to the status quo, has robbed the individual of the energy and confidence to discover goals better befitting the need to transform the new Japan. Nowhere does Ozu consider the option of his characters' creating an environment that would again fulfill the abiding needs of its people.

At the beginning of *Tokyo Twilight* Takako has left her husband, taking refuge with her baby daughter, Michiko, at the home of her banker father (Chishu Ryu, who epitomizes the Ozu patriarch in so many of these films). Takako's husband, Numata, a scholar, has become a heavy drinker, arriving home late every night. He is even abusive to the baby. It is alto-

Tokyo Twilight: Through Akiko, Ozu dramatizes the turmoil of the younger generation in contemporary Japan.

gether as infelicitous an arranged marriage as one is likely to find in the entire Ozu *oeuvre*. In contrast, the patriarchal parental home, despite the absence of the absconding mother, is all order and calm. It is an incomplete home, but one still retaining the graces made possible only through family members' maintaining the manners appropriate to the continuation of such a traditional style of life. When her father asks her how things are at home, Takako replies, "Shall I make tea?" Her old-fashioned reticence is as effective an answer as Ozu believes could be framed.

Ozu also endorses Takako's comment that Numata is "that way." "Neurotic" as he is, he will never change. As Masahiro Shinoda has remarked,[2] Japanese films exhibit little interest in psychology and little strength in psychological analysis. Certainly this is true of Ozu's treatment of human nature as unchangeable. When Takako returns to her husband so that her child, unlike herself and her sister Akiko, will grow up with both parents present, it is in recognition that her irritable, unpleasant husband, who has called the child "a nuisance" and parental love "a primitive animal instinct," will remain so. Ozu offers a totally negative portrait of the intellectual in Numata, one of the few men of ideas to appear in his films, although there are many "professors" and "doctors." In the intellectual, Ozu senses a disrupter, one who would arbitrarily and nihilistically attack traditional values. Ozu's "intellectual" Numata knows nothing of where true values lie, is discontented when he should be counting his blessings, and is disrespectful to those he would do better to revere. He is a singularly repulsive figure.

Through Akiko, Ozu dramatizes the turmoil of the younger generation in contemporary Japan. The loss of her mother has led Akiko to despise herself as a human being of no value. Unlike all the good Ozu girls, she engages in sex outside of marriage. In Japan, where it is extremely difficult for women to purchase contraceptives, the only method of birth control available to them is abortion. It is a course that Ozu finds as repellent as would the staunchest Roman Catholic in the West. Abortion, for Ozu, is symbolic of a social disease afflicting all of Japan after the war. In Akiko's case it is viewed as a direct consequence of her mother's flight from her responsibilities in search of egoistic self-gratification. Shamelessly, Akiko pursues the father of her unborn child, unable to accept his indifference. Facing filthy Tokyo Bay, in smog so thick that Ozu's focus must become exceedingly shallow, Akiko informs her lover of her pregnancy. He, an *après-guerre* creature like herself, asks whether the child is his, an inconceivably rude question to be put to a woman of good family in the old, or new, Japan.

Their mother now lives with the proprietor of a Mah-Jongg parlor; the man with whom she had originally run away has long since died in a prisoner-of-war camp. And at this seedy, run-down Mah-Jongg den where Akiko is searching for her elusive lover, she meets, instead, her mother.

---

[2] Joan Mellen, "Interview with Masahiro Shinoda," *Voices from the Japanese Cinema*, p. 242.

A sweet-faced woman, the mother feels genuine love for her daughters now, which Ozu, no childish moralist, does not doubt. In Isuzu Yamada's facial expressions, she beautifully conveys this mother's sufferings; freely-chosen love has brought her no peace. In Ozu, arranged marriages have as much chance as any, if not more, of being happy, since greater effort is required of the participants than in those in which the husband and wife have "chosen" each other.

But the mother's present concern, says an insightful Ozu, his psychological perception meeting that of Freud, cannot undo the child Akiko's primal loss. "She grew up without ever knowing a mother's love," says Takako in defence of the sister she has had to retrieve at the police station after Akiko has been arrested for loitering very late at a coffee bar. "That's why she's lonely." Their father has done his best, but it has not been enough. The absence of maternal love has led, in Akiko, to a perverse dissoluteness; the destruction of her character is expressed by Ozu in a sharp cut from Akiko's abortionist closing the curtain on her patient-victim to baby Michiko cooing and occupying herself with childish games. Thus does Ozu contrast the diseased with the healthy, implying at the same time that Akiko was once as pure and innocent as baby Michiko. Having been robbed of the warm circle of love that only a stable family life can provide, Akiko's character has been irrevocably soiled, permanently stained by the absence of emotional security during crucial years.

Both sisters, Takako in kimono and Akiko, the postwar woman in sweater and skirt, are victims of the breakdown of the family. Both cannot forgive their mother and both are cruel to her. Their point of view diverges somewhat from Ozu's here, for although he too finds the mother's behavior unforgivable, he pities this guilt-ridden, unhappy woman. Ozu refuses to condemn her out of his feeling that life itself punished her for living for herself.

Yet Ozu also accepts the logic of the anger felt by Akiko and Takako. Akiko screams at her mother: "I'll never have a baby! If I do, I won't abandon it the way you did. I'll love it with all my heart . . . I hate you!" Takako is equally brutal. Dressed in funeral kimono after Akiko's suicide, she visits her mother only to blurt out three words: "You're to blame!" Ozu may agree intellectually, but he also sustains to the end his sympathy for this worn-out woman. In the train sequence the mother, now leaving Tokyo since there is nothing to hold her, pathetically wipes the carriage window, hoping that Takako, her only surviving child, will come at the last moment to see her off, a universal custom in Japan and one full of feeling. She doesn't.

Life proceeds, its strange ironies abounding. The train watchman, unjustly blamed for Akiko's "accident," is arrested for not quickly enough issuing a warning of the oncoming train in whose path we know she threw herself. Takako returns to her husband Numata because she doesn't want Michiko "to be lonely like Akiko." She sacrifices forever her own hopes for personal happiness, or even for a life of calm and order. The film clearly implies her mother should have made the same decision, especially since she was married to a man far superior in every way to Numata. "I'll try very hard this time," says Takako.

Her father thoroughly approves of this decision, although her departure from his house means that he will now be left completely alone. Ozu's characters are given the choice of the pursuit of self-fulfillment, which is likely to fail, or the upholding of traditional values, like that of the family. Those who are most pure and most good choose the latter, knowing the transcendent meaning of the restoration of order.

Takako never entertains the possibility of locating a second, more congenial, husband; Ozu's answer would be that she has no guarantee of ever finding such a man, or of finding another man at all. The divorced woman in Japan bears the aura of having failed at a critical life task. By implication, marriage is seen as a lifelong feudal obligation. Demonstrating one's inability to make it work, in full view of the entire community, by seeking a divorce is tantamount to having failed to observe a quasi-religious feudal obedience. The divorced in Japan do not so frequently remarry, whatever the reasons for the original separation, as if the scars of the first marriage cast a lifelong shadow over the individual, man or woman. Like the company man who entertains thoughts of seeking a new employer, a very rare occurrence in Japan, a country of lifetime employment, leaving one "position" renders the woman suspect and tainted. Her father admits to the mistake of having persuaded Takako to marry Numata, when she preferred a man named Sato, but such errors are inevitable, irrevocable—and forgivable. Ozu does not dwell upon them.

The patriarch survives, filling the last scene with his presence. He is reconciled to his now empty life, as all mature people in Ozu must accept the circumstances of their existence. In an otherwise dark and gloomy film, with so many scenes occurring at night, the last sequence takes place on a bright sunny morning, Ozu's means of applauding the father's obedience to an authentic Japanese spirit, regardless of his personal discomfort. He is thus blessed because he has lived by caring for others more than for himself, whatever his failures of judgment. His effort to sustain his little family, although it ultimately failed, has been heroic. It is a touching ending with the resonance, nonetheless, of an unmistakable message.

The End of Summer (*Kohayagawa-ke no Aki*, 1961), his next-to-last film, finds Ozu arguing that quite a large emotional and behavioral range has been permissible within the traditional Japanese family structure. Accepting the inevitability of the family's historical demise, in this film he views with nostalgia the death of the patriarch, symbolizing the death of the institution itself. The climax is the grand funeral of the Kohayagawa family's head, a lovable, affable Osaka brewer, whose last days have been spent in the sympathetic company of his mistress, much to the chagrin of his married daughter. "The heat of late summer is severe," says the "old master," as he is called. As the literal translation of the film's title, "The Autumn of the Kohayagawa Family," tells us, it is the autumn of the family as a flourishing institution, which coincides with the end of the brewer's life. In the heat of changing times, people have become irritable and intolerant. They have returned to an egotism which, for Ozu, the family has always held in check. The daughter and her husband, who is in the family business, but is less strong and capable than his father-in-law, worry about the inheritance the old man will leave, as though he were already dead. Materialism has invaded the very household, greed supplanting affection. The selfishness of the old man's heirs is crucial to Ozu's brilliant association in this film between the passing of the family as a viable institution and the monopolization of business in the society by giant conglomerates, the *zaibatsu* which devour small enterprises like that begun by the brewer.

This old merchant has lived with a resonance of his own which changing times—he calls them "disgusting"—have been unable to weaken. A chance choice of a tram one day brings him together with a mistress he has not seen for nineteen years. The constancy of love enduring over time is established. Never has she forgotten the night when he changed her "from a girl to a woman." The daughter of the brewer's former mistress, who may or may not be his child, is an *après-guerre* modern girl like Akiko of *Tokyo Twilight*, but much more crass and insensitive. She is totally despised by Ozu. This girl dates Americans (an unspeakable violation of her integrity for this director), speaks snippets of English which make her sound ridiculous, and seeks to extract a mink stole from the old patriarch, who thwarts her by dying first. "I'll consider him my father until he buys that stole," she decides. As "autumn" sets in, the fabric of the younger generation's character has weakened to a point beyond redemption.

Every moment of the dying brewer's life becomes precious to us, as Ozu contrasts his humanity with the crass world he will be leaving behind, a world which was, to some extent, redeemed by his continuing existence. That his hypocritical daughter, evoking her dead mother, calls him a sinner to his face because he has taken up with his mistress once again serves only, through Ozu's silence, to endear him to us all the more. The family, Ozu suggests in *End of Summer*, was not meant to be an emotional or— at least for men—a sexual prison. The daughter's puritanical rigidity would destroy the harmonious Japanese family; her father's freedom to express a renewed feeling for a woman he once loved is presented by Ozu as right and good, the prerogative of the patriarch. What holds the family together is not an iron discipline—or moral righteousness—but good feeling, which will inevitably be expressed in all one's close relationships. It is not to be confined to the four walls of a single household. Ozu, of course, evades the question of whether he means to extend this freedom to actual adultery by making his hero a widower. Meanwhile, the old brewer's value is enhanced by Ozu through the humility with which he helps his former mistress scrub her floors. The small tasks of life please him now, at the end of summer, as they always did Ozu.

And he dies, not in the bosom of his selfish family, as his first heart attack had led them all to expect he would, but at the house of his mistress, Sasaki. Her daughter immediately blurts out, "there goes my mink stole!" The old merchant himself says only, exactly like the old man in *Tokyo Story* upon the death of his wife, "so this is the end." Even grand and seemingly eternal institutions die with scarcely a whimper. "Life is so fleeting, isn't it?" says the mistress, for lack of anything better. Two peasants in a field observe the flight of crows and conclude that someone must have died. "New lives replace the old," says the man, Chishu Ryu in a cameo role. "How successfully nature works," echoes the woman (Yuko Mochizuki). People face the inevitabilities with utterly unpersuasive clichés and platitudes.

The brewery must now merge with a big company and the son-in-law become a salaried man. The death of the patriarch means the end of an earlier era of free enterprise and individualism, which Ozu does not view as having been irreconcilable with the maintenance of a strong family. The freedom of the old brewer to take up once more with Sasaki has been included in the film precisely because Ozu wishes to suggest, paradoxically, a compatibility between the strong traditional family and a world where individualism cannot help but affect the characters of all. Economic in-

The End of Summer: Two peasants in a field observe the flight of crows and conclude that someone must have died. "New lives replace the old," says the man.

The End of Summer: Ozu mourns the loss of all that he has loved. The parade
of figures in black in the funeral sequence crosses a bridge as if into a new
epoch.

dividualism, expressed in Kohayagawa's creation of the brewery, did indeed
demand a certain degree of personal individualism, expressed in this
continuing love affair. But in *End of Summer*, recognizing that the chaos
of capitalist life has been used in arguments to suggest that the traditional
family could not survive in such an environment, Ozu replies that the
strong family, if its internal restraints were ever so gently lessened, might
yet have survived. Early capitalist society, in which meaningful family
life was still possible, is contrasted with the depersonalized epoch of
monopoly capitalism, which, with the death of the old brewer, assumes
total control of the society in Ozu's film. With the ascendance of this
new era, Ozu finally relinquishes his hope for the survival of the traditional Japanese family. *End of Summer* becomes Ozu's most historically
resonant film as he brings to the foreground of the action the inextricable
relationship between the economic structure of the society and social
institutions like the family.

Thus, in this film, does Ozu mourn the loss of all that he has loved.
The parade of figures in black in the funeral sequence crosses a bridge as
if into a new epoch. The people themselves may not register that the death
of the old man means the final passing of one way of life and the triumph
of a far less human alternative, but we, and Ozu, do.

Unlike Keisuke Kinoshita in such late family chronicles as *The River Fuefuki* (*Fuefukigawa*, 1960), Ozu is never guilty of a mindless traditionalism which argues that all the emotional gratification a human being could desire is to be found within the bosom of the family. But he is far more skeptical about the new postwar freedoms than a Naruse, who could make such a confused family film as *Herringbone Clouds* (*Iwashigumo*, 1958) precisely because he could not reconcile his own ambivalence toward the weakening of family bonds with the younger generation's insistence upon living solely according to its own wishes. Ozu can even partially applaud the new when it means, in *End of Summer*, that the youngest daughter, Noriko, will be free at last to marry for love. He recognizes the destructiveness of the old ways that leave her widowed sister, Akiko, thinking herself an old woman when she is only in her thirties. And he does not approve of Akiko's determination to remain alone for the remainder of her life.

But Ozu includes so many arranged marriages that work out well in his films because he always regarded the price of the new freedom (he might call it "license") as too high for the Japanese to pay. At stake always is the authority of the family and its value as a source of solace which, once lost, could never be retrieved. Ozu creates numerous repetitive plot situations all designed to form a plea to his audience that it not recklessly cast away this gem of Japanese civilization. For Ozu, the Japanese family alone makes possible a nuanced appreciation of one person for another, which for him belongs among the highest achievements of the Japanese national character.

Ichikawa's Wholesome and Unwholesome Families

Ototo (*Younger Brother*) takes place in the Taisho era, before the War, about forty years ago, but today we still have much the same problem in our family system. I hold the opinion that each family should be accustomed to respecting the individuality of every member.
Kon Ichikawa[1]

In contrast to the paeans of Ozu are Kon Ichikawa's biting assessments of the Japanese family's suffocating, insidious emasculation of the individual. Of all Japanese directors, Ichikawa affects the most aesthetic distance from his subject matter. But much more than in anti-war films like *The Harp of Burma* or *Fires on the Plain* are the characters in Ichikawa's films about the Japanese family treated as though they were insects beneath a clinician's microscope. Ichikawa would anatomize that sanctified institution of the family as if, by observing its workings as he would the tentacles of an insect, he could free us all of its deadly grasp. In Ichikawa's bitter satires about the Japanese family there is rarely a character wholesome enough to be entrusted with the director's point of view, as the patriarchs played by Chishu Ryu serve Ozu. Stifled by the family, Ichikawa's people fall into two categories; they are either weak and puerile or strong and domineering. Both types are treated as equally repulsive. For Ichikawa, in the best and most honest of his films, the Japanese family seems to possess a particular capacity to cultivate the most unsavory qualities of human nature.

The inbred, insulated Japanese family is the scene, in many Ichikawa films, of oddities of psychological and sexual perversion. Having become inverted in the isolation imposed by the authoritarian family, Ichikawa's characters in their frustration frequently turn destructive impulses against themselves and each other. In the Japanese manner, their world is always divided between insiders and outsiders, those belonging to one's own group (most particularly one's family) and the remainder of humanity, toward whom one feels no obligation to abide by even the most elementary courtesies. Family members invariably become deeply dependent upon each other's actions with little opportunity for recourse or even companionship outside of the narrow family circle.

[1] Joan Mellen, "Interview with Kon Ichikawa," *Voices from the Japanese Cinema*, p. 127.

Conflagration: His mother is a coarse woman of loose morals, her vulgarity a further reflection for Mizoguchi of his own lack of value.

With this degree of power over its members, the Japanese family is viewed by Ichikawa as a nurturer of madness and a cultivator of the dark places of the human soul. Repression—politely if inaccurately termed *enryo,* or "reserve," and justified by Japanese as permitting the emotional privacy of the other—also breeds its opposite, as Ichikawa well knows. The more circumscribed expected behavior becomes, the more likely it is to produce its opposite: actions violent, perverse, meaningless, and destructive, both of the self and of others. In the finest of Ichikawa's "home dramas" the family closes in unrelentingly on the individual.

Among Ichikawa's attacks on the family system may be counted the brilliant *Conflagration (Enjo,* 1958), an adaptation of Yukio Mishima's novel *The Temple of the Golden Pavilion.* Its subject, based upon a true story, is the burning down by a Buddhist acolyte of a beautiful Kyoto temple, the Kinkakuji or Golden Pavilion. The desperation of the boy, which culminates in his destruction of this building of incomparable loveliness, is attributed in part, both by Mishima and by Ichikawa, to the influences of his family upon the youth, a boy tormented by a stuttering problem and a sense of his own unworthiness.

That his father had always accorded such fulsome praise to this temple has led the boy, Mizoguchi, to contrast its grace with his own physical weakness and inadequacy, epitomized by his stuttering. He comes to see the Kinkakuji as a threat to his very existence, as if it were a living thing. His mother is a coarse woman of loose morals, her vulgarity a further reflection for Mizoguchi of his own lack of value. She is, unlike any mother in the canon of Ozu, her child's chief tormentor: "You fool," she calls him at one point in the film, "if they start taking stutterers like you into the Army, Japan is really finished." Having been taught, almost literally, by his parents to hate himself, Mizoguchi responds by hating the world.

In Ichikawa's film, the traumas of Mizoguchi's family life bear an even closer connection to his hysteria than they do in the Mishima novel. As the film opens, he has already burned down the Kinkakuji. Scenes of his childhood are then revealed in flashback, as if to provide some explanation of why this boy would perform so senseless and destructive an act. In the most revealing of these returns to his past, Mizoguchi's father places his hand over the boy's eyes so that Mizoguchi will not observe that, almost in their very presence, his mother is making love to another man. This is the primal scene of Mizoguchi's life, the degrading memory that leads him to seek revenge on the beautiful temple.

Only a few moments after the flagrant adultery of his mother, Mizoguchi and his father stand by the sea in dark silhouette. At this point his father introduces the subject of the beauty of the Kinkakuji, as if its mere existence could wipe out the shame and humiliation of their lives. But the Golden Temple can ultimately only remind Mizoguchi of his own pain, as the prostitution of his mother has made him feel sullied and inadequate. The Golden Pavilion itself, with its pristine clarity of form, comes to seem to Mizoguchi as if it were a silent reproach and a reminder of his own disgrace, since he first heard of its splendor when, shocked, he had just witnessed the whoredom of his mother. He identifies himself, of course, far more with his mother's corruption than he ever could with the inaccessible Golden Temple.

Visiting him after he has become an acolyte at the Kinkakuji, his mother advises Mizoguchi to "make good" so that he may one day be head priest at the temple. That so disgusting a mother could have such an ambition for him serves only to remind Mizoguchi of his own inadequacy and, indeed, of the sacrilege of his residing at the temple at all. When, later in the film, his mother persists in her obsession that he one day preside over the temple, he finally becomes emboldened enough to express at least part of what he feels as her son. He accuses his mother of not caring about him at all, as indeed, the film makes clear, she does not. As Ichikawa zooms in on Mizoguchi, he tells his mother that he knows about her lover; immediately he associates this knowledge with his physical imperfection which, he now says, will forever prevent him from becoming a great priest. "With this stutter I couldn't become a great priest," he shouts, "so you had better give up your stupid dreams." By juxtaposing Mizoguchi's informing his mother that he knows of her lover with this reference to his stutter, Ichikawa brilliantly has Mizoguchi reveal his conviction that his mother's lasciviousness, which unconsciously he sees as externalized in his stuttering, has rendered him unworthy of the Kinkakuji. His later discovery of the head priest's liaison with a geisha compounds his sense that filth and degradation, originally bestowed upon him by his mother, pervade the entire world, as they do his life. It is his accusation of his superior, a repetition of his earlier accusation of his mother, that will be the immediate cause of his loss of the right to succession at the Temple.

In a flashback to his father's funeral, Mizoguchi, in keeping with custom, lights the fire to the corpse. The coffin top opens and for a surreal moment flames leap up covering the entire wide screen, suggesting that at this moment the horror of conflagration became fixed in Mizoguchi's mind. This flashback to his father's cremation thus indisputably links the burning of the Golden Temple with Mizoguchi's relationship with his parents. In lighting the funeral pyre of his father, Mizoguchi is destroying the best of himself, what he will also be doing when he burns down the Golden Temple which, like his feelings for his father, he both loves and hates. He is punishing his father for having reminded him so irrevocably of his own shortcomings by introducing him to the Temple. Burning this Temple, in his sickened mind, will become a means to survival. Out of his neurosis, Mizoguchi seeks to create a world in which the Kinkakuji would no longer exist as a constant reminder of his weakness.

Mothers in Ichikawa, as in life and as opposed to the idealized, mannered world of Ozu, call their children "monsters." When Mizoguchi commits the unspeakable act of burning down the Temple of the Golden Pavilion, an act for which his mother bears considerable responsibility although she is far too unconscious of her effect on her son ever to realize it, she sends the message that she will never see him again.

Mizoguchi emerges as if of his own volition, a boy whose family never saw him as an individual with needs and handicaps deserving of greater sympathy and personalized attention than is perhaps common in that supposedly holy sanctuary, the Japanese family. It is almost impossible not to conclude from this film Ichikawa's belief that the source of Mizoguchi's dementia lay in those first family relationships which offered him so little. Not being valued by his parents for himself rendered Mizoguchi victim to a loneliness and self-hatred mocked by the self-sufficient magnificence of the Golden Temple.

Several of Ichikawa's films are about families whose members are deeply at war with each other. These works directly challenge Ozu's view that the traditional Japanese family not only preserves but makes possible the most profound feelings of love and concern among its members. The people of *The Key* (*Kagi*, 1959) may be related and live together, but they are all incapable of the concerned affection idealized in the home dramas of Ozu.

The family—and in particular a matriarchal family—is the subject of a virulent Ichikawa satire, *Bonchi*, made the following year in 1960. The title, as Donald Richie has pointed out, is an untranslatable Osaka dialect word "used to affectionately designate the eldest son."[2] Despite the fact that his screenwriter is so frequently Natto Wada, his wife, Ichikawa has

---

[2] *Japanese Cinema: Film Style and National Character* (New York: Anchor Books, 1971), p. 186.

been accused in Japan, on the basis of a film like *Bonchi*, of misogyny, a particular distaste for powerful women.

In *Bonchi* Ichikawa focuses on a matriarchal family, through which he observes the absurdities of the family system in general. In particular, in *Bonchi* Ichikawa finds the Japanese family plagued by an egomaniacal drive, above all other considerations, to perpetuate itself. The leaders of this family, a grandmother and her daughter, a mother, demand of their one scion, who happens, unfortunately for him, to be a male, that as soon as he reaches manhood he marry and produce a daughter. This reversal of traditional expectations, in which sons are demanded with no less hysteria, allows Ichikawa with sly humor equally to satirize the absurdity of the patriarchy in Japan. In *Bonchi* a granddaughter must be produced so that power in the family can be continued through the female line. The husband of this daughter would be adopted into the family, the couple living within the matrilineal household. But Ichikawa's real point is that the institution of the family, whether dominated by men or women, places its own survival ahead of the needs and feelings of individuals.

Lest one persist in the view that Ichikawa is primarily criticizing women and dreading the resurgence of the matriarchy, which disappeared from Japan with the creation of the Emperor system, rather than satirizing the traditional family, one has only to examine another of his family films, *Younger Brother* (*Ototo*, 1960), made in the same year as *Bonchi*.

Within an authoritarian, *patriarchal* family live a seventeen-year-old sister and her spoiled, lazy younger brother of fourteen or fifteen. Throughout the film she seems to live only to sacrifice herself to his whims. He takes his sister's generosity for granted, having grown up to believe that women

Bonchi: The institution of the family, whether dominated by men or women, places its own survival before the needs and feelings of individuals.

were born to serve him, a notion absorbed from their stern, self-centered father. When he contracts tuberculosis, she becomes his nurse, wearing herself out laboring at his side. After his death, she is left, at the moment she is entering womanhood, exhausted and worn out, lacking the energy to assume a life of her own.

Coldly, and as far removed from the narrative as he is, Ichikawa implicitly blames the insularity and attitude of patriarchal superiority of this family for the unhappiness brought to both brother and sister. The father's wife, not their natural mother, is hostile to both brother and sister, as well as hypocritically religious. She, too, has internalized the dictum of the patriarchy that women exist to minister to the comfort of others; at every chance she attempts to turn the daughter into a household servant. Meanwhile the father, when he is at home, sits alone in his own room, his back assertively turned to the room in which the others founder. He remains determined not to become involved in any of the petty affairs of the household. His concerns are solely with his own comfort—an ample supply of cigarettes and warm *sake*.

The "younger brother" becomes more and more wayward. And his sister is left to deal by herself with his scrapes at school, his stealing, and his generally wild behavior. Such a family, in which formalities make it impossible for the others to communicate with the tyrannical father, allows its weaker members, especially its women, no recourse when the inevitable problems of life arise. In one scene the sister is accosted by a man pretending to be a policeman chasing her brother. Ichikawa demystifies the idea

Younger Brother: Ichikawa demystifies the idea that the patriarchal family accords the individual protection in exchange for his loyalty and subservience.

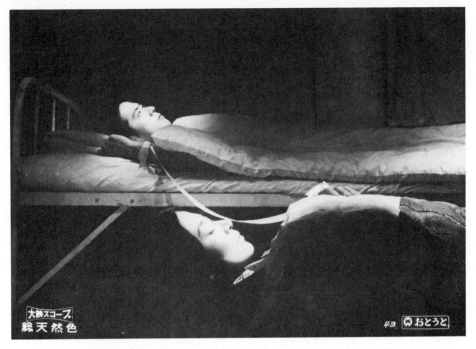

Younger Brother: Her helpfulness has become entirely compulsive; she is now incapable of being anything but sister to this brother.

that the patriarchal family accords the individual protection in exchange for his loyalty and subservience, as Ozu would have us believe.

When a marriage proposal arrives, the sister chooses to reject it. She feels an obligation to keep watch over her brother, who has now quit school and grown more irresponsible than ever. What begins as the sincere need to protect him becomes, in this sister, a perverse and self-destructive need to be needed. Her subservience and inability to consider her own future, as well as the strain of the responsibility which the parents refuse to share, lead her now to sacrifice herself irrevocably.

Selfishly, her brother, sensing this weakness in her, seeks to bind her to him even more tightly. After his tuberculosis sets in, he deliberately goes boating to exacerbate his illness so that she will not accept the marriage proposal. She, in turn, adorns herself for her visits to him in the hospital in a manner befitting a wedding, thus perverting natural impulses to what Ichikawa, unlike Ozu, sees as the unwholesome response of self-renunciation. "Marriage isn't every woman's fate," she says. Predictably, the father encourages her to live at the hospital, and work hard at nursing her brother. The son he urges, as he has always, to do exactly as he pleases, which at one point, to the delight of the sardonic Ichikawa, clearly means masturbation: "Do anything you want to in bed."

When her brother dies, the sister, bereft and now anemic, rushes out of the room where she has been resting in a temporary respite from her duties by his bedside. Her helpfulness has become entirely compulsive;

she is now incapable of being anything but sister to this brother. She dons her apron, ready to serve him once more, unable to register that he is dead. She has ceased entirely to exist for herself.

We are left uncertain as to what will happen to this sister. But it is clear that "the sins of the fathers," a term used at one point by the son, are further exaggerated in the tightly-knit Japanese family system. For Ichikawa, they last long in the life of the individual; we are given the feeling that the sister's deteriorating psychic health will not soon or easily improve.

In *Ten Dark Women* (*Kuroi Junin no Onna*, 1961) Ichikawa again attacks the myth of the supportive Japanese family, this time in a black comedy about a married man who has nine mistresses. The women eventually form an alliance against this weak man, who has proven to be so capable of using them all. They band together, plotting his murder, and gather at a party where his wife, in the presence of all, will shoot him. She, however, plans only to pretend to kill him so as to keep him exclusively for herself, a game to which he, knowing himself defeated, assents. Ichikawa and screenwriter Natto Wada thus satirize and condemn the unlimited prerogatives afforded the Japanese male. Part of their argument is that the Japanese man, having been emasculated precisely by his unlimited sexual license, is now unworthy of the privileges afforded him by male-chauvinist Japanese society. The hero seems to lack all sensuality and we can only wonder, as they come to, why all these strong, beautiful women (and the array of mistresses includes some of Japan's most glamorous stars, from Fujiko Yamamoto, who plays the wife, to Keiko Kishi) should want such a man. The film asks at the same time what would happen if all women exploited by Japanese men were to join together. Its plot becomes a fantasy of retribution, a threat to all Japanese men should all Japanese women organize together on the basis of their mutual grievances.

Ten Dark Women also reflects Ichikawa's abiding pessimism, his persistent refusal to believe that things can be any different than they are. The women, despite their greater strength in both character and numbers and their awareness of how little this man offers them, nevertheless continue to compete among themselves for his favors. As the man himself says: "If I'm so terrible, why do you care for me so much?" In this sense, they are no better than he, although somehow we believe, almost in spite of the director, that they should be. But the plot—Ichikawa's making the man helpless, pathetic, and outnumbered—forces us willy-nilly to side with him and hope that he escapes the clutches of these voracious females.

In Ichikawa's films there is the pervasive sense that most things will remain forever unknowable, impenetrable to our inquiries. Particularly mystifying is the attraction between men and women. Ichikawa would no more think of asking why the ten women want this man than he would how the old grandmother in *Bonchi* became the kind of person who would be willing to go to any lengths of cruelty. And for Ichikawa, knowing the origins of our motives—even if we could—would not help us because we

Ten Dark Women: The film asks what would happen if all women exploited by Japanese men were to join together.

cannot change anyway. The miseries of the Japanese family appear to be so much more endemic in his films than in those of any other Japanese director because of Ichikawa's predilection to see both social life and human nature as immutable. Such a view allows him brilliantly to explore the perversities nurtured by obsessional personalities, like the daughter in *Younger Brother* or Mizoguchi in *Conflagration*, although it sometimes considerably weakens the range of his art.

Because Ichikawa is so skeptical about the viability of our holding for long any convictions at all, he refuses to confine himself exclusively to the role of opponent of the Japanese family system. Thus could the same director also make a semi-sentimental, pro-family film like *Being Two [Years Old] Isn't Easy* (*Watashi wa Nisai*, 1962). Ichikawa has termed this film his "hymn to life," created "in the hope of making a little imprint on my heart,"[3] indicating that, although it may contain some satiric elements, in this film he is also offering positive values in which he personally believes. The endorsement of the family in *Being Two Isn't Easy* reflects, Ichikawa says, his own point of view.

Actually, *Being Two Isn't Easy* is an uneven film reflecting an ambivalence within Ichikawa regarding the Japanese family. Told from the point of view of a baby who reaches the age of two by the end of the film, it separates into two distinct halves. The first part brilliantly and satirically

[3] "The Uniqueness of Kon Ichikawa," from *Chuo Koron* (Tokyo), May 1963, reprinted in *Cinema*, 6, no. 2 (Fall 1970): 30. Translated by Haruji Nakamura and Leonard Schrader.

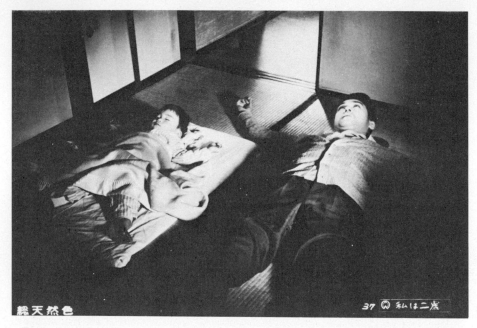

Being Two Isn't Easy: Bewildered, knowing nothing of sexual differentiation, Taro silently answers his father, "I don't know whether I'm a boy or not, but I'm a human being."

exposes how children's personalities are distorted by parents' imposing on them their own needs, a theme perfectly in keeping with the entire Ichikawa canon. But instead of sustaining this point of view, in the second half of the film Ichikawa moves toward an endorsement of family life. By the end, Ichikawa is exalting the sanctities inherent in the family through the love of the child for his now-dead grandmother, a love which is so elevated in this film that it allows the baby to form his first connection with the outside world and even, Ichikawa implies, makes it possible for him psychically to grow up to be a man.

In voice-over, almost as soon as he sees his first shadows, baby Taro already feels "all alone and unhappy." If such conceptualizing on the part of an infant departs from narrow realism, Ichikawa's recognition that these emotions date from our earliest days is brilliant and true. His father all but forces Taro to walk, insisting that he must "keep at it" because he is "a boy." Bewildered, knowing nothing of sexual differentiation, Taro silently answers his father, "I don't know whether I'm a boy or not, but I'm a human being." In a patriarchal society the mystique of maleness is cultivated almost from the moment of birth. Ichikawa darkly views such invocations to the baby's "manhood" as absurd, although he doesn't remain with this theme long enough to measure its full destructiveness or to challenge the patriarchal structure of the society which so early and so vigilantly inflicts such views on us all.

Taro's loss of his treasured freedom begins as his father builds a gate, ostensibly to keep him from falling down the stairs. The baby senses that the real function of the gate is to contain him. Taro's ego is bruised as his father calls him a liar because he seems to be asking to go to the potty too often, the father showing no awareness that Taro's understanding of his own body is as yet incomplete. Worse, Taro begins to blame himself and doubt his own worth when he becomes the cause of dissension between his parents. His father petulantly complains that before Taro was born, they could go out on Sundays. His mother, equally insensitive to the feelings of the helpless being who is so dependent on them both, feels herself a martyr because it takes four and one-half hours each day to make Taro's food. Her complaining is like a knife to the child's heart. Ichikawa's distance keeps him coldly analytical toward these parents who seem so unaware that their child is a human being whose feelings can easily be hurt.

Ichikawa reveals how, in the nuclear family, the child is made to feel guilty for his very existence. Such experiences lead Taro to the desperate decision to "grow up fast." Imagining himself climbing out of his crib, he laughs. His father believes the child is admiring him, which is obviously why he needed to have this child in the first place. Taro has come into the world, not to be treated as a separate person with rights to which every individual is entitled, but to provide an ever-ready source of balm to his father's ego. The father feels his boss does not appreciate him and has therefore created a being who will, even if Taro's "appreciation" must be gained by means of terror or violence. His father objects jealously to Taro's having a dog: "aren't parents enough?" as if Taro were a slave forced to yield all his affection to these two people. Yet despite their insatiable demands for affection, his parents do not want to be particularly inconvenienced by this newcomer whom they have brought, through no choice of his own, into their family. When Taro is sick, he is given painful injections, not to cure the illness (for which they are known to be ineffective) but solely to prevent him from coughing at night and keeping everyone awake. The injections Taro so dreads turn out to be mere tranquilizers. The family becomes the first and most powerful threat to our freedom and well-being.

The climax of *Being Two Isn't Easy* comes with the death of the grandmother who has lived with the family. When Taro, unaware, asks for her, he is told that she's watching to see if he's a good boy. Although the grandmother, in the Japanese manner, has fomented many quarrels in the household, the father admits that he understood the meaning of family ties only when he saw the old lady and Taro together. Her appreciation of her grandson's existence taught them the value of having offspring. They agree it would be a sad world indeed if there were no children, and they decide to have another.

At his second birthday party Taro looks through the window at the moon and imagines that he sees the face of his grandmother. "Grandma," he says. He believes she can see him from the moon and speculates on how many candles his grandmother's cake would have had on her next birthday. It would have been brighter than the moon, Taro decides. Ichikawa cuts to a shot of a cake with a huge number of candles, a shot exclusively from the point of view of the child and linking, as if on an unbroken chain of being, his few years with the full ones of his grandmother.

His parents blow out the two candles as if propelling him through his childhood by their strength. And Taro, again in voice-over, shares with us a new sense of his identity which he never before displayed, and which is inspired by the memory of his grandmother: "I am Taro. This is my father. This is my mother. I used to be a baby. I was born from my mother . . . I will become a man."

In *Being Two Isn't Easy* Ichikawa locates value in the natural processes of life and in the links of love between the generations. The family is revealed to provide life-giving, essential strengths in exchange for the freedoms it necessarily and inevitably extracts from us, freedoms we would have lost anyway through living in the world as it is. Not only is it unavoidable that we grow up within the nuclear family, but this institution allows us love and continuity available nowhere else.

We thus leave Ichikawa with the family intact. That, albeit with reservations, he returns to an institution he so bitterly satirized in films like *The Key*, *Bonchi* and *Younger Brother*—that he so contradicts himself—is not, however, an unusual quality in directors of his generation and older. These artists, while recognizing its abuses of the individual, have ultimately found it impossible to conceive of Japan without the family at its center. *Being Two Isn't Easy* brings Ichikawa close to the spirit of Ozu, who also approaches the family with a full understanding of how it limits us. The argument of this film, as of so many of Ozu's, is that the enrichment the family provides far outweighs any limitations it may impose.

Susumu Hani: *The Family as Betrayer*

[*Bad Boys*] is about the spirit of totalitarianism, which is still deep rooted in modern Japanese behavior. At the beginning of the film, there is the appearance of a modern, stable society. It all seems democratic. What I found out was that even those delinquents who revolted against society behaved like their old feudalist fathers. Through my film *Bad Boys*, I wanted the Japanese audience to sympathize with the bad boys. Because the film showed the totalitarian insides of the delinquents, the audience then, I felt, would be led to see their own insides.

Susumu Hani[1]

From the beginning of his career, when he made documentaries like *Children in the Classroom* (*Kyoshitsu no Kodomotachi*, 1954) and *Children Who Draw* (*Eo Kaku Kodomotachi*, 1955), Hani's point of view has been that of the young. For the poor and working-class families which are his focus, Hani shares with Shohei Imamura a compassion based upon their having been "deserted" in Japan's struggle for economic prosperity. Among these families, who have never recovered from the deprivations of the postwar period, the dissolution of the family and the fact that its value to Japan and the Japanese has been a fable appear indubitable. Maintaining traditional discipline on behalf of a society that no longer offers the security and protection originally at least partially granted by feudal power, these families expose for Hani the negative value of the institution as it continued into the new Japan after the Second World War.

The families of Hani offer their lonely children and lonelier adolescents no positive values on which to build their lives, neither spiritual comfort nor moral direction. In this, as with the families of Kon Ichikawa, they duplicate the dilemma of the society at large. Feeling economic pressure much more acutely than the white-collar middle class, Hani's working-class families frequently abandon their young, leaving them alone and ill-equipped to face the closed bourgeois world which Hani finds bearing down upon all Japanese.

Hani's young people are always at war with neo-feudal Japan, just as they are at war with their families, who never seem to place the interests and needs of their children first. The troubled children in Hani are always

[1] "Susumu Hani Interviewed by James Blue," *Film Comment*, 5, no. 2 (Spring 1969): 30.

forced to depend solely on their own resources, as if they had all been orphaned at birth, condemned to grow up, willy-nilly, through their own efforts. These young people, neurotic and tormented, pay the price for the moral default of the society. They perceive what is wrong in their elders, but they lack the means and the ideas to change anything. And, as social drop-outs, they succeed only in making themselves even more vulnerable to the abuses of a society with long-refined methods of punishing those who refuse to conform.

Bad Boys (*Furyo Shonen*, 1960), Hani's first feature film, is based upon real-life experiences of what used to be called "juvenile delinquents," youths gone astray. In voice-over before the credits, a boy confides, "I've seen the Ginza only through the window of a police van," immediately establishing the cultural deprivation afflicting the characters we are to meet in this film. For "actors" Hani chose actual former reform school boys, who would be re-experiencing events similar to those in which they had actually participated. Hani's premise in *Bad Boys* is that only outcasts can convey to us how outcasts truly feel.

The protagonist is an eighteen-year-old named Asai. His father died during the war; Asai himself went to work in a factory after Middle School (junior high). The point of view of the film is wholly his. As *Bad Boys* opens, Asai has been identified by the father of a friend as the "bad one," one who "isn't like my son," the ringleader who engineered the jewel robbery in which both boys took part. With no father to defend him, Asai faces the unmediated wrath of the law. Through chronicling the influence of Asai's broken family on his behavior, Hani introduces a theme which had as yet been insufficiently recorded in the Japanese film. In flashback we watch Asai in Asakusa, a working-class amusement section of Tokyo, instructing a snake charmer: "You've got to hold him gently. It's love that counts." The snake, of course, is Asai, unconsciously speaking of himself. He, like the snake, is simultaneously dangerous and vulnerable. Asai is a boy in need of a love that has been denied him and of approval from a society which has made no provision for helping individuals, like himself, who could remind Japan only of the inhumanity of its social order.

It is not surprising that Asai winds up in reform school. Offering him no compassion, like the society, his mother, full of shame, covers her face as she leaves the police station, more concerned with herself and her own "reputation" than with the problems facing her son. Her appearance is recorded in so understated a manner that we are barely aware that she has come and gone, that she has been there at all. Her behavior is symbolic of the perfunctory character of her entire attitude toward her son.

Over a close-up of the reformatory gate as he enters, Asai tells us that had he known that this would be his destination, he would never have promised to go straight. He had offered to change his life only as a bribe to facilitate his being let off for this petty crime. The older generation, represented by the officials who have control over Asai's life,

Bad Boys: In the mini-society they construct within the reformatory, a feudal power structure reigns which Hani has compared to that prevailing within the Japanese army.

arc characterized by lies and hypocrisy, justifying his distrust of them. For all their psychological testing and interviewing, their goal remains to lock Asai up as a threat to property and middle-class order. He is refuse, to be tossed aside like the cockroaches he throws into the rice that is his daily prison fare. There is no attempt to understand Asai as a human being, to discover the causes of his anti-social behavior, to help him to build a satisfying life.

Among Asai's fellow prisoners a hierarchy of power prevails, exactly like that operating in the world outside, against which these boys are revolting. Their rebellion is mere defiance, as in stealing a pearl necklace from a jewelry store, because they lack any means of understanding how the feudal society in which they have grown up has oppressed them. They know only that they hate it. Yet in the mini society they construct within the reformatory, a feudal power structure reigns which Hani has compared to that prevailing within the Japanese army.[2] New recruits to the prison are initiated by the other boys. Extreme physical punishment is the means by which loyalty to the group is demanded as an absolute. The body is glorified to the exclusion of the mind.

Hani's youths, culturally deprived, uneducated, and isolated, have no way of attributing their discontent and maltreatment to feudal institutions. As drop-outs, they have no means of making contact with the student movement. Pathetically, they duplicate among themselves the very values that have been oppressing them. The hand-held camera

[2] *Ibid.*, p. 30.

records the beatings Asai suffers at the hands of those exactly like him who, like the child Asai recorded in flashback, must also have wandered the streets of postwar Tokyo stealing food when and where they could. Hani photographs Asai in the prison with affection as he enjoys learning the skills of carpentry. Asai is a touching figure, if one without a future in Japan, as he confides to us in voice-over: "I don't know how I'll end up."

Asai is finally released from the reformatory. He is paid 320 yen (300 yen are equivalent to one dollar) for his labor. He turns to face the hall now behind him and yells "Thanks!" The unsteady, hand-held camera, reflecting his precarious future, follows him to the gate. There are several ramifications to Asai's unusual offering of "thanks" to the oppressive reformatory. Hani sees it as a declaration of Asai's having grown up, his having become a man as a result of this experience. Paradoxically, the unsympathetic reformatory has given Asai something positive, the opportunity to mature. The manner in which Asai says "thank you," according to Hani, involves a sophisticated term that Asai had never before used.[3] This, too, marks his having matured. He has transcended his past life sufficiently to communicate with the world outside in a new manner.

Such "thanks" is in direct opposition to Asai's previous attitude toward the external world, which had been one of unqualified hostility. Of course, it is also an ironic "thank you" because the prison has, in fact, exploited him for his labor. In this sense, it should be the prison which thanks Asai. But his internal resistance to its authoritarian atmosphere is what has given Asai maturity by permitting him to become aware of his own inner strength. In the last shot we view Asai through the bars of the gate, as if he were still imprisoned. The society into which he re-emerges, like the family he never had, continues in its unfeeling way to offer little to the weak and the unconnected.

Hani's critique of the Japanese family is inseparable from his criticism of all of Japan's social institutions. His attack on social injustice seems oblique because he focuses on the consequences of inequity among the young rather than on a more direct depiction of social abuse. Hani struggles for an authentic sense of the damage that has been and is being done to Japan's young people. Part of the authenticity Hani evoked in *Bad Boys*, for example, was the result of his filming in an actual institution. The authorities were very much afraid of contact between actual prisoners and outside boys, the "actors," and the government gave Hani permission to shoot only because through his earlier documentaries he had already been recognized as a person interested in new modes of education.

Frequently we meet Hani's young people in the classroom, only to watch as they are shaped by the predominant values of the culture. At home they are encouraged to conform to whatever they are told at school. Hani likes to make films about young people because he believes

[3] *Ibid.*

they possess the potential to be different from their parents; despite the militarism we see among the "bad boys," their sensibilities have not yet been totally corrupted by the pressures within Japanese society for a middle-class form of success.

The undermining of the young, of course, begins much earlier than adolescence, and in *Children Hand in Hand* (*Te o Tsunagu Kora*, 1962) Hani returned to a much younger group. This film is a beautiful parable about Japanese society—its potential and its decadence—as seen through the interactions among the children in an elementary school class. Fierce competition sets these children against each other. Already a cruel domination by the strong of the weak can be observed. Hani suggests, however, that relations between Japanese need not be based on this principle; cooperation and mutual understanding are possible as well. In this view lies Hani's idealism and the source of the title of the film, "children hand in hand."

There is a particular uneasiness in Japan toward the afflicted, the deformed, and the handicapped, a tendency primitive and almost animistic in the frequent impulse to shun such people, as if the spirit of their affliction might be communicable. Compassion gives way to fear. The weak are a reminder to all that success, however struggled for, may turn out to be an illusion, strength temporary, hard work not always enough to ensure survival.

At the center of *Children Hand in Hand* Hani places a boy named Nakayama who is slower than the others, both intellectually and physically. He then watches what happens, as if, by revealing to the audience the moral flaws of these children, the Japanese might be given some insight into their own. The children of the film reveal for Hani some of the best but also some of the most destructive tendencies in the national character. He would offer his Japanese audience, through this excursion into an ordinary classroom, a vision of who and what they are.

Yet Hani's style seems totally uninfluenced by so strong a point of view. He makes his film seem as if it were a spontaneous expression of life unmediated by the artist's hand. The camera seems merely to observe. Never does Hani impose upon his films an artificially constructed, Aristotelian-style plot. Rather, they seem to be composed, like life, of a series of happenings structured according to the psyches, left free and unbridled, of his characters. *Children Hand in Hand* ends on the semi-finality of an elementary school graduation, but most of the film seems a recording of what happens in a typical Japanese classroom, unalloyed by the intervention of the adult consciousness of the director.

In the opening sequence the slow Nakayama is at once singled out for us as a problem; on the class trip to Nara, he is late for the bus. Meanwhile, among the others—unlike Nakayama destined for high positions in the corporate structure of the society when they become adults—mutual distrust reigns. Each child fears another will copy his answers on an arithmetic test. "Life's like a race," says one, "if you don't win, you lose." These children have already been corrupted by the world in which they will later have to function, their heads filled with visions of "big pay checks" and "good jobs." There is also strong pressure in the group for all to cheat, since they are already well aware that success is all that counts.

The children, treated by Hani as prototypic Japanese, are also fiercely chauvinistic, incommensurately angry when they refuse to grant the superiority of American-made pencils: "What's so different about them? Same as ours." The Hani-like teacher tries to encourage cooperation among his pupils but they refuse, and especially will not yield to his suggestion that they tolerate the weaker Nakayama: "Group work slows us down." They display little sympathy for his slowness, cruelly making it difficult for him to value himself. The behavior of his classmates fills Nakayama with a sense of his own inferiority and worthlessness. Comparing himself to the others, who so insist upon emphasizing their intellectual superiority, he cannot help but find himself a lesser human being.

Hani implies that a place for Nakayama could be found within the group, as it could within the society at large, if only the others were tolerant enough to permit it. One boy does try to teach Nakayama to write and derives pride from so helping another, an example the kind of altruism that Hani suggests is being lost in Japan. The majority persist in tormenting Nakayama, refusing to allow him to play baseball with them because any team with him on it will surely lose: "Let him pick up the balls . . . picking up balls is good enough for him."

Sadistically, the other children exploit Nakayama's weakness and they torture him. The boys bury him in an enormous hole up to his head because since "the television tower is stuck in the dirt, dirt must make you smart." They know that the simple, trusting Nakayama will believe such "logic," although they are laughing at him all the while. They run off, leaving him helpless and alone, unable to move. The sun sets. People pass him on their way home from work. "I'm getting smart," he tells the sister of one of his classmates passing by. She promptly digs him out. When Nakayama cannot learn to read, the class laughs.

In another vignette, reflecting Hani's brilliance as a psychologist, the teacher and the mothers of the pupils complain about the children into a tape recorder. The children are then permitted to listen to the tapes and are encouraged to talk into the recorder, replying to their parents with words they wouldn't dare use to their faces. One child argues that if his mother would "let him alone," he could do better at school. This progressive method of encouraging self-expression among the children is an attempt to exorcise their frustrations. It necessitates a transcendence of traditional modes of behavior, particularly the obedience to authorities. In this sense it is healthy and a meaningful attempt to overcome the stultifying pattern by which inferiors in Japan always must repress their discontent or anger at those above them. The scene also affords us the opportunity to hear Nakayama's attitudes toward himself. It provides no surprises: "I'm no good . . . being in the hole didn't make me smart. How can I get smart?" Nakayama learns to read, but he still cannot write, a task, of course, enormously more difficult for Japanese than for Western children.

But Nakayama does have talents, and although these are not traditional academic abilities, they must be cultivated, just as Nakayama must learn to accept himself and be aware of his own value. Nakayama is tricked into helping one of the boys steal a family antique. He is used, but the experience reveals him as possessing a strong capacity for solidarity. His staunch character will not permit him to inform on his friends, even when he knows that they are making a fool of him. Nakayama is also good with his hands; he excels at electricity and carpentry. He says at one point that he would like to be a teacher when he grows up, a psychologically credible ambition because the teacher is the only person who has been kind to him. This he can never be. The teacher gently suggests that he "do something that you like and that suits you." "Like the repair work?" Nakayama asks. Nakayama, so encouraged by the patient and understanding teacher, can discover this answer for himself, producing one of the loveliest moments of the film.

In the deeply moving graduation scene, Hani dollies in to the teacher and to Nakayama's mother as, with pathos, they look at the little boy being given his personal farewell by the school principal: "I appreciated your seriousness and perseverance," Nakayama is soberly told, "Continue!" Nakayama's mother treats him with pity and kindness, if with worry. Hani does not place responsibility for the difficulties faced by such children on the family alone, as if it were an entity capable of preserving pure values despite the corruption of the rest of the society, as Ozu would have us believe. For Hani in *Children Hand in Hand* the family alone, even at its sympathetic best, can do little for its young because outside values in Japan are at once so overwhelming and so antithetical to human development. This is an insight Kinoshita expressed for the 1930s in *Twenty-four Eyes* and it is no less true for Hani's postwar "peaceful" Japan.

When Hani does depict detailed scenes of family life, however, they are sometimes filled with torment, as in *The Inferno of First Love* (*Hatsukoi Jigoku-hen*, 1968), sometimes called *Nanami*. Shun and Nanami are two young people trying to consummate their love for each other. Nanami, who works as a nude model although she is barely out of her teens, is the more experienced partner. Shun is a virgin. In their first encounter he finds himself impotent.

Shun is, in fact, one of the most troubled of Hani's young people. His neurosis, the film reveals, has resulted from an unsavory family life in which he has been exploited and sexually abused. As a modern psychologist, whose premises are similar to those of Western therapists, Hani recognizes that we can understand ourselves only by examining the past. In the first sequence Shun and Nanami are in bed together. Nanami tells Shun, "I want to know more about you." Immediately, by means of a straight cut, Hani moves to a flashback, as if there were a strong, uninterrupted link between past and present.

We witness Shun as a child. His father had died when he was seven and he is being abandoned by his mother, a not atypical occurrence among the poor, as witnessed by the growing rate of infanticide in the Japan of the 1970s. The mother—soft focus and echo chambers reminding us that we are in the past—is shown with her lover, a boxer. She walks away from her child while he stands helplessly watching her.

Shun soon becomes, like Asai, a reform school boy. He is labelled "hopeless," and his foster parents selfishly refuse to adopt him. The foster father is a metalworker. In a series of stills we observe him teaching Shun this trade. The boy is not paid for his labors, the seeming reason why this couple has consented to take him in. We are yet unaware of the man's homosexual advances toward Shun, which Hani reserves for a later revelation and which more fully account for Shun's presence in this household. Parents in Hani behave very differently than they do in Ozu. They participate much more actively in the despoliation of the young than even Ichikawa's parents in his satiric films. Hani insists upon focusing on such families precisely in reaction to an Ozu or a Kinoshita, who persist in mythologizing about the virtues of the Japanese family.

Trauma, in Ozu, is resolved at home or nowhere. Even late in the 1950s no one in *Tokyo Twilight* conceives of the idea of providing psychological therapy for the troubled Akiko. Ozu's failure to introduce the idea of dealing with Akiko's anxiety as if it could be treated and relieved like a physical ailment is, however, realistic for Japan. The Buddhist-influenced view that the personality, like society, is somehow immutable has prevented a liberated attitude toward psychiatry from gaining widespread support. Even Shohei Imamura, who is well aware of the distortions of the personality prevalent in contemporary Japan, prefers to treat insanity in a mystical manner, and even suggests[4] that we return to viewing the insane as blessed and closer to an invisible spiritual world from which we "normal" ones have become alienated. Nagisa Oshima, a radical critic of Japanese social institutions, seems to lack all faith in the transformation of the personality, and his characters, often stiff and unrealized, sometimes suffer from this rigid point of view. It is Hani alone who has suggested that we need not be hopelessly bound by the neuroses bestowed upon us by an unwholesome family life. Nor should the troubled be locked away in some dark corner of the household until they are ready to function once again, as is a frequent custom among Japanese families when an individual develops neurotic symptoms which prevent him from conducting a normal social life.

Hani believes that the state of psychiatry, where it does exist in Japan, leaves much to be desired. In *The Inferno of First Love* he bitterly satirizes the Japanese approach to psychological aberration. Hardly unexpected, given his past, Shun becomes morose and withdrawn. The foster parents then send him to "Laughing School," which Hani photo-

---

[4] Conversation with the author, Tokyo, November 1974.

The Inferno of First Love: Shun develops a semi-perverse, semi-paternal relationship with a little girl of five or six named Momi whom he meets in the park. Shun both adores and sexually molests Momi.

graphs with a wide-angle lens, flattening out into grotesque caricature the faces of master and pupils attempting to laugh.

The consequences of Shun's neurosis and the failure of such farcical and destructive behaviorist approaches to therapy are serious. Shun's anxiety begins to take a distorted sexual form. He develops a semi-perverse, semi-paternal relationship with a little girl of five or six named Momi whom he meets in the park. Shun both adores and sexually molests Momi. With her he feels free and happy, able at last to escape from his life. Misplacing and misdirecting his sexual drive, he uses her in a way neither he nor she can understand, but which is, of course, destructive for them both.

Yet Hani treats what amounts to Shun's sexual abuse of the little girl with gentle understanding and without horror or self-righteousness.

There is an innocence about the molestation, as if Shun were not aware of what he was doing. In the first sequence of Nanami and Shun in bed together, Hani overlapped the sound of the tapping of metal in Shun's foster father's shop. What our families do to us finds expression in our self-destruction, in Shun's molesting of Momi as well as in his sexual inadequacy with Nanami. Such neurosis, for Hani, inevitably comes to all who have been systematically taught that they are worthless. By means of very high overhead shots of Shun in the metal shop Hani conveys his character's absolute powerlessness and hence his lack of full responsibility for his problems, even for what he does to Momi.

Hani suggests in all his films about the young that the family and the entire society have defaulted on their moral obligation to provide an environment in which children can accept themselves. Instead, the police pursuing the army deserter Oki in *Morning Schedule* (*Gozencho no Jikanwari*, 1973) demonstrate that the world of authority is one only of threat and punishment. Left to their own devices, thrown back upon paltry inner resources, Hani's young people frequently succumb. It is never their own fault.

The Structures of Oshima

The idea of the father as the ruler of the family could be considered an analogy to the rulers of the state itself, which for two thousand years has been ruled by an emperor who represents power.[1]

Ceremonies are a time when the special characteristics of the Japanese spirit are revealed. It is this spirit that concerns and worries me, my own spirit which wavers during such occasions. One might easily reject, both intellectually and emotionally, militarism and xenophobic nationalism in daily life. But these forces, once beyond the realm of daily life, are not so easily denied.[2]

Nagisa Oshima

Oshima's *Boy* (*Shonen*, 1969) is one of the bitterest satires ever to be made on the Japanese family. Based upon an actual event reported in the Japanese press, a father and mother instruct their son, a boy of ten, to fling himself in front of moving cars and pretend to be injured. The parents then appear, demanding compensation or "silence money," and threatening, if they are not appeased, to report the incident to the police. They travel throughout Japan perpetrating this scheme, reaching the northernmost tip of Hokkaido before they are apprehended for fraud. Oshima argues, not that he is realistically representing a typical Japanese household, but that the entire situation symbolizes the essence of family life in Japan. The power relationships between parents and children, exaggerated through the outrageous fraud, are nevertheless meant to suggest those beneath the surface of all Japanese families.

The father of this family, a war veteran, uses fake (or real, since it doesn't quite matter) war wounds as an excuse for not maintaining regular employment. This is the reason he offers for forcing his son to risk his life daily for the family's sustenance. Angrily, Oshima satirizes all such people who call themselves "victims" as an excuse for moral lethargy. Sometimes the father gives his ten-year-old son, the "boy" of the title (the word is used as a name, suggesting how pathetic and alone this child is), injections so that bruises will appear on his skin and the "accidents" thus seem more credible. As the film progresses, the boy is actually hit by a few of the cars and his scrapes and bruises become "real." We are in the presence, Oshima tells us, of the highly touted

[1] "Nagisa Oshima Interviewed by Ian Cameron," *Movie* (United Kingdom), no. 17 (Winter 1969–70), p. 14.
[2] "Why *The Ceremony?*" press release published in the United States by New Yorker Films, its American distributor.

Boy: As the film progresses, the boy is actually hit by a few of the cars, and his scrapes and bruises become "real."

Japanese family, one of the glorious manifestations of the "Japanese spirit."

Like Hani, Oshima used a non-professional, an actual orphan, to play the boy. When members of the crew offered to adopt him after the film was completed, Oshima has related, the boy refused, preferring to return to the orphanage; he had had too sour an experience with families to want to become a member of one.[3] The experience of acting in this film could only have confirmed his belief that freedom is inconceivable within the Japanese family as it is structured.

For this father is more than a scoundrel. He is the Japanese patriarch exposed. He demands, like the Emperor as whose surrogate he functions, absolute power over his vassals, wife and children. When the wife and boy attempt to break away from him, if only to do the same "work" on their own, the wife being motivated to save money for a coming baby the man does not want, he beats her mercilessly. That she is pregnant makes no difference, especially since she has violated his orders by refusing to undergo an abortion. This man is clearly destructive to all in his "care." But the father could not be so dangerous were not the culture as a whole endorsing his behavior. Oshima includes so many Japanese flags in the shots of *Boy*—they seem to appear everywhere—to indicate the intimate relationship between the individual family and

[3] "Nagisa Oshima Interviewed by Ian Cameron," p. 14.

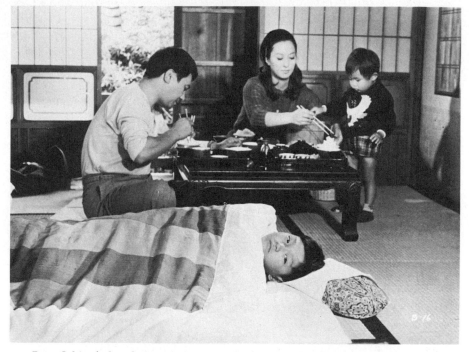

Boy: Oshima's boy hero experiences each day a total violation of his personal integrity.

the State, which could not survive as it is were not each of its separate households perpetuating its values.

The psychology of the typical young Japanese, as in the films of Hani, is characterized by frustration and repression of one's deepest longings. Oshima's boy hero experiences each day a total violation of his personal integrity. He hates the cheating and fraud he is forced to perpetrate. But, recognizing the power of the family over his·life, he says nothing. Pathetically, he is also intensely loyal to his parents. At first this may seem unrealistic, given their vicious exploitation of him. But they are all that he knows. His very dependence leads him to protect them, and hence himself against the entire outside world. When he does object to running in front of cars, his parents threaten not to feed him. He runs away at one point but his powerlessness, particularly economic powerlessness, forces his return to the family.

The boy's only escape lies in the fantasy life he constructs and which he shares with a baby brother too young to understand. Oshima's choice of a ten-year-old was well calculated. By the age of ten the boy has already learned the extent to which he must conform; he has absorbed the rules of what it means to belong to a Japanese family. Yet he is young enough still to long for self-definition.

Oshima's use of atonal music creates a sense of discordance, another facet of this film's subtle departure from realistic naturalism. The music denotes a universe where natural order has been distorted. The shot compositions also contribute to this mood of disorder. In one shot, the entire family and one of the drivers they are cheating occupy only one-third of the frame, while the other two-thirds remains empty of human habitation. The people, as *lumpen*, semi-working-class outcasts, are peripheral to this post-war Japan whose worst values they, like Hani's reformatory boys, frantically perpetuate in their struggle for survival, As such, they are even peripheral to the shots of a film in which they are the central characters.

The hopelessness and the predestined suffering of the children of such people are reflected in the information Oshima includes about the family backgrounds of the parents. The man lost his father at the age of five. The wife, actually the boy's stepmother, was abandoned at the age of four by her mother, a mother who had married four times. Like the boy they victimize, these parents have themselves been victims. The society will readily punish such people for their transgressions, but Japan will provide them with no opportunity to break out of the cycle of misery into which they have been cast. Japan's prosperity appears in *Boy* in the profusion of cars driven by people with somewhere to go, unlike our family, homeless and traveling from one end of Japan to the other staging these phony accidents.

Out of his fear and the impulse to escape, the boy develops the fantasy of being from outer space. He is a wise boy, explaining the world of fish to his baby brother, "the big ones eat the little ones," another parable of life in Japan interpolated by Oshima. The boy, of course, is one of the "little ones." All he can do is pretend to be a man from outer space, "come to save the world." By the age of ten he already knows that Japan is in need of saving. In the shot in which he speaks of saving the world, a Japanese flag blows in the wind, lest anyone doubt that, through the wretched life of this boy, Oshima is describing the wretched lives of all his countrymen.

Later, on the street, the boy watches as two older children accost and rob a younger, accusing him of "bumping into them." The victim, relinquishing his money for "hospital bills," is then pushed into the mud. Our boy approaches the victim to help him, but the humiliated victim only hits him and steps on his beloved baseball cap, grinding it into the mud. Learning nothing from his own exploitation, the victimized boy now immediately picks on someone smaller than he. Oshima observes the violence of competition, in which "the big fish devour the little," occurring every day on the streets and byways of Japan. Angry at finding the boy wandering alone in the streets, the mother throws the baseball cap, which the boy has carefully washed at an open faucet and dried in steam, into the mud a second time. He is assaulted in equal measure by his family and by the world.

Like Hani, Oshima thus insists that the family provides no sanctuary, and, in fact, this boy's family inflicts on him far greater cruelty than comes to him in his experiences in the uncaring, essentially indifferent society. For the father is also a sadist. In one scene he pursues the boy into the toilet, a refuge where the boy innocently sings about the friends he once had when he lived with his grandparents. The grandparents wouldn't be pleased to see him again, says the father. They wrote they were glad he left, a lie that would be obvious to all but this vulnerable boy. His friends, the father goes on, won't remember him. The father concludes by telling the boy that his desk at the school he attended is now occupied by another. So that he can survive by the boy's risking his life, this father literally tells his son that he is a dispensable human being, easily replaceable. The unspeakably cruel implication is that, were he to die in one of the staged automobile accidents, his absence would go unnoticed, would change nothing. In the character of the father Oshima offers not psychological realism but the spirit of the Japanese patriarch. In most households the sadism would not, of course, be so overt, but for Oshima it would be no less real. Behind the patriarch's authority Oshima finds the destruction of the young, inevitable in the family at this stage of Japan's social development.

The boy's psyche becomes so damaged that he begins to welcome the pain that comes to him from the accidents. So perverse has been his life experience that only suffering assures him of his normality, and indeed that he exists at all: "Even an ordinary child can say it hurts when it really hurts." Only pain allows him to feel like an ordinary child; the perverse has become the normal. In this scene the boy lies in a fetal position, highlighting the motif of his desire to return to the womb and so end his suffering. It involves a death wish as well, for if he ceased to exist, his suffering would thereby also end.

Oshima insistently rejects the sentimental approach to such subject matter adopted by his predecessors in the Japanese film. For us to weep for this boy would permit an easy catharsis. It would allow the audience relief without accepting the necessity of remedy, a fault, according to Oshima, shared by Japanese filmmakers from Kinoshita to Shindo. The instances of child abuse, constant in this film, are presented without heart-rending music or pathos. It is inconceivable in fact to find in any of Oshima's films the "Auld Lang Syne" of Kinoshita's *Twenty-four Eyes* or even the "There's No Place Like Home" of Ichikawa's *The Harp of Burma* and Ozu's *Early Summer*. The strongest comment Oshima will make is dispassionately to reveal that such abuse exists.

The airplane trip to Hokkaido the family takes near the end indicates that the fantasy life of the boy has all but encompassed his consciousness. He explains to his little brother, and seems almost to believe it, that the clouds are "monsters out of which men from outer space will appear." More than ever he reveals his need to be rescued. Their arrival in Hokkaido, the northernmost point of Japan, is treated by Oshima as a positive event. "Is this the end of Japan?" the boy asks in double entendre. "Only outer space is left." From the point of view of this child, the wish to be rid of Japan has been rendered wholly desirable.

With nowhere left for them to flee, and decreasing opportunities to ply their "trade," the violence within the family becomes more extreme. Oshima records the man striking his wife, her blood spurting onto the snow, in black-and-white rather than color. As with sentimentality, he renounces spectacle, which he sees as antithetical to the ability of film as a medium to confront us with the truth. Attempting to create sympathetic pain in himself for his bleeding mother, the boy scratches his arm with a watch she had bought him. Chaos ensues and, in a clever use of irony, Oshima has the baby, unnoticed, step accidentally in front of a car which cannot stop on the ice. The meaning of their staged accidents is expressed in the family's actually becoming the victims themselves of a real accident, although only the boy is humane enough to face its consequences.

The car slams into a telephone pole, killing the driver, a young woman. For this real accident and death, however, only our boy, and not his parents, assumes responsibility, as if at an unconscious level he believes that his having tortured drivers with fake accidents and unreal wounds has brought down upon him, with this death, a just retribution. What he feels as he flings himself angrily on his father, the real culprit, is an acute sense of responsibility for the suffering of others, which his own pain has taught him in spite of the amorality of the environment provided by his family. The red boot in the snow, now photographed in color, reiterates the colors of the Japanese flag, red sun on white. For Oshima this symbol returns guilt and responsibility to where they finally belong, not solely to the man, part victim and part victimizer, but once more to the State and its institutions.

The boy builds a snowman "from outer space, all the way from Andromeda," the red boot forming its face. He calls it a messenger of justice, unafraid of monsters, trains, and cars. It is, of course, what the boy himself would like to be: "He never gets hurt, he never cries, he doesn't even have any tears, he has no parents, he's all alone." And "when he's really afraid, other men from outer space come and save him." In frustration at being "just an ordinary boy," unable to do anything about the evils surrounding his life, our hero destroys the snowman. It is too painful a reminder of how things ought to be. It makes his suffering unbearable.

Oshima takes measure of·the psychic damage done to this boy in the last moments of the film. When the police show the boy a photograph of himself, he calls it "a man from outer space." He is bereft of a personal identity, the price of having had to serve in a Japanese family. But when the policeman remarks that it must have been nice to ride on a plane, a tear runs down the boy's cheek as Oshima cuts to the images recording the thoughts that have led this otherwise highly controlled child to cry: the snowman with its boot, the head of the accident victim stained with blood. Suddenly the boy admits that he went to Hokkaido. He cannot escape responsibility for the girl's death. No matter what has been done to him, he survives with his moral sense intact. It is in this final response of the boy that Oshima pleads for the valuable humanity being trampled and ignored in today's Japan. The slowness of Oshima's last fade informs us of the permanence of the boy's memory of this gratuitous death. His sense of himself as a murderer, irrational though it may be, is the only legacy for the future bequeathed him by his now dissolved family.

Oshima's great epic of the fall of the Japanese family, and how deeply

The Ceremony is Oshima's great epic of the fall of the Japanese family and how deeply this institution has been intertwined with Japanese imperialism and militarism.

this institution has been intertwined with Japanese imperialism and militarism, is *The Ceremony* (*Gishiki*, 1971), his finest film to date. The title derives from the importance in Japanese life of ceremonies like weddings and funerals, for these have traditionally been occasions when a uniquely Japanese spirit is believed to manifest itself. But the deaths in *The Ceremony* are primarily suicides or murders, the weddings, farcical. The patriarch of the Sakurada family at the center of the film, a grandfather, rules with an iron hand. He is a man who has committed a form of incest with a woman who would have been his daughter-in-law had he agreed to relinquish her to his son. This act becomes symbolic of the hypocrisy lying behind the pretensions to dignity of the Japanese family as a social institution.

Oshima presents *The Ceremony*, the history of a typical upper-middle class family from the Second World War to the present, as, simultaneously, a history of Japan. The question the director poses through the action is whether the Japanese people, emerging from the militarism and xenophobic nationalism of the war period, have discovered new values to replace the old. Oshima's answer, resonant throughout this film, is that they have failed to do so.[4]

The hero of the film is named Masuo, his name the result of his having been born in Manchuria during the Japanese occupation of that territory.

[4] In the *Tokyo Shimbun* for January 18, 1971, Oshima wrote of *The Ceremony*: "My film will only be my own personal answer to these questions, a clinical example as it were. And at present I am inclined to answer that, superficial aspects aside, the Japanese people have undergone almost no basic change."

He is simultaneously a product of his country's history and a reminder of its aggression (in 1931 Japan had invaded Manchuria, setting up a puppet colony, Manchukuo) and defeat. Masuo's father committed suicide at the end of the war, losing his entire *raison d'être* with the Emperor's shocking declaration that he was a man and not a God. Wildly fanatic, Masuo's father feared a Communist takeover of Japan which would have to be defeated at all costs. But in the destruction of the idea of the Emperor's divinity, he saw the end of Japan and took his own life, refusing to fight any longer for the Japanese spirit since its core had already been destroyed with Emperor Hirohito's abdication of his true role.

The younger generation is comprised of Masuo, his cousin (and possibly his half-sister) Ritsuko, his male cousin Terumichi, the family heir, and another male cousin named Tadashi, a Mishima-like figure.[5] The events of the film include Masuo's sexual initiation by his aunt, Setsuko, the mother of Ritsuko, and his arranged marriage and wedding at which the bride fails to appear, an event simultaneous in time with the neo-fascist Tadashi's death in an automobile "accident." The film concludes with the suicide of Terumichi, which he arranges solely as a means of ending, once and for all, the Sakurada family line.

It is essential to Oshima's purpose that the Sakuradas be "mainstream" Japanese. The grandfather had been a government official in the Ministry of Home Affairs before being purged, temporarily, after the War. The men of the older generation have all been soldiers in the Imperial Army. One of Masuo's uncles, Isamu, has left-wing, but Stalinist, sympathies which are treated by Oshima with appropriate ridicule.

At the mercy of such a family, such a Japan, Masuo grows up as a man without a future. The legacy of the Sakurada family is as amoral a set of values as that predominating in the lower-class family of *Boy*. Although he is not above incest himself, the grandfather will even murder Masuo's aunt, Setsuko, rather than have Masuo sacrifice his responsibility to the family name with an incestuous love affair. For Oshima in this film the extremes of Japan's history require an expressionism of form. The murders and the incest, suicides, and betrayals become symbolic of an even worse offense: Japan's failure of moral renewal after the War and its consequent abandonment of its younger generation to so continuingly feudal a society as to make life in Japan scarcely worth living.

Radically departing from the traditional Japanese film, Oshima rejects chronological narrative, opening *The Ceremony* with Masuo's receiving a telegram from his cousin Terumichi, now living on a deserted island. It is 1971. In this message Terumichi announces the fact of his own death, causing Masuo and their cousin Ritsuko, whom both have loved, to leave for this island. Throughout the film Oshima intercuts shots of their journey. The end is thus contained in the beginning. Oshima's plot structure suggests that the destruction of the Sakurada family (the name means

---

[5] Mishima's ritual suicide occurred after the writing of the scenario of *The Ceremony*, although before the film was shot. Oshima's conception of the character of Tadashi was, therefore, somewhat prescient.

"Cherry Blossom," a traditional if platitudinous emblem for Japan), like that of the traditional society itself, will be accomplished from within by its own contumely, arrogance, and chauvinistic neo-fascism.

The most uncompromising critic among Japanese directors of his nation's structures,[6] Oshima remains obsessed by Japan and the Japanese, in himself and in those around him. The heightened emotion in his films comes not from any climactic dramatic developments in the action but from the director's continuous, silent lament over the default of a corrupt nation he yet loves. The tone of his films, particularly of *The Ceremony*, is as strikingly ambivalent as that of the American novelist William Faulkner toward the benighted denizens of Yoknapatawpha County, Mississippi.

Early in *The Ceremony*, Ritsuko remarks to Masuo, "We see each other only at weddings and funerals," introducing the central image of the film. The Japanese communicate with each other and feel that they are wholly themselves primarily at these highly formal ceremonial occasions at which behavior is highly prescribed and hierarchy rigorously maintained. The action flashes back to 1947. Masuo and his mother have evaded the Russians, who are repatriating Manchuria. But they are seized by Japanese whom Oshima will characterize as the worst enemies of the younger generation. These Japanese have been commissioned by the grandfather, after the death of Masuo's father, to return mother and son to the bosom of the Sakurada family; toward this end they take Masuo and his mother "prisoner."

Masuo, says Oshima, running an allegorical second story-line alongside that of his characters, represents all young Japanese forced after the War to submit to the institutions of the old Japan rapidly undergoing resurrection. Masuo, as a child, is already a participant in the first ceremony of the film, funeral rites for his dead father. The boy's hand is guided by his grandfather's in making the offering, a magnificent allegorical expression of the reconstituted old *zaibatsu*, or ruling class, appropriating the energies of all young Japanese almost at the moment the War ended. Momentarily we will learn that, having been de-purged, the grandfather has become once more the head of a big *zaibatsu*.

Like Hani, Oshima sees distorted sexuality as the inevitable consequence of political and social repression. The seductive aunt, Setsuko, insisting on washing the eleven-year-old Masuo, has herself been seduced and sullied by the grandfather. Oshima makes it clear that she never washes her own daughter, Ritsuko, so feelingly. Setsuko finds an unnatural outlet for her thwarted sexual energies among her young nephews, for her opportunities for relationships with eligible men are as negligible as those of women under feudalism. Angry and jealous, Ritsuko calls Masuo the "Manchurian brat."

---

[6] Oshima's politicization of film narrative has been justly admired by Western filmmakers. When asked which directors among his contemporaries he feels an affinity for, Bernardo Bertolucci immediately replied, "I feel close to the structures of Oshima" (Jonathan Cott, "A Conversation with Bernardo Bertolucci," *Rolling Stone*, June 21, 1973, p. 46).

All are deformed by the suffocating patriarchy. Masuo's cousin Tadashi feels intense shame at being the "son of a war criminal," and to compensate for this humiliation will become a neo-fascist. To the child Masuo, as yet pure, all his uncles look like war criminals, as indeed they are. His uncle Isamu is seemingly more liberated. But allegiance to the Communist Party, which has been the only alternative available to dissenting Japanese of his generation, has made him no better than a fool. He tries to coax Masuo into testifying to the kindness of the Russian soldiers he had encountered in Manchuria.

No one, least of all the supposed socialist Isamu, suggests that the Japan of the future should be different from that of the past. The young are particularly ineffectual. All that the most outspoken and intelligent, Terumichi, can do is, at a semi-surreal moment, to spray disinfectant on the whole assembled family in a wild, symbolic gesture that speaks directly for Oshima and the degree of regeneration he believes the Japanese are in need of.

Baseball games punctuate Masuo's youth, symbolic of the Westernization and so-called "democratization" of Japan. These baseball games, which allow him to escape from himself, like the fantasies of the boy in the earlier film, suggest an emotional detachment and inability to form meaningful relationships that already characterize Masuo's boyhood. He plays baseball on the first anniversary of his father's death. When his mother dies, he decides to give up baseball, which he was also playing at the moment of her death. Just as his mother had not been present when his father died, he is not present at her deathbed. The family has ceased to be a place where devotion of one person to another can flourish. Women, in any event, are of no consequence to this patriarchy. What is important, says the grandfather when Masuo's mother dies, is not where women are buried, but "the reform of a nation debased by defeat." By this he means the reconstitution of all the old institutions, from the family to the *zaibatsu*. The funeral of Masuo's mother must take second place to the greater consideration.

On the night of his mother's death, Masuo burns his baseball uniform and learns that his aunt Setsuko and his father were lovers. Taking advantage of the fact that Setsuko was both an illegitimate child and a relative, the daughter of his stepsister, the grandfather had seduced her himself, refusing to permit her to marry his son, Masuo's father, although the two had been in love. He had then arranged her marriage to a Chinese. In China, Setsuko still saw Masuo's father.

Asserting his power over them both, the grandfather interrupts Setsuko's confession to Masuo of her love for his father by grabbing and undressing her, as if to destroy the truth by brute force. At first, listening to the two, the grandfather, his motives selfish, secret, and his own, is shot from behind a veiled screen. Setsuko, his lifelong victim, appears unshielded, in full light. Oshima stresses the inbred quality of the Japanese. The frequency of incest among this homogeneous people is seen by the director as a violation of the spirit of the individual. The grandfather seems about to rape Setsuko. But once he asserts his power, he walks away, uninterested, his political, physical, and moral supremacy having been established.

Masuo, observing this entire scene, which has been enacted for his benefit by the grandfather to establish that Setsuko has been no more than a whore, a person of no value, does nothing to aid his aunt as she passively makes ready to succumb to his grandfather's advances. And by not intervening he commits his first act of moral default. In voice-over, recalling this event at a future moment when Setsuko is already dead, he tries to justify his unforgivable behavior: "Setsuko, I didn't have the courage to save you—or to save myself." Similarly, Masuo will be too weak to combat the old forces that have taken command in postwar Japan and against which he and all those of his generation would have had to wage unrelenting, undivided warfare should they have succeeded in forging a new and better society.

Masuo begs Setsuko to make love to him. Unable to find any other means of providing solace or peace for either of them, he would unite himself with her sexually, as his father and grandfather had done before him. Setsuko exists for this family as a sexual object to be abused and discarded. Before long, having ceased to be of use in this regard, she will be found murdered, thrust through with a sword, another symbol of the resurgence of the old feudal values. Yet, her mutilated humanity rendering her always a victim and never an exploiter, Setsuko is the most appealing member of the family and the only one ever to have shown Masuo any love.

More ceremonies follow the reconstitution of the *zaibatsu*. In 1956 uncle Isamu marries and fittingly, given his Communist Party sympathies, sings at his wedding a "song of labor." Its theme is how the Russians use their hands to satisfy their demands. The laughable triteness of this ditty, as well as its unmistakable, simplistic, socialist-realist propaganda, immediately inaugurates this sequence as the most humorous in the film. At this wedding Susumu, another uncle (Tadashi's father), who had been in a Chinese prison, sings "China Night." The war continues to haunt all those who had taken part in it. And the bride sings, of all things, the "Internationale." Each member of the family sings a song expressive of himself. Terumichi's exalts anarchy. Tadashi, choosing "Under the Red Sun of Manchuria," glorifies the 1931 annexation with the purpose of taunting with his fierce nationalism his father, Susumu, who had been impressed by Mao's China. Masuo, so passive that he never gets a chance to participate at all, would, he tells us in retrospect, have had to sing about banning the bomb. In him and in Terumichi, who at least were concerned about the Japan of the present, there might have been a hope for a regenerated society which has, however, failed to come into being.

The most grotesque of all the ceremonies in the film is Masuo's "wedding" in 1961. The bride in this arranged marriage, refusing to be a pawn in the hand of two families who would dispose her for their own ends, fails to appear at all, sending instead a hasty and obviously fraudulent excuse about "appendicitis." We never see her at all. Having felt nothing at all for this woman, Masuo is relieved. But his grandfather, in a surreal departure from realism, insists that the wedding ceremony go forward without the bride. Important guests have been invited; the forms must be maintained regardless of the reality. Tadashi attends the wedding in a police uniform, now considering himself "on duty twenty-four hours a day" and refusing to obey his grandfather's order to change clothes. Japan, rapidly undergoing remilitarization, says Oshima on the level of his allegory, cannot help but reveal its tendencies toward neofascism even at its ceremonial occasions.

In a wedding speech, the absent bride is praised for being a pure Japanese girl "free of the taint of foreign postwar influences." In a brilliant insight Oshima recognizes that a real bride is not needed at all; the idea of one will suffice. What is real is what those in power, symbolized by the grandfather, decide is real, as they are shown to control every facet of the lives of their Japanese subjects. The master of ceremonies announces that the bride and groom will cut the cake, no matter that everyone will observe Masuo doing it alone. The bride's empty chair is held, as word comes that she will now retire to change. Neither Masuo's humiliation nor his sexual frustration are of concern to his elders, who desire only that he conform to whatever travesties they deem necessary.

At this wedding, refusing to recognize any impropriety and taking advantage of the chaos of the situation, Tadashi insists on standing up and reading his *New Manifesto for the Reconstruction of Japan*. Its title is not accidentally a parody of Ikki Kita's 1919 *An Outline Plan for the Reorganization of Japan*, which inspired and nourished the intense militarism culminating in the Second World War. Tadashi wishes to subsume the "political and financial vipers" under a resurgent military. He is ushered out of the reception room only because the moment is not propitious, not because his elders will ultimately be in basic disagreement with his ideas nor because the "political and financial vipers" of which his grandfather is, of course, one, would not serve a new military as they did the old.

On this same night Tadashi is hit by a car and killed, and there is the suggestion that he has been assassinated, another indication that his ideas are being taken very seriously indeed. Only his Communist Party member uncle, Isamu, refuses to admit that Tadashi's views had gained any credence among the Japanese, as Oshima satirizes the organized left's continuing blindness and ineffectuality before the resurgence of fascism. "Tadashi's ideology was stupid, so he died, of course," says Isamu, placing ideology always ahead of feeling, and revealing not the slightest sorrow at the death of his nephew.

At home after the wedding, Masuo, the abandoned man of Manchuria, an innocent now symbolically paying the price for its annexation by Japan, breaks down and cries. He grabs a pillow and pretends to make love to it, as if it were a bride, coaxing it, as a virgin, to relax. Despite his hysteria, an outbreak of madness caused by the grandfather's having put him through the cruel wedding ceremony, no doctor is called because people might hear about it, face be lost. A bizarre humor pervades *The Ceremony*.

With impeccable logic, Masuo now grabs his grandfather himself and mounts him, calling him, in bitter irony, a "pure Japanese girl." It is as if the grandfather were responsible for Masuo's loss of a normal life, as indeed he is. Oshima juxtaposes Ritsuko's sudden reading of Tadashi's manifesto calling for capital punishment of all government ministers with Masuo's mad mounting of the grandfather who was himself once a minister, as if the two events were intimately connected. The neo-fascist document asserts the grandfather's guilt, for which he deserves Masuo's attack.

Having been emasculated by the architects of the new Japan, Masuo's next action is also fitting. He removes Tadashi's white-bandaged body from its box and enters the coffin himself, pulling Ritsuko, possibly his half-sister, in with him. In his semi-conscious state between life and death, he would at last make love to her, Masuo is already a dead man. All his grandfather can do now is sit alone in the half-dark, sobbing and banging his fist on the floor in rage. The family is rapidly disintegrating, and it is becoming clear that—with Tadashi dead and Masuo, Ritsuko, and Terumichi all unmarried and childless—the Sakurada family will cease to exist upon the death of the old patriarch.

After this melodramatic orgy of recrimination and self-hatred, the remainder of the action becomes anticlimactic. The grandfather dies. Masuo, curling up in a fetal position at the funeral, is clearly incapable of assuming the family leadership, although his uncles beg him to assume these responsibilities. "The earth is falling on me," Masuo says, "I'm being buried. I am buried." Finally, Ritsuko, more out of pity than desire, makes love to him, but incest is, for Oshima, always a dead end and a symbol of decay, not renewal. Terumichi has disappeared to his island. Soon he will send the telegram that opens the film.

When Ritsuko and Masuo arrive on the island, blood is splashed everywhere, a legacy, even in Oshima, of the *chambara*. Terumichi has written: "I am the only one capable of continuing the Sakurada family. By killing myself, I destroy the Sakurada family." This is true, although Oshima finds Terumichi's suicide a futile, individualistic gesture, an escape from the need to struggle against the kind of oppression represented by his grandfather. Masuo is guilty of even greater moral impotence. Just as he had once failed to prevent his grandfather from almost raping his aunt Setsuko, he now fails to prevent her daughter's suicide. Ritsuko decides to end her life beside the dead Terumichi. She binds her legs in traditional fashion, observing, ironically, one last cere-mony from samurai days. She then takes poison which she has brought along for this purpose.

Masuo now descends into complete psychosis. He pretends to be pitch-ing a ball as if he were once again, as in his childhood, escaping from reality by playing baseball. Setsuko is the umpire, as she once was. Ritsuko

The Ceremony: The past, engulfing the Japan that should have been theirs to rebuild, has sapped the energy of the young.

is at bat. Tadashi retrieves balls in the outfield. All these people, come to life through Oshima's camera, are now dead, resurrected only in Masuo's imagination. At the very end Masuo puts his ear to the ground, listening for the cries of his baby brother, immersing himself totally in the memory of the baby who had been buried alive in Manchuria. He has ceased totally to live in the present.

According to Oshima's allegory, Masuo, Terumichi, and Ritsuko have been buried alive in the new Japan. Immediately after the War, their elders lost no time in regaining power and in preserving the old values intact. Beside so strong a comeback of feudal norms, the young lacked the will—and the health—to offer an alternative vision. The past, engulfing the Japan that should have been theirs to rebuild, has sapped the energy of the young. Lacking the moral strength, self-confidence, and unshakable convictions of their oppressors, they have proved themselves powerless to thwart the resurgence of a neo-feudal society out of the ashes of the War. Before the character for "The End" appears, Oshima allows the screen to go black, offering no image. Any hope for a different, freer Japan has been lost. Moral defeat, like a dark cloud, has finally consumed those who saw the need for change. *The Ceremony*, like Imamura's *History of Postwar Japan,* chronicles the moral consequences of a neo-feudal epoch of prosperity following the early postwar period. And it is finally only Oshima who has placed the story of the Japanese family in its appropriate historical context.

Others of Oshima's young people, contemporaries of Masuo, are equally doomed, equally victims. Some became active in the Zengakuren, later the Zenkyoto, and still later the Zengakuto, the group associated with the attack on Lod airport in Tel-Aviv. Bewildered, Oshima's students stand by, as Masuo stood by in the presence of his grandfather's violence, as the movement they have tried to build falls to pieces. First devoted to such issues as thwarting the renewal of the security treaty between Japan and the United States, and later encompassing other diverse and equally important issues, such as the terms of the reversion of Okinawa to Japan, the movement eventually splintered into sects finally devoted more to abusing each other than to opposing social injustice. In Japan, as in Europe and the United States, the New Left also created a counter-culture. It was centered in Shinjuku, a student quarter of Tokyo. Yet even where they seemed capable of creating alternate life styles, Oshima found the young unable to surmount the problems inflicted upon them by the family and the authoritarian society at large.

In *Diary of a Shinjuku Burglar* (*Shinjuku Dorobo Nikki*, 1968) Oshima depicts the spirit of political and sexual liberation attained by the student movement in 1968. At the end of the film a demonstration of hippies, street people, students, and ordinary residents flares up on the streets of Shinjuku, a testament to the widespread discontent and boundless energy of Japan's young people seeking an outlet for impulses toward freedom denied within the normal channels of social life. It was especially important to Oshima that he portray a demonstration not arranged by one of the organized political parties of the left, such as the Socialists or Communists. For Oshima, these groups, stagnant and reformist, their spirit later to be symbolized by the slogans and empty rhetoric of Uncle Isamu in *The Ceremony*, have only set back Japan's desperately needed transvaluation of values. The spontaneity of the student rebellions of the 1960s and the revolutionary energy they express are seen by Oshima as providing at least a glimpse of a radical constituency hopefully, if perhaps only at some point in the future, no longer to be deceived by what came to be known, in Japan as in the United States, as the "Old Left."

Accompanying this political renewal was a determined drive among Japan's youth to be permitted a freer expression of their sexuality; the New Left, as represented in *Diary of a Shinjuku Burglar*, seeks freedom from traditionally imposed definitions of what it means to be a man or a woman. Oshima has in fact said that "a male figure being a female figure was the most significant aspect or spirit of that time, the era of the demonstrations from 1968 to 1969."[7] The liberation of the male from traditional Japanese ideas about masculinity thus becomes analogous to the political protest. The movement recognizes, at least implicitly, that once Japanese society begins to be immersed in political upheaval with its end a more democratic society, the Japanese could also begin to

[7] Joan Mellen, "Interview with Nagisa Oshima," *Voices from the Japanese Cinema*, p. 270.

free themselves psychologically from rigid, traditional, and repressive attitudes toward sexuality.

The two young people at the center of *Diary of a Shinjuku Burglar* cannot physically consummate their relationship, a failure similar to that which Hani depicts in *The Inferno of First Love*. The boy, whose name is Birdey Hilltop, is impotent. Oshima has explained this failure, which, like that of Hani's character, Shun, is never resolved in the film, in terms of needs which Japanese society's definition of "male" and "female" has rendered immune to fulfillment:

> . . . the boy needed maternal characteristics in the girl. But Japan as a country cannot have the characteristic of being a mother. No Japanese girl could have such a motherly quality, and so Japanese men are constantly dissatisfied at not being able to get what they are looking for, which means also the girls aren't satisfied.[8]

At the end of the film, in a tent in Shinjuku, Birdey Hilltop and his girlfriend, Umeko, become involved in a street theater production which reproduces Japanese Kabuki as it was at the moment of its origins. Birdey and a real-life street theater performer, Kara Juro of the Situation Players, enact the role of a figure in Japanese history named Yui Shosetsu, who attempted a coup d'état during the feudal period. In having Birdey act this part, "stealing" it from Kara Juro to whom it belonged, and in becoming absorbed in the enactment, Oshima attempts, rather unsuccessfully and obliquely, to suggest that Birdey Hilltop can forget himself and his problems. Allegorically, the film makes much more sense. Oshima claims that in any act of rebellion, in Yui Shosetsu's or in that of the student revolt occurring in Shinjuku at the same moment as the theatrical presentation, the frustrated hero can find some measure of emotional release. By inference Oshima suggests that in revolutionary struggle may be discovered a respite from repression. By acting out long-buried impulses, we may be able to transcend inhibitions that have proven immune to more conventional modes of psychological therapy.

The last scene, recorded with a hand-held camera, depicts the huge street demonstration. Policemen proliferate. Screams resound, windows are broken. And a red blob on the wall of Shinjuku Station is called "the Cherry Blossom of Japan's lost virginity." One demonstration does not a revolution make. But, for Oshima in this film, if the student revolts accomplish only for a moment a demystification of Japan's "cherry blossom" identity, they have achieved something positive. Birdey and Umeko are not yet sexually free, just as Japan has not yet been liberated from her past. In how the two are inextricably connected lies the logic of *Diary of a Shinjuku Burglar*. But the film remains a minor work because the allegory is so much more interesting than its surface action.

Oshima also portrays the lost youths of the student movement in *The Man Who Left His Will on Film*. Self-referential in style, its circular plot at once suggesting inhibition that can find no release,

---

[8] "Nagisa Oshima Interviewed by Ian Cameron," p. 13.

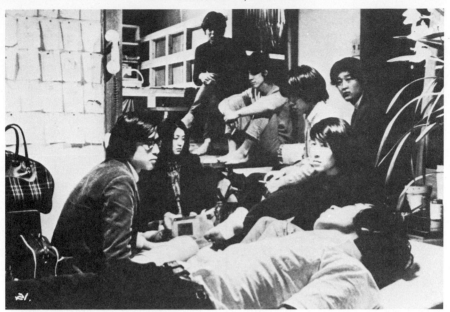

The Man Who Left His Will on Film: The boy's death comes to parallel the demise of the student movement itself, which, having failed to achieve any of its demands, has turned Japan's youth once again back upon themselves.

the "story" is that of a student filmmaker who films his own suicide and then kills himself at the end of the film by jumping from a building. Oshima's only apparent "contribution" lies in the shot of the boy's actual death. Throughout the film the illusion is maintained that the hero of the film has shot it all, including his suicide, and that Oshima's work is therefore a film produced by this boy as a last will and testament which explains his suicide. The effect is as if Oshima were offering us so authentic a work that it was actually entrusted to him by his own central character.

Any causal explanations for the death, however, as in Godard, must be provided through active participation by the audience itself in piecing together the boy's footage, which is randomly projected. Oshima leaves the chronology of events in as subtly elaborate a disarray as Alain Resnais did his in *Last Year at Marienbad*. He demands of his Japanese audience that it confront what has befallen the restless youths of the New Left, who have moved without purpose or direction through the new Japan despite the fury of their political protests. The boy's death comes to parallel the demise of the student movement itself, which, having failed to achieve any of its demands, has turned Japan's young people once again back upon themselves with no outlet for their discontent.

At the end of *The Man Who Left His Will on Film* a hand grabs the camera from the dead boy. Another man is about to assume the task of filming the meaning of his life. Just as the demonstrations at the end of *Diary of a Shinjuku Burglar* did not mean that the revolution was at hand, this film equally suggests the need for a permanent, ongoing struggle in which the first step must be attainment of greater self-knowledge on the part of these students. The man who picks up the camera and would take the hero's place may not end his life in an ineffectual suicide. His quest for truth may not fill him with the hopelessness experienced by Motoki, Oshima's hero. The camera's new owner may in fact see the revolution through to a further stage.

Oshima leaves us with a cacophony of images, debates, dreams, and fantasies. They reveal the trauma of the young in Japan, desperately opposed to the policies of an authoritarian state, yet incapable of creating a meaningful political opposition with which ordinary Japanese could identify. For such a bewildered generation, who have turned to tormenting each other, suicide becomes a ready option. Even the landscape of the revolution now seems uncertain, whether it will occur on the quiet middle-class streets photographed by Motoki, or amid violent demonstrations, as his radical friends would have us believe. Chronology has been so reversed as to make it impossible for us to reconstruct the action in a linear manner because any single solution to Japan's problems does not seem ready to hand. Like the deserted highway on which Motoki's girlfriend is raped and beaten, Japan has become a no-man's land. Everyone has been cast forth in isolation and without solace, with even the would-be revolutionaries sufficiently diverted to believe that their enemies are each other rather than the all-powerful State.

The Family Anatomized:
Imamura's *The Pornographer*

If you think of life as an unending series of cycles, it is less threatening.
Shohei Imamura[1]

An incomparably more witty and perceptive appreciation of the "perverse" and a brilliant satire on the history of the psyche in Japan emerge in Shohei Imamura's *The Pornographer*. The hero, Ogata, makes pornographic movies for a living, catering to the voyeuristic urges of men with waning sexual capacities. The goings-on in the real environment of Ogata's life, however, turn out to be far more bizarre than anything recorded in his pathetic, essentially innocent, soft-core pornographic films. *The Pornographer* is also given two framing scenes by Imamura, at the beginning and at the end. These involve a screening of the very film we are looking at, an event at which Imamura himself is besieged with questions about the meaning of the film. This distancing effect, paradoxically, serves only to heighten the reality of Ogata's strange travail.

Ogata has lived for many years with a widow named Haru and her teen-aged children, a son, Koichi, and a daughter, Keiko. The behavior of this "family" at home serves Imamura as a means of exposing the absurd myths that have been embedded in the psyches of ordinary Japanese. Ridiculously, according to Imamura, Haru has refused to marry Ogata because her husband, before he died, ordered her to remain a widow, a universal injunction visited upon the Japanese woman throughout the past and continuing into the present. Haru is convinced, in this hilarious comedy, that the huge fish she keeps in a tank, ugly and seemingly sentient, contains the spirit of her husband, since she bought it on the day he died. Imamura shoots Haru and Ogata through the fish tank, as if from the point of view of the jealous fish-husband, watching their every move. He is satirizing the entire notion of ancestor worship, as well as the unnecessary waste and pain resulting from the injunction that widows not remarry.

Within this family, Oedipal relationships flourish. The son, Koichi, fondles and caresses his mother, with Imamura cutting to an extreme close-up of the ever-jealous fish, its mouth opening and closing in disapproval. Ogata has lusted incestuously after Keiko since she was a child,

[1] Conversations with the author in Tokyo, October, 1974.

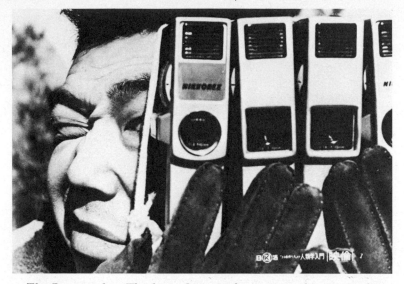

The Pornographer: The hero, Ogata, makes pornographic movies for a living, catering to the voyeuristic urges of men with waning sexual capacities.

and in the course of the film, after several funny abortive attempts, he finally robs her of her virginity. Especially exciting to him is a long scar on her leg, a consequence of a childhood accident when, having exclaimed, "I don't like you," she ran away from Ogata and was hit by a truck.

About to seduce her, Ogata first caresses Keiko's scar, a preference Imamura refuses to view as perverse, treating it as merely funny. Just as Ogata is about to rape Keiko, Imamura cuts to a flashback of Ogata at the scene of the accident, rushing to pick up Keiko in obvious concern. Love is intermingled with lust in all of us, good motives with selfish ones. Although his middle-aged aficionados of pornography are voyeurs, Imamura is not. Human sexuality, Imamura finds, is infinitely complex. Value judgments by the director would be absurd in the face of man's rich nature. *The Pornographer*, despite its ostensible preoccupation with incest, voyeurism, virginity, and lust, offers one of the most liberated views toward the question of sex in Japanese cinema.

Other psychological configurations typical of the Japanese also succumb to Imamura's biting satire. The chauvinism of the Japanese is ridiculed during a screening of a pornographic film which features as one of the actors "a real American." "The penis looks just alike!" someone calls out in wonder. The pretensions of the American Occupation and the utterly superficial degree to which its edicts were implanted in the consciousness of the Japanese are equally ridiculed. In a conversation about the desirability of a man's making love to his own daughter, someone interjects a complaint about the "intrusion of democracy," with the implication that, guilty as it was of so many violations of Japanese mores, the Occupation must also have been responsible for the taboo against incest, which, according to this reasoning, presumably flourished unchecked in Japan until after the Second World War.

"Democracy" is experienced by these Japanese as "restraint." Their contact with the Occupation has taught them that "democracy" no longer bears the slightest resemblance to its original meaning, that it has no connection whatsoever with "freedom," a sense hardly likely to have been conveyed by the conquering American army. The incest taboo is treated by Imamura's characters, accustomed to a more wholesome and freer approach to sexuality, as an inconvenience and a source of annoyance. Continuing the association between incest, the American Occupation, and freedom, when Ogata discovers the teen-aged Keiko reading an erotic book, he tells her to read chemistry, the autobiography of Albert Schweitzer, or—in a hilarious juxtaposition—a book about democracy! At this point, clearly as a bribe for his silence, Keiko offers Ogata a kiss.

All the characters in *The Pornographer*, like Tome in *The Insect Woman*, live by their instincts. Their morality is that of expediency. Haru agrees one night to sleep with Ogata as a bribe, so that he will finance a separate apartment for Koichi. Daughter learns from mother, the psychological cycle unbroken. But the people have learned to buy and sell their feelings from a more corrupt society. Keiko's private high school insists that Ogata donate 100,000 yen before she will be admitted. Like one of the voyeurs, the camera in so many of the shots in this film is stationed outside the window, peering in on the goings-on between the characters, but without comment or moral judgment.

Priests in this film tell people that evil is inside them, but Imamura does not believe it. The meaning of life, if such a thing exists, eludes us and it is best, therefore, that we live out our impulses unhindered by absurd restraints. In this way Imamura addresses himself to the puritanical repressiveness of Japanese society. Whatever our tastes, he urges that we fulfill them. For Imamura the world has become so insane that no one has the right prudishly to condemn the actions of another.

Psychological equilibrium can, in fact, be achieved only if we act out how we feel, ignoring mystifying restraints such as those ordering widows not to remarry, or people not to commit incest. After the death of Haru, her daughter, Keiko, takes up with a wild *yakuza*, only later to assume a conventional life style as the proprietress of her mother's beauty salon. Unburdened by rigid moral codes, she lives at each moment according to her desires; the balance of her life is maintained naturally, without censorious, repressive injunctions from a hypocritically puritanical society whose people have felt so sexually confined that they cannot help but become exactly what the society seems most to fear: absorbed by sex, a preoccupation symbolized by Ogata's flourishing trade in pornographic films. The instinctual is, for Imamura, always a welcome change from what has come to be known as "civilized." This is the major theme of all his films and it allows him a radical approach to human psychology.

When Haru falls ill, Imamura offers another extreme close-up of the ubiquitous fish, confirming the woman's own analysis that the evil spirit of the fish has caused her illness out of a desire for revenge over her sexual infidelity. If she believes this is true, then it is. The fish accompanies Haru to the hospital. The censoring eye of her dead husband will not allow her to live in peace but, by taking the fish with her, Haru is shown to have acquiesced in her own torment by her malicious husband, who clearly does not deserve her lifelong fidelity to his memory. Haru's acceptance of her dead husband's right to censor her behavior is a repressive force deeply rooted in her being. It causes her death.

No strict Freudian, Imamura in the typical Japanese manner sees the personality as immutable. Long-implanted feelings, like Haru's belief that her husband is watching her, remain with us up to the last moment. Haru finally goes mad, destroyed by the puritanical censorship of a society which places so many obstacles in the way of fulfilling basic needs. From her hospital bed she now sings obscene songs. As she is embraced by either Ogata or her son Koichi—we can't quite distinguish which man it is—the fish executes a deep dive, with the camera appearing to be right there with it in the tank.

As he mourns the dead Haru, Ogata's mind turns in flashback to when, as a child of four or five, he himself was sensually fondled by his mother. The two women, Haru and his mother, coalesce in his mind, Imamura's means of indicting the Japanese mother for so lavishing her frustrated affections on her sons as to bind them to the need for a mother for the rest of their lives. The scene recalls Oshima's remark that Japanese men bear an ungratifiable need for the maternal in women.

Ogata concludes that man, as long as he lives, will always be the same, a view echoing Imamura's own. He finally throws the husband-fish into the canal, for it was nothing but a fish all along. Toward the end of *The Pornographer* a wild orgy of eroticism, expressing the raging images within Ogata's mind, is presided over by Ogata as a guest at his own nightmare. He declaims: "Your life flourishes until you lose your eroticism," indicating his growing fear that his own powers have begun to fail. A naked leg suddenly appears, with a long scar identifying the body as Keiko's, still the object of his desire. And in this dream sequence Ogata makes love at last to his mother.

It is at this supposedly climactic moment that the orgy begins to lose all interest. The human mind is a source of endless amusement for Imamura, who constantly cautions us not to take ourselves too seriously. The Oedipal desire turns out to have been far more exciting than its actual fulfillment. Even possessing the body of his mother is disappointing to Ogata once it occurs, which is why, Imamura tells us, it is best that we not be overly concerned with the "danger" and the "sin" of incestuous impulses. Oedipal passions are safe because, like all the rest of our lusts, they are incapable of satisfying us.

"I don't understand the relations between man and woman," muses an Ogata restored to "reality." A friend casually remarks that a machine is better than a woman since it's honest, obedient, and not greedy. At once the scene is set for Imamura's surreal ending. Mother, wife, and daughter have failed to gratify Ogata sexually. He moves onto a houseboat and declares his "male liberation" by constructing an artificial wife, a life-sized doll who will never resist him and through whom he can declare his freedom from women.

Five years pass. The architect of such a doll must know the physiology of women and Ogata studies in order to create a perfect facsimile. From Keiko's beauty parlor he obtains real human hair to implant in his new "wife." He fondles the doll as if it were a real woman. We are victims of mechanical impulses anyway, says Imamura. Ogata in his madness is only personifying what, in the depth of our psyches, we have all been reduced to.

One day the rope holding Ogata's houseboat breaks away from its moorings and he is set afloat down the canal. Too busy conversing with the doll he has named Haru, he doesn't notice this change in his condition. Down the river he floats, and out to sea. For scale, the little houseboat is photographed beside a giant luxury liner, an image as awesome as that in Fellini's *Amarcord*. A zoom back shows us the boat on a television-sized screen. The sound of a projector running indicates that we are once more at Imamura's screening. Voices break in, demanding of Imamura whether he means by this ending that Ogata is going to die.

It couldn't matter less. The "story" is at an end because the feelings of "anthropos," man, have now totally been anatomized. Ogata has gone the way of us all, from Oedipal childhood through insatiable middle years to the bewilderment of old age. His rudderless houseboat reflects the unguided, directionless course we all pursue through the channels of sexuality. In Imamura's depiction, it is a vital, frightening, and very funny voyage.

PART

6

ALTERNATIVES

The Civilized and
the "Primitive"

> At the gate he stopped me, asking: "Where are you riding to, master?"
> "I don't know," I said, "only away from here, away from here. Always
> away from here, only by doing so can I reach my destination." "And so
> you know your destination?" he asked. "Yes," I answered, "didn't I say
> so? Away-From-Here, that is my destination."
> Franz Kafka, "My Destination"

That Japan is a culture which feels itself doomed is nowhere better
expressed than in the enormous financial success in 1974 of a disaster epic
called *The Submersion of Japan*.[1] The shifting of the earth's crust induces
a series of earthquakes and tidal waves which cause the sinking into the
sea of the entire Japanese archipelago. Tokyo burns, and high-rise buildings fall, as a mob fights its way onto the grounds of the Imperial Palace
in the revealing belief that safety is to be found there. Fuji erupts, and one
doomsday after another results finally in the entire disappearance of Japan.

Potboiler though it is, *The Submersion of Japan* baldly expresses the
sense of crisis and panic in Japanese culture. In the audience it awakens
an already strongly entrenched sense of helplessness nurtured by authoritarian centuries and confirmed by an economy with a thirty percent rate of
inflation compounding a history of actual earthquakes and natural cata-
clysms. An emotion forever latent in the Japanese, and aroused by this film,
is that all lies outside the control of the individual. The very need of the
culture to create the desire for security reflected in a lifetime employment
system betrays the sense of precariousness and impending disaster which
so many feel, as if their own disallowed desire for confidence born of a real
mastery of social events is a potential detonating force.

Recognizing the prevalence of these impulses, *The Submersion of Japan*
attempts but fails to reassure a disturbed audience. It sanctifies an old
prince, a member of the Imperial family who is firmly and indubitably the
benevolent paternalist. Its forty-five-year-old Prime Minister (Tetsuro
Tamba) is presented as concerned only with "the people"; it is he who
opens the gates of the Imperial Palace to the masses during the first of the
film's disasters. *The Submersion of Japan* bespeaks Japan's ruling group's
fear of popular upheaval, epitomized in the storming of the Imperial

---

[1] Released in the United States as *Tidal Wave*.

Palace with its evocation of Eisenstein's Winter Palace sequence in *October*.

The film thereby obliquely avows that Japan is desperately in need of drastic change. Indeed, the devastation of the established society serves as an unconscious metaphor of the widespread awareness that the current stability of Japan is based upon repression of deep and powerful impulses for self-expression which must, as a consequence, be all the more explosive and overwhelming upon their release. The very fetish with security is a psychological clue. People who suppress either spontaneous feeling or autonomy over decisions and events are guarding against their own, long-denied needs. It is they, the Japanese people, and their centuries-old, internalized renunciation of challenge to an oppressive social order, who are the potential source of upheaval and not any shifting in the earth's crust. The subterranean shifting in this film is but a metaphor for the tumult that will erupt once Japan's people are released to full expression.

Revealingly, this formula film can find no alternative but a scientist-cum-samurai who chooses to go down with Japan rather than save himself. The Prince makes the same despairing decision, evoking not only Mishima but the death syndrome at work in the defenders of a decaying order. The entire film, made by the Toho Company and thus offering an official and established view, nonetheless reveals the utter moral barrenness of Japan today. It betrays an Armageddon mentality on the part of Japan's rulers. Should upheaval occur, they would rather sink the archipelago and go down with it than accept or anticipate new values and a different social order. Yet, as always, the attempt to reject something reveals both its force and its presence. We can see that, without new values, Japan is lost. Nothing less than the spiritual survival of the nation is at stake.

Neo-feudalism at the heart of the "new" urban, industrialized Japan has led some directors to reject the entire notion of "civilization," as if the Japanese people had been betrayed by the process of history which has led only to pollution and injustice. At the same time they have felt that the industrial progress of Japan has alienated her people from their original and authentic culture, to which it may yet be possible to return. Director Koichi Saito, who considers himself a disciple of Shohei Imamura, has said that he moved the action of his films *Journey into Solitude* (*Tabi no Omosa*, 1972) and *Tsugaru Folksong* (*Tsugaru Jongara Bushi*, 1973) to the countryside, "because there is a real Japan still intact in rural areas like Tsugaru and Shikoku . . . people there still have the true Japanese feeling and I see them as 'Japan.' "[2] There is a shared feeling among such directors that there are two Japans, one authentic and one inauthentic. The "true" Japan remains close to its origins, to oneness with nature and to the instincts as opposed to the intellect. In urban areas, however, openness has been replaced by hypocrisy.

Many set the date of the loss in the culture of what was truly Japanese at the moment of the ascension to power of the samurai class in the

[2] Conversation with the author, New York, May 1974.

twelfth century; others choose the victory of the particularly harsh and repressive Tokugawa clan in the 1800s. Nyozekan Hasegawa is adamant in his insistence that the culture of ancient times, if rediscovered, would lead to an understanding of long-buried, highly positive attributes of the Japanese character: "The Japanese of ancient times showed an extremely internally-minded, tolerant disposition in their development . . . yet in the Tokugawa period . . . they were given a completely opposite, exclusionist character. In ancient times one aspect of the national character was active, in Tokugawa times another, completely different aspect."[3]

There is not only nostalgia behind this quest for morality from among the ancients, but genuine urgency. It has been a search laden with conviction and it has attracted, in its various manifestations, thinkers from both the political right and the political left, Mishima as well as Imamura. Returning to the past, for a director like Imamura, has meant a return to a pre-feudal Japan, while to people like Mishima it has meant a rediscovery of feudal elements inherent in the origins of life in Japan but coming to the fore in their full majesty only with the ascent of the samurai.

Certainly the rhythms of pre-industrial Japan are idealized in Mishima's novel *The Sound of Waves*, filmed as *Shiosai* in 1954 by Senkichi Taniguchi. The scene is a small island named Kami-Shima where all the people earn their living as fishermen. *Kami* means "gods" and *Shima* means "island." It is suggested that only the simple residents of Kami-Shima are capable of living in harmony with the spirits ruling over Japan. The body of the young hero, Shinji, who might be a cousin of the garden boy, Saburo, in that other Mishima adaptation, *A Thirst for Love*, is idealized by Taniguchi's camera. Inspired by Mishima, he does for his simple, pure, wholly physical hero what Leni Riefenstahl did for her Aryan athletes in *Olympia*. A fascist-inspired camera attempts to convince us that those who do not think, who live within nature and who respond to life in purely physical terms, bask in the favor of the gods. The rhythm of the men's bodily movements is sanctified in this film and much time is spent in observing them at their physical labors.

Not all the returns to primitive island life in the postwar Japanese film signify a return to feudal values, however deeply they share a rejection of the moral anarchy of "civilized" life. In *The Island* Kaneto Shindo, unlike Mishima and Taniguchi, does not idealize the lives of Japan's impoverished island people living below subsistence level in the third wealthiest country in the world. In a bitter irony, the family of his film lives on a tiny island surrounded by the sea and yet is totally without the water necessary to sustain life, just as this family's poverty exists within a sea of Japanese prosperity.

Twice each day, morning and evening, husband and wife row to a nearby island for the day's supply of water. Over and over we watch as they trudge up the hill of their island to the house perched on top. The man and woman neither look at each other nor utter a word throughout the film.

[3] *The Japanese Character: A Cultural Profile* (Tokyo: Kodansha International, 1965), p. 7.

The Sound of Waves: A fascist-inspired camera attempts to convince us that those who do not think, who live within nature and who respond to life in purely physical terms, shine in the favor of the gods.

Nothing they could say would alter their condition. Even music is frequently omitted from their trudging up the cliff with their buckets, as if any sound might disturb them and cause some of the precious water to spill. Some of this water is thrown onto the parched ground to nourish a few pathetic plants. Shots of the couple and their two sons eating are intercut with those of animals, as if their lives were no better, if not worse, than those of the beasts.

When the woman accidentally spills a pail of water, the man strikes her across the face so hard that she falls down. Survival is at every moment an issue in an area where technology has yet to ameliorate the harshest of living conditions. In Japan's achievement of a material culture filled with gadgets and thirty million television sets servicing ninety-nine percent of the population,[4] Shindo finds that not all Japanese by any means are sharing in the new-found wealth.

One of the two children dies in the course of the film, the doctor having arrived on the remote island too late. The day after the burial, the couple are again carrying water. Life must go on. But, for the woman, it is too much. Angrily she dumps a pail of water on the ground and tramples on all the plants, throwing herself down and clawing the sand. Yet hers

[4] For an amusing look at this phenomenon see Susumu Hani's fine television documentary *TV TV Nippon* (1973).

can only be a rebellion that bears no fruit. She soon lifts herself up and begins watering the fragile plants, as she will continue to bow beneath the weight of the buckets of water. Shindo's last helicopter shot pictures the rocky island in the midst of the sea as small and insignificant, barely, worthy of notice, or so the authorities deem, inhabited as it is by people on the periphery of the prosperous, "civilized" Japan.

And yet Shindo is also exalting the primitive in locating so much strength and endurance among these island people. This is how the Japanese once were, he implies; impoverished but living with an integrity and closeness to nature denied to those of the "mainland," who are educated and well-fed but weak and lacking in energy, both physical and spiritual. The children of these island people are self-sufficient, feeding the animals and themselves, preparing breakfast for their parents returning with the morning's supply of water, or diving into the sea for fish. They are unburdened by self-consciousness, vanity, or self-importance. The woman truly enjoys the simple luxury of her bath, taken last, after husband and sons, at the end of the day. There is also a festival scene in which the people of the area dance in harmony with nature and the seasons.

Shindo is thus constantly pointing to the heroism of his islanders who have so much in common with the original Japanese. By implication, he rejects the style of existence, burdened by nihilism and anxiety, of the rootless city dweller. The ritualized lives of his four characters are contrasted with the seedy life style they observe on their one visit to the "mainland" (another, larger island), where they try to sell a fish the boy has caught. Unimpressed, unmoved, and impassive, they watch a dancer on television. Television—all the seeming pleasures the mainland can provide —has little to offer them.

Shindo uses choral music at the end as the woman once more assumes her burden; it grows louder as the plants are watered and is meant to grant transcendence to the lives of these people. Shindo never suggests that their lives embody an ideal to which it is possible, or even desirable, for all Japanese to return. But he sees grandeur even in what seems to be the futility of their struggle for existence. And while for once avoiding sentimentality, if not some degree of romanticism, he does direct us through this primitive island setting to vital, precious qualities once part of the Japanese character and now lost.

As a positive alternative to the world from which his character, Oshima, in *A Man Vanishes* (*Ningen Johatsu*, 1967) flees, Imamura proposes in *Kuragejima: Tales from a Southern Island* a rural, primitive style of life. The island of Kurage still retains its oral traditions, including the myth of its creation by a brother god and a sister goddess. Incest at once defines the original experience of the homogeneous Japanese. In the course of Imamura's film, engineers and modernizers descend upon the island, disturbing its traditions and littering its landscape with the debris of civilization, which includes jet planes, taxis, and billboards advertising Coca-Cola. The wild, retarded girl, Toriko, who represented the spirit of the island, is now dead. The engineer who once loved her returns to Kurage because he can no longer bear modernized Japan. But the island itself, its identity in constant danger of extinction, can now offer only a temporary and flawed refuge.

Kuragejima is full of legends, myths, and folklore, with Imamura here, more than in any of his films, functioning as a cultural anthropologist whose subject is the Japanese. In the first shot a pink-fleshed pig falls overboard from a boat. A shark swims into view and the pig goes under—shades of *Jaws*. Kurage Island is still a place where the laws of nature, for Imamura infinitely superior to those of man, continue to reign.

The family at the center of the film, the Futoris, retain the ancient customs of their forefathers. Where the Futoris fail to observe the rituals that governed behavior on the island in the past, the culture falls into jeopardy. The island is already on the verge of modernization, and Imamura in part accounts for the island's cultural decimation in terms of its being a punishment for the greed of the Futoris. One of them, named Nekichi, has begun to kill fish with dynamite, rather than using the old methods. In this way he earns the wrath of all those on the island who would continue to live in symbiosis with nature, taking only what they need. With Oshima, Imamura suggests that the corruption of the Japanese, no longer issuing solely from without, from an unjust society, has now become internalized. It is not only the engineers sent by Japanese *zaibatsu* who are destroying Kurage Island but her own people, who have become alienated from their traditions. The islanders will, of course, be overcome by the superior force of technology, but they are also shown by Imamura as cooperating in the demise of a culture they have not sufficiently cherished.

The beginning of the end comes with the arrival of technicians to establish a sugar factory on Kurage Island. One of the Futoris is selected as the engineer's assistant. The islanders instruct him to subvert the project by teaching the engineer to respect the way of life of the original inhabitants. The plan is for the engineer first to be seduced by one of the women. But the problem is that the islanders have lost their power to protect their own way of life. Long years of abuse of the population by destructive customs have contributed to replacing its traditions with the Coca-Cola culture of the ending. There is a ravine where, to control the population, pregnant women were made to jump into the rocky sea. Those who were late to work were killed for the same reason. Nekichi now kills fish with dynamite, an act for which he is beaten as a lawbreaker. His sister-in-law Uma loves him, but contact with the mainland has made the islanders ashamed of their natural impulses. They fear the condemnation of outsiders for such acts as incest and have even come to believe that the views of the mainlanders are superior to their own. The Futoris were once priests, but the confusion created by repeated invasions by people from the mainland has caused them to lose confidence in their culture and has rendered them human beings who have outlived an epoch in which they could flourish.

The engineer's primary task is to locate a source of fresh water for the factory. But the best place where water flows is located at the island shrine. Refusing to lay a long pipeline and bring in water from some other source, he insists on using this supply, although it means destroying the shrine. The people object because "God is the whole creation—even the grass. If you take away the laws of the Gods, nothing is left here." But such protest is of no avail.

Thus does Imamura chronicle the last moment of transition when the original island culture is giving way before the fanatical impulse to industrialize for profit at any price. What is offered in place of the old culture are things of no value, Coca-Cola and jet planes. And, finally, the islanders are not blamed by Imamura for their defeat. It is the new Japan that has made them self-conscious and diffident about their customs. They ask the engineer what those on the mainland think of them, while the point of view of the film is that they shouldn't care, since their ways are superior. Nekichi even begins to use bullets to kill fish, but he has discovered such methods from a world in which planes flying overhead are said to be "going to Vietnam." He is not to blame.

By the time Uma is asked to seduce the engineer in order to initiate him into island ways and make him sympathetic to their traditions, it is already too late. There are, however, some moments of victory. The engineer tries to force his assistant, Kametaro, to cut down a sacred tree. Kametaro refuses and the engineer, trying to do it himself, falls into a gigantic hole. It is as if the gods were still active on the island, accomplishing their own revenge. Falling in love with the wild, incestuous girl, Toriko, the engineer learns that the gods may be alive within her.

But, by the end, the island cannot be sustained as it once was. The people are forced to sell their land to the sugar factory. The bulldozer moves through the jungle, unmindful of the life it destroys in its wake. It slices a lizard in half. Only Nekichi Futori refuses to sell his land, wishing to remain in harmony with the gods. He and Uma are now attacked by the other islanders, who are on their way to becoming paid laborers. Progress necessitates the destruction of the old traditions. When, like Nekichi, someone proves recalcitrant and wishes to retain his continuity with the past, lies are used to destroy him. Because he will not sell his land, the other islanders conspire with the representatives of the factory to accuse him of a murder he did not commit.

In flight from sure death, Uma and Nekichi set out from the island in a small boat laden with their possessions. They are pursued by vigilante islanders who don the masks traditionally employed in acts of ritual murder. Uma and Nekichi would "start a new island," like the brother god and sister goddess of legend who founded Kurage, but it is no longer possible to live as the gods once did. The islanders raise their spears. Nekichi is drowned amid a sea of sharks, recalling the imagery of the first sequence. Uma is left tied to the sail of their boat under a bright sun and an orange sky. She will starve to death. The misguided people, alienated from their traditions, put on their masks once more and row home, having killed the wrong man. They have ceased to know who they are.

Five years later, a huge jet sets down on Kurage Island. Coca-Cola is sold to thirsty tourists. In front of the tiny train linking the center of the island with the airport runs the ghost of Toriko, seen only by her brother Kametaro, once her husband and also once her engineer-lover's assistant. She runs along the tracks as his memory of what was once a wild, free, pure island. The engineer, who has brought his wife back to the island with him, has been too deeply corrupted by civilization and consequently cannot see Toriko's ghost. In the last long aerial shot, the boat with Uma tied to the red sail still floats aimlessly on the wide blue sea. It is Imamura's final symbol of the defeat of the islanders and the death of their traditions. The death blow to their way of life has been by their own hands.

Kuragejima is a very difficult film. Imamura forces us to view the action through alienated eyes already corrupted by moral judgments we have absorbed through having ourselves been born "on the mainland." Our revulsion at Toriko's uninhibited sexuality, for example, is a function only of our having been "civilized." Kurage Island was once a life-renewing place and at moments we are awarded glimpses of its passion and sense of completeness. But the steady influx of the point of view of the mainland has already, by the film's beginning, rendered it corrupt and we can witness only vestiges of the old culture.

In the rush to technological progress Imamura believes that Japan has sacrificed its closeness to the gods. He emerges in *Kuragejima* as a highly religious, almost mystical filmmaker who believes that the original Japanese were once able to live in harmony with the gods of nature, and that this ability is rapidly being lost to his people. Never didactic, he can only

Kuragejima: Tales from a Southern Island: They are pursued by vigilante islanders who don the masks traditionally employed in acts of ritual murder.

Journey into Solitude: There is a tendency among some of Japan's directors to find a source of escape from the chaos of modern life in the rural byways where an "old Japan" still exists.

point by implication to the need for the Japanese, before it is absolutely too late, to struggle back to their increasingly vanishing cultural heritage. The danger is that this culture may soon recede into being only a vague memory, as ghostly as the once-vibrant Toriko. For Imamura, the mythic is an alternative to Japan's crisis of values, a source of the identity and strength through which, if only they would, the Japanese could face their future with confidence.

Koichi Saito, the cinematographer for Imamura's *The Insect Woman* and *Kuragejima,* has also made two films reflective of the view that a reprieve for today's Japanese who lack moral direction may be located in a return to a primitive, non-industrial Japan. Both *Journey into Solitude* and *Tsugaru Folksong* are rather pedestrian films, lacking the wit and intelligence of Imamura's works. But they do participate in the tendency among some of Japan's directors to find a source of escape from the chaos of modern life in the rural byways where an "old Japan" still exists. In these films emotional restoration lies in returning to one's origins, which are the origins of all Japanese. But whereas in Imamura's *Kuragejima* we feel we are in the presence of far-reaching truths, in the hands of Saito the return to the primitive too often results in extreme oversimplification. In soft-focus the heroine of *Journey into Solitude* washes her face in a stream. Straining, Saito tries, but fails, to convince us that through such actions people can be brought back in touch with their primal, lost selves.

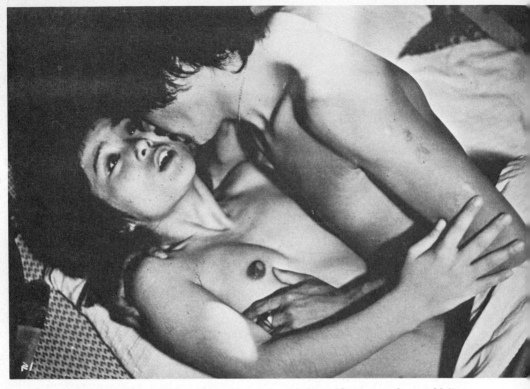

Tsugaru Folksong: Saito endorses the notion of the noble savage who would live
a free and pure life so long as he is not subverted by corrupt "civilizing" forces.

Saito proposes a highly traditional alternative to the amorality plaguing
contemporary Japan. Quite explicitly, he suggests a return to nature.
He endorses the notion of the noble savage who would live a free and pure
life so long as he is not subverted by the corrupt, "civilizing" forces of
what, in so many of these films, is referred to as the "mainland." In the
West, these views suggest Rousseau, Thoreau, the William Morris of
News from Nowhere. They imply that industrialization has taken from us
more than it has added. They would have us return to more uncomplicated
modes of existence, ways of life unblemished by logic and free of dissatisfaction. As responses to Japan's postwar surge into prosperity based upon
unrestrained industrialization, these films seem quixotic, religious, nostalgic
dreams of those who have abandoned the task of coping with modernized Japan as it is.

Not all the films that re-examine the rural remnants of Japan's original
culture propose that the Japanese could hope to return to an insular purity
now lost. Much more than Imamura's *Kuragejima* or Saito's *Tsugaru
Folksong,* Toichiro Narushima's *Time Within Memory* is highly critical
of the rural islanders who long to be assimilated within the corrupt Japanese mainland. The hero, Minoru, is a young man in his thirties who
returns to the primitive island where his mother died when he was eight

years old, attempting to come to terms with her memory. Narushima's intention, as he has said, is "to contrast the corrupt mainland with the relatively tranquil life of the island."[5]

But Narushima simultaneously creates an allegory in which the primitive island represents Japan itself and "the islanders' ways recapitulate the Japanese experience in general."[6] It is this aspect of his treatment of the subject that prevents Narushima from idealizing the "primitive island" as distinct from the "corrupt mainland." The islanders, for example, have "an egoistic, self-defensive fear of foreigners"[7] so expressive of attitudes toward outsiders in Japan today and one reason, according to Narushima, why feudalism has lasted so long in Japan. Unlike such people as Mishima or Imamura, Narushima does not set his film on a primitive island in order to recommend that the Japanese as a people return, even in spirit, to an original rural culture now in danger of extinction. His aim in *Time Within Memory* is in part to help the Japanese locate themselves within their island mentality, which has functioned as a mixed blessing. Their isolation has accorded them a homogeneous moral code. But it has also insulated the Japanese, emotionally if not technologically, from the strengths of the world outside. In returning to the island where his mother died, Minoru seeks an understanding of who he is. Simultaneously, Narushima suggests who the Japanese are and have been.

Most of *Time Within Memory*, however, does explore the dualism between island and mainland, primitive and civilized, pure and corrupt. On mainland Kagoshima, Minoru's mother was badly treated. His grandfather's mistress saw to it that the widow was not taken in by the family and she was separated from her child. To convey the alienation this caused in Minoru, Narushima sometimes photographs within the same shot the child Minoru and the now mature man. Unable to purge himself of the traumas of his boyhood, the adult Minoru carries them with him. The psychology of the man is still based upon the primal pain of his having been separated from his mother, not only by his grandfather but also by her sailor second husband, who refused to adopt the child and admit him into their home.

When Sawa, the mother, contracts tuberculosis, she is deserted by the sailor. She and Minoru spend a few last months together on her island home, Okinerabu. Sawa is fully aware of her imminent death. On Okinerabu, the island women are brown and healthy in contrast to the pale and sickly people of the mainland like Sawa. Because she is already ill, Sawa is afraid to touch her son. The pain of not receiving her physical affection remains with Minoru into his manhood.

Folk customs are kept alive on Okinerabu and Sawa takes part in the harvest moon festival. The islanders move together in harmony. Sawa is the

[5] Joan Mellen, "Interview with Toichiro Narushima," *Voices from the Japanese Cinema*, p. 214.

[6] *Ibid.*, p. 215.

[7] *Ibid.*, p. 217.

Time Within Memory: Having lived so long on the mainland, Sawa has lost her own closeness with nature.

most beautiful dancer of all. Yet the meaning of her dance is to express the desire of the islanders to emigrate to the mainland. Although the island is a source of health, its people do not want to be cut off from modernized Japan. In their dissatisfaction with their lives lies the origin of the loss of their original culture.

Having lived so long on the mainland, Sawa has lost her own closeness with nature. She and Minoru go fishing, only to have the unusual island tides suddenly overwhelm them because she has forgotten how suddenly they can rush in. Weakened by her illness, she clings to a rock, sending the boy for help with the stipulation, as in "Orpheus and Eurydice," that he not look back. A stalwart boy, he stumbles to safety. By the time he reaches the shore, the rock to which she had been clinging has been completely submerged in the sea.

The adult Minoru lifts three skulls from a common grave in a final attempt to communicate with his mother. According to island mythology, if he cuts his finger, his blood will stick to the one that is hers. He holds her skull, says "Mother," and her image appears to him. Feeling her bones had been deserted, she explains, she had called Minoru all the way from Tokyo.

Only through original island customs can Minoru make contact with his mother and his own deepest feelings, an aspect of the plot of *Time Within Memory* that links Narushima with Imamura. It required this ancient ritual to rid him of his discontent; only by means of primitive customs could he speak with his lost mother and hence with himself. In a fire he cleanses his mother's bones. For this Japanese man, the act expresses a therapeutic purging of himself as well.

Narushima never suggests that the Japanese can go back to an original island life. The "bottomless hell" of the mainland has become too powerful, having engulfed almost all of Japan. What he does suggest is that for the Japanese to understand themselves, they must return as much as possible to the rituals of their original culture, which permitted an abiding continuity between the living and the dead. It is an aspect of Japanese culture that seems to have been unrealized by other peoples, certainly those of the West, and yet remains one of the most beautiful values of the Japanese experience.

In Minoru's communication with his dead mother, one to be sustained throughout his life, lies the meaning of "ancestor worship," a living, growing, comforting emotion, a palliative against loneliness and alienation, and an always accessible affirmation of one's identity. Like Imamura, Narushima does finally locate solace for the Japanese among their earliest customs. Psychically, if not socially, he too proposes a return to origins.

Only in Shinoda's *Himiko* are we given a truly harsh view of Japan's beginnings. *Himiko* seems almost to have been made in answer to the views of people like Imamura who would suggest that a meaningful culture existed in Japan's past. Shinoda sees in Japan's earliest history the simultaneous birth of Shintoism and the Emperor system, both built upon bloodshed. To gain hegemony over the Japanese, the "original" religion of Shinto and the Emperor system first had brutally to enslave the first inhabitants of Japan, who worshipped "mountain gods" or "gods of the earth."

The setting of *Himiko* is the second century. The Yamatai tribe has conquered those who worship the gods of the earth whose spiritual leader is a priestess named Himiko. She is said to be in contact with the God of the Sun, whom she reaches by means of a copper mirror, later to be reified as one of the artifacts of Shintoism. Political expediency reigns, and when considerations make it necessary, Himiko is replaced by another priestess, said also to possess the power to communicate with the sun.

At the end of *Himiko* a helicopter tours the sacred burial places around Osaka where Japan's emperors, ostensibly descendants of the sun god, are buried. The helicopter hovers over these oases as if urging that now at last, in the twentieth century, they be opened. Once exposed, many believe and Shinoda suggests, they would reveal the origin of Japanese culture as stemming from those violent foreign people who came to Japan from Korea and subjugated her native peoples shown in the film as slaves. Such a suggestion implies an impurity in the Imperial line. Boldly, it proposes that Japan's emperors were not descendants of the original Emperor

Jimmu, said to be a great-grandson of the sun goddess Amaterasu. It is not an idle anthropological point Shinoda is making, for he is claiming that those in political power in Japan have used the Emperor and his supposedly sacred character to perpetuate their own power.[8] To open the tombs over which Shinoda's helicopter hovers might damage forever at last the myth of the Emperor's divinity, might accomplish what General MacArthur's political machinations after the war prevented. Shinoda believes that, were these tombs to be opened, the consequence would be an immediate challenge to the present Emperor Hirohito's claim to be an emperor at all.[9]

Shinoda proposes a Korean ancestry for the Japanese Emperor and sees the shaman Himiko as a half-caste, part Korean and part Japanese. His purpose in making these outrageous claims is to free people from such traditions as those demanding that they worship the Emperor, Himiko, the tombs of dead emperors, or the Japanese flag—all of which he sees as interrelated parts of a single destructive culture which led directly to the Second World War.[10] Such a purpose links him in intention, if not in style, to such political filmmakers of his generation as Oshima and Yoshida much more than to the Imamura of *Kuragejima*, despite the return to the past in *Himiko*.

At the end of the third century a Chinese scholar left two thousand words about the real-life Himiko. Before Japan had a written language, the Chinese were already writing realistic historical accounts. From these sketchy notes, Shinoda constructed his imaginary re-creation of Japan's earliest history. Shinoda sees Himiko as a goddess created by human beings, as are all gods. In the film her reign continues peacefully until the arrival from abroad of her half-brother, Takehiko.

Japan is at this point at a transitional moment, about to advance from a religious to a scientific age. Excavated sacred bronze bells are hidden because their discovery might undermine Himiko and those sharing power with her. The group led by Himiko, one which will create the "Emperor system," is cruel and exploitative. It violates the laws of nature and the "mountain gods" of the original inhabitants of Japan by killing does and fawns as well as stags. Violence and brutality are thus traced by Shinoda to Japan's early moments. The invading group already plans to kill all rebels who side with the beleaguered original inhabitants. Repressive authoritarianism is shown, in Shinoda's vision, to have been simultaneous with the ascension of the first emperors.

Himiko at this transitional moment is something of a split personality. By day she functions as a prophetess; by night she is a woman who must be provided with male slaves to gratify her sexually. This situation changes when she falls in love with her half-brother, Takehiko. Shinoda structures his plot around the incest motif because he sees inbreeding as a persistent

---

[8] Conversation with the author, Tokyo, October 1974.
[9] *Ibid.*
[10] *Ibid.*

Himiko: By day she functions as a prophetess; by night she is a woman who must be provided with slave men to gratify her sexually.

and destructive characteristic within the Japanese experience.[11] The incestuous affair defeats Himiko, causing her to lose her relationship with the sun god. She turns to the god of the land at the moment of her union with Takehiko. This makes her an ordinary woman, and hence no longer of use to the Emperor's party.

Himiko's suggestion that the people now worship the land god favored by her brother is particularly upsetting to the Emperor's sons because they have subdued their people under the cult of the sun. It is, therefore, politically necessary to retain a shaman like Himiko to perpetuate this mythology. When Himiko proves unreliable, a little girl named Toyo, mentioned in the original Chinese manuscript as the successor to Himiko, is set up in her place. Where a goddess or god does not exist, one can easily be created by those in power.

Toyo, a mere child with a callow, childish voice, also calls herself

[11] *Ibid.*

"Himiko." According to instruction, she utters prophecies about sending one thousand slaves and presents to Korea, presaging Japan's many conquests of that nation under the Emperor system. What Toyo lacks in spirit, she makes up in will. The new Emperor, who has ascended the throne by killing his brother after the death of their father, has no illusions that either he or Toyo has descended from the gods.

The incest taboo is used politically as a means of dethroning Himiko, who has been rendered unpredictable by her passion. All traditions and beliefs in this film are seen as functions of politics and the need of those in authority to perpetuate their power. Shinoda contradicts Japanese mythology by having the land god exist first, only to be replaced in Japan by sun worshippers. It is another means of suggesting that other cultures existed in Japan before the one that came to be known as "purely" Japanese. Takehiko knows this because he has traveled abroad. The implication is clearly that Himiko and her party came to the area later than those who worshipped the god of the earth. And these people, therefore, have more right to live undisturbed in Japan than those led by Himiko, flaunting and abusing their power.

The cruelty inherent in this tradition is expressed in Himiko's brutal revenge against Takehiko for making love to another woman, one of her priestesses. She accuses him of intriguing with someone from the "land-god country." But it is jealousy that leads her to have him banished and beaten. From the moment that she has Takehiko tortured, his nails torn out, his blood dripping onto the white sand of the sacred garden where Himiko's communications with the sun god had taken place, Himiko's own decline, and that of Japan, begins. It is as if cruelty from within, a violence endemic to human nature, was inflicted upon Japanese culture from the beginning.

Himiko destroys Takehiko out of jealousy. The Emperor's sons, after the death of their father, struggle for power and a system is created that has nothing whatever to do with spirituality or religious conviction. The copper mirror is made into an object of worship by the conniving sons precisely because they fear that their god may be weaker than the god of the earth. Thus does "Japan" come into being. Himiko is stabbed through the vagina with a blunt instrument; her murder is accomplished by enslaved mountain people who serve the Emperor's party as executioners. Himiko can be worshipped only when she is dead, just as the Emperor system can be maintained only so long as the sacred tombs remain unopened.

The priest Nashime, who stood by Himiko's side, has grown old and lonely, bitter in the knowledge of his own role in obeying the Emperor's sons and betraying and supplanting her. He looks up as Shinoda's helicopter makes its first ascent, the camera angle still low. Higher, it carries us over modern Japan and over the sacred burial places standing out from among highways full of cars. In this context the tombs are seen as ridiculous, like their inhabitants who have been designated, contrary to history, as an unbroken line of descendants from the sun. For Shinoda the so-called holy traditions of early Japan contain no meaning for people today, desperately in need as they are of liberation from precisely such an unwholesome and hypocritical ideology. Shinoda's starting point for this liberation is *Himiko*'s deliberate contradiction of the idea of the sanctity of the Imperial house. It is a bold and absolutely necessary first step toward that transvaluation of the "uniquely Japanese" value system which all these directors view as so urgent.

The Political
Cinema in Japan

I feel that, unless we make clear the secret of the spirit of the Japanese, who hurry to live and hurry to die, Japan will soon be led to war again. It may be too late to be making clinical experiments in film, but, as I have nothing else to do, I can only make my films in silence, dreaming of the distant day when the State will perish.

Nagisa Ōshima[1]

Political cinema is characterized by a perception of endemic social injustice. At times, description alone of repressive social institutions has defined the political film, as in *Bicycle Thieves, The Conformist*, or *The Godfather, Part Two*. Other political films argue the need to change such institutions or the entire society itself, as with *Potemkin, The Battle of Algiers*, or even, in spite of itself, *Mr. Smith Goes to Washington*. In *Mr. Smith* Frank Capra points to a system that fails to respond to the needs of people. Only at the end does he offer the weak palliative, in essence an apologia for the social order, of a change of heart coming from those in power.

Of course, not all political cinema has been *critical* of social injustice. Propaganda on behalf of a state justifying its policies has also been part of the history of the political film, from *The Triumph of the Will* in support of German fascism to the Japanese *War at Sea from Hawaii to Malaya* celebrating Japan's imperialistic ambitions during the Second World War.

In Japan, while the historical film has flourished, the political film, either in fictional or straight documentary form, has not. Until the 1960s, which witnessed such films as Shinsuke Ogawa's *Sanrizuka* series and Noriaki Tsuchimoto's *Minamata* films, Japan had not developed a strong documentary tradition. And before the emergence of the generation of Oshima and Yoshida, Japan had not produced strong political films of any kind.

Given the anti-feudal perceptions of the preponderance of Japan's intellectuals and artists, this may seem surprising. But the degree of their personal commitment notwithstanding, to many Japanese artists, even those on the left, Japanese society has seemed intractable. The absence of a tradition which assumed or expected individual rights for which most people would be prepared to struggle has disheartened many. The Buddhist view of the world as transitory and full of pain has suffused the entire

[1] *Tokyo Shimbun*, January 18, 1971.

culture, inducing a sense of resignation in the presence of political brutality. This reluctance to struggle is expressed best, perhaps, in Miss Oishi's automatic resignation from her teaching job in Kinoshita's *Twenty-four Eyes*. It does not occur to her actively to oppose the repression she loathes, let alone take steps to save her students who are being prepared for slaughter in the Imperial war. All she does is politely suggest that they would do better to remain at home. The lack of faith among Japanese artists in a mass movement of any kind has led, throughout the history of the Japanese film, to an idealization of individuals who struggle, but always within the director's clearly articulated stricture, that, however heroic the effort, failure must follow. This sense of preordained defeat was enormously reinforced by the stunting of the trade union movement from the end of the nineteenth century to well after the Second World War. Without confidence that common effort could sustain a social struggle, Japanese directors have felt authority to be too pervasive to oppose, except in personal, quixotic ways wherein the rebel demonstrates nobility because he knows he is engaged in moral witness rather than serious political battle.

It is also true that when a director wished to express political views, censors were ready and waiting within the studio to prevent it. And, as always, in the knowledge that certain views were tolerable and others not, artists practiced self-censorship, feeling out the limits of the permissible. Political repression in Japan was the norm long before the birth of the film industry, and directors from Ito to Mizoguchi were forced to mediate whatever political statements they desired to make through the oblique avenue of the historical or "samurai" film. This allowed only a very limited, symbolic illumination of the particular situations faced by Japanese in the twentieth century.

Only with the rise of the student movement did the political film truly begin to emerge in Japan. It is not that Oshima was the first to understand and address political realities. Because his path was prepared by directors working under far more difficult circumstances in a less favorable period and climate, his attacks on Kurosawa and others are particularly offensive. Like Mizoguchi, Kurosawa, having observed the disintegrative, inhuman results of the marriage between feudalism and capitalism in Japan, always recognized and demonstrated that the individual had a *right* to expect equity and justice and to fight for them. These two finest of Japanese directors advanced in their work the concept of inalienable rights as defined in the Western tradition by men like Tom Paine. It was the repression throughout the twentieth century that prevented these ideas from being placed in a contemporary political context in their films.

Thus all political films in Japan were made not merely after the Second World War but after the Occupation. Those most vital were produced during the 1960s. They take as their theme not the war, nor the poverty and depression occasioned by its aftermath, but postwar society itself. Political filmmakers in Japan today address themselves to those Japanese social institutions which developed after the war in a feudal pre-war manner and which continue into the present. They are more interesting, if occasionally less realized, than the anti-war films discussed earlier because they would enjoin Japanese to re-examine their society in all its fundamentals. They pose alternative values and a radically new political direction for Japan. They portray the postwar "lumpenization" of the urban poor wherein *yakuza* flourish at the top of the caste of outcasts while, at the bottom, stray youths for whom there is no place begin to populate the society. A scandalizingly co-opted press and police are attacked, their violation of rights far more dangerous than that which occurred during the 1930s because there is a pretense of democracy. Thus, the very abuse of rights suggests that so-called democratic processes, which ought to preserve them, are inadequate. The remedy, because it exists in form only, since Japanese political life has not been democratized, is mistaken for the ailment. The pervasive racial prejudice in Japan against *burakumin* and Koreans comes under unrelenting attack. Japanese imperialism today, in Southeast Asia and beyond, is exposed. The pollution, not only of the natural environment but of the quality of life and of the entire society, by the reconstituted *zaibatsu* conglomerates has been a major focus of young filmmakers, who are very mindful that Japanese cartels rule the nation every bit as much as they did in the pre-war period.

There is an important difference in tone, therefore, between the political cinema of older directors like Shindo, Imai, and even Kurosawa and that of Oshima and Ogawa. Younger directors refuse to countenance the easy illusion that reform works or holds out any promise but that of deception designed to abort serious change. That injustice can be righted by the acts of any single individual is also perceived as a chimera or a demonstration of futility.

Where Kurosawa would offer acts of individual conscience in sacrifice to an unjust society, as in *High and Low*, Yoshida argues in *Coup d'État* that every Japanese educated during the first half of the twentieth century grew up indoctrinated in, and assimilating, fascist ideas; in the absence of overt group resistance, all, he suggests, were witting or acquiescent participants in a fascist culture. The failure of Kurosawa's individualist heroes in such political films as *The Bad Sleep Well* (*Warui Yatsu Hodo Yoku Nemuru*, 1960) has influenced documentarists like Ogawa to reject the crusading hero as a viable character. The objects of attack in the new political films are far broader, including at times the entire culture, but, paradoxically, the struggle fails less frequently and absolutely than it does in the films of older directors like Imai.

In style, the new films refuse catharsis. Resistance to sentimentality is always a sign of a mature political cinema. In *Twenty-four Eyes* Kinoshita resolves our pain in tears. Oshima and Yoshida never permit pity for their characters, not even for so touching a subject as Oshima's exploited child in *Boy*. Tsuchimoto and Ogawa ask their audience to address itself to the society beyond the world of their films, and to change it. They enjoin an end to suffering through means shown to be viable in their films. These directors demand unabashedly direct political participation in Japanese society by their viewers, something Imai or Kurosawa never did. Yet the films of these young documentarists argue by example as opposed to injunction. Their films escape the pitfalls of didacticism because in their work it is neither slogans nor correct sentiments that influence us, but the felt life of people whose condition makes their acts necessary and compelling. If we are moved to emulate them, it is because these films capture a reality sufficiently persuasive not to require overt invocation.

Japan's earlier political films, such as Kaneto Shindo's *Gutter* (*Dobu*, 1954), sometimes had as their sole object a depiction of urban proletarian life. *Gutter*, in fact, takes as its primary theme only the atmosphere of poverty, the gray world of unskilled workers and *lumpen* figures scrounging out an existence on the fringes of society. Foremost among the exploited in *Gutter*, and personally symbolic of their oppression, is a woman named Tsuru, played by Nobuko Otawa. Starving and seemingly retarded, she is a pathetic figure, her tongue flailing wildly and uncontrolled in her mouth. Only after spending considerable time with her do we discover that she is kind, guileless, and dying of a physical disease that seems to have affected her mind.

Such people, Shindo asserts, with truth if without nuance, belong to the proletariat, to be distinguished psychologically as well as morally from the big bosses and capitalists who exploit them. In *Gutter* there are strikes that inevitably degenerate into brawls between workers and strikebreakers. Tsuru herself, in a flashback, is shown lying in the mud, a casualty of a strike at the textile mill where she had worked. In wide-angle lens the boss glares at us with a cigarette dangling from his lips. If Tsuru seems like an animal, greedily devouring rice by pushing it into her mouth with her hands, Shindo argues that it is because Japan's working classes have been reduced by inhuman living conditions to the rudiments of survival in slums where poverty is so severe that people are driven daily to abuse each other as a misdirected reflex against their misery. These, the truly innocent victims of the perpetrators of Imperial war, are the ones who pay most dearly for Japan's defeat.

In Shindo's political cinema the mere depiction of pain substitutes for analysis. Style serves only to emphasize Shindo's simplistic dichotomy between the "good" and the "bad," a far cry from Oshima's insistence that the exploited must bear part of the responsibility for their continuing degradation. Thus Shindo can give us a montage sequence in which images of the men who have abused her flash before Tsuru's eyes: the boss whose cigarette dangling from his lips made it seem part of his anatomy (a borrowing, no doubt, from Hollywood of the 1930s), the man whom, as a prostitute, she had solicited and who threw her out of his car because he suddenly feared venereal disease.

At the end Tsuru, in frustration and with no particular target in mind, picks up a gun. At once she is shot dead by the police, her blood slowly draining into the dry earth of the "gutter." And with her death *Gutter* passes into extreme sentimentality as Shindo exhorts the exploiters of people like Tsuru to appreciate the goodness of Japan's working class. The policeman who shot her even begs Tsuru's corpse for forgiveness, pleading

Gutter: Shindo exhorts the exploiters of people like Tsuru to appreciate the goodness of Japan's working class.

that it was only duty that forced him to kill her. Those in authority, temporarily misguided, are really good people at heart. The ultimate message of what Shindo may have thought was a politically daring film can be only that political action on the part of those like Tsuru and her friends (and, by indirection, the audience) is not required. Once those most cruel see what harm they are doing, they will of their own volition cease and desist from tormenting the weak.

On the surface it would seem as if actor-turned-director So Yamamura's

Crab-Canning Ship (*Kanikosen*, 1953) avoids the pitfalls of Shindo's *Gutter* by introducing, in the manner of Eisenstein's *Potemkin* which it closely resembles, a collective hero. At the film's center are all the sailors condemned to slave labor on a canning vessel. The villain is not only the cruel foreman but also those above him who insist that he force the men to fulfill superhuman quotas. Yet we never see these superiors, who are also protecting *Russian* canning ships against their own because power politics demand at the moment that rivalry with Russia be subordinated to an early variety of "détente."

Finally, as in *Gutter*, we are confronted primarily with stereotypes, the "good" sailors and the "bad" foreman against whom they will finally mutiny. The very use of stereotypes in the political film indicates, however unconsciously on the part of the director, that the personage dramatized is a ubiquitously recognizable type. If he is the exploiter, we partake of a sense that we have met him in the past and will surely meet him in the future. His cruelty is rendered invincible and immutable; the implication is that, should one of these villains, whether the cruel foreman of *Crab-Canning Ship* or the factory boss in *Gutter* be displaced, another just like him would take over. Such stereotypes indicate a defeatism on the part of the director, a sense of universal exploitation afflicting all by a ruling group and of endemic impotence on the part of the weak. And Yamamura's oppressor is grotesquely caricatured, refusing to rescue men washed overboard or to go to the aid of another ship sending out an S.O.S.

Crab-Canning Ship: We are confronted primarily with stereotypes, the "good" sailors and the "bad" foreman, against whom they will finally mutiny.

Yamamura, with his seemingly revolutionary film about a mutiny of abused workers, is also guilty of a further defeatism. Although he made his film in 1953, after the departure of the American Occupation, he sets it in the distant 1920s, in keeping with the proletarian novel that was its source. The time is that of the depression, the struggle of the sailors for their rights marked by the atmosphere of Japan's preparations for imperialistic war and its concern with markets, resources, and supplies of cheap labor. The Second World War—and Japan's defeat—are, of course, known to be irrevocable facts of history. And this defeat, by inference, suggests that the repression of the mutinying sailors was—and is—equally unavoidable. The message of Yamamura's only seemingly bold film is that such efforts, now as then, are equally doomed. And at the end, like Shindo, Yamamura seeks only pity from the audience, rather than solidarity with his suppressed sailors. He refuses to mediate their defeat with any hope of future revolt or demonstration of how the sailors' experience may be a harbinger of larger efforts against injustice.

Yamamura's imagery is often powerful, as at the end when he superimposes a bloodstained flag of the rising sun over the corpses of the sailors who have died at the hands of the State. In Japan, where the national flag is identified both with the Emperor and with a near-sacred past, its association with murder makes a powerful comment on the imperial regime which took Japan into World War Two. Loyalty is demanded by Yamamura, not to the flag but to its wronged victims, a politically resonant moment even for postwar Japan.

But finally, like Shindo's, Yamamura's effort at political cinema is emasculated by its reduction to a simple paean to the oppressed. Its application to postwar Japan is barely hinted at. By failing to unfold how the events of Crab-Canning Ship are related to the present, Yamamura confines its meaning to the past. It was a safe, though wholly unsatisfactory, decision and it severely restricts the range and merit of his film.

Equally disappointing as political cinema have been Tadashi Imai's efforts to expose the injustices within Japanese society. Susceptible as a member of the Japanese Communist Party to platitudes about "the people," and influenced by the aesthetics of socialist realism, he, far more than Shindo, works close to the sentimental, suggesting too often that there is a special nobility among the oppressed. With Imai, political cinema is reduced to a dramatization of suffering for its own sake with only the weakest sense of either its cause or remedy.

Imai's strongest political film is Darkness at Noon (Mahiru no Ankoku, 1956) about proletarian boys whom Imai has called "juvenile delinquents" or "bad boys."[2] They are framed by the police and forced to confess to a murder they did not commit. Despite a pro forma disclaimer that the film does not refer to real people, its origin is an actual event. While the case was still before the court, Imai made his film, clearly urging acquittal. It was swiftly suppressed by the Toei company, which, as Anderson and

[2] Joan Mellen, "Interview with Tadashi Imai," Voices from the Japanese Cinema, p. 109.

Richie indicate, had "allegedly received threats from high government sources."[3]

Imai's tone in *Darkness at Noon* is one of willed outrage but, like Shindo or Yamamura, he is far more concerned with eliciting sympathy for his victims than with indicating or soliciting plausible action on the part of the Japanese people against such social injustice as that described in his film.

Darkness at Noon is weakened to the degree that it persists in focusing overly long on the victims and only superficially on their executioners. Imai spends more time, as did Shindo, around the slum dwellings of his victims than in systematically exposing the nature of police power in Japan, as Costa-Gavras would do so successfully for Greece in *Z*. It is as if Imai had felt his subject matter was realized once he stated that the boys were innocent. Never does *Darkness at Noon* face the much more important problem of the nature of a state which seems to have no room for its young men.

Imai's message is that Uemura, his central figure, has been framed because he is poor and on the fringes of society, an embarrassment to the authorities. The injustice, isolated as it is from a richer critique of Japanese society, comes to seem arbitrary. It is possible even to view it as the result of unlucky circumstances, such as the fact that the one policeman who did see the boys at 10:40 p.m., a time which makes it impossible for them to have committed the murder, is too cowardly to testify because he fears losing his promotion if he tells this unpopular truth. Imai's impulse is always to wring his hands and lament that such things could be permitted to happen.

By far the best sequence of the film is a surreal, comic enactment of the crime, done with Dutch angles and varying freeze-frames, slow-motion, and speed-ups, to show that these boys could not have committed the crime in the short space of time alleged. The judge, bored, cleans his glasses in a set piece borrowed from Pudovkin's *Mother*. Jump-cuts are inserted to make a mockery of the official version of the murder. But all is resolved in melodrama as the hero, sentenced to death, yells to his mother, "Supreme Court! Not yet!" while the police brutally restrain him. Technique in the last half of the film, effective as it seems, serves primarily to obfuscate. *Darkness at Noon* asserts the innocence of the five accused, but fails in any serious way to transcend the particularities of this individual case.

When he is dealing with topical as well as inherently explosive political themes, Imai's substitution of sentimental catharsis for social or historical nuance becomes particularly infuriating. *Kiku and Isamu* (*Kiku to Isamu*, 1959) is about the half-breed children left behind in Japan as a legacy of the American Occupation. Kiku and Isamu, whose mother, now dead, was a Japanese, are being raised by their nearly seventy-year-old Japanese grandmother, having been abandoned by the black G.I. who was their father. The film chronicles the abuse of these two sweet children by

[3] *Japanese Film: Art and Industry*, p. 284.

the Japanese population. The inhabitants of the rural area where they
live seem physically offended by the very sight of these mixed-blood children, especially by the stocky, eleven-year-old Kiku, whose skin is so dark
and who is so strikingly different in appearance from the Japanese children
of her age.

Imai deplores the racism of the Japanese who, inflated by a sense of
their own racial superiority, are unable to accept these innocent, unlucky
children, hapless products of the war. It is not that their presence reminds
the rural residents around Tsugaru, where the film takes place, of the Japanese defeat and humiliation, but that a bigotry which is part of Japanese
culture and the national sensibility comes into play as these half-castes attempt to survive in the only home they know. Kiku and Isamu are Japanese children, but it will be impossible for them to lead normal lives in
Japan because, as if they were foreigners, they can never be accepted.

Unfortunately, Imai is content merely to state the problem, never
reaching toward conclusions or universal truths and never moving the
problem beyond the small village setting of his film. His perspective is limited to the fact that these children are abused. He never explores why such
racism has become so deep-seated a facet of the Japanese character, or what
the origin of this bigotry is in terms of Japanese history. Nor does he even
comment in this film, made in the fifties, on the quality of the Occupation itself. As in *Rice* (*Kome*, 1957), Imai instead deals only with
symptoms, never with either cause or remedy, focusing, albeit with a compassionate camera, solely on how the children are treated in this one
isolated rural area.

Within this limited range, *Kiku and Isamu* is a successful film. We
watch as the racism of the Japanese toward blacks resembles the racism
of the very Americans toward whom the Japanese in this film feel so
superior, culturally and spiritually. Her classmates call Kiku a "gorilla"
and make monkey sounds at her. Isamu, outraged, reports to his teacher
that one of the members of his class has called him a "nigger." Kiku and
Isamu might just as well have been the first black children in a white school
in the American South.

In her innocence, Kiku cannot understand why there must be differences
between the races. And Imai is sophisticated enough to handle with considerable irony the scene in which Kiku's teacher tells her that all people
are "equal." In the face of the kind of cruel discrimination faced by Kiku,
the Occupation-originating platitudes of would-be Japanese liberals can
provide no solace. Kiku herself remains unsatisfied by these words of consolation. At another poignant moment, Kiku is bewildered by the news
that she will never be able to marry in Japan, that she will never be
accepted. A boisterous, high-spirited, energetic girl, her ambition is to be
a "good mother." Gently, her grandmother and the teacher try to warn her
that this may never come to pass. Racism in Japan will prevent any family
from accepting her as a suitable wife for their son. The teacher encourages Kiku to learn a trade because "women should be independent." Kiku
cannot understand why.

Having had her first menstrual period and, now that she has reached maturity, faced with the prospect of being sequestered in a Buddhist nunnery, Kiku attempts suicide. She is too heavy, however, and the attempt is unsuccessful. The rope breaks and she only falls down. In a marvelous evocation of country wisdom, Imai then has the toothless, wizened old grandmother (played to the hilt by Tanie Kitabayashi) welcome Kiku's entrance into womanhood. She is desperately aware that she must somehow restore this injured and betrayed child to the living.

What she wisely chooses is to make Kiku proud of the fact that she has become a woman. The prospect of the nunnery is abandoned and her grandmother tells her that she will now be initiated into the secrets of being a farmer. She will be instructed in all the techniques, the mysteries, of cultivating the land. Through this experience she will be permitted the experience of living as a human being in Japan. Delighted with the new dignity conferred on her, Kiku, armed with the tools of her new trade, proudly struts by her former schoolboy antagonists. In supreme triumph she informs them that she is now a woman, no longer subject to their taunts.

If this is a satisfying ending, it is also a facile one. Kiku, absorbed into rural Japan, is still faced with being a half-caste; the uplifting ending tends to obscure this truth. Imai leads us to purge our pity and our horror at the racism permeating Japanese society through tears—first of sorrow, as when Isamu, adopted by a black family in the United States, leaves Kiku behind, and then of satisfaction, as Kiku goes off to till the land. He thus absolves his Japanese audience of the task of even seeking a remedy for this racism, having found so easy an answer for Kiku. And he refuses to confront the audience, as will Oshima in taking up the same theme, with the fact of its own racism.

As in Kinoshita's *Twenty-four Eyes*, which is infamous in this sense, our anger at the apparent injustice is effectively dispersed through tears. Imai finally has more in common with the apolitical Ozu, who rarely takes up social questions, than he has with Oshima, a political filmmaker seemingly like himself. For in Imai, as in Ozu, we are left with the message always to make the best of things as they are. However intolerable the suffering afflicting us, "it can't be helped" and "no one is to blame."

Film in the hands of a great artist like Kurosawa always differs radically from the work of such lesser artists as Shindo and Imai. Yet Kurosawa's two most political films, *The Bad Sleep Well* and *High and Low*, retain some similarities in the treatment of social questions to the work of these directors.

The Bad Sleep Well seems boldly to concern itself with the corruption of Japan's entire ruling class, a corruption in which the giant corporations, the press, and the police work in tandem. As such it is much more courageous than any of the films of Imai, even *Darkness at Noon* which contains its "good" policeman along with its "bad." Kurosawa's hero, Nishi (Toshiro Mifune), seeks to avenge the death of his father, whom corporation vice-president Iwabuchi (Masayuki Mori) had driven to suicide.

The Bad Sleep Well: Nishi is dangerous because he will not acquiesce in yielding to the domination of these so-called superiors. But as a single rebel, he is harmless.

His revenge begins in the first sequence, when he marries Iwabuchi's lame daughter, not for love but to insinuate himself in the Iwabuchi household.

By the end of the film Nishi has fallen in love with his wife, and the demands of human feeling cause him to jeopardize his plan to expose Iwabuchi's crimes. That Nishi loves Iwabuchi's daughter renders him vulnerable to his father-in-law, who does not hesitate to give his *yakuza* the order for Nishi's murder as soon as he perceives Nishi's aim.

But the political thrust of the film as an attack on the collusion between government, press, police, and *zaibatsu* had already been lost two-thirds of the way through the film, when Kurosawa began more and more to focus on the psychology of Nishi. The political satire is abruptly abandoned as Kurosawa confines himself to exploring Nishi's personality. His single-minded hero is made politically ineffective by the normal assertion of love. The "bad" of the title (it literally translates as "the worse you are, the better you sleep") are those who would resort to any means to perpetuate their power, those who rule Japan. But Kurosawa seems suddenly to lose heart, as if he finds the theme of how to overcome such a ruling order too disturbing to pursue.

This sense of futility before the crucial question at the heart of his own subject was actually latent in *The Bad Sleep Well* almost from the start. That Kurosawa has chosen a single individual to combat so vast a hierarchy roots in defeat, from the start, the idea of how to struggle against "the bad." Because his conception of how to combat such a system is therefore inadequate, and he does not make the inherent inability of a single "hero" to combat social evil his theme, Kurosawa is forced, by the end of the film, to make a statement only about Nishi's personal loss. He is left with a film less about power in Japan than about thwarted love between husband and wife. And because the plot of *The Bad Sleep Well* is so confined to the impossible effort of one man to expose the nature of Japan's *zaibatsu* to the world, Kurosawa is also forced, willy-nilly, to surface the apolitical theme that to defeat evil one must oneself become evil, a truism effective only because the odds are so stacked and a single man is pitted against an entire social system.

At one point Nishi says, "people won't do anything, [that's] why they're [the executives] so powerful." But neither Nishi nor Kurosawa carries this idea to its logical conclusion—that a defeat of the Iwabuchis requires an entirely different approach. Thus Kurosawa's real theme, implied but never realized, cannot emerge: that the chain of corruption extends from the presidents of corporations to the Japanese government itself.[4] At the beginning of the film Iwabuchi plans to go into politics, hoping to become a minister. We know that there are nameless superiors from whom he himself takes orders, but this is as far as the political theme reaches. And it is dispersed, along with Iwabuchi's political ambitions, once Nishi falls in love with his wife, Iwabuchi's daughter.

At the end, Iwabuchi bows to the telephone, as Kurosawa bitterly satirizes the absurdity of the feudal relationships that prevail in Japan today. There are those higher up than he who are guilty of worse crimes. Kurosawa refrains from exposing them and these figures remain nameless. The best point Kurosawa makes in the film is that a feudal submissiveness governs all relationships in official Japan. When a minor official named Miura receives a message from the company president that he is "trusted completely," he immediately kills himself in obedience to the real meaning of this message. Nishi is dangerous because he will not acquiesce in yielding to the domination of these so-called "superiors." But as a single rebel, he is harmless, reduced to a scheme of "punish[ing] men who prey on people who can't fight back," but unable even to damage the reputations of those who, at the end, will continue to sleep undisturbed.

Iwabuchi murders Nishi by hiring *yakuza* who inject alcohol into Nishi's veins, tie him up, and place his car on a railroad track. The real "Nishi," whose name Iwabuchi's son-in-law took to conceal his identity, can only yell impotently, "Should things be this way? Is it right?" The theme of the film has been reduced, unfortunately, to the notion that the enormous power of the Iwabuchis has defeated Nishi, not that Nishi's strategy was inadequate. There remains an unfinished quality to *The Bad Sleep Well*, a sense that not all that needs to be said has in fact been said.

High and Low is a much more sophisticated political film. Based on a pulp detective story called *King's Ransom* by Evan Hunter writing under the pseudonym of Ed McBain, it takes as its starting point a mistaken kid-

---

[4] Kurosawa himself has mourned this fact: ". . . maybe the picture would have been better if I had been braver. At any rate, it was too bad I didn't go further. Maybe I could have in a big country like America. Japan, however, cannot be this free and this makes me sad." (Quoted in *Films of Akira Kurosawa*, p. 143.)

The Bad Sleep Well seems boldly to concern itself with the corruption of Japan's entire ruling class, a corruption in which the giant corporations, the press, and the police work in tandem.

napping. Instead of seizing the son of the wealthy shoe executive whom he wishes to punish for the arrogance of his privileged existence, the kidnapper grabs the child of the man's chauffeur.

The moral question governing the first half of the film is whether the executive should pay the enormous ransom, which would ruin him financially and permit his rivals in the shoe company to squeeze him out, for a mere chauffeur's son. Fortunately, this rather obvious moral dilemma is replaced in the second half of *High and Low* by Kurosawa's much more interesting treatment of the personality of the kidnapper. Once the child is rescued, because the humane Kurosawa hero could never hesitate long over such a choice, the director devotes himself to an analysis of Japanese society. Exposing a corrupt police department and press, *High and Low* comes close to developing into one of the finest critiques of the inequitable class structure of Japan ever offered in a Japanese film.

Kurosawa finds the inequity between "high" and "low" a much richer theme than the kidnapping and shifts our attention quite soon from Gondo, the shoe executive (Toshiro Mifune), to the kidnapper himself. It is not because the kidnapper was played by a fresher and more energetic actor (Tsutomu Yamazaki), as Kurosawa has suggested,[5] that he begins to occupy the center of the film, but because this man raises a question that at once indicates Kurosawa's power as a political filmmaker.

At the center of *High and Low* is the question of what the individual has a *right* to expect from the society in which he lives. In Japan, where, as Chie Nakane reminds us, a vertical hierarchy governing all relationships persists and one is always first subject to a predetermined status within a collective; to demand a style of life different from that afforded by one's allotted place in the system constitutes extreme rebellion. In a social order which functions only so long as everyone accepts his place, to challenge one's position amounts to a revolt against the organization of the entire society. Ironically, Kurosawa makes his rebellious kidnapper an interne studying to be a doctor, a person who will soon enter the medical profession; this kidnapper is soon to share in the benefits enjoyed by the privileged within Japanese society. Yet, according to Kurosawa, it is just such a man, about to escape his poverty, who revolts, a man who knows he will soon enjoy a better station in life.

It is a brilliant insight on Kurosawa's part that it is precisely a man soon to escape it who would find his poverty so intolerable that he would jeopardize his entire future by becoming a kidnapper. History confirms that those who become revolutionaries are usually not the poorest and most hopeless, but exactly those who have begun to taste the fruits of prosperity and thus are much more aware of the pain of inequity. Japanese critics like Tadao Sato, who have insisted that an interne would never become a kidnapper and that therefore *High and Low* is based upon an incredible premise,[6] reveal themselves as simply incapable of grasping the depth of Kurosawa's social vision.

In the last scene of *High and Low* the kidnapper faces Gondo, the man he ruined, from behind his prison bars. He asserts his *right* not to have had to live in "a three-tatami room, freezing in winter, stifling in summer." It is a challenge to the class structure of Japan, because the kidnapper was inspired to his crime by the sight of Gondo's white mansion high on a bluff, overlooking with supreme indifference the entire city of Yokohama, including the slums below where he himself lived. "Your house looked like heaven," he tells Gondo.

Gondo has asked, "Must we hate each other?" and the implied answer is

---

[5] Joan Mellen, "Interview with Akira Kurosawa," *Voices from the Japanese Cinema*, p. 48.

[6] Most recently at a panel discussion in Kyoto in 1972.

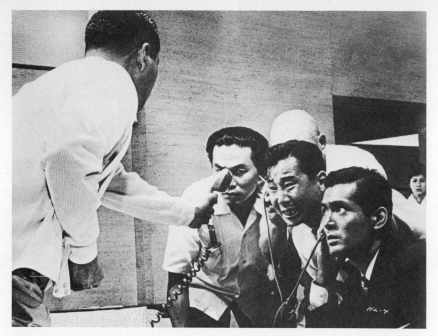

High and Low: Through the police, with their willingness to use any methods necessary to catch the kidnapper and their preference for law and order over justice, Kurosawa begins to tell a secondary story about Japanese society.

that they are both more than individuals. They each also represent the inequity between rich and poor. As men, they might have been friends. As fellow Japanese, victimized by living in a society that makes life heaven for some and hell for others, they can only hate and fear each other. The arbitrariness of class differences is expressed by Kurosawa as he has Gondo's face reflected in the glass behind which the kidnapper views him. Gondo's face is as if superimposed upon that of this impoverished man, driven to drug addiction and murder by an intolerable existence. The point is plain. One could as well have been the other.[7]

That he wishes to end the film on the theme that as long as there are class differences, there will be crime and brutality, however "good" individuals like Gondo may be, is reflected in a shot earlier in this prison sequence. As Gondo and the chief detective, Tokura, walk down the corridor on their way to the kidnapper's cell, the heads of workers washing the floors are bent low in a shot borrowed from Michael Curtiz' *Mildred Pierce*, a variation of which Kurosawa had also used in the field sequence of *Throne of Blood*. The disparity between rich and poor, high and low, appears in the very composition of the shot, foreshadowing the theme of the dialogue between Gondo and the kidnapper shortly to follow. Despite his having lost everything, Gondo, we are confident, will be restored to

[7] The original McBain novel, which contains a similar incident, lacks any of Kurosawa's political resonance. McBain's kidnapper speaks only in terms of personal gain: "I'm saying I *had* nothing, and I *still* got nothing—even after all the lousy cheap stickups. Don't I ever get nothing?"

prosperity. He is already making shoes again, if for a small company. But there are also those who will never break out of the closed circle of their hopelessness, and whose pain is expressed in the kidnapper's anguished scream that follows his last words: "My life's been like hell since I was born!"

Kurosawa's disenchantment with contemporary Japan is seen as well through his characterization of Gondo as a good man unable to survive in the cutthroat corporate world. In many ways he is a carryover from the conception of Nishi in *The Bad Sleep Well*, the one man who would live rightly in defiance of the evil going on around him. Gondo would make finely constructed shoes as distinct from the shoddy products preferred by his fellow executives concerned only with quick profits. Capitalism is, in fact, compared by Gondo to war: "It's either win or lose."

What saves *High and Low* from the central weakness of *The Bad Sleep Well* is that midway through the film Kurosawa leaves behind the isolated, noble hero, not only to focus on the kidnapper but also to comment on the police pursuit of this victim of social injustice. Through the police, with their willingness to use any methods necessary to catch the kidnapper and their preference for law and order over justice, Kurosawa begins to tell a secondary story about Japanese society. The satire of the police is a minor theme, perhaps, and one Kurosawa treats almost unnoticeably. But it is present in *High and Low* through much of the middle of the film and it confirms the kidnapper's sense of hopelessness at the end.

The police, in their own words, become "bloodhounds," led by their chief, "Boss'n," who in his physical appearance, bald and fat, very much resembles a bloodhound. At one point "Boss'n" jokes, "Are we police or are we criminals?" Just as Gondo and the kidnapper are interchangeable by the end of the film, so are the police and their victim. The final logic of *High and Low* is that it is the established order that has led to all the acts of violence in the film, from the kidnapping to the murder of a girl in an "opium den," where the kidnapper tests out the potency of the drugs with which he hopes to kill his accomplices, now that the police are on his trail.

The police are as guilty of this murder as he. Spotting him on the street, they could easily have picked him up before he met the girl. They choose to allow him to remain free so that they may catch him at a more serious crime than kidnapping. "The kidnapper deserves capital punishment," decides detective Tokura (Tatsuya Nakadai, against whose personal affability Kurosawa runs the counter-theme of police ruthlessness), "if we arrest him now he'll only get fifteen years." It is the police who indirectly permit the murder necessary for them to catch the kidnapper at a capital offense. And when they do apprehend him, and the kidnapper attempts to use the poisonous heroin on himself, they stop him by force, keeping him alive almost sadistically for a further and more painful punishment.

These police, while working for a state shown in this film to be built on an unjust inequity between rich and poor, are themselves "have-nots," like the kidnapper uneasy at Gondo's supreme wealth. "Usually I waste no

love on the rich," says the "Boss'n." Later the police, working at the low
angle of the kidnapper's view of Gondo's palatial house, remark that "it
seems as if it's looking down on us." They thus directly echo the kidnapper's anguish, repeating the same emotion he felt, which differs from
theirs in degree but not in kind. Yet, unlike Gondo, they fail to show any
sympathy whatsoever for the victim of social injustice who turns to a life
of crime. And in this blindness to the pain of the criminal they express
the logic of the policeman as a tool of the ruling class which would preserve
order at all costs, willfully unmindful of the causes of crime.

Class pain permeates this film. At Gondo's old factory, workers on the
assembly line are sympathetic with this fallen executive, their good natures
set in contradiction to the rude, peremptory behavior of their superiors.
Even Aoki, Gondo's chauffeur, whose son has been ransomed, is permitted
by Kurosawa to interject what seems to be an irrelevant remark, "I don't
like bosses, but I brought this on." Kurosawa's real theme is not kidnapping and the horror of such an act, but the injustice of a class system and
the suffering inherent in a society where some are "high" and others "low."

High and Low is a brilliant political film, although its artistic premises
remain a generation away from the political films to emerge from directors
like Nagisa Oshima and Yoshishige Yoshida. High and Low does indeed
attack the entire structure of Japanese society, its aim as profound a social
criticism as any that could be conceived by Kurosawa's younger antagonists.

Yet there are also fundamental differences between the approaches to
the political film of these two generations. High and Low, as a typical
example of Kurosawa's later work, is a quest film. It proceeds as an inquiry
into the truth about modern Japan, moving as if we were from the first
unaware of the feudal vestiges characterizing this brutally unjust society.
In this search, the police are our guides. By the end we have discovered
how deeply injustice pervades Japanese society.

Oshima and Yoshida, from the first shots of their films, have abandoned
this quest as unnecessary. They begin from the premise that the quest has
long ago been completed, the result as severe an indictment of Japan as
could be made. Because Kurosawa would still pursue the journey to understanding of the nature of Japanese society and culture, his films retain
a linear, chronological structure. Because he is interested now in how feudal
Japan has invaded our psyches, long ago having discovered its essential corruption, Oshima in particular frequently departs from narrative realism.

Japan's film directors, like her other artists and intellectuals since the
Second World War, have pursued moral, political, and spiritual solutions
to the painful experience of living in an essentially valueless society. Beyond exposés of conformity and adherence to predetermined obligations,
moral quest has not flourished in this culture. Yet the moral anarchy of
postwar Japanese society has appalled intellectuals of wide-ranging political
persuasion.

Nagisa Oshima, as a filmmaker and intellectual, differs markedly, however, from Japan's pre-war Marxist dissenters. As Frank Gibney and others
less reactionary have pointed out, the degree of commitment of Japan's

supposedly Marxist professors, novelists, and journalists has been superficial, rarely manifesting itself in any direct or serious attack on the ruling
class with which these "left" thinkers appear to be personally quite satisfied. "Barring the core communists," says Gibney, "the average Japanese
progressive is the socialist equivalent of a 'rice Christian'."[8] The "core communists," or party members, have been, of course, the *least* likely to challenge Japanese history, as their postwar performance within the student
and worker movement amply reveals. Moscow had, in fact, most specifically
forbidden them to do so. But Gibney is essentially correct, certainly about
the generation preceding Oshima's. (He was born in 1932.)

Oshima is representative of an entirely new breed of Japanese intellectuals
who came to the fore during the postwar confusion, willing to risk much in
a direct challenge to the ruling order. In defying the power structure of
the Japanese state so directly, Oshima has jeopardized his opportunities
to make films. He has demonstrated a sincerity and commitment rare for
leftist intellectuals in a society insinuating at every turn its insistence upon
consensus and conformity. Oshima and a new group of his film contemporaries, such as Yoshishige Yoshida and Shinsuke Ogawa (both born in
1933), have demanded in their films, despite institutional obstacles, that
the Japanese people take a long, unrelenting, and brutal look at who they
are and what they have become.

But it is not only people of the left like Oshima who have agitated for
a social and psychological transformation of Japan. A right-wing novelist
and parliamentarian, the militarist Shintaro Ishihara, also speaks of a
"nation without morality."[9] Ishihara is no less alarmed than Oshima by "a
spiritual void at the core of the Japanese nation, a moral degeneration that
characterizes everything that goes on in this society."[10] Ishihara is a member of the neo-fascist *Seirankai*, a strongly financed current within the
ruling Liberal-Democratic Party, yet much of his description of Japanese
social decay could have been employed by Hani or Oshima. Ishihara, of
course, absolves capitalism and established authority from responsibility for
this crisis, implying that insufficient moral resolve is a result of the
weakening of the power of the state. But the problem is perceived by all;
only the solutions differ.

When someone like Ishihara speaks obliquely of the need "to gain an
awareness of the past which will show us how long our reservoir of morality
has been left empty and dry,"[11] we may infer that, like Mishima, he is
arguing for a return to feudal institutions as the source of a value system
which would restore Japan to that presumed sense of purpose and identity she had lost since the War. Others, like Oshima, have sought to
liberate the Japanese from the remaining vestiges of feudalism so essential
to the authoritarian rule of the corporate few.

[8] *Japan: The Fragile Superpower* (New York: W. W. Norton & Co., 1975), p. 236.
[9] "A Nation Without Morality," *The Japan Interpreter*, 9 (Winter 1975): 276–291.
A translation of "*Nippon no dogi*," from *Jiyu*, April 1974.
[10] *Ibid.*, p. 276.
[11] *Ibid.*, p. 291.

In film an avant-garde cinema developed in the late fifties, parallel to the rise of the *Zengakuren*, the largest student organization of the time. Film again served in Japan as a source of cultural regeneration. The "new wave" movement in cinema was represented by Hani, Yoshida, and Oshima, the last-named arguing that the struggle against the Japanese-American Security Treaty marked a turning point in the fate of postwar Japanese art.[12] Faced with the opposition of the Communist Party, the movement failed and the security treaty was signed. The financiers of film applied pressure against young avant-garde and radical filmmakers, who began to have an increasingly difficult time making films for big companies like Shochiku, Toho, and Daiei, where their predecessors, Ozu, Naruse, Kurosawa, and Mizoguchi, had thrived.

In 1960 Oshima reached a turning point in his career with *Night and Fog in Japan*, an important film which examines why the student movement failed. Its title is borrowed from Alain Resnais' "Night and Fog," a documentary about Nazi concentration camps. Within the student organizations there had been repeated clashes between those influenced by the Communist Party, which favored accommodation with the ruling power, and those who, as members of a "New Left," recognized that Stalinism had been a prime force in defeating all revolutionary movements in their epoch.

The brutal police states of Eastern Europe and the authoritarianism of the official Communist parties were repellent to people with democratic, socialist, and revolutionary convictions in Japan as elsewhere. Equally appalling was the fact that the Stalinist rulers in Russia used all national struggles as ploys for exacting diplomatic and trade concessions from the United States in exchange for aborting open challenges to the established order by indigenous Communist parties and those they could influence. The *Zengakuren*, like the New Left elsewhere, at first resisted the conservatism of the Communist movement. But it failed to compete with the Communist Party for the support of the working class, and thereby caused its own isolation. This isolation led in turn to the substitution of terrorist confrontations for a developing support in the populace. Indeed, the less this support was sought or in evidence, the more extreme the tactics became; and the more confrontationist the tactics, the more the New Left was isolated from the public. By failing to advance a program both democratic and free of control by the Soviet Union or China, the student movement in Japan defaulted on the task of building a mass opposition in the populace and enabled the established order to crush it.

Oshima focuses *Night and Fog in Japan* at the moment when the New Left came to believe that success for a movement in Japan could come only by rejecting the restraints and compromises Stalinism would have imposed upon it. But Oshima goes on to argue that the ultimate responsibility for the failure of the movement to abrogate the security treaty with the United States had to rest, finally, with the participants themselves, who were guilty

12 *"Situation et Sujet du Cinema Japonais," Positif* (Paris), no. 143 (October 1972), p. 30.

of timidity, nihilism, and a failure to observe the insidious influence of the Communist Party upon their movement. In *Night and Fog in Japan* Oshima has said that he was accusing, most specifically,

> those who possessed the qualities of leadership yet failed to utilize them, abstaining from the struggle, those who, having once faced up to the struggle, were disheartened by setbacks and those who secretly harbored pleasure in the chaos for its own sake.[13]

Night and Fog in Japan opens with another of Oshima's ceremonies, this time a wedding. But what should be an occasion of harmony rapidly degenerates into a political debate between opposing forces of two generations, both of which have seen the mass demonstrations in which they were involved come to nothing. Ota, one of the younger militants wanted by the police, calls the previous generation "Stalinist zombies," and the wedding more like a "funeral." The stage is set for a fascinating glimpse of the internal debate within the student movement.

The characters are often set out by Oshima in shallow focus against a black background, as if it were a theatrical rendition. *Night and Fog in Japan* is a film about consciousness, the consciousness of these militants who have seen efforts for which they were willing to give their lives degenerate into bitter reproach and failed political ends. The task of the film is not to entertain, but to explore why this has occurred. It was, in part, a reflection of the times not only that Shochiku finally decided to suppress this explosively honest and revolutionary film but that a major studio should have financed it in the first place. Only the commercial success in Japan of Oshima's previous film, *The Tomb of the Sun* (*Taiyo no Hakaba*, 1960), and the potential student market can account for Shochiku's decision to grant Oshima carte blanche in making *Night and Fog in Japan*.

The bridegroom, Nozawa, had been involved ten years earlier in the Stalinist left, participating in the "bloody May Day" demonstrations called in protest against the Korean War and the American assault on political autonomy in Japan. The bride, Reiko, a generation younger, is a member of the New Left which, in 1960 when the action takes place, has just been defeated in its struggle against the renewal of Japan's security treaty with the United States, known as AMPO. Nozawa had become a journalist, guilty over his abstention from the struggle; he and Reiko had met at an AMPO demonstration.

Their wedding becomes a battlefield as forces belonging to each generation grapple with the reasons why their respective movements failed. The master of ceremonies at the wedding, Nakayama, is the central figure in the film; he is the former leader of Nozawa's group and a member of the Communist Party. Feelings at the reception are as strident as they were on the barricades; even at a wedding, they rise to the surface and engulf the participants. Politics invades every facet of life because issues that touch

[13] Appended by Oshima to the script of *Night and Fog in Japan*. Translated by Keiko Mochizuki.

the very survival of Japan as a conscious, vital culture have come to a head. Escape from this moment of crisis proves impossible, nor can a private world of family obligation or domesticity serve any longer as a barrier to personal involvement, as the couple who are marrying had assumed.

The most significant episode recounted among the interpolated flashbacks concerns the suicide of Takao, a member of Nozawa and Nakayama's dormitory. Takao's "crime" was to set free a young worker whom the dormitory had labelled a "spy." Nakayama sits in a darkened room, a light flashing into Takao's face as if they were enacting a G.P.U. interrogation for Stalin. Caught stealing "documents," the young worker, different from the others in not being a student, had been locked into a closet until he "confessed." The film never establishes whether the worker was a "spy." But even if he had been, his acts could have had little bearing on the real cause of the movement's failure.

Oshima uses this image of locking the "spy" into the closet to indicate that the police state methods projected by the Communists, like the tactics adopted by Nakayama, were responsible for the isolation of the movement. In their isolation they had sought scapegoats and had intensified repression within their own ranks, the very things responsible for popular disaffection from them in the first place. Oshima suggests that Nakayama uses the method of the "witch hunt" precisely to conceal the real reasons for his failure to lead a successful movement, as well as to prevent examination of his own behavior.

Oshima is totally on the side of Takao who, in a moment of doubt, lets the accused boy go free, genuinely concerned that he may well be innocent, as he claims. Oshima stresses how the Communist Party insists that a man

Night and Fog in Japan: Betrayals within the movement are seen by Oshima as more pernicious than anything the police could do.

is a spy without presenting any evidence, thus capturing the entire role of the party in these events and its major responsibility for the movement's failure. That a "worker" is chosen as the scapegoat makes a mockery of all Nakayama's Marxist pretensions, his hypocrisy symbolized by the photograph of Stalin on the wall of his room.

Thus, betrayals within the movement are seen by Oshima as more pernicious than anything the police could do. First, in a cynically terrorist phase, the Communist Party had ordered weapons to be used against the police. Then, suddenly, it had sabotaged the movement by ordering the demonstrations to cease. The purpose underlying both the ultra-left and the reformist policies was to prevent a mass movement from developing that could bring to Japan a revolution at once socialist, democratic, and outside the control of the Stalinist states. It was such Stalinism, Oshima shows, that caused disillusionment and the consequent depoliticization of so many former student radicals in Japan and elsewhere. The relative prosperity of Nakayama, in contrast to the extreme poverty of the other students, is a telling visual indictment of his character and his politics.

When Takao sincerely asks Nakayama why he was so sure that the young worker was a spy, he is accused by Nakayama of refusing to submit to "united opinion." Takao is given not an answer but a sentence, ordered to confess in turn to having also been a spy, as a "lesson" to the movement. If he refuses, the leadership threatens to denounce him as an "imperialist." Takao chooses suicide. The iron hand of Nakayama is such that not one of the others sides with Takao or offers him support.

The wedding serves as a confessional during which all clarify and attempt to understand this tragedy. The pervading atmosphere is one of futility. The security treaty has just been signed, and the militants have no choice but to turn to the past to learn why they failed so profoundly. Oshima deplores the easy rhetoric of Nakayama, who had never once participated in the demonstrations yet who insists that Takao died because of "American imperialism." It becomes clear that the prosperous Nakayama, representing the Communist Party, sought primarily to protect the position of the party as a legal entity with the right to participate in the Diet. His motives were thus very different from those of the sincere partisans of the movement.

Nozawa, confused and disillusioned, questions whether he himself ever was a revolutionary. In 1960 he wished to throw himself into the struggle once again, but was haunted by the futility of it all. He stands for all the youths of Oshima's generation. As the movement died, he lost his personal relationship with Misako, a fellow militant who married Nakayama. She was seduced by Nakayama's facade of culture (he played Shostakovich on a record player) and by the financial security he alone could provide. Participating in the AMPO struggles became for Nozawa a means of renewing his spirit; in these bloody battles he met and took care of Reiko, a wounded girl who would become his wife.

The two generations come together finally when the traitor to the earlier movement betrays the second as well. Just as the Communist Party called off the first demonstrations in the 1950s, so it also sabotages the anti-security treaty movement. Nothing had been learned by the younger generation from the failure of their elders. The official parties again call for abstention from the struggle.

The film ends on a marvelous, surreal note. In the midst of all the confusion and recriminations, Nakayama gets up at the wedding to speak, taking charge and assuming the pose of rhetorician as he has always done. He is the master of the slogan. A new demonstration is planned by the younger generation protesting the arrest by the police of Ota, the fugitive who turns up at the wedding.

At once Nakayama demands that those under his sway refuse to participate; he is still in a position of leadership. He calls those who would join "irresponsible rabble rousers" and addresses his fellow guests as if he were at a rally, denouncing "petit-bourgeois demonstrators" who do not understand the problem "of the unions" although it is he who has betrayed the one worker in the film, denouncing him as a "spy." He tells them as they stand, immobile as statues, that they don't understand what "unity" is, that they are "enemies of the people."

All the Stalinist clichés, historically used to repress indigenous revolutionary struggles, are resurrected; it becomes clear that Nakayama, speaking mechanically, as if he were a robot, is merely following the official line handed down by Moscow to the Japanese, as it has to other foreign Communist parties. The camera tracks from one spellbound guest to another as they stand, powerless to stop him now, as they have always been, and unable to offer an alternative strategy or inspiration. His voice fades on the sound track although he continues speaking, still in power at the end of the film in 1960 as he had been ten years earlier in wielding his insidious influence over the anti-Korean War demonstrations. For Oshima, the Communist Party has maintained a stranglehold on the movement and has been the single major force in its demise. But the other, equally destructive element has been the failure, due to personal and political inadequacy, of those who should have known better to do anything to stop it. *Night and Fog in Japan* is one of the most courageous political films ever made in any country. It provides the explanation for the loss of optimism about meaningful social change in postwar Japan.

In *Night and Fog in Japan* Oshima asserted his solidarity with the movement while articulating powerful criticisms of it. On October 12, 1960, four days after Shochiku released the film, the head of the Socialist Party, Inejiro Asanuma, was assassinated by a right-wing fanatic while making a speech. Shochiku immediately shelved the film with the feeble excuse that it had not been grossing enough. An angry student reaction to the assassination and a resurgence of the movement were obviously feared. Petitioning Shochiku, as many student organizations did, proved futile. The film was never re-released.

The following year Oshima became an independent filmmaker, only to be forced in the early 1970s to disband his company, Sozosha, because of financial difficulties. Japan's young filmmakers have thus been intimately connected with the tumultuous political events of the postwar period. From the first, Oshima saw cinema as a link between intellectuals and the Japanese people. And he saw, as his own immediate task, the differentiation of his work from that of directors before him, like Kurosawa and Ozu (who reigned at Oshima's own Shochiku). For Oshima, the traditional Japanese cinema had always pitted the "good individual" against a "corrupt society." It was from this view that he wished to distinguish himself: "I insist that the situation is not that simple. The corruption outside has become the corruption within . . . this cycle never ends. We have to blame ourselves as we blame outer factors."[14]

Oshima became a filmmaker partially to use the medium as a means of exploring how to renovate a society fatally unclear about its motives. The consciousness of having been victims of war, a pacifism shared by so many Japanese, led to wide support for the student movement. Oshima feared, wisely, that so narrow a base was inadequate, in part because this emotion would not move people too young to have experienced the war. Further, an appeal to feelings of war victimization, common to older directors, was often sentimental and politically unclear and did not address itself to the specific issues of a given struggle such as that against the Red Purges (Japan's McCarthyism), the Korean War, the Japanese-American Security Treaty, or, later, the terms of the reversion of Okinawa to Japan.

Through the 1960s and into the 1970s Japan continued to make use of the "nuclear umbrella" of the United States, facilitating an initial vast economic expansion. The hegemony of the highly conservative Liberal-Democratic Party, backed by the United States, wielded an ever-increasingly armed Self Defense Force which effectively maintained the status quo with respect to all social issues. The student movement was defeated in every one of the struggles in which it engaged, leading to terrorist solutions and internecine warfare between rival left-wing political sects. A director like Oshima, who in the 1950s had been vice-chairman of the Student Union Committee at Kyoto University, could not help but dissociate himself from the fanatic, ragged remnants of what the student movement had once been.

Especially potent as contributions to a Japanese political cinema are Oshima's films dealing with the plight of the Korean in Japan and in Asia: *Death by Hanging* (*Koshikei*, 1968), *Three Resurrected Drunkards* (*Kaettekita Yopparai*, 1968), and *Diary of a Yunbogi Boy* (*Yunbogi Nikki*, 1965). The most successful of these is *Death by Hanging*. Like *Boy*, it is based on a true story, that of an actual Korean resident imprisoned in Japan for murder. From this starting point, Oshima explores the psychology of a Korean in Japan, asking why he would become a criminal. Simultaneously, he exposes the attitudes of the State toward such a person.

Death by Hanging begins with the hanging of the prisoner, a hanging he miraculously, surrealistically, survives. From this moment on the film moves interchangeably on the levels of fantasy, allegory, and symbol, as if

[14] "Ideas of Crisis," *The Discovery of Contemporary Society* (Tokyo: Bungei-Shunju-Sha, 1960), 7: 9. Translated by Keiko Mochizuki.

only in this manner could Oshima expose to the Japanese the racism
and injustice inherent in their legal system. *Death by Hanging* offers a
plethora of styles, beginning as a documentary with titles enquiring of
Japanese people whether they are for or against the death penalty. We are
told that seventy-one percent of the population is against its abolition. To
these people Oshima addresses himself: "Have you ever seen an execution
chamber? Have you ever seen an execution?" In voice-over the chamber is
then described, down to the presence of a toilet for men only. To further
dramatize the horror of capital punishment, Oshima hangs his hero.

In *Death by Hanging* Oshima abandons such narrative conventions as
plot, psychology of character, and anything remotely resembling a causal
structure upon which his action would be based. In his hands political
cinema becomes an attack on Japan from within and without, on feudal
psychic patterns assimilated by the Japanese as well as on the injustice of
its social institutions. Only an unconventional aesthetic can serve so unconventional an aim. Documentary techniques are left behind once the
Korean survives the hanging; allegory becomes Oshima's most effective tool.
But if directors of Kurosawa's generation also included allegory in their
films, Oshima totally abandons all surface realism, relying on allegory alone.

When the authorities decide to hang the Korean a second time, the
chaplain in residence, a Catholic since the Korean is a Catholic, finds himself forced to report the reverse of his usual pronouncements: "His soul has
departed, but his body lives." That the Korean is made a Christian, having
chosen a non-Japanese religion, reflects his alienation within a society so
hostile to him because he is different. As the Korean's executioners try to
decide what to do with him, Oshima hurls one irony after another at us.
They cannot execute an unconscious person because that would be breaking the law. (Official murder is not considered unlawful!) They need him
to re-express his guilt before they can hang him again, an irony because they
assume, although we are not sure, that the Korean, R., is guilty of the
crime for which he was hanged. He will be revived only so that he can be
forced to admit to his crimes a second time and the State can then execute
him again in good conscience.

The psychic exploration of R.'s consciousness, Oshima's depiction of
how a Korean resident in Japan must feel about himself, given the daily
abuse he suffers, opens with the title: "R. does not accept being R." The
Korean lies naked, a body, an object on which his tormentors can now
work. In another title Oshima asks: "Is this R. the R. who committed the
crime and confessed?" offering us now the information that the man had
once actually confessed to the rape and murder for which he was sentenced
to be hanged. But even if the Korean were originally guilty, once having
been "executed," he is not the same man. The horror of capital punishment is expressed in its being not a punishment for a heinous crime (R. has
already been punished) but a sadistic form of revenge by the State.

Only the chaplain opposes the antics of R.'s official executioners, one of
whom would even pretend to be the woman R. strangled in a staged
re-enactment designed to produce another confession. The policemen

salaciously enjoy the very thought of the rape, guiltier by far than R. of sexual violation because they trade in human violations of every kind every day. Far more than R. is the State guilty of crimes against humanity. The police also refer to "war criminals," unwittingly describing themselves, all veterans of the Second World War.

Meanwhile, the chaplain ridiculously opposes the second execution on the ground that God must have taken R.'s soul in the first hanging. It is the soul and not merely the body that must be punished; hence there is no need for a second execution. If God did not take R.'s soul in the first execution, then God does not exist, a possibility a Catholic could not admit. The chaplain must therefore, Jesuitically rather than out of compassion, insist that R. not be killed again since his soul is gone. The chaplain thus opposes further torture of R. to keep his personal ideology intact, and not because hanging is inhumane and State murder no less a violation of the teachings of Christ than any other killing.

Once he regains consciousness, a new R. emerges, a reborn human being who, through amnesia, has been freed of the knowledge of the harshness of his prior life in Japan as a member of a severely persecuted minority. "What is *Chosanjin* [a Korean]?" he asks. Since so many Koreans are born in Japan, it is meaningless to say that they are from *Chosan* (Korea). Oshima's point is that of course there are no differences between Japanese and Koreans. R. goes on to say he knows nothing of rape or carnal desire or what is meant by the term "family."

The police then attempt to depict his previous environment, affording Oshima the opportunity to describe the lives of Koreans in Japan. R.'s father was a drunkard, his mother deaf and dumb. Bright "for a Korean," he had tried to go to night school. At the age of thirteen he had even won a speech contest about Abraham Lincoln. Oshima is deeply ironic as he has one of the officials say, "If you'd graduated, you might have become a civil servant," for, however intelligent the Korean, such jobs in government, as well as even jobs as skilled workers in factories, are denied to Koreans in Japan. The enactment of R.'s home life has the police revealing their own racism. One instructs him: "Eat more like a Korean would. Be more vulgar!" The re-enactment serves finally only to repoliticize R., to reawaken his consciousness of himself as a Korean, and to inspire him to rebel—the inevitable response of the oppressed minority to those in authority.

The scene moves to the locale of the crime. A girl appears on the roof of the school where R. ostensibly raped and killed his victim. She is introduced to us as his "sister." This woman argues that R. killed as a Korean in revenge against the Japanese, as Eldridge Cleaver in *Soul on Ice* describes raping white women as a means of exacting some revenge upon his oppressors. R.'s "sister" thus expresses the view of the orthodox Left toward Koreans; that she stands for the traditional Left is also revealed in her outspoken opposition to capital punishment.

Although Oshima of course shares in the latter, R's "sister" does not by any means express the director's own point of view regarding the situation

Death by Hanging: The "sister" first seems to be a savior, symbolizing the spirit of the Korean people.

of Koreans in Japan. The "sister" first seems to be a savior, symbolizing
the spirit of the Korean people. She is the soul, we learn, of older women in
South Korea beaten by their husbands. Yet she is a propagandist, urging R.
to work for the improvement of "Korean-Japanese relations," a position
which at once places her with such organizations of the Left as the
Japanese Communist Party and light-years away from the feelings of
Oshima. Finally, she has no concern for the needs of R. as a suffering
individual.

Oshima is especially hostile to the woman when she resorts to slogans
which are as dehumanizing of R. as the racism of the police. "R.," she
asserts, "didn't choose to be born in Korea." "You Japanese," she goes
on, "will never understand us Koreans. Japanese imperialism forced him to
do this." She thereby absolves all individuals of responsibility for their acts,
viewing everything in abstractions unrelated to the concrete situation of
any single person like R.

A doctor, who has been present throughout, presumably to determine whether or not R. in fact dies in the hanging, replies, not without some of Oshima's endorsement: "That gives license for 600,000 Koreans to commit murder." "The Japanese made *us* bleed," the "sister" goes on, finally exposing her position as an ethic of revenge. And even R. dissociates himself from her by indicating that her description of his situation is "less and less like R." He did not commit the crime as a political act at all. At once his "sister," hardly a comrade, rejects him as "not being a Korean."

Yet even R.'s "sister" is infinitely preferable to the vulgar constables, now drunk and exposing more and more of their corruption. The doctor reveals himself to have been something of an Eichmann during the war. His tongue loosened, he defensively asserts that he had only the job of saying who was alive and who dead. The functionaries of the Japanese state are seen by Oshima as its deepest criminals. In a fantastic revelation, the doctor admits that if death by hanging were abolished in Japan, he would go to Vietnam or Korea to ply his trade.

Oshima's use of imaginary characters like the "sister," symbolizing Korea, is aesthetically fitting because his hero, a culturally deprived Korean, long ago retreated to his fantasy life for gratification. Unable to satisfy his desires, sexual, social, or intellectual, he resorted to the world of the imagination which, of course, could never fulfill his needs. The frustration attendant upon the failure of fantasy to satisfy him resulted in the rape and murder. R. confides to his "sister" that when he thinks of his crimes, he feels more confident. Strength for R. is perversely derived from the fact that some of his imaginings came true, even if they involved the atrocities of rape and murder. His psyche has been distorted by oppression. His crimes were a means for him to feel, as a non-person in Japanese society, that he was in fact alive and real. Simultaneously with this attainment of self-knowledge by R., his executioners, the real criminals, continue their war stories, confiding that they had been sexually aroused by the act of killing their enemies. Official crime, for which there is no justification, is contrasted by Oshima with the desperate, completely understandable crimes of R.

All dissolves in farce. One of the policemen suggests the solution of exterminating all 600,000 Koreans in Japan; another would favor killing only the Communists among them. Still another fears that the "Red Flag of Pusan" will march into Japan in revenge, resulting in the rape of Japanese women. Thus Oshima chronicles the guilt within the Japanese psyche over the much-abused Korean population.

At last R. admits his guilt, thereby accepting who he is. As Oshima dollies away, a Japanese flag is on the floor in front of R. while a noose hangs overhead. R. is once more about to resume his identity as a victim of the Japanese state, for which flag and noose stand as symbols. Oshima cuts to a boy and girl. They roll over and over on the grass in innocent pleasure. The boy is R. as he would have liked to have been, had he been able to transcend being a "Korean" and live a normal life. On a tiny island in the water, the setting sun high above them, the boy and girl in R.'s fantasy, having escaped from Japan, embrace.

R., his face framed by the Rising Sun flag, now becomes himself. In very extreme close-up he admits to the crimes, but insists that he doesn't feel guilty. He argues that if it's wrong to kill, it must be wrong for these officials to kill *him*. Postwar education is blamed by his executioners for this anti-feudal impertinence, but R. persists. He insists on naming these representatives of the State as his murderers. But the logic of his life dictates that R. be executed. Because he accepts himself, and the consequences of the damage done him as a Korean living in Japan, he must also accept his appropriate destiny.

R. also dies because, having asserted that "a nation cannot make me

Death by Hanging: Because he accepts himself, and the consequences of the damage done him as a Korean living in Japan, R. must also accept his appropriate destiny.

guilty, I remain innocent," he cannot be permitted by the State to survive. He would be denying the brutality of official Japan were he not to allow it to martyr him. At last a "good job" is made of the hanging and R. succumbs. A voice confronts the audience, accusing it of complicity in the brutalization of this Korean.

In Oshima's political cinema the battlefields exist within the damaged psyches of the oppressed and in the zeal of their would-be defenders like R.'s "sister" as much as they are located in the representatives of the State. Constantly he chastizes the well-meaning Japanese audience for its passivity, its willingness to be conditioned to injustice, its failures to rebel and to defend the weak. R. is an unwinning, impassive figure throughout *Death by Hanging*, but a man no less deserving of defense for that. That his personality seems so unappealing is only further evidence of the damage inflicted upon him as a Korean in Japan.

A much more personal and compassionate treatment of the Korean is found in Oshima's short film *Diary of a Yunbogi Boy*. In 1964 Oshima made his first trip outside of Japan. "A very un-international human being," as he has described himself,[15] he visited South Korea, former colony of Japan and present reminder of the role of Japan in Southeast Asia in this century. There he observed and took snapshots (which comprise most of this film) of boys on the streets, shining shoes, selling sticks of gum, begging, barely surviving.

The small documentary film that resulted was based on the diary of a Korean boy named Yunbogi which had been published in Japan. It was shown for eight nights only in Tokyo, and only on the condition stipulated by the theater manager that at each viewing Oshima himself would make a speech about the film. *Diary of a Yunbogi Boy*, Oshima has said, derives from his "deep love for those peoples [of Asia]"; it might be seen as a "lamentation" of a person "torn by a feeling of sin as an assailant Japanese."[16]

The voice-over narration of *Yunbogi* is full of rhetorical laments and exhortations, expressing Oshima's own pain as he observes the starving, lonely children of South Korea, their family life disrupted by extreme poverty, their prospects in life negligible:

> Yunbogi! Where is your mother? Is she peddling something somewhere? Or maybe she's working as a house servant, or drawing water in heavy, heavy water buckets, or carrying a baby that belongs to someone else. . . .
> But still, it's easier for a woman to find work. For a man, it is very difficult. Yunbogi! Don't criticize your father because he is ill and out of work. Don't criticize your father!

Periodically, children like Yunbogi are gathered up from the streets like stray dogs and cats and taken to the "Garden of Hope," a reformatory from which, just as often, they run away. The end of the film contains ten-year-

---

[15] "About *Yunbogi's Diary*," pamphlet published by the Shibata Organization, Tokyo, distributors of Oshima's films, April 1972.
[16] *Ibid.*

old Yunbogi's own lamentation for his absent mother, heart-rending but not sentimental because no amount of feeling evoked by such a forgotten child could be in excess:

> Mama! I don't mind not eating! I don't mind dying! I wouldn't care if I starved or died, if only I could be with you! Why did you go away and leave us behind, Mama? Mama! Mama! I call to you again and again, but you never answer me.

The very last words of the film, however, belong to the narrator, hopeful because, as a suppressed Korean newspaper in 1940 had said in speaking of the resistance of the Koreans to the Japanese during the Second World War, "boiled red peppers get hotter. Beaten wheat pushes out new shoots." And Yunbogi, too, is "a stalk of beaten wheat that will push out new shoots."

In his denunciation of Japanese imperialism in Asia, Oshima, like Imamura, makes a very different kind of political film from those of his predecessors. Calling for an end to the lethargy of the oppressed, he urges to action all his besieged people, even the motherless child Yunbogi. In them he sees a future, no matter that, for the moment, we are looking in extreme close-up at the swollen belly of a starving Korean child or hearing on the sound track "Sometimes I Feel Like a Motherless Child."

Yunbogi's sister, Sunna, who leaves home at the age of eight to sing for people at bus stops, will no doubt soon become a prostitute. Yunbogi must beg for food on the streets like a dog. But Oshima is confident that such people will some day rise up. Shots of demonstrations during which an active student movement overthrew Syngman Rhee offer Oshima further cause for hope. "You will be throwing stones one day," Oshima first asks and then asserts to Yunbogi. Over a shot of Yunbogi's face we hear the roaring sounds of a demonstration.

Oshima's sympathy is colored by his sense of personal guilt as a Japanese, another aspect of his cinema that separates him from his predecessors. In voice-over he records thirty-six years of Japanese pillage, domination, and massacre in Korea; we hear the loud marching of soldiers. In this context Oshima applauds the projected rebellion of Yunbogi and of "all Korean boys" for whom he stands. It is the Japanese director's means of apologizing for the behavior of his country toward the rest of Southeast Asia, particularly during the Second World War. As such, films like *Death by Hanging, Three Resurrected Drunkards,* and *Diary of a Yunbogi Boy* become political acts in themselves. They are made in opposition to what Oshima sees as a renewed assault Japan has been making on the peoples of Asia who remain unable to defend themselves. Their sense of urgency and strength of conviction make them unique for political cinema anywhere.

Japan's Revolutionary
Documentarists

Through the *Sanrizuka* films we were trying to be the voice of the oppressed.

Shinsuke Ogawa[1]

Although they can't change the world, movies can give encouragement to people . . . the process of making *Minamata* encouraged people to go to the stockholders' meeting.

Noriaki Tsuchimoto[2]

With the defeat of the student movement, Oshima's films have become less popular in Japan and there have been long lapses of time, such as from 1972 to 1975, when he made no feature films at all, working only for television.[3] The freshest films of the late 1960s and the 1970s in Japan have been the work of the young documentarists chronicling the struggles of rural peoples against the pollution that has decimated Japan's countryside. Although, as indicated in the first chapter of this book, these anti-pollution movements reveal feudal responses permeating the revolutionary, they remain the most positive political and social signs in Japan today of a culture in transition. Incorporating such feudal attitudes as the demand that the company and the government cease departing from sincere and benevolent paternalism, these movements have also begun to chronicle the progress of the Japanese from feudal subservience to action on behalf of their right to control their lives. Japanese documentarists are recording this process on film.

Ogawa's *Sanrizuka* films, as well as his *Dokkoi Ningen Bushi*[4] (1975) about the plight of day laborers on the Yokohama docks, and Tsuchimoto's *Minamata* series deal very little with the psychology of the participants. Not even implicitly do they refute the view that submersion in the group and a group mentality have led to a stultification of the psyches of ordinary Japanese. Seemingly unaware of how the individual's constant identification of himself in terms of a group has led to such psychological problems

---

[1] Conversations with the author, Tokyo, November 1974.

[2] Conversation with the author, Tokyo, October 1974.

[3] The 1976 French co-production, *Empire of the Senses* (*Ai no Corrida*), marked Oshima's return to active filmmaking.

[4] The title means, literally, a song of earthy, common people uttering the sound "dokkoi" as they carry heavy loads that require a great deal of physical exertion.

as the inability to assume personal responsibility for an action, Ogawa and Tsuchimoto seem to be suggesting that it is through group solidarity that an individual can express his needs.

The weakness of their work is that they define these needs solely in social terms, as in the Sanrizuka peasants' determination to retain the land earmarked for the new international airport. Neither director is particularly concerned with psychological needs which the traditional group in Japan has always made subordinate to the prerogatives and perpetuation of a collective. And therefore they do not test whether the resurgent power of decentralized peasant or citizen's groups may not, in fact, involve a further submersion of the personality of the individual at the same time that it effectively challenges either the mammoth Kajima Construction Company, as in the case of the Sanrizuka peasants, or the equally mammoth Chisso Chemical Corporation, as in the case of Minamata.

In this sense their work, while it is of immediate social significance, does not deal with the central dilemma at the heart of the culture: how democratic social institutions are to be freely chosen and sustained if the concepts of the individual and individual decision-making have not yet been made fundamental elements of one's experience as a Japanese. It is not a matter of either glorifying individualism for its own sake or applying Western standards to Japanese culture. Rather, it seems that individual self-confidence and self-expression may be prerequisites to a truly democratic form of group action. It may be that only when a person has attained full consciousness of himself as a unique human being, with potential specific to himself, can the fulfillment of the needs of the person and those of the larger entity of which he is a part become simultaneously possible. Ogawa and Tsuchimoto seem to be suggesting that rural groups driven by oppression to resurrect ancient forms of group organization and ritual have shortcut this process. It is a spurious premise indeed, given the authoritarian quality not only of social but of personal life in Japan.

Dealing exclusively with urgent political problems facing specific sectors of the population, documentarists like Ogawa and Tsuchimoto, ignoring, unlike Oshima, the larger questions involving the destiny of the culture itself, see their films primarily as political acts designed to strengthen the determinaton of the peasants who are their subjects to resist the giant conglomerate *zaibatsu*. In the struggles of the villagers around Narita, the projected site of the new international airport, or those of the citizens of Minamata City, directors Shinsuke Ogawa and Noriaki Tsuchimoto see cause for hope that the Japanese people will not remain forever passive in feudal subservience to authority. To paraphrase Stanley Kauffmann's subtle remark about Fernando Solanas' *Hour of the Furnaces*, among their virtues, these documentarists don't pretend to be objective.[5]

Since 1968 Ogawa has made six films depicting the resistance of the rural villagers around Sanrizuka to the new airport: *Summer in Narita, Winter in Sanrizuka, The Three-Day War in Narita, Peasants of the Second*

---

[5] *Living Images: Film Comment and Criticism* (New York: Harper & Row, 1975), p. 195.

Fortress, The Building of the Iwayama Tower, and *Heta Village.*[6] Since 1966, when the Narita airport plan was accepted from the Kajima Construction Company, the government has faced continual opposition to its construction, a resistance that has seen the building of towers by the farmers to prevent planes from landing. The peasants are tenant farmers and under Japanese law a landowner is never under virtually any circumstance allowed to evict a tenant. It was this fact that gave the tenant farmers who had lived for generations on the land proposed for the airport the determination to struggle to preserve their homes and their way of life. For the Japanese, whom people as different as Chie Nakane and film director Toichiro Narushima have declared incapable of revolution, the Narita struggle represents a turning point in history.

In addition to building the tower, which the government could have torn down but was afraid to, the peasants opposed the pipeline system that was intended to carry jet fuel from port to airport. They proved that chemicals from the pipeline system had infected their drinking water. Pipeline construction was stopped, only to have the courts declare that the chemical was not dangerous. The Sanrizuka peasants found themselves in opposition to the entire structure of Japanese society. The government shielded and supported companies like Kajima while accepting their bribes; the legal system served to protect the interests of both business and government.

Documentarist Shinsuke Ogawa completely identified himself with this struggle; he has said he has such feeling for the defiant Iwayama tower that, should he see it torn down, it would be as if he were watching the rape of a woman he loved.[7] His crew stayed at Sanrizuka, living exactly as did the peasants, completely trusted by the participants. Ogawa photographs the people in acts of violence against the police, deeds in which they could easily be identified from the evidence of Ogawa's films, and for which they could be arrested. But these peasants have long since passed the point when this could matter.

Thus the *Sanrizuka* films differ from most traditional documentaries. They were made with the collaboration of farmers who were shown rushes and who castigated Ogawa when they felt he had directed a scene without feeling. Ogawa's films have made the Sanrizuka struggle better known throughout Japan, suggesting that all the anti-pollution groups are fighting for a common goal and against the same enemy. The implication, never didactically specified in any of the films but nonetheless apparent, is that all these groups should organize into one, the better to render their voices more powerful. While this has not as yet happened, meetings have been held between, for example, the Narita farmers and the victims of Minamata disease. These dialogues were held in front of the symbolic, almost mythic Iwayama tower. With this remarkable resistance, the Japanese people, as

---

[6] *Nihon Kaiho Sensen: Sanrizuka no Natsu,* 1968; *Nihon Kaiho Sensen: Sanrizuka,* 1970; *Sanrizuka: Daisanji Kyosei Sokuryo Soshitoso,* 1970; *Sanrizuka: Daini Toride no Hitobito,* 1971; *Sanrizuka: Iwayama ni Tetto Ga Dekita,* 1972; and *Sanrizuka: Heta Buraku,* 1973.

[7] Conversation with the author.

Peasants of the Second Fortress: People who have always lived by traditional norms have now begun to challenge such concepts as "nation,"
"law," and "police."

Ogawa points out,[8] have at last transcended an instilled obedience to any
idea that could be labeled by authority as "for the sake of the country."
They have been pressed to sell their land in the same manner in which they
were once sent to war. The invocation no longer works.

The Sanrizuka struggle has not been without casualties. Peasants who
have refused to accept the money offered by the government, insisting on
the right to continue to farm their land, have been arrested. Chaining
themselves to the very trees, they have repeatedly been beaten by the
police. Out of such experiences, people who have always lived by traditional
norms (the peasantry in every country tends to be conservative) have now
begun to challenge such concepts as "nation," "law," and "police."

[8] *Ibid.*

Ogawa believes that Sanrizuka is politically important precisely because its challenge comes from people's direct experience of oppression and not from imported ideologies, as easily discardable as they are superficially embraced. Maoist or Leninist slogans find no place in the *Sanrizuka* films because, for Ogawa, they do not pertain to the experience of the Japanese. It is revealing that the Communist and Socialist parties have been reluctant to involve themselves in Sanrizuka, recognizing at once that its challenge to State power is in direct conflict with their own policies of accommodation with the State. Only the student movement and individual radical workers have allied themselves with the warriors at Sanrizuka.

The central assertion of all the *Sanrizuka* films is that, paradoxically, the peasants discover the source of revolutionary action from within their own heritage, through long-ingrained traditions of cooperation and collective effort which have always been part of the way of life of rural Japanese. This is the seeming contradiction at the heart of *Sanrizuka*; feudal traditions themselves, if utilized in new ways to meet new situations, can lead people, whose survival has in fact always depended on collective action, to revolutionary rebellion against the State. This mediation between the feudal and the politically rebellious, whereby familiar and accepted traditions are transformed to work on behalf of present needs, invalidates the criticisms of the Narita struggle made by some leftists in Japan. Some have suggested that the movement of the peasants is reformist, since they seek only to protect their own land and property. Indirectly, therefore, they are upholding the property system itself and their struggle thus lacks any political significance.

But this argument seems facile. It is not only that life-and-death events have occurred at Sanrizuka. More important is the degree to which the consciousness of the participants has been transformed as a result of their challenge to the highest authority, the State itself. As a woman actually says in *Summer in Narita*: "Struggle changes a human being's values." In *The Three-Day War in Narita* a peasant sums up the outrage of the Sanrizuka residents in highly revolutionary terms:

> It's the end for Japan! Taking everything away from us—the Corporation is a thief! The police are bodyguards of thieves. Me, I'm going to protect my own land by myself. Anyone who comes to destroy my place is going to get cut up with a sickle or something. The government never consulted us and now is trying to take my land away. It was just after I was repatriated at the end of the war that I first broke the soil here.[9] I pay my debts and then, all of a sudden—the airport!

Such a view hardly bespeaks a selfish concern for "private property."

[9] Before World War Two, the area comprising Sanrizuka was a forest. People left homeless by the war and the second and third sons of poverty-stricken peasants were lent a small sum of money by the government and encouraged to cultivate the area at the time of the food crisis after the war. The people had to cut down the trees and dig up the tree stumps, the latter incredibly arduous work, to begin farming. It was only after ten years that the Sanrizuka farmland became productive and the people full-fledged peasants.

Ogawa has been in quest of a film language based directly on the ripening political consciousness of the Japanese. His earlier films like *Sea of Youth* (*Seinen no Umi*, 1965), *The Oppressed Students* (*Assatsu no Mori*, 1966), and *Report from Haneda* (*Gennin Hokokusho*, 1967) dealt with struggles of the student movement. In *The Oppressed Students* Ogawa concentrates on two thousand students at Takasaki College of Economics at Takasaki City who, as he says, "shocked" the authorities by disclosing that the college administrators had unfairly accepted the sons of local bosses, conservative politicians, and corporation heads. Their demonstrations were against the intervention of the government in questions of academic freedom.

Report from Haneda is a news-style documentary dealing with a confrontation between students and riot police on the occasion of then Premier Eisaku Sato's visit to the United States. During this demonstration, held at Haneda Airport, still the only access to Tokyo, a student was killed and his death attributed by the police to another student. Ogawa's role at once became to undermine this falsity by informing the public, through footage he had shot, of the police brutality which pervaded the incident. He gave a photograph to the police as evidence that the victim must have died at the hands of the police rather than through the excesses of his fellow demonstrators.

As in the case of Noriaki Tsuchimoto and all these documentarists, the commercial distribution system for films in Japan is closed to Ogawa; he

The Oppressed Students: Their demonstrations were against the intervention of the government in questions of academic freedom.

must personally show his films before community organizations or student groups and at union meetings. The political act of showing the films thus completes the political impulse from which they were originally made.

A typical example of the *Sanrizuka* series is *Peasants of the Second Fortress*. There are no overviews, no helicopter shots, no zooms. Ogawa's camera remains close to the participants, as though it were one of them, patiently holding its own and refusing to yield to the police, no matter how long it takes. It is this mood of waiting and refusing to surrender that pervades the film, making it seem static to some. Ogawa does not cut away from peasant council meetings even when the talk becomes dreary and repetitious. His search is for authenticity and the flavor of the struggle rather than for falsely imposed Aristotelian unities, dramatic climaxes, and easy resolutions.

Student groups arrive on the scene, but we remain uncertain of what tendency they represent, and Ogawa tells us nothing beyond what we see. The students initiate more extreme actions and violent responses to the police. Ogawa refrains from commenting, for any judgment from the film-maker would immediately introduce the political consequence of isolating one element of the struggle from another. In this spirit Ogawa often refrains from using even the one source of comment that directors of the purest of documentary films permit themselves, namely, the cut. Ogawa's *cinéma vérité* interviews among the peasants sometimes seem interminable, but their very length serves further to validate his aim. He would dignify the Sanrizuka struggle by recording it in all its minutiae. The long takes convey that Ogawa himself accepts the exigencies of such strenuous activity with patience, as the real participants have done. To share their experience, we too must endure all the boring moments of waiting and planning, of just surviving and continuing.

The theme, as in all the *Sanrizuka* films, is that "the development of Japan proceeds only at the cost of human sacrifices." By 1971, when *Peasants of the Second Fortress* opens, the State has already expropriated much of the land. Many peasants have sold their land to the government. The remaining combatants now dig tunnels in the fields and build underground fortresses. All decisions are made by the peasants themselves; each person has a separate function, recorded by the hand-held camera. The peasants organize this phase of their struggle in a military manner, prepared to fight to the end.

Staying with the action as he does, Ogawa is able to come up with such marvelous shots as those of two women chaining themselves together to a tree with combination locks. Keeping the camera so close to the participants sometimes prevents Ogawa from expressing clearly what is happening in the overall situation, as when the police suddenly attack the peasants. But this is not as important to him as aligning the camera with the peasants who demand of their leaders that they, unlike the Communist Party leadership notoriously absent from the large demonstrations of the late 1950s and 1960, be constantly present on the front lines—in this case within the tunnels. By remaining with the peasants Ogawa gains some very good shots of the airport personnel, hired at seventy dollars a day to break up the peasant protests. All sound is recorded asynchronously and indiscriminately.

Thus, despite the enormous amount of physical action, *Peasants of the Second Fortress* is undramatic. We don't even witness any communication between the peasants and their student supporters. The two groups appear to act independently, as in some deepest sense they did. Another important facet of the *Sanrizuka* series, and of *Peasants of the Second Fortress* in particular, is the appearance of strong peasant women at the forefront of the struggle. When young peasants are about to be arrested, the women's committee pushes forward to defend them. The women figure prominently in all decision-making sessions; often their voices are the loudest and their will to accelerate the struggle, greatest. The Sanrizuka struggle has for the first time brought these peasant women into the political world, at last human beings to some extent in charge of their own destinies.

Any political "meaning" in *Peasants of the Second Fortress* arises solely from discussions among the participants themselves. These are frequent and as direct as any statements the director himself could make:

> In the old days people were resigned to oppression . . . we have a proper constitution now . . . yet they rob us of our land. . . . How can we believe in this corrupt government? . . . The government is afraid we'll revolt and overthrow it. They're going to exterminate us. . . . The blood will remain. They can't exterminate our peasant spirit.

An old man, in a full, close shot, speaks of wanting to be part of the struggle even if he can't contribute anything directly. It is he who provides Ogawa with an important truth. These people have no political party or group on which to rely, certainly not the Socialists who, this old man reveals, have told the peasants to defend their rights through a lawsuit and through quiet lobbying in the Diet. The peasants have been able to rely only on themselves.

The long *cinéma vérité* interview with the tunnel leader, which includes such particulars as the quality of the toilets in the tunnels and problems with insects and rats, becomes important, too, as a testament to the peasants' political and physical self-sufficiency. This self-reliance, which is part of peasant tradition, has also grown from the need to cope with the daily demands of their revolution. Ogawa includes a discussion of the uses of the sleeping bag to indicate the steady advance of their process of self-education and determination to solve the smallest of problems.

The peasants made the tunnels, unaided, without any prior scientific knowledge; only they were permitted to use them, in fear that the tunnels would be too dangerous for the students. In the end, cranes and dynamite may destroy the tunnels, their "second fortress," but Ogawa's faith that there will be third, fourth, even tenth fortresses has been justified by the indomitable wills of these people and their extraordinary resilience. As the film closes, young peasants are again working at enlarging the tunnels, now symbolic of their determination not to be defeated. That they prevented the opening of Narita International Airport for nearly ten years is itself an unparalleled triumph.

A deeper, more personal look at the peasants is provided by *Heta Village*. The farmers, protecting their hamlet, are shown to be doing so in quite specific keeping with the ancient rituals and traditions they maintain. The film brings Ogawa close to Imamura, for whom he had earlier worked as an assistant.

In *Heta Village* Ogawa proposes to answer the question of how it was possible for the peasants to sustain their struggle for so long. In their oldest customs and in the very cultural patterns passed down through generations, which had heretofore sustained the status quo, he discovers the source of the revolutionary energy of the residents of Heta Village. It is a measure of the power of a revolutionary process that when it is ripe, all the experiences and ingrained ways of people become mobilized on behalf of their opposites. If, in the past, these people were slow to challenge authority, they are now slow to yield to it. Their stubborn will is now in the service of a new perception.

At the base of their movement is the revitalization of the concept of the *ko*, or group meeting, a theme that lies at the heart of *Heta Village*. The *ko* began as a Buddhist prayer meeting and later developed many forms, including that of the town meeting. An *obisha ko* is a women's meeting. There are also old people's *ko* and youth *ko*. The *ko* is a historical means among Japanese peasants of uniting people horizontally, rather than vertically by rank. Ogawa shows how this ancient communal tradition provides the backbone of the Sanrizuka movement, sustaining it by drawing on established, familiar, and revered patterns of social organization. *Heta Village* refutes through historical fact Chie Nakane's narrow, schematic dicta on the vertical hierarchical structure supposedly inherent and pervasive in all of Japanese society, a structure which, in her view, renders revolutionary struggle among the Japanese people psychologically and socially impossible.

In the face of adversity Heta Village functions as a commune, helping the people to be impervious to police lies. The camera at these *ko* meetings generally focuses on the group as a whole rather than on individual speakers, reinforcing the revolutionary solidarity which the peasants manifest and which has become part of Ogawa's technique as well as his theme. The women are proud to have sought action instead of crying over the fate of their sons. It is an indirect comment from within Japanese life on the kind of political cinema offered by Imai or Kinoshita, in which injustice is responded to by a flood of tears, among both the characters and the audience.

Undermining the communal effort to keep the village intact was the sale of the land and adjacent cemetery of one of the residents by his heirs after his death. The man's son, having been compelled by financial necessity, is bitterly sorry for this betrayal, as he bows his head to the camera in shame. Ogawa is sympathetic. "You couldn't help it?" he asks. "That's right" is the response. The man had then asked the villagers to help him retrieve the family tomb from the sold cemetery and in *cinéma vérité* style we watch as they debate whether or not to aid him. The issue is complicated because the man who died, whose name was Meiji Ogawa, had himself been a strong supporter of the struggle; it was his survivors who sold out. Should then Meiji-san's household be removed from the alliance?

Many of the young men of the village are now in prison. The villagers wish to encourage them, since these youths had fought so hard to keep this cemetery, now lost. Generously, the peasants assert that the spirit of the struggle was represented by the dead Meiji Ogawa. They decide to move his tomb so that it will not rest on government land.

The women participate most effectively in this film. One confronts the police, declaring, "You look like human beings, but you don't have the hearts of human beings . . . you are like gangsters." A policeman taps nervously on his shield. None can meet the eyes of the people, let alone the fierce women with their strong language. Ogawa also photographs "Women's Day" rituals, a New Year celebration. A woman carves a horse-radish into the shape of a phallus to bring to the local shrine to pray for safe births and healthy children. For testicles, potatoes are added to the horseradish with toothpicks, and grass becomes pubic hair. The women compete to make the most original lifelike replica. "Without testicles," one confides to Ogawa, "it won't work."

New arrests occur and more meetings are held at which the people consider how to respond. Families from which the young people have been taken must be helped in their work. Someone remarks that too much *enryo*, or self-restraint, will crack the solidarity of the village. The people must not be afraid to impose on each other. Thus, not all traditional responses are of use in the struggle, only those that foster cooperation and communal effort. The peasants decide to bring food to the prison, if only to demonstrate to the police their continuing solidarity with the young people.

Ogawa ends *Heta Village*, one of the most moving and effective of these new documentary films, with a question printed on the screen as a title: "Are they going to come to destroy this *buraku* [village]?" Who could fail to respect or to declare deeply felt solidarity with Ogawa's Sanrizuka peasants? Who could not admire the warfare they have waged so tenaciously against an oppressive corporation out to destroy them through the force of an even more oppressive institution, the Japanese state, which it, with other corporations, essentially controls?

Similar to Ogawa's *Sanrizuka* films, if on a far more modest scale, were two films by Kiichi Hoshi: *Trenches: The Sunagawa Anti-war Movement* (*Zango*, 1971) and *The Trenches, Continued* (*Zoku Zango*, 1971). The subject is the efforts of students and local revolutionaries to block expansion of the Tachikawa American Air Force Base located but an hour's drive from Tokyo. Underground trenches, serving as barracks, were constructed by the local peasants; thus the source of Hoshi's title.

In part one, *Trenches*, the protest is directed against the Americans who use Tachikawa Base to transport aircraft to Vietnam. It was in the service of this purpose that the original runway at the airfield was found to be

Heta Village: Who could fail to respect and declare deeply felt solidarity with Ogawa's Sanrizuka peasants?

too small and expansion became necessary. The expansion became the target of the students and anti-war workers whose efforts provide the subject of Hoshi's film. On the north side of the runway, a bamboo pole with a flag was placed so that aircraft couldn't land. The students guarded it from a trench, trying to convince the landowner, Aoki, to permit them to remain. The Japanese government counters by offering Aoki ten million yen for this small piece of land. But Aoki refuses to sell as he, too, is opposed to the Vietnam War. In part two, the Japanese Self Defense Force comes to Sunagawa. To stop their activities and prevent their planes from landing, the students construct a thirty-meter-high steel tower, like that later to be built at Sanrizuka.

Hoshi's hand-held camera introduces us to an inside view of the Sunagawa movement. The slogans are those of the 1960s: "Smash AMPO [the Security Treaty with the United States]" and "Stop S.D.F. [the Self Defense Forces]." Round table discussions are included, in which strategy is discussed. The students live on the land, supporting themselves through cultivation and hiring themselves out as manual day-laborers. The music is lyrical. Like Ogawa, Hoshi minimizes conventional dramatic structure, his film leaving events unorganized in any thematic or aesthetic sense. Students seek means of communicating with local people, but are not always successful. The students are accused by some local, more "proper" residents of never taking a bath.

The Trenches, Continued contains more action because of the confrontation over the building of the tower. Landlord Aoki decides that he wants his land returned and is against the construction of such a tower. He had accepted the trenches, but this time he fears putting himself in jeopardy with Japanese law, which would be invoked with respect to obstructing the Japanese Self Defense Force, where as it could be ignored when the acts were against the Americans.

The students begin to construct the tower from inside the trenches so that it won't be discovered immediately. Only when Aoki is away do they remove the trench roof. Aoki sues the students in court for return of the land. He is in a strong position because they neither have a contract nor do they pay rent; their occupation of the land has been dependent upon Aoki's promise that they would fight together. But the population itself was so vehemently opposed to the arrival of the Self Defense Forces in the area that, although of course the S.D.F. did come, the tower was left standing from 1971 until 1974, long after the students had abandoned the trenches.

There are fascinating shots of the construction of the tower. The electricity has been cut off and there is no longer any water. The students dig in the dark; because of Hoshi's limited equipment, we are barely able to see them. But this actually heightens our sense of being there and involved in the struggle. Aoki, dressed in a T-shirt, yells at the students, denouncing them as "thieves" for occupying his land. He walks around demarcating the boundaries of his property with a rope. The students try to communicate with him. Hoshi's camera pans up the tower, as Ogawa's will the Iwayama later, quietly conveying the tenacity and commitment of the students.

Hoshi records a local popular movement which arose from a history of disenchantment by ordinary Japanese with the remilitarization of their country. In essence, the struggle against this base had begun in 1955, when American construction was first undertaken. Hoshi's aim is to reach as large an audience as possible with the visual drama of the Sunagawa movement. He does not conceal internal conflicts between students and villagers, inevitable concomitants of the highly difficult task of building a strong united front against the government among distinct social groups and classes. The Communist and Socialist parties, Hoshi points out,[10] offered no concrete help whatever, other than the distribution of petitions, in preventing the advent of the Self Defense Force in Sunagawa. Nor would any of the labor unions become involved, since where union leadership tends to the left, it is heavily influenced by the Communist Party.

The films are made in support of the intervention by the students, many of whom later worked on the construction of the tower at Sanrizuka. Both parts of Trenches are small, 16mm. documentary films, made on a shoestring outside the commercial theatrical distribution system. Yet, like the work of Ogawa, they represent the movement in Japan in the late 1960s and the 1970s of films conceived as direct tools in political resistance. And

[10] Conversation with the author, Tokyo, November 1974.

Hoshi considers himself not a "film director," but a man of the locality, a "community person," using film as a weapon against repression.

Of a magnitude and merit equal to the work of Ogawa are the films of Noriaki Tsuchimoto. These concern the people of Minamata City and environs, who were poisoned when they ate fish from a mercury-polluted sea in which the Chisso company had dumped its chemical waste. Minamata disease has been aptly described by photographers W. Eugene Smith and Aileen M. Smith, who worked to attract international attention to the plight of these victims:

> Chisso-Minamata Disease: The nervous system begins to degenerate, to atrophy. First, a tingling and growing numbness of limbs and lips. Motor functions may become severely disturbed, the speech slurred, the field of vision constricted. In early, extreme cases, victims lapsed into unconsciousness, involuntary movements, and often uncontrolled shouting. Autopsies show the brain becomes spongelike as cells are eaten away. It is proven that mercury can penetrate the placenta to reach the fetus, even in apparently healthy mothers.[11]

The mercury was a catalyst used in the production of acetaldehyde, which is necessary in photography. When the chemical was discarded in the sea, the result was thousands of cases of Minamata disease in humans and the death of virtually every cat in the area. Chisso, Eugene Smith reports, paid experts for a long time to refute the evidence that the mercury, which it could not deny was part of its industrial waste, was the cause of the "new" disease. It paid the severely injured and the dying minuscule sums of "consolation," refusing to acknowledge any responsibility for the victims and continuing to pour mercury waste into the sea throughout the 1960s, despite the epidemic of Minamata disease in 1956. Finally, a mass movement of victims and their supporters confronted the Chisso executives. Their demand was for reparations and lifelong medical care for the victims, whose cases could only grow progressively worse, since there is no cure for Minamata disease. Equally important was their determination to force Chisso to accept responsibility and to admit that its indifference had caused the torment and destruction of so many lives.

The obstacles faced by the Minamata militants included a government-created Central Pollution Board which, though established to assess whether indemnities were called for, basically confined itself to apologies to the victims! It was a brazen attempt by State and corporation to prevent any effective challenge to their authority; what they conceded amounted to little more than cynical and empty words. They seemed well aware that the Minamata movement might serve as a catalyst to such other rebellious groups in Japan as the Sanrizuka peasants.

Another difficulty confronting the Minamata leaders was the traditional reluctance among the Japanese to engage in so direct a confrontation with

[11] *Minamata*, An Alskog-Sensorium Book (New York: Holt, Rinehart & Winston, 1975), p. 18.

authority, as opposed to meek acceptance of token words of regret and of patronizingly granted nominal sums. Only the most courageous of the Minamata patients, the "Direct Negotiations" Group, were willing to initiate the lawsuit which finally resulted, in 1973, in a reasonably generous settlement, although to "acknowledged" cases only. The settlement was for a base figure of $60,000 to each. But the government continued to refuse to certify victims born after 1960, despite their obvious affliction with Minamata disease. The government contended that the disease had "ceased" in that year. The Chisso company, with government support, used every possible method to defeat its victims. Chisso union members, turned *yakuza* on behalf of the company, had no qualms about using the most extreme violence against members of the Minamata movement; they also assaulted Eugene Smith, almost maiming him for life.

By far the most moving expression of the Minamata travail has been Noriaki Tsuchimoto's documentary, *Minamata: The Victims and Their World*. Susami Hani, for whom Tsuchimoto worked as assistant director on *Bad Boys*, has called this film the finest documentary made to date in postwar Japan.[12] Its climaxes comes when the Minamata victims confront the executives of the Chisso company at their annual stockholders' meeting. There they seek not money, the only form of restitution available to them, but recognition of what has occurred. They do not demand confessions from Chisso but an admission of responsibility, accompanied by preventive measures for the future. Still well within the system, the victims confront their oppressors with the need for moral "leadership," knowing all the while that this would be at best a symbolic restriction on Chisso. They have long since lost faith that this system of supposedly benevolent paternalism actually functions in accordance with the myth; they recognize that it is a facade, used by those in power ever since feudal times, to palliate and exact submission from the populace. But if the victims perceive that the corporate executives abdicate their pretended role of "protecting" the people, or of "acting in their interest," the protesters nevertheless invoke the old feudal codes. So ingrained are feudal ways, the cartilage of the entire authoritarian structure of power in Japan, that what they ask of Chisso's executives is the admission that they have failed to live up to their obligation to care for the people. Yet for all that, the effect of mass action is to burst these mental bonds, exposing to the victims the real nature of the corporation and showing the villagers that only their own efforts can be relied upon to create that change which is increasingly a prerequisite of survival in Japan. Filmed as it happened, this confrontation becomes one of the most significant film moments in Japanese cinema since the war.

Before this climactic encounter, we meet the Minamata victims in *cinéma vérité* interviews and see them demonstrating outside the gates of the Chisso company. Many have concluded that they could not survive unless the Chisso plant was physically destroyed. Others express the pain

[12] Joan Mellen, "Interview with Susumu Hani," *Voices from the Japanese Cinema*, p. 185.

of their isolation in a Japan still steeped in that feudal mode of thought epitomized in the code of *bushido*, which scorns weakness. Many Japanese are embarrassed by the sight of handicapped, disfigured, injured, or maimed people. The victims were thus further afflicted by the psychological discomfort of many Japanese before physical disability. "It's nothing to those who haven't suffered it," a child bitterly declares. Some try pathetically to be philosophical: "He's not pitiful unless we think he's pitiful." As the film opens, we already see people buying stock in Chisso, one share each, so they will earn the right to attend the stockholders' meeting.

Tsuchimoto is careful to distinguish between two groups of victims, those who continued to trust the government and its blandishments, and those who filed the history-making lawsuit. Deeply conservative, these rural Japanese are conditioned to ask their oppressors to take care of them; direct, opposing action was, to many, unthinkable. Tsuchimoto reveals, in the most important and the most powerful testament of his work, that the Japanese people, challenged by so flagrant an insult to their humanity, were moved, finally and ineluctably, to revolt. They set themselves against Chisso, mobilizing the support of people throughout Japan, making known through marches, displays, exhibits, and the most simple of personal accounts what had happened to them. It was the magnitude of national support for the people of Minamata that prevented Chisso from continuing to dismiss accounts of the disease as "radical," "exaggerated," and "untrue." It was popular outrage that forced a recalcitrant, establishment court to award the victims the final settlement.[13]

Tsuchimoto does not hesitate to portray the callousness and cruelty of many Japanese toward the Minamata victims. A woman is banished from her husband's house because she has the disease; his family fears she will jeopardize the marriages of her sisters-in-law. She has a three-year-old child and is already partially blind. This is a society in which the handicapped or the mentally ill have traditionally been hidden at home, confined and shut away from the eyes of the world. Their existence humiliated the family, which was expected to bear the pain of such "deformity" in silence and, above all, without outside help.

The Minamata victims are frequently treated as outcasts and untouchables, long after it has become known that the disease is not contagious. To many in Japan, it is the victims who are the shame of Minamata. In a society long inured to repression, it is psychologically impossible for many to face open suffering and need. Hurt and vulnerability upset psychic equilibrium. Such suffering demands of strangers an open expression of compassion, which is not part of the Japanese sensibility. And, were one to allow oneself truly to register and feel what has happened in Minamata, it demands revolutionary anger, also an uncharacteristic response for the Japanese, given their social history.

Part of Tsuchimoto's intent, therefore, is to humanize and individualize the Minamata victims. To this end he introduces us to several of them.

[13] "By early 1975, Chisso would pay out indemnities of more than eighty million dollars." Smith and Smith, *Minamata*, p. 135.

One is Eiichi, to whom a shopkeeper gives a powerful stereo recorder, enjoyed as well by his deaf-mute brother, also a victim, who senses the sound through the vibrations of the speaker. Another, a child, declares that he hates baseball and wrestling. A Japanese boy, in the best macho tradition, is expected to excel at sports. This youth hates those who say behind his back that he is sick, and tells us that he knows what "pollution" is. He must wear diapers which have to be changed for him because he has lost sphincter as well as other muscular control. Had he been able to grow up in normal health, he would have been too bright to be a fisherman. Tsuchimoto now asks him what will happen to him if he doesn't get better by the time he grows up. The child suddenly falls silent and then calls a halt to the interview. He throws Tsuchimoto out of his house. The director has gone too far, summoning up too much pain. "No more, no more, goodbye," the boy tells him. The scene is almost unbearable.

The second part of the film concerns what is to be done. Tsuchimoto focuses on the "one-share movement" aimed at forcing Chisso to admit responsibility and cease emitting poison. He does not mention that the Chisso trade union actually sided with the company against the victims, taking no part in the struggle. This omission may be partly based upon Tsuchimoto's feeling that introducing the issue of the neo-feudal role of so many trade unions in Japan would distract from the central issue of the Minamata victims. It was a mistaken decision, for a solidarity strike against Chisso, not to mention other corporations, might have been decisive on behalf of the victims. But, then, we would not be speaking about contemporary Japan as it is. The failure of Japan's trade unions to conduct such struggles lies at the heart of the feudal residue in Japan and is an important barrier to social change.

Nowhere is this better illustrated than in the default of the Chisso trade union. Japan's trade unions in general have a long history of identifying with management, the "superiors" of the "group," i.e. the company, to which they, too, belong. Tsuchimoto remains content to locate an authentic revolutionary response solely among the victims themselves, just as Ogawa shows that only the Sanrizuka peasants whose lands were in danger of confiscation knew the urgency of sustaining their struggle and were capable of doing so.

The date is November 28, 1970. The place is the Chisso stockholders' conference and the question is whether the Minamata patients will be permitted to speak. Tsuchimoto pans the victims praying and uttering sad lamentations from the gallery. When the president of Chisso introduces himself from the dais, bedlam breaks loose. The patients and their supporters yell that if they are not allowed to speak, there will be no meeting. Company bodyguards push a movement leader off the stage.

Only after open resistance are the patients even granted the right to be heard. The patients are alive, vital, full of fervor and passionate energy despite their disease. The president, under the floodlights, is waxlike and pallid. He looks like a mummy or a corpse, as indeed, morally, he is. He offers perfunctory words of sympathy, but the people do not accept them. "Bring the forty-one [dead] back to life!" many scream. A woman rushes to the platform and positions her face nose-to-nose with the president's: "Words don't make any difference. I lost both my parents!" Tsuchimoto, with his hand-held camera, tries to keep the scene in focus. The woman continues: "Children want their parents . . . can't you understand my feelings . . . you can't buy lives with money!"

Tsuchimoto cuts to a large bird in the sky swooping down into the sea for fish. Fishing boats go out once more as they will in Tsuchimoto's later *The Shiranui Sea* (*Shiranui Kai*, 1975). A song is heard: "Weeping, we offer our hearts to the deceased. Yet they will be saved by the Lord Buddha." There are no illusions in *Minamata: The Victims and Their World* about the success of the demonstrations. The people must go on fishing because they have no other means to survive, whether mercury poisons the fish or not. Tsuchimoto's appended note that in 1973 Chisso was ordered to pay damages of 1,500,000 pounds sterling is emphatically anticlimactic.

Tsuchimoto's three 1974 documentaries about the medical nature of Minamata disease[14] were made, he has said,[15] so that the world would not forget the patients. In 1974 there were only 788 officially designated cases, with 2,600 pending. Tsuchimoto is seen in these films as an investigator setting out, in one scene, with a fisherman on Minamata Bay.

Part Two of this medical trilogy concerns the disease's pathology and is the most interesting. Extreme close-ups reveal eyeballs moving uncontrollably. The film seeks to prove that new victims are continually being created, and to make the plight of these people internationally known. Tsuchimoto found that the process itself of making *Minamata: The Victims and Their World* encouraged the patients to attend the stockholders' meeting filmed at the end.[16] Thus the film itself had a revolutionary effect on the movement it was made to encourage. The medical films are meant to do the same.

Can such companies as Chisso and such a government be brought under humane laws? Minamata becomes, in Tsuchimoto's films, a microcosm of Japan and the entire industrialized, capitalist world, indifferent to the incurable diseases its production processes inflict upon the helpless. As long as the people of the area—which has grown to include Niigata and other cities—continue to eat fish, there will be more cases of Minamata disease. The tide spreads the mercury in the water throughout the Japanese islands, yet throughout *The Shiranui Sea* the bay is full of fishing boats and shots abound of lush, thick-fleshed fish caught in this area and soon to be marketed. This film was made specifically to alert the fishermen in outlying areas who have not yet had direct contact with the dread disease.

---

[14] *Minamata Disease—A Trilogy* (*Igaku to Shiteno Minamata-byo*): Part One, *Progress of Research* (*Shiryo: Shogen-hen*); Part Two, *Pathology and Symptoms* (*Byori: Byozo-hen*); Part Three, *Clinical Field Studies* (*Rinsho:Ekigaku-hen*).

[15] Conversations with the author, Tokyo, October 1974.

[16] *Ibid.*

Works such as Tsuchimoto's, with the psychological pressure they place on the government and on Chisso, play their small part in revolutionizing Japan and its people—as perhaps no films have in the nation's history. If their subject is the hopeless, they themselves, by their very existence, offer hope. The works of Ogawa and Tsuchimoto should perhaps be seen less as films, art objects, than as political documents. Tsuchimoto certainly is concerned not so much with constructing well-wrought works of art as with instructing his audience that the enemy is not only a company president seeking to preserve company funds but the neo-feudal government behind which organizations like Chisso stand protected and unafraid.

On an airfield abandoned by the United States military, the peasants of Okinawa, in concerted action, break up the concrete, plow the land, and convert it back into sugar cane fields. Over the head of a woman working in the fields with a hoe, F105 jet fighter planes descend, fire, and ascend again in practice outings. Such images at once express the central theme of Yoichi Higashi's powerful documentary *People of the Okinawa Islands* (*Okinawa Retto*, 1968). A shadow has been cast over the lives of these people by both the presence of the American base on the island and the ever-encroaching American and Japanese corporations polluting the environment and enslaving the local people by seeking to convert them into a cheap labor force. Higashi chooses as the political moment of his film the reversion of Okinawa to Japan so that he may explore what has happened to Okinawa as a result of the American military presence, and what the future may hold. Before he made his film, Higashi says, he asked many Okinawans what they wished most; their response was directed far more against the American military presence than it was against the islands' reversion to Japan, nationalist Okinawan sentiment notwithstanding. The majority of those to whom he spoke wanted most to be rid of the Americans. In this spirit he made his film, despite the accusation by some on Okinawa that it was not radical enough because it did not treat *Japanese* imperialism, its past colonization of Okinawa, and the renewal of this through the projected arrival of Japanese Self Defense Forces after the island's reversion to Japan.[17]

Beginning on the Okinawan "mainland," the camera journeys to all the islands of the Okinawan archipelago, each with its unique problems. *People of the Okinawa Islands* is aesthetically the single finest example of the new documentaries emerging from Japan. Tightly constructed, the film is replete with powerful images which Higashi had to photograph with a hidden camera since picture-taking is forbidden in the proximity of the American installations.

Higashi opens in a glass-junk factory producing glassware from discarded Coca-Cola bottles. In voice-over the narrator begins at once his denunciation of the Japanese government for "selling us to America." Okinawa is compared to a girl sold by her father into whoredom, not once but twice. The first shot after the credits is of an American submarine off the coast

---

[17] Conversation with the author, Tokyo, November 1974.

of Yokosuka (Japan). The time is that of the reversion of Okinawa to Japan, in honor of which student demonstrators come to Okinawa on the ship *Himeyuri* with banners reading "Withdraw the B52's." In commemoration of the occasion they burn their passports, as American students had once burned their draft cards. Passports are now no longer needed for travel to Okinawa. But reversion has not meant that the Americans have departed.

Higashi cuts at once to the barbed wire fence surrounding the American base, using extreme close-ups and diagonal pans. Inside, American children play football. Two narrators, echoing each other, comment upon the contribution of the Americans to life on Okinawa:

A. We have been educated under freedom, peace, and democracy.
B. Behind the netting is the America that taught them to us.
A. America has 400 overseas military bases for peace, of which 117 are concentrated in Okinawa.
B. Anywhere on Okinawa, there are ramparts of democracy defended by wire netting.

In miraculously clear shots, given the difficulties of shooting the film, the camera manages to peer through the barbed wire at Green Berets.

Higashi finds the lives of the people of Okinawa permeated by their contact with the Americans. He dollies in to a huge piece of scrap metal, lugged by Americans from Vietnam and now decorating a coffee shop. A girl tells us how she wishes to go to a beauty school in Tokyo but that they refuse there to teach how to cut the hair of the black G.I.'s who will form a large portion of her clientele. A prostitute screams in the middle of the street in impotent rage at not having been paid for her services by an American soldier. She is ignored by the M.P.'s. Noticing Higashi, she puts her hand over the lens of the camera.

Meanwhile, an American-financed rally in favor of continuing the base proceeds with the slogan, "Let's protect our land from the Reds." As in Minamata, there are those who are influenced by monetary considerations or unwilling to face the larger issues. Their argument is that without the American bases, the people of Okinawa would not be able to support themselves. Girls in miniskirts adorn the rally, accompanied by American soldiers. The camera returns to the barbed wire, this time encircling a reformatory adjacent to the Kadena Air Force Base. The boys there are regimented and militarized, as Higashi conveys that the spirit of repression inherent in the American Occupation since the Second World War governs all aspects of life on Okinawa:

A. They study about peace, freedom, and democracy surrounded by wire netting. But the boys seem to train their bodies only for revolt, only for adventure, and for escape.

A voice comments that everything on Okinawa is used solely for military purposes. A girl relates the story of an American who ran over a little girl and then did nothing to help her, not even inquiring whether she was still alive. She herself, without any prompting, associates the American's indif-

ference with the killing in Vietnam. An amateur acting group called
"Creation" and composed of students, housewives, and other non-actors
puts on a play against American imperialism, finding therein an outlet for
their concerns. A public bath has its water contaminated by jet fuel which
has entered the well servicing it. Such is life on Okinawa.

Higashi takes time to document, through statistics, the extent of the
American military presence. Kadena Air Force Base is three times larger
than Tokyo's Haneda International Airport, with 2.5 miles of runways and
military planes landing and taking off every three minutes. It employs
3,200 Okinawans. A giant B52 moves into view, large enough, "A" tells
us, to carry two twenty-four-megaton hydrogen bombs. The B52's are
photographed as grey monsters:

> **B.** Doesn't this mean that we, who allow the United States to use these
> bases, are helping Americans kill the people of Vietnam?

We learn as well that Okinawan divers, inspecting boat bottoms, now
suffer from radiation disease, as Higashi proves (if proof is still needed)
that the United States has long been secreting nuclear weapons within
Japanese territory in violation of their agreement under the terms of
AMPO, the mutual security treaty between the two countries.

Higashi also captures a demonstration *against* the B52's and the coming
of nuclear submarines to Okinawa. Demonstrators zigzag down "International Street" in Naha, the capital, and are immediately attacked by
helmeted police. Higashi cuts to a B52 taking off with a deafening roar.
Slogans include "The U.S., Get Out of Asia!" and "Remove the B52's!"
Workers also demonstrate, unable to negotiate with management, the
American army. The International Anti-war Day demonstration is broken
up by the ubiquitous M.P.'s. (In *Youth*, concerned on the surface with
photographing a baseball tournament game at Naha Stadium, a dispassionate if fully aware Kon Ichikawa focuses on blue-eyed American G.I.'s
in the crowd. Having prepared us, he follows with a shot of a B52. In an
otherwise apolitical context, we are reminded even by Ichikawa that
Okinawa has become synonymous with the American military presence, for
which the B52 stands as symbol.)

With the reversion of Okinawa, Okinawans fear that the United States
and Japan have secretly agreed to increase the number of bases in order
to solidify military ties between Japan and the United States. The Socialists, to resounding cheers, defeat the ruling Liberal-Democrats in a local
election. Women in straw hats cavort uninhibitedly in an impromptu
"*Kacharashi*" dance. The political struggle is to restore control of the
economy to the Okinawans.

Higashi now leaves the mainland for the outlying islands of the archipelago. On the sugar cane lands of Henzajima (Island), Gulf Oil has asked
for a lease to build a storage base. Views are once again divided because
some see this as an opportunity for a bridge to be built to the mainland,
permitting electricity to be installed on the island for the first time and,
with it, the possibility of television! "A" envisages giant tanks, rows of

smokestacks. Higashi focuses on a dead tree and an abandoned Marine truck.

The destruction of the environment, Higashi shows, will be the first consequence. Refused by Henzajima, Gulf approaches Miyagijima. Large numbers of slogans on the walls are eloquent in their response to Gulf's offer:

> The hazards of oil combines bring death.
> Fires and explosions await us.
> Our crops will wither away.
> No more drinking water for us; the sea will be
> polluted.
> Edible fish, there'll be none.
> No man can inhabit such an island.

The sounds of the traditional samisen are heard, reasserting the identity of the people. Movements like those at Sanrizuka and Minamata are springing up on Okinawa and all over Japan. The constant demand of the people is for control of their own lives. The leader of the Miyagijima movement asks Gulf how many Okinawans from Miyagijima they will employ. To the figure 3,000 he replies sarcastically, "For as long as the world lasts?" Persisting, he discovers that Gulf actually intends to hire only one hundred people and declares, "We can't sustain the lives of four thousand islanders on the wages of one hundred workers!"

The hated Green Berets come to Miyagijima to work on the roads. The people work beside them, hoping thereby to use their more powerful enemy, even in small ways. These, Higashi tells us, are people once suppressed by the Ryuku Dynasty which had taxed them according to their height. Later, the conquering Satsuma Clan from southern Japan continued the unjust tax. Since then, the islanders of Miyagijima have had a long history of being exploited for their labor. Now their farmers' movements face the carbines of the police.

We see as well "silent Sisyphuses" in the pineapple fields of Ishigakijima, where girls from Taiwan are imported to work in the canning factories for 19 cents an hour. Finally, *People of the Okinawa Islands* compares the Americans to "poisonous snakes." Some of the Okinawan people have been corrupted. A taxi driver longs to return to the Self Defense Forces where he felt "manly": "It's so . . . sort of masculine, manly, and I find that kind of active life very attractive." But most are appalled by such American behavior as the dropping of miniature hydrogen bombs filled with "junk" on the Okinawans in symbolic "tests." Having brought petitions to their legislature, the islanders have discovered their politicians to be afraid of the Americans. They, without fear and with nothing to lose, are the stronger.

The samisen plays. The Okinawans have faith that they will one day reclaim their land and drive out the Americans completely, these foreigners who have tried, like the Japanese government at Sanrizuka, to evict them from their own land. Higashi's narrator, serving as his surrogate,

People of the Okinawa Islands: The Okinawans have faith that they will one day reclaim their land and drive out the Americans completely: foreigners who have tried, like the Japanese government at Sanrizuka, to evict them from their own land.

urges on his determined people in repetitive rhetorical declamation similar to that used by Oshima in addressing Yunbogi and all the boys like him. "Don't decelerate the speed. Don't stop. Don't be distracted by the complex shadow which will repeatedly appear over you. Don't get frightened by it. Take a deep breath and don't look back." *People of the Okinawa Islands* is a very powerful film.

Such documentaries, as Ogawa states, are not "bombs."[18] Film, even militantly political film, does not by itself change the world. But the documentaries of directors like Ogawa, Tsuchimoto, and Higashi expose a suppurating Japan at one of the rare moments in its history when the Japanese people are banding together against feudal harassment. It is at once unique and a consequence of the postwar student movement now in eclipse that at such a time there are filmmakers able to chronicle and lend their aesthetic support to these efforts waged against a callous, still neo-feudal social order.

Only *yakuza*, pornographic, and American as well as Japanese disaster films are making money in Japan today. Their popularity may well be symptomatic of the general sense of directionless alienation afflicting the culture. But the documentarists, however limited their audiences of the moment, may be far more significant, not only for politics but for Japanese film art of the future. The gangster and sex films merely feed an escapism that cannot be sustained. But the documentarists, with directors like

[18] Conversation with the author in Tokyo, October 1974.

Oshima, Imamura, Hani, and Shinoda, are doing what the finest Japanese filmmakers have always done. In writing the history of postwar Japan on film, they are marrying their art with the urgent need for moral and spiritual self-renewal of their society itself.

The Japanese psyche, beset by feudal habits and stridently recalcitrant in the face of change, remains in many ways as it once was, despite the surface appearance of a pluralist society and the existence of such dissidents as Ogawa and Oshima. It is, in fact, against these seemingly impenetrable patterns, feudal both in their origin and in their persistence, that Oshima, Yoshida, and Shinoda have worked. Their efforts add a dissident and democratic dimension to a culture so beset by confusion and so often induced, as with Mishima, to revert to what was once at least a stable and viable set of values, even if those values were authoritarian and repressive for the individual. In resurrecting the *ko*, or community council meeting, a borrowing from feudal days, Ogawa seems unaware that this same social mode which makes possible collective struggle also encourages the subsuming of individual potential before the needs of the group, and this weakens both his art and his politics. Missing from his films is any suggestion that the Japanese may have to reject the entire concept of the supremacy of the group before group action that embodies democratic rights for the individual will be possible.

History, contrary to popular cliché, does not produce a future in replica of the past. The nostalgia among Japanese artists for the elegance of the code of *bushido* or, as in the case of Imamura, for pre-samurai and pre-industrial times will also pass. But as long as the serious artists of the Japanese film continue to work, we shall at least in this area be in the presence of a culture actively engaged in the process of confronting itself, even at the risk of exposing old wounds and admitting to the difficult truth that they have yet to heal. Japan's filmmakers have sought to minister to the pain of their culture and in so doing have forged perhaps the most unique and remarkable film art of any nation. They have conjoined their perceptions with the future of the national life. And they have produced an art containing a hope and an example.

Index

Page numbers in italics refer to photographs.

About the Author

Joan Mellen is Associate Professor of English at Temple University, where she teaches courses on Japanese and American film. She is the author of *Marilyn Monroe, Women and Their Sexuality in the New Film, A Film Guide to "The Battle of Algiers,"* and *Voices from the Japanese Cinema.* She is currently completing a book on male sexuality in American films.